Library of Congress Cataloging in Publication Data
Main entry under title:

Surveys in parapsychology.

"Includes papers selected from parapsychological jour-
plus one from a related field."
Includes bibliographical references and index.
       Psychical research--Addresses, essays, lectures.
White, Rhea A., 1931-   [DNLM:
. S94   133.8   76-119
8108-0906-0

SURVEYS IN PARAPSYCHOLOGY:

Reviews of the Literature,
with Updated Bibliographies

by

RHEA A. WHITE

The Scarec

Metuche

To

A pair of extraordinary editors,

Laura A. Dale (JASPR) and

Dorothy H. Pope (JP)

CONTENTS

Acknowledgments   vii

Foreword, by Montague Ullman   ix

Introduction   xi

I.   Some Basic Areas of Parapsychological Study   1

     1.   The Problem of Precognition
          W. G. Roll   3
     2.   Is There a Case for Retrocognition?
          W. H. W. Sabine   22
     3.   The Case for Psychokinesis
          J. G. Pratt   50

II. Psi in Special Subject Populations   71

     4.   Psi and Animal Behavior: A Survey
          Robert L. Morris   73
     5.   Psi Abilities in Primitive Groups
          Robert L. Van de Castle   95
     6.   Medical Parapsychology
          Carroll B. Nash   120

III. Insights into How Psi Operates   139

     7.   Psi-Missing Re-examined
          J. B. Rhine   142
     8.   ESP over Distance: A Survey of Experiments
               Published in English
          Karlis Osis   180
     9.   Position Effects in Psi Test Results
          J. B. Rhine   204
     10. Hypnosis and ESP Performance: A Review of
               the Experimental Literature
          Charles Honorton and Stanley Krippner   227

11. State of Awareness Factors in Psi Activation
      Charles Honorton   272
12. Scientific, Ethical, and Clinical Problems in
      the "Training" of Psi Ability
      Rex G. Stanford   288

IV. Theories of Psi Phenomena   307

13. Consideration of Some Theories in Para-
      psychology
      K. Ramakrishna Rao   309
14. Psi Phenomena and Biological Theory
      John L. Randall   333
15. ESP and Memory
      W. G. Roll   351
16. The Challenge of Psi: New Horizons of
      Scientific Research
      C. T. K. Chari   382

V. Criticisms of Parapsychology   399

17. Recent Criticisms of Parapsychology: A
      Review
      Champe C. Ransom   401
18. A Scientific Critique of Parapsychology
      James C. Crumbaugh   424
19. Telepathy and Other Untestable Hypotheses
      J. B. Rhine   441

Appendices   459

A. Parapsychological Periodicals   459

B. Locating Articles on Parapsychology   464

C. Information about the Authors   465

D. Abbreviations of Parapsychology Periodicals
      Cited in Additional Readings   474

Name Index   475

Subject Index   481

ACKNOWLEDGMENTS

I would like to thank Jean Spagnolo for many labors on my behalf and Irving Adelman for his excellent advice. I also want to express my gratitude to Stephanie Becker, typing assistant, and to Marty Bowe, faithful photocopier. And special thanks go to Jane and Walter Martin, and again to Jean and Marty, for saving me the time I so badly needed to get this volume completed.

R. A. W.

FOREWORD

There are many indications that a new era is dawning with regard to both public and scientific interest in the claims and methods of parapsychological research. A number of simultaneously converging influences seems to have brought this about. There is more research going on now than ever before. The research is international in scope and there is a greater degree of communication and collaboration, particularly between Eastern and Western countries. Technological advances have opened up new and fruitful avenues of research, bringing us closer to the century-old goal of reproducing so called paranormal events in the laboratory in a qualitative way as well as on a quantitative and statistical basis. There has been more exposure of the work going on in the professional literature as well as in the mass media. A great deal of skepticism on the part of many leaders of the scientific community has been replaced by interest in and in some instances by a commitment to parapsychological research. Add to this a push from below in the form of the growing interest of young people in the field and what emerges is the picture of a new science on the move.

Movement on this large scale creates problems as well as possibilities. The problems arise in connection with the spread of misinformation, in which case they are due to a lack of accurate and sufficient information. They also may come about as a result of the deliberate exploitation of public interest. In either event there is a need for sufficient and reliable information. This book addresses itself to both of these needs.

There is a clear focus to the book. How would someone developing a serious interest in parapsychology go about familiarizing himself with the research that has gone on and that is going on? Where would he turn for reliable information concerning the research members in the field, the work they are doing, the centers and laboratories where the work is carried out, the books that have appeared, and the periodical literature where research reports are published? These are the questions that led to the design and content of this book. The articles selected are broad in scope and represent a sampling from the writings of many of the leading researchers. The reader is presented with a good deal more than factual laboratory data. The intent of the author is to stimulate the further interest of the serious student. There are carefully selected additional reading lists for each of the areas covered. The reader will emerge with a familiarity with the periodical literature available and, even more important, with a working knowledge of how to locate articles and reports of particular interest.

A word about the author's qualifications for the task she has undertaken is in order. Miss White has been closely associated with the modern era of parapsychology. She has brought to the field her talents as experimentalist, scholar and librarian. She herself has made numerous contributions to the literature and is the co-author with Laura A. Dale of an important reference book, Parapsychology: Sources of Information. Her name is associated with some of the classical experiments in parapsychology on the determining influence of attitude on the results of ESP tests with children. For many years, she has been the librarian and Director of Information for the American Society for Psychical Research. She has used her diverse skills and rich background in both fields well in the selections she has made and the help she offers for further study.

Montague Ullman, M. D.
Director
Division of Parapsychology and
    Psychophysics
Maimonides Medical Center
Brooklyn, New York

INTRODUCTION

This collection includes papers selected from parapsychological journals plus one from a related field. An effort was made to choose articles which would provide reliable, in-depth information on parapsychology and encourage serious students to turn to the periodical literature of the subject. Although everyone is aware that a vast quantity of books on parapsychology is being published today, fewer people realize that almost all of the important and reliable work is published in specialized periodicals, and even fewer know what these periodicals are. Yet no one who has a serious interest in the subject, especially those who want to try their hand at research, can afford not to be familiar with the contents of the major journals, at least. Thus this sampler is aimed at providing information on parapsychology, stimulating interest in the subject, and encouraging students to turn to the all-important periodical literature.

In selecting articles to serve these ends, emphasis was placed on solid, meaty papers primarily of the review type which deal with specific aspects of parapsychology and contain bibliographies of some length to guide the user to further sources of information. Unfortunately, review articles on all aspects of parapsychology have not appeared in the periodical literature, despite their importance to researchers, to say nothing of students. As Dr. Robert L. Van de Castle pointed out in a provocative paper entitled "Is there a madness to our methods in psi research?" published in the Proceedings of the Parapsychological Association, 8, 1971: "One way to become oriented to where important directions can be found is through a wide-ranging review article. By comparing a large number of studies placed side by side and noting points of similarity in experimental variables and scoring patterns, it becomes possible to formulate new hypotheses about interrelationships that may have been previously overlooked. However, such literature reviews are extremely rare" (p. 43).

Although it was considered important to choose fairly recent papers, it was not always possible, and for purposes of this book it was not considered necessary to omit papers simply because they were not recently published. This is because, although some areas of parapsychology are expanding rapidly, thus making earlier work obsolete, in many instances no major innovations have occurred in some years. It is hoped that this book will encourage budding researchers to update these areas with their own original work.

As a further guide to reading, additional and more recent sources will be listed at the end of each article. In most cases these additional items were published after the article which they update. However, in a few instances earlier work is cited if it is considered important and if it was not mentioned in the article which the additional readings are supplementing.

The papers in Part I cover some of the basic areas of parapsychological study. The papers selected are primarily reviews of the evidence for a particular aspect of psi phenomena, such as psychokinesis and retrocognition. The articles in Part II are reviews of psi phenomena in special populations, such as animals and primitives. The third part is on the way in which psi operates. Some selections review patterns of psi expression in experimental results while others describe some of the conditions favoring or affecting psi test results. Part IV presents some theoretical approaches to psi. Two of the selections are general review articles while two deal theoretically with specific aspects of psi. The final part consists of three critical approaches to psi: a survey of recent criticisms, a criticism of parapsychology on the grounds that it lacks a repeatable experiment, and a criticism of the choice of parapsychological research topics and the interpretation of results in psi research. These last two critical reviews are by parapsychologists themselves.

Readers who want to go beyond this book and become acquainted with the periodical literature at first hand may consult the two appendices for further information on the periodical literature of parapsychology and how to locate it.

Rhea A. White
Director of Information, A. S. P. R. , and
Assistant Reference Librarian,
East Meadow Public Library, N. Y.

PART I

SOME BASIC AREAS OF PARAPSYCHOLOGICAL STUDY

INTRODUCTION

The papers in this first part are reviews of some of the basic types of psi phenomena. Psi is the general term used in parapsychology for any type of phenomenon considered to be parapsychological, i.e., phenomena for which there is no known physical explanation. Psi phenomena fall into two major categories: extrasensory perception (ESP), or the cognitive forms of psi, and psychokinesis (PK), or the motor forms of psi.

ESP may be subdivided further into two categories: clairvoyance, or the ability to obtain information about an event or object directly; and telepathy, or the ability to obtain information about the contents of another person's mind. When the target information exists both in another person's mind and independently of it, then the term general extrasensory perception (GESP) is used.

It is also claimed that there is a temporal dimension to psi, one aspect of which is precognition, or the ability to obtain information about the future which is not otherwise available. The evidence for precognition, however, is not considered to be as compelling as that for the contemporaneous forms of ESP.

The first paper in Part I, "The Problem of Precognition" by W. G. Roll, is one of the few attempts made to survey both the evidence for precognition and theories offered to explain it. Since Roll wrote his paper, the literature deal-

ing with precognition has expanded tremendously. This is
because tests for precognition are often employed by parapsychologists not only to establish beyond all doubt that precognition occurs, but also because it is the easiest type of
test in which to control for sensory cues, since the targets
have not yet been determined. The list of additional readings
at the end of the article is limited to experimental reports
and theoretical contributions.

Roll's paper presents the evidence in favor of precognition, or the ability to know future events before they happen. Does a corresponding ability to be directly aware of
past events exist? Some persons have had experiences indicating that such is the case, and it has been called retrocognition. However, if precognition is the easiest form of psi
in which to rule out all sensory cues, then retrocognition is
the most difficult, and some say, impossible. For how can
one rule out the possibility that knowledge of the past, even
if not obtained by normal means, was not obtained by clairvoyance of existing records and written accounts of the past?
The second article in this section, "Is There a Case for
Retrocognition?" by W. H. W. Sabine, is a review of the
evidence for retrocognition and of ways of interpreting it.

The foregoing papers deal with cognitive aspects of
psi functioning. The final paper in this part is concerned
with the motor aspects of psi, or psychokinesis (PK). Many
people who are willing to accept the evidence for the existence of ESP remain skeptical about PK. Dr. Pratt's paper,
which was originally delivered at a symposium on parapsychology under the sponsorship of the Canadian Physiological
Society, was selected because, even though dated, it is one
of the best surveys of the laboratory evidence for PK. Since
it was delivered, the area of PK investigation has expanded
tremendously. In particular, during the last decade there
have been a number of persons such as Nina Kulagina and
Uri Geller who have apparent abilities to mentally move objects and bend keys. Unfortunately, it is very difficult to
get the people who make such claims to submit to laboratory
investigation.

After Pratt's paper was published a critical survey of
the evidence for PK by Edward Girden appeared in the American Psychological Association journal, Psychological Bulletin.
It sparked a lively controversy in the literature. References
to these articles as well as to later laboratory studies and
some theoretical approaches are given in the lengthy list of
additional readings.

Chapter 1

THE PROBLEM OF PRECOGNITION*

by W. G. Roll

Introduction

In a lecture at Duke University dealing with psychoanalysis and parapsychology the speaker characterized the
former as "theory without facts" and the latter as "facts
without theory" (21). Whatever may be said about the first
assertion, it is certainly true that intelligible explanations of
psi phenomena are conspicuously lacking.

It is probably also the case that much of the reluctance
of other members of the scientific community to consider seriously the findings of psychical research is due to the absence
of an explanatory model and, more particularly, a model that
makes sense to them. That is to say, one that links up with
more familiar ones or at least employs similar basic concepts. As Dr. George G. Simpson remarked in Science,
"the claims will not carry conviction unless some credible
explanation is produced" (22).

It is not the first task of the psychical researcher to
be a public relations man. His main concern is to gain understanding and control of the phenomena. For this undertaking, however, he needs to relate the observations to those
in other areas of science. It is known that to some extent
at least, psi phenomena are influenced by familiar physical
and psychological conditions. In the search for added means
of understanding and control, the parapsychologist is hopeful
that the overlapping fields will broaden. In selecting the
building blocks for his theories, therefore, he knows that a
useful explanation is likely also to be an intelligible one.

*Reprinted by permission of the author and publisher from
the Journal of the Society for Psychical Research 41:115-28
(Sept. 1961).

Attempts to talk sensibly about psi are frustrated by the phenomenon of precognition, the "cognition of a future event which could not be known through rational inference," as one source defines it (9). Prima facie, the precognitive experience is a response to, and hence, effect of, events which have not yet come about. The alleged process is conspicuously out-of-step with other natural ones and the task of reconciliation seems a hopeless one. Several skilful philosophers have attempted it (e.g., see the discussions of Professor Broad, Ducasse, and Flew in The Philosophy of C. D. Broad [20]). Leaving linguistic niceties aside, we can say that they accept the definition of precognition quoted above; that is to say, they operate from the premise that in cases of precognition, future events affect the present. Their special contribution is to define words as "cause," "time," and "cognize," so that this assertion will make sense. But these operations do not bring precognition into closer alignment with the world-picture of present-day science: they imply that whatever semantic status the future is given, it somehow exists in the present. The remainder of science (excepting parts of micro-physical theory, where brief temporal reversals enter into the equations) rests on the assumption that it does not, but is created through present actions.

In this paper I shall attempt to show that there is no need to suppose that the phenomenon we have come to know as precognition involves a reversal of the cause-effect relationship.

Experimental Work

Experiments in precognition began in 1933 at Duke University. The targets were packs of cards, shuffled by hand after the subject made his forecast. It was soon realized that the person who mixed the cards might arrange them with the aid of ESP to match the subject's guesses. A shuffling machine was therefore introduced which mechanically randomized the cards before their order was compared with the responses. A new difficulty soon arose. When results began to accumulate from the experiments, begun in 1934, in which the subjects "willed" falling dice to show certain sides, the possibility had to be faced that the card scores were produced similarly. Perhaps the subjects used PK on the cards in the machine and thereby caused them to appear in the predicted order.

The Duke parapsychologists then conducted a series of experiments

> in which the subjects attempted to predict the order
> of cards as they would be after being shuffled and
> cut mechanically, the number of shuffles and the
> point of cutting being determined by printed tempera-
> ture reports in a specified newspaper for a speci-
> fied day in the future. It was believed that this
> would at least reduce the force of the counterhy-
> pothesis of PK sufficiently to put it out of consider-
> ation. Two experimental series conducted on this
> plan gave significant results (19).

The PK hypothesis was the less likely explanation since,

> the temperature itself would have to be modified by
> the hypothetical effect in question and this seems
> considerably more incredible than that the machine
> might be influenced directly (18).

Professor C. W. K. Mundle, in his review of the evidence
for precognition raises two objections (13).   First of all, he
points out that the results in the two series in question (8,
18) are not impressive.   The evidence for the occurrence of
precognition does not consist in the number of hits, but only
in their distribution, and even this is not highly significant.
Secondly, Mundle says that, had the findings been more convincing, PK might still explain them.   For,

> the temperature readings were presumably deter-
> mined by someone looking at a thermometer and a
> thermometer is a mechanical device no more com-
> plicated than a card-shuffling machine. If we ad-
> mit, as Rhine does, that shuffling machines may be
> influenced by PK, why should we assume that ther-
> mometers are immune from such influence? In
> Rhine's experiment, a difference of one degree in a
> temperature reading would make a vast difference
> to the final order of the pack (13).

Dr. S. G. Soal and Mr. F. Bateman make the same
point (23) and one might also speculate that PK (or ESP) could
have influenced some of the human or mechanical processes
involved in printing the temperature in the newspaper.

In the same paper, Mundle considers the Soal and

Goldney experiments (24) and comes to a similar conclusion.
The forward displacement effect might have been the result
of a psi influence from the subject directed to the mind or
brain of the person who determined what the next card would
be. Soal himself recognizes this possibility (23).

However, in Mr. Whately Carington's drawing experiments (4, 5) Mundle finds something which goes beyond nonprecognitive ESP and PK. This has to do with the clustering
of hits around the target. An inverted "U" or rather "W"
curve was produced which represents the distribution of correct responses. The guesses which were intended to correspond with the target and which did so, constitute the central dip of the curve. The responses which were made for
the drawings which came before or after the actual target,
but which nevertheless resembled it, constitute the two caps
of the curve. The highest scores were on pictures twice removed from the targets, though the hits on the latter were
also significant. The only way in which we can account for
the curve in terms of ESP and PK, Mundle suggests, is by
saying that the "efficacy of this complex waxes and wanes in
phase with the 'hit curve'." He prefers to regard the temporal clustering of hits "as the several effects of a single
known event which occurred at the (temporal) centre of the
cluster," and draws an analogy with wireless transmission to
explain his idea:

If a number of radios were tuned to a certain wave
length at a certain time, an observer would be able to witness
similar events, say, transmissions of music from a symphony
orchestra, in the vicinity of them all. From this he would
conclude "even if he were completely ignorant of the modus
operandi of wireless transmission, that they were causally
connected." Furthermore, by taking notice of the volume of
receivers at different locations, he might infer the existence
and even the location of the transmitter.

Mundle says it might be argued that " 'Spatial (or spa-
tio-temporal) clustering around a central event or process of
a set of events or processes which are, structurally and/or
qualitatively, similar to each other'--is part of what we mean
by 'causal connection'." He goes on to suggest that "Carington's results reveal another criterion of causal connections:
a purely temporal clustering, around a central event or process, of a set of events or processes which are, structurally
and/or qualitatively similar to each other."

Whatever the merits of such a criterion may be, there are several ways to account for Carington's curve without adopting this view of time and causality. One of the subjects, rather than Carington, might have been the actual agent. It is evident from the description of the experimental procedure that much was left to the arbitrary choice of the experimenter in the matter of selecting targets (namely in deciding which words in the dictionary were "reasonably drawable," and how to draw them). If one of the subjects was the agent, Carington (and the other percipients) might have drawn a picture which would have features in common with the subject's drawing for that day, with the picture the subject made previously, and with those he consciously or unconsciously intended to produce later. If this is what took place, a comparison of responses and targets would give rise to a curve such as Carington's.

Another explanation for the hit distribution has been advanced by Mangan (12). The person who judged the degree of similarity between originals and responses might have created the effects by ESP guessing of which drawings were intended for which targets. The displacement effect produced by matching originals with responses would then be of the nonprecognitive type shown by a card-calling subject who responds to the symbol one or two cards down in the pack instead of the one the experimenter is holding. Finally, as Mundle, himself, realizes, Carington's W-effect may not have been produced by many individual curves: perhaps some of the subjects contributed the cap of the curve, another section, one leg, and a third, the other. If this happened, the distribution of scores can again be explained in terms of contemporary ESP. In brief, Carington's results have little, if any, bearing on the precognition question.

Since these tests, four experimental series with a more advanced design have been carried out at Duke University (1, 2, 12, 16). Before we discuss them, it should be pointed out that the results, though statistically significant, fade somewhat when seen against the background of unpublished insignificant work. After the completion of the first two, the combined result reached $P = 0.06$, which is little better than chance (17). Though the two later series will have improved this figure, the evidence from precognition testing is not yet nearly as convincing as the results of the nonprecognitive ESP work.

In these tests a calculating machine was used to arrive

at the targets. The cards were arranged according to series
of numbers printed in tables of random numbers. The crucial question is how the place in the tables was selected
from which to copy the card-order. The procedure used in
all these series (with minor variations) is described as follows by Mangan:

> A place of entry into tables of random num-
> bers is determined on a calculating machine in the
> following manner. Four three-digit numbers are
> obtained by throwing 'bridge' dice (with ten faces)
> and are multiplied together. This product may in-
> clude the billion values. This is then multiplied by
> the digits in reverse order. The resulting product
> is divided by a four-digit number made up of the
> middle digits of the four original three-digit num-
> bers. The individual digits of the quotient are
> added and the resulting sum is used as an index
> number to select a specific place in a table of ran-
> dom numbers (12).

This was done after the subject made his guesses.
Mangan writes, "The complexity of the computations would
appear to place the determination of the point of entry into
the tables beyond the range of human control" (12).

But, the human brain contains a calculating machine
which is much more powerful than the parapsychologist's. It
is not generally under conscious control (when it is, we say
about a person that he is a "calculating genius"). It works
below the threshold of awareness and furnishes rapid guidance
to the highly complex perceptual and motor activities of everyday life. Dr. K. Lorenz suggests that it is this calculator
which underlies "insight" or "intuition" (8), the sudden understanding of problems which often are highly complicated. He
notes the difference between these operations and those of
conscious logical inference, and says about the former that
"they are, in very many respects, much more akin to the
functions of mechanical calculating machines."

Lorenz proposes that it is this "computer" which underlies intuition, thereby accounting for the speed of the process,
and for the fact that it is unconscious. He says,

> the unconsciously working computer of our Gestalt
> perception is distinctly superior to all consciously
> performed computations. The superiority is due to

the fact that intuition, like other highly differentiated types of Gestalt perception, is able to draw
into simultaneous consideration a far greater number of premises than any of our conscious conclusions. It is the practically unlimited capacity for
taking in relevant details and leaving out the irrelevant ones which makes the computer of this highest
form of Gestalt perception so immensely sensitive
an organ (11).

According to this theory, everybody is a potential calculating prodigy. When the "computer" is applied to tasks
other than perceptual and motor coordination, this potentiality
is realized, providing a startling example of intuition or an
instantaneous solution to complex mathematical problems of
the type incorporated in recent precognition experiments.

We need not suppose that all the calculations start
from scratch. It is possible that the subject in the past has
solved some of the problems which make up the new one. It
would be a matter of recognizing the known elements in the
new situation, to recall the solution to them, and then to carry out whatever additional calculations are called for. This
seems to have been the method of Finkelstein, the Polish calculating genius (3).

There are, needless to say, likely to be many series
in a book with random numbers which will give statistically
significant correlations if matched with the subject's guessing
columns. If the person is to be able to use one of these
series, he must calculate which four three-digit figures
manipulated as shown above will eventually produce the number corresponding to one of the desired places of entry in
the tables. Again, there are, of course, several sets of
four-digit figures which will produce the same final sum.
Finally, he must by PK (or skill) cause the dice to fall so
that they show the required figures.

The calculating machine is only one of the barriers
incorporated into precognition tests. The die throws form
another. It seems that the person who is responsible for
the final results must be an exceedingly good PK subject.
But the physical influence on the dice need neither be strong
nor accurate in its aim to achieve significant correlations.
For instance, let us suppose that no psi influence is exerted
till the throw of the last of the twelve dice (to obtain the
four three-digit numbers). Each of the ten faces of this die

would be likely to lead to a different place in the table and
approximately half of these entries would give a positive deviation if matched with the subject's guesses, and about half a
negative deviation. Say, the 1, 4, 6, 7 and 0 faces of the
last die might result in positive deviations, and if such were
his aim, he would try to have the die come up with any one
of these faces. Consequently, this person would not have to
be unusually good at PK in order to obtain a significant total
score. He need only be able to score some hits with this
last die where he has a 50-50 probability of success by chance.

The die throws and the calculations are always done
after the guesses have been made, and generally at a time
unknown to the subject and at a remote location. It is not
known at present whether PK results can be obtained at a
distance. Exploratory researches indicate that a short separation between subject and dice is no impediment (7). However, the process is roughly the same whether we suppose
that it is the distant subject or the present experimenter who
is responsible for the results. In the former case this person would have to know by ESP which columns in the book of
numbers would match his guesses and then aim for the die
faces which he calculates will give the correct entry point.

If the experimenter is the actual subject in the test,
the selection of the die face would be determined by two
sources of information, one from the tables of random numbers by ESP or unconscious memory, and the other from the
guesses of the "subject" which are ascertainable only by ESP.
This type of combination of information from two sources is
not unknown in the literature and was demonstrated by the
"split agents" experiments with Mrs. Stewart in which she
used her ESP to draw on information from two persons to
make one response (23).

Our exposition is based on the assumption that the
"PK targets," i.e., the most advantageous die faces, can be
known with the aid of ESP. It is suggested by a series of
exploratory PK tests with concealed targets that ESP can assist PK. In trials with cup thrown dice, the subjects of Dr.
Karlis Osis obtained significant results when aiming for concealed targets (15). PK experiments indicate, also, that subjects do not know when they are performing. It is not difficult to suppose that a person may not even realize that he is
the "subject" in a PK test. The fact that results in precognition runs hug the ground in the manner of psychokinesis and
never reach the heights of ESP trials, tends to confirm the
argument that the process is based on PK.

Non-Experimental Cases

The term "spontaneous," as a description of psi in everyday life, is misleading. Spontaneity is as characteristic of laboratory phenomena as of psi in ordinary situations. Conversely, also intended or anticipated occurrences are encountered in both areas. It would be more accurate to distinguish between anticipated experimental cases, anticipated non-experimental cases, spontaneous experimental cases and spontaneous non-experimental cases.

Though it is questionable whether non-experimental cases constitute proof of psi, they indicate it sufficiently to be given serious attention in a discussion of the nature of parapsychological processes. Careful studies have been published by the London and New York Societies, and the Duke Laboratory has a quantity of cases received from apparently sane and serious persons.

Non-experimental cases of precognition have little in common with laboratory work except that they, too, rely on ESP and PK. An examination of the non-experimental material requires some comments on the modus operandi of these familiar forms of psi. The two main types of ESP are clairvoyance and telepathy. In a successful clairvoyance experiment the subject produces a description (or significantly avoids it) of some physical event or state. His report appears to be due to a response to the physical characteristics of the object in question. But in many clairvoyance tests there are no known physical stimuli to which a percipient could respond. In the common "down through" (DT) test, for example, the cards are left in the pack undisturbed, in this way precluding the operation of their light-reflecting properties as the effective stimuli.

Similarly, in telepathy we are not dealing with familiar stimuli. This is true whether we suppose that the target consists of non-physical mental occurrences or of brain processes reflected in or by mental events. In the latter case we are faced with a situation similar to the DT trials and in the former we say, in effect, that the subject responds to other causal agents than those known to belong to living brains.

This gap in our conceptual picture can be filled by postulating the existence of psi fields along with the electromagnetic and gravitational ones. These fields are composed of psi elements whose function is analogous with the electrons and other constituents of electromagnetic fields. As with known fields, the psi field of an object does not lie in it but in a surrounding spatial continuum. It interacts with the psi fields of other bodies (or is part of a whole embracing them all, which is saying the same), and it also interacts with the object's more familiar fields. In ESP the physical fields of the target object (inanimate, as the cards in a clairvoyance test or animate, as in telepathy) influences its psi field, the latter affects the psi field of the percipient whose physical fields are consequently changed, resulting eventually in a response that reflects the target situation. In PK, the modification of the brain's physical fields, induced by a person's volitions or intentions, brings about the change in his psi field which, in turn, interacts with the psi fields of objects in his environment, e.g., dice, whose physical fields are then also affected.

The reduction of all psi phenomena to one is a by-product of this addition to our terminology. It is primarily intended to focus attention on certain spatial and temporal relationships in the data which have escaped notice or been regarded as anomalous. These will be discussed elsewhere.

In precognition, psi elements are effective twice, first, as they affect a person's nervous system, causing him to have the precognition and secondly, as their influence is exerted on other physical systems, resulting in the "verfication" of the precognition. The temporal lag, which is due to the time it takes these forces to build up an observable effect on the physical conditions may vary. Though the verifying events in precognition are influenced by psi fields, the reports of non-experimental cases do not refer to anything unusual with regard to the means by which precognitions are fulfilled. If the PK-type force has escaped notice, it is likely to be small. This raises the question, how the gross incidents arise.

The following case (14) was reported to Myers by Mrs. Atlay, wife of the Bishop of Hereford.

> I dreamt that the Bishop being from home, we were unable to have family prayers as usual in the chapel, but that I read them in the large hall of the Palace, out of which, on one side, a door opens into the dining room. In my dream, prayers being ended, I left the hall, opened the dining room door, and there saw, to my horror, standing between the table and the sideboard, an enormous pig. The dream was very vivid, and amused me much. The Bishop

being from home, when dressed I went down into
the hall to read prayers. The servants had not
come in, so I told my governess and children, who
were already there, about my dream, which amused
them as much as it had done me. The servants
came in and I read prayers, after which the party
dispersed. I opened the dining room door, where
to my amazement, stood the pig in the very spot
in which I had seen him in my dream. With regard to your question as to whether I could have
heard the pig in my sleep, he was then safely in
his sty. . . . It got into the dining room in consequence of the gardener being engaged in cleaning
out the sty while the servants were at prayers;
they having left every door open, the pig met with
no obstacle on his voyage of discovery.

Myers' report includes a statement from the governess
to the effect that Mrs. Atlay told her the dream before the
service, that the sty was a considerable distance from the
palace, and that the pig got loose while Mrs. Atlay was reading prayers; the gate had not been locked securely.

Perhaps the psi elements originated with Mrs. Atlay:
things may have been a bit dull in the household. A pig in
the palace might be a welcome diversion! But how can psi
elements, whatever their origin, have brought about the animal's escape to the dining room? Non-experimental cases
seem to present a stronger physical force than we encounter
at the PK machines. For a short period of time it appears
that Mrs. Atlay applied as great PK abilities as an alleged
poltergeist agent. A physical effect of this magnitude would
have been observed easily. Yet, in this as in other precognition cases, no one reported anything uncanny or otherwise
unusual accompanying the verifying event.

Nor is there evidence that anyone associated with the
precognition had noticeable PK powers. However, the physical effect of the psi elements need not be stronger than that
responsible for laboratory results. The PK we meet in the
laboratory emerges when other causal processes cancel each
other out, as with tumbling dice which, if not biased, are
under equal "pull" from their six sides. But the devices constructed by parapsychologists and statisticians are not likely
to be the only (macro-) physical systems in the world which
generate random events. There are probably numerous instances where two or more physical forces cancel each other

out, leaving it to chance variations--or perhaps a psi effect
--to tip the scales.

In the Atlay case and similar ones, we need not suppose that there was an effective psi influence on the stable
physical systems. The psi elements affected only the weak
parts of the barriers which confined the pig. The gatelock
may have been on the verge of giving way, requiring only a
small effect to do so; a slight influence on the animal's brain
may have stimulated its desire to escape and directed its
path. In this and similar precognition cases it is possible
to assume that the actual (verifying) events were shaped by
the same type of minute physical forces as operate in experimental PK. The rarity of veridical precognitions is accounted
for by the hypotheses that the influences are no stronger and
as erratic as laboratory PK, and that they are likely to be
effective only on unstable physical systems.

At present there is no way of knowing when an effective series of psi elements has been launched or which dreams
or other mental experiences are psychically caused. Psi elements seem to activate existing neural pathways and to draw
on the percipient's private stock of mental images. This accounts for the fact that precognitions and other ESP experiences are usually indistinguishable from those with a wholly
subjective origin. It has puzzled some investigators that a
percipient occasionally seems to know or suspect that a particular experience was parapsychological. A study of the
cases reveals that this conviction is based on a secondary
rational judgment and varies with the subject and circumstances under which the experience arises.

In the Dommeyer case (6) the precognition presented
itself as a dream (of excreta) which the percipient, Mrs.
Dommeyer, reserved as a symbol for a particular occurrence
(the unexpected arrival of money). Whenever she experienced
the image, Mrs. Dommeyer knew that the event would follow.

A second type, of which the Levyns case (10) is an
example, consists of experiences in which a hunch or image
intrudes on the subject's attention and, not making sense in
terms of current thoughts or activities, is regarded as parapsychological. In February, 1949, Mr. J. E. Levyns, Chief
Accountant of the Cape Provincial Administration, South Africa, accompanying the Under Secretary, Mr. E. A. Bouchier,
journeyed by car to Bloemfontein. Shortly before 3 p.m., at
the outskirts of Laingsbury they passed a bus. Mr. Levyns
recalls:

As I slowed down to pass the bus, a small Coloured
girl dashed out from between two of the houses,
making for the bus. I saw that the only chance of
avoiding running over her was to accelerate, which
I did. The car being large and new leapt forward
and the child passed unharmed behind us. It was
the closest escape from killing a human being that
I had ever had in my motoring experience, which
began in 1930.

On 5 March, when he returned home, Mrs. Levyns
asked whether he had been involved in an accident, explaining
that on 28 February, shortly before 2 p. m. when relaxing
after lunch, she suddenly heard his voice saying clearly, "My
God! I nearly hit that child. " The events were reported by
Mr. and Mrs. Levyns and confirmed by Mr. Bouchier.

In a third type, actual events begin to duplicate an
earlier mental experience and from this the percipient infers
what will follow. The Lady Z incident (14) reported to Myers,
is of this kind. The night before a visit to a relative, planned for the next day, Lady Z dreamt that her brougham turned
up one of the streets north of Piccadilly and then that she was
herself standing on the pavement, holding her child and watch-
ing the old coachman fall off the box and hit his head on the
road. The next day when they reached Piccadilly on the
homeward journey, Lady Z noticed that the coachman was
leaning back in his seat as if the horses were pulling. As
they turned up Down Street, she suddenly remembered the
dream. She jumped out of the brougham, caught hold of the
child, and called a policeman who caught the coachman before
he fell off the box. He was saved from falling and striking
his head on the ground, and came to no harm.

This account is of interest also because it is an example of a quite large group of cases in which the subject
successfully prevented part of the precognized situation from
taking place. Lady Z predicted the probable course of future
events. The precognitive dream was responsible for her interference with the events as they were foreseen. Precognitions of this kind are a special form of inferential prediction.

In the three cases mentioned above there is no reference to the source of the operative psi elements. Research
on non-experimental cases can be described as investigations
to discover what was omitted from the reports. Something

has escaped notice or we should not still be groping for
means to control and understand the phenomena. I suggest
that the undercover agents are psi elements generated by
motivational factors. In the Levyns case, for example, the
girl may have been the subject of feelings of aggression (perhaps even self-directed or masochistic). Such wishes, transformed into a PK-like force, may be as fleeting and shallow
as those which govern the fall of a laboratory die, and, like
these, still produce results. In some instances the effective
psi elements may be triggered by a collective effort. Further work on joint agency in psi tests will have to be carried
out before this idea can be pursued.

Precognitions often consist not only in foreseeing an
event such as a death, but the event may occur in a situation which is reproduced with photographic exactness by the
veridical occurrence. The Levyns case would have been typical if the impression had come in terms of an accurate visual image of the car incident.

It is difficult to suppose that the agent's desire incor-
porates such details. Moreover, the precognitive experience
may include a setting, as a house or landscape which exists
at the time of the precognition, though (normally) it is unknown to the subject. It cannot reasonably be postulated that
this background situation is molded by a PK influence since,
as a rule, the desire expressed in the central event could
not have been in existence early enough to shape the surroundings by PK. Precognitive experiences of this kind benefit
from the feed-back mechanism which results from the interaction of the two psi fields. The psi elements from the a-
gent, which are aimed towards, say a certain person are
"corrected" by the psi field belonging to the situation selected as the scene for the event.

Concluding Remarks

This discussion is divided into two sections. In the
first I show that experimental precognition results can be understood in terms of conventional psi processes assisted by
biological mechanisms. In the second part I discuss non-
experimental cases in the light of a closer scrutiny of ESP
and PK. It is shown that the precognitive experience and the
verifying event can be the two effects of the same psi forces.

The question how psi works must be approached from

two complementary points of view.   In one, the emphasis is
on psi stimuli and influences, in the other, on the response.
Psychical researchers have neglected the stimulus object in
favour of the responding subject.   The response-orientation
has not been barren; it has led to a large body of tests which
show persistent though slight relations between ESP responses
and psychological factors.

Current concepts in the field relate to the psychological programme.   Further steps towards control and explanation will benefit from the recognition that the abilities discovered by psychical research imply extensions of the physical world.   On the theoretical side the concept of psi field
and its corollaries provides a framework within which psi
phenomena are made intelligible.   On the empirical side it
will enlarge the scope of investigation by focusing on aspects
of the psi process which have been overlooked.

REFERENCES

1. Anderson, M. "A Precognition Experiment Comparing
   Time Intervals of a Few Days and One Year."
   Journ. Parapsychol., 23, 1959, 81-9.
2. Anderson, M., Gregory, E. "A Two-Year Program of
   Tests for Clairvoyance and Precognition with a
   Class of Public School Pupils." Journ. Parapsychol.,
   23, 1959, 149-77.
3. Blousfield, W. A., Barry, H. "The Visual Imagery of
   a Lightning Calculator." Amer. Journ. of Psychol.,
   45, 1933, 353-8.
4. Carington, W. "Experiments of the Paranormal Cognition of Drawings." Proc. of the S. P. R., 46, 1940,
   34-151.
5. Carington, W. "Experiments of the Paranormal Cognition of Drawings." Proc. of the S. P. R., 46, 1941,
   277-344.
6. Dommeyer, F. C. "Some Ostensibly Precognitive
   Dreams." Journ. of the A. S. P. R., 49, 1955, 109-
   17.
7. Fahler, J. "Exploratory 'Scaled' PK Placement Tests
   with Nine College Students, With and Without Distance." Journ. Parapsychol., 22, 1958, 303.
8. Humphrey, B. M., Rhine, J. B. "A Confirmatory
   Study of Salience in Precognition Tests." Journ.
   Parapsychol., 6, 1942, 111-43.
9. Journal of Parapsychology, 24, 1960, 158.

10. Levyns, J. E. P. "Precognition of a Near Accident."
     Journ. of the S. P. R., 40, 1960, 419-21.
11. Lorenz, K. "The Role of Gestalt Perception in Animal
     and Human Behaviour." Aspects of Form, edited
     by L. L. Whyte, London, Lund Humphries, 1951.
12. Mangan, G. L. "Evidence of Displacement in a Precog-
     nition Test." Journ. Parapsychol., 19, 1955, 35-
     44.
13. Mundle, C. W. K. "The Experimental Evidence for PK
     and Precognition." Proc. of the S. P. R., 49, 1950,
     61-78.
14. Myers, F. W. H. "The Subliminal Self." Proc. of the
     S. P. R., 11, 1895, 334-93.
15. Osis, K. "A Test of the Relationship Between ESP and
     PK." Journ. Parapsychol., 17, 1953, 298-309.
16. Osis, K. "Precognition Over Time Intervals of One to
     Thirty-Three Days." Journ. Parapsychol., 19,
     1955, 82-91.
17. Pratt, J. G. "Survey of Precognition Tests with the
     Use of an Electric Calculator in Target Selection."
     Unpublished manuscript, 1957.
18. Rhine, J. B. "Evidence of Precognition in the Covaria-
     tion of Salience Ratios." Journ. Parapsychol., 6,
     1942, 111-43.
19. Rhine, J. B. "Precognition Reconsidered." Journ.
     Parapsychol., 9, 1945, 264-77.
20. Schilpp, P. A., ed. The Philosophy of C. D. Broad.
     New York, Tudor, 1961.
21. Scriven, M. "The Improbability of ESP." A public
     lecture presented at Duke University on April 13,
     1960, under the auspices of the Parapsychology
     Laboratory.
22. Simpson, G. G. Science, 131, 1960, 966-74.
23. Soal, S. G., Bateman, F. Modern Experiments in
     Telepathy. London, Faber and Faber, 1954.
24. Soal, S. G., Goldney, K. M. "Experiments in Precog-
     nitive Telepathy." Proc. of the S. P. R., 47, 1943,
     21-150.

ADDITIONAL READINGS ON PRECOGNITION

Beloff, J. and Bate, D. "An attempt to replicate the Schmidt findings." JSPR 46: 21-30 (Mar 1971).

Brier, R. M. and Tyminski, W. V. "Psi application: Part I. A preliminary attempt." JP 34: 1-25 (Mar 1970).

_____. _____. "Psi application: Part II. The majority-vote technique--analyses and observations." JP 34: 26-36 (Mar 1970).

Broad, C. D. "The notion of 'precognition.'" In Smythies, J. R. (Ed.). Science and ESP. N. Y., Humanities Press, 1967. Ch. 7. Also IJP 10: 165-96 (Sum 1968).

Buzby, D. E. "Precognition and a test of sensory perception." JP 31: 135-42 (Jun 1967).

_____. "Precognition and clairvoyance as related to the draw-a-man test." JP 32: 244-47 (Dec 1968).

_____. "Precognition and psychological variables." JP 32: 39-46 (Mar 1968).

Carpenter, J. C. "Two related studies on mood and precognition run-score variance." JASPR 32: 75-89 (Jun 1968).

Chari, C. T. K. "Precognition, probability and quantum mechanics." JASPR 66: 193-207 (Apr 1972).

_____. "W. G. Roll's PK and precognition hypotheses, an Indian philosopher's reactions." JSPR 41: 417-21 (Dec 1962).

Dobbs, H. A. C. "Time and ESP." PSPR 54: 249-361 (Pt 197, Aug 1965).

Fahler, J. and Osis, K. "Checking for awareness of hits in a precognition experiment with hypnotized subjects." JASPR 60: 340-46 (Oct 1966).

Feather, S. R. and Brier, R. "The possible effect of the checker in precognition tests." JP 32: 167-75 (Sep 1968).

Flew, A. "The challenge of precognition." In Angoff, A. and Shapin, B. (Eds.). Parapsychology and the Sciences. N. Y., Parapsychology Foundation, 1974. Pp. 174-85.

Freeman, J. "Boy-girl differences in a group precognition test." JP 27: 175-81 (Sep 1963).

Freeman, J. A. "An experiment in precognition." JP 26: 123-30 (Jun 1962).

_____. "A precognition experiment with science teachers."

JP 33: 307-10 (Dec 1969).

_____. "A precognition test with a high-school science
club." JP 28: 214-21 (Sep 1964).

_____. "The psi-differential effect in a precognition test."
JP 33: 106-12 (Sep 1969).

_____. "Sex differences and target arrangement: High-
school booklet tests of precognition." JP 30: 227-35
(Dec 1966).

Garnett, A. C. "Matter, mind, and precognition." JP 29:
19-26 (Mar 1965).

_____. "Matter, mind, and precognition. Comments."
JP 29: 185-203 (Sep 1965).

Haraldsson, E. "Subject selection in a machine precognition
test." JP 34: 182-91 (Sep 1970).

Honorton, C. "Creativity and precognition scoring level."
JP 31: 29-42 (Mar 1967).

Krippner, S., Honorton, C., and Ullman, M. "A second
precognitive dream study with Malcolm Bessent."
JASPR 66: 269-79 (Jul 1972).

Krippner, S., Ullman, M., and Honorton, C. "A precognitive
dream study with a single subject." JASPR 65: 192-
203 (Apr 1971).

Meerloo, J. A. M. "Man looks into the future: a psychological analysis of prognosy." IJP 10: 165-96 (Sum
1968).

Morris, R. "Obtaining non-random entry points: A complex
psi process." In Rhine, J. B. and Brier, R. (Eds.).
Parapsychology Today. N. Y., Citadel, 1968. Pp. 75-
86.

Mundle, C. W. K. "Does the concept of precognition make
sense?" IJP 6(2): 179-98 (Spr 1964).

Nielsen, W. "Relationships between precognition scoring
level and mood." JP 34: 93-116 (Jun 1970).

Orme, J. E. "Precognition and time." In Angoff, A. and
Shapin, B. (Eds.). Parapsychology and the Sciences.
N. Y., Parapsychology Foundation, 1974. Pp. 186-97.

Owen, A. R. G. "Time and prediction." IJP 8: 341-66
(Sum 1966).

Rhine, J. B. "The precognition of computer numbers in a
public test." JP 26: 244-51 (Dec 1962).

Roll, W. G. "The problem of precognition. Comments by
C. J. Ducasse, C. W. K. Mundle, C. Zorab, and
G. F. Dalton." JSPR 41: 173-83 (Dec 1961).

_____. "The problem of precognition. Comments on his
critics by W. G. Roll." JSPR 41: 6-15 (Mar 1963).

_____. "The problem of precognition. Notes and com-
ments evoked by C. D. Broad." JSPR 41: 225-33 (Mar
1962).

Ryzl, M. "Precognition scoring and attitude toward ESP."
JP 32: 1-8 (Mar 1968).

Sanders, M. S. "A comparison of verbal and written responses in a precognition experiment." JP 26: 23-34
(Mar 1962).

Schmeidler, G. R. "An experiment on precognitive clairvoyance. Part I. Main results." JP 28: 1-14 (Mar
1964).

_____. "An experiment on precognitive clairvoyance.
Part II. The reliability of scores." JP 28: 15-27
(Mar 1964).

_____. "An experiment on precognitive clairvoyance.
Part III. Precognition scores related to the subjects'
ways of viewing time." JP 28: 93-101 (Jun 1964).

_____. "An experiment on precognitive clairvoyance.
Part IV. Precognition scores related to creativity."
JP 28: 102-08 (Jun 1964).

_____. "An experiment on precognitive clairvoyance.
Part V. Precognition scores related to feeling of success." JP 28: 109-25 (Jun 1964).

_____. "Note on precognition with and without knowledge
of results." Psychological Reports 11: 486 (No 2,
1962).

Schmidt, H. "Precognition of a quantum process." JP 33:
99-109 (Jun 1969).

_____. "Psi tests with internally different machines."
JP 36: 222-32 (Sep 1972).

Sheargold, R. K. "An experiment in precognition." JSPR
46: 201-08 (Dec 1972).

Struckmeyer, F. R. "Precognition and the 'intervention'
paradox." JASPR 64: 320-26 (Jul 1970).

Targ, R. "Precognition in everyday life--a physical model."
In Angoff, A. and Shapin, B. (Eds.). Parapsychology
and the Sciences. N.Y., Parapsychology Foundation,
1974. Pp. 251-65.

Thouless, R. H. "Experiments on psi self-training with Dr.
Schmidt's precognitive apparatus." JSPR 46: 15-20
(Mar 1971).

Chapter 2

IS THERE A CASE FOR RETROCOGNITION?*

by W. H. W. Sabine

Retrocognition has been defined in S.P.R. literature
as "Perception or awareness of past event not known to or
within the memory of the perceiver."[1] The word is not given
in the Oxford English Dictionary or its Supplement, and so
far as I can ascertain, its first use was by F. W. H. Myers
in 1892.[2] The case is very different, it may be noted, with
the word "precognition," in illustration of which the O.E.D.
cites several passages from seventeenth-century writers who
used the word to denote the absolute foreknowledge of God.

Though the name is new, the general idea of retrocognition is ancient. The opening passage of the Book of
Genesis can, by its nature, be based on nothing but a claim
to retrocognition; and Socrates, at the beginning of the ninth
book of Plato's Republic, stresses the power of the soul of
the dreamer "to apprehend what it knoweth not, either something of what hath existed, or of what now exists, or what
will exist hereafter."

It is obvious that telepathic awareness of the kind now
almost universally accepted as proved must be regarded as
applicable to cases of apparent retrocognition of events whenever the actors concerned in those events are still living; and
therefore retrocognition, if it can be established at all, must
be established in relation to historical events--events outside
living memory.

It is equally obvious that if retrocognition is a fact,
no such limitation of its application has to be assumed: it
could, in its turn, have bearings of fundamental importance

---

*Reprinted by permission of the author and publisher from
the Journal of the American Society for Psychical Research
44: 43-64 (April 1950).

on the real nature of "telepathy." But until we know more
about extrasensory perception in general we are bound to
tread very gingerly in dealing with apparent retrocognition.

The conception of historical retrocognition, as it has
existed during the past sixty years or so, cannot be properly
evaluated merely by consideration of the very interesting but
few cases that have been published during that period. Just
as our ideas about precognition have been confused by traditional beliefs or disbeliefs in "prophecy," so is the conception
of retrocognition largely the product of a traditional background. To determine what retrocognition really is--if reality it has--requires attention to the background. There is a
certain type of visionary experience which seems to have particular relevance to the current view of retrocognition, and I
will quote two curious instances.

The first is preserved in Sir Walter Scott's Letters on
Demonology and Witchcraft (1830), and is introduced and followed by the humorous remarks with which the great and be-
loved novelist unfortunately deemed it necessary to sustain
his character as a man of "common-sense" when dealing with
the supernormal. Scott ascribes the account to "Peter" Walker, who appears to be identical with Patrick Walker. [3] The
following is the account in Walker's words:

> In the year 1686, in the months of June and July,
> many yet alive can witness that about the Crossford
> Boat, two miles beneath Lanark, especially at the
> Mains, on the water of Clyde, many people gathered
> together for several afternoons, where there were
> showers of bonnets, hats, guns, and swords, which
> covered the trees and ground; companies of men in
> arms marching in order upon the waterside; com-
> panies meeting companies, going all through other,
> and then all falling to the ground and disappearing;
> other companies immediately appeared, marching
> the same way. I went there three afternoons to-
> gether, and, as I observed, there were two-thirds
> of the people that were together saw, and a third
> saw not; and, though I could see nothing, there was
> such a fright and trembling on those that did see,
> that was discernible to all from those that saw not.
> There was a gentleman standing next to me who
> spoke as too many gentlemen and others speak, who
> said, 'A pack of damned witches and warlocks that
> have second sight! the devil ha't do I see'; and im-

mediately there was a discernible change in his
countenance. With as much fear and trembling as
any woman I saw there, he called out, 'All you that
do not see, say nothing; for I persuade you it is
matter of fact, and discernible to all that is not
stoneblind. ' And those who did see told what works
(i. e. locks) the guns had, and their length and wide-
ness, and what handles the swords had, whether
small or three-barr'd, or Highland guards, and the
closing knots of the bonnets, black or blue; and
those who did see them there, whenever they went
abroad, saw a bonnet and a sword drop in the way.

There was not necessarily any relation to the past in
this instance of mass-hallucination as it may be termed. The
marching men, the guns, bonnets, etc., are not described as
being other than contemporary with the spectators. If the
phenomena had not continued on "several afternoons" one
would conclude that some event distant in space had been seen
in mirage form. The importance of a case like this to the
development of ideas about retrocognition lies mainly in its
suggestive character; it inevitably suggests to the modern
reader the idea of seeing historic objects, and in reprinting
the story Scott ensured its universal dissemination.

The second incident I wish to quote occurred on June
28, 1812, and the scene was a piece of wild moorland in a
part of Yorkshire well known to me. The percipients concerned were two farmers named Anthony Jackson and Martin
Turner, and their experience was recorded at the time in the
county press. The following is a summary of the account,
as given by a local historian:

They saw at some distance what appeared to be a
large body of armed men in white uniform; in the
centre of which was a person of commanding aspect, dressed in scarlet. After performing various
evolutions, the whole body began to move forward in
perfect order towards the summit of the hill, passing the two terrified spectators, crouched among
the heather at a distance of one hundred yards. No
sooner had this first body, which extended four deep
over an enclosure of thirty acres, attained the hill,
than a second body, far more numerous than the
former, dressed in a uniform of a dark color, appeared and marched after the first to the top of the
hill, where they both joined, and passing down the

> opposite slope, disappeared; when a column of thick
> mist overspread the ground where they had been
> seen. The time from the first appearance of this
> strange phenomenon to the clearing away of the mist
> was about five minutes, as near as the spectators
> could judge, though they were not in a 'proper mood
> of mind' for forming correct estimates of time or
> numbers. They were men of undoubted veracity,
> and utterly incapable of fabricating such a story. [4]

It will be noticed that there is a similarity between
this experience and the Scottish one, in so far as bodies of
marching men were again involved. Moreover, the time of
year, June 28th, approximates to Walker's "June and July. "
The mist may suggest an atmospheric condition in which
some unusual type of mirage occurred. But it is very difficult to say what body of men in white uniform, commanded
by a man in scarlet, could have been miraged in the England
of 1812. On the site of this affair (which is now covered by
the waters of a reservoir) three ancient tumuli then existed,
but it is doubtful whether the farmers would have the slightest
idea of the nature of these mounds, nor is there anything in
local tradition that could have suggested to them the particular kind of impressions described above. The story of the
two men was widely circulated through being included in
Catherine Crowe's Night Side of Nature, the first edition of
which appeared in 1848.

Such (irrespective of their validity) are records of a
type which, perused by several generations, have affected
the modern idea of historical retrocognition.

Important, too, have been the numerous accounts of
individual "ghosts" in historical costume, such as apparitions
of monks seen in ruined abbeys, or of highwaymen at the
scene of their crimes. But in considering the real value
of such accounts to the evidence of retrocognition, it is necessary to distinguish between the appearance of an historic figure which acts in the present, and one which is seen acting
in the past.

Thus when the long-deceased father of the Duke of
Buckingham, clad in outmoded garments, appeared in a dream
on three successive nights to the officer of the king's ward-
robe in Windsor Castle, commanding him to warn the Duke
that his life was in danger, [5] retrocognition was not involved
as it might have been had the Duke's father been seen engaged
in some action of his own life.

Following these traditional stories has appeared the
type of historical romance, serious or humorous, in which
the hero is transported back into an earlier age. Mark
Twain's <u>A Connecticut Yankee at King Arthur's Court</u> (1889)
is a familiar example. The impression produced on the minds
of numerous readers of such works of fiction has no small
bearing on the development of recent ideas about retrocognition.

By far the most important work of imagination bearing
on retrocognition was Camille Flammarion's <u>Lumen</u>, originally published at Paris in 1873. The first <u>English</u> edition appeared in 1897, when it was stated that 52,000 copies of the
French original had then been sold.

Lumen is a man who died in 1864, but in pursuance
of a promise returns to inform his friend Quaerens of his
experiences, and in particular relates how he witnessed the
past. "I beheld in 1864 events actually present before me
which had taken place at the end of the last century." He
has the thrilling experience of seeing some incidents of the
French Revolution taking place, including the scene in the
Place de la Concorde just after the execution of Louis XVI.
Expressed very briefly, the explanation is that Lumen has
arrived at a star so distant from the earth that the light reflected from the earth in 1793 is only reaching the star seventy years later. Nothing magical, but a telescopic instrument
of immense power enables the star inhabitants to see the
earth events of seventy years earlier.

Flammarion's beautiful blending of imagination with
science never fails to hold its readers. Whereas a mere
romance makes its time-transported hero actually participate
in historic events (ignoring the physical effects he thus produces) <u>Lumen</u> falls into no such fantasy. The past events are
viewed, but in no sense participated in or altered by the view-
er. The importance of <u>Lumen</u> to later theories about retrocognition and precognition is evident to its reader.

We now arrive at the first case of apparent historical
retrocognition of which modern psychical research has taken
notice, namely, the case of "Miss A."

The identity of Miss A does not seem ever to have
been revealed to the public. 6 At the time when her published
experiences took place she was described as being "a young
lady." It appears from the narratives that she was closely

associated with the Countess of Radnor, who attested most of her experiences; and identity of Miss A was certainly known to F. W. H. Myers and probably to other contemporary members of the S. P. R.

It was Myers who, at p. 498 of Vol. VIII of the Proceedings, published "Case III--Miss A," and in the course of his commentary used the word "retrocognition" for, apparently, the first time. Certainly retrocognition seems a very appropriate word to apply to this account by Miss A (p. 499):

"I saw a large modern room change into the likeness (as shown afterwards by independent record) of what it was 200 years ago; and I saw persons in it who apparently belonged to that date." Lady Radnor, in attesting the above, noted that the room in question was the Long Parlour at Longford, which in 1670 was used as a chapel. Longford Castle, near Salisbury, was the home of Lord and Lady Radnor.

On August 17, 1889, Miss A had an experience in Salisbury Cathedral which some months later was recounted by Lady Radnor to Sir Joseph Barnby, the musician. This is what Sir Joseph told Myers (p. 504):

Miss A's statement was to the effect that she had seen vast processions of gorgeously apparelled Catholic ecclesiastics with jewelled crosses carried before them, gorgeous canopies and baldachinos held over them and clouds of incense filling the place. Amongst the dignitaries was one who came near them and gazed at them with a singularly sad expression of countenance. On being asked why he looked so sad, he said [the reply, it appears later, was obtained by automatic mirror-writing]: 'I have been a great sinner. I was greatly responsible for the beheading of Anne Boleyn. What adds to the sadness of it, her father and I were boys together, and our homes were in close proximity to each other.' On being asked his name, he said: 'My name is John Longland.' On being further questioned he replied: 'Mr. Barnby's music brought me here. I often hear it in Eton Chapel.'

Investigation showed that John Longland had been Dean of Salisbury in Henry VIII's reign, and also that his body had been buried in Eton College Chapel, though this fact was not

locally known because the brass which covered the tomb had
been destroyed by an act of vandalism in the seventeenth century.

Miss A also saw in the Cathedral a monk in a brown
gown, and on a third occasion the ceremony of the induction
of a seventeenth-century bishop, Brian Duppa. At Longford
Castle, this time in the crystal, she saw a carved fireplace,
secret passage, etc. By the aid of the crystal Miss A was
able to obtain many other apparently retrocognitive scenes.
In all the cases mentioned above, the details were subsequent-
ly verified in books or documents which it is most improbable that Miss A could have seen previously. The full details
will be found in the volume already named.

In the case of Miss A, therefore, it will be recognized
that the idea of historical retrocognition had come to full
flower.

In Vol. XI, p. 338 of Proceedings Myers again took
up the subject of retrocognition, contrasting it with precognition in the following words: "On the one side there is
retrocognition, or knowledge of the past, extending back beyond the reach of our ordinary memory; on the other side
there is precognition, or knowledge of the future, extending
onwards beyond the scope of our ordinary inference."

As was logical, Myers sought to apply the idea of
retrocognition to cases of extra-normal knowledge of events
in the recent past, participants in which were still living.
He cannot be said to have been successful, for all the cases
in Vol. XI are capable of being attributed to telepathy/clair-
voyance. Myers was evidently aware of this, and near the
end of his chapter he speaks of "true retrocognitions involving scenes and histories in which men long departed have
played their part."

In his Human Personality (1903), Myers repeated several of the Miss A cases, but added no new matter, and it
was not until the publication in 1911 of An Adventure that
visionary retrocognition again came to the fore. This book
made an enormous sensation at the time of its publication,
not only because of its contents, but because the integrity of
the authors was guaranteed by the publishers, Macmillan and
Company, London.

The authors of An Adventure were given in 1911 as

"Elizabeth Morison" and "Frances Lamont," acknowledged
pseudonyms which were abandoned in the fourth edition, published in 1931. [7] The real names of the authors, with important particulars respecting them, were:

> Miss Charlotte Anne Elizabeth Moberly.
> Born 1846. Died 1937. 7th daughter of Dr. George
> Moberly, Head Master of Winchester, later Bishop
> of Salisbury (1869-85). Among her brothers and
> brothers-in-law were 4 heads of schools or colleges,
> and 2 Bishops. In 1886 she became Principal of
> St. Hugh's College, Oxford.
> Miss Eleanor F. Jourdain. Born ? Died
> 1924. Daughter of the Rev. Francis Jourdain.
> Head of a girls' school at Watford. Later an M. A.
> of Oxford, and a Doctor of the University of Paris.
> Distinguished for learning, music, and knowledge of
> the French language. Became Vice-Principal to
> Miss Moberly at St. Hugh's College, Oxford.

On the afternoon of Saturday, August 10, 1901, these
two ladies were visiting Versailles as part of a sight-seeing
holiday in Paris and environs. The retrocognitive experiences which apparently befell them in the grounds of the Petit
Trianon fitted into their surroundings in such a way that neither lady passed any comment at the time, and it was only a
week later that they suddenly spoke of the matter and came
to realize that something very mysterious indeed had happened
to them. Their entire book, An Adventure, needs to be read
to evaluate their story, and to appreciate their scholarly and
able commentary. The following extract from Miss Jourdain's
contribution gives an idea of the nature of the experiences
themselves:

> We went on in the direction of the Petit Trianon,
> but just before reaching what we knew afterwards
> to be the main entrance I saw a gate leading to a
> path cut deep below the level of the ground above,
> and as the way was open and had the look of an
> entrance that was used, I said: 'Shall we try this
> path? it must lead to the house,' and we followed
> it. [8] To our right we saw some farm-buildings
> looking empty and deserted; implements (among oth-
> ers a plough) were lying about; we looked in, but
> saw no one. The impression was saddening, but
> it was not until we reached the crest of the rising
> ground where there was a garden that I began to feel

as if we had lost our way, and as if something
were wrong. There were two men there in official
dress (greenish in colour), with something in their
hands; it might have been a staff. A wheelbarrow
and some other gardening tools were near them.
They told us, in answer to my enquiry, to go
straight on. I remember repeating my question,
because they answered in a seemingly casual and
mechanical way, but only got the same answer in
the same manner. As we were standing there I
saw to the right of us a detached solidly-built cottage, with stone steps at the door. A woman and
a girl were standing at the doorway, and I particularly noticed their unusual dress; both wore white
kerchiefs tucked into the bodice, and the girl's
dress, though she looked 13 or 14 only, was down
to her ankles. The woman was passing a jug to
the girl, who wore a close white cap. [9]

Now neither the plough, nor the two men in official
dress, nor the solidly built cottage, nor the woman and girl
had any physical existence in 1901; and the same comment
applies to many other persons and objects seen in the grounds
of the Petit Trianon while the two women were walking slowly
through them, talking of friends in England and similar matters, each noticing but concealing from the other a feeling
of depression, even of "heavy dreaminess."

Prolonged research in the French national archives
proved to the satisfaction of Miss Moberly and Miss Jourdain
that the people and things they saw, and which had no physical existence in 1901, had all existed in or about the year
1789. Their case is supported not only by evidence drawn
from rare printed books, engravings, and charts, but from
MS records and account books, sometimes covered with dust
and apparently unopened for a century. The minutest details
were investigated, extending even to the personal appearance
and pronunciation of the persons spoken to. [10]

The experiences in the grounds of the Petit Trianon
culminated when one of the visitors, Miss Moberly, saw a
fair-haired lady sitting close to the house in a dress which,
as subsequent researches showed, corresponded exactly to a
dress belonging to the Queen, which her modiste repaired in
1789. Miss Jourdain, though walking at Miss Moberly's side,
did not see this lady. Similarly Miss Moberly had not seen
several things noted by Miss Jourdain.

The hallucinatory period (as I think it must be termed)
concluded when a young man, who looked "inquisitively a-
mused," showed the two visitors out of the garden through
what was in 1901, and for long before, a solid stone wall.
An old chart, however, reveals that in the Revolutionary period a roadway had existed at that point.

An Adventure was reviewed at length in the Proceedings of the S. P. R. (Vol. XXV, pp. 353-360). The review
was entirely unfavorable to the authors' claims. 11 Whether
the review was written by Professor F. C. S. Schiller, whose
name appears at the foot of the immediately following review,
or by Mrs. Henry Sidgwick, as has been stated elsewhere, I
have not been able to determine. Much irony was directed
at the authors' theory of an "act of memory," or survival of
Marie Antoinette's thoughts, a theory which they later discarded. Of course, the implied passing through the stone
wall was indicated as conclusive evidence of delusion (see
Footnote 27).

The replies made to the two ladies by various officials,
and especially the "inquisitive smiles" and "peculiar smiles"
directed at them, were cited as proving that they were not
witnesses of true historical scenes, which ought to have re-
enacted themselves without taking any notice of the seers; nor
could these circumstances be reconciled with participation in
the mind of the Queen.

These adverse criticisms, together with many others,
were repeatedly made without causing the authors to modify
any statement which they had put forward as factual. Finally,
in 1938, just after the death of Miss Moberly at over ninety
years of age, J. R. Sturge-Whiting published The Mystery of
Versailles, a critical examination of the whole account, largely based upon a close study of the locale made by Mr. Sturge-
Whiting in person. His conclusion was that An Adventure, so
far as concerned its supernormal claims, was throughout a
"pathetic illusion." But Mr. Sturge-Whiting treated his subject from a purely external point of view. He seems to have
assumed that if he could find any grounds for saying that what
the claimants believed to have been objective may not have
been objective, they must be convicted of illusion; but he
showed little or no awareness of those subjective experiences
which are classified under the general head of "extrasensory
perception," and which psychical and parapsychological researches have shown to be no illusions but mental processes
as real as they are inexplicable.

Most of that which Miss Moberly and Miss Jourdain recounted is in accord with their having had visions, hallucinations, or waking dreams of the type generally associated with the Highlanders and some other northern peoples, but which have been recorded in the annals of every nation under the sun.[12] That these visual experiences are purely subjective is highly probable, and the records of the psychical research societies show that in many cases they have been proved to be one of the forms under which telepathy, clairvoyance, and precognition manifest to the conscious mind. Readers of this Journal are familiar with the extent of the evidence to that effect, and it is hardly necessary to stress the point here.

Because of its possible bearing on retrocognition, however, and because the experience, like that claimed by Miss Moberly and Miss Jourdain, befell more than one person at the same time, I may briefly cite an interesting case from the records of the S. P. R. In W. H. Salter's Ghosts and Apparitions[13] we read that on a sunny afternoon in December, 1897, three sisters aged 21, 18, and 12 saw an apparition near the old manor house in which they lived, and six and a half years later the eldest and the youngest wrote independent accounts of it, while their mother wrote a third account based on what the second sister had told her. The girls had seen a man by an oak tree in a fence, but their dog growled and refused to approach the spot.

> 'Walking closer,' recorded the youngest sister, 'I saw that it was a man, hanging apparently from an oak tree in front of some railings over a ditch. He was dressed in brown, rather brighter than the colour of brown holland; he did not seem to have a regular coat, but more of a loose blouse. One thing I most distinctly recall is his heavy clumsy boots. His head hung forward, and the arms dropped forward too. Coming within about 15 yards I saw the shadow of the railings through him, one bar across the shoulders, one bar about his waist, and one almost at his knees, quite distinct but faint. I have a remembrance of a big, very black shadow in the background. At about 15 yards the whole thing disappeared suddenly. We went to the railing and looked over a clear field beyond, which would give no possible cover to anyone trying to hide. Walking back by where we had first seen it we saw nothing but an oak tree by railings in a fence. When I

saw it my only feeling, I remember, was intense
curiosity to see what it was--one seemed impelled
to go forward; afterwards, sickening terror. [7]

Now this experience may or may not have been precisely of the same character as that of Miss Moberly and
Miss Jourdain, but the fact that it was shared by three young
girls walking across familiar fields near their own home may
well suggest to the critic that he had better shift his ground
from kindly pity for the "pathetic illusion" of two middle-aged
spinsters sightseeing in Paris!

The Trianon couple were as subject to occasional illusion as other people. In the matter of the position of rocks,
etc., they may have been misled by their recollections of a
complicated terrain. But unless we are going to allege (which
no one ever has done) that they published, not a mere literary
hoax, but an untrue record sustained to their last days, then
their testimony cannot be disposed of by reiterating that at
every point they substituted imagination for fact; that, for example, despite their learning, they were so stupid as to trans-
mute two ordinary gardeners of 1901 into officials of the
eighteenth century wearing uniforms and three-cornered hats.

Did not the behavior of these officials indicate their
dream-like character? In dreams visual images are more
frequent than auditory; and dream people, if not silent, may
speak briefly, sometimes evasively. So the minds that created the two officials could put into their mouths only mechanical responses of little utility. Had normal invention been at
work, Miss Jourdain's fluent French could have supplied appropriate "evidential" answers.

Moreover, the circumstances in which An Adventure
came to be written do not require the dream theory to be
confined to the possibility of an extraordinarily prolonged
"waking dream" of the kind to which allusion has been made.
Since the two women exchanged no comment on the experience until a week later, [14] a week which was fully occupied
with other matters, the possibility arises that the recollection
of the visit to the Petit Trianon had become insidiously blended with the recollection of a telepathic dream while asleep,
one embodying clairvoyant and/or precognitive images. This
dream may have taken place the night before the visit, and
something of its hidden springs may perhaps be gathered
from the Baedeker guide to which reference was made in footnote 8, p. 49. The description of the Petit Trianon in the

guide is very brief. Only ten lines are in large type, including this passage:

> A visit should be paid to the Jardin du Petit Tria-
> non, which is laid out in the English style and con-
> tains some fine exotic trees, an artificial lake, a
> 'Temple of Love,' and a 'Hamlet' of nine or ten
> rustic cottages, where the court ladies played at
> rustic life.

When the eye of the English-speaking reader lights on
the word 'Hamlet' (so printed), it suggests to him the tragedy,
although a moment later he realizes that the celebrated
Hameau is intended. But an image of Hamlet has been called
up, a picture of the solitary and melancholy man in conjunction with the "Temple of Love." Does this account for the
sinister cloaked figure, seen by the two women, sitting close
to the pillared "kiosk"? All who have had personal experience of the precognitive dream know that such images may
arise before the physical sense experience as well as after.
The physical sense experience here concerned was the reading of the above-quoted passage, and it makes little difference
to the argument whether the women read that part of the guide
the previous evening or during the visit itself.

What follows in their account is surely very significant
to any dream theory. This definitely "bad man" who is a-
waiting the women in a lonely spot has to be escaped from.
So--as though in response to the wish--on the scene runs the
young and handsome page, quite an incipient story-book hero,
and the two ladies are saved from a most disagreeable encounter. Nothing unusual in that if it was all a dream!
What is unusual--perhaps unique so far as accurate reporting
goes--is that these dream figures and their surroundings
should be clothed with characteristics built from the results
of future historical research.

Now let us look at what Miss Moberly and Miss Jourdain said of themselves in the course of their commentary:

> One of us [Miss Jourdain] has to own to having
> powers of second sight, etc., deliberately unde-
> veloped, and there are psychical gifts in her fam-
> ily. She comes of a Huguenot stock. The other
> [Miss Moberly] is one of a large and cheerful party,
> being the seventh daughter and of a seventh son;
> her mother and grandmother were entirely Scotch,

and both possessed powers of premonition accompanied by vision. Her family has always been sensitive to ghost stories in general, but mercilessly
critical of particular ones of a certain type. [15]

Add to this self-revelation that Miss Moberly's father
was Bishop of Salisbury till 1885, and that it was only a few
years later that Miss A had, in Salisbury Cathedral and near
it, those vivid and apparently retrocognitive visions which
Myers recorded and published in 1892. Miss Moberly can
scarcely have been ignorant of the fact that such remarkable
claims had been made publicly and associated with a Cathedral so familiar to her.

A further circumstance which may be no less significant is that it was in 1897, just four years before the experiences at the Petit Trianon, that the English translation appeared of Flammarion's Lumen. It will be recalled that the
initial episode in this work is one in which Lumen sees the
French Revolution in progress seventy years after it has happened. So far as concerns Miss Jourdain, who was fluent in
the French language, she may have read the French original
long before 1897.

It seems, therefore, a reasonable conclusion that the
women were not unacquainted, when the Trianon experience
occurred, with the idea that seeing the past might be possible.

A very important statement bearing on this subject has
been made public since Miss Moberly died in 1937. It is to
be found in Four Victorian Ladies of Wiltshire[16] by Edith
Olivier, a close friend of Miss Moberly, and an advocate of
her cause in the Trianon case. "There exist," states Miss
Olivier, "several other stories of Anne Moberly's second sight
which are less generally known." For the good reason that
there would be little evidential value in stories written down
some years after the subject's death, Miss Olivier confines
herself to two cases. The first she heard from Miss Moberly's lips, but bases it also on "a written account of it from
a member of her [Miss Moberly's] family." This merits a
brief outline.

When visiting the picture gallery of the Paris Louvre
in 1913, Miss Moberly saw "a tall, commanding, yet grace-
ful man. He must have been of unusual height, for he equalled
the height of a child sitting on its father's shoulder close by
in the crowd. The man had a small golden coronal on his

head, and wore a loose toga-like dress of some bright colour.
I looked at him and he looked at me. Our eyes literally
seemed to meet. It was not a face or a figure to forget;
for his whole bearing was one of unusual nobility, and grace-
fulness. He looked from side to side, as though taking it
for granted that he was being noticed."

None of the officials had seen the man, despite his
height, etc., and Miss Moberly inferred he must have been
an apparition. First she thought of Charlemagne, but discovered "that the pattern of the toga, the shape of the coronal, and the rather unusual way in which the straps of the
sandals were wound round the leg, all indicated a Roman emperor of the fourth century." Her researches seem to have
been as thorough as those in the Trianon case. Medallions,
etc., of Constantine the Great were found to resemble the
man. Moreover, a ceremonial Roman road had passed over
the site of that part of the Louvre, and Constantine is said
to have used it in procession on two known occasions.

The second account is more important because it is
transcribed from Miss Moberly's own record, written immediately after the initial experience, which took place, as she
particularly notes, "between sleeping and waking." The entire
record is too long to be quoted in full, but the following gives
an adequate idea of its nature.

'As I have never seen Cambridge,' wrote Miss Moberly, 'I mean to go there this week. We[17] planned
this on Saturday, June 21st, and yesterday, June
23rd, between sleeping and waking in the early
morning, I saw a vivid picture of an open space
with some buildings, which I called King's College,
though I have no doubt that it was entirely unlike
the real King's College.... We went to this chapel
(which was small) and at the door was a man in
some sort of dark cassock, who told us that we
could go in. A funeral service in Latin was just
coming to an end, and I noticed among the congre-
gation of dark-gowned men, scarlet and purple robes,
as well as white surplices. As the service was
nearly over we went outside to see the procession
pass ... first, some acolytes and censer boys
came out, then a few clerics, followed by two car-
dinals (?) in scarlet; one was tall, and had white
lace on the skirt and the undress cap. He was
pompous and seemed important. The other suggest-

ed a university professor.... The coffin was more
square and seemed more ornamented than one sees
to-day. There was some coloured painting on it,
and on the end where the feet would be was the
name: ARNOLPHUS M_____ I could see no more.
Behind it came some men in dark gowns, and last
of all a group of tall thin women in white woolly
cassock-like skirts, with dark pointed hoods over
their heads. I thought one of them (who had an old
face) might have been the mother. The procession
wound from the chapel ... towards the little church-
yard, which sloped considerably away.... Afterwards I heard someone say that the second word on
the coffin was "Magister." Written June 24, 1913.'

When Miss Moberly arrived in Cambridge she found
that the present buildings of King's College in no way suggested those in her vision. Enquiries about a graveyard, however, elicited the fact that one belonging to the church of
Saint John the Baptist (long disappeared) had extended from
the centre of the nave of the present King's College Chapel
to Clare College on sloping ground. An old map showed
buildings in the position of those seen in the dream. Miss
Moberly thought these may have been in connection with a
Carmelite monastery established nearby towards the end of
the thirteenth century, and wondered whether her dream "women" were not really white friars. The heads of national
groups of this Order were termed "Magister," and were under
the General of the Order. One who died a General after having been Magister "was named Radulphus which is another
version of Arnolphus. 18 He was renowned as a very holy
man. Celestial lights were seen over his head. His body
was sent to England for burial in 1277, but it was not known
where it was laid. The Carmelites' habit, regularly black
with a white hood, was changed for a time in the latter part
of the thirteenth century to be white with a black hood, like
the figures in the procession. "

The foregoing account by Miss Moberly, even in the
abbreviated form in which I have had to quote it, will probably be deemed a very careful one, devoid of exaggerated
claims or suppositions. It differs from the Trianon experience in several important respects: it did not take place on
the actual historic scene assigned to it; it was not shared;
and the percipient was aware of the unusual nature of her experience. Whether the fact that it occurred "between sleeping
and waking" is also a point of difference it would be very en-
lightening to know for certain.

In considering all the cases[19] it is hard to see any indication that other than purely subjective creations of the mind
are involved, images built up not only from unconscious
knowledge acquired since infancy in environments impregnated
with historical associations, but also from extra-normal awareness of the sources of additional knowledge. These apparently retrocognitive visions or dreams seem to owe their general character and direction to the normally acquired contents
of the percipients' minds, but at the same time they precog-
nize the results of future research, which research would not
have been undertaken but for the visions. That they contain
also, or alternatively, a truly retrocognitive element must, I
think, remain an open question.

Besides the comparatively rare visual form there is
the much more frequent form of apparent extra-normal knowledge of the historic past occurring in automatic writings or
oral statements which purport to be inspired by discarnate
personalities. One of the best known cases of this kind, that
of "Patience Worth," was discussed recently in the Journal of
the A. S. P. R. [20] by Mr. C. W. Clowe, who propounded a theory of hereditary memory to explain the character of the writings produced. In the course of his discussion Mr. Clowe
put this very important question: "Excepting those who were
known in this life and who purport to be communicating with
us through mediums, has any soi-disant control in the history of psychic research furnished details of his or her earth-
ly life which could be or have been investigated and found correct?"

As some measure of reply to that question I would
mention the records contained in a book called Voices From
Another World, [21] by F. Gurtis, a German writer whose real
name was Willibald Franke. Several of the sixty-four communications which he recorded as purporting to come from
historical characters, mostly obscure or forgotten, were
proved correct in names and dates when the public records
were searched. It is interesting to note in this connection
that, despite the title of his book (probably not his own
choice), Franke was not a spiritualist, and indeed emphati-
cally asserted that "intercourse with the spirit world does
not take place."

Franke obtained the writings by means of the psychograph, an arrangement having some general resemblance to
the ouija board, and controlled by several sitters at the same
time. The following is a fair specimen of the results obtained, the words written by the psychograph being [underlined]:

At this sitting, in addition to one of our artist
friends who frequently joined us in our experiments,
we had with us a poet, Tyrolese by birth, and at
that time resident in the Rhine district.

'Will you tell us a good deal to-day?'
Yes.

'Who is it?'
Prosper von Langendorf.

'From what part?'
Wied, Neuwied.

'When did you live?'
1584, the year of grace 1584.

'Can you talk to us in verse?'
From the serpent I was forced to escape,
Both the camp and the court left behind;
Then my ermine and silk were exchanged,
Through the world in monk's habit I ranged,
But God's peace nowhere did I find.
Through the fields and the meadows I wandered,
(Oh maiden, so lovely and dear!)
At last now mine eyes God hath opened,
He has ta'en me to dwell with Him here.

The poet above mentioned, whose first experience
of the psychograph it was, desiring to test how far
the communications might be influenced by his own
subconscious (which the announcement of Neuwied as
the place of origin seemed to render likely), now
left the instrument and went to a distant corner of
the room, asking what it was that he was writing
at the moment. The answer came:
Light still is light, e'en when thou art blind.

The astonished questioner admitted that although he
had left the psychograph, there was indeed still
some connection, for the book he had begun (which,
however, was not published after all), was to be
called 'The Light of the Seas.' To none of those
present was this title, or even the intention of the
writer, known. He now took his place at the table
again, and the following statement appeared:

Martinus said, Be not a fool; write German and

love English.

'Where did you live?'
Erdfurth [the old spelling of Erfurt], Wittenberg,
Worms, Wartburg are celebrated, where Martinus
Lutherus rested, God honours him.

We imagined that Prosper von Langendorf had finished speaking, and asked for further information
about him.

Hang the washing in the sun and don't ... it!

'Why are you so coarse?'
Remember my disastrous life and forgive me!

'How was it disastrous?'
Thirty years of war and misfortune.

'When did you die?'
I died in February 1584. Frederick built the town
of Neuwied, God gave me life in 1584 and granted
me rest in 1654. Agnes my lovely lass, the sweet
maid of Cologne seduced me with her charms. Oh
pretty one, thy crimson gown. --God bless thee!
Prosper is putting on his armour.

'What do you mean by that?'
The evening glow and the roses shine like her crimson gown.

The contradiction in the date of birth must be regarded rather as the correction of a slip in speaking. Since our friend living at that time in the
Rhine province was not sure when Neuwied was
founded, we looked the matter up and discovered
that in 1653 Count Friedrich von Wied founded the
town in place of Langendorf which had been laid
waste. This fact (hitherto unknown to any of the
participants in the sitting) imparted by Prosper von
Langendorf therefore proved to be correct, and his
name too was interesting from the information that
on the site of the present Neuwied there had formerly been a place called Langendorf, which was then
in ruins. Whether a race of nobles had existed,
and this Prosper Langendorf was a scion thereof,
or whether we are meant to read the name as

Prosper from Langendorf, we have no means of as-
certaining. 22

Franke came to the conclusion that the supposed communications originated in the subconscious minds of the sitters, with the important addition (here agreeing in general
with Mr. Clowe's theory in the case of Patience Worth) that
the subconsciousness (Unterbewusstsein) must include some
kind of inherited memory. He held that the historical knowledge, linguistic endowments, and poetic capabilities displayed
in the productions of the psychograph hardly admitted of any
other explanation. Such a theory of inherited memory, besides its disregard of current biological teaching, must take
into account the memories of deceased ancestors from the
remotest times. During only the past 400 years each person
now living may be able to count some 8,000 deceased ancestors (less according to the extent of common ancestry shared
by the couples), and this figure swells to millions when several more centuries are added. It is hardly logical to contend that hereditary transmission of this vast field of memory
is proved by historical statements which, despite Franke's
opinion, do admit of other explanations. Remarkable as they
are, they yet do not display that degree of knowledge of foreign and ancient languages, of dialects, customs, and so forth,
which the theory of the hereditary transmission of memory
requires.

The invention of a discarnate personality might be
thought to be a preferable theory if really satisfactory evidence were given of historical knowledge not contained in
books, records, or living minds. One kind of such evidence
might be in this order. Some years ago I knew an archaeologist who had made a special study of "Roman Triple Vases."
He published a monograph discussing the possible uses to
which the Romans may have put these three-necked vases,
but he could come to no definite conclusion on that point.
Yet in the days of ancient Rome the vases were so common
that everyone must have known their use. If spirit communi-
cators were to clear up even small problems of this kind we
should have excellent evidence of their authenticity. It is true
that the evidence would not be final, since there are hardly
any circumstances to cover which some aspect of extrasensory
perception cannot be brought in. For example, in the above
hypothetic case it could be said that some other archaeologist
may have solved the problem, and though he may have written
nothing down, his mind would be open to the telepathic perception of the seer or medium. None the less, if the solu-

tion of historic problems was repeatedly due to communications ascribed to spirits, if gaps in the archives were filled (instead of the archives merely being confirmed), the case for that ascription would be immensely stronger than it now is.

But when we contrast the psychographic writings, writings which do not evade any aspect of life, with the rather school-story-book type of visions of the English ladies mentioned above, both the spirit hypothesis and that of inherited memory seem equally unsatisfactory. Do not the beheaded queens, Anne Boleyn and Marie Antoinette, perhaps represent a lingering schoolgirl sentimentality, and the sweet maid of Cologne the more masculine outlook? If the mind of a Prosper von Langendorf could reveal itself through artists and poets, why not through schoolmistresses on vacation, or young lady guests in ancient castles? One may fairly assume that everyone has a wide assortment as well as a vast number of ancestors. As against this criticism it may reasonably be contended that the mind will, consciously or unconsciously, act as a filter of the contents of the subconscious, rejecting whatever the individual's ideas of the bienséances may judge unfitting.

The further suggestion may be made that what is involved is not memory in the form of physically transmitted effects on the brain cells, but telepathy from one generation to another. The mental impressions of a couple living in 1584 telepathically transmitted to (or perceived by) their children, and by those children to their children, etc., would explain knowledge of the past existing in the subconscious of a living person without assumptions which orthodox biological science denies. Indeed, such a telepathic theory might, in its turn, have a vital bearing on the evolution of species.

Besides the possibilities of (1) communication from the spirits of deceased people, (2) the possession of memories inherited from ancestors, and (3) parent-child telepathy, there are several other theories which may be considered to account for knowledge of the past, including apparent retrocognition. They are: (4) Memory of previous lives (i. e., through reincarnation, not inherited memory); (5) Telepathic awareness of historical knowledge in the minds of living people (apart from parents); (6) Clairvoyant awareness of documents and books; (7) Precognition of the experience of acquiring the information when the search comes to be undertaken; (8) Observation from another dimension.

It is not necessary to comment here on theories 4 to 7, because, like the preceding three, in purporting to account for extra-normal knowledge of the past they dispense with any need for such a word as "retrocognition." Proof of theory 8 would alone sustain retrocognition in the sense in which Myers used the word in 1892. Retrocognition means that the percipient, at the present time, and not through his own or anyone else's memory, or by means of any existing record has extra-normal awareness of the past, whether it takes the vivid visual form attributed to Miss A or some other form. Retrocognition, in fact, is proposed as the opposite of precognition.

The existing view of precognition is that it is extra-normal awareness of a future event. On the hypothesis that, relatively, all future events exist as present events to other-dimensional observers, it is logical to make the same assumption about past events. Indeed, the acceptance of precognition in such a sense may be said absolutely to entail a corresponding theory of retrocognition.

Of the greatest importance, therefore, to the problem of retrocognition is the true nature of precognition. In Second Sight in Daily Life[23] I have advanced reasons for the view that precognition is "Perception or awareness, not attributable to information or rational inference, which corresponds to the future sense perception of the subject, or of another person." It is the coming individual experience which is precognized, and not the event. Has not this elementary truth been overlooked in the fascination of attempts to link the problems of the mind with the problems of astrophysics?

Individual experience of an event may consist of personal participation in it, hearing news of it, seeing a film or photograph of it, and so on. The impressions made on two persons by the same event are never the same. This is true even when both are direct witnesses of the event, but for the present purpose it is only necessary to envisage a case in which A is a direct witness of an event, and B hears of it by a verbal message. The two sets of mental images thus arising will obviously be entirely different from each other, even though embodying some common general idea such as, "a car has collided with a wall."

The important point here is that any precognition which each man may have had of his coming experience corresponds to that experience, not to the experience of the other man, nor to any "event." An analysis of each man's dream, or other precognitive experience, will show that it relates to his coming physical sense perception, and to concepts arising therefrom peculiar to his mind, and including his errors and misunderstandings. No evidence will be found of extra-normal perception unrelated to physical sense perception, nothing that betokens a "reaching out" to cognize a "future event."

Precognition thus appears to be a "memory before-hand," as strictly individual as ordinary memory. Its individuality is not lessened by the almost certain fact of tele-pathic awareness of the precognition in other minds.

If this view is correct, [24] if precognition is "memory beforehand," the place which was allotted to retrocognition is one that is already occupied by ordinary memory, conscious and unconscious. There is our memory of the past, and our "memory" of the future--our individual past and our individual future.

Though the word "retrocognition" is not applicable to the individual memory of the past, it would be possible to apply it to individual access to a universal memory, one in which are stored all the mental impressions of all the minds of all time. Such a collective memory would amount to the permanent existence of all past events that had been known to any mind, and access to such a memory would be as effective retrocognition as perception of the event itself. The existence of an "akashic record" of past events is asserted by modern occultism, but evidence such as psychical research requires has not, so far as I am aware, been made public.

As was remarked at the outset of this article we are not justified in classifying as retrocognitive, cases of the pos-session or acquisition of normally inexplicable knowledge of the past so long as any person is living who has the knowledge by normal means. Nor can we regard as conclusive any cases of apparent historic retrocognition when the information concerned exists in books, manuscripts, hidden articles, bur-ied foundations of buildings, and so on. Such instances are attributable to forms or aspects of extra-normal cognition which have been accepted as conclusively proven by many qualified investigators.

Thus the hallucinatory visions of Miss A, and of Miss Moberly and Miss Jourdain, did not contain any information not ascribable to clairvoyant awareness of documents and books, and/or precognition of the coming experience of looking them up. Miss A saw in Salisbury Cathedral "a monk, dressed in dull sort of muddy brown." An engraving of a Franciscan which she and Lady Radnor found afterwards in Steven's Continuation of Dugdale's Monasticon corresponded exactly with what Miss A had seen.25 Likewise, Miss Moberly saw Marie Antoinette in a green silk bodice, and seven years later she and Miss Jourdain found a colored illustration of the bodice in De Reiset's Modes et Usages, accompanied by the Queen's measurements.26 Effectively, therefore, the content of the visions was existing in a normal sense at the time of the visions.

It is evident that the difficulty which confronts us in the case of apparent retrocognition is similar to and even greater than that presented by apparent spirit communications. Precisely what information of the past could we accept as satisfactory?

If we were told that a retrocognitive vision revealed that the crew of the Marie Céleste had been carried off by pirates and murdered, how should we know whether it was true? And if we arrived at proofs as a result of the vision, could it not be said that those proofs had already been discovered by extrasensory perception which then manifested itself in the form of the vision? Again, if some lost art of manufacture were recovered, or if some mysterious hieroglyphics were explained by seeming retrocognition, it might be held that the explanation would rather be found in extrasensory awareness of the minds of living persons who had been engrossed by the problems in question, and whose unconscious minds had arrived at the solutions.

These difficulties serve to reinforce the need to consider anew whether there is a prima-facie case for retrocognition. It was propounded as a supposed necessary corollary of the existence of precognition. But, as indicated above, the necessity depends upon the view taken of the nature of precognition.

Since the present writer believes that the real nature of precognition gives no support to the view that it arises from perception of a physical future event existing at the time of the precognition, he is bound to conclude that the place assigned to the corresponding theory of retrocognition is already occupied by the individual memory.

NOTES

1. E. G., <u>Foreknowledge</u>, by H. F. Saltmarsh, G. Bell &
   Sons, London, 1938.
2. Proc. S. P. R., Vol. VIII, 1892, p. 501.
3. Scott's reference is "Walker's <u>Lives</u>, Edinburgh, 1827,
   Vol. I, p. xxxvi." Patrick Walker published lives
   of Peden, Cargill, and other Presbyterian martyrs
   between 1727 and 1732. These were collected and
   republished at Edinburgh in 1827 as <u>Biographia Pres-</u>
   <u>byteriana</u>. The B. M. Catalogue shows an <u>1800</u>
   <u>chapbook</u> edition of a life of Cargill by Peter Walker; this may indicate that the same Walker was
   known by both Christian names.
4. <u>History of Harrogate and the Forest of Knaresborough</u>,
   by William Grainge, 1871, p. 348.
5. <u>History of the Rebellion and Civil Wars in England</u>, by
   Edward, Earl of Clarendon, 1674, Book 1.
6. Mr. G. N. M. Tyrrell informs me that his identification
   of Miss A with Miss A. Goodrich-Freer (<u>Science</u>
   <u>and Psychical Phenomena</u>, p. 51) was a slip resulting from the confusing use of initials, and that
   Miss A was not Miss Goodrich-Freer. The latter's
   pseudonym was "Miss X." In Vol. VIII of the
   S. P. R. Proc. Myers refers (p. 484) to "Case II--
   Miss X," and later (p. 498) to "Case III--Miss A."
   In Vol. VI of the <u>Journal of the S. P. R.</u>, p. 3, he
   names Miss X and Miss A in the same sentence as
   separate individuals.
7. With a Preface by Edith Olivier and a Note by J. W.
   Dunne. Published by Faber & Faber, London,
   1931 and by Coward-McCann, New York, 1935.
8. It is worth noting that the plan of Versailles in the then
   current Baedeker's <u>Paris and Environs</u> (14th ed.,
   1900) is lettered in a highly misleading manner,
   one which gives the impression that the Petit Trianon lies in a direction quite different from the
   true one. The word "Château" would seem to a
   stranger to apply to buildings far to the left of the
   house. It was towards these buildings on the left
   that the two women turned. That they were using
   Baedeker's map is expressly stated by Miss Moberly (p. 2). Whichever edition they had, the plan was
   the same, for it appears in all preceding editions
   (1898, 1896, etc.).
9. <u>An Adventure</u>, 1011 Ed., pp. 16 f.
10. The evidence collected, published and unpublished, to-

gether with the original letters exchanged between
Miss Moberly and Miss Jourdain from the beginning
of their enquiries, has been deposited in the Bod-
leian Library, Oxford.

11. "... it does not seem to us that, on the evidence before
us, there is sufficient ground for supposing anything supernormal to have occurred at all. The
persons and things seen were, we should judge, the
real persons and things the seers supposed them to
be at the time, probably decked out by tricks of
memory (and after the idea of haunting had occurred
to them, pp. 11, 20), with some additional details
of costume suitable to the times of Marie Antoinette
(p. 24). No detailed account of the experiences was
apparently written down till three months later, Nov.,
1901, and it is unusual to be able to rely on one's
memory for details of things seen after even a much
shorter interval of time," Proc. S. P. R., Vol. XXV,
1911, pp. 353 f.

12. "I [Miss Jourdain] began to feel as if I were walking in
my sleep." An Adventure, 1011 Ed., p. 18.
    "He saw him ... by a waking dream, which
I take to be the best definition of second sight."
William MacLeod, A Treatise on the Second Sight,
Edinburgh, 1763, p. 47.

13. G. Bell & Sons, London, 1938, pp. 104 f.

14. An Adventure, 1911 Ed., pp. 11 and 20.

15. Ibid., p. 100.

16. Faber & Faber, London, 1945.

17. It is not explained to whom "we" refers.

18. Miss Moberly's early friend, Charlotte M. Yonge, in
A History of Christian Names, 1863 (Vol. II, pp.
281, 414), explained Arnulf as "eagle-wolf," and
Radulf or Randulf as "house-wolf." This does not
support Miss Moberly's identification of the names,
but it does indicate how Radulphus could be transformed into Arnolphus in her mind.

19. Since we have only a second-hand account of the Constantine the Great case, it should not be stressed.
However, the addition of an alleged experience involving a famous Roman emperor to one involving
a beautiful and ill-fated queen must be remarked
on. We learn from Miss Olivier that Miss Moberly was descended from a natural son of Peter the
Great. The associative connections between the
Russian Emperor Peter the Great, and the Roman
Emperor Constantine the Great will be noticed.

20. Vol. XLIII, 1949, pp. 70-81.

21. Translated by Lillian A. Clare, and published by George
     Allen & Unwin Ltd., London, 1923.

22. Ibid., p. 109. Both the verses and the prose, it may
     be as well to point out, are part of Miss Clare's
     excellent translation.

23. Coward-McCann, New York, 1950, pp. 39-43.

24. The view is based on personal experience. Laboratory
     experiments in precognition have not only been of
     the greatest value in demonstrating that precognition
     is a fact, but have borne out views derived from a
     study of the more complex sphere of spontaneous
     precognition. An examination of the accounts of the
     many valuable series of experiments which have
     been conducted on the basis of cards bearing sim-
     ple designs, does not yield proof that the percipient
     precognizes a "future event" (in this case the card
     to be chosen). He precognizes his future experience
     in seeing the card or being told the result; or,
     where that is ruled out--as now it generally is--he
     precognizes the future perception of the agent or of
     someone else who will know the card to be chosen.
     Thus Dr. S. G. Soal, in his report of his 1941-
     1943 series of experiments, defined precognitive
     telepathy as, "The prehension by a Sensitive, by
     means of his psi faculty, of the future contents of
     the Agent's mind," Proc. S. P. R., Vol. XLVII, p.
     22.

25. Proc. S. P. R., Vol. VIII, p. 507.

26. An Adventure, 1911 Ed., pp. 75 f.

27. After this paper was ready to go to press I learned from
     Mr. W. H. Salter's article, "An Adventure: A Note
     on the Evidence" (S. P. R. Journal, January-Febru-
     ary, 1950, pp. 178-187), that it was Mrs. Henry
     Sidgwick who reviewed the book when it first ap-
     peared in 1911.

ADDITIONAL READINGS ON RETROCOGNITION

Bentley, W. P. "Research in 'psychometry' in the U.S. and England." IJP 3(4): 75-104 (Aut 1961).

Dean, E. D. "Precognition and retrocognition." In Mitchell, E. D., et al. (Eds.). Psychic Exploration. N.Y., Putnam's, 1974. Ch. 6

Ellwood, G. F. Psychic Vistas to the Past. N.Y., New American Library, 1971.

Hastings, R. J. "An examination of the Dieppe Raid case." JSPR 45: 55-62 (Jun 1969).

Lambert, G. W. "Antoine Richard's garden: A postscript to 'An Adventure.'" JSPR 37: 117-54 (Jul-Oct 1953).

_____. "Antoine Richard's garden: A postscript to 'An Adventure.' A supplementary note." JSPR 38: 12-18 (Mar 1955).

_____. "Antoine Richard's garden. A postscript to 'An Adventure.' Part III." JSPR 37: 266-79 (Mar-Apr 1954).

_____. "Antoine Richard's garden: Some further notes." JSPR 38: 365-69 (Dec 1956).

_____. "Richard's garden revisited." JSPR 41: 279-82 (Jun 1962).

_____. and Gay, K. "The Dieppe Raid case." JSPR 36: 607-18 (May-Jun 1952).

Leary, F. W. "Time and Trianon: Analysis of An Adventure." JASPR 33: 216-34 (Oct 1945).

MacKenzie, A. Apparitions and Ghosts. London, Barker, 1971. Pp. 40-43, 136-45, and 166-67.

_____. The Unexplained. N.Y., Abelard-Schuman, 1970. Pp. 58-89.

Murphy, G. "Direct contacts with past and future: Retrocognition and precognition." JASPR 61: 3-23 (Jan 1967).

_____. and Klemme, H. L. "Unfinished business." JASPR 60: 306-20 (Oct 1966).

Roll, W. G. "Pagenstecher's contribution to parapsychology." JASPR 61: 219-40 (Jul 1967).

Chapter 3

THE CASE FOR PSYCHOKINESIS*

by J. G. Pratt

Introduction

      Perception and motor action are two functions that are closely associated with each other. In the normal individual, perception guides motor adaptation, and action without perception is only so much motion.

      Ordinarily, of course, we think of perception as involving the sense organs, and of motor reaction as depending upon the use of the muscles. But the evidence reviewed in the preceding paper by Dr. Murphy indicates that information is sometimes acquired without the use of the senses. Because of the interdependence of perception and response in ordinary behavior, the experimental establishment of ESP suggested that there might be a corresponding capacity of thought processes to exert a direct influence on physical systems.

      Clairvoyance, for example, can be described as a direct influence of matter upon mind. Might there not be a

*Reprinted by permission of the author and publisher from the Journal of Parapsychology 24: 171-88 (Sept 1960).
      This paper is adapted from one of the same title which was presented at the Third Annual Meeting of the Canadian Federation of Biological Societies at the University of Manitoba, Winnipeg, on June 9, 1960. The occasion was a symposium on parapsychology sponsored by the Canadian Physiological Society, and the program consisted of a paper by Dr. Gardner Murphy on "The Investigation of Extrasensory Perception" followed by this survey of the evidence for psychokinesis. The author wishes to express his appreciation to the Society, particularly to Prof. J. Doupe and Dr. R. J. Cadoret, and to the Parapsychology Foundation which provided funds to cover travel expenses.

reciprocal capacity--an effect of mind upon matter? The
laboratory evidence for ESP gave a hint, at least, of the occurrence of psychokinesis.

But the PK hypothesis did not originate through logical
considerations alone. There are on record many spontaneous
occurrences which appear to indicate that PK may be a natural, even though rare, basis of experiences in everyday life.
These spontaneous occurrences which pose the question of PK
are not so common as those which seem to be manifestations
of ESP. But they are sometimes impressive in nature and
they are sufficiently numerous to deserve attention as the
raw stuff of experience and observation to which the research
in PK is related.

These unexplained physical happenings with an apparent psychological aspect range from isolated occurrences such
as a picture falling from the wall or a clock stopping at the
time of a death to recurrent physical disturbances of the sort
popularly referred to as poltergeists and unexplained physical
effects associated with rare individuals. Such happenings
have received a large amount of serious study in the past,
but they have not provided the necessary basis for a scientific conclusion. Rather, they serve to raise and to keep open
the question of whether man might possess an ability for psychokinesis. At the same time, however, efforts to study
them showed that a different kind of evidence, based upon an
experimental approach, would be required to answer this
question.

I shall be concerned with the experimental evidence
for PK which has been produced over the past 25 years. In
preparing this paper, I listed the periodical literature on PK
(see end of this chapter). This list, still not complete, contains 74 reports on original research, 11 papers presenting
new evidence based upon further analyses of existing data,
and 23 reviews or discussions of the PK problem. It is obvious that I will not be able to communicate all of the details.
Rather, my aim will be to give you an introductory impression of the nature and strength of the experimental case for
PK.

Experimental Establishment of PK

There is, as I have already pointed out, a close logical and psychological link between ESP and PK. Yet, by

1934, the experimental study of ESP already had a long history, while very little had been done toward bringing the investigation of the PK hypothesis into the laboratory. After the publication of his ESP monograph in that year, Dr. J. B. Rhine thought the time had come for trying to deal experimentally with the PK hypothesis. But what method should one choose for undertaking such a study? Dr. Rhine credits the answer to this question to a casual visitor who claimed that he could successfully will dice to fall so that they would give winning numbers. This confident boast brought to mind the fact that many experienced players of the game of craps feel that they are sometimes able to control the dice.

Would the ancient and simple gaming die provide a suitable means of experimentally testing PK? Dr. and Mrs. Rhine, using themselves and a few friends and students as subjects, set out to find the answer empirically. The first tests were made by throwing two dice for designated sums of the uppermost faces: high dice (8 or more); low dice (6 or fewer); or sevens. The first work was exploratory, and the dice were thrown under a variety of circumstances. Some of the trials were made as in ordinary dice games: the cubes were shaken in cupped hands and rolled upon a blanketed surface or bounced off a vertical barrier before they came to rest. For other tests, the dice were shaken in a cup before they were thrown. In still others, the dice were rolled down an inclined chute onto a horizontal table or floor area.

These first PK tests yielded results that were highly significant statistically. The subjects obtained only a slight average excess of the designated target, but this success was maintained over a large number of throws and the odds against chance were very great. While the experimenters had confidence in their own observations and recording, they wanted the results confirmed before publishing such startling findings. Dr. Rhine therefore quietly informed a few people about the results and encouraged them to undertake PK tests. Several of them did so.

This stage of quiet research on the PK hypothesis lasted from 1934 through 1942. Very early during this period, variations in testing procedure were made. For example, some subjects preferred to try to get as many as possible of a designated target face. This kind of test was more adaptable than that based on the sum of two faces, since it allowed the subject to throw any number of dice at the same time. Tests were actually made with from one to 96 or more dice per throw. Adequate safeguards were introduced to control against physical bias of the dice by throwing equally for every face, and machines were introduced to provide automatic throwing, which eliminated all handling of the dice.

Most of the series which were done yielded statistically highly significant results. As the experiments were completed, the results were noted in terms of the overall scores, and the records were added to the files of accumulating PK evidence. This process continued over the eight-year period before the experimenters felt that the degree of confirmation justified publication of the results.

Then, in the course of re-examining the data preparatory to reporting the findings, a new type of internal evidence was discovered which provided a clear-cut basis for the exclusion of counter-hypotheses to PK even in the more exploratory series. This evidence was the discovery of rhythmic changes in the level of success in relation to the subject's progress through the PK test. More specifically, it was found that as the subjects had worked their way through the assigned trials to be recorded on the record page their success had varied in a systematic way.

No one had anticipated or noticed any regular variation in performance while the separate series were being conducted. Consequently, no one gave any thought to position effects. It may therefore be said that neither the experimenters nor the subjects were consciously motivated in one part of the record page more than in another. The position effects made it possible to consider as evidence for PK the results of even the more informal exploratory experiments, such as those in which subjects made their choice of targets instead of throwing equally for each face of the die. Even though the six-face, say, was used as target throughout an experiment, a statistical test based upon the difference between the scores in two different sections of the record page would be free of any possible effect of physical bias in the die. The six-face would not be favored during the throws made at one particular moment while being disfavored in the throws occurring at the next moment.

What were the unexpected position effects found in the PK records? When the first series was being re-analyzed, it was observed that there was a general decline of success between the top half and the bottom half of the record page. Similarly, there was a decline of success between the data

recorded in the lefthand columns of the page and those recorded in the righthand columns. As a means of getting a
statistical test of these two trends, the page was divided into four equal quarters by means of horizontal and vertical
center lines. Then a statistical evaluation was applied to
the difference in the hits scored in the upper left and the
lower right quarters of the page. This statistical test was
labeled the "quarter distribution" or QD analysis.

   Having discovered a decline effect in the first records
examined, the experimenters proceeded to apply the QD analysis to all of the series in the files. A total of 18 separate
experimental series were found to be suitable for evaluation
by this method.

   In 12 of these series the subjects had been throwing
for a designated face of the die as target. In all but one of
these the QD analysis showed a higher rate of scoring in the
upper left quarter than in the lower right quarter of the page.
Statistically, a difference as large as that observed between
the total score of the upper left quarter for all 12 series and
that of the lower right would be expected on the basis of random sampling about three times in a hundred million such
sets of data.

   The other six series were experiments in which the
subjects threw a pair of dice for a designated sum of the two
faces. The QD results revealed in this case as well that in
all but one series the upper left quarter had given a higher
score than the lower right. Here the difference between the
total scores had the probability of chance occurrence of less
than 1 time in 150.

   The QD results for the PK record page were discovered and reported by J. B. Rhine and B. M. Humphrey of
the Duke Parapsychology Laboratory. Recognizing this evidence as crucial for the PK hypothesis, they issued an invi-
tation to any qualified scientists to come and recheck the results for themselves. When no one else accepted the invita-
tion, I myself took the opportunity. Although I was a member of the staff, I was not at the laboratory when these
analyses were made, and thus I was qualified to make a completely separate recheck. In the time available, I was able
to re-analyze completely the 10 out of the 18 series which
contributed the most to the statistical significance of the complete QD analysis. A few minor errors of tabulation were
found, but these did not make any appreciable difference in

the results. Thus my own findings verified the Rhine and
Humphrey report.

The QD analysis was carried through two further
stages to see if the decline effect was present in structured
units of the records smaller than the page. The final stage
was one that was completely independent statistically of the
results that had already been found. This was a study involving the quartering of record units lying wholly within the
four quarters of the page, a sort of quarter distribution analysis of the original page quarters.

Out of the original 18 series, only 8 were found to
lend themselves to this third QD study. These showed the
predicted decline effect. In the series in which a designated
target face was the objective, the difference between the first
and fourth quarters gave a P-value of . 0005; in the section
involving high-dice and low-dice results from a pair, this
difference yielded a probability of . 00043. A combination of
these two results by Fisher's method yields the probability
value of . 000005.

So far in this paper I have restricted the statistics to
a few crucial probability values. But I should like to mention here two other figures--figures which show the truly impressive scope of the work involved in this research effort.
The 12 series for target faces analyzed in the QD studies
contained a total of nearly 700, 000 die readings. The six
series in which a pair of dice were thrown for a specified
sum of the two faces contained a total of just over 37, 000
readings of the two dice.

In March, 1946, Dr. Rhine published an article sur-
veying the PK evidence as it appeared at that time. The
case for PK was conclusive--as conclusive, at least, as it
could be on the basis of work largely centered in or directed
from one laboratory. The publication of this survey of the
evidence marked the end of the first stage of PK research.
From this point on, the hypothesis had scientific status, commanding the close attention of research workers in parapsychology. The emphasis shifted to the question of confirmation of the evidence by investigators in other research centers.

Independent Confirmation of PK

Since 1945, there have been many confirmatory PK

experiments, but I will be able to present only the basic details regarding three of them at this point and of a fourth one
near the end of the next section.

In 1946, L. A. Dale reported in the Journal of the
American Society for Psychical Research a PK experiment
which she had conducted as the research officer of that organization. The experiment was rigorously planned from the
outset to guard against conceivable non-PK factors. Each of
54 college students who were used as subjects was present
for a single session in which 96 die-throws were made for
each of the six faces of the die in turn. The dice were
shaken in a cup and poured into the open upper end of a
three-foot inclined plane. After falling under the force of
gravity, the dice spread out over an enclosed horizontal surface at the bottom. Both the incline and the target area
were covered with glass. The experimenter and the subject
independently observed and recorded the upper faces of the
dice after each trial. In case of any discrepancy between
the two records, the lower score was counted. Since the experiment as a whole gave a positive deviation, errors were
thus interpreted on the safe side.

The trials for each target face were recorded on a
separate record sheet in four columns, two at the top of the
sheet and two near the bottom. As planned before the experiment was begun, tests for significance were applied to the
total deviation of successes from mean chance expectation and
to position effects among the four columns on the page. The
31,104 die readings of the total experiment yielded a positive
deviation of 171 hits. This is significant, with a probability
of .005. There was also a regular decline among the four
columns on the page. Taking them in order, the deviations
were +100, +55, +12, +4. The difference between the first
and fourth columns is of marginal significance, with P=.04.
The position effects follow closely the pattern of those reported for previous series. On the basis of the total deviation
and position effects, this work confirmed the earlier PK results.

Another formal effort to repeat the PK results was
made in the Department of Biophysics of the University of
Pittsburgh. This experiment by McConnell, Snowdon, and
Powell was reported in the Journal of Experimental Psychology in October, 1955, though the work itself was completed
a few years earlier.

The experiment involved the making of about 170,000 die-throws by 393 subjects, and the research extended over a period of approximately 18 months.

Each subject made throws of two dice to complete three record sheets of six columns each, three across the top of the page and three across the bottom. For the first page the dice were shaken and thrown from a roughened cup into a padded tray. For the other two pages the dice were thrown by an automatically-operating electrical apparatus, and the results were recorded photographically after each throw as well as by the experimenter. The automatic photographic recording of the dice make it possible to recheck the scores from the films and thus to find any errors in the experimenters' records.

The investigators planned to analyze their results in terms of both the total score and position effects. The total score of the experiment was not significantly different from chance expectation, but the analysis for a decline effect within the page revealed a drop in performance which was significant, with a probability of .002.

The third example of a confirmatory experiment was one conducted by G. W. Fisk and D. J. West in England with a selected high-scoring PK subject. An unusual feature about this work was the fact that the subject was not informed which face of the die was the target for any given set of trials. Thus the entire experiment involved a condition which Dr. R. H. Thouless had earlier introduced in his PK research --the subject's success depended upon using ESP to get the target and PK to make the dice fall to match it.

In the first series of tests, done in 1951-52, Mr. Fisk selected at random each day a digit from 1-6 as the target face and pinned this number on the wall of his study in Surrey, England. During the course of the day, the subject in her own home a number of miles distant threw the dice to match the unknown target. Throughout the course of the series, the subject completed 10,000 trials in which she scored 117 more hits than chance expectation. This result yields a probability value of .0016.

In three further series with this subject, consistently positive scores were obtained under similar conditions of working (requiring both ESP and PK). These further results

(15,032 trials with a positive deviation of 172) were significant, with a probability level of .00017.

The three experiments chosen as examples of independent confirmations were selected on the basis of the ade-
quacy of the experimental conditions, not because of the results. In fact, a number of other series could be cited
which reached higher levels of statistical significance. But
on the basis of both the safeguards imposed and the results
obtained, these three should offer reassurance to any open-
minded scientist who might have wondered whether the case
for PK rested on work done in the laboratory from which the
discovery was first announced.

PK Placement

In 1951, W. E. Cox reported an experiment in which
subjects attempted to use PK on a tumbling die in two ways
simultaneously: one, to get designated target faces; and secondly, to make the dice stop on those squares on a checker-
board surface which were marked with the target-face number. Both the target-face data and the placement data were
statistically significant.

This beginning on the investigation of PK placement
was followed up by other investigators, and the results of
two other researches were published in the Journal of Parapsychology simultaneously with the Cox report. One was the
work of Mr. Haakon Forwald, an engineer in Sweden.

Since 1951, Forwald has been the most active investigator of PK placement. By the end of 1957, eight reports
on his research had been published. In this work the investigator, serving as his own subject, mechanically released
cubes to roll down an inclined plane and spread out on a
horizontal throwing surface. A center line divided the horizontal surface into equal right- and lefthand areas. The subject's aim was to influence the falling objects to stop on the
side designated as the target.

During the first series, the results were scored only
in terms of the division of objects between the target and
non-target sides. The two sides were used as target the
same number of times, and thus any physical bias in the apparatus was controlled. Nevertheless, the number of objects
falling within the target area was highly significant.

Forwald then introduced a simple change in his apparatus with the purpose of achieving a more sensitive measure of the PK placement effect. He drew lines parallel to the center line of the table at one centimeter intervals and numbered them to provide a scale. Thereafter the cubes were scored to show the actual degree of displacement.

The experimenter released six cubes on each trial and 10 releases were recorded together as a set, the first five for the righthand or A-side of the table as target and then five for the lefthand or B-side. The data were evaluated by a Student's t-test of the difference between the cube distribution when A was target and that for B as target.

As Forwald continued his research, two general facts became clear. One was that he was getting, with almost marvelous regularity, an effect upon the placement of the dice in the direction of his wishes. The second was that this effect was not uniformly distributed throughout the set, but it was concentrated in the first throw of the set for each target side. As evidence that something more than chance was operating, his data were unequivocal. Because the placement effect was concentrated in the first throw of the set, it became standard procedure to single these results out for separate analysis.

Parapsychologists have long been subjected to criticisms not encountered by scientists in other fields. When any investigator working alone has obtained significant results, it has been commonplace to hear that he could have made errors of observation and recording and thus have deceived himself. To forestall such criticism, it was necessary for Forwald to repeat his tests in the presence of a witness and independent recorder.

This need was met in the fall of 1957 during a visit by Forwald to the Duke Parapsychology Laboratory. The purpose of the visit was tacitly understood but not overtly stressed. It was recognized that any PK subject would be placed at a psychological disadvantage if he felt "put on the spot." Consequently, we were interested to approach the crucial stage of his visit by slow degrees.

As a starting point Forwald worked through two series entirely alone as he had done in Sweden. These series gave significant results for the first throw of the set (the basis of the statistical test, selected in advance on the strength of Forwald's previous work), with P-values of .007 and .017.

He then tried repeating this success when a member
of the laboratory staff was assigned as an independent observer and recorder. Two series done under this condition
were totally without statistical significance.

In the next stage, three different members of the laboratory staff in separate series participated as co-subject as
well as independent observer and recorder. With one of
these laboratory members, Mr. Forwald's results were significant, with the P-value of . 006. Up to this point the results were merely exploratory as far as the real purpose of
the visit was concerned.

Finally, plans were made for a confirmatory test set
up on the basis of the work done up to that point. In this
test, Mr. Forwald had as his co-subject the member of the
laboratory with whom he had previously worked successfully
in this capacity in an exploratory series. This member of
the laboratory also made an independent record of the cubes.
The two records were compared on the spot and agreement
was reached before the cubes were disturbed. The results
reached a level of significance represented by a P-value of
. 0002. Thus, in spite of the psychological difficulties which
had to be overcome, a confirmation of this subject's abilities
was obtained under conditions excluding subjective errors of
observation and recording.

But Forwald's objective in his work as a whole has
not been limited to piling up more and more evidence for a
PK placement effect. Almost from the beginning of his research, he has been trying to gain some insight into the dy-
namics of the PK process. He has, for example, compared
cubes of different kinds of materials, weights, roughness,
and surface coatings. At the same time, he has worked out
mathematical formulas for converting the effect obtained (taking into account the relevant aspects both of the cube movements and of the cubes themselves) into the physical energy
equivalents for bringing about the result. It is too soon to
attempt to make any general scientific evaluation of these research efforts, since they are still at an early stage of development. I mention them only as an indication of the fact
that the investigators of the PK effect are aware of the need
of finding ways of relating this function to more familiar scientific principles. Parapsychologists not only want to know
whether PK occurs; as soon as this conclusion is reached,
they turn to the much more difficult task of trying to learn
something about the nature of the effect.

Other investigators have also continued to contribute
to the study of the PK placement effect during the past decade. There has been further research from Mr. Cox, who
was the originator of this type of test, as well as by others
whom I will not have time to mention here. But thus far it
is the work of Mr. Forwald which stands out in this area,
and it is work which presents some very challenging questions
for future investigators of PK.

Concluding Remarks

The emphasis in this paper has been placed on evidence for the occurrence of PK. This seemed appropriate,
because the establishment of a direct, extramuscular influence of subjective factors upon physical systems would--even
more than perception independently of the senses--have revolutionary implications for psychology and biology. The general acceptance of the PK effect would require a reorientation of scientific thinking regarding the nature of the organ-
ism--a reorientation in which the influence of mental factors
would be recognized in fact and not in name only. But I
need not, before a group of biological scientists, dwell on
the importance of the discovery that thought processes have
real force.

But something should be said regarding the secondary
problems--questions about the nature of PK--which have received some attention in the research. A start has been
made toward finding out whether the PK effect is limited by
the space and mass aspects of the physical situation. Thus
far, no differences have been found in relation to the number, mass, shape, and distance of the objects the subject
was attempting to influence. Also, a range of types of objects have been used with apparent success, including dice
and cubes, coins and other discs, spheres, roulette, a spinning pointer, and the swimming of paramecia. On many of
these points the present results are inadequate for final conclusions, but the findings encourage further explorations in
search of the scope and limits of PK in relation to the physical world.

Some progress has also been made on the investigation of the psychology of PK. Motivation has been found to
be a factor of paramount importance. Subjects who succeeded in their first series of tests have often failed in later efforts to demonstrate their PK abilities: the excitement and

eager curiosity which marked their first experience could not
be recaptured. Thus investigators have learned that success
in a test for PK--as with ESP--is not to be taken for granted.
In general, successful replication of experiments has been
found to be as difficult for PK as for ESP. Even when successful subjects have been performing at their best average
level, a trial-by-trial analysis of their scoring rate has revealed high peaks of PK influence separated by valleys of
chance results within the test structure.

The findings of parapsychology form but a beachhead
on a new continent of the natural order. The facts with
which I have been dealing show that PK, like ESP, is a part
of that beachhead. The uncertainties in the situation are not
concerned with the evidence for the occurrence of the phenomena, for it is clear that a landing has been made and a
foothold secured. They relate, rather, to what we will find
as we extend our lines of exploration and discovery. They
are the challenge to further research.

PERIODICAL LITERATURE

Averill, R. L. , and Rhine, J. B. "The effect of alcohol
        upon performance in PK tests. " J. Parapsychol. ,
        1945, 9, 32-41.
Binski, S. R. "Report on two exploratory PK series. " J.
        Parapsychol. , 1957, 21, 284-95.
Cox, W. E. "The effect of PK on the placement of falling
        objects. " J. Parapsychol. , 1951, 15, 40-48.
        . "A comparison of spheres and cubes in placement
        PK tests. " J. Parapsychol. , 1954, 18, 234-39.
        . "Three-tier placement PK. " J. Parapsychol. ,
        1959, 23, 19-29.
Dale, L. A. "The psychokinetic effect: the first A. S. P. R.
        experiment. " J. Amer. Soc. Psych. Res. , 1946, 40,
        123-51.
Dale, L. A. , and Woodruff, J. L. "The psychokinetic ef-
        fect: further A. S. P. R. experiments. " J. Amer. Soc.
        Psych. Res. , 1947, 41, 65-82.
Fahler, J. "Exploratory 'scaled' PK placement tests with
        nine college students with and without distance. " J.
        Amer. Soc. Psych. Res. , 1959, 53, 106-113.
Fisk, G. W. , and West, D. J. "Psychokinetic experiments
        with a single subject. " Newsletter of the Parapsychol-
        ogy Foundation, November-December, 1957.
        . "Dice-casting experiments with a single subject. "

J. Soc. Psych. Res., 1958, 39, 277-87.

Forwald, H. "A further study of the PK placement effect."
J. Parapsychol., 1952, 16, 59-67.

_____. "A continuation of the experiments in placement
PK." J. Parapsychol., 1952, 16, 263-83.

_____. "Chronological decline effects in a PK placement
experiment." J. Parapsychol., 1954, 18, 32-36.

_____. "PK placement and air currents." J. Parapsy-
chol., 1954, 18, 41-42.

_____. "An approach to instrumental investigation of psy-
chokinesis." J. Parapsychol., 1954, 18, 219-33.

_____. "Experiments with alternating PK placement and
control tests." J. Parapsychol., 1955, 19, 45-51.

_____. "A study of psychokinesis in its relation to phys-
ical conditions." J. Parapsychol., 1955, 19, 133-54.

_____. "A continuation of the study of psychokinesis and
physical conditions." J. Parapsychol., 1957, 21, 98-
121.

_____. "An experimental study suggesting a relationship
between psychokinesis and nuclear conditions of matter."
J. Parapsychol., 1959, 23, 97-125.

Gatling, W., and Rhine, J. B. "Two groups of PK subjects
compared." J. Parapsychol., 1946, 10, 120-25.

Gibson, E. P. "Note on an impromptu experiment in psychokinesis." J. Amer. Soc. Psych. Res., 1947, 41, 22-
28.

_____. "An exploratory PK experiment based upon throw-
ing twenty-four dice." J. Parapsychol., 1948, 12,
289-97.

Gibson, E. P., Gibson, L. H., and Rhine, J. B. "A large
series of PK tests." J. Parapsychol., 1943, 7, 228-
37.

_____. "The PK effect: mechanical throwing of three
dice." J. Parapsychol., 1944, 8, 95-109.

Gibson, E. P., and Rhine, J. B. "The PK effect: III.
Some introductory series." J. Parapsychol., 1943, 7,
118-34.

Greene, F. M. "The feeling of luck and its effect on PK."
J. Parapsychol., 1960, 24, 129-41.

Herter, C. J., and Rhine, J. B. "An exploratory investigation of the PK effect." J. Parapsychol., 1945, 9,
17-25.

Hilton, H., Jr., Baer, G., and Rhine, J. B. "A comparison of three sizes of dice in PK tests." J. Parapsychol., 1943, 7, 172-90.

Hilton, H., Jr., and Rhine, J. B. "A second comparison of
three sizes of dice in PK tests." J. Parapsychol.,

1943, 7, 191-206.

Humphrey, B. M. "Help-hinder comparison in PK tests."
J. Parapsychol., 1947, 11, 4-13.
_____. "Simultaneous high and low aim in PK tests."
J. Parapsychol., 1947, 11, 160-74.

Humphrey, B. M., and Rhine, J. B. "Position effects in
the large Gibson series." J. Parapsychol., 1943, 7,
238-51.
_____. "PK tests with two sizes of dice mechanically
thrown." J. Parapsychol., 1945, 9, 124-32.

Humphreys, L. G. "Note on 'Wishing with Dice.'" J. Exp.
Psychol., 1956, 51, 290-92.

Knowles, E. A. G. "Report on an experiment concerning
the influence of mind over matter." J. Parapsychol.,
1949, 13, 186-96.

Lossky, N. "Extrasensory perception and psychokinesis: an
explanation in terms of intuitivist epistemology and
personal metaphysics." J. Soc. Psych. Res., 1952,
36, 702-708.

Mangan, G. L. "A PK experiment with thirty dice released
for high- and low-face targets." J. Parapsychol.,
1954, 18, 209-218.

McConnell, R. A. "Why throw dice?" J. Parapsychol.,
1952, 16, 187-91.
_____. "Remote night tests for PK." J. Amer. Soc.
Psych. Res., 1955, 49, 99-108.
_____. "Further comment on 'Wishing with Dice.'" J.
Parapsychol., 1958, 22, 210-15.

McConnell, R. A., Snowdon, R. J., and Powell, K. F.
"Wishing with dice." J. Exp. Psychol., 1955, 50,
269-75.

McMahan, E. "PK experiments with two-sided objects." J.
Parapsychol., 1945, 9, 249-63.
_____. "A PK experiment with discs." J. Parapsychol.,
1946, 10, 169-80.
_____. "A PK experiment under light and dark conditions."
J. Parapsychol., 1947, 11, 46-54.

Mitchell, A. M. J., and Fisk, G. W. "The application of
differential scoring methods to PK tests." J. Soc.
Psych. Res., 1953, 37, 45-60.

Mundle, C. W. K. "The experimental evidence for PK and
precognition." Proc. Soc. Psych. Res., 1949-52, 49,
61-78.

Nash, C. B. "PK tests of a large population." J. Parapsychol., 1944, 8, 304-310.
_____. "Position effects in PK tests with twenty-four
dice." J. Parapsychol., 1946, 10, 51-57.

_____. "Psychokinesis reconsidered." J. Amer. Soc. Psych. Res., 1951, 45, 62-68.

_____. "The PK mechanism." J. Soc. Psych. Res., 1955, 38, 8-11.

_____. "An exploratory analysis for displacement in PK." J. Amer. Soc. Psych. Res., 1956, 50, 151-56.

Nash, C. B., and Forwald, H. "Discussion of interpretation of Forwald's PK placement results." J. Parapsychol., 1956, 20, 53-58.

Nash, C. B., and Richards, A. "Comparison of two distances in PK tests." J. Parapsychol., 1947, 11, 269-82.

Nicol, J. F., and Carington, W. "Some experiments in willed die-throwing." Proc. Soc. Psych. Res., 1947, 48, 164-75.

Osis, K. "A test of the relationship between ESP and PK." J. Parapsychol., 1953, 17, 298-309.

Pope, D. H. "Bailey's comparison of a coin and a die in PK tests." J. Parapsychol., 1946, 10, 213-15.

Pratt, J. G. "A reinvestigation of the quarter distribution of the (PK) page." J. Parapsychol., 1944, 8, 61-63.

_____. "Lawfulness of position effects in the Gibson cup PK series." J. Parapsychol., 1946, 10, 243-68.

_____. "Target preference in PK tests with dice." J. Parapsychol., 1947, 11, 26-45.

_____. "Dice bias and manner of throwing." J. Parapsychol., 1947, 11, 55-63.

_____. "Rhythms of success in PK test data." J. Parapsychol., 1947, 11, 90-110.

_____. "Restricted areas of success in PK tests." J. Parapsychol., 1947, 11, 191-207.

_____. "The meaning of performance curves in ESP and PK test data." J. Parapsychol., 1949, 13, 9-22.

_____. "The Cormack placement PK experiments." J. Parapsychol., 1951, 15, 57-73.

Pratt, J. G., and Forwald, H. "Confirmation of the PK placement effect." J. Parapsychol., 1958, 22, 1-19.

Pratt, J. G., and Woodruff, J. L. "An exploratory investigation of PK position effects." J. Parapsychol., 1946, 10, 197-207.

Price, M. M., and Rhine, J. B. "The subject-experimenter relation in the PK test." J. Parapsychol., 1944, 8, 177-86.

Reeves, M. P., and Rhine, J. B. "The PK effect: II. A study in declines." J. Parapsychol., 1943, 7, 76-93.

_____. "The PK effect: the first doubles experiment." J. Parapsychol., 1945, 9, 42-51.

Rhine, J. B. "Dice thrown by cup and machine in PK tests."
J. Parapsychol., 1943, 7, 207-217.
_____. "The PK effect: early singles tests." J. Para-
psychol., 1944, 8, 287-303.
_____. "'Mind over matter,' or the PK effect." J. Amer.
Soc. Psych. Res., 1944, 38, 185-201.
_____. "Early PK tests: sevens and low-dice series."
J. Parapsychol., 1945, 9, 106-115.
_____. "The psychokinetic effect: a review." J. Para-
psychol., 1946, 10, 5-20.
_____. "Hypnotic suggestion in PK tests." J. Parapsy-
chol., 1946, 10, 126-40.
_____. "The Schwartz PK experiment." J. Parapsychol.,
1946, 10, 208-212.
_____. "The Forwald experiments with placement PK."
J. Parapsychol., 1951, 15, 49-56.
Rhine, J. B., and Humphrey, B. M. "The PK effect: the
McDougall one-die series." J. Parapsychol., 1943,
7, 252-63.
_____. "The PK effect: special evidence from hit pat-
terns. I. Quarter distributions of the page." J.
Parapsychol., 1944, 8, 18-60.
_____. "PK tests with six, twelve, and twenty-four dice
per throw." J. Parapsychol., 1944, 8, 139-57.
_____. "The PK effect with sixty dice per throw." J.
Parapsychol., 1945, 9, 203-218.
_____. "The PK effect: special evidence from hit pat-
terns. II. Quarter distributions of the set." J.
Parapsychol., 1944, 8, 254-71.
_____. "Position effects in the six-by-six series of PK
tests." J. Parapsychol., 1945, 9, 296-302.
Rhine, J. B., Humphrey, B. M., and Averill, R. L. "An
exploratory experiment on the effect of caffeine upon
performance in PK tests." J. Parapsychol., 1945, 9,
80-91.
Rhine, J. B., Humphrey, B. M., and Pratt, J. G. "The
PK effect: special evidence from hit patterns. III.
Quarter distributions of the half-set." J. Parapsy-
chol., 1945, 9, 150-68.
Rhine, L. E. "Placement PK tests with three types of ob-
jects." J. Parapsychol., 1951, 15, 132-38.
Rhine, L. E., and Rhine, J. B. "The psychokinetic effect:
I. The first experiment." J. Parapsychol., 1943, 7,
20-43.
Richmond, N. "Two series of PK tests on paramecia." J.
Soc. Psych. Res., 1952, 36, 577-88.
Rose, R. "Some notes on a preliminary PK experiment with

six dice." J. Parapsychol., 1950, 14, 116-26.

_____ . "Experiments in ESP and PK with aboriginal subjects." J. Parapsychol., 1952, 16, 219-20.

Steen, D. "Success with complex targets in a PK baseball game." J. Parapsychol., 1957, 21, 133-46.

Thouless, R. H. "Some experiments on PK effects in coin spinning." J. Parapsychol., 1945, 9, 169-75.

_____ . "A method of correcting for dice bias in evaluating PK test data." J. Parapsychol., 1947, 11, 231-35.

_____ . "A report on an experiment in psychokinesis with dice and a discussion on psychological factors favoring success." Proc. Soc. Psych. Res., 1951, 49, 107-130. Condensed version in J. Parapsychol., 1951, 15, 89-102.

Van de Castle, R. L. "An exploratory study of some personality correlates associated with PK performance." J. Amer. Soc. Psych. Res., 1958, 52, 134-50.

Vasse, P. "Expériences de germination de plantes." Rev. Métapsychique, New Series No. 12, 223-25, 1950.

Vasse, P., and Vasse, C. "A comparison of two subjects in PK." J. Parapsychol., 1951, 15, 263-70.

Wilbur, L. C., and Mangan, G. L. "The relation of PK object and throwing surface in placement tests: I. Preliminary series." J. Parapsychol., 1956, 20, 158-65.

_____ . "The relation of PK object and throwing surface in placement tests: further report." J. Parapsychol., 1957, 21, 58-65.

"Confirmatory experiments in PK research." (Editorial) J. Parapsychol., 1946, 10, 71-73.

"ESP, PK, and the survival hypothesis." (Editorial) J. Parapsychol., 1943, 7, 223-27.

"ESP and PK as 'psi phenomena.'" (Editorial) J. Parapsychol., 1946, 10, 74-75.

"Independent discoveries of target preference in PK data." (Editorial note) J. Parapsychol., 1948, 12, 148-50.

"The mind has real force!" (Editorial) J. Parapsychol., 1943, 7, 69-75.

"'Physical phenomena' in parapsychology." (Editorial) J. Parapsychol., 1943, 7, 1-4.

"A PK experiment at Yale starts a controversy." (Editorial note) J. Amer. Soc. Psych. Res., 1952, 46, 111-17.

"The PK research at the point for decision!" (Editorial) J. Parapsychol., 1944, 8, 1-2.

"Significance of the PK effect." (Editorial) J. Parapsychol., 1943, 7, 139-43.

ADDITIONAL READINGS ON PSYCHOKINESIS

Andre, E. "Confirmation of PK action on electronic equipment." JP 36: 283-93 (Dec 1972).

Barry, J. "General and comparative study of the psychokinetic effect on a fungus culture." JP 32: 237-43 (Dec 1968).

Brier, R. M. "PK on a bio-electrical system." JP 33: 187-205 (Sep 1969).

Brookes-Smith, C. "Data-tape recorded experimental PK phenomena." JSPR 47: 69-89 (Jun 1973).

————. and Hunt, D. W. "Some experiments in psychokinesis." JSPR 45: 265-80 (Jun 1970).

Cox, W. E. "Clairvoyant PK." (Abstract) JP 38:239-40 (Jun 1974).

————. "The effect of PK on electromechanical systems." JP 29: 165-75 (Sep 1965).

————. "PK on a pendulum." In Rhine, J. B. (Ed.). Progress in Parapsychology. Durham, N. C., Parapsychology Press, 1971. Pp. 97-101.

————. "PK tests with a thirty-two channel balls machine." JP 38: 56-68 (Mar 1974).

————., Feather, S. R., and Carpenter, J. C. "The effect of PK on electromechanical systems. II. Further experiments and analysis with the PK clocks machine." JP 30: 184-94 (Sep 1966).

Forwald, H. Mind, Matter, and Gravitation. N. Y., Parapsychology Foundation, 1970. (Parapsychological Monographs No. 11).

Girden, E. "A postscript to 'A review of psychokinesis (PK)'." Psychological Bulletin, 59: 529-31 (Nov 1962). Reprinted in IJP 6(1): 89-92 (Win 1964).

————. "A review of psychokinesis (PK)." Psychological Bulletin 59: 353-88 (Sep 1962). Reprinted, together with a rebuttal by G. Murphy, a reply by Girden, and discussion by J. Beloff, J. Eisenbud, A. Flew, J. Rush, G. Schmeidler, and R. Thouless, in IJP 6(1): 25-137 (Win 1964).

Honorton, C. and Barksdale, W. "PK performance with waking suggestions for muscle tension versus relaxation." JASPR 66: 208-14 (Apr 1972).

McConnell, R. A. and Forwald, H. "Psychokinetic placement: I. A re-examination of the Forwald-Durham experiment." JP 31: 51-69 (Mar 1967).

Metta, L. "Psychokinesis on Lepidopterous larvae." JP 36: 213-21 (Sep 1972).

Morris, R. L. "The measurement of PK (psychokinesis) by electric clock." In Rhine, J. B. and Associates. Parapsychology from Duke to FRNM. Durham, N.C., Parapsychology Press, 1965. Ch. 10.

_____. "PK on a bio-electrical system." In Rhine, J. B. and Brier, R. (Eds.). Parapsychology Today. N.Y., Citadel, 1968. Pp. 63-74.

Murphy, G. "Report on paper by Edward Girden on psycho-kinesis." Psychological Bulletin 59: 520-28 (Nov 1962). Reprinted together with Girden's paper, a postscript by Girden, and discussion by J. Beloff, J. Eisenbud, A. Flew, J. Rush, G. Schmeidler, and R. Thouless, in IJP 6(1): 25-137 (Win 1964).

Pratt, J. G. "The Girden-Murphy papers on PK." JP 27: 199-209 (Sep 1963).

Rhine, L. F. "PK in the laboratory: A survey." In Rhine, J. B. (Ed.). Progress in Parapsychology. Durham, N.C., Parapsychology Press, 1971. Pp. 72-85.

_____. Mind over Matter. N.Y., Macmillan, 1970.

Schmeidler, G. R. "PK effects upon continuously recorded temperature." JASPR 67: 325-40 (Oct 1973).

Schmidt, H. "PK experiments with animals as subjects." JP 34: 255-61 (Dec 1970).

_____. "A PK test with electronic equipment." JP 34: 175-81 (Sep 1970).

_____. "PK tests with a high-speed random number gen-erator." JP 37: 105-18 (Jun 1973).

_____. "Psi tests with internally different machines." JP 36: 222-32 (Sep 1972).

_____. "Psychokinesis." In Mitchell, E. D. and others. Psychic Exploration. N.Y., Putnam's, 1974. Ch. 7.

Stanford, R. G. "'Associative activation of the unconscious' and 'visualization' as methods for influencing the PK target." JASPR 338-51 (Oct 1969).

_____., Zenhausern, R., Taylor, A. and Dwyer, M. A. "Psychokinesis as psi-mediated instrumental response." JASPR 69: 135-49 (Apr 1975).

"Symposium: Psychokinesis on stable systems: Work in progress." RP 2: 121-36, 1973.

Tart, C. T., Boisen, M., Lopez, V. and Maddock, R. "Some studies of psychokinesis with a spinning silver coin." JSPR 46: 143-53 (Sep 1972).

Wadhams, P. and Farrelly, B. A. "The investigation of psychokinesis using P-particles." JSPR 44: 281-88 (Jun 1968).

Watkins, Graham K. and Watkins, Anita M. "Possible PK
    influence on the resuscitation of anesthetized mice."
    JP 35: 257-72 (Dec 1971).

PART II

PSI IN SPECIAL SUBJECT POPULATIONS

INTRODUCTION

Two of the three selections in this section deal with psi phenomena in special populations. The first is "Psi and Animal Behavior," by Robert L. Morris. He is primarily concerned with the evidence for psi in animals other than man (termed anpsi by parapsychologists). Although there are indications, both anecdotal and experimental, that many animal species, if not all, possess some psi ability, the standard fields devoted to the study of animal behavior, such as ethology and comparative psychology, rarely make mention of it. Morris surveys this evidence and also reviews the methodological problems likely to be faced by anpsi researchers.

It has often been suggested by parapsychologists and anthropologists alike that primitive peoples would be more likely to express psi than civilized subjects because of their greater openness toward altered states of consciousness in general. However, with a few exceptions, these have been armchair speculations. Anthropologists rarely study psi phenomena in the primitive cultures which they investigate for other purposes, and parapsychologists, though theoretically in favor of psi tests of primitives, prefer to conduct their parapsychological investigations in the civilized countries of the world. An outstanding exception has been Robert Van de Castle, who has not only expressed a theoretical interest in psi in primitive societies, but has actually conducted experiments with natives. The second paper in this section was his presidential address to the Parapsychological Association in 1972. Although it is in part an experimental report, it is in-

cluded here because of the thorough review of the literature
which it contains.   Until recently, Van de Castle was virtually the only person actively engaged in this subject area, as
the list of additional readings attests.   However, an anthropologist, J. K. Long, organized a conference on parapsychology and anthropology at the 1974 meeting of the American
Anthropological Association and is making a brave attempt to
convince anthropologists that they should investigate psi in
primitive cultures.   Because so little has been written on
parapsychological anthropology, or paranthropology, as it has
been suggested it be called, both a review article and a book
on the subject by Long have been cited in the additional readings even though they have not yet gone to press at this writing.

        The final paper in this section is not so much a re-
view of parapsychology in a special population as a survey of
psi applications in a specific subject area: medicine, including psychiatry and psychotherapy.   A number of excellent review articles have appeared recently on psychiatry and parapsychology, particularly those by Montague Ullman cited in
the additional readings.   Dr. Nash's paper was selected,
however, because it touches on all the possible applications
of psi to both medicine and psychiatry.

Chapter 4

PSI AND ANIMAL BEHAVIOR: A SURVEY*

by Robert Lyle Morris

Introduction

The study of animal behavior has been undertaken in
the past by two fairly discrete groups of scientists: (a) ethologists, who mainly studied the behavior of animals under
natural conditions and focused upon the relatively inflexible
"innate" components of behavior, and (b) comparative psychologists, who were more interested in flexible behavior patterns
such as those the animal "learns" as it performs a task for
reward under controlled laboratory conditions. The resultant
dichotomy between "innate" behavior and "learned" behavior
is generally considered today to be more apparent than real.
Behavior is now seen to be the outcome of extremely complex interactions between genes and environment. A good introduction to these topics is provided by Klopfer and Hailman
(10). The serious student will find more comprehensive cov-
erage in two recent books, one by Marler and Hamilton (15)
and the other by Hinde (8). The former should probably be
read first.

The possibility of psi abilities in animals (anpsi) is
rarely considered in the animal behavior literature. A passage from a recent book by N. Tinbergen, one of the leading
proponents of the ethological school, probably reflects the attitude of most present-day animal behavior researchers:

> ... If one applies the term [ESP] to perception by
> processes not yet known to us, then extrasensory
> perception among living creatures may well occur
> widely. In fact, the echo-location of bats, the func-

*Reprinted by permission of the author and publisher from
the Journal of the American Society for Psychical Research
64: 242-60 (July 1970).

tions of the lateral line in fishes and the way electric fishes find their prey are all based on processes which we did not know about--and which were
thus 'extrasensory' in this sense--only twenty-five
years ago (37, p. 44).

Taken literally, of course, such a statement is quite
acceptable to parapsychologists and animal behavior researchers alike. However, does such a statement simply indicate
that animal behavior researchers are interested in recognized
but poorly understood phenomena such as bird migration and
the responses of certain animals to magnetic fields, e.g.,
Brown, et al. (3)? Or does it indicate that they are genuinely open to the possibility of investigating those cases of
reported animal behavior which more clearly resemble the
phenomena of parapsychology? So far, the former would
seem to be much more likely than the latter. Only two researchers with real backgrounds in animal behavior have developed sufficient interest in psi to make firm contributions
to parapsychology: Dr. J. G. Pratt, who took his degree
under D. K. Adams in comparative psychology at Duke and
who is certainly no stranger to readers of the Journal of the
ASPR; and Dr. Remi Chauvin, who is a leading French eth-
ologist and frequent contributor to parapsychological journals.

One reason why so little interest in anpsi has been
shown by comparative psychologists and ethologists may be
that no concise survey of the present evidence bearing on
this question is available. The following section will attempt
to rectify this situation.

SURVEY OF THE EVIDENCE FOR PSI IN ANIMALS

In this paper, evidence for psi in animals is taken to
mean evidence for the presence of some means of general information acquisition above and beyond those mechanisms already known or specifically postulated to be present. This
definition is quite general, but should suffice for the discussion of research that will follow. More specific characteristics may or may not be available from the data at this
time.

Homing and Psi-trailing

One of the most puzzling phenomena of animal behavior

is the ability of certain animals to "home"; that is, to return
to a place of origin after having been removed from it and
released at some distance. Pigeons, for example, have been
used to carry messages from one loft to another since early
Greek and Roman times, and they have been raced for sport
for over a hundred years. The distance involved must be
great enough to eliminate the possibility that the animal is
using recognition of familiar landmarks in accomplishing its
task. Also, the means of removal must be such as to eliminate the possibility that the animal is picking up environmental cues along the way.

Recently the problem of how homing is accomplished
has produced extensive research, especially with pigeons and
certain migratory birds. Matthews (16) provides the best recent summary of these studies.

Since some species are able to home from any direction, it is generally considered that homing involves two components: (a) selecting the correct initial direction, and (b)
maintaining that direction long enough to bring the animal
within the range of familiar landmarks. There is now extensive evidence that celestial cues, such as the positions of the
sun, moon, and certain star configurations, are involved in
direction maintenance. However, no adequate theory has yet
been developed to explain how the proper direction is initially
chosen. This is true not only for birds, but for many other
animals that appear to home. Such widespread occurrence of
an unexplained ability led Sumner (36) in 1939 to suggest that
psi may be involved in the homing process. Later, Rhine
(28) and Pratt (22) speculated along similar lines and initiated
interaction with some of the leading researchers in the field.
A research program was begun in cooperation with the Office
of Naval Research. Pratt (23) has provided a summary of
the research that followed, in which he and a number of co-
workers, including the Cambridge parapsychologist R. H.
Thouless, attempted to find an experimental design with
pigeons that would provide a clear-cut test of the "psi hypothesis." Several attempts were made to use a mobile loft
in these studies. However, this was rendered difficult by the
pigeons themselves, who were reluctant to respond to it as a
normal loft. Pratt finally decided that the best design would
make use of lofts located at sea on ships. The pigeons would
be familiarized with the loft location and taught to home to it.
Then they would be presented with a test situation in which
the loft was at a new location. In such a situation, if the
pigeons go to the loft in its new location, psi is involved; if

they do not, then subtle learned cues are responsible. This study would require extensive funds and time, and it has not as yet been carried out for these reasons. Consequently, there is at present no experimental evidence bearing directly on the question of the involvement of psi in animal homing ability.

A somewhat related phenomenon is "psi-trailing." The following is a generalized example. A family moves to a distant location, leaving behind a favorite pet. Some time after the family has left the pet becomes very upset and soon disappears. A few days or even weeks later, an animal very closely resembling the pet arrives at the new home of the family and shows definite signs of recognizing them as its old owners. If, in such cases, the pet really has negotiated the distance to the new home of its former owners, it has not done so through the use of learned information acquired in the usual way, since it has never traveled the route before, nor has it ever been located at the destination before.

Rhine and Feather (31) have presented the only serious attempt to assess the validity of the psi-trailing phenomenon. For their analysis they drew upon the Duke Parapsychology Laboratory's collection of cases involving possible ESP in animals sent in by people all over the world. Four criteria for appraisal of psi-trailing cases are suggested: (a) a reliable source of information about all the salient aspects of the case; (b) a sufficiently specific characteristic by which the animal is recognized, e.g., a name-tag, license number, or unusual scar; (c) an assessment of the general circumstances of the case--whether they make sense, are internally consistent, etc.; and (d) adequate supporting data, such as independent corroborative testimony from others involved, availability of the pet (with identifying characteristics) for inspection, and so on.

Fifty-four cases were judged by the authors to meet the above criteria adequately. Included were cases involving twenty-eight dogs, twenty-two cats, and four birds. Long-range trailing cases (over thirty miles) involved ten dogs, twelve cats, and three birds. These cases provide the best evidence for psi-trailing as a phenomenon. As the authors point out, however, they do not conclusively demonstrate psi-trailing. One does not know how many pets were left behind that tried to find their owners and failed; one does not even know how to evaluate the likelihood of psi-trailing occurring by "chance," i.e., without information of any sort, psi or

otherwise, being utilized, other than that it would decrease
with distance. Also, some have argued that a heightened
sensory capacity could have been used, such as smell. If
this is to be seriously considered for cases involving several
weeks of elapsed time and over a hundred miles in distance
covering well-traveled major highways, then we are dealing
with a phenomenon of sensory acuity just as unknown as any
other possibilities encompassed by the psi rubric. Sensory
physiologists should in this case become quite interested in
"psi-trailing. "

At any rate, as in the case of homing, an adequate
experimental test of the psi hypothesis has not yet been done.
Rhine and Feather propose two studies: (a) Test the ability
of a pigeon to locate its mate over gradually increasing distances. Pigeons maintain bonds to their mates and seek them
when separated. The suggestion here is that psi is not mo-
dality-specific, and that a bird good at locating its own loft
(a homing situation) should also be good at locating a separated mate (a psi-trailing situation). (b) Study the initial
orientation of the animal as it sets out after its owner, using an apparatus that would allow the collection of a fair a-
mount of data. These suggestions are good, but until they
or others have been carried out, no conclusions can be reached
about either homing or psi-trailing.

Hive Behavior

Several early naturalists and students of animal behavior were impressed by the unusual precision in the activities of social insects, especially those living in hives. Eugene Marais, a South African naturalist, in the early 1900's
wrote about the coordination in the behavior of the workers in
termite colonies (14). He postulated a network of higher-lev-
el communication that facilitated the social activities of such
simple creatures. Maeterlinck (13) took up Marais' ideas and
repeated them in later work. He felt that the simultaneous
performance of complex behavior patterns by so many simple
insects could not be adequately explained in terms of inherited
traits or learned behavior patterns. His term for the communication mechanism was "spirit of the hive," although he
admitted that this term had no explanatory value and merely
served to show that he did not understand how the communication was effected.

Edmond Selous (quoted in Hardy, 7), an early orni-

thologist, postulated that some sort of thought-transference
was involved in the coordination of the sudden turns of large
flocks of birds.   Theodore Reik (26), a psychoanalyst, presented a discussion of psi communication not only in social
insect hives, but also in groups of caterpillars.   Reik mentioned the zoologist Degener's assumption of a "hyperindivid-
ual group soul" in animal societies.   He also called attention
to Freud's notion that the original presence of a "group will"
in hive societies has been replaced in social evolution by the
superior method of communication through external sign-
stimuli.

These theories were formulated during the early stages
of the science of animal behavior.   Recent developments in
our understanding of the roles of high-frequency sounds and
external chemical information transmitters (e.g., pheromones),
as well as advances in our understanding of the evolution of
social behavior, have made such theories less necessary to
our comprehension of hive behavior.   Additionally, there is
as yet no experimental evidence that would strongly suggest
the presence of psi in such behavior.   Consequently, we cannot say that hive behavior itself provides strong evidence of
anpsi.

Thinking Animals

Occasionally one hears of an animal that can talk, add
and subtract, and read the future.   Upon investigation, such
an animal generally turns out to be a horse or a dog that has
been taught to respond to verbal questions by barking, tapping,
or pawing an appropriate number of times, or by selecting
an appropriate lettered block from a tray.   It soon becomes
evident that for the animal to succeed someone in the room
must know the answer and that this person is providing a
subtle cue which tells the animal when to stop responding or
when its paw is above the appropriate block.   Several extensive reports of such cases exist (e.g., 1, 9, 12, 32), the
most famous of which is Clever Hans (21).

Three hypotheses have been put forward to explain
"clever" animals: (a) genuine intelligence, (b) psi ability,
and (c) subtle cues from the environment.   The first hypothesis has been ruled out by the consistent failure of such animals to succeed when no one present knows the correct answer, together with the findings of comparative psychologists
regarding the limitations of animal intelligence.   The second

hypothesis is the one which is under consideration in this paper. The third hypothesis has been demonstrated to be applicable to most cases. There are certain cases (e.g., 12) in which the animal succeeded when the person who knew the answer was supposedly not visible to it. In none of these instances, however, does the description of the situation seem sufficiently detailed to allow the reader to draw firm conclusions. A possible exception is one of the five cases of clever dogs investigated by White (38), but even here one would like more information. Both Rhine (28) and White have concluded, as a result of their own experiences, that work with selected outstanding animal subjects trained to respond to questions posed by the trainer or owner is extremely difficult. Here one is generally working with a complex trainer-animal relationship that has been gradually built up and is easily disrupted by external influences. Moreover, environmental cues appear to be involved in these cases at some part of the training process, and animals such as dogs and horses are quite used to responding to subtle cues from their owners during their daily interactions.

Only once has an adequate experimental procedure been imposed upon a clever animal, but since this case (that of the dog Chris) closely resembles other experimental studies involving forced-choice responses, it will be considered below in the section dealing with experimental studies. The present section must be concluded with the statement that no definite evidence for anpsi can be found in the published accounts of investigations of clever animals.

Additional Non-experimental Evidence

Rhine and Feather (31), in their discussion of the non-experimental cases collected at their laboratory, have described three categories of behavior suggestive of psi in addition to homing and psi-trailing: (a) behavior which suggests a reaction to impending danger to the animal itself or to its owner; (b) behavior which suggests a reaction to the death of the distant owner; and (c) behavior which suggests anticipation of a positive event such as the return home of the owner after a long absence.

Some of these cases are quite striking. In one instance, a dog was left at a veterinarian's while the owners went to Florida. One morning the dog started howling at 10 A.M. and continued for a full hour. This behavior prompted

the veterinarian to mention this unusual event to the family
upon their return.   They were astonished, since on that morning they had been marooned in a flash flood from 10 A. M.
to 11 A. M.   Such coincidences, although striking, are admittedly difficult to deal with in other than a descriptive manner.
The safest policy appears to be to continue collecting information from real-life situations and to examine them closely for
suggestions which may lead to adequately controlled experimental designs.   Accordingly, the rest of this section will be
devoted to the experimental literature.

Experimental Evidence Based on Choice Behavior

        The investigations to be discussed in this section can
all properly be called parapsychological research.   Each study
was designed specifically to test for psi ability in the animals used.   The researchers were all people who considered
themselves at least part-time parapsychologists.

        The first work to be considered is that of Osis and
Foster (20).   They did a series of experiments with cats involving a simple two-choice maze apparatus.   The cats were
run one at a time, and were required to select which of two
cups at the end of a runway contained food.   Several series
under different conditions were carried out, all under a two-
experimenter plan in which the handler and scorer did not
know where the food was.   In preliminary runs, it was found
that some cats did better than others and that positive conditions (e.g., handling the cats affectionately) produced better
results than negative conditions in which distractions were
present, such as rubbing the cats' fur the wrong way, darken-
ing the room, and so on.   Consequently, some of the series
were predicted high-aim (expected successful scoring) and others were predicted low-aim (expected significant avoidance of
the correct target, or psi-missing).   The high-aim series,
taken together, produced significant positive results (P < .01).
The low-aim series were more variable, with negative results in all but one and no overall significance.   When trials
showing a strong bias to one side (four or more consecutive
responses to one side) were eliminated, the overall results
improved.   The experimental design appears adequate to have
eliminated visual cues (the food was out of sight of the cats
until their response was made) and unconscious cues from the
experimenter.   Olfactory cues were minimized by having a
fan above the apparatus blowing air toward the food cups.
The authors felt that the increased success when biased trials

were removed was additional evidence that no olfactory cues
were present, since such cues should operate equally on biased and unbiased trials.   However, it is possible that certain trials may have provided barely above-threshhold olfactory cues, and that these cues were sufficient to compel the
cat's attention and break any existing side bias.   For this
reason, and also because the results were not as good when
analyzed directly, series by series, these data cannot be
considered as strong evidence for psi in animals.   Two main
points are raised by this work, however: (a) the need to
consider side habits when dealing with forced-choice material,
a point also noted by Rhine (28); and (b) the possibility that
consistent target avoidance, or psi-missing--a phenomenon
present in human ESP responses (e.g., 29)--may also occur
in animals. (For evidence of psi-missing to be legitimate,
of course, it must be predicted in advance.)

        The next forced-choice experiment to be discussed was
done by Wood and Cadoret (39), using Chris, a "clever" dog
owned by Wood, as the subject.   Chris had a history similar
to the other clever animals mentioned above.   Preliminary
studies by another investigator (6) showed that Chris was responding to experimenter cues.   Later on, at Cadoret's suggestion, Chris was taught by his owner to do a standard ESP
card-guessing task by converting the number of times the dog
pawed to a standard symbol call (e.g., one paw for circle,
two paws for square, etc.).   Soon a procedure was developed
whereby Chris responded to ESP cards that were enclosed in
opaque envelopes and unknown to the experimenter, having
been prepared by a second party the night before.   Under
these conditions, Chris responded well above chance (P <
.0001) during a pre-set series of 500 trials, in blocks of ten
to twenty trials per day.   When Cadoret was called in to witness this high level of performance, Chris produced a significant negative deviation under a variety of conditions.   The
authors were unable to account for this, other than to suggest
that the dog may have shown psi-missing as a result of the
stress of Cadoret's visit and the pressure to do well for him.
Pratt (23) also did some work with Chris, and has recently
suggested (24) that Chris may have been responding to unconscious experimenter cues all along, with the experimenter
functioning as the psi subject.   Because of this possibility,
and because of the inconsistency in Chris' results, one is reluctant to consider this experiment as strong evidence for psi
in animals.   It does represent, however, the best attempt so
far to deal with "clever" animals experimentally, and the
strength of the results under reasonably tight conditions suggests that some psi was involved, either by animal or man.

Another forced-choice experiment is one carried out
by Bestall in South Africa (2). His studies dealt with precognition in laboratory mice. The mice, all males, were run
in a two-choice maze situation. If they made the correct
choice, as determined by a random process that occurred
after the choice was made, they were rewarded six hours
later by access to a female. Incorrect choices were pun-
ished by death. Bestall obtained significant results by this
procedure, and also some evidence for cyclic variation in
hitting. Later experiments by Bestall, however, did not produce clear-cut results. It is difficult to conclude much from
Bestall's work other than that the precognition procedure appears sound, so long as the actual determination of the target is not under the influence of the experimenter. The
cyclicity of scoring is of interest only in proportion to its
consistency, which is difficult to assess from the information
available.

A recent project of much interest also involved precognition in mice. The authors are a well-known French bi-
ologist and a colleague who for the present wish to remain
anonymous, but who have published an account of their work
under pseudonyms (4). These investigators employed a shock-
avoidance task. Periodically an electric current was passed
through the floor of one half of the animal's cage. A few
seconds before each occasion, a light signaled the mouse that
a trial was beginning. By precognizing which half would receive current, the mouse could escape to the other side and
avoid the shock. A low barrier separated the two sides.
Both the side the mouse was on at any given time and the
side to which current was administered were recorded automatically. In the main study so far reported, four mice
were run for twenty-five sessions each, with one hundred
trials comprising a session. The overall results of this experiment were not statistically significant. However, when
only those trials were considered in which the mice crossed
from one side to the other following non-shock, the results
became statistically significant. These trials were selected
by the authors for special analysis because they appeared to
be the only ones in which the animal's crossing behavior was
not either rigidly stimulus-bound or highly stereotyped. Such
trials, the authors reasoned, would be more likely to show
psi than the rigid or stereotyped trials because they would
not be so likely to have been determined by external, sensory
stimulation. This appears to be legitimate reasoning and procedure. However, it places a specific burden on the randomizing device used to determine the side to be shocked, in this

case a device using radioactive decay as its noise source.
A hit can only be scored when the side to be energized is
not the side energized on the previous trial.   Likewise, a
miss can only be scored when the side to be energized is the
same as the side energized on the previous trial.   Consequently, any tendency for the randomizing device to generate
more alternating target sequences than non-alternating target
sequences would provide more opportunities for hits than
misses.   An analysis of the target order which I myself carried out revealed no such tendency on the part of the randomizing device.

Another possibility is that the randomizing device may
have favored one side over the other, thereby providing the
mouse with a probability learning task which would artificially
increase the proportion of hits.   No such overall bias was
evident, nor did the analysis of the target order show a daily
bias in excess of expected random deviation.

This study stands as the best available evidence for
psi in animals primarily because it was a tightly-designed,
automatically-recorded experiment yielding significant results.
However, because the significance was not obtained on the
overall results, but rather on a secondary (although logical)
analysis, one is reluctant to draw firm conclusions until replications are in print.   The investigators are continuing their
research and have presented confirmatory findings in a recent
convention report (5).   An independent attempt at replication
by American investigators has yielded encouraging results,
but is not considered a confirmation at this time by these researchers (11).

An early study involving attempts by trained dogs to
locate underwater mines with the aid of ESP has now been
declassified by the U.S. government.   The method and results
were recently presented by Rhine (30), who was one of the
investigators.   Since this study has not yet been published,
complete evaluation will not be undertaken here, other than
to note that sensory cues and psi on the part of the trainer
may not have been adequately eliminated.

Finally, we come to a series of studies in which a
human (hereafter referred to as the agent) attempted to influence solely by his own thoughts the actions of an animal
in a forced-choice situation.   Richmond (33) attempted to influence the direction of locomotion of paramecia viewed by
him under a microscope.   This study produced interesting

results, but was not done with a blind observer and recorder. Morris and Warren (18) tried to influence rats and fish to go left or right in a simple T-maze. Both studies involved blind handlers and recorders for the animals and produced marginally significant results. However, in both cases the agent was visible to the handler and could conceivably have provided unconscious cues either to the animal or the handler. Stump and Morris (35) attempted to influence two kittens in a T-maze and obtained a consistent and significant difference between the two kittens in their performance, one scoring positively and the other negatively. Once again, the agent was physically present and could have provided cues. Osis (19) also attempted to influence kittens in a two-choice situation. In the main series reported, the agent was screened from the animal and the handler, and the handler was blind. As in the work described above by Osis and Foster (20), there were predicted high runs and predicted low runs, depending on whether or not running conditions were favorable and free of disturbances. The predicted low runs produced marginally significant negative results and the predicted high runs produced positive but non-significant results. An analysis of scoring changes over time per cat revealed a significant decline in scoring from the first hundred trials done by each cat to the second hundred. This decline had also been found in earlier series, and was considered by the authors as good evidence that no learning based on external cues was taking place. This study is the best-designed of those examining the possibility of man-animal psi communication. Its main drawback is that the results were not obtained on an overall psi-hitting basis, but are present only on internal analyses or analyses of psi-missing. Conclusions are difficult to reach until similar results are obtained in a replication of the design and procedure.

Experimental Evidence Based on Emotional Behavior

A few anpsi studies of a preliminary nature have been designed to examine somatic, or emotional responses rather than fixed-choice responses.

Morris (17) did two experiments in which the locomotor activity of an animal was monitored over a period of time and then used as an indicator of whether or not the animal anticipated through psi what was about to happen to it. In the first study, nineteen rats were inserted one at a time into an open field maze and a count taken of the number of floor squares traversed by each rat during a two-minute time interval. Following this, a second experimenter either killed the rat or spared it, according to whether an odd or an even digit had been assigned to the rat by a random number table in the possession of this second experimenter. Thus the procedure was double-blind. The expectation was that rats about to die would show less activity than those that would live. Results were positive but not significant. Three of the rats had been run in the maze several times previously and were all extremely active. When their scores were removed, the scores of the remaining sixteen rats showed a marginally significant difference in the expected direction between those to die and those to live.

The second Morris study (17), done with the aid of Miss Kendra Matthew, involved using the relative locomotor activity of three goldfish as an indicator of stress anticipation. For each trial, the activity of all three was rated by an observer for two consecutive thirty-second intervals. Following this, the observer threw two dice to determine which goldfish was to be held aloft in a net. The expectation in this case was that the most active animal would be the one to be picked up. Analysis of the results showed that the most active goldfish was to a significant extent more likely to be picked up than the least active. These results were stronger when there was a long interval between trials than when there was a short interval. This finding confirmed expectations, since the fish would be more likely to habituate and dampen their responses if the intervals between trials were short. The first of these two studies would have provided strong evidence for psi if the results had been obtained on all the animals run and if the number of animals run had been larger. The second study used only one experimenter and the results could have been due to her own psi as she threw the dice. Conclusions therefore cannot be drawn until further studies have been carried out, with refinements of design in the latter case. It is interesting to note that the activity level shown by the rats anticipating stress was low, whereas for the goldfish it was high. This difference was anticipated by the experimenters, as it conforms to the natural responses of these two species in the presence of stress. Rats freeze when threatened, whereas goldfish try to escape when the net enters the water.

Reitler (27) conducted exploratory experiments in which he noted that a colony of sea worms, Tubifex, gave regular responses to the presence of a human observer apparently with-

out the mediation of known sensory cues. However, the possibility of sensory cues from unanticipated sources may not
have been adequately excluded, and conclusions are difficult
to draw for this reason.

At a recent conference in Russia, mention was made
of some experiments conducted on mother rabbits and their
young (34). Reportedly, the mother showed psychophysiological responses when her young were harmed while at some
distance from her. Until this report is published in accessible form, one cannot assess its value.

Summary of the Evidence

None of the studies presented above can stand alone
as conclusive evidence for psi in animals. In each case,
either the design was lacking or the results obtained were
not sufficiently clear-cut. Studies which rely on internal or
indirect effects for their significance fall in the latter category. When considered collectively, the body of evidence is
fairly impressive, yet there is a certain inconsistency and
ambiguity present which dulls the overall effect.

Much of the uncertainty could be removed if more research were done. Several studies deserve to be repeated,
most notably those of the French workers, and those of Osis,
Bestall, and Morris. (The Wood and Cadoret study with
Chris is omitted from this list because it centered on a specific individual animal trained in a certain way, which makes
repetition practically impossible.) Such attempts at repetition, not only by the original workers themselves but also by
others, are essential throughout the field of parapsychology.
Any unanticipated results obtained by indirect or internal
measures cannot stand on their own unless repeated, since
the question of improper selection of analysis will inevitably
arise in any discussion of the results.

It has often been pointed out that parapsychology as a
whole has been plagued by nonrepeatability. Several factors
may be involved, but two stand out. First, workers in the
field seem reluctant to repeat their own and each other's experiments. Either no attempt at all is made, or else the
attempted repetition differs in some crucial way with respect
to subjects, experimental procedure, nature of the testing
situation, and so on. This reluctance may be accounted for

in part by the increased amounts of time and money that are
necessary for adequate work. Second, many researchers report that a crucial factor in obtaining evidence of psi is the
relationship between subject and experimenter. Such relationships can easily change from one session to another, or within a session. Rao (25) reviewed several studies showing that
different experimenters under the same conditions can produce
dramatically different results.

If subject and experimenter variables are in fact responsible for the lack of repeatability in parapsychology, then
perhaps work with animals may acquire additional significance
for parapsychologists. Subject and environmental variables
would be more easily controlled, whereas experimenter variables could conceivably be eliminated through use of standardized automated apparatus. Consequently, experimental
work done with animals may be easier to replicate than work
with humans. Of course, if animal work results in just as
much nonrepeatability as human work, then the experimenter
can no longer fall back on his conventional excuses and will
be forced to look elsewhere.

My plea for an increase in research into the problem
of anpsi is thus aimed not only at established animal behavior
investigators, but also at parapsychologists. The research
cited above should provide evidence to animal behavior researchers that there may be an entirely new aspect to animal
behavior and that this possibility deserves careful attention.
The advantages of anpsi research should provide stimulation
for parapsychologists to overcome their objections to such research in terms of expense, time, and equipment because of
the potential rewards it offers in consistent results. The fact
that no conclusions have thus far been reached should not be
a deterrent to either the animal behavior researcher or the
parapsychologist, for it is in those areas in which conclusions
have not been reached that the best opportunities arise for exciting and innovative research.

SOME CONSIDERATIONS OF METHOD

The final section of this paper will deal with methodological problems likely to be faced by anpsi researchers.
The following suggestions are merely to be taken as guidelines and are by no means to be construed as fixed
rules.

Forced-Choice Experimentation

Choice of species: The species chosen for anpsi research should be (a) a species mentioned often in spontaneous
cases, since such animals have already given indications of
psi ability; (b) a species that is easy to motivate and that can
readily be induced to seek rewards or avoid punishment, since
such responses may serve as good objective indicators of the
functioning of the psi process in a variety of situations; (c) a
species for which psi would seem to be especially adaptive in
nature, such as one constantly involved in violent predator-
prey relationships; (d) a species that fits the practical requirements of tightly-controlled laboratory research such as reasonably small size, ease of handling, freedom from disease,
and so on; and (e) a species about whose behavior and physiology a fair amount is already known.

Choice of motivator: In a forced-choice experiment
the animal is induced to choose among alternatives, each one
of which is equally likely to lead to a reward; i. e. , something
sought after by the animal because it is motivated to do so.
Avoidance of unpleasant stimulation can function as a reward
in this context. Some of the studies described above used
response-outcome contingencies that were already fixed at the
time the animal made the choice (GESP or clairvoyance paradigm). Others used response-outcome contingencies that were
fixed only after the animal had finished making its choice
(precognition paradigm). The feature common to both situations is that the information linking the reward to a specific
response is not available to the animal through known channels of information transmission.

Some general considerations regarding the kind of motivation to be used in these situations are as follows: (a)
They should be motivators that occur often in spontaneous psi
cases involving the species; (b) they should have been shown
by previous research to function as motivators for the species
involved, and (c) they should be administrable in a fairly easy,
clear-cut, unambiguous way without providing sensory cues.
Since almost all animals have deceptively good abilities with
at least one sense, often that of smell, many researchers
prefer to use the precognition paradigm so as to eliminate
all possibility of sensory cues.

Choice of experimental situation: For forced-choice
studies, the following requirements should be met: (a) The
animal should be able to acquire its reward by making a fairly

simple, easy to recognize, and easy to score response.   (b)
The animal should have available to it some number of similar alternative responses, only one of which will lead to the
reward on a given trial.   (c) The situation should be one
which is natural to the animal, so that the surroundings and
the responses to be made are not new to it and therefore do
not require a great deal of time-consuming learning before
usable trials can begin.   The animal should be allowed to
familiarize itself thoroughly with all aspects of the situation
before it starts the ESP trials, unless the stress of being in
a new situation is itself part of the experiment.   (d) The situation should have a response-reward contingency built into
it so that the animal is aware (through previous learning)
that one of the alternative responses it can make will lead to
the reward on any given trial.   (e) The initial ESP trials
should be fairly well balanced among alternatives, as animals
sometimes show perseveration at the site of initial success.
Once the animal seems free of perseveration, a more completely random order of correct alternation can be used.

     Some general procedural considerations: Preliminary
studies with a given animal can be loosely carried out to take
advantage of the spontaneity of occasions in which full experimental precautions are not practical or would be psychologically inappropriate.   Studies from which scientific conclusions will be drawn must have adequate controls.   All observers and scorers should be completely unaware of the precise target situation in order to prevent unconscious biasing
of the results.   The target order (order of choices leading
to the reward) should be properly randomized.   This means
that each choice should have an equal likelihood of being associated with the reward on any given occasion.   Standard
random number generating devices and tables of random numbers are available for this purpose.   If one's own device is
used rather than a table that has already been tested for randomness, then the device should be periodically checked for
randomness.   This will insure that the animal is receiving no
information that it could use in making its choices.   Also,
any selection of trials for special analysis should be made
with a specific logic in mind (as in the case of the French
investigators) and done in such a way as to avoid the possibility of introducing an artifact into the results.   (These rules
are inserted only for the sake of completeness since most
readers are undoubtedly already well aware of them.)

Emotional or Somatic Response Experimentation

Much of what was stated above for forced-choice work also holds true for emotional response work. Consequently, only those aspects peculiar to emotional response experimentation will be discussed.

Choice of species: The species should have a readily measurable emotional response pattern. If psychophysiological recording techniques are to be used, they should be thoroughly understood as they apply to the species at hand before experimentation has begun. Often this implies taking a considerable amount of time to familiarize oneself with the techniques appropriate for the species.

Choice of motivator: The motivator should be an event known to produce an emotional response in the species involved, such as the onset of stress.

Choice of experimental situation: There are two main requirements involved: (a) The animal should be placed in a situation in which its emotional responses can be easily recognized and scored with respect to intensity and duration. This means either attaching the animal to physiological measuring devices such as a modified plethysmograph or respirometer, or else having the animal in an open field where a trained observer or recording device can assess the animal's known emotionally-related behavior patterns, such as amount of activity and defecation. (b) The emotion-provoking stimulus can occur in two ways: either as an incident occurring while the animal is being observed but out of range of its senses (GESP or clairvoyance paradigm), or an incident occurring to the animal itself shortly after it is observed (precognition paradigm).

CONCLUSIONS

The guidelines offered above are intended to bring together the methodologies of animal behavior research and parapsychology. Each has much to offer the other. I have tried to show earlier how both disciplines can benefit from good research on the question of psi in animals.

Most of the studies cited above were lacking in some aspect of methodology. Few if any of them were carried out under the optimal conditions undoubtedly desired by the experimenters themselves. As better-trained personnel becomes interested in the field, and as more space, equipment, and animals are made available to those desiring to do anpsi work, this situation will change. Only through such change and through constant improvement in technique and research sophistication can progress be made in our understanding of the possible presence and function of psi in subhuman species.

REFERENCES

1. Bechterev, V. M. " 'Direct Influence' of a Person upon the Behavior of Animals." Journal of Parapsychology, Vol. 13, September, 1949, 166-176.

2. Bestall, C. M. "An Experiment in Precognition in the Laboratory Mouse." Journal of Parapsychology, Vol. 26, December, 1962, 269. (Abstract.)

3. Brown, F. A., Bennett, M. F., and Webb, H. M. "A Magnetic Compass Response of an Organism." Biological Bulletin, Vol. 119, 1960, 65-74.

4. Duval, P., and Montredon, E. "ESP Experiments with Mice." Journal of Parapsychology, Vol. 21, September, 1968, 153-166.

5. _____. "Further Psi Experiments with Mice." Journal of Parapsychology, Vol. 32, December, 1968, 260. (Abstract.)

6. Erickson, R. Personal communication.

7. Hardy, A. "Biology and ESP." In J. Smythies (Ed.), Science and ESP. New York: Humanities Press, 1967.

8. Hinde, R. A. Animal Behaviour. New York: McGraw-Hill, 1966.

9. Kindermann, H. Lola, or the Thought and Speech of Animals. (Trans. from the German by Agnes Blake, with a chapter on "thinking animals" by Dr. William Mackenzie.) New York: Dutton. (No date; first German edition, 1919.)

10. Klopfer, P., and Hailman, J. An Introduction to Animal Behavior. New York: Academic Press, 1967.

11. Levy, W., Mayo, A., and Andre, E. Personal communication.

12. Mackenzie, W. "Rolf of Mannheim: A Great Psychological Problem." (With notes by J. H. Hyslop.) Proc. A.S.P.R., Vol. 13, 1919, 205-284.

13. Maeterlinck, M. The Life of the White Ant. (Trans. by A. Sutro.) London: Allen and Unwin, 1928.

14. Marais, E. The Soul of the White Ant. (Trans. by

W. de Kok.) New York: Dodd, Mead, 1937.
15. Marler, P., and Hamilton, W. Mechanisms of Animal
     Behavior. New York: Wiley, 1966.
16. Matthews, G. V. T. Bird Navigation. (2nd ed.)
     Cambridge: Cambridge University Press, 1968.
17. Morris, R. L. "Some New Techniques in Animal Psi
     Research." Journal of Parapsychology, Vol. 31,
     December, 1967. 316-317. (Abstract.)
18. _____., and Warren, L. Unpublished manuscript.
19. Osis, K. "A Test of the Occurrence of a Psi Effect
     between Man and the Cat." Journal of Parapsychol-
     ogy, Vol. 16, December, 1952, 233-256.
20. _____., and Foster, E. B. "A Test of ESP in Cats."
     Journal of Parapsychology, Vol. 17, September, 1953,
     168-186.
21. Pfungst, O. Clever Hans. (Ed. by Robert Rosenthal.)
     New York: Holt, Rinehart and Winston, 1965.
     (1st Am. ed, trans. by C. L. Rahn. New York:
     Henry Holt, 1911.)
22. Pratt, J. G. "The Homing Problem in Pigeons." Jour-
     nal of Parapsychology, Vol. 17, March, 1953, 34-
     60.
23. _____. Parapsychology: An Insider's View of ESP.
     New York: Dutton, 1966.
24. _____. Personal communication.
25. Rao, K. R. Experimental Parapsychology. Springfield,
     Illinois: Thomas, 1966.
26. Reik, T. Listening with the Third Ear: The Inner Ex-
     perience of a Psychoanalyst. New York: Farrar,
     Straus, 1949.
27. Reitler, R. "ESP in a Primitive Animal." Indian Jour-
     nal of Parapsychology, Vol. 3, 1962, 1-11.
28. Rhine, J. B. "The Present Outlook on the Question of
     Psi in Animals." Journal of Parapsychology, Vol.
     15, December, 1951, 230-251.
29. _____. "The Problem of Psi-missing." Journal of
     Parapsychology, Vol. 16, June, 1952, 90-129.
30. _____. "Experiments with Dogs." Paper presented
     at the Winter Review Meeting of the F. R. N. M.,
     Durham, North Carolina, January 2-3, 1970.
31. _____., and Feather, S. R. "The Study of Cases of
     'Psi-trailing' in Animals." Journal of Parapsychol-
     ogy, Vol. 26, March, 1962, 1-22.
32. _____., and Rhine, L. E. "Second Report on Lady,
     the 'Mind-reading' Horse." Journal of Abnormal
     and Social Psychology, Vol. 24, 1929, 287-292.
33. Richmond, N. "Two Series of PK Tests on Paramecia."

Journal S. P. R., Vol. 36, March-April, 1952, 577-588.

34. Stevenson, I. Personal communication.
35. Stump, J., and Morris, R. L. Unpublished manuscript.
36. Sumner, F. B. "Human Psychology and Some Things that Fishes Do." Scientific Monthly, Vol. 49, 1939, 245-255.
37. Tinbergen, N. Animal Behavior. New York: Time Inc., 1965.
38. White, R. A. "The Investigation of Behavior Suggestive of ESP in Dogs." Journal A. S. P. R., Vol. 58, October, 1964, 250-279.
39. Wood, G. H., and Cadoret, R. J. "Tests of Clairvoyance in a Man-Dog Relationship." Journal of Parapsychology, Vol. 22, March, 1958, 29-39.

ADDITIONAL READINGS ON ANPSI

"Animal research and psi. A panel discussion." Participants: D. B. Lindsley, J. Kamiya, W. G. Walter. In Cavanna, R. (Ed.). Psi Favorable States of Consciousness. N. Y., Parapsychology Foundation, 1970. Pp. 189-98.

Artley, B. "Confirmation of the small-rodent precognition work." (Abstract) JP 38: 238-39 (Jun 1974).

Extra, J. F. M. W. "GESP in the rat." JP 36: 294-302 (Dec 1972).

Harris, S. and Terry, J. "Precognition in a water-deprived Wistar rat." (Abstract) JP 38: 239 (Jun 1974).

Metta, L. "Psychokinesis on Lepidopterous larvae." JP 36: 213-21 (Sep 1972).

Morris, R. L. "The psychobiology of psi." In Mitchell, E. D. and others. Psychic Exploration. N. Y., Putnam's, 1974. Ch. 9.

_____., Janis, J. M., Levin, J., and Harary, B. "Human-animal communication during out-of-the-body experiences." (Abstract) JP 38: 242-43 (Jun 1974).

Randall, J. "An attempt to detect psi effects with protozoa." JSPR 45: 294-96 (Jun 1970).

_____. "Biological aspects of psi." In Beloff, J. (Ed.). New Directions in Parapsychology. London, Elek Science, 1974. Metuchen, N. J., Scarecrow Press, 1975. Ch. 4.

_____. "Experiments to detect a psi effect with small animals." JSPR 46: 31-38 (Mar 1971).

_____. "Recent experiments in animal parapsychology." JSPR 46: 124-35 (Sep 1972).

_____. "Two psi experiments with gerbils." JSPR 46: 22-29 (Mar 1972).

Schmidt, H. "Animal PK tests with time displacement." (Abstract) JP 38: 244-45 (Jun 1974).

Schouten, S. A. "Psi in mice: positive reinforcement." JP 36: 261-82 (Dec 1972).

Chapter 5

PSI ABILITIES IN PRIMITIVE GROUPS*

by Robert L. Van De Castle

Primitive Belief Systems

The word "psi" has been used to cover the entire range of psychic or parapsychological phenomena. There is general agreement that the processes involved in clairvoyance, telepathy, precognition and psychokinesis clearly fall within the psi boundaries. Agreement also exists that spiritualism and reincarnation are areas where psi factors are involved although disagreement arises as to whether the previously-mentioned processes are sufficient to account for the phenomena or whether an additional explanatory construct involving a discarnate personality is required. Some uncertainty has been expressed whether dowsing, psychic healing and physical stigmata are manifestations of psi since they are phenomena that may only represent exaggerations of normal perceptual or physiological processes.

We parapsychologists therefore have some rather definite ideas regarding the boundary lines between psi and non-psi, parapsychological and psychological, extrasensory and sensory. The rationale for drawing such boundary lines is based upon whether the phenomena are explicable in terms of prevailing scientific laws or theories. We all share some common notions about what is possible or impossible because of similar exposure to contemporary scientific thinking. By using various types of consensually agreed-upon criteria, we make phenomenological distinctions between facts and fantasies

---

*Reprinted by permission of the author and publisher from the Proceedings of the Parapsychological Association No. 7: 97-122, 1970.

This paper is the Presidential Address presented at the Thirteenth Annual Convention in New York City on September 10, 1970.

and between waking and dreaming experiences. It is often
difficult to realize how culturally ingrained our thinking on
these matters has become and the extent to which reality has
become structured for us by social learning and reinforcement.

        Some appreciation of our ethnocentric bias can be
gained by turning our attention to the conception of reality
held by primitive man. All the various boundary lines previously mentioned do not exist for him, and no distinction between subjective thought and objective deed is drawn. His
dream world is not something set apart, as if in parentheses,
from his waking world--both fuse together and form an uninterrupted experiential sequence in which every component is
accorded equal validity. If a Cherokee Indian dreamed he
was bitten by a snake, he was treated exactly the same as
if he had actually been bitten by a snake. When an Ashanti
in Africa had a dream involving adultery, he was required to
pay an adultery fine. A Huron warrior who dreamed he had
a finger cut off by the enemy promptly cut off his own finger
upon arising. The dream, for the primitive, was as sub-
stantively real as the rock upon which he might stub his toe--
perhaps even more so because some rocks were in actuality
transformed spirits or the domiciles of dreaded devils. Jackson Lincoln (1935) documents many examples of how completely dreams were accepted by primitives and concludes
that this acceptance influenced every major facet of primitive
culture.

        An extended treatment of the types of thought processes
engaged in by primitives has been provided by Heinz Werner
(1948) and by Sir James Frazer (1967). Frazer's book, The
Golden Bough, discusses two types of sympathetic magic.
One type, described as homeopathic or imitative magic, involves the principle that like produces like. A familiar example would be the attempt to injure a person through inserting pins into a doll that possesses some likeness to the
intended victim. By the use of imitative magic, various positive benefits can also be realized such as securing a plentiful
supply of game through enacting dances in which the desired
animals' activities are mimicked as well as those of the successful hunter. Imitative magic also leads to the erection
of taboos. For example, Eskimo boys must not play the
string game of cat's cradle because as men their fingers
might become entangled in the harpoon-line while hunting.
A pregnant Ainu woman must not spin or twist ropes for two
months before her delivery lest the umbilical cord become
twisted around the embryo.

The second type of sympathetic magic is contagious magic. This is based upon the assumption that things which were once joined together possess a permanent linkage; consequently, an act rendered to one unit will affect the other unit even though they are physically separated. Should an evil-intentioned sorcerer obtain some hair or fingernail clippings from a person, he can work his malevolent will upon the person to whom they once belonged. The manner in which the placenta is handled carries important implications for the child's future; should it be burned, the individual would suffer the same fate in the future. Even footprints can be effectively used: in Southeastern Australia it is believed a man can be made lame by placing sharp pieces of quartz or bone in his footprints.

Frazer (1967) makes an interesting comment about the belief in telepathy among primitives:

> Belief in the sympathetic influence exerted on each other by persons or things at a distance is of the essence of magic. Whatever doubts science may entertain as to the possibility of action at a distance, magic has none; faith in telepathy is one of its first principles. A modern advocate of the influence of mind upon mind at a distance would have no difficulty in convincing a savage; the savage believed in it long ago, and what is more, he acted on his belief with a logical consistency such as his civilized brother in the faith has not yet, so far as I am aware, exhibited in his conduct. For the savage is convinced not only that magical ceremonies affect persons and things afar off, but that the simplest acts of daily life may do so too. Hence on important occasions the behavior of friends and relations at a distance is often regulated by a more or less elaborate code of rules, the neglect of which by the one set of persons would, it is supposed, entail misfortune or even death on the absent ones. (pp. 25-26)

Since primitives are so totally committed to a belief in the existence of telepathy and other psi functions, some parapsychologists have proposed that careful studies be carried out to evaluate more adequately the psi abilities of primitives. An attempt to review the material that has actually been published in the parapsychological journals or other sources bearing upon the question of psi abilities of primitives is provided in the following section.

Review of the Literature

Before the turn of the century, Andrew Lang in his
book, Cock Lane and Common Sense (1894), pointed out that
descriptions of psi events were distributed on a world-wide
basis and had appeared throughout recorded history. He suggested that this universality was found because the phenomena
did exist in objective reality in such abundance that every
group of people had been forced to acknowledge its presence.
E. R. Dodds (1931-32) published an article entitled "Supernormal occurrences in classical antiquity" which reviewed accounts from Greece and the Middle Ages.

An article on spiritualism in Madagascar by Besterman in the Proceedings of the Society for Psychical Research
(1928-29) was followed by an appendix containing a listing of
all the reports dealing with psychic phenomena in primitive
groups that had been published prior to 1928 in either the
Proceedings or the Journal of the Society for Psychical Research. A perusal of this one-page listing reveals that the
most frequently cited phenomenon (eight references) was firewalking; following in frequency were the Indian rope trick,
Indian conjuring and spiritualism. Only four reports included
firsthand accounts of possible telepathy or clairvoyance. Two
of these were from British officers in South Africa describing
incidents in which natives reported information about occurrences up to 300 miles away before the officers received any
official word of the occurrences (Besterman, 1926). Another
account involved an old Australian black woman treating a
sick white girl who reported a conversation with a spirit who
said the sickness was the result of the girl bathing in a sacred place and being stung by spirit bees. The girl confirmed
having bathed by herself in a secluded spot that matched the
description provided by the old woman (Parker, 1899). The
remaining account dealt with a report from the Bahamas of
young girls accurately describing distant events while in
trance (Matthews, 1886). This report also mentions that
many members of this special cult would go into trance states
at the same time even though they were widely separated geo-
graphically and the times of entering trances were not related
to any scheduled occasion.

Besterman's survey covering the literature up to 1928
is therefore not very impressive in terms of providing scientific evidence for psi in primitive cultures. Most of the reports dealt with firewalking, a phenomenon probably more related to psychophysiology than to parapsychology, or with ac-

counts of other phenomena of only tangential parapsychological interest. The few reports clearly dealing with possible
psi events did not include any detailed information about the
circumstances surrounding them, nor was any effort made to
repeat the events under controlled conditions.

An area that could have important implications for survival research in parapsychology is that of possession and
trance phenomena. No effort has been made to cover the anthropological literature on this topic but the following references have been reviewed or noted in parapsychological journals: Belo, 1960; De Vesme, 1931; Freed and Freed, 1966;
Huxley, 1966; Oesterreich, 1966. Unfortunately, few of these
sources attempt to deal with the phenomena as having any
veridical basis and most of them are more interested in the
abnormal psychology aspects.   Zorab (1957, pp. 106-109),
however, lists a number of papers that apparently deal with
ethnology and parapsychology. Witchcraft (Kluckhohn, 1967)
and shamanism   (Eliade, 1964) are also universal in primitive cultures but the emphasis of investigators in the field has
been on understanding the psychodynamic patterns underlying
the personality of these practitioners. A good bibliographic
source for such an ethnopsychiatric approach is Margetts
(1968).

Occasionally an anthropologist will mention having observed a successful prediction by a native diviner.   Firth
(1967) describes a Tikopia possession case in which the spirit
said that he arrived to announce the coming of fish and the
next morning a shoal of fish appeared. Hallowell (1942) reported that some predictions from a Saulteaux diviner about
the welfare of his father and other members of his party
were consistent with later information obtained about them.
Callaway (1884) sought out a South African diviner who used
animal bones to indicate accurately that he was concerned
about a pregnant female black goat, and who also correctly
predicted that she would deliver a white and grey kid by the
time he returned home. A West African diviner correctly
predicted to Prince (1967) that one of his Canadian companions would have a male child one year later.   Prince felt
that many of the characterological analyses sketched out by
the diviner were extremely insightful. A consultation with a
woman diviner in the French Cameroons was reported by
Egerton (1938) as yielding rather vague information although
he did not attempt to confirm the diviner's statement that his
wife and children in England were well.

Gorer (1935), in a more impressive report, stated that a West African diviner provided a very specific description of his home and companions in Dakar 1,000 miles away that proved to be accurate. In working with the Negas in India, Hutton (1921) mentioned that on three occasions inquiries were made of him as to whether certain relatives in a regiment located in France were dead. In each instance, confirmation of the deaths of these persons was obtained several months later. Thus, when anthropologists have been willing to maintain an open mind toward the possibility of psychic phenomena, they have frequently noted field material that seems suggestive of psi abilities.

Such reports, although encouraging, still lack the persuasiveness that characterizes carefully controlled studies. Probably the first example of an effort to test experimentally the claims of a native diviner was that of Laubscher (1938), a psychiatrist at Cape Town University. One day he buried a purse wrapped in brown paper in the ground, covered it with a flat brown stone, and placed a grey stone on top of the brown one. No one witnessed this act. Laubscher immediately set off in an automobile and travelled 35 miles an hour to a Tambu diviner 60 miles away. In a seance dance, Solomon Daba, the diviner, described the purse, the paper and the stones in accurate detail. He was also amazingly accurate in describing the appearance of some missing cattle from a distant region and accurately predicted the exact date that Laubscher would return to England even though this date was several months beyond the official date that passage had already been booked for. The only other attempt that I know of scientifically to examine the claims of conjurers was that mentioned by Chari (1960). On the basis of laboratory studies with them in India, he concluded that no evidence was found to substantiate their claims.

The first investigation employing the traditional ESP cards with an unselected native group was that of Foster (1943). He trained a teacher at an Indian school in Manitoba to administer a screened touch matching test to 50 pupils, most of them girls, aged 6 to 20 years. Thirteen of these Plains Indian children were classified as being from primitive backgrounds, 14 from semi-primitive backgrounds and the remaining 23 were considered relatively advanced. The designation "primitive" was used to indicate that such children came from families primarily engaged in hunting, fishing or trapping activities and that they had never seen cars or trains. The testing was carried out during the winter of 1940-41.

Each subject individually completed 125 trials. The overall positive deviation above chance expectation produced a CR of 3. 07. Unfortunately, no breakdown was given for the scoring levels of the three groups differentiated on the basis of acculturation, nor were sex differences analyzed. A new type of ESP test was included later in the study involving several shifting tasks which I had difficulty in understanding from the published report. Although a positive deviation was obtained on these series, the results were not statistically significant.

In an article describing some of his observations in Jamaica and Haiti, Pobers (1956, p. 107) claims, "There have been a few attempts of cards and dice experiments in Haiti, in French Equatorial Africa, etc. " However, he does not supply any references for this statement.

A brief report describes some testing with a group of New Guinea natives (Pope, 1953). A native school headmaster used ESP cards to test a group of nine males averaging slightly over 21 years of age and a group of six native teachers. The combined number of runs for both groups was 147. Although a positive deviation of 39 hits above chance was obtained, the results were not statistically significant. A drawing task was also attempted; the target picture was a concealed photograph of an American-style living room. Seven of the nine drawings "were more or less boxy-looking likenesses of the exterior of a native house. " These drawings were interpreted as reflecting a rigid reponse to a set task rather than as evidence for ESP.

The most extensive testing program carried out with primitive groups is that reported in several publications by Ronald Rose and his wife Lyndon. Two of these (L. Rose, 1951; R. Rose, 1952a) contained anecdotal information about the psi abilities of Australian aborigines obtained from the natives and from settlement managers. The Roses indicate that additional observations on psychic manifestations among the aborigines are detailed in a book by Elkins (1944).

The Roses' first testing expedition was carried out in August, 1949, to the settlement of Woodenbong where the natives were half-castes who had not engaged in tribal living (L. Rose & R. Rose, 1951). A GESP design was adapted for field conditions. Ronald Rose served as agent while his wife recorded the subjects' verbal calls. Subjects were tested individually although onlookers were frequently present at

the scene. The agent was able to hear the subject's call and
used this cue to turn the cards. After completing a run,
Ronald Rose would call out the target order so that his wife
could record it on the sheet containing the subject's calls.
A total of 296 runs were obtained from 23 subjects and their
positive deviation of 226 hits produced a CR of 6.57. One of the
subjects was a 75-year-old woman who was diabetic and crippled;
in addition, she was frequently tested while trying to manage an
unruly two-year-old grandson. Despite these problems, Lizzie
Williams completed 68 runs and achieved such high scores that
she earned a CR of 9.03.

The Roses also carried out some PK tests with six-
sided plastic dice that had different colors on each side.
Twelve of these dice were placed in a shaker and thrown onto a blanket-covered table. Each color was the target face
an equal number of times. The 20 subjects tested completed
1,896 runs but the overall deviation, although positive, was
not significant. It was pointed out by the Roses that the
average aborigine did not believe that he could influence psychokinetic phenomena since that was a prerogative of the
"clever men" or witch doctors.

The next testing (R. Rose, 1952b) was carried out
several months later in Central Australia with one group that
was detribalized and another that was almost tribal. A total
of 25 subjects were tested and their positive deviation of 52
hits for 171 runs gave a CR of 1.99. The deviation of the
nearly tribal natives was independently significant (CR=2.96)
while that of the detribalized natives was not. Two of the
subjects were "clever men" but their scores were not remarkable. PK tests were again administered, this time using 12
dice from the Duke Laboratory. The 1,128 PK runs produced
an insignificant positive deviation of seven hits.

The Roses returned to Woodenbong four years later to
retest the same natives (R. Rose, 1955). Twelve subjects
were tested of whom all but one had been tested previously.
Seven of the subjects obtained individually significant scores.
Lizzie Williams, who had been bedridden for the last four
years, was the highest-scoring subject with a CR of 6.72 for
32 runs. The combined group's total of 243 hits for 139 runs
yielded a CR of 10.31. Using the Duke dice, a total of 312
PK runs were completed, but the positive deviation of six hits
was insignificant.

A book summarizing the data obtained on all the testing expeditions was published by Ronald Rose (1956). He in-

dicated that slightly over 50 Australian subjects had been tested and completed a total of 665 runs. The overall positive deviation of 545 hits produced a CR of 10.57。 The PK results were at the chance level for the 3,504 runs carried out。

With reference to testing expeditions in other Pacific locations, Rose's book has a single sentence indicating that two series of GESP tests were carried out with Maori subjects from New Zealand which yielded a CR of 9.25 for 279 runs。 They also conducted some testing in Samoa but with insignificant results: the positive deviation for 200 GESP runs was 27 and for 1,080 PK runs, 24. The different psychological attitudes encountered by the Roses in Samoa were attributed to the repressive efforts of the missionaries since 1830 to stamp out any native beliefs in psychic matters。

The large-scale program of testing primitive subjects undertaken by the Roses has added an extremely important chapter to the history of parapsychology. Their methodology might seem a little rustic to those who have dwelled only in laboratory settings but the Roses appear to have attempted to be as careful as possible under the difficult conditions imposed by testing in the field. They were consistently unsuccessful in obtaining any results compatible with a PK hypothesis, which might be related to the fact that the natives apparently did not accept the possibility that such powers could reside in anyone who was not a "clever man." Their overall GESP results were above chance to an extremely significant degree but, here too, psychological factors played a role。 In the Samoan culture, where belief in magic or psychic possibilities had been ridiculed and attacked for well over a century, only chance scores were obtained. The Australian and Maori natives, who were more familiar with and accepting of a belief in telepathy, were able to achieve scores that provided evidence for ESP。 Marked individual differences were present, however, and subjects seemed able to improve their scores during retesting when it may be presumed that they felt more familiar with the task and more comfortable in their relationship to the experimenters。

The San Blas Expeditions

Through a continuing series of grants from the Parapsychology Foundation I have been able to undertake testing expeditions to the San Blas Islands in 1968, 1969 and 1970.

These 360 or so islands are located off the eastern coast of
Panama and approximately 18,000 Cuna Indians live on the
40 inhabited islands.   The Cunas have begun to accept some
degree of Panamanian authority during recent decades but remain fairly independent and steeped in traditional beliefs.
As a result of close inbreeding, they have acquired a distinct
somatotype consisting of powerful shoulders and chests with
spindly-appearing legs.   They are among the world's shortest
people and have attained the world's highest percentage of al-
binos.

The mythology of these people is too complex to attempt any simple summary.   Their most important deity is
the Earth Mother.   A great deal of magic and ritual is practiced, and belief in evil spirits and ghosts is widespread.
Special individuals, born with a caul or placental membrane
over their head at birth, are called neles.   A nele is a person who can make contact with supernatural forces, diagnose
illness, prescribe treatment, and interpret dreams because
of his special training and frequent inhalation of cacao bean
smoke.   This latter procedure gives him direct access to
spiritual realms.   For more detailed accounts of Cuna culture
and magical practices, the works by Keeler (1960), Nordenskiöld (1938) and Stout (1947) should be consulted.

During an earlier visit in 1964, I had carried out
some informal GESP tests with conventional ESP cards and
obtained encouraging results.   In order to make the testing
materials more relevant for this culture, I prepared colored
pictures the size of playing cards depicting five objects that
would be familiar to Cunas, and pasted these on individual
pieces of cardboard.   The five objects were: a jaguar in a
jungle setting; an underwater view of a shark; a conch shell
on sand; a large canoe with a sail; and a propeller airplane
in the sky.   Fifteen duplicates of each of these five stimuli
were prepared, making a deck of 75 cards.   These cards
were used for the testing sessions in 1968, 1969 and 1970.

The subjects were adolescents attending the Junior
High School on Nargana Island.   Their ages ranged from 12
to 18 years.   The school was the highest-level school established by the Panamanian Government and served, because of
its central location, all the San Blas Islands.   The teenagers
spoke in Indian dialect in their homes and in their Nargana
residences although classroom instruction was carried out in
Spanish.   Classroom size varied from about 20 to 30 pupils;
the school as a whole contained about 200 pupils.   The school

was utilized because it allowed a large number of subjects to
be tested in a short period of time and because the pupils
would be able to comprehend and follow the testing instructions.

The testing procedure involved a group GESP task.
Each pupil was supplied with a strip of paper consisting of
two CALL-CARD columns cut from a standard ESP record
sheet. Stapled to this strip was an identical testing form
with a piece of carbon paper placed in between. As the testing proceeded, the student wrote down his guesses for the
target cards in the CALL column. Two runs of 25 trials
apiece were completed at each testing session. When all 50
trials were finished, the student tore off the top strip and
wrote some identifying information on the back. After these
strips were collected, the target order was read to the pupils,
who recorded it in the CARD column on their duplicate copy
in order to provide them with feedback concerning their performance. For official scoring purposes, only the original
copies in the experimenter's possession were used.

I served as agent for all testing sessions. During
1968 and 1969 my two oldest sons, Brett and Lance, helped
as recording and testing assistants, and in 1970 Brett again
served in this role. A session would begin with an explanation of the task in Spanish to the students. This orientation
was given by one of the two English-speaking teachers after
I had explained it to him. During 1970 the orientation was
frequently given by a Peace Corps Volunteer, Mac Chapin,
who was assisting me. After all questions were answered,
I stationed myself outside the classroom while the recording
assistant sat at a desk next to me. The deck of 75 cards
was shuffled face down and the top 25 cards were removed
to make up the first target deck. As I looked at each card
for a period of about 20 seconds, I would first call its number aloud in Spanish so that the students could coordinate
their calls with the target order. After finishing with each
card, it would be placed face down on the desk and the accumulating pile would be kept in place by the recording assistant until all 25 cards had been placed on the stack. The
stack was then turned over and the target order was recorded
under the joint scrutiny of the recording assistant and myself.
The 25 cards were returned to the large deck and reshuffled
for a few minutes. As before, the top 25 cards were removed to make up the target order for the second run. The
procedure for completing the second run was identical to that
described for the first run.

After the target order for both runs had been recorded, I entered the classroom and instructed the students to
remove their top testing strip and to write their name, sex
and age on the back of this form. These original sheets
were collected and placed in a storage envelope before the
target order was slowly read aloud so that students could in-
formally check the number of hits they got on the carbon copies in their possession. During the remainder of the classroom period, students frequently wrote out their most recent
dream on a special form provided them. Two or three class-
rooms were generally tested per day and it usually took three
days to complete the testing program.

The attitude of the students toward the testing seemed
to be a blend of humor and perplexity. There was usually
some laughter after the procedure was explained, and there
was considerable banter back and forth between the students
as they commented upon the unusual request made by the
visting American. Sometimes the boys' responses were quite
loud; the situation seemed to offer them an opportunity for a
bit of attention-getting in front of their classmates. Although
a few individuals would persist in their noisiness during the
testing session, the overall level of cooperation was good.

The records were scored by a laboratory assistant
after my return to Charlottesville. Approximately five percent had to be discarded because it was apparent that the instructions had not been followed. Bases for exclusion included such errors as failure to record the proper number
of trials or using scoring symbols that had not been part of
the instructions. The subjects' method of recording their
guesses was to use the initial letter of the object portrayed,
so that the letter "T" was used for "tigre" (jaguar), the letter "B" for "barco" (canoe) and so on.

A total of 456 usable records were obtained for the
three-year period involved. Since all subjects completed two
runs apiece, this resulted in 912 runs available for evaluation. The overall results produced an insignificant deviation
of 50 hits above chance expectation. Since it appeared that
there was a different test-taking attitude between the girls and
boys, it was decided to examine the results to discover if different patterns might be associated with the scores of the
girls and boys. The results of this analysis are shown in
Table 1.

As can be seen by examining Table 1, the girls ob-

Table 1

Mean GESP Scores in Chronological Order for Cuna
Girls and Boys

Year	Girls		Boys		CR diff.
	Runs	Average	Runs	Average	
1968	54	5. 80	258	4. 93	2. 94
1969	52	5. 27	190	4. 95	. 99
1970	80	5. 54	278	4. 92	2. 40
Total	186	5. 54	726	4. 93	3. 76
					$P < .0002$

tained a mean score above chance for each of the three years.
Their positive deviation of 100 hits gave them a CR of 3. 67.
The boys obtained mean scores slightly below chance for each
of the three years but their overall negative deviation was not
significant. The CR of the difference between the mean
scores of the girls and boys is 3. 76 which is significant at
the . 0002 level.

In order to check on the consistency of these scoring
patterns, the data were arranged in a two by two contingency
table. Scores of 11 or above were placed in one group
while scores of 10 or below were placed in the other group.
These analyses are shown in Table 2. It will be noted that
for each of the three years the majority of the girls had
scores above chance expectation while the majority of the
boys obtained scores at or below chance expectation. Only
the scores for the 1970 results were independently significant
although the combined results for all three years gave a chi
square value of 13. 06, which is significant at the . 0004
level.

The basis for the difference in scoring pattern between
the sexes is unclear. One possible interpretation might be
that the girls appear to be more cooperative and attentive
than the boys. Another might involve the explanation given
to the class about what the task involved. Frequently the
teacher would explain this as an effort to determine who might
have the powers of a nele. Although neles occupy an extremely high social status, they are also viewed with some appre-
hension because of the tremendous supernatural forces they
are believed to control. In earlier years the eyes of the
nele were plucked out after his death in order that his spirit

Table 2

Sex Differences in Number of Subjects Scoring
Above Chance and At or Below Chance

Year	Girls		Boys		Chi Square
	11+	10-	11+	10-	
1968	15	12	51	78	2.35
1969	15	11	37	58	2.93
1970	23	17	44	95	8.86
Total	53	40	132	231	13.06 P=.0004

would not be able to find the villagers should it desire to do
so for some malevolent purpose in the afterlife. Since almost without exception neles are male, it is possible that
this explanation may have carried more of a frightening implication for the boys than would have been the case for the
girls.

In looking over the scores more carefully, it was noted
that some difference in scoring occurred in relation to age
level. The girls scored above chance at all age levels; the
boys in the 14 to 17 year group obtained scores considerably
below chance while the scores of the younger boys were a-
bove chance. Since it was the older adolescent boys who
usually made the boisterous and flippant remarks, this finding would seem more supportive of the interpretation that cooperation was positively associated with scoring level. Scores
on a Perceptual Maturity Scale that I had constructed and validated in another context several years earlier (Van de Castle, 1965) were available for several girls, but no relationship was found between these scores and their ESP scores.
No attempt has been made so far to examine the types of
dreams reported by students differing in ESP scoring level.

When I examined the data more closely, I noted that
several subjects had been tested during consecutive years.
An interesting pattern emerged when the retest scores of
these subjects were tabulated. Twenty girls had been tested
during two adjacent years. Although they scored above
chance on both occasions, their scores for the first testing
were considerably higher than for the second testing. The

reverse pattern was present in the 67 boys, whose negative
scores improved slightly during the second year that they
were tested. The difference in mean scores between girls
and boys was significant for the first testing (P < .004), but
not for the second testing. These results are shown in Table
3. The consistency of the scoring pattern for the results on
the first testing was evaluated by means of a 2 x 2 contingency table. It was found that 13 of the 20 girls had scores
of 11 or higher while only 26 of the 67 boys scored at this
level. The chi square value for this contingency table is
4.26, which is significant at the .04 level.

Table 3

Mean GESP Scores of Subjects Tested
During Two Consecutive Years

Subjects	N	First Testing	Second Testing
Girls	20	5.80	5.42
Boys	67	4.77	4.88
CR diff.		2.86 P < .004	1.50

Pursuing this question of year-to-year results further,
an analysis was carried out to see whether the absolute level
of scoring was similar from year to year for those students
who had been retested. Pearson correlation coefficients
were calculated separately for girls and boys comparing the
ESP scores obtained in 1968 with those obtained in 1969,
and comparing those in 1969 with those in 1970. These correlation coefficients are shown in Table 4. For both sexes
there was a positive correlation between the level of ESP
scoring in 1968 and 1969. Only the correlation coefficient
for the girls was independently significant, however, and
their results account for the significant correlation found for
the two sexes combined. Both coefficients are significant at
the .02 level. The coefficients comparing the 1969 and 1970
scores were negative for both sexes but not to a significant
degree.

Table 4

Correlation Coefficients
Between Mean GESP Scores for Adjacent Years

Years	N	Girls	N	Boys	Total
1968-1969	12	+.67*	49	+.19	+.30*
1969-1970	13	-.22	38	-.13	-.12

*P < .02

The results in Table 4 indicate that similar scoring levels were obtained from students during the 1968 and 1969 years but that some shift occurred in patterning from 1969 to 1970. Although only 20 girls and 67 boys were tested repeatedly, some of these were tested in all three years, so that the number of paired scores was 25 for the girls and 87 for the boys. The testing procedure was the same for all three years but there were some slight differences associated with the 1970 testing. First, the testing during that year took place in April whereas in the two preceding years it had taken place in June. School had opened up just two days before our arrival in April and the students may not yet have settled into a regular schedule. Another difference was that only my oldest son accompanied me during the 1970 expedition whereas both sons had been present during the earlier two years. Finally, in 1970 the testing procedure was frequently explained by the American Peace Corps volunteer who had not been present earlier.

In an attempt to clarify the psychological conditions which might be associated with higher scoring levels, I recorded some notes during 1969 and 1970 about my moods and the conditions surrounding the testing sessions for each class. These notes were recorded on the storage envelopes and written out before the target order was read to the class. For the first group tested in 1969, I predicted that the scores on the second run would be higher than those on the first run because I felt I achieved better concentration during the second run. However, there were 30 more hits obtained on the first run than on the second, and the difference in mean scoring level between the two runs was significant at the .05 level. During the second testing session in 1969 I made the prediction that the overall scores would be above chance because I felt that I had excellent concentration for that session. The 23 hits below chance expectation obtained for that session were significant at the .02 level. There was a basketball game going on during the third testing session and I noted that my concentration was poor. The scoring level for that session produced a deviation of 6 hits above chance expectation. There were no notes made during the fourth and fifth testing sessions, but during the sixth session I recorded that one of my sons was hiccoughing during the second run and that this distraction interfered with my concentration. A total of 31 more hits were obtained on the second run than on the first, and this difference in scoring was significant at the .01 level.

When the results mentioned above were combined, a very interesting pattern emerged. For the 71 runs on which I had recorded that my concentration was very good, a deviation of 46 hits below chance expectation was obtained which was significant at the .007 level. For the 83 runs in which I had noted that I was distracted to a minor degree, a deviation of 44 hits above chance expectation was obtained which was significant at the .02 level. The CR of the difference between these two sets of conditions was 3.65, a value significant at the .0004 level.

Notes had also been made during the 1970 expedition but the results were much less impressive. The notations generally dealt with predictions as to which of the two runs would be expected to yield a higher score or whether the first half or the second half of a given run would be more likely to yield a higher score. Higher scores had again been predicted for those runs in which I felt that I had achieved a high level of concentration while low scores were predicted for those runs in which I had been distracted. Distracting conditions involved events such as sounds from a nearby generator, hearing my son rocking in his chair, and experiencing some feeling of time pressure because the bell signalling the end of class had rung while testing was underway. There were a total of 133 runs for which high scores had been predicted: these yielded a negative deviation of 13 hits, while a positive deviation of 20 hits was found for the 133 results were in the same direction as had been obtained during the preceding year, they were not statistically significant.

These findings suggest that better results are obtained when I, serving as agent, do not become too intensely pre-

occupied with the target stimulus and when some components
of my attention are shifted toward awareness of peripheral
activities. The state of relaxed attentiveness was much more
effective than making a fierce effort to fuse with the card and
trying to force a vivid image of the stimulus into the fore-
front of consciousness.

In addition to the GESP series, testing for psychokinesis was also carried out during 1968 and 1969. The apparatus contained a wooden platform measuring approximately
two feet by two feet surrounded by three side walls about
four inches high. An inclined chute lined with a piece of
corrugated rubber led into the open side of the platform. At
the top of the chute was a small metal box large enough to
hold twelve plastic dice. One half of the testing apparatus
was painted red and the other half black. The test was a
placement task in which subjects were instructed to attempt
to influence the dice, after they had been released, to land
on either the red side of the platform or the black side. A
total of 12 releases of the 12 dice were completed for each
subject, making a total of 244 trials per subject. These were
treated as six runs of 24 trials each.

Three experimenters were involved in the testing procedure. One of my sons shuffled a stack of twelve playing
cards and exposed these cards one at a time to the subject.
If the card displayed a black suit, the subject attempted to
influence the dice to fall on the black side of the platform;
if a red suit was displayed, the red side of the platform became his target area. Neither of the other two experimenters could see the target-designating card. My other son
served as dice handler: he loaded the dice into the metal
box and released them for each trial. I recorded the number of dice that landed on each of the two sides of the platform. After the results of each trial had been recorded, a
new target card was exposed to the subject and the whole
procedure repeated. Both sides of the platform served as
target area an equal number of times. The order of the target cards was preserved by inserting them into numbered
plastic envelopes attached to a board. After the six runs
were completed, the order of the target cards was recorded
and the hits tabulated under the joint scrutiny of all three
experimenters.

A total of 108 subjects were tested individually during the two years. Their 648 runs yielded an insignificant
deviation of 27 hits below chance expectation. Most of these

subjects were children or women who came from islands
where the traditional culture was generally stronger than on
Nargana Island.   After each subject was tested, a small gift
was given such as a necklace or mirror for the girls and a
harmonica or plastic flute for the boys.   Similar types of
gifts were given to adults when they participated.   Since gifts
were given regardless of the subject's scoring level, word
quickly spread that if you sat near the American and his box
you would receive a gift.   Once the procedure was started,
I did not feel it was possible to change it because the Cunas
have strong feelings that everyone must be treated the same
and share equally in any presents that are distributed.   Their
attention became directed to the gift box and they frequently
glanced toward it during the session.

Subjects had a great deal of difficulty in grasping the
requirements of the testing situation and did not seem to
comprehend readily what the task involved.   They would stare
at the playing card designating the target side continuously
and seldom even glanced toward the platform to observe where
the dice had fallen.   Cunas become extremely embarrassed if
they become the center of attention, and they were frequently
uncomfortable during the sessions because others crowded a-
bout them and considerable laughter would frequently emanate
from the bystanders.   It was not possible to avoid this latter problem because no privacy exists on the islands.   If
testing was carried out inside a hut, the villagers would gath-
er about and peek through the slotted walls while making jok-
ing remarks.

No differences in PK scoring were found in relations
to sex or age variables, and overall scoring was at chance
level.   My failure to obtain any evidence for PK was similar to findings reported by the Roses.   They felt their chance
results had occurred because their primitive subjects did not
have any confidence that they could succeed at such a task
since such phenomena were the prerogative of the "clever
men." A similar factor was probably operative among the
Cunas since only a nele is considered powerful enough to influence physical events.   In addition, it is extremely difficult
to appeal to any competitive motives among the Cunas for
such a task since personal ambition is not encouraged in their
mores.   Their dreams seem to be totally lacking in any
achievement imagery and reflect their interest in group mem-
bership.   In their dreams, Cunas do not seem to make many
self-initiated efforts to cultivate social contacts but they are
generally affiliated with others during the entire dream.   In

the Cuna afterlife, everyone is considered equal in value and
people must even be identical in height.   This latter requirement is accomplished by measuring everyone in a golden coffin; those who are too long will have their legs cut to whatever length is needed to insure fitting the required size.   Attempts to exhort the subject to try to exceed someone else's
PK scores thus fall upon unreceptive ears in this noncom-
petitive society.

Efforts to arrange GESP or PK testing sessions with
neles were not successful.   Since there were only nine or
ten neles, they were in constant demand for diagnostic or
curing ceremonies, each of which could last several days.
Thus the neles were seldom at home when I attempted to contact them, and would explain that they were busy preparing
medicines if a request for a testing appointment were made.

On a few occasions neles mentioned that they knew I
was coming to visit them because they had recently had a
dream informing them of my imminent arrival.   News travels
rapidly from island to island, however, and my whereabouts
could be easily known at any time.   Since I had established
a reputation for always seeking out any nearby neles, they
could predict a forthcoming visit from me with considerable
confidence.   On another occasion, I had made a present of
an alabaster egg to a nele.   When he saw me two days later,
he told me he had experienced a dream in which his egg had
talked to him and said that I was also carrying several other eggs, one of which was pink, another blue and another
black.   This information was correct but I am not sure that
a paranormal explanation is required.   It is possible that
some conversation about the eggs might have been overheard
or that our baggage might have been inspected in our absence.
Although they are scrupulously honest and would never steal
any object, the Cunas would not hesitate to thoroughly explore
the interesting and curious contents of an American's unlocked
suitcase.

One nele was willing to attempt a diagnosis of my
physical condition as well as that of Dr. Peter Hauri, a colleague from my laboratory who was assisting in the administration of the Perceptual Maturity Scale.   Dr. Hauri requested information concerning the source of a nasal drip from
which he suffered.   After inhaling the smoke of eight cacao
beans burning in an incense pot, the nele peered at Dr.
Hauri and told him that his problem was of congenital origin
but that he could be cured with one month of treatment in

medicine baths that would be prepared by the nele. I did not
indicate any specific problems, but at the time was suffering
from a mild degree of pain associated with a blocked sinus
cavity near my nose that had developed after some recent
skindiving activities. The nele's diagnosis indicated that I
was experiencing stomach or intestinal problems and that
some slight cardiac difficulties existed. No mention was
made of the sinus pain. The first diagnosis was correct but
was a fairly safe bet, because most Americans experience
problems with diarrhea as a result of drinking the river
water transported from the jungle mainland. About a year
later, I had a thorough cardiac examination at the University
of Virginia Hospital because of some slight chest pains, but
no abnormalities were found.

It is difficult to assess the diagnostic prowess of the
nele on the occasion just described. One could say that he
was accurate in assessing my current intestinal and future
cardiac complaints but, on the other hand, one could also say
that such assessments were likely problems on the basis of
actuarial probabilities. Since, with the exception of the temporary sinus condition, we did not offer the nele any unusual
or specific symptomatology with which to work, it could be
argued that we presented him with a minimal opportunity to
demonstrate his skills. The question of whether neles possess any demonstrable psi abilities remains unanswered and
must await further investigations.

My research with the Cuna Indians indicates that significant GESP results can be obtained from individuals who
are members of non-western societies. I feel that these results can be accepted with considerable confidence since no
alternative explanations, except for chance or fraud on the
experimenter's part, would seem to account for the patterning of scores which was found. Any contribution from sensory cues or biased target orders is ruled out because the
overall deviation was not significantly above chance. The
significant results which were found came from within-class-
room differentiations based upon sex and age classifications.
It does not seem reasonable to assume that if sensory cues
were available, they would have been employed only by girls
or young boys and ignored by the older boys sitting in adjacent seats.

The area of anthropological parapsychology is surely
one deserving of further study. The literature to date has
been so scanty as to be almost nonexistent. Humphrey's

(1944) review of the firsthand reports up to that time ended
with a plea for further research, but with the exception of
the project undertaken by the Roses and the present Cuna project, this plea has not led to any systematic or controlled
studies during the subsequent quarter of a century.

It is to be hoped that anthropologists will become sensitized to the important contribution they could make
to our understanding of the psi process by undertaking investigations in the field to assess the validity of the psychic
claims made by shamans, witchcraft practitioners, diviners,
and so on. Perhaps a fruitful approach would be to examine
the type of cultural pattern found in societies where psi occurs most frequently. Mead (1961), for example, has classified social systems as competitive or cooperative. She
notes that different concepts of the supernatural are held by
members of each kind of system. Those raised in a competitive society feel they are engaged in an antagonistic struggle with the supernatural while those from a cooperative system feel the universe is an ordered one and that it can be
influenced to an individual's advantage. Similarly, D'Andrade
(1961) has hypothesized on the basis of anthropological records from 57 societies that there is more effort to control
supernatural spirits and to employ magical helpers if the
society is one where offspring must abandon the parent's
household after marriage and reside in a different group or
village.

Unless we quickly take advantage of the possibility of
studying psi in these primitive settings, we will find that the
opportunity will have passed forever. Our position could
then be likened to that of an ornithologist desiring to study
the behavior of the passenger pigeon.

REFERENCES

Belo, J. Trance in Bali. New York: Columbia University
        Press, 1960.
Besterman, T. "Savage telepathy." J. Soc. Psych. Res.,
        1926, 23, 2-4.
_____. "Evocation of the dead and kindred phenomena
        among the natives of Madagascar." Proc. Soc. Psych.
        Res., 1928-29, 209-222.
Callaway, H. The Religious System of the Amazulu. Lon-
        don: The Folk-Lore Society, 1884.
Chari, C. T. K. "Parapsychological studies and literature

in India." Int. J. Parapsychol., 1960, 2, 24-36.

D'Andrade, R. G. "Anthropological studies of dreams." In
F. Hsu (Ed.), Psychological Anthropology. Home-
wood, Ill.: Dorsey Press, 1961.

De Vesme, C. A History of Experimental Spiritualism.
Vol. I: Primitive Man. Vol. II: Peoples of Antiquity. London: Rider and Co., 1931.

Dodds, E. R. "Supernormal occurrences in classical antiquity." J. Soc. Psych. Res., 1931-32, 27, 216-221.

Egerton, F. African Majesty. London: Routledge and Sons,
1938.

Eliade, M. Shamanism: Archaic Techniques of Ecstasy.
New York: Pantheon Books, Bollinger Series 76, 1964.

Elkins, A. P. Aboriginal Men of High Degree. Sydney:
Australasion, 1944.

Firth, R. Tikopia Ritual and Belief. Boston: Beacon Press,
1967.

Foster, A. A. "ESP tests with American Indian children."
J. Parapsychol., 1943, 7, 94-103.

Frazer, J. G. The Golden Bough. New York: Macmillan,
1967 (1 volume, abridged edition).

Freed, S. and Freed, R. "Spirit possession as illness in a
North Indian village." Int. J. Parapsychol., 1966, 8,
105-132.

Gorer, G. Africa Dances, a Book about West Africa Ne-
groes. New York: Knopf, 1935.

Hallowell, A. I. The Role of Conjuring in Saulteaux Society.
Philadelphia: University of Pennsylvania Press, 1942.

Humphrey, B. M. "Paranormal occurrences among prelit-
erate peoples." J. Parapsychol., 1944, 8, 214-299.

Hutton, J. H. The Sema Negas. London: Macmillan, 1921.

Huxley, F. The Invisibles. London: Rupert Hart-Davis,
1966.

Keeler, C. Secrets of the Cuna Earthmother. New York:
Exposition Press, 1960.

Kluckhohn, C. Navaho Witchcraft. Boston: Beacon Press,
1967.

Lang, A. Cock Lane and Common-Sense. London: Longmans Green and Co., 1894.

Laubscher, B. J. Sex, Custom and Psychopathology, A
Study of South African Pagan Natives. New York: R.
McBride and Co., 1938.

Lincoln, J. S. The Dream in Primitive Cultures. London:
Cresset Press, 1935.

Margetts, E. L. "African ethnopsychiatry in the field."
Canad. Psychiatr. Assoc. J., 1968, 13, 521-538.

Matthews, F. B. "An account of an outbreak of religious

hallucinations in the Bahamas, West Indies, with a
brief sketch of some phenomena connected therewith."
J. Soc. Psych. Res., 1886, 2, 485-487.

Mead, M. Cooperation and Competition Among Primitive
Peoples. Boston: Beacon Press, 1961.

Nordenskiöld, E. An Historical and Ethnological Survey of
the Cuna Indians. Göteborg: Museum of Ethnography,
1938.

Oesterreich, T. K. Possession: Demonical and Other, A-
mong Primitive Races, in Antiquity, the Middle Ages,
and Modern Times. New Hyde Park, New York: University Books, 1966.

Parker, K. L. "An Australian witch." J. Soc. Psych. Res.,
1899, 9, 69-71.

Pobers, M. "Psychical phenomena among primitive peoples."
In G. E. Wolstenholme and E. C. Millar (Eds.),
Ciba Foundation Symposium on Extrasensory Percep-
tion. Boston: Little, Brown, 1956.

Pope, D. H. "ESP tests with primitive people." Parapsychol. Bull., 1953 (May), No. 30, 1-3.

Prince, R. "IFA: A West African divination technique."
Int. J. Parapsychol., 1967, 9, 141-144.

Rose, L. "Psi patterns amongst the Australian Aborigines."
J. Amer. Soc. Psych. Res., 1951, 45, 71-76.
_____. and Rose, R. "Psi experiments with Australian
Aborigines." J. Parapsychol., 1951, 15, 122-131.

Rose, R. "Psi and Australian Aborigines." J. Amer. Soc.
Psych. Res., 1952, 46, 17-28. (a)
_____. "Experiments in ESP and PK with Aboriginal sub-
jects." J. Parapsychol., 1952, 16, 219-220. (b)
_____. "A second report on psi experiments with Aus-
tralian Aborigines." J. Parapsychol., 1955, 19, 92-
98.
_____. Living Magic: The Realities Underlying the Psych-
ical Practices and Beliefs of Australian Aborigines.
New York: Rand McNally, 1956.

Stout, B. San Blas Acculturation: An Introduction. New
York: Viking Fund Publications in Anthropology, No.
9, 1947.

Van De Castle, R. L. "Development and validation of a perceptual maturity scale using figure preferences." J.
Consult. Psychol., 1965, 29, 314-319.

Werner, H. Comparative Psychology of Mental Development.
New York: International Universities Press, 1948.

Williams, J. Psychic Phenomena of Jamaica. New York:
Dial Press, 1934.

Zorab, G. Bibliography of Parapsychology. New York: Parapsychology Foundation, 1957.

ADDITIONAL READINGS ON ANTHROPOLOGY AND PSI

Angoff, A. and Barth, D. (Eds.). Parapsychology and Anthropology. N.Y., Parapsychology Foundation, 1974.

Boyd, Doug. Rolling Thunder. N.Y., Random House, 1974.

Emerson, J. N. "Intuitive archaeology: A psychic approach." New Horizons 1: 14-18 (Jan 1974).

Harner, M. J. Hallucinogens and Shamanism. New York, Oxford University Press, 1973.

Huxley, F. "Anthropology and ESP." In Smythies, J. B. (Ed.). Science and ESP. N.Y., Humanities Press, 1967. Ch. 13.

Lester, D. "Voodoo death: some new thoughts on an old phenomenon." American Anthropologist 74: 386-90 (Jun 1972).

Long, J. K. "Anthropology and parapsychology." Current Anthropology. In preparation.

———. (Ed.). Parapsychology and Anthropology (tentative title). Hanover, N.H., University Press of New England. In preparation.

———. "Shamanism: trance, hallucinogens, and psychical events. IX International Congress of Anthropological and Ethnological Sciences, Chicago, 1973." In Bharati, A. (Ed.). The Realm of the Extra Human. v. 1. The Hague, Mouton. In press.

Rao, K. R. "Psi in communities and other interpersonal situations in the Eastern world." In Cavanna, R. (Ed.). Psi Favorable States of Consciousness. N.Y., Parapsychology Foundation, 1970. Pp. 74-83.

Van de Castle, R. "Anthropology and psychic research." In Mitchell, E. D. and others. Psychic Exploration. N.Y., Putnam's, 1974. Ch. 11.

———. "The Cuna Indians of Panama." Journal of Communication. 25: 183-90 (Win 1975).

———. "An investigation of psi abilities among the Cuna Indians of Panama." (Abstract) JP 38: 231-32 (Jun 1974).

———. "Some possible anthropological contributions to the study of parapsychology." In Schmeidler, G. R. (Ed.). Parapsychology: Its Relation to Physics, Biology, Psychology and Psychiatry. Metuchen, N.J., Scarecrow Press, 1976.

Weiant, C. W. "Parapsychology and anthropology." Manas 13: 1-2, 7-8 (1960).

Chapter 6

MEDICAL PARAPSYCHOLOGY*

by Carroll B. Nash

Not the least among the disciplines to which medical
men have contributed is the science of parapsychology. In
fact, the medical implications of parapsychology have increased
to the point where the overlapping fields of medicine and parapsychology constitute the distinct entity of medical parapsychology. While further knowledge concerning paranormal phenomena is still obtainable by the use of cards and dice, parapsychological experiments are also performed with apparatus
which may be found in the medical laboratory, e.g., the
plethysmograph,[1] the polygraph,[2] and the electroencephalograph. The electroencephalograph, which was first employed
in the study of ESP by the Canadian physical Cadoret,[3] has
been more recently used in parapsychology at the Jefferson
Medical College.[4] Here it was applied in an experiment with
fifteen pairs of identical twins who were tested for the appearance in one twin of an alpha brain wave when it was produced in the other by the closing of his eyes. This apparent
phenomenon of extrasensory communication was demonstrated
in two of the fifteen pairs, even though the two members of
each pair were in separate rooms six meters apart. Experiments indicating a relationship between ESP scores and alpha
wave productivity were performed at the University of Virginia School of Medicine,[5] and attempts were made at the
Maimonides Medical Center to improve the subject's ESP
scoring level by conditioning him to increase his output of
alpha waves.[6]

That ESP could be of practical value to the physician
is the opinion of the Austrian neuropsychiatrist Urban.[7] He
believes that the physician by using telepathy to reach the
correct diagnosis and therapy might avoid long interrogation

---

*Reprinted by permission of the author and publisher from
Parapsychology Review 3: 13-18 (Jan-Feb 1972).

of the patient.   Trained ESP sensitives are employed as assistants in a number of hospitals and clinics in Brazil. [8]
Their diagnoses are confirmed by standard methods, such as
x-ray findings, fluoroscope examinations and laboratory tests,
and treatment is in the hands of a registered physician who
follows his own scientific and empirical judgment.   Due to
this combination of the two methods, satisfactory clinical results are obtained in many cases.

The French physiologist Richet, who won the 1913 No-
bel Prize in Physiology and Medicine for his work on ana-
phylaxis, studied phenomena in the séance room and became
convinced that at times psychokinesis or movement at a distance occurred. [9]   Many objects including tables were dis-
placed and sometimes moved from one place to another even
though the medium was controlled so that normal contact with
the objects moved was impossible.

The Swiss psychiatrist Jung had two experiences which
could be attributed to spontaneous psychokinesis. [10]   The first
incident involved a heavy walnut table, an heirloom, that
split with a sound like a pistol shot.   The second phenomenon
involved a bread knife, stored inside a drawer, that, in some
inexplicable manner and with deafening report, split into four
pieces.   To explain parapsychological phenomena, Jung postulated a noncausal relationship between two events, linking
them together in a meaningful way.   This meaningful coinci-
dence he called synchronicity. [11]

That the terminal positions of randomly rolling dice
can be mentally controlled by psychokinesis has been established experimentally. [12]   Similarly, the mind may influence
the body by psychokinesis to produce illness or to alleviate it.
Psychosomatic effects such as the removal of warts by suggestion, hypnotically induced blisters, and stigmata are presently without medical explanation.   Psychokinesis may be the
modus operandi in cases where communication between brain
and organ by means of nerves or hormones is inadequate to
explain the psychosomatic effect.   This may be the explanation of the hypnotic cure by an English medical doctor of
congenital ichthyosiform erythroderma or "crocodile skin. "[13]
Previously the patient had been treated at various hospitals
without avail, and skin grafting had proved ineffective.

In faith healing, ESP, as well as psychokinesis, may
be responsible.   Illness may be functional and caused by the
mind or it may be organic and have a physical cause.   How-

ever, even where the disease is functional rather than organic, its healing is paranormal if conducted through ESP.
Some hypnotic phenomena indicate that faith healing does not
depend upon suggestion through sensory channels but instead
may occur through ESP. The French doctor Bertrand described experiments in which he verbally commanded his entranced subject to do one thing while willing her to do the
opposite.[14] Unable to solve the conflict, the subject showed
signs of increasing agitation which Bertrand could not resolve
except by making his willed and verbal commands coincide.
The English physician Elliotson reported the ability of a hypnotized subject to experience tastes, smells and experimentally induced pains that he himself was experiencing, with no
obvious contact between himself and the subject.[15]

Hypnosis at a distance is particularly indicative of
ESP since the possibility of sensory cues is precluded. The
French psychiatrist Janet published reports of 16 successful
attempts out of 22 trials of hypnosis at distances of at least
500 meters in which the time for each trial was randomly
determined.[16] Even posthypnotic suggestions were carried
out, such as carrying a lamp into another room and lighting
it in broad daylight. More recently the Soviet physiologist
Vasiliev accomplished telepathic hypnosis of three subjects
in a distant room separated from him by two intervening
walls.[17] As in the tests by Janet, the moment for hypnosis
was randomly determined.

In some cases the cure effected by faith in the healer
may be the removal of pain. The British medical doctor
Knowles performed experiments in relieving the pain of patients by his mental concentration.[18] Although he succeeded
only when the patient was aware of his attempt, he was out
of sight of the patient, did not apply suggestion verbally, and
did not succeed except when he willed that the pain would
cease. His greatest success was in cases of osteoarthritis,
and he was unsuccessful in alleviating pain that was artificially induced. He believes that the physician's expectation profoundly affects the patient's welfare not only through suggestion but also through telepathy. Variations in telepathic ability between physicians may be one of the reasons for the differences in their therapeutic accomplishments. Similarly,
the diagnostic ability of the physician may vary with his extrasensory perceptiveness.

Miraculous cures have some relationship to faith heal-
ings although they may be considered to be in the realm of

the supernatural rather than the paranormal. In a study of the eleven cures pronounced miraculous at Lourdes between 1946 and 1956, the English psychiatrist West concluded that lack of adequate medical investigations made a complete appraisal impossible.[19]

A few apparent cures of organic illness have been disclosed by investigations of the results of healers. The British medical physician Rose carried out a study of 90 persons claimed to have received benefit from healers.[20] Demonstrable organic disability was relieved or cured in one instance. In this case a physician had a small but definite hernia diagnosed by a surgeon and two other doctors. The hernia completely disappeared after four or five treatments by a healer, and there has been no trouble since.

The two German physicians Enke and Marx made evaluations of objective changes in 247 patients treated by a healer.[21] While improvement was greater in the predominantly functional diseases, it also occurred in ten patients with predominantly organic disease.

The British psychoanalyst FitzHerbert refers to two cures of organic illness of persons attending healing services.[22] One was an instantaneous disappearance of an inoperable goiter and the other the instantaneous development of a sizeable piece of new bone. Psi must be considered as a possible causal mechanism for the phenomenon of spontaneous cure.

Paranormal healing has also been reported in animals, the wounds of mice having been healed in this manner in one experiment.[23] This was accomplished through the coordinated research of the Medical School of the University of Manitoba and the Medical School of McGill University. Ten cages, each containing ten wounded mice in separate compartments, were held between the hands of a healer for two 15-minute periods a day. Without looking at the mice or cage, the healer either inserted his hands into an open paper bag concealing the cage or held the cage after it was sealed in the paper bag. A second group of wounded mice was treated the same way except that each day a different individual held the cage, while a third group of wounded mice remained unhandled. Each group consisted of 100 mice in ten cages. In the group held by the healer the rate of healing was significantly greater than in the other two groups, and there was no significant difference between the rates of healing in the latter two.

In addition to the evidence that positive thinking may have a beneficial effect on another organism, there are indications that negative or abnormal thinking may have a harmful effect. The writer performed an experiment with 19 psychotics in which each held a bottle of glucose solution. [24] When poured on suspensions of yeast cells the solutions were found to inhibit the growth of this organism.

The psychiatrist today would be deficient in his practice without some knowledge of paranormal phenomena. A poll of specialists in psychiatry and neurology[25] revealed that 23 percent of those replying answered affirmatively to the question: Have you ever observed, in your general experience or professional practice, anything which would indicate an extrasensory awareness? Some importance should be credited to this affirmation of ESP made by 163 American neuropsychiatrists.

Several psychiatrists have come to the conclusion that some paranormal phenomena may have a psychotic basis. The British psychiatrist Bendit reported that a good number of mental patients had ESP as a part of their make-up. [26] The perception of unknown or ambiguous objects and the experiencing of uncontrolled impulses are the typical causes of morbid anxiety. Therefore, in order to deprive these phenomena of their threatening character, he taught the patient to understand that they may have a rational source in ESP.

In some Brazilian hospitals the ESP faculty is developed when it is found to be at the bottom of a neurosis or psychosis. [27] When an individual is disturbed by voices and visions of an hallucinatory nature, he is trained to hear and see these hallucinations more clearly. It is claimed that the ESP faculty is developed under the full control of the individual, who returns to normal life completely cured.

Such treatment is a far cry from the orthodox handling of the mentally ill in most civilized parts of the world. It may be possible to employ it in Brazil because of that country's different sociocultural attitude toward the paranormal. According to the American psychiatrist Ehrenwald, any reference to the occurrence of telepathy should be avoided for the advanced schizophrenic who may use interpretations involving psi as confirmation of his delusional trend. [28] The paranoiac frequently alleges that he is being subjected to telepathic influences and claims to possess supernatural powers of thought or action. For this reason, the psychiatrist

regards with suspicion the sanity of a person making such
assertions.

Nevertheless, many psychiatrists believe that the paranoiac may use ESP in his keen discernment of the thoughts
of others which refer to him. Even mentally well patients
may unconsciously perceive meaningful sounds which occur
during surgical anesthesia. This has been revealed by studies of patients under hypnosis conducted by the American
physician Cheek, who found indications that ESP may have
been occasionally involved. [29] This might be of even greater
occurrence in paranoidal patients. According to Ehrenwald,
the paranoiac is telepathically sensitive to the repressed
sadistic-aggressive tendencies in the unconscious minds of
his fellow-men. The telepathic sensitivity is still present in
the patient at the stage of schizophrenic deterioration, and
his irrational behavior results from his attempts to ward off
his uncanny experiences which arise partly through telepathy.
Ullman, another American psychiatrist, has frequently encountered paranormal expression in very ill individuals who
were teetering on the brink, but not yet over on the psychotic side. [30] He has found that once schizophrenia is en-
trenched, the psi ability seems to be lost.

Psychotic patients have not been found to obtain higher ESP scores than those achieved by normal persons.
Card tests given by the Austrian psychiatrist Urban failed to
indicate that paranoid patients claiming telepathic persecution
are endowed with greater ESP sensitivity. [31] Actually, he
found that, during or after electroshock, insulin shock or
narcoanalysis, the ESP scores of mental patients increased
temporarily to above their pretreatment level.

The writer found no evidence of greater ESP scoring
ability in subjects with stronger neurotic or psychotic tendencies. [32] I obtained negative correlations between the ESP
scores of 165 subjects and the several psychiatric categories
of the Minnesota Multiphasic Personality Inventory, which is
frequently used as an index of neurosis or psychosis.

The hysteric as well as the schizophrenic may utilize
ESP. Ehrenwald is of the opinion that the hysteric may
actually be a much better ESP subject than the schizophrenic
because he shows much less resistance. [33] Hysteric in origin is the mediumistic trance which is induced by suggestion
or autosuggestion. It provides an outlet for tendencies whose
expression is being withheld in ordinary life. Because of

this, the productions of the mediumistic trance are comparable to the symptoms of hysteria and especially of hysteric
multiple personality.   Personalities produced during trance
appear to result from the integration, elaboration and drama-
tization of mental material some of which may be extrasensory in origin.

Hysterical dissociation of an infantile part of the psyche
in which severe conflicts are kept repressed may be the explanation for poltergeist phenomena.   According to the American psychoanalyst Fodor, a torn-off part of the mind, that is
conditioned by conflict-material which the main personality
has repressed, utilizes psychokinesis to produce paranormal
physical phenomena. [34] Successful psychoanalysis would cure
the underlying pathology and remove the cause of the poltergeist.

An alternative hypothesis to dissociation as the cause
of some psychic phenomena is spirit possession.   Whether
psychiatrists are really open-minded on the possession issue
is questioned by the South African psychiatrist Hurst. [35] In
some Brazilian hospitals mediums are used to effect a cure
when there is evidence of spirit possession. [36] Through a
medium, contact is made with the supposed parasitic spirit
and the manifesting secondary personality is made to understand that he has died and is no longer inhabiting his own
body.   In the United States, the American neuropsychiatrist
MacRobert cites two cases of psychical healing in which the
attending physician engaged a medium to expel the obsessing
spirit. [37]

Hallucinations provide a means by which paranormally
obtained information may be manifested in the consciousness.
The British neurologist Walter believes that, although a physical disturbance is necessary for an hallucination, the neu-
ronic complexity of the brain is so vast and its metabolic
economy so intricate that physical conditions giving rise to
hallucinations must occur quite often in everyone. [38] The
English psychiatrist West distinguishes between the hallucinations of psychotics and the ostensibly psychic hallucinations
of the mentally sound. [39] He states that pathological hallucinations tend to be auditory, stereotyped, repetitive and
vague.   They take place during a manifest illness and are
accompanied by other symptoms, particularly by disturbances
of consciousness and loss of awareness of the normal surroundings.   The psychic hallucination, on the other hand,
tends to be visual and to be unique, or almost unique, in the

life of the subject. It is realistic, and is remembered with
greater certainty and described with more precision than the
pathological hallucination. It is disconnected from any illness
or known disturbance, and is not accompanied by any loss of
contact with the normal surroundings.

Osis conducted a poll of doctors and nurses concerning the hallucinations of over 35,000 patients on their deathbed. [40] In contrast to hallucinations of the healthy, there
was an overwhelming preponderance of apparitions of dead
persons, usually relatives of the dying patient. Most typically, the experience had a calming effect on the dying patient
who interpreted the apparition as a spirit come to help his
transition into the next world. The great majority of such
experiences occurred in conscious, lucid patients who were not
confused by drugs or fever. The frequency of these experiences was not related to the nature of the patient's illness
nor to his educational and social background. The ratio of
apparitions of dead to living persons was greater in patients
in a state of clear, as opposed to impaired, consciousness
and the calming effect of the hallucination was much more
frequent. The proportion of apparitions interpreted as having "come to take the patient away" was much larger in those
instances which occurred very close to the moment of death.

Stevenson, a professor of psychiatry at the University
of Virginia School of Medicine, described 35 cases of spontaneous impressions about distant persons. [41] He personally
investigated most of these cases and believes ESP is the best
interpretation for them. He concludes that the fully developed
impression consists of an awareness that a particular person
is in distress. This is followed first by an emotion appropriate to that awareness, and then by an impulse to help the
distressed person. He has found that the percipient can bring
additional details to consciousness after he has had an initial
general impression.

A limited number of experiments have been performed
in which the effects of drugs on parapsychological phenomena
have been tested objectively. In tests of ESP or of psychokinesis the use of a moderate quantity of alcohol caused significantly higher scoring, [42] while the administration of 100
ml. of gin resulted in a significant decline in scoring. [43]
Subjects did significantly better after caffeine was administered, [44] and it also countered the effect of sodium amytal
which was found to lower the score. [45] The Canadian physician Cadoret examined the effects of the stimulant dexedrine

as well as the depressant sodium amytal on ESP performance. [46] While sodium amytal decreased the performance,
dexedrine had a positive effect with free response material
(pictures cut from magazines) and a negative effect with limited response material (standard ESP cards). Huby and the
English physician Wilson found that dexedrine caused a decline
in scoring as did the depressant quinalbarbitone. [47] In contrast, Dartalan, a chlorpromazine-like tranquilizer, appeared
to raise the scoring ability.

LSD treatment offered possibilities for parapsychological studies in a pilot study of six terminal cancer patients
according to the psychiatrist Pahnke. [48] A few reports of
ESP under LSD were given by the physician Levine, but it is
not clear that the frequency of occurrence was greater than
in spontaneous drug-free states. [49] The Italians Cavanna and
Servadio, biochemist and psychiatrist working in conjunction,
tested four subjects with doses of LSD and psilocybin (an
hallucinogen found in mushrooms) for similarity between their
described imagery and covered photographic color prints. [50]
While some of the results might be indicative of ESP, there
was no indication of higher scoring with the hallucinogens.
Paranormal phenomena produced by persons after eating hal-
lucinogenic mushrooms were reported by the Americans Wasson[51] and Puharich. [52] Apparently paranormal effects of
mescaline and LSD were reported by the Canadian physicians
Blewett, Hoffer and Osmond. [53] In a further paper, Hoffer
compared ESP sensitivity with the effects of LSD. [54] In both
ESP and in LSD intoxication, he believed there is an increase
of adrenalin production followed by its being overbalanced by
the production of its metabolites. Osmond, who participated
in the above study, suggests that in the hypertribal society
which may arise in the future, ESP will become a necessity
for survival. [55] He assumes that, where nonverbal communication is depended upon, extrasensory capacities will be am-
plified in the struggle to make one's feelings known to his
fellows.

Several psychoanalysts have found evidence of ESP in
analyzing the dreams of their patients. The study of telepathic dreams has reached the experimental stage at the
Maimonides Medical Center in Brooklyn. [56] Subjects' dreams
were compared with paintings viewed by an agent in a room
40 feet distant. In blind experiments, the dreams were found
to correspond with the paintings more often than expected by
chance, regardless of whether they were ranked by the subjects or by outside judges. The American psychiatrist Ull-

man, who participated in this research, reported that target
material threatening the preservation of the dreamer was most
likely to be incorporated into the dream. [57] He concluded
that the dreamer scans for external events that have a special meaning for him.

The Viennese psychiatrist Stekel was first to bring
telepathic dreams to psychiatric attention. [58] He cited a number of presumptively telepathic dreams observed in his work
with neurotic patients and saw that love, jealousy and anxiety
predisposed the agent and the percipient to the telepathic
event.

Freud wrote on the subject of telepathy on six occasions. [59] He believed that it is feasible for psychoanalysis
to reveal a possible telepathic event when it would otherwise
not have been recognized as such. It was his conclusion that,
if telepathy were a fact, the laws of unconscious mental action
would apply to telepathically perceived data. As a result of
his own studies, he believed that emotionally emphasized complexes might take on telepathic activity in their transition
from the unconscious to the preconscious.

In his last contribution to parapsychology, Freud cited
publications in apparent telepathy by two other well-known analysts, Deutsch and Burlingham. Deutsch described a telepathic action by her patient and attributed it to her failure to
give the patient full attention because of being preoccupied
with her own affairs. [60] Burlingham reported telepathy between mother and child, both of whom were being analyzed
at the time. [61]

Eisenbud, an American psychoanalyst, described telepathic occurrences between two patients who did not know one
another. [62] Occasionally this took the form of competition in
telepathy between the patients in an attempt to gratify the
analyst and gain his love.

The Hungarian psychoanalyst Hollos reported observing
over 500 instances of telepathy in his analytic work. [63] He
found that telepathy is a frequent occurrence between analyst
and patient, especially during a difficult period in the analyst's life. He concluded that in the telepathic process, as
it manifests itself in analysis, there is a return of what the
analyst has repressed, but the return occurs in the mind of
the patient and is subject to his rules of distortion. He supported Freud's thesis that wishes in a state of imperfect re-

pression are subject to telepathic transmission. Servadio, an Italian psychoanalyst, confirmed the views of Hollos. [64] He concluded that the telepathically transferred material is subject to the process of repression which takes place in the analyst and is related to the special complexes of the patient.

The American psychoanalyst Fodor stated that the clue to a complete understanding of a patient's dream sometimes lies in an event which is not revealed through the patient's associations alone but which in some instances can be found by analysis of the analyst's dreams in relationship to his patient. [65] He concluded that the telepathic dream reflects like a mirror the contents of the analyst's unconscious.

Ehrenwald, an American psychiatrist, expressed the opinion that some of what a therapist finds in a patient's mind he has telepathically implanted there himself. [66] This is exemplified by the correspondence in the dream content of patients with the prevailing idea of the schools of their analysts, which he called doctrinal compliance.

The American psychoanalyst Pederson-Krag reported cases displaying the frequently aggressive nature of telepathy. [67] She concluded that human speech had to be invented because telepathic communication revealed too much of man's aggressive and erotic impulses.

Schwarz, an American psychiatrist, presented a record of 91 apparent telepathic phenomena between his daughter --when she was between one and three and one-half years of age--and either him or his wife. [68] Most events took place when both child and parents were in a state of rapport, and while either the agent or the percipient was preoccupied in a passive trance-like state.

The British psychoanalyst FitzHerbert wrote that lack of memory of the first few years of one's life may be caused by the free flow of telepathy from mother to child. [69] If the child did not later forget the material, it would confuse his identity. She also concluded that the continuous presence of a single mother-figure is important to a child during his early years because, through ESP, the child receives much of the mother's mental content. The sudden appearance of a different "mother" with a completely different mental content results in emotional shock and confusion to the child.

Opposition to parapsychology by analysts as well as by other scientists results partly from the fact that science has tried hard and long to dispel belief in the type of phenomena whose existence is now being asserted by parapsychology. It also results from the fact that primitive, animistic and magical ideas have been thrown aside in the development of the ego, and psychological defenses have been set up against them. When we are confronted with paranormal experiences, these defenses against magical thinking are endangered and are reinforced to avoid the anxiety that develops when the ego's bulwarks are threatened. As a result, our rational selves deny the evidence for parapsychology in an irrational manner.

Despite these forces, many psychoanalysts accept the existence of ESP. Gillespie, former President of the British Psychoanalytic Society and former President of the International Psychoanalytical Association, concluded that the reason so few analysts have published material on the subject is that paranormal phenomena involve the analyst personally as much as the patient. [70] Publication of the phenomena is made difficult or impracticable because the events are intimately mixed up with the analyst's private life and personal problems. He writes, "I have found, in fact, both in public and private discussion, that not a few analysts took it for granted that such things occur; I found myself in the position of the little boy who was the only one to mention what everyone else knew about the Emperor's clothes."

Nevertheless, ESP occurs only emotionally and often decreases in frequency as it is pursued. For example, the American psychoanalyst Eisenbud states that his observations of telepathy in his patients have become less frequent during his career. At least a partial explanation of the poverty of ESP and its chronological decline may be offered by a medical analogy made by Rushton. [71] It is a well known fact that, in order to maintain its individuality, the human body is generally impervious to foreign proteins, and repels any of these bodies that successfully invade it. Similarly, in order to maintain its personal integrity, the human organism generally precludes the entrance of extrasensory information, and any successful entry builds immunity against its repetition. Perhaps, psychic sensitives are individuals who possess low immunity to psychic penetration and have a weak immune response mechanism for the prevention of paranormal incursion.

REFERENCES

1. Dean, E. D. and Nash, C. B. "Plethysmograph Results under Strict Conditions," J. Parapsychol. 27
   (1963): 281-82.
2. Backster, C. "Evidence of a Primary Perception in
   Plant Life," Int. J. Parapsychol. 10 (1968): 329-
   48.
3. Cadoret, R. J. "An Exploratory Experiment: Continuous EEG Recording during Clairvoyant Card Tests,"
   J. Parapsychol. 28 (1964): 226.
4. Duane, T. D. and Behrendt, T. "Extrasensory Elec-
   troencephalographic Induction between Identical
   Twins," Science 150 (1965): 367.
5. Stanford, R. G. and Stanford, B. E. "Shifts in EEG
   Alpha Rhythm as Related to Calling Patterns and
   ESP Run-Score Variance," J. Parapsychol. 33
   (1969): 38-47.
6. Honorton, C. and Carbone, M. "A Preliminary Study
   of Feedback-Augmented EEG Alpha Activity and
   ESP Card-Guessing Performance," J. Amer. Soc.
   Psych. Res. 65 (1971): 66-74.
7. Urban, H. J. "Parapsychological Research at a Psychiatric Clinic," in Proceedings of the First International Conference of Parapsychological Studies
   (New York: Parapsychology Foundation, 1955).
8. Rodriguez, L. J. "Brazil: African Heritage," Tomorrow 8 (1960), No. 4: 79-84.
9. Richet, C. Thirty Years of Psychical Research, trans.
   Stanley DeBrath (New York: Macmillan, 1923).
10. Jung, C. G. Memories, Dreams, Reflections (New
    York: Pantheon Books, 1963).
11. Jung, C. G. and Pauli, W. The Interpretation of Na-
    ture and the Psyche (New York: Pantheon Books,
    1955).
12. Rhine, J. B. and Pratt, J. B. Parapsychology (Spring-
    field, Ill.: Charles C. Thomas, 1957).
13. Mason, A. A. "A Case of Congenital Ichthyosiform
    Erythrodermia of Brocq Treated by Hypnosis,"
    Brit. Med. J. 4781 (1952): 422-23.
14. Bertrand, A. Traité du Somnambulisme (Paris, 1823).
15. Elliotson, J. Remarkable Cure of Intense Nervous
    Affections, etc.," Zoist 5 (1847-48): 234-53.
16. Janet, P. "Sur quelques phénomènes de Somnambu-
    lisme," Bull. de la Soc. de Psychologie de Paris.
    Revue Philosophique 21 (1886): 190-98.
17. Vasiliev, L. L. Experimental Research in Thought

Suggestion (Leningrad: Univ. Leningrad Press, 1962).

18. Knowles, F. W. "Psychic Healing in Organic Disease," J. Amer. Soc. Psych. Res. 50 (1956): 110-17.

19. West, D. J. Eleven Lourdes Miracles (London: Gerald Duckworth, 1957).

20. Rose, L. "Some Aspects of Paranormal Healing," J. Soc. Psych. Res. 38 (1955): 105-20.

21. Strauch, I. "Medical Aspects of Mental Healing," Int. J. Parapsychol. 5 (1963): 135-65.

22. FitzHerbert, J. "The Nature of Hypnosis and Paranormal Healing," J. Soc. Psych. Res. 46 (1971): 1-14.

23. Grad, B., Cadoret, R. J., and Paul, G. I. "The Influence of an Unorthodox Method of Treatment on Wound Healing in Mice," Int. J. Parapsychol. 3 (1961), No. 2: 5-24.

24. Nash, C. B. and Nash, C. S. "Effect of Paranormally Conditioned Solution on Yeast Fermentation," J. Parapsychol. 31 (1967): 314.

25. MacRobert, R. G. "Current Attitudes of American Neuropsychiatrists toward Parapsychology: A Survey," J. Parapsychol. 12 (1948): 257-72.

26. Bendit, L. J. Paranormal Cognition (London: Faber and Faber, 1943).

27. Rodriguez, L. J. "Brazil: African Heritage," Tomorrow 8 (1960), No. 4: 79-84.

28. Ehrenwald, J. Telepathy and Medical Psychology (London: George Allen, 1947).

29. Cheek, D. B. "Unconscious Perception of Meaningful Sounds during Surgical Anaesthesia as Revealed under Hypnosis," Amer. J. Clin. Hypn. 1 (1959): 101-13.

30. Ullman, M. "The Nature of Psi Processes," J. Parapsychol. 13 (1949): 59-62.

31. Urban, H. J. "ESP Tests with the Mentally Ill," Parapsychol. Bull. 14 (1949): 1-2.

32. Nash, C. B. "Relation between ESP Scoring Level and the Minnesota Multiphasic Personality Inventory," J. Amer. Soc. Psych. Res. 60 (1966): 56-62.

33. Ehrenwald, J. Telepathy and Medical Psychology, loc. cit.

34. Fodor, N. On the Trail of the Poltergeist (New York: Citadel Press, 1958).

35. Hurst, L. A. "Parapsychology and Some Potential Relations," Publications of the South-African Soc. Psych. Res. 3 (1958): 6-13.

36. Rodriguez, L. J. "Brazil: African Heritage," loc. cit.
37. MacRobert, R. G. "When Is Healing 'Psychic'?" Tomorrow 3 (1955), No. 3: 47-55.
38. Walter, W. G. The Neurophysiological Aspects of Hallucinations and Illusory Experience (London: Society for Psychical Research, 1960).
39. West, D. J. "Visionary and Hallucinatory Experiences: A Comparative Appraisal," Int. J. Parapsychol. 2 (1960): 89-100.
40. Osis, K. Deathbed Observations by Physicians and Nurses. Parapsychological Monograph No. 3 (New York: Parapsychology Foundation, 1961).
41. Stevenson, I. "Telepathic Impressions: A Review and Report of Thirty-Five New Cases," Proc. Amer. Soc. Psych. Res. 29 (1970): 1-198.
42. Brugmans, H. J. W. "Some Experiments in Telepathy Performed in the Psychological Institute of the University of Groningen," in Compte-rendu du Premier Congrès International des Recherches Phychiques, 1921 (Copenhagen, 1922): 396-408.
43. Averill, R. L. and Rhine, J. B. "The Effect of Alcohol upon Performance in PK Tests," J. Parapsychol. 9 (1945): 32-41.
44. Rhine, J. B. and Humphrey, B. M. "An Exploratory Experiment on the Effect of Caffeine upon Performance in PK Tests," J. Parapsychol. 9 (1945): 80-91.
45. Rhine, J. B., et al. Extrasensory Perception after Sixty Years (New York: Henry Holt, 1940).
46. Cadoret, R. J. "The Effect of Amytal and Dexedrine on ESP Performance," J. Parapsychol. 17 (1953): 259-74.
47. Huby, P. M. and Wilson, C. W. M. "The Effects of Drugs on ESP Ability," J. Soc. Psych. Res. 41 (1961): 60-66.
48. Pahnke, W. "The Psychedelic Mystical Experience in Terminal Cancer Patients and its Possible Implications for Psi Research," in Psi and Altered States of Consciousness; Proceedings of an International Conference on Hypnosis, Drugs, Dreams, and Psi, 1967, ed. R. Cavanna and M. Ullman (New York: Parapsychology Foundation, 1968).
49. Levine, J. "Psychopharmacology: Implications for Psi Research," in Psi and Altered States of Consciousness; Proceedings of an International Conference on Hypnosis, Drugs, Dreams, and Psi, 1967, ed. R. Cavanna and M. Ullman (New York: Parapsychology

Foundation, 1968).

50. Cavanna, R. and Servadio, E. ESP Experiments with LSD 25 and Psilocybin, Parapsychological Monograph No. 5 (New York: Parapsychology Foundation, 1964).

51. Wasson, V. P. and Wasson, R. G. Mushrooms, Russia and History (New York: Pantheon Books, 1958).

52. Puharich, A. The Sacred Mushroom (Garden City, N. Y.: Doubleday, 1959).

53. Blewett, D. B. "Investigating the Psychedelic Experience," in Proceedings of Two Conferences on Parapsychology and Pharmacology, 1958, 1959 (New York: Parapsychology Foundation, 1961).

54. Hoffer, A. "Pharmacological Stimuli to Sensitivity," in Proceedings of Two Conferences on Parapsychology and Pharmacology, 1958, 1959 (New York: Parapsychology Foundation, 1961).

55. Osmond, H. "Psi and the Psychedelic Movement," in Psi and Altered States of Consciousness; Proceedings of an International Conference on Hypnosis, Drugs, Dreams, and Psi, 1967 (New York: Parapsychology Foundation, 1968).

56. Ullman, M., Krippner, S. and Feldstein, S. "Experimentally-Induced Telepathic Dreams: Two Studies Using EEG-REM Monitoring Technique," Int. J. Neuropsychiat. 2 (1966): 420-37.

57. Ullman, M. "The Experimentally-Induced Telepathic Dream: Theoretical Implications," J. Amer. Soc. Psych. Res. 64 (1970): 538-74.

58. Stekel, W. Der Telepathische Traum (Berlin: Johannes Baum, 1920).

59. Devereux, G. Psychoanalysis and the Occult (New York: International Universities Press, 1951).

60. Deutsch, H. "Occult Processes Occurring during Psychoanalysis," Imago 12 (1926): 418-33.

61. Burlingham, D. T. "Child Analysis and the Mother," Psychoanal. Quart. 5 (1935): 69-92.

62. Eisenbud, J. "The Dreams of Two Patients in Analysis Interpreted as a Telepathic Rêve à Deux," Psychoanal. Quart. 16 (1947): 39-60.

63. Hollos, I. "Psychopathologie Alltäglicher Telepatischer Erscheinungen," Imago 19 (1933).

64. Servadio, E. "Psychoanalysis and Telepathy," Imago 21 (1942): 489-97.

65. Fodor, N. "Telepathic Dreams," Amer. Imago 3 (1942): 61-85.

66. Ehrenwald, J. Telepathy and Medical Psychology, op. cit.

67.   Pederson-Krag, G.   "Telepathy and Repression," Psy-
        choanal. Quart. 16 (1947): 61-68.
68.   Schwarz, B. E.   "Telepathic Events in a Child between
        1 and 3 1/2 Years of Age," Int. J. Parapsychol.
        3 (1961), No. 4: 5-52.
69.   FitzHerbert, J.   "Extrasensory Perception in Early
        Childhood," Int. J. Parapsychol. 3 (1961), No. 3:
        89-95.
70.   Gillespie, W. H.   "Experiences Suggestive of Para-
        normal Cognition in the Psychoanalytic Situation,"
        in Ciba Foundation Symposium on Extrasensory Per-
        ception (Boston: Little, Brown and Co., 1956).
71.   Rushton, W. A. H.   "First Sight--Second Sight," Proc.
        Soc. Psych. Res. 55 (1971): 177-88.

Alberti, G. "Psychopathology and parapsychology--some possible contacts. " In Angoff, A. and Shapin, B. (Eds.).
Parapsychology and the Sciences. N. Y. , Parapsychology Foundation, 1974. Pp. 225-37.

Ehrenwald, J. History of Psychotherapy: From Healing
Magic to Encounter Groups. N. Y. , Aronson, 1975.

Eisenbud, J. Psi and Psychoanalysis. N. Y. , Grune and
Stratton, 1970.

Grad, B. "Healing by laying on of hands: Review of experiments and implications. " Pastoral Psychology 21:
19-26 (Sep 1970).

_____ . "The biological effects of the laying on of hands
on animals and plants: implications for biology. " In
Schmeidler, G. R. (Ed.). Parapsychology: Its Relation to Physics, Biology, Psychology and Psychiatry.
Metuchen, N. J. , Scarecrow Press, 1976.

_____ . "The 'laying on of hands': implications for psychotherapy, gentling, and the placebo effect. " JASPR
61: 286-305 (Oct 1967).

_____ . "Some biological effects of the 'laying on of
hands:' A review of experiments with animals and
plants. " JASPR 59: 95-129 (Apr 1965).

Hudesman, J. and Schmeidler, G. R. "ESP scores following therapeutic sessions. " JASPR 65: 215-22 (Apr
1971).

Kelsey, M. T. "Healing ministry within the church. " Journal of Religion and Health 9: 105-22 (Apr 1970).

LeShan, L. The Medium, the Mystic and the Physicist.
N. Y. , Julian Press, 1974.

Melton, J. G. A Reader's Guide to the Church's Ministry of
Healing. Evanston, Ill. , The Academy of Religion and
Psychical Research, 1973.

Neff, H. R. Psychic Phenomena and Religion: ESP, Prayer,
Healing, Survival. Philadelphia, Westminster Press,
1971. Ch. 4.

Rejdak, Z. "Still healing in the shadow of legal regulations?"
Osteopathic Physician 41: 83-98 (Apr 1974).

Rogo, D. S. "Psi in the clinical framework of abnormal
psychology. " In Angoff, A. and Shapin, B. (Eds.).
Parapsychology and the Sciences. N. Y. , Parapsychol-

ogy Foundation, 1974. Pp. 52-67.
Servadio, E. "Psychoanalysis and parapsychology. " In
    Angoff, A. and Shapin, B. (Eds.). Parapsychology
    and the Sciences. N. Y. , Parapsychology Foundation,
    1974. Pp. 68-82.
Ullman, M. "Psi and psychiatry. " In Mitchell, E. D. (Ed.).
    Psychic Exploration. N. Y. , Putnam's, 1974. Ch. 10.
Ullman, M. "Psychiatry and parapsychology: The Consum-
    mation of an uncertain romance. " In Schmeidler,
    G. R. (Ed.). Parapsychology: Its Relation to Phys-
    ics, Biology, Psychology and Psychiatry. Metuchen,
    N. J. , Scarecrow Press, 1976.
Wells, R. and Klein, J. "A replication of a 'psychic heal-
    ing' paradigm. " JP 36: 144-49 (Jun 1972).

PART III

INSIGHTS INTO HOW PSI OPERATES

INTRODUCTION

The papers in this section are centered primarily on questions concerning the way psi operates or in delineating the characteristics of psi.

Although at first glance it may appear that the sole purpose in conducting standard ESP tests is to locate subjects who can guess significantly more targets than would be expected by chance, in actual fact this aspect of psi testing represents only the tip of the proverbial iceberg. It is very likely, as J. G. Pratt has pointed out, that "judged by what the data show, the calling is not a series of separate efforts to identify individual targets as they are presented. It is, rather, a process of mental associations made within certain constraints as defined by the assigned task and oriented toward the sequence of targets" (p. 149). [1]

In the first paper in this section J. B. Rhine surveys an aspect of psi that persons not familiar with the literature of experimental parapsychology may well not be aware of: psi-missing. When psi-missing occurs in a psi test, the subject fails to respond correctly to the targets significantly fewer times than would be expected if only chance factors were operating. This form of psi expression is one of the most intriguing, elusive, and yet at the same time potentially revealing clues we have to the nature of psi. Dr. Rhine has been concerned with this problem from the earliest days of his research, and in this overview he discusses what is known thus far about psi-missing and when it is likely to occur.

The second paper, "ESP over Distance," is a survey by Karlis Osis who attempts to assess the role of distance on ESP test results. Although it has become commonplace in the literature to say that ESP transcends both space and time, this is the first complete survey aimed at determining whether or not that statement is correct.

In the third paper, "Position Effects and Psi Test Results," J. B. Rhine surveys a large block of the data Pratt refers to--that which is indicative of position effects, or the tendency of hits in psi tests to be distributed systematically according to the position of the trial on the record sheet. In other words, he is describing the evidence indicating that the subject is responding to the entire run as a unit, not simply to individual trials.

Hypnosis has long been considered a likely tool for the induction of psi-conducive states or as a means of enhancing psi test results. In "Hypnosis and ESP Performance," Honorton and Krippner review the experimental studies of hypnosis and ESP, describe some methodological considerations in contemporary hypnosis research, and discuss the possibility of training ESP by means of hypnosis.

Until recently parapsychological experimentation for the most part has either been directed toward obtaining evidence that psi exists or in discovering correlates of ESP and PK performance. But the generation of parapsychologists who have come into their own during the last decade have not been content with these goals. Several of them have had the courage and the ingenuity to look into ways of activating psi in controlled experimental situations. The advent of improved instrumentation for studying subjective states, especially the EEG, has also provided the impetus for this new research. Charles Honorton has been a leader in these explorations and in "State of Awareness Factors in Psi Activation," he reviews the salient points that the research has revealed thus far.

The final paper in this section, "Scientific, Ethical, and Clinical Problems in 'Training' of Psi Ability" by Rex Stanford, differs from the others in this book because it is being published here for the first time. It was presented at the symposium, "The Application and Misapplication of Findings in Parapsychology," at the 1975 annual meeting of the American Association for the Advancement of Science. It is included here even though it was not previously published in a periodical because of its timeliness and importance and because it contains the best review to date of attempts to train psi ability. Stanford also offers cogent criticisms of the psychic development claims of commercial mind training courses. Because of its recency, only a few items could be included in the list of additional readings.

REFERENCE

1. Pratt, J. G. "Some Notes for the Future Einstein for Parapsychology. " JASPR 68: 113-55 (Apr 1974).

Chapter 7

PSI-MISSING RE-EXAMINED*

by J. B. Rhine

Since the effect known as psi-missing was described
and named in 1952 (40), it has become the topic of a fairly
large literature and has taken on increased importance in
parapsychology. This type of missing, as most of you know,
is not the mere lack of success, or chance missing. Psi-
missing is the systematic avoidance of the targets (when hitting is intended) to an extent that chance missing cannot explain. Accordingly, it is a definite finding in its own right,
and, although only sixteen years have passed since it was
expressly identified, it has now become for some workers in
parapsychology one of the pressing problems of psi research.

One reason for this urgency is the difficulty psi-missing creates for the average investigator. As is now well
known, the subject in a psi test is generally unaware of whether or not he is hitting or missing the targets. Because of
the uncertainty this produces, the experimenter cannot confidently depend on getting psi ability to register dependably; or
if he is able to do so for a time, this can well be followed
by a period of missing that will cancel his earlier gains.

On the other hand, psi-missing has actually been the
source of much of what is known today about parapsychology
and has greatly enriched the rational conception of how psi
operates. But to appraise the problems and the values of
psi-missing calls for a new survey of progress at this stage.
Accordingly, I shall briefly outline (1) the way the concept
of psi-missing developed, (2) the conditions under which such

---

*This article, based on a paper presented at the Autumn Re-
view Meeting held by the Institute for Parapsychology in September 1968, is reprinted by permission of the author and
publisher from the Journal of Parapsychology 33: 1-38 (Mar.
1969).

missing occurs, (3) what is known about how it occurs, and
(4) the methods by which it is measured. Finally, there will
be a section on the nature and bearing of the psi-missing effect.

I. FIRST INDICATIONS

At the Duke Parapsychology Laboratory, where the
concept developed, the initial encounter with a probable psi-
missing effect was with the first high-scoring subject, AJL.
It was in 1932 when, after a period of high scores in card-
guessing tests of clairvoyance, I inadvertently kept him over-
time, and his scores abruptly dropped to a level below chance
for the few test runs made before I had to release him. In-
trigued by the sudden shift, I watched for later occasions on
which AJL seemed under strain, and I even deliberately introduced such conditions now and then. Eventually I gathered
enough trials (1,650 guesses) of this type to give a significant
drop of scoring rate below the chance average, thus providing
a tentative basis of judgment--a kind of pilot study (42, p.
85).

I suspected at the time that AJL was, in some half-
conscious sort of way, trying to use ESP to avoid the targets.
These results called to mind an earlier report by Estabrooks
(9) of a puzzling case of negative deviation in ESP tests with
playing cards. In the last of four test series, the subjects
reversed their earlier high-scoring trend and dropped significantly below mean chance expectation. Estabrooks reported
that they had needed urging to do this additional series, and
also that in this series they were separated from the target
cards by greater distance than earlier (which may have made
the test seem harder). Estabrooks proposed "adverse autosuggestion" to explain the reversal.

In order to see what the "will-to-miss" would do, I
asked two of the better subjects who were available at the
time (HP and CES) each to do a series of tests of clairvoyance in which they deliberately tried to miss the targets.
Both of them obtained significant negative deviations. In each
case the drop below chance was approximately equal to the
normal positive deviation of the subject (42, pp. 95, 113).

The negative motivation idea, however, did not last
long as a general hypothesis of what causes negative deviations. The first challenge came from the clairvoyance test

results of another Duke subject, HLF, a graduate student in
psychology (42, p. 188). He had carried out a series of self-
tests in which he tried to identify the suits of playing cards
in long runs of 100 calls per day for a period of nine days.
The pooled results were close to chance, but when they were
broken down into total scores of the five 20-trial segments of
the run, they showed a steep decline giving the following segment deviations from chance: +13, +5, +3, -7, -9. The
difference between the first two segments and the last two is
acceptably significant. [It is assumed that psi-missing is reasonably likely to be involved when, as in this case, a significant difference is found and approximately half of it (or more)
is contributed by the negative deviation. Here it is -16 as
against +18.] This raised the question as to how to explain
the drop below chance in the last two segments. Negative
motivation did not seem applicable in this case.

Soon after HFL did this work, a similar case came
in from a well-controlled experiment with AJL (42, p. 188).
In this experiment the subject was given clairvoyance tests
with long, comparably slow runs of 50 trials each, with target cards enclosed in sealed opaque envelopes (requiring slow
recording of the envelope number with each guess). He, too,
obtained a total score close to chance; but again, when the
total scores were broken into five run-segments (10 trials
each), they gave a decline like that of HLF: +7, +1, +3,
-3, -8. Here, too, the first two segments differed significantly from the last two, and again motivation did not seem
to be the differentiating factor.

But whatever the explanation, the immediate effect of
these negative deviations was alarming to the experimenter
of that period. The canceling effect of these negative deviations was destructive to the total score, the main basis of
the test significance. At the same time, in cases where they
had been evaluated, these unplanned negative deviations were
found to indicate as much evidence of psi as the normal positive deviations. It was really a case of pitting psi against
itself, and the effect was disconcerting in one way and intriguing in another.

The question was raised in 1936 as to the propriety
of the use of the binomial test of significance in dealing with
these negative deviations (in appropriate samples). [The occasion was that of a visit of about 25 mathematicians to the
Duke Laboratory incidental to a convention being held at the
University.] One of the leading statisticians of the day, Dr.

Thornton Fry, not only gave his approval but even presented a case of similar target avoidance from his own observation. As a member of a Scientific American committee investigating the claims made for the "Abrams Diagnostic Box," he had helped to test a practitioner's claim of the ability to determine whether a microscopic slide (completely hidden in the box) contained water or blood; the 10 trials given were all misses. Since no known physical basis of identification existed, it looked as though the man was using ESP to give consistently wrong guesses, perhaps because he was under extreme pressure. It was a significant finding (although the committee did not know how to handle it and did not report it).

But the mid-thirties at the Duke Laboratory was no time to consider calmly and deliberately what might be causing such unexplained negative deviations in psi tests. Parapsychology at that time was in the thick of the great controversy with the psychologists over ESP. The primary question for everyone working in the new field was how strong a case could be made for the occurrence of that capacity. However interesting these negative deviations might be theoretically, the demand on every hand was for more and better evidence; at such a stage, negative deviations that canceled the positive results were simply agonizing. Besides, it was not easy to sell ESP and the importance of negative deviations together to a critical psychological profession. Attention had to be directed toward more practical considerations.

The first practical step was to try to avoid conditions in testing which would cause negative deviations. A rule was worked out that would safely permit the experimenter to discontinue working with a subject if the trend of his scoring shifted downward below mean chance expectation. This automatic selection system, as it was applied, was proper enough but it did not work very well.

A second practical method proved to be much better: This plan made use of negative deviations under certain proper conditions and made them work for the research program instead of against it. But this development belongs with the later section on the measurement of psi-missing. I will turn now, much as we began to do back in the forties, to look at the conditions under which the scoring rate shifted to the negative side of the mean. It had become clear that progress depended on the discovery of the conditions responsible for psi-missing. Such information was necessary in the planning of new experiments if any control over psi-missing and its consequences was to be gained.

II. THE CONDITIONS OF PSI-MISSING

To make a complete summary of the conditions under which psi-missing has been found would be a large task today. However, it will suffice for the present purpose to identify and illustrate the three main categories of these conditions. All three of these are primarily psychological in type, since even where physical conditions are involved, it is the individual's subjective reaction to them that is important.

First will be those conditions associated with psi-missing known as <u>position effects</u>, that is, variations of scoring rate due to the position of a trial on the record sheet. Second will come what I referred to in 1952 as dual-task experiments, but which I will now call <u>two-aspect test conditions</u>. The third type will consist of <u>conditions of stress</u>. It is difficult to think of these three categories as completely independent of each other; rather, since the same type of effect (psi-missing) is produced in all three, one expects at least one or more common factors to be found among all. However, I think these broad types of conditions are sufficiently distinctive for the present examination of the material.

Psi-Missing Associated with Position Effects

On this set of conditions, a beginning has already been made by the cases of subjects HLF and AJL, whose decline of success in lengthy runs of card-guessing tests of ESP led to psi-missing at the end of the run. The number of such examples is not large, probably for the very good reason that the lesson was learned early that a long, tedious test run tended to produce negative deviations at the end; these of course tended to cancel the hits of the first part and thus to reduce total scores. Long runs, therefore, were generally avoided by experienced testers.

Exceptions have occurred, however; and as it happens, you heard one such decline mentioned in the paper by Adrian Parker (32) yesterday. You may recall that he mixed up 25 card-guessing trials in ESP with 25 trials of marginal visual perception (using a sort of tachistoscope to present the targets

of both types). The mixed deck of 50 targets was divided
into two runs of 25 each (each run containing 12 of the one
type and 13 of the other). These mixed runs were made at
one long session, with two control runs of standard BT tests
of clairvoyance alternated with the mixed runs. Since checkup of the mixed runs was made during the session, the 50
mixed trials in effect represented one long run with a break
in the middle, the whole requiring over an hour for completion. The score average for the second half gave a negative
deviation approximately as large as the positive deviation of
the first part. The difference between the two halves of the
experiment was significant.

Declines of scoring in psi test performance have, however, been quite common. In fact, this effect has been so
general that it is now regarded as one of the earmarks of the
psi process, although it is recognized as an effect of the
structure of the record sheet. I have mentioned thus far only
the decline within the run; but there is a fairly common tendency to decline from left to right on the record page as well
as from top to bottom. This is particularly likely when the
same subject is going through a long, repetitive series of un-
varied tests in which a number of record sheets are involved.

Generally the ESP record sheets contain from 2 to 10
vertical columns; and under certain conditions (for example,
with a subject repeatedly filling out record sheets) a left-
right decline is likely to occur giving a sufficiently negative
deviation in the second half to be considered psi-missing.
For easy illustration, let me draw attention again to the paper
by Parker, in this case to the two 25-trial ESP control runs
given to each of his subjects. These were alternated with
the sections of the long, slow run (of mixed cards) I described
earlier, but in this case the checkup occurred after each run.
By the time of the second control run, the subject had been
through either half or all of the long, tedious mixed run and
had been working from about an hour to an hour and a half.
In the second of these two standard runs the subjects as a
group gave a negative deviation approximately as large as the
positive one which the first run produced. Again, the difference was significant, as it had been with the ESP portion of
the mixed pack. Here, then, was a decline into psi-missing
from one run to another on the same record sheet.

Incline curves of scoring rate in psi tests are, as I
have mentioned, quite rare--that is, those beginning with psi-
missing and converting to a positive deviation later on the

record page.   In all these cases of psi-missing at the start,
it seems clear we do not have the same effect of mere position as it appears in the case resulting from a decline.
Rather, the situation looks more like a condition of temporary stress from which the subjects recover later, a condition suggesting that the subjects are not ideally prepared for
the test or the test situation.

One general location of psi-missing due to position remains, and it is the one where the missing is most easily
overlooked.   This is found within the run itself and is not
caught in the usual decline analyses of top-bottom, left-right,
or diagonal-decline breakdowns.   It is probably safe to conjecture that this "internal psi-missing" is the most prevalent
type and, at least up to this point, has been the most difficult to discover and competently handle.   It was first encountered, so far as I recall, in the analyses Humphrey and
I made at Duke (26) on the early results of Schmeidler's
"sheep-goat" comparisons (51).   We found that Schmeidler's
missing goats (or skeptics) actually averaged above chance in
the first and last segments (of 5 trials each) of the 25-trial
run; but they fell so low on the three internal segments
as to make a total negative score.   On the other hand, the sheep
(or believers) continued scoring above chance through all five
segments.   But this is only half of the story.   We found a
quite similar effect in the structure of the 5-trial segment
itself, of which there were five in the run.   I will return to
this finding later when I review the methods of analysis needed to handle such internal effects.   But whatever else may
be involved in these attitude tests, this psi-missing inside
the segment and the run appears to be a response to the
structure of the record sheet itself.

One is tempted also to consider displacement hitting
and missing as "position effects," although displacement (mis-
taking the target adjacent to the intended one) strictly belongs
in a class by itself.   However, psi-missing may also occur
in the displacement results, just as in scoring on the regular target.   This is reported by Osis and Turner (31) as backward displacement in one section of their distance-ESP experiment, although the main significance depends on positive deviations in forward displacement.

To sum up this section on position effects, I will suggest that psi-missing seems often to be an effect of position
itself--a consequence of the subject's reaction to the structure
of the record page.   The association with position effects is

at any rate clear in many researches. It might be mentioned in passing, however, that all the examples cited have been in ESP tests. There are position effects as well as psi-missing in PK work, too, but I cannot recall an example of the two combined in a PK experiment. I shall come back to this point in later discussion.

Psi-Missing under Two-Aspect Test Conditions

In 1952 we were already somewhat aware of the two-aspect effect as it related to psi-missing, but there is today a much more varied lot of findings with which to deal in this connection. The effect itself is this: When in a psi test the subject is confronted with two features in a comparative way, he tends to react differentially to the two in his psi responses; that is, he generally scores above chance on one and below on the other with significant consistency, if he shows psi ability at all.

This differential response by the same subject to two elements in the test is not to be confused with the use of the psi-differential method in comparing two sections of a group of subjects--let us say two levels of ranking on a mental test, or two contrasting attitudes toward ESP, such as Schmeidler's sheep-goat comparison. Rather, on two-aspect tests the differentiation is in the individual subject's own response to two distinct elements in the test situation.

In the two-aspect tests there may in some instances be a frank preference on the part of the subject for one of the two conditions, and for this reason the result has been called by Rao a "preferential effect" (33). A clear-cut example of this is Sanders' precognition tests (50). Sanders had his subjects register their preference between two methods of response, calling or writing, and obtained a significant difference which was preponderantly due to the negative deviation.

However, in many of the experimental situations involving two-aspect conditions, there is no reason to consider that an effective preference exists. For example, in Freeman's oft-repeated booklet tests of precognition with children as subjects (12, 13, 14, 15, 16), the differentiation between arrangements of targets, resulting in reverse directions of differentiation by the two sexes, would hardly seem to fit the preference category. Mere action in scoring positively is not

an adequate basis for using the term "preferential. " "Differential" has long been the more appropriate neutral term,
and it still allows, of course, for the fact that in some two-
aspect experiments a definite preference has been indicated.

It is interesting to see that in some instances the mere
suggestion of the experimenter in characterizing one of two
conditions as "first" is enough to differentiate it in the production of two directions of deviation; for example, in one of
Cox's (4) PK experiments with dice, a comparison was made
between hits on the target face and those on the location of
the cubes on a designated one of six numbered squares. Thus
"face" and "place" represented the two aspects of the target
comparison, and alternately the experimenter would designate
one of the two as "primary" for a given period of the test.
A significant difference was produced by the subjects, one in
which the primary target was favored, even though the two
types of targets were balanced off equally in the series. Psi-
missing was shown on the secondary targets.

In other experiments the subjects may shift the sign
of deviation as they observe one of the two conditions under
comparison succeed better than the other; and there may be
other features of the experiment that affect their attitudes.
In another of Cox's experiments involving placement PK (5),
marbles were compared with dice, both being released together. The more mobile marbles gave a positive deviation,
while the dice gave marked psi-missing. The results did
not conform to original preferences, but such rankings are
naturally labile.

In some cases the two aspects are quite closely identified. For example, in ESP experiments involving two elements in the same response, both Foster (11) and Hallett
(23) in separate experiments found the subjects differentiating
to a significant degree. In the work of Foster, the two-aspect test required a response involving both a symbol and
color choice; and in Hallett's experiment, the combination
was symbol and target position. In much of Freeman's work
already mentioned (his booklet tests of precognition), both
place and target are closely combined, but the differential
effect is quite consistent.

On the other hand, it is possible, as Cox (6) has found
in a more recent experiment, to unify two elements in a test
to such a degree that the subject's response integrates the individual elements. This recent work involved a two-clock test

of PK in which the experimenter emphasized the importance of the joint effect; that is, influencing the two together. The point seems to be that if the subject mentally unifies the two elements, there is no differential effect; and if not, there usually is. This seems psychologically normal enough.

It has been suggested that in some way, perhaps in making more of a game of the test, the subject responds more successfully if he is confronted with a two-aspect test condition, especially if the dual aspect is fairly well focused: probably a subtle element of contest is introduced. Yet, even if the two elements are effectively united, there may be an enhancement effect. The Cox experiment last referred to (with the two clocks) gave results on the two at a level somewhat above that of either of the individual clocks.

The two-aspect test is a challenging area for further research, with fair promise of improved scoring as well as better understanding of how the psi-differential effect operates. It has already probably added more to the collection of cases of psi-missing than any other condition. Some large bodies of data are based almost entirely on the two-aspect test. I have mentioned Freeman's work, which has extended over several years. The considerable range of two-aspect tests by Rao and his associates would also come in this classification (33, 34, 46). In fact, the psi-missing effect in a two-aspect test is the most common type of finding in recent years and can almost be counted on when the proper conditions are provided.

Psi-Missing under Conditions of Stress

Most examples of psi-missing that do not belong in the two preceding sections are grouped together in this one. Yet this is more than a mere collection of leftovers; there is at least one common condition that appears to characterize this group of psi-missing series: the condition of "stress" or mental strain in the subject. The classification is necessarily a tentative one, especially since there is no objective evidence of the stress involved; but this term will serve the present purpose of exploration.

For most of these examples of psi-missing attributed to stress, the fit will appear reasonable enough, I think. To use a now familiar example, we can all agree that in Dr. Fry's case, the practitioner who made the 10 straight misses while demonstrating the Abrams Box to a critical committee was most likely under considerable tension. Similarly, the highly publicized dowser from Maine, Henry Gross, along with another dowser, also gave a significantly negative deviation in a series of short tests given him by an investigating group to see if he could tell whether or not water was flowing in an underground pipe (39).

Very similar to these public demonstrations are some recent experiments conducted by Rao and his associates in India (37). He and his associates gave ESP tests to two groups of applicants who were awaiting important interviews, and in both cases the groups produced negative deviations on their pre-interview tests. (These were significant when combined; whereas in comparable post-interview tests the subjects gave a significantly positive total deviation.) [The statement in parentheses is based on my own combination of the two series.]

While one cannot be so confident about the mental state of the individual in some of the other experiments which produced large negative deviations, there is at least the exploratory advantage of trying to see how small a stress effect it may take to produce this magical psi-missing effect. Take, for example, the case of Lottie Gibson (17), who started off with a positive deviation when she was subjected to doing PK tests in darkness. Her scoring rate in normal light had been significantly positive up to this point. In the tests in the dark a flashlight had to be turned on and the record made after each throw of six dice from a cup. Soon after the beginning of the session with this condition, the rate began to fall and in the end produced a significantly negative total deviation for the darkness series (more than canceling the positive beginning). Undoubtedly the procedure was slower, more tedious, and probably frustrating after the novelty wore off.

But it is clearly the subjective reaction to the physical situation that matters. In a somewhat comparable case of PK testing done by McMahan (28) the effect of darkness was reversed. The experiment was based on the throwing of discs by means of a rotating wire cage, and the groups of young people who took part as subjects gave every indication of enjoying the test in darkness more than in the light. The discs had luminous faces, the test went smoothly, and the experimenting in the dark was a bit of a lark. The result was that the darkness test got the positive deviation and the light test a (somewhat larger) negative one, with a significant difference

between the two conditions. It would seem that the less exciting tests in the light came to appear like "controls" to the
subjects, something to be endured and gotten over with; there
is no proof, of course.

In the ESP researches, too, certain physical limitations have been reported to have produced negative deviations.
Bevan's ESP experiment (1) with the subjects being tested
while alone in an experimental darkroom will illustrate.
Woodruff (61) obtained a similar effect in later work after
the subject had been in an aviation test chamber two hours
or more.

But the limitation need not be one of physical confinement; any sort of separation involving delay in learning about
one's results would seem to have something like the same effect upon many subjects. When, for example, the Canadian
Broadcasting Company carried out a precognition test in 1961,
the more than 30,000 responses sent in by mail yielded a
significantly negative deviation (41).

It may not require a confining or delaying situation to
induce subjective conflict in participation in a psi test. For
some subjects, the mere approach to such a test might be
expected to generate a certain amount of more-or-less sub-
merged protest. The somewhat consistent tendency to negative deviation by the skeptics in Schmeidler's clairvoyance
tests (52) might serve as an example of this. The "goats"
in her classes who registered their doubts about ESP before
the tests began are likely to have experienced at least some
mild resistance, conscious or unconscious.

Other classifications of personality states or traits,
if they have been correlated with ESP test performance,
might also be similarly interpreted without stretching the
stress concept too far. Humphrey's (24) use of the subjects'
drawings for personality clues will illustrate. The drawings
were rated as to whether they were expansive or compressive. As might be expected (if a significant difference were
shown), the more compressive drawings were associated in
these clairvoyance tests with negative deviations, while the
expansive subjects tended to give positive deviations. There
was enough consistency and significance to justify continued
study.

These main types of stress-generating conditions, I
think, will serve to illustrate stress as an acceptable working

hypothesis for most of what is left of the still unclassified
psi-missing. The chief distinction of this third section on
conditions is that in all cases a more-or-less obvious strain
or stress seems reasonably inferable. On the other hand, in
position-effect cases of psi-missing, as well as in most of
the two-aspect examples, the shift back and forth from hitting
to missing generally on a trial-by-trial basis would appear to
work too fast for changes of mood or affect to account for
the differential effect. The other types of psi-missing seem
to call for something other than a state of tension.

III.   HOW IS PSI-MISSING PRODUCED?

Earlier Suggestions

We have already seen that the suggestion of unconscious
negative motivation to account for AJL's negative deviation did
not fit psi-missing as a position effect.

I had suggested in 1952 that since a psi test response
had to involve a cognitive judgment as to which target was
correct, psi-missing was a cognitive error, not of course
conscious. While it was clear by that time that the psi process was essentially unconscious, it was regarded as responsive to some degree of conscious guidance. For example,
the subject was at least consciously oriented toward a specific target in the test situation, and he usually made a
conscious choice of the target in each trial. Yet success
depended upon access to the unconscious psi process.

It seemed to be at this focal point of relative uncon-
sciousness, therefore, that the psi differential function was
exercised, the function that determined whether, if psi occurred, it was psi-hitting or psi-missing that would register.
Motivational factors were not necessarily excluded; in some
cases they could well be alternative or joint influences. In
fact, it could be supposed that bias, preference, or other influences could affect these unconscious cognitive judgments
much as they do conscious ones; but there were situations in
which motivation did not seem identifiable as a probable de-
terminant.

Just how this cognitive error might operate in a psi
test response was therefore a further question; but in trying
to answer this, I did not at that time attempt to hypothesize
very far. I suggested only that the subject could be (prob-

ably inadvertently) departing from his usual way of exercising
psi and that this alone might lower his scoring rate below
chance.   For example, if a subject normally scores highest
by taking the first symbol that comes to mind and later shifts
over to the practice of waiting for the most vivid one, he
may automatically miss the target simply by rejecting the
first choice.   (This will be called the "change of method"
suggestion of psi-missing.)

A second way of getting significant negative deviations,
mentioned in the same review, was called the "displacement
missing" effect.   If a subject produced significant displacement and (as some do) avoided calling doubles (that is, suc-
cessively repeating the same guess) his scores would be expected to average below chance on the direct target.   I mentioned earlier that Humphrey (27) found what is probably a
case of that, with Soal and Goldney's subject BS; but his
order of displacement seemed far too rare to account for
much of the psi-missing that has been encountered.   Also,
it is doubtful whether it constitutes true psi-missing, since
it is only indirectly produced by psi.

Psi-Missing and Consistent Missing

In 1950 Cadoret and Pratt (2) at the Duke Laboratory
reported an effect called "consistent missing. " By this was
meant systematically wrong guessing (for example, repeatedly calling a circle a star.) They found the effect, however,
only in the high-scoring runs of the results examined and not
in those below chance.   They mentioned the point that consistent missing should be expected to produce negative deviations, but they failed to find evidence.   (However, they did
not have significant psi-missing data under analysis.)

This failure of Cadoret and Pratt to find consistent
missing in their low-scoring runs accounts for our not thinking further at the Duke Laboratory of consistent missing as
actually involved in psi-missing results and for my omission
of it as a likely possibility in 1952.   Accordingly, the examples I offered to illustrate "systematic cognitive error"
were such as would tend to suggest free (or inconsistent)
missing, with no necessary patterning implied.

But the idea did not remain overlooked.   In 1955, in
a short article, Nash (29) mentioned the consistent-missing
effect as a hypothesis of psi-missing, and in 1965 Louisa E.

Rhine (46), in likening the psi-missing effect to the blocking
of information in spontaneous ESP, implied the consistent-
missing concept.   In an article on psi-missing in 1965 (35),
Rao suggested that consistent missing might be a special case
of psi-missing.   While no testing of the idea was done, these
suggestions kept it under consideration.

At the time I began this fresh examination of the psi-
missing evidence, it seemed to me increasingly logical that
consistent missing should be an important factor, at least in
some of the psi-missing effects, and that it was clearly worth
a test; furthermore, it had the advantage of being subject to
comparatively easy test if suitable data could be obtained incidentally from past experiments.

Fortunately, at this stage of my re-examination of the
consistent-missing hypothesis a paper on that very topic had
already been submitted by Dr. Ulrich Timm (56) for the Parapsychological Association Convention in Freiburg.   It was evident at once from this paper that Timm had already applied
a consistent-missing analysis of the Cadoret and Pratt type
to a series of results already at hand that seemed to show
definite psi-missing.   Timm reported significant evidence of
consistent missing--or, as he calls it, the "mixing-up of targets"--in the (probably) psi-missing records which he analyzed.

Timm's treatment seems to me to provide an adequate
first test of the hypothesis of the consistent confusing of targets in psi-missing.   The method is thus clearly opened up
for further examination of psi-missing records to determine
to what extent consistent missing is present.   Timm properly
does not claim to have the whole explanation of the negative
deviation even in the case he examined.   He indicates that
the amount of "mixing-up" he found is far from large enough
to account for the entire negative deviation of the block of
data under examination; but it is enough to initiate a new attack on this important question.

One limitation of the consistent-missing hypothesis of
psi-missing is that it can not apply if only two targets are
used; in that case missing of either kind (chance- or psi-)
has only one wrong choice, and the missing is "consistent"
of necessity.   However, most of the psi testing has been done
with more than a two-target range.   This is fortunate in view
of the provision it makes for exploratory study of where the
psi judgment goes when it gets off the track.   Tracing these
consistent wanderings should be a profitable line of study.

The Psi-Missing Operation in Focus

It would appear, then, that psi-missing may or may not be the result of consistent missing; it may register as excess of wrong ESP guesses or wrong PK effects, on the direct target or in displacement, and it may occur with a conscious preference or with no obvious or known subjective differential ranking.

The irreducible residuum of fact that seems to remain is that the test subject is trying to hit the target, to register his psi effect, and more often than not makes mistakes. Neither his psi hits nor his psi misses are very far from chance; he is mostly failing to register psi either way except as a small percentage. His effort is lost in the unconscious system psi has to transcend. But he keeps up a repetitive guessing operation (in ESP tests), generally using mental habits and patterns of association that are even obstructive to psi. When psi does get past this line of conscious judgments, it emerges as a right or wrong conscious selection for the test record. But what makes it so often significantly wrong?

Here the study of spontaneous psi experiences offers an insight in conjunction with test results. Louisa E. Rhine (46) drew the parallel between incomplete psi experiences that indicate mental blocking and the psi-missing effect in the tests. While one experiencing person may receive a fully detailed picture of a distant or future scene, another one gets only suggestive fragments of a message. LER calls this second type a "blocking" experience, one in which most of the fuller meaning is barred from the subject's experience, allowing only a fragment to be received.

This does not go far enough for psi-missing as it stands; mere suppression is not missing, of course. But such blocking is probably a first condition of that type of missing. What makes the test situation give a pile-up of excess misses is the fact that the subject has to continue forcing himself to guess (or throw the dice) until the test is over. This forces him to produce errors whenever blocking occurs. In the spontaneous situation it would merely give an incomplete positive experience. Under the requirements of test conditions a negative deviation results.

All this makes it worth a still larger look for the rare cases in which the spontaneous experience turns out to

have contained meaningful errors. As LER has pointed out,
those which come to mind have familiar parallels in the pro-
tective substitutions known to general psychology. For example, a prominent federal judge (a Protestant) once dreamed
of an elaborate Catholic funeral with many distinctive features,
including even the exact day of its occurrence. The corpse
in the dream was that of President Franklin Roosevelt. But
when, 30 days later, the designated day came, the details of
the dream were fulfilled by the accidental death of the dreamer's own mother.

One reason for the return to the search for more such
spontaneous cases that may involve psi-missing is that they
may help in better localizing the point and process of the unconscious cognitive error in these effects. Probably to understand what goes wrong in psi-missing will bring us closer
to grasping what goes right in psi-hitting. Advances in science have often progressed via the oddities and errors of nature.

IV. THE MEASUREMENT OF PSI-MISSING

Psi-missing as an operation is not dependent on measurement or it would be some sort of artifact; however, it does
have to be measured in order to be detected. Like most
scientific knowledge, the discovery of psi-missing depended
on mathematics. If the effect occurred spontaneously it would
pass unnoticed. Even in practices that are assumed to depend to some extent upon psi, the occurrence of psi-missing
would be overlooked unless systematic measurements were
applied to a sufficient series of attempts under adequate conditions of observation. As I mentioned earlier, I found evidence of psi-missing in work with two Maine dowsers, but
only in the series of controlled tests to which evaluative
measurement could be applied. The complete lack of success
with them under other conditions could also have been due to
psi-missing, but there was no way to tell.

Likewise, Thornton Fry's case of the missing of 10
successive trials in the blood and water test by the Abrams
Box practitioner was another case of a practice yielding psi-
missing in a rare moment of careful measurement. How
much of the same thing went on in the practitioner's general
routine the world will never know.

There is one widespread human practice, however, that
is exceptional in that it has had to depend (when it is honest)

upon reasonably accurate measurement. Moreover, this practice at times most probably involves psi-missing and at others psi-hitting. I refer to the practice of gambling, a practice that provides a surprisingly relevant background to the
measurement of psi-missing. Parapsychology owes its first
and most used mathematics as well as some of its test materials (for example, cards and dice) to the practices of the
casino. The methods of card-guessing and dice-throwing
(with the essential aim of winning against chance) were adopted
by psi workers in their original basic tests and the long-con-
tinuing use of these methods (and their adaptations) indicates
their usefulness. What is uniquely important here is that
these game-tests were equally well suited to the measurement
of psi-missing. This is because they offered chances of "losing" that were near enough to those of winning to make this
differential effect easy to observe. It could be measured as
precisely as winning.

The games themselves naturally needed this balance
of two-way chances to provide the gamble--make it a "game
two could play." Parapsychology, on its part, also needed
the same elements of gaming, first of all, of course, to test
the hypothesis that chance could be outguessed; psi is one of
the hypotheses for the explanation of luck. Parapsychology
profited also from the casino's use of small numbers of targets (in psi testing two, four, five, and six targets were generally used). Not only did the smaller number of choices
appear to make for better (more encouraging) results in psi-
hitting, but psi-missing would hardly have been discovered
with a larger number of targets; there would have been too
little opportunity for impressive negative deviations. With
$p=1/2$ per trial, the chances of hitting and missing are of
course equal. But they are still not too unequal for a fair
balance with $p=1/5$. It was fortunate, then, for these and
still other reasons, that psi testing began with its most valuable heritage from the casino.

The Binomial Method

The binomial method of testing the significance of the
results of the tests with cards and dice had first been developed for gambling practice. It had been used in some of
the earliest nineteenth-century tests of telepathy and clairvoyance (for example, by Richet in the mid-eighties), and
was used by Coover (3), Estabrooks (9), and in the early
Duke work (42). The critical ratio measured the deviation

of total hits from theoretical chance, and as soon as the procedure of treating negative deviations in essentially the same
way as the positive ones had been approved, negative deviations began to be taken seriously when the experimental situation and design made this permissible. The practice was
early adopted (40, p. 91) of correcting the probability of an
experimental result (multiplying it by 2). I have mentioned
my application of this binomial procedure to AJL's work done
under a certain selected condition of strain; but when this
reached the point of significance, I regarded the finding as
only a "suggestive" pilot study, alerting us to look further
for the effect obtained.

When, in 1941, I found in preliminary series (38) that
adult subjects, confronted for the first time with group precognition tests, produced negative deviations, I carried through
a lengthy confirmatory series of similar tests with a number
of groups and presented the significant negative deviation as
evidence of precognition. At the same time, a parallel series
with children and adolescents in essentially identical tests
produced a significant positive deviation.

As I have indicated earlier, there were situations in
which the positive and negative trends were shown by the
same subjects in two different sections or aspects of the experiment. The simplest of all were those cases of long runs
I have mentioned, produced by HLF and AJL, in which it
seemed desirable to test the significance of the difference between the first part and the last. The same binomial method
lent itself to the evaluation of a difference between the positive deviation of the first two segments of the run and the
negative deviation of the last two. Where the two opposite
signs of deviation could properly be set off against each other and compared statistically, the binomial method was available. The crucial ratio of the difference (CR_d) offered an
effective test of significance when the conditions permitted.

But psi-missing was not always so clearly segregated
as to permit such easy identification. In those early years
at Duke, new research workers were being introduced without previous training. We were beginning to work with unselected subjects and at the same time we were trying out
many new exploratory conditions. One of the results of
these innovations was a collection of negative deviations
mingled with a lot of positive ones. It meant that there was
heavy internal cancellation within a series, sometimes with
chance totals as a result.

This led to the attempt to avoid the psi-missing problem by the use of a device called the "salience ratio" (SR),
a method that needs a bit of explanation since it had not been
a standard method hitherto. Although it has been in little
use for 25 years, it did play an important role at a very difficult stage.

The Salience-Ratio Method

Let me point out first that nearly all ESP record
sheets have columns of 25 spaces, divided by double horizontal lines into five segments of five trials each. It was
observed that the end segments tended to show greater deviations than the middle segments and more often than not went
in the opposite direction from the middle. We found that the
hits of these two end segments (10 trials) could be set off
against the three middle segments (15 trials), and the CR_d
obtained. These salience ratios (SRs) for the run could be
readily combined, by the chi-square method, for the results
of a given subject or for an entire series (18, 38). The
salience differences, of course, measured position effects
occurring within the structure of the run, and so long as the
terminal segments differed significantly from the middle segments, it did not matter at all which was positive and which
negative. In a word, psi-missing did not matter. Generally
there were salience differences; and if so, when these were
evaluated they showed evidence of ESP that would probably
have been lost in pooling the data in one grand total.

It was important to find that the SR method could also
be applied just as well to position effects within the five-
trial segment itself. By setting off the two end trials of
each segment against the three middle ones, a segmental
salience ratio (SSR) was obtained which was independent of
the run salience ratio (RSR). (Of course the SSRs of the five
segments in the run were combined for evaluation, just as
the RSRs were combined for the runs of the series.) The SR
statistic, devised with the supervision of Dr. J. A. Greenwood, statistical editor of the Journal of Parapsychology,
supplied us with this first statistical means of by-passing
the psi-missing problem. A number of researches were
evaluated by means of the SR device in the early 1940s, most
of them by Humphrey and me. The SR offered some definite
advantages, especially in throwing light on the position effects
in segment and run, but it also added considerable work to
the analysis of data, and it never became widely used.

The Critical Ratio of the Difference

Actually, the main reason the salience-ratio method was laid aside was that in the early forties we began to realize that we could, with certain conditions, use psi-missing as part of the experimental design. It was merely the CR_d method built into the design of the research project. As with most advances in method, we half-stumbled into the adoption of it. In this case, we first found ourselves applying the CR_d technique retroactively on occasion; for example, to test the significance of the difference between the first and second halves of a long series, one having a positive deviation and the other, as a rule, a negative one.

About the same time, group comparisons introduced another use for the CR_d test of significance. In the early forties, Schmeidler (51) began reporting the results of her sheep-goat comparisons in clairvoyance tests. The CR_d method served the purpose of this comparative study, and this differentiation increasingly became the evaluative procedure in the design of this type of investigation. Whenever an attempt was made to correlate any other measurement with psi test scores, it was commonly found that the most convenient method of preliminary measurement was to divide the subjects into groups on the basis of the non-ESP criterion and to compare the two resulting groups of subjects as to their ESP scoring rates by the CR_d method.

But while the critical ratio of the difference has been the most common procedure in these situations, it is not-- and of course should not be--the only one nor the best one for all occasions and purposes. It has been particularly important to test the consistency of performance among the subjects, and tests for consistency have become a matter of general routine, with several standard methods in use. [See reviews of statistical methods in parapsychology by Greenwood (19; 45, Ch. II), Greenwood and Stuart (20), Greville (21, 22), and by Rhine and Pratt (44, Ch. 9).]

These CR_d measures of psi in relation to other mental states had another value besides being tests of significance. They showed something about psi itself. Eventually it became clear that the non-psi measures that were used to separate the subjects gave results that were related only to the direction of deviation and not, after all, to the amount of psi ability manifested by the subjects; the psychological test merely served to divide those who, under the circumstances, were

psi-hitters from those who were psi-missers. It was plain
that those who gave negative deviations often had as much or
more psi ability than those who scored above chance. Psi
itself was apparently not correlated with the general mental
measures at all!

This realization that all of the personality studies
were related only to secondary differences, as indicated by
the sign of deviation, and that they were probably not giving
much if any information directly on the psi process itself
came at first as something of a jolt. However, the importance of this general distinction has grown in magnitude as
the psi-missing problem itself has taken on urgency. The
psychological relations discovered did indeed reveal important things about the nature of the psi-missing effect and
of course about the psi process itself. The appraisal of
these belongs in a later section. At this stage we are still
concerned with the CR_d as method.

The Psi-Differential Effect as Method

The increased use of the CR_d led to the adoption of
the terms "psi differential" and the "psi-differential effect"
(PDE) as identifying the sign difference as a research device.
The experimenter who planned a research project would, if
he were wise, add to his design a condition aimed at splitting
the results differentially. Such a device could well utilize
an attitude test (after the Schmeidler type) with a plan to test
the significance of the evidence by means of the CR_d (44, p.
175).

Or, after observing the differentiating influences of
position effects, a psi worker might plan to break his experimental results into a first-half versus second-half differential within some such unit as the record page or the entire
series itself. The general tendency of psi to decline in scoring rate within the various units of an experiment furnished
a convenient basis for planning.

Also, most subjects, when confronted with two parts
or aspects of an experiment, tend to show differential rates
of scoring, one part giving a positive deviation and the other
a negative one. Eventually it became more or less the standard design to set up a dual-task or two-part (perhaps two-
target or two-technique) design as insurance of getting extra-
chance results. This systematic planning to utilize psi-miss-

ing by means of the PDE has been responsible for much of
the real progress in the research conducted in recent years.

Among the many researches already carried out with
the use of the PDE design, at least three general types may
be designated: First, two groups of subjects may be compared as to psi ability in relation to some differentiating
measure such as subject attitudes. Second, the subjects, individual or group, may each be given a two-part (or two-
condition) experiment with the anticipation of a PDE between
the two parts. Third, the subjects may be exposed to test
conditions (for example, long runs, boredom, darkness) that
will produce a negative shift of deviation in contrast to a part
of the experiment using normal conditions. These are only
the main types of PDE usage, but they illustrate how psi-
missing has been put to work as a research instrument in
itself.

A still further use has been made of the psi-missing
tendency: it has sometimes been employed as a psychological
device as well as the statistical one (as in the PDE) I have
been discussing. The most effective effort of this type is the
playing-up of the comparison of two features of an experiment
in such a way that together they seem to activate the subject
to produce larger deviations in both directions; that is, it
looks as if the proximity itself (at least up to a point) en-
genders more psi-differential effect--as if the two aspects
"compete" and accentuate the difference. The closer the two
elements of a test are in focus (so long as the subjects do
not integrate them), the better the results are differentiated.
Several experimenters--and I have mentioned Cox (4) and
McMahan (28)--have helped subjects to focus on the two-aspect tests by deliberately specifying one aspect as primary
at one stage and later reversing the rank as a control. At
any rate, it is now possible to design tests that play to advantage upon this differential reaction.

The method, if generally valid, will raise important
questions as to underlying psychological factors; thus far it
has been an empirical matter, but it does suggest that the
"magic" may consist of making the test a contest and thus
adding the quality of a game. Perhaps there is an unconscious type of judgment involved--one that goes beyond conscious control. It can now be explored more readily with
PDE techniques combined with others now available.

Test of Score Frequency and Variance

Another interesting problem in the measurement of psi-missing arises from its spotty localization; for example, it may be hidden within a run in such a way that the run score shows nothing very unusual. The run may have one or more segments below chance while the other segments are above, and all cancel to chance. Psi-missing may, as indicated earlier, even be concealed within the segment itself.

But this hidden psi-missing, too, has recently been recognized and measured by a number of methods, one of which is the evaluation of the frequency of the different run scores. If (because of cancellation, let us say) too many of these scores approximate the chance mean (five hits in a 25-trial ESP run), this effect can be detected by means of a chi-square test of goodness-of-fit, which compares the frequency of the scores with chance frequency (45, Appendix 2). A significantly high frequency of scores close to 5 would suggest internal cancellation in the run, a good clue to localized psi-missing. Actually the goodness-of-fit test has been used mainly to test for significance where there is wide variance of scores, some runs showing unusually high scoring and others falling well below. The goodness-of-fit method tests this exceptional scattering of high and low scoring that would cancel if the scores were totaled. Thus, the test gets around the psi-missing problem effectively up to a point. However, it has not been widely used. It tells too little beyond mere overall significance; and it measures only the frequency of score variation.

Another of the well known ways of measuring run scores has come into greater use in recent years; that is, the chi-square test of score variance (from the theoretical mean), dealing with score size instead of frequency (20; 45, Appendix 3; 49). If the scores cluster around chance they show small variance; whereas if they vary widely on either side, the variance is large. The chi-square test of run-score variance gives a sensitive measure of how far the scores vary from chance either way, and even if they vary subnormally. This tool of inquiry has in recent years become very useful and has revealed evidence of psi in many places that would normally have been overlooked.

The Variance-Differential Effect

         The run-score variance test has recently grown into
a still more complicated device. It has been observed that
in a psi test of the two-aspect type where different conditions
are compared, the difference between the run-score variances
of the two parts of the experiment is usually an even more
sensitive test of significance than the CR_d of the pooled deviations. Where the score variance in one of the two test conditions is large (above the expected variance) and that in the
other is depressed, this variance-differential effect (VDE)
can itself be tested for significance by the variance-ratio
(F-ratio) method. The run-score variance test and the VDE
appear to provide the most sensitive psi test procedures yet
found for getting around the psi-missing effect (when that is
desired). And at the very least they add to the other tests
of significance in the field an additional set of useful tools.
[Some of the recent uses of these methods may be seen in
the Journal of Parapsychology beginning in 1966 with papers
by D. P. Rogers and J. C. Carpenter (49), D. P. Rogers
(47, 48), and R. G. Stanford (55) and continuing in later
volumes.]

         Moreover, the very idea of significantly small vari-
ance (i.e., very little fluctuation of scores) as an experimentally induced effect is a challenging one. Rogers (47,
48) has reported success in inducing this subchance variance
by psychological methods. Thus far the only way of accounting for such constriction of scoring is by internal cancellation
of localized hitting by localized missing within the run (for
example, the terminal segment deviations might cancel the
deviations of the middle ones). However, it happens that the
variance test and VDE method can be applied to whatever
units are of interest--the segments of the run, the trials in
the segment, or other subdivisions.

         The addition of the VDE method of by-passing the psi-
missing problem will probably in time be as useful as the
PDE device has been over the years. While differing widely,
they supplement each other in a remarkable way, the VDE
converting the psi-missing effect to a common measure about
as efficiently as the PDE enables the researcher to make use
of that effect when he wants it. The PDE was a vital necessity at one stage of the research; the VDE may be more essential to the anticipated period of development and use.

Odds and Ends on Measurement of Psi-Missing

        In this section I have followed in outline the trail of
the explorers in psi measurement as they tackled psi-missing.
I have left out some steps merely for brevity (possibly some,
too, by oversight). For example, I have not gone into the
evaluation of psi-missing in tests based on free target material, although some of those tests gave strong negative deviations in certain two-aspect target combinations. Also, from
time to time over the last 25 years the more elaborate analysis of variance has been used, sometimes with a view to
"getting around" psi-missing effects, but also with a view to
revealing possible correlations of a more complex nature
than were identified by the usual procedures. Analysis of
variance has not been found especially appropriate for the
simple experimental designs necessary in psi research at
the present exploratory stage. In all the evaluative devices
simplicity seems to hold an advantage for parapsychological
explorations. This advantage is related to the comparative
unpredictability of psi test performance as yet and the presence of uncontrolled variables. There is a timing for grades
of complexity of methodology in a new field that should be
judged from the viewpoint of the problems themselves--and
not that of what the methods can do in some other field.

        As I have said, the recognition of psi-missing and the
continuing study of it have depended upon mathematical methods, and it will have to remain that way on into the indefinite
future. The figures had to come out with a significantly
minus deviation (from a theoretical mean chance expectation)
before we knew there was something there to investigate further. But with the right combinations of test conditions and
with measured test results, the hidden processes of psi communication have been further detected and traced on into unconscious levels where they would otherwise have remained
beyond the reach of science and understanding.

                    SOME GENERAL INDICATIONS

Psi-Missing as a Minor Abnormality

        From this review of psi-missing it appears that the
systematic avoidance of targets is a mild abnormality in the
expected functioning of psi ability. Schmeidler (51, p. 121)
suggested this in 1944 when referring to below-chance scoring in discussing position effects in her sheep-goat compari-

sons in ESP tests: "Such low scores are strikingly analogous
to the lapses of memory and slips of the tongue that have so
convincingly been shown to be indicators of unconscious resistance." Perhaps it would not be too inappropriate to refer
to this type of missing as "psi-illusion."

For the present the most important aspect of this similarity would seem to be the increased identification it gives
to the two areas of human response, the sensorimotor and
the extrasensorimotor. From the psi research viewpoint one
wonders about what other generalizations might be made across
the borders of the psi field, what might be learned from related explorations going on in the sensorimotor domain that
could be borrowed for a tryout in the psi laboratory.

On the other hand, it is too early as yet for the psychologist to consider the advantages to be borrowed from
progress in parapsychology; but there are points on which
this field seems to have pushed ahead in methodology and in
some specific findings concerning unconscious behavior.
These should be of interest to psychology eventually.

The Relative Stability of Psi

The second major point of this review is one of contrast between psi and psychology rather than of positive relationship. From this review of psi-missing it is clear that
the factors that make test scores vary the most are the subjective conditions of the person under test. Long, monotonous runs, competition between two types of target, and tension or frustration of the subject--such factors are familiar
psychological conditions, and yet it is right here that we must
look for what makes psi performance so unstable. The elusive character of psi ability under test is generally attributable to variation of these mental states.

What is equally clear is that psi itself, if we take both
signs of deviation and both large and small variance into account, is pretty much of the same strength throughout these
many differences of mental states. In a word, it is psi that
is stable and psychological factors that are the source of uncertainty. It is not psi that is difficult to manage; it is the
psychology of the subject.

This distinction between psi ability and psi test performance could only have been possible as a result of the

psi-missing investigations. The importance of this point may
be indicated by the fact that this is a reversal of the picture
that has prevailed hitherto. I myself have always before
characterized psi as an uncertain, fugitive function. Quite
plainly, however, it is psi testing and the exercise of this
capacity that are lacking in stability. This makes a great
difference conceptually; it should have important consequences.

It is true, the recognition that it is upon these well
known psychological variables that the demonstration of psi
must depend helps to make common cause with a number of
other subtle and obscure mental abilities. Swinging full circle, we are back once more at the point where we can say
there is no valid line of complete distinction between psi exchange on the one hand, and sensorimotor or other cognitive
communications on the other. [There are, however, still
differences enough to warrant the independence of parapsychology as suggested in my earlier paper "Psi and Psychology" (43).]

At least one point of insight into the psi-missing operation has resulted from this survey, one that links that effect to spontaneous psi experiences. While it still seems best
to describe psi-missing as unconscious cognitive error, Louisa E. Rhine added something new to the picture by likening
psi-missing to what she calls "blocking" (46). This blocking
effect takes place in spontaneous ESP experiences of the "incomplete" type. In such a case, only a fragment of the full
potential message is communicated and the rest repressed,
and we can now see how this blocked-off positive message
might be turned into psi-missing--provided the subject is required to respond trial by trial. Such forced response, combined with mental blocking on an unconscious level, should
be expected to distort the delicate unconscious judgment involved and thus multiply misses (cognitive errors). It is
somewhat analogous to being pressed into repeated responses
in trying to recall a name on which one experiences temporary blockage. The very forcing, however gentle, becomes
an impeding factor in itself. Psi, of course, is still more
hidden and blind than memory.

At this point someone may think of the possibility that
psi-missing is pure artifact since it is certainly a product of
the subject's reaction to conditions in the test situation.
Every experiment necessarily has artificial elements; Franklin's kite was artificial but the lightning was not. The psi in
psi-missing is as verifiably actual as it is in psi-hitting.

The good fortune of psi workers in catching this missing effect is definitely due to the design of approach, as we have
seen in the review of measurements. With other methods
psi researchers might have found only limited psi-hitting,
when and if it occurred. Blocking could only have added to
the chance scoring. As it was, blocking was forced into becoming psi-missing which, with a technique that measured
extrachance misses, was in time processed into psi evidence.

Psi-Missing versus Chance Missing

          The survey of psi-missing brings into the clear anoth-
er competing effect which psi-hitting has in the tests, and
that is chance itself. With the ability to evaluate both psi-
hitting and psi-missing, only chance hits and misses are left.
Subjects respond in tests of ESP by guessing habits and target associations against which psi must compete. Chance
presumably takes over when the subjective state is unsuited
to a psi response (either hit or miss). Conscious guidance
which controls so wide a range in sensorimotor exchange,
can only partially and very delicately control this selective
psi judgment.

          If, however, the experiment can be so designed as to
make it possible, after the test is over, to select those portions of the run under which the conditions were manifestly
not right for psi, conditions that were not genuine psi tests
because they did not allow for the possibility of psi function,
then the rest of the run could be evaluated separately and
should yield high results. While some efforts have been made
to get accompanying physiological (or other) indices such as
the electroencephalograph that would permit selection of valid
psi trials, the only success to date is in the area of psi research with animals. Esther Foster, working with Osis (30),
first drew attention to the side-habit formation in ESP tests
with cats, and the fact that these gave only chance scoring
rates whereas in the switch-over tests there was evidence of
ESP. In recent years, two French biologists working under
the assumed names of Duval and Montredon (8) have successfully used this selection of trials, which they call "random
behavior," to segregate the valid psi trials of the series in
ESP tests with mice. Animal habits are likely to be simpler
than human ones, and the choice of only two targets makes
the selection simpler. It is only a beginning, but at least a
new outlook has been given psi research by this move to bring
measurement one step further into the analysis of the elements

operating in the psi test runs. With random behavior isolated and psi-missing as measurable as it is, psi testing and even better control over it may be anticipated.

Dependence of Psi-Missing on Method of Measurement

The review of the ways in which psi-missing has been measured brought out its close dependence on the particular methods used. Added to this was the similarity between the two-way deviations of psi and the winning and losing streaks in games of chance. Finally, linked up with these points, were some basic similarities between the psychological conditions of the hitting-missing differential and the winning-losing contrast.

This opens up questions as to possibilities of further advantage: Does the science need a "proving ground" which could be adopted from the gambling world or some phase or branch thereof? Or would the effective use of psi offer an essential threat to the casino and its commercialization of the psi-missing potential?

How Psi-Missing May Be Avoided

Can psi-missing now be controlled? We have seen on the one hand that there is a considerable range of conditions that are known to have produced psi-missing, and some of them are controllable. Nothing has yet been said about conditions that prevent it, although there are some facts of interest. To begin with, one of the papers you have heard will serve as a starting point. Dagel and Puryear (7) reported ESP test results from runs of 100 trials each with no declines in the run or negative deviations at the end. As you know, this differs from earlier results of similarly long runs. They used a GESP test, a mechanical test device, and the subject had immediate knowledge of success after each trial. Second, at two of the Review Meetings last year Schmidt (53) reported no declines or psi-missing in 100-trial units; instead of GESP his tests were for precognition. But he did use a mechanical test device and the subject did have immediate knowledge of his score.

Tyrrell (54, 57, 58, 59, 60) in the late 1930s, reporting work with his ESP test machine, did not (so far as I can discover) mention declines or psi-missing. His subject did have immediate knowledge of results.

What is perhaps most interesting is the fact that the results of PK tests have not shown as much psi-missing as those of ESP. I have mentioned reports of it such as the work, mentioned earlier, carried out in the dark-light comparisons and in two-aspect experiments. But while there are plenty of declines and U-curves in the PK researches, they have with one exception not gone over to significant negative deviations. [The one exception, however, is too ambiguous to prove or disprove the rule. Forwald (10) once withheld from two subjects he was testing for PK with dice the fact that he wanted a negative deviation in the second of the two sets, and they produced a significant negative deviation. (Or was Forwald himself the real subject?) Then when he explained to them the true value of their results, the scoring, though nonsignificant, was reversed in direction.] The one differentiating characteristic for all this PK work is that it is routine to give the subject immediate knowledge of success.

It looks as though immediate knowledge may be an effective damper on psi-missing, at least when the conditions are not too favorable to it. How far and how reliably this feedback factor may go to prevent psi-missing (and of course not interfere with hitting) will be important to explore further.

Methods of Handling Psi-Missing
Help toward Reliable Control

Obviously if these various lines of progress keep on and we find out enough about (1) the conditions producing psi-missing, (2) ideal ways to utilize it (or if preferable, either to avoid or ignore it), and (3) the way to select random behavior trials in advance of checking, the field should soon be ready for the important stage of development for reliable application. As you heard Carpenter's paper yesterday on a successful (preliminary) use of a combination of methods for making assured predictions of the identification of psi targets, you must have realized that there is now some fresh attention to this practical objective. There are at least more technical aids, improved methods, and verifying devices than ever before.

The best forward step, however, is in the fact that we now have a better inside look into the psi process through the window of these mild aberrations that produce negative deviations. As the subject shifts from missing to hitting and back again in U-curves, as he goes from trial to trial in the

segment and from one segment to another in the run, we see
that these unconscious successes and errors are only a delicate shade apart. The conditions involved in the mere structure of the run and the test are responsible, and now we can
fairly well suspect what they are; more than that, they are
manipulable, and perhaps we can soon train subjects to do
the manipulating. The puzzle of psi-missing, and along with
it the mystery of psi-hitting, seems closer to our inquiring
scrutiny than ever before. This is not psi control, of course,
but if better psi understanding comes, can control be far behind?

A General Unconscious Judgmental Error

With psi-missing so closely tied up with methods and
conditions of the test, I should not expect much of it to occur
outside of the laboratory. But similar unconscious cognitive
error might occur over the entire range of subliminal functions of life whenever such blocking and stress are encountered by the individual as produce psi-missing--and especially
if the individual is forced into reaction by his environment.
I am much inclined to think we are dealing in psi-missing
with a general unconscious tendency to judgmental error and
that the methods we have found useful in psi research might
be generally helpful if applied to similar problem areas outside the psi field.

But I prefer another emphasis that is necessarily a
little conjectural; namely, that in finding these facts about
psi-missing we are uncovering something more than the mainly negative and disruptive features that the research has had
much to do with. It seems reasonable to say that in psi-
missing we have come upon the limits which conscious control
can exercise in psi testing (psi-missing is still a limited reaction to the conscious target it is avoiding). We are finding an outer range of limited (that is, unconscious) control.
In other large areas of nature, for example, in life, in
growth, and in volitional action, comparable limits and similar negative reactions (misses) may occur, as easily unnoticed as psi-missing is in life. These limits and their extent would be extremely important to know, at least from a
research point of view.

Here it looks as if we have now penetrated in psi research to the edge of the consciously controllable personal influence over the unconscious constituent processes underlying

at least some of the behavior of the organism; and we can
by these reversals of intended reaction move back and forth
across this line, finding on the one hand that we can produce
psi-hitting as desired and, because of the nature of the test,
can get it reversed and even measure the operation of psi
when it is still working under limited guidance. In cases
like consistent missing, we can even see what it is doing
when it is going wrong.

Position Effects Next

Finally, it has become necessary to find out to what
extent psi-missing and position effects are mutually involved,
if only in the understanding of one of these two large by-
products of psi research. Such a study has had to be undertaken in dealing with psi-missing itself. A later paper will
present a progress report on the study of this dual relation,
as seen from the viewpoint of position effects.

REFERENCES

1. Bevan, J. M. "ESP tests in light and darkness. " J.
       Parapsychol. , 1947, 11, 76-89.
2. Cadoret, R. , and Pratt, J. G. "The consistent missing
       effect in ESP. " J. Parapsychol. , 1950, 14, 244-
       56.
3. Coover, J. E. Experiments in Psychical Research at
       Leland Stanford Junior University. Stanford: Stan-
       ford University Press, 1917.
4. Cox, W. E. "The effect of PK on the placement of
       falling objects. " J. Parapsychol. , 1951, 15, 40-
       48.
5. _____ . "A comparison of spheres and cubes in
       placement PK tests. " J. Parapsychol. , 1954, 18,
       234-39.
6. _____ . "Double hits in PK tests with electric stop
       clocks. " Awaiting publication.
7. Dagel, Lou T. , and Puryear, Herbert B. "Effect of
       immediate reinforcement in GESP tests. I and II. "
       Master's thesis, Trinity University, San Antonio,
       Texas, May 1968.
8. Duval, Pierre and Montredon, Evelyn. "ESP experi-
       ments with mice. " J. Parapsychol. , 1968, 32,
       153-66.
9. Estabrooks, G. H. "A contribution to experimental

telepathy. " J. Parapsychol., 1961, 25, 190-213.

10. Forwald, H. "Chronological decline effects in a PK placement experiment. " J. Parapsychol. , 1954, 18, 32-36.

11. Foster, Esther B. "Multiple-aspect targets in tests of ESP. " J. Parapsychol., 1952, 16, 11-22.

12. Freeman, John A. "Boy-girl differences in a group precognition test. " J. Parapsychol. , 1963, 27, 175-81.

13. _____ . "A precognition test with a high-school science club. " J. Parapsychol., 1964, 28, 214-21.

14. _____ . "Sex differences and target arrangement: high-school booklet tests of precognition. " J. Parapsychol., 1966, 30, 227-35.

15. _____ . "Sex differences and target arrangement, and primary mental abilities. " J. Parapsychol. , 1967, 31, 271-79.

16. _____ . "Sex differences and primary mental abilities in a group precognition test. " J. Parapsychol. , 1968, 32, 176-82.

17. Gibson, E. P., and Rhine, J. B. "The PK effect: III. Some introductory series. " J. Parapsychol. , 1943, 7, 118-34.

18. Greenwood, J. A. "The statistics of salience ratios. " J. Parapsychol., 1941, 5, 245-49.

19. _____ . "The role mathematics has played in ESP research. " J. Parapsychol. , 1942, 6, 268-83.

20. _____ , and Stuart, C. E. "Mathematical techniques used in ESP research. " J. Parapsychol., 1937, 1, 206-25.

21. Greville, T. N. E. "Symposium on ESP methods: A summary of mathematical advances bearing on ESP research. " J. Parapsychol. , 1939, 3, 86-92.

22. _____ . "A survey and appraisal of the statistical methods used in parapsychological research. " J. Parapsychol. , 1949, 13, 4-8.

23. Hallett, S. J. "A study of the effect of conditioning on multiple-aspect ESP scoring. " J. Parapsychol. , 1952, 16, 204-11.

24. Humphrey, Betty M. "Success in ESP as related to form of response drawings: I. Clairvoyance experiments. " J. Parapsychol. , 1946, 10, 78-106.

25. _____ , and Pratt, J. G. "A comparison of five ESP test procedures. " J. Parapsychol., 1941, 5, 267-92.

26. _____ , and Rhine, J. B. "The evaluation of salience in Doctor Schmeidler's ESP data. " J. Para-

psychol., 1944, 8, 124-26.

27. _____., and _____. "Position effects in the Soal
     and Goldney experiment." J. Parapsychol., 1944,
     8, 187-213.

28. McMahan, Elizabeth A. "A PK experiment under light
     and dark conditions." J. Parapsychol., 1947, 11,
     46-54.

29. Nash, Carroll B. "An hypothesis of psi-missing based
     on the unconsciousness of psi." J. Amer. Soc.
     Psych. Res., 1955, 49, 75-76.

30. Osis, Karlis, and Foster, Esther. "A test of ESP in
     cats." J. Parapsychol., 1953, 17, 168-86.

31. _____., and Turner, Malcolm E., Jr. "Distance
     and ESP: A transcontinental experiment." Proc.
     Amer. Soc. Psych. Res., 1968, 27, 1-48.

32. Parker, Adrian. "Attempted induction of ESP using a
     tachistoscope." Awaiting publication.

33. Rao, K. Ramakrishna. "The preferential effect in
     ESP." J. Parapsychol., 1962, 26, 252-59.

34. _____. "Studies in the preferential effect: I. Tar-
     get preference with types of targets unknown." J.
     Parapsychol., 1963, 27, 23-32.

35. _____. "The bidirectionality of psi." J. Parapsy-
     chol., 1965, 29, 230-50.

36. _____. Experimental Parapsychology. Springfield,
     Ill.: Charles C. Thomas, 1966.

37. _____., Kanthamani, B. K., and Sailaja, P. "ESP
     scores before and after a scheduled interview."
     (Abstract) J. Parapsychol., 1968, 32, 293.

38. Rhine, J. B. "Terminal salience in ESP performance."
     J. Parapsychol., 1941, 5, 183-244.

39. _____. "Some exploratory tests in dowsing." J.
     Parapsychol., 1950, 14, 278-86.

40. _____. "The problem of psi-missing." J. Parapsy-
     chol., 1952, 16, 90-129.

41. _____. "The precognition of computer numbers in
     a public test." J. Parapsychol., 1962, 26, 244-51.

42. _____. Extra-Sensory Perception. 2nd ed. Boston:
     Bruce Humphries, 1964.

43. _____. "Psi and psychology: conflict and solution."
     J. Parapsychol., 1968, 32, 101-28.

44. _____., and Pratt, J. G. Parapsychology: Frontier
     Science of the Mind. Springfield, Ill.: Charles C
     Thomas, 1957.

45. _____., et al. Extra-Sensory Perception After Sixty
     Years. New York: Henry Holt, 1940.

46. Rhine, Louisa E. "Toward understanding psi-missing."

J. Parapsychol., 1965, 29, 259-74.

47. Rogers, David Price. "Negative and positive affect and ESP run-score variance." J. Parapsychol., 1966, 30, 151-59.

48. _____. "Negative and positive affect and ESP run-score variance: Study II." J. Parapsychol., 1967, 31, 290-96.

49. _____., and Carpenter, J. C. "The decline of variance of ESP scores within a testing session." J. Parapsychol., 1966, 30, 141-50.

50. Sanders, M. C. "A comparison of verbal and written responses in a precognition experiment." J. Parapsychol., 1962, 26, 23-34.

51. Schmeidler, Gertrude R. "Position effects as psychological phenomena." J. Parapsychol., 1944, 8, 110-23.

52. _____., and McConnell, R. A. ESP and Personality Patterns. New Haven: Yale University Press, 1958.

53. Schmidt, Helmut. "Clairvoyance tests with an electrically operated machine." Awaiting publication.

54. Smith, B. M. "The Tyrrell experiments." J. Parapsychol., 1937, 1, 63-69.

55. Stanford, Rex G. "The effect of restriction of calling upon run-score variance." J. Parapsychol., 1966, 30, 160-71.

56. Timm, Ulrich. "Mixing-up of symbols in ESP card experiments as a possible cause for psi-missing." Awaiting publication.

57. Tyrrell, G. N. M. "Some experiments in undifferentiated extrasensory perception." J. Soc. Psych. Res., 1935, 29, 52-71.

58. _____. "Further research in extra-sensory perception." Proc. Soc. Psych. Res., 1936-37, 44, 99-168.

59. _____. "The Tyrrell apparatus for testing extrasensory perception." J. Parapsychol., 1938, 2, 107-18.

60. _____. Science and Psychical Phenomena. New York: University Books, 1961.

61. Woodruff, J. L. "ESP tests under various physiological conditions." J. Parapsychol., 1943, 7, 264-71.

ADDITIONAL READINGS ON PSI MISSING

Carpenter, J. C. "The differential effect and hidden target differences consisting of erotic and neutral stimuli. " JASPR 65: 204-14 (Apr 1971).

Crumbaugh, J. C. "Variance declines as indicators of a stimulus-suppressor mechanism in ESP. " JASPR 62: 356-65 (Oct 1968).

Freeman, J. A. "Differential response of the sexes to contrasting arrangements of ESP target material. " JP 251-58 (Dec 1965).

_____. "The psi-differential effect in a precognition test. " JP 33: 206-12 (Sep 1969).

Johnson, M. and Nordbeck, B. "Variations in the scoring behavior of a 'psychic' subject. " JP 36: 122-32 (Jun 1972).

Kanthamani, B. K. "A study of the differential response in language ESP tests. " JP 29: 27-34 (Mar 1965).

Kelly, E. F., Child, I., and Kanthamani, H. "Explorations in consistent missing. " (Abstract) JP 38: 280-31 (Jun 1974).

Kelly, E. F., Kanthamani, H., Child, I. L., and Young, F. W. "On the relation between visual and ESP confusion structures in an exceptional subject. " JASPR 69: 1-32 (Jan 1975).

Kelly, E. F. and Kanthamani, B. K. "A subject's efforts toward voluntary control. " JP 36: 122-32 (Jun 1972).

Kreitler, H. and Kreitler, S. "ESP and cognition. " JP 38: 267-85 (Sep 1974).

Nash, C. B. "Opposite scoring direction in ESP. " JASPR 29: 122-26 (Jun 1965).

Palmer, J. "Scoring in ESP tests as a function of belief in ESP Part I. The sheep-goat effect. " JASPR 65: 373-408 (Oct 1971).

Rao, K. R. "The differential response in three new situations. " JP 28: 81-92 (Jun 1964).

_____. "Studies in the preferential effect. III. The reversal effect in psi preference. " JP 27: 242-51 (Dec 1963).

_____. "Studies in the preferential effect. IV. The role of key cards in preferential response situations. " JP 28: 28-41 (Mar 1964).

Rhine, L. E. "The establishment of basic concepts and

terminology in parapsychology." JP 35: 34-56 (Mar 1971).

Sailaja, P. and Rao, K. R. Experimental Studies of the Differential Effect in Life Setting. N. Y., Parapsychology Foundation, 1973. (Parapsychological Monograph No. 13).

Stanford, R. G. "A further study of high- versus low-scoring sheep." JP 29: 141-58 (Sep 1965).

_____. "A study of high- versus low-scoring goats." JP 29: 159-64 (Sep 1965).

Timm, U. "Mixing-up of symbols in ESP card experiments as a possible cause for psi-missing." JP 33: 109-24 (Jun 1969).

Chapter 8

ESP OVER DISTANCE:
A Survey of Experiments Published in English*

by Karlis Osis**

The Problem and Its Perspective

One of the most fascinating characteristics of ESP is
that it can overcome long distances in space, and seemingly
in time also, penetrating the future. A puzzling aspect of
man's personality is that by just closing his eyes he may on
occasion envision correctly what is happening on the other
side of the world or what will occur in the future. The available evidence from experiments and spontaneous cases seems
to justify the assumption that ESP can reach around the globe
(5, 21, 26, 31, 32, 38).

This apparent sovereignty of ESP over space and time
has, over the centuries, spurred the creative imagination of
researchers and philosophers (9, 13, 20, 37, 54, 55). Many
able individuals have rightly considered the spatial and temporal properties of ESP to be among the most important keys
to the riddle of the nature of human personality. For them,
the "reach of the mind," with its virtual omniscience of far
lands and the distant past and future, gives back to man
some of the dignity and grandeur lost in modern scientific
concepts of personality. I believe that this line of thought

*Reprinted by permission of the author and publisher from
the Journal of the American Society for Psychical Research
59: 22-42 (Jan 1965).
**I am very grateful to Dr. Malcolm E. Turner, Jr., of
Emory University, who challenged my conventional ideas a-
bout ESP over distances and so instigated this survey. His
help as consultant and collaborator in the evaluations is highly valued. The late Dr. E. B. Foster, Mrs. M. J. Mason,
Mrs. J. E. Nester, and Mr. J. M. Smith also gave valuable assistance which is deeply appreciated.

is sound and constructive, but only up to a point.

The space-time problem has proved to be one of the most dangerous pitfalls in parapsychology because it has tempted researchers to speculate far beyond what our factual knowledge of ESP warrants. We know for certain only a few facts about ESP as related to space and time, and even these facts are entangled with a multitude of other variables inseparably interwoven in the data. Let us beware of constructing gigantic castles with just these few solid bricks of knowledge, added to a whole warehouse of building materials from philosophies of the past. There is no reason why we shouldn't speculate if we admit that this is what we are doing; however, it becomes dangerously confusing if strong empirical evidence which simply does not exist is claimed as a basis for these lofty castles.

I am fully aware of the controversial nature of this topic and, in fairness to the reader, I want to state my own bias. When, as a young student, I wrote my dissertation on the hypothesis of ESP, I believed that the independence of ESP from distance in space and time was an established fact. I took it as the cornerstone of my thesis. After coming to the United States, the original sources became available to me; I checked there the validity of claims for clear-cut empirical evidence for ESP's independence of space. To my horror I found none.

The power of our cultural heritage, or Zeitgeist, to distort thinking in parapsychology is clear in the case of the distance problem. I believe, therefore, that we definitely need clarification of the available empirical facts about ESP over distances; this is the purpose of the present survey. In order to escape the spell of the Zeitgeist, I went straight to the primary data in the published experiments sampled and by-passed the opinions of the experimenters. This was necessary in order to clear the ground for new creative theoretical thinking and better future experimentation.

Delineation of the Problem

The ESP communication system clearly has three parts. At one end is the internal functioning of the percipient, who acquires information by ESP. At the other end is the stimulus; for example, an ESP card, an accident, or an idea in a friend's mind. The system's third part, to which this paper

is devoted, is the unknown factor which brings both ends of
the communication system together. In my opinion no one
yet knows what this factor is. Among other possibilities, it
might be visualized as analogous to the light rays which connect our eye with the object seen, or to the sound waves
which connect the tones of a violin and the listener. Modern
communication theories are accustomed to calling this mediating factor a "channel." I think we can adopt the term for
ESP also. Let us bear in mind that this channel does not
have any spatial properties, such as those of a pipe or canal.
Radio waves are called a channel in spite of their being distributed around the globe. This paper is concerned only with
the channel in the ESP communication system, whatever it
might turn out to be, and not with the stimuli or the subjective, internal factors. Further, as I have already said, I
will survey and evaluate only the experimental data pertinent
to the channel factor, and not the hypotheses and speculations
which have been based upon these data. Theoretical discussions are very necessary, of course, but I will wait to develop some of my own in another paper.

Procedure

        For relevant empirical material on distance in ESP
the parapsychological literature in English was surveyed:
this included research journals and books. The literature in
other languages was touched upon only lightly because of
linguistic limitations.

        In ESP research two basic types of stimuli are used:
(a) alternative-choice, e.g., ESP cards, in which the subject
knows the alternative stimuli, but must ascertain the order
of presentation; and (b) free stimulus material, e.g., drawings, in which the subject does not know the stimulus population and must indicate the nature of the stimuli. These
two types of research are reviewed separately, with primary
emphasis on alternative-choice methods and visual stimuli.
Experiments with ESP cards (or other targets with one-fifth
probability for guessing correctly) form the backbone of the
survey, and special attention is given to research in which
the same subject did ESP tests involving different distances
within the same experiment. A few distance experiments
were found where playing cards, numbers, letters, and clock
cards were used, but these will be mentioned only rather
briefly since there were too few instances to permit grouping
in distance classes. Some of the distance experiments using

free stimulus material are reviewed, but with emphasis only
on those in which quantitative evaluation was carried out.

Excluded from the survey are all experiments not designed for distance comparisons and in which little-known
response methods (ESP in dreams, map dowsing, hypnosis
induced by ESP, etc.) were used. Mediumistic and so-called
psychometry experiments were also excluded since their results are open to other interpretations than ESP over distances. Broadcast experiments were sampled but not included
in the tabulations since none in which distances were evaluated were found to have been performed under acceptable conditions. Experiments in which distance ESP was coupled with
precognition or psychokinesis were not deemed suitable for
inclusion because of the obvious confounding of variables.
Finally, no tabulation of spontaneous ESP experiences was attempted; this would be a herculean task in itself and would in
any case involve great difficulties of interpretation in terms
of the distance factor.

Having decided on the type of research material to be
included in the survey, another problem arose. What is the
minimum distance between subject and target in an experiment which will warrant its being called a "distance experiment"? Subjects usually experience little change in attitude
if they are separated from the targets by only a few yards;
but they seem to consider it a "real distance" if the cards
are placed in another building. Therefore, in order to min-
imize the possible effect of the attitude factor, a hundred
yards--the distance assumed to separate two buildings--was
chosen as an arbitrary lower limit.

The distance within the first mile seems to be rather
interesting as a factor in the transmission of known energies.
Therefore, the distance from a hundred yards to one mile
was used for the first "distance class." The range of the
other classes is a thousand miles. If the original source
reported the data within a distance range of, say, 500-1400
miles, the middle of the range--in this case 950 miles--was
taken as the basis for classification in the present survey.

Distances were measured as around the globe; that is,
on the circumference. Of course, the distance through the
globe, the diameter, is somewhat smaller, but as the known
energies used for communication, e.g., radio waves, bounce
around the globe, it was decided to use this same distance
measure for ESP in order to permit direct comparison.

The minimum length of experiments accepted for evaluation in the survey is twenty runs (500 guesses). However, this rule was liberalized for some experiments which are mentioned, but not included in the main evaluations.

No special measures were taken for selection in terms of the quality of the experiments as I wanted to include all the data from which the claims of no lawful relationship between ESP success and distance had originated.

In a sense this survey will give rather inaccurate information because of limitations in the data. Approximately half of the tabulated material involves multiple calling for the same set of targets, and this could not be taken into account in our evaluations. Experiments 1 and 2 (in Table 1 below) are insufficiently described in the original publications. Some experiments involved highly selected subjects and others unselected groups. Conditions varied widely. However, we simply do not have anything better to stand on in evaluating claims of evidence for the independence of ESP from distance.

RESULTS

Card Experiments with Five Alternative Choices

Experiments in which cards with five alternative choices were used as stimuli are summarized in Table 1. The scoring levels according to the distance classes are distributed in definite non-chance fashion. When the distance increases, the class average decreases consistently from class to class without exception (Figure 1). Most decline is registered between the first two classes; that is, between the 100-yards-to-1-mile class and the 1.1-mile-to-1000-mile class. Actually, the first of these classes ranges only from one hundred yards to a quarter of a mile, as there are no data for the rest of the range.

Dr. Malcolm E. Turner, Jr., Professor of Statistics at Emory University, has developed a statistical model for evaluation of the problem of ESP over spatial distances (see Appendix). [Ed. note: Appendix has been omitted but is cited in the list of additional readings.] He is the sole author of this model. The basic idea of the model is to express in mathematical terms any lawful relationship that ESP might have to distance. The model utilizes modern information theory, as well as the latest advances in statistics.

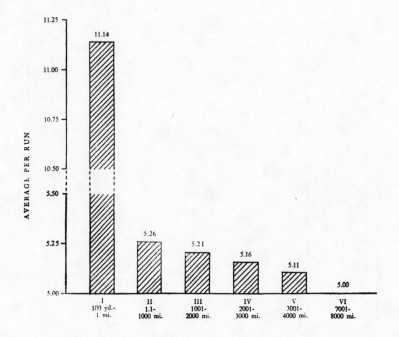

Fig. 1. ESP scores according to distance classes (only experiments with five alternative choices are included).

The gist of the procedure in over-simplified, non-mathematical terms is this: ESP scores are transformed by means of appropriate statistical operations into amounts of information transmitted, as expressed in "natural units" or "nits." This is necessary in order to provide a basis for calculating statistics which describe important trends in the relationship of ESP to distance. One of these statistics is π, which Turner defines in the Appendix: "π is a constant we may term the 'extrasensory perceptivity' and is a measure of the 'power' of the object-subject system in a particular situation." It is necessary to calculate this "extrasensory perceptivity" in order to describe, by another statistic, δ, precisely the way in which ESP declines over distances, if indeed it does.

Table 1

ESP Scores According to Distance Classes*

No.	Experiment	I 100 yd.-1 mi. Runs	I Avg.	II 1.1-1000 mi. Runs	II Avg.	III 1001-2000 mi. Runs	III Avg.	IV 2001-3000 mi. Runs	IV Avg.	V 3001-4000 mi. Runs	V Avg.	VI 7001-8000 mi. Runs	VI Avg.
1	Rhine: *Extra-Sensory Perception* (35)												
2	Rhine: Tarkio Series (36)			34	6.38								
	Duke Series (36)			1045	5.52	28	4.93						
3	Rhine, Pratt: Pearce-Pratt Series (39)			402	5.22			527	5.16				
4	Gibson (16)	74	7.54			190	5.25						
5	Riess: Series A (40)	74	18.24										
	Series B (40)	10	5.30										
6	Soal, Bateman: Telephone Series (50)	40	6.15										
	Cambridge Series (50)			64	4.66								
	Antwerp Series (50)			48	7.19								
7	Rhine, Humphrey: Marchesi Series (38)									353	5.07		
	Duke Subjects (38)									1000	5.09		
8	McMahan, Rhine: Marchesi Exp. (26)									244	5.22		
9	McMahan, Bates: Marchesi Exp. (24)			339	4.77								
10	Skibinsky: Names (48)			299	4.72								
	ESP Symbols (48)			301	5.16								
11	Kahn: Harvard Exp. (18)			854.56	5.25								
12	Osis: Haeckel Exp. (31)									100	5.24		
13	Osis, Pienaar: Slow Rate (32)											24	6.17
	Rapid Rate (32)											24	3.83
	Totals	198	11.14	3386.56	5.26	218	5.21	527	5.16	1697	5.11	48	5.00

* Only experiments with five alternative choices are included.

This statistic, δ, or "proportionality constant," is Turner's basic tool for pinning down mathematically any distance law. With it one can sweep across all the major possibilities of a distance law to find precisely that one which fits the data best. For example, if δ is found to be 0, ESP is not related to distance; if δ is equal to -2, the result is the inverse square law characteristic of known energies when radiating in all directions. Other values of δ would show, for example, whether ESP decreases over the distance rapidly or slowly; uniformly over any distance; with a rapid decline at first, leveling off to a slight decline, etc.

Dr. Turner kindly volunteered to evaluate the survey data represented in Table 1. The evaluations were done in accordance with his model, and the steps are outlined in the Appendix. He found that the following trends occurred:

1. ESP scores are significantly related to distance.
2. "Extrasensory perceptivity" or "power constant" $\hat{\pi} = 0.608$.
3. "Proportionality constant," which "indexes the class of distance laws," $\hat{\delta} = -0.398$.
4. Some chance variation (error variance) could, of course, affect the magnitude of δ. Its true value most likely is within the usual statistical confidence limits. At the 95% confidence limit, the true δ should be somewhere between the following values: $P\{-.409 \le \delta \le -.387\} \cong .95$. At the 99% confidence limit, which is more conservative, the finding is: $P\{-.416 \le \delta \le -.380\} \cong .99$.
5. Turner calculated on the basis of these statistics the way in which the average run score would vary with distance. The predicted mean run score, as a function of distance x, is: $\hat{m}_i = 5e^{0.608x_i^{-0.398}}$, where e is the base of the natural logarithm.

Turner concludes that $\delta = -.4 = -2/5$ seems to be as good a choice as any for describing the ESP distance law; in other words, ESP obeys the inverse two-fifth's law in the data of Table 1.

Let us sum up: In the data evaluated, there is a significant relationship between ESP scores and the distance between subject and stimulus. The relationship indicated is not of the usual inverse square type, but more like that of an inverse two-fifth's. In other words, in these experiments the ESP scores decreased somewhat less than by the inverse square root of the distance.

The crucial question arises: Can we generalize from the results of this survey sample that ESP effects are inversely related to distance? The limitations and weaknesses of the published data have been pointed out above. In my opinion the data are too scant and defective to warrant safe conclusions as to ESP in general.

These same data have been the basis for the Zeitgeist interpretation that ESP is independent of distance. Obviously Turner's analysis does not support the independency hypothesis at all; if anything, what is indicated is the dependency of ESP on distance. However, Turner's evaluations set a challenging example of what can be extracted from the data of better-designed future experiments, aimed at the channel factor in ESP.

Comparison of Scores of the Same Subject over Two Different Distances (five alternative choices)

In the data presented in Table 1 variables associated with the subjects (individual differences, attitudes, etc.) are neither balanced nor statistically controlled. The first distance class is filled exclusively with the scores of some of the best subjects ever known in parapsychology. This factor alone might explain the high scores in this class.

If we could sufficiently balance factors other than distance influencing ESP scores, and at the same time vary only the distance between subjects and targets, much more dependable information would be obtained. I do not know of any published experiment where this requirement was fully met. The closest approximations to it are the cases in which the same subject has guessed cards at two different distances within one experiment.

There were seven such cases in the surveyed publications (see Table 2). In cases 1 and 2, and in the Antwerp Series of 3, near and far distances were not used in the same session. In the Cambridge Series of case 3, and in case 4, the long-distance calls were done in the favorable first half of the session and the near-distance calls afterwards.

Table 2

ESP Scores of the Same Subject over Two Different Distances+

No.	Experiment	Near Distance			Long Distance			Average Differences++	CR_d++
		Distance	Runs	Avg.++	Distance	Runs	Avg.++		
1	Gibson: Subject 1 (16)	0	50	6.12	700-2000 mi.	72	5.58	.54	1.47
	Subject 5 (16)	0	25.4	5.80	700-2000 mi.	42	4.74	1.06	2.11*
	Subject 11 (16)	0	24	6.46	700-2000 mi.	68	5.20	1.26	2.65**
2	Rhine, Pratt: Pearce-Pratt Series (39)	100 yd.	30	8.77	250 yd.	44	6.70	2.06	4.36**
3	Soal, Bateman: Cambridge Series (50)	0	64	6.23	70 mi.	64	4.66	1.58	4.47**
	Antwerp Series (50)	0	48	7.27	200 mi.	48	7.19	.08	.20
4	Osis: Haeckel Exp. (31)	0	55	6.13	4000 mi.	100	5.24	.89	2.64**
	Totals		296.4	6.60		438	5.52	1.08	7.16**

+ Only experiments with five alternative choices are included.
++ The average scores, average differences, and CR_d's were rounded for sake of convenience in presentation; hence, they will not check exactly.
 * Significant at the .05 level.
** Significant at the .01 level.

In case 1, the procedures are only sketchily described. In case 3 (Cambridge Series) some synchronization errors might have interfered with the distance part of the experiment. (If we exclude case 3 (Cambridge Series) from the analyses, the findings will not change.) Only in case 3 (Antwerp Series) did the same agent look at the targets at both distances.

This kind of comparison clearly indicates the same trend as in the previous analyses. In all cases the scores at the longer distance are lower than the scores for the near-by targets (Table 2 and Figure 2). In five out of seven cases the scoring differences are individually significant (in one case $P < .05$; in four cases $P < .01$). The CR of the difference of the total is 7.16. The consistency of the trend is obvious.

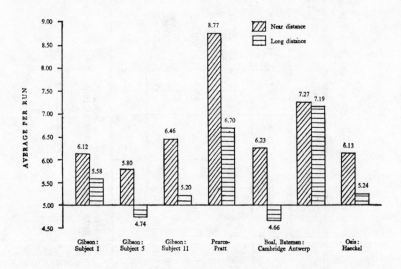

Fig. 2. ESP scores of the same subject over two different distances (only experiments with five alternative choices are included).

There is in Table 2 a considerably smaller number of variables that could account for the differences observed than there is in Table 1. Nevertheless, these differences still might be explained in terms of the subjective variables only.

The most serious counterhypothesis is raised by J. B. Rhine and others (36, 50, 59) to the effect that the subject's attitude toward the distance condition could in itself explain any scoring trends observed. This is a sound hypothesis, but it still lacks empirical validation. For example, if the subject feels challenged and alerted by the task of "overcoming distance" by ESP, he might on this account score best on distance targets. On the other hand, if he is adversely affected by the frustrating situation of distance ESP, the scores might go down. The importance of the attitude factor in distance telepathy was already recognized by E. M. Sidgwick and A. Johnson in 1892. At that time they called it ".. the effect of the distance on the imagination of the agent or the percipient" (46, p. 547).

The obvious way out of this difficulty would be to set up experiments in which the variables of distance and attitude are controlled. We could ascertain the subject's attitude and take it into account in statistical assessment; and by the same token we could also find out what the subject habitually does when confronted with a frustrating situation, since distance ESP targets are frustrating for most subjects.

Alternative-Choice-Tests Not Included in the Main Evaluations

In addition to the standard card tests with five alternative choices, playing cards, clock cards, numerals, letters of the alphabet, etc., have been used in distance experiments, with the number of alternatives varying from two to eighty. Scores on these tests are not directly comparable, nor do the tests provide enough data to permit grouping in distance classes. Furthermore, very few of these experiments satisfy the minimum requirement of twenty runs. Nevertheless, I want to mention some of this work even though its relevance to the distance problem is slight.

Experiments with separate scores on two distances provide more useful material for comparisons: we can easily detect the general trend; that is, which of the two scores is lower. However, unified statistical treatment is not possible here because the probabilities of hitting are so heterogeneous and the reported statistics so varied. Therefore, only a simple tabulation of the higher and lower scores is noted.

In 1938 R. Shulman (45) performed ESP experiments

using sound stimuli with five alternative choices over distances from a hundred to four hundred yards. These were compared with tests using screened color ESP cards, where distance was not involved. Unfortunately, there is very little known about ESP and auditory stimuli, as nearly all ESP experiments have utilized visual stimuli. We cannot include Shulman's data in the main evaluations because stimulus and distance variables were confounded. However, his results follow the general trend of decline already observed in the survey: 345 runs, no distance, average score: 5.17; 223 runs, over distance, average score: 5.08.

Some experiments with ESP cards (25) and with other types of cards (14, 15, 29) obviously involved distances, but either the data were not separated into distance categories or the distances were not stated.

F. L. Usher and F. P. Burt (56) in 1907 performed a pioneering experiment with playing cards over distances ranging up to 960 miles. The number of trials was very small: 36 trials, in the same room, 9 complete hits; 60 trials, over distance, 4 complete hits. (This involved multiple calling of some cards.) The trend is obvious.

J. E. Coover (11) reported in an appendix to his larger work a brief experiment using playing cards with the face cards omitted ($P=1/40$). The distances varied from twenty-seven to ninety miles. He obtained 5 hits in 149 trials. The scores on the various distances are not clearly separated in the report.

S. G. Soal (49) performed distance tests involving free material and a few playing card trials in the early 1930's. His evaluations are much too complex for this review, but he concluded that in his data there was no evidence that ESP functions at any distances.

In 1932 T. Besterman (2) published the results of an experiment between London and Athens. The stimulus material consisted of pictures with twenty alternative choices. There were 674 guesses: deviation was -4.7. No distance comparisons were made.

C. B. Nash (30) in 1961 followed up the star subjects in Chesebrough-Pond's ESP television contest with distance tests using the numbers 0-9 as stimuli. In 180 runs he obtained a deviation of -41, associated with $P=.04$. Further,

twenty subjects at a distance ranging from 6 to 520 miles had
a deviation of -16, and nineteen subjects at a distance from
680 to 2400 miles had a deviation of -25. A very slight non-
significant decline effect seems to be present, but the numer-
ically larger negative deviation is associated with the greater
distance. Nash's test was meant to be a test of GESP; however, the instructions to the subjects were like those devised
for precognition tests, emphasizing future comparison.

D. Michie and D. J. West (27) performed in 1957 a
mass television ESP test, and followed up their star subjects.
Clock cards were used as stimuli in the follow-up. One high-
scoring subject, Mr. Downey, was extensively retested. His
"mean divergence score deviation" over a distance of approximately a hundred miles was 0.8125; at no distance, 0.7627.
The difference is extremely small and in the opposite direction from the general trend of this survey.

In 1963 A. E. H. Bleksley (3) reported an experiment
on long-distance ESP during sleep. This involved the subject's awakening each night at a certain time randomly selected by the experimenter in Johannesburg, South Africa.
During the first series the subject was traveling from South
Africa to Holland; distance varied and were quite great, up
to five thousand miles. During the main series the subject
remained in South Africa at a distance of nearly a thousand
miles. Bleksley's evaluations are too involved to describe
in this survey, but more ESP success was reported at the
constant, but shorter distance. Bleksley gives plausible psychological explanations for this difference: He met the subject only after the series at the longer distances was completed.

G. L. Mangan (21) performed a distance experiment
over approximately 2150 miles. He used dual-aspect targets
with 1/5 probability of hitting each aspect and 1/25 for hitting the whole card. The subject was instructed to make one
guess a day for a hundred days. Ninety-five trials were
scored and resulted in 13 complete hits, with 3.8 expected
by chance. This result is associated with P=.000002. Partial hits, as well as displacements, were also evaluated.
The number of trials is too small for inclusion in the main
evaluations. However, the rate of ESP scoring over so long
a distance is very high indeed and this small experiment
stands out as very impressive evidence for long-distance
ESP.

Experiments Using Free Stimulus Material

Distance experiments with free material are numerous, but difficult to evaluate. Most reports do not include quantitative evaluations. In cases where quantitative evaluations are given, subjective judgment on the part of the judges is always involved, leaving room for an alternative interpretation--the judge's own ESP exerted during the judging process. Of course, the judge's ESP influence is less likely to be a factor in experiments where complete similarity between response and stimulus is demanded, as in M. C. Marsh's main evaluations (22, 23).

Distance tests with free stimulus material were attempted as early as the 1880's by S. P. R. researchers, and F. Podmore's book (33), published in 1902, contains an entire chapter summarizing the results of many attempts to produce "telepathic effects at a distance." The Miles-Ramsden series (28) was a later long-range exploration of the same type. R. Warcollier's experiments (58) in the 1920's and 30's with free material made many useful contributions to the field of parapsychology, but their lack of quantitative assessment makes them useless for distance comparisons. The same is true for the Sinclair experiments (34, 47).

Methods of evaluating free stimulus material did not reach maturity until the 1940's (5, 6, 7, 8, 51, 52). The first distance experiment of sophisticated design (drawings as stimuli) was published by W. Carington in 1940 (5) and further similar research in subsequent papers (6, 7, 8, 10). The statistical assessments yielded several highly significant measures. The distances between target material and subjects varied widely from rather small to transatlantic.

Carington did not seem to be particularly interested in the distance factor and evaluated it only in a small, highly-selected portion of his data, Duke Group, Series IV-A (5). The twelve Duke subjects (longer distance) scored significantly better than the rest of the 105 participants, located in England and Holland. This result certainly falls in line with the Zeitgeist, but it does not reflect on the experiment as a whole because we do not know what distance trends may be hidden in the data. Moreover, Carington's methods, particularly his catalogue technique, have been severely criticized by S. G. Soal and F. Bateman (50) and by the Board of Review of the Journal of Parapsychology (4). In the face of these difficulties, I refrain from stating my personal position and present Carington's own conclusion: "Distance makes no difference" (9, p. 69).

Carington's experiments were repeated twice by A. S. P. R. experimenters. The first repetition, by E. Taves, G. Murphy, and L. A. Dale (53), a large-scale experiment with 272 subjects and 8723 responses, did not yield significant results on the main measures taken. No distance breakdown was performed.

G. R. Schmeidler and L. W. Allison (44) undertook a second repetition in which they followed Carington's method more closely. His catalogue method, which has not withstood later criticism (50), was used. The experiment as a whole gave significant results (P=.012). When the agents and subjects were in the same building, the average score was .484; when the subjects were in "the New York area," the average score was .125; and when the subjects were scattered over the U. S. A. (including some in New York), the average score dropped to .062.

J. H. Rush and A. Jensen (42) performed a reciprocal drawing experiment of fifty trials over distances of 200-500 miles. Assessment gave P=.002. No distance comparisons were made.

M. C. Marsh developed a well-designed experiment with drawings as stimuli, and used a distance of 470 miles. This is documented in his Ph. D. dissertation (22) and also in a brief published report (23). Marsh's 371 subjects achieved "133 raw A hits on the targets used in the experiments, as against 37 hits on the unused control targets" (23, p. 8). Marsh used several statistical assessments which proved to be highly significant. No distance comparisons are possible.

On the whole, in distance experiments with free stimulus material the quality of the evaluation methods is very uneven; in many of them evaluation is inadequate by modern standards or lacking altogether. Therefore, this area of research is not a particularly fruitful one for probing the distance problem, although it does seem to give us some clues.

Trends in the Data Not Included in the Main Evaluations

The experiments not included in the main evaluations

(Tables 1 and 2), but which have been briefly described, are
so heterogeneous that unified quantitative analyses seem impossible. For that reason this section was nicknamed the
"Tidbit Basket!" However, the experiments in which two distances were used lend themselves to comparison by a ranking
method; that is, it is possible to determine which score at
which distance within each experiment ranks higher. Table
3 summarizes the ranking effects. Of the seven experiments

Table 3

EXPERIMENTS USING TWO DISTANCES, NOT INCLUDED IN MAIN EVALUATIONS

| Experiment | No. of Alternatives | Higher Score | | Qualifying Comments |
		Near	Far	
Shulman (45)	5	×		Sound stimuli for far targets, visual for near
Usher, Burt (56)	52	×		96 trials only
Nash (30)	10	×		Negative deviation numerically larger for far subjects
Michie, West (21)	12		×	Comparison between successful (Fisk) and unsuccessful (West) experimenters
Bleksley (3)	various methods	×		Personal contact with subject only after far series
Carington (5)	free material		×	Slanted selection of data: only one group (Duke) in one series evaluated for distance
Schmeidler, Allison (44)	free material	×		Use of Carington catalogue method

included in this table, five yielded higher scores on the near-
distance targets, and two gave higher scores on the long-distance targets. Difficulties of interpretation are summarized
in qualifying statements in the right-hand column of the table.

DISCUSSION

In a careful analysis of the relevant experimental data
it was noted that ESP scores seem to decrease quite uniformly with increased distances. On the other hand, in sampling opinions about the relationship between ESP and distance,
we find that most researchers express a view opposite to the
direction the data take. W. Carington's statement is quite
representative of published opinion: "Distance makes no dif-

ference. All workers seem to be agreed on this" (9, p. 69).
A few leading experimenters, however, such as S. G. Soal
(50) and D. J. West (59), insert cautious clauses to the effect that it is likely, but not definitely established, that distance makes no difference. In the French school there have
been dissident voices, among them those of R. Kherumian
(19) and R. Amadou (1), who said: "Our conclusion would,
then, be simple and prudent. It has not been proven whether
distance affects or does not affect the intensity or the intel-
ligibility of a telepathic message..." (1, p. 223).

What is the reason for this discrepancy between the
trends in the data and the majority of opinions? In part, as
I pointed out above, it seems to be caused by our cultural in-
heritance, or Zeitgeist. Philosophers such as Kant, Schopen-
hauer, von Hartmann, and others have stressed the idea that
ESP goes beyond the subjective forms which we call space
and time. In part, the confusion seems to arise from our
expectation that a decrease in ESP scores is an either/or
situation: that a decrease in scores over distances either will
be tremendous or will not occur at all. The logical possibility that a decrease in ESP efficiency could, in fact, be
quite moderate has usually been overlooked. G. R. Schmeidler clearly perceived the difficulty of detecting such a decrease: "If, for example, psi is really proportional to distance or time raised to some fractional power, where the
value of the fraction is small, very wide experimental variations will be necessary to detect any effect" (43, p. 111).

Another possible root of confusion may lie in unsys-
tematic interpretations of the data. A logical way to deal
with the results would be to ascertain carefully the trends in
the data when distance between the stimulus and the percipient
is introduced, and only thereafter to look into the causative
factors responsible for the trends. For example, if the
scores do decline with distance, we cannot tell immediately
whether to ascribe this decline to subjective factors, such as
attitudes, beliefs, feeling "on the spot," etc., or to the channel factor--the hypothetical energy which connects stimuli and
percipient. In practice, we tend to jump quickly to this second level of interpretation without carefully and thoroughly investigating at the first level. Very little work, if any, has
been done on the third level of interpretation; that is, evaluating jointly the subjective factors and the channel factor, and
their interactions; nor has much effort been made to analyze
in a reliable way either the components of the subjective factors or the possible components of the channel factor. Some

quite sharp theoretical analysis of the channel factor has been
done, such as that of H. A. C. Dobbs (12), B. Hoffmann (17),
J. H. Rush (41), and L. L. Vasiliev (57). Their hypotheses,
however, have not been followed up experimentally, except in
an often sporadic way by Vasiliev.

The need for clearly restating the problem and devising
sharply-delineated hypotheses and modern means for testing
them is great indeed. Turner's model (see Appendix), upon
which the main evaluations in this paper are based, is one attempt. Let us remember that Turner's approach keeps strictly within the data description level; that is, the first order
of interpretation. So far as I know, he is the first to propose such a detailed and mathematically sound description of
data concerning ESP over distances. He has carefully avoided
any confounding of the first-order interpretation by the other
higher-order interpretations mentioned above. I think this is
a desirable approach.

It is possible to design experiments in which variables
are ascertained that will permit mathematically precise data
descriptions and also will generate second- or third-order interpretations. For example, in my forthcoming paper, to be
published in the next issue of this Journal, I describe an experiment incorporating statistical control not only of some of
the attitudes and personality variables, but also of some of
the components of the channel variables, i.e., distance in
space and time and their interactions. This is just a small
beginning. Nevertheless, the twin problems of ESP over distance in space and time and of ESP orientation (how to find
a particular point in space) present themselves as very challenging and promising tasks. A sound and systematic approach to these problems will probably establish clear-cut
trends in the ESP channel factor. This would permit a definitive and precise theoretical analysis in scientific terms,
which is not possible at present. Only when enough bricks
are properly made can one build a sound structure.

There are breath-taking possibilities for a future theory
of the ESP channel factor. For example, will an unknown energy be pinpointed with the aid of modern communication-
theory tools such as precise energy expansion curves, signal-
to-noise ratios, etc.? Will a new additive dimension be found
in line with the hypotheses of Chari, Hart, and Smythies?
Or will a qualitatively different structure-giving principle
emerge such as Driesch's Seelenfeld, Jung's "other-valued
reality," or Tyrrell's "Elsewhere"? There is plenty of room

for a variety of approaches to the channel factor. It seems
to be a "many splendored thing. "

This survey does not pretend to give final answers to
questions concerning ESP and distance, or to the specific
question of the relationship between distance and the channel
factor in ESP. But it has succeeded, I hope, in its intent
to clear the ground and establish the available empirical trends
as a basis for new creative thinking and better future experiments.

REFERENCES

1.   Amadou, R. La Parapsychologie. Paris: Editions
        Denöel, 1954.

2.   Besterman, Theodore. "An Experiment in Long-Distance
        Telepathy. " Journal S. P. R. , Vol. 27, April, 1932,
        235-236.

3.   Bleksley, A. E. H. "An Experiment on Long-Distance
        ESP During Sleep. " Journal of Parapsychology,
        Vol. 27, March, 1963, 1-15.

4.   Board of Review. "Letters to the Editors. " Journal
        of Parapsychology, Vol. 4, June, 1940, 153-155.

5.   Carington, Whately. "Experiments on the Paranormal
        Cognition of Drawings, I. " Proc. S. P. R. , Vol.
        46, 1940, 34-151.

6.   _____ . "Experiments on the Paranormal Cognition
        of Drawings, II. " Proc. S. P. R. , Vol. 46, 1941,
        277-344.

7.   _____ . "Experiments on the Paranormal Cognition
        of Drawings, III. " Proc. A. S. P. R. , Vol. 24,
        1944, 3-107.

8.   _____ . "Experiments on the Paranormal Cognition
        of Drawings, IV. " Proc. S. P. R. , Vol. 47, 1944,
        155-228.

9.   _____ . Thought Transference. New York: Creative
        Age Press, 1946.

10. _____ , and Heywood, Rosalind. "Some Positive Re-
        sults from a Group of Small Experiments. " Proc.
        S. P. R. , Vol. 47, 1944, 229-236.

11. Coover, John E. Experiments in Psychical Research.
        Palo Alto, California: Stanford University Press,
        1917.

12. Dobbs, H. A. C. "Review of L. L. Vasiliev's Experi-
        ments in Mental Suggestion. " Journal S. P. R. , Vol.

42, March, 1964, 229-248.

13. Dodds, E. R. "Telepathy and Clairvoyance in Classical
    Antiquity." Journal of Parapsychology, Vol. 10,
    December 1946, 290-309.

14. Fisk, G. W., and West, D. J. "ESP and Mood: Report
    on a 'Mass' Experiment." Journal S. P. R., Vol.
    38, September, 1956, 320-329.

15. _____. "Towards Accurate Predictions from ESP
    Data." Journal S. P. R., Vol. 39, December, 1957,
    157-162.

16. Gibson, Edmond P. "A Study of Comparative Perform-
    ance in Several ESP Procedures." Journal of Para-
    psychology, Vol. 1, December, 1937, 264-275.

17. Hoffmann, B. "ESP and the Inverse Square Law."
    Journal of Parapsychology, Vol. 4, June, 1940,
    149-152.

18. Kahn, S. David. "Studies in Extrasensory Perception:
    Experiments Utilizing an Electronic Scoring Device."
    Proc. A. S. P. R., Vol. 25, 1952, 1-48.

19. Kherumian, R. "Anticipations." Revue Métapsychique,
    1950, 137-142.

20. Ludwig, A. F. Geschichte okkultistischen (metapsychi-
    schen) Forschung, I. Pfullingen: Johannes Baum,
    1921.

21. Mangan, G. L. "An ESP Experiment with Dual-Aspect
    Targets Involving One Trial a Day." Journal of
    Parapsychology, Vol. 21, December, 1957, 273-
    283.

22. Marsh, M. C. Linkage in Extra-Sensory Perception.
    Unpublished Ph. D. thesis. Grahamstown, South
    Africa: Rhodes University, 1958.

23. _____. "Three ESP Experiments Using Drawings as
    Target Material." Publications of the South African
    S. P. R., No. 5, 1962.

24. McMahan, Elizabeth A., and Bates, E. K., Jr. "Report
    of Further Marchesi Experiments." Journal of
    Parapsychology, Vol. 18, June, 1954, 82-92.

25. _____, and Lauer, Joan. "Extrasensory Perception
    of Cards in an Unknown Location." Journal of
    Parapsychology, Vol. 12, March, 1948, 47-57.

26. _____, and Rhine, J. B. "A Second Zagreb-Durham
    ESP Experiment." Journal of Parapsychology, Vol.
    11, December, 1947, 244-253.

27. Michie, D., and West, D. J. "A Mass ESP Test Using
    Television." Journal S. P. R., Vol. 39, September,
    1957, 113-133.

28. Miles, Clarissa, and Ramsden, Hermione. "Experiments

in Thought-Transference." Proc. S. P. R. , Vol. 21,
1907, 60-93.

29. Murphy, Gardner, and Taves, Ernest. "Covariance
     Methods in the Comparison of Extra-Sensory Tasks."
     Journal of Parapsychology, Vol. 3, June, 1939, 38-
     78.
30. Nash, Carroll B. "Retest of High Scoring Subjects in
     the Chesebrough-Pond's ESP Television Contest."
     Journal A. S. P. R. , Vol. 57, April, 1963, 106-110.
31. Osis, Karlis. "ESP Tests at Long and Short Distances."
     Journal of Parapsychology, Vol. 20, June, 1956,
     81-95.
32. _____, and Pienaar, D. C. "ESP Over a Distance
     of Seventy-Five Hundred Miles." Journal of Para-
     psychology, Vol. 20, December, 1956, 229-232.
33. Podmore, Frank. Apparitions and Thought-Transference.
     New York: Charles Scribner's Sons, 1902.
34. Prince, Walter Franklin. "The Sinclair Experiments
     Demonstrating Telepathy." Bulletin 16, Boston So-
     ciety for Psychic Research, 1932.
35. Rhine, J. B. Extra-Sensory Perception. Boston:
     Bruce Humphries, 1934.
36. _____ . "The Effect of Distance in ESP Tests."
     Journal of Parapsychology, Vol. 1, September, 1937,
     172-184.
37. _____ . New World of the Mind. New York: Wil-
     liam Sloane Associates, 1953.
38. _____, and Humphrey, Betty M. "A Transoceanic
     ESP Experiment." Journal of Parapsychology, Vol.
     6, March, 1942, 52-74.
39. _____, and Pratt, J. G. "A Review of the Pearce-
     Pratt Distance Series of ESP Tests." Journal of
     Parapsychology, Vol. 18, September, 1954, 165-177.
40. Riess, Bernard F. "A Case of High Scores in Card
     Guessing at a Distance." Journal of Parapsychol-
     ogy, Vol. 1, December, 1937, 260-263.
41. Rush, J. H. "Some Considerations as to a Physical
     Basis of ESP." Journal of Parapsychology, Vol.
     7, March, 1943, 44-49.
42. _____, and Jensen, Ann. "A Reciprocal Distance
     GESP Test with Drawings." Journal of Parapsy-
     chology, Vol. 13, June, 1949.
43. Schmeidler, Gertrude R. "Research Projects in Para-
     psychology." Journal of Parapsychology, Vol. 12,
     June, 1948, 107-113.
44. _____, and Allison, Lydia W. "A Repetition of Car-
     ington's Experiments with Free Drawings." Journal

A. S. P. R., Vol. 42, July, 1948, 97-107.

45. Shulman, R. "Research Notes: An Experiment in Ex-
     tra-Sensory Perception with Sounds as Stimuli. "
     Journal of Parapsychology, Vol. 2, December,
     1938, 322-325.

46. Sidgwick, Mrs. H., and Johnson, Miss Alice. "Experi-
     ments in Thought-Transference. " Proc. S. P. R.,
     Vol. 8, 1892, 536-596.

47. Sinclair, Upton. Mental Radio. Monrovia, California:
     Upton Sinclair, 1930.

48. Skibinsky, Morris. "A Comparison of Names and Sym-
     bols in a Distance ESP Test. " Journal of Parapsy-
     chology, Vol. 14, June, 1950, 140-156.

49. Soal, S. G. "Experiments in Supernormal Perception
     at a Distance. " Proc. S. P. R., Vol. 40, 1932,
     165-362.

50. _____, and Bateman, F. Modern Experiments in
     Telepathy. New Haven: Yale University Press,
     1954.

51. Stuart, C. E. "An ESP Test with Drawings. " Journal
     of Parapsychology, Vol. 6, March, 1942, 20-43.

52. _____. "An ESP Experiment with Enclosed Draw-
     ings. " Journal of Parapsychology, Vol. 9, Decem-
     ber, 1945, 278-295.

53. Taves, Ernest, Murphy, Gardner, and Dale, L. A.
     "American Experiments on the Paranormal Cogni-
     tion of Drawings. " Journal A. S. P. R., Vol. 39,
     July, 1945, 144-150.

54. Tischner, R. Geschichte okkultistischen (metaphychi-
     schen) Forschung, II. Pfullingen: Johannes Baum,
     1924.

55. Tyrrell, G. N. M. The Personality of Man. Balti-
     more: Penguin Books, 1947.

56. Usher, F. L., and Burt, F. P. "Thought Transfer-
     ence. " Annals of Psychical Science, Vol. 8, 1909,
     561-600.

57. Vasiliev, L. L. Experiments in Mental Suggestion.
     Church Crookham, Hampshire, England: Institute
     for the Study of Mental Images, 1963.

58. Warcollier, René. Experimental Telepathy. Boston:
     Boston Society for Psychic Research, 1938.

59. West, D. J. Psychical Research Today. London:
     Gerald Duckworth, 1954.

ADDITIONAL READINGS ON DISTANCE
AND PSI PHENOMENA

Bleksley, A. E. H. "A further study on long-distance ESP during sleep." (Abstract) JP 33: 321-22 (Dec 1969).

Dean, E. D. "Long-distance plethysmograph telepathy with agent under water." (Abstract) JP 33: 349-50 (Dec 1969).

Krippner, S. and others. "A long-distance 'sensory bombardment' study of ESP in dreams." JASPR 65: 468-75 (Oct 1971).

Mitchell, E. D. "An ESP test from Apollo 14." JP 35: 89-107 (Jun 1971).

Osis, K. and Fahler, J. "Space and time variables in ESP." JASPR 59: 130-45 (Apr 1965).

Osis, K. and Turner, M. E. Jr. "Distance and ESP: A transcontinental experiment." PASPR 27: 1-48 (1968).

_____, _____, and Carlson, M. L. "ESP over distance: Research on the ESP channel." JASPR 65: 245-88 (Jul 1971).

Ruderfer, M. "Note on the effect of distance on ESP." JASPR 63: 197-201 (Apr 1969).

Turner, M. E., Jr. Appendix to Dr. Osis' article: "A statistical model for examining the relation between ESP and distance." JASPR 59: 43-46 (Jan 1965).

Chapter 9

POSITION EFFECTS IN PSI TEST RESULTS*

by J. B. Rhine

Parapsychology is best identified as a branch of natural science by the accumulated knowledge that the psi process, while still distinctive in nature, operates in a measurably lawful way. Probably none of the findings in psi research have shown this lawfulness more clearly than have position effects, or PEs, the systematic distribution of hits according to location of the trial on the record page. The most common of these PEs are either declines in the scoring rate (across the page from left to right, down the column from top to bottom, or diagonally) or U-curves of success within one of the units of the record page (the set, run, or segment of the run).

But although PEs have been a familiar phenomenon in experimental parapsychology almost from its beginning and have almost reached the status of being a criterion of evidence of psi activity, the attention given to them has been largely limited to their practical aspects; that is, to their use as a basis for testing the extrachance significance of data. On the other hand, their bearing on the nature of psi has not hitherto been actively investigated.

However, in today's revaluation of parapsychology, the PEs take on a new importance, not only for the understanding of the psi process, but also for the effort to bring it under increased control. If indeed the mere position of the trial on the record sheet can measurably affect the rate of success (as we now know it can), the PE becomes more than

*Reprinted by permission of the author and publisher from Journal of Parapsychology 33: 136-57 (June 1969).
        This article is based on a paper presented at the Winter Review Meeting of the Institute for Parapsychology on January 3, 1969.

204

a statistically useful device for testing significance. It can
with some success be converted into an experimental tool for
the manipulation of psi performance.

Yet, while one need hardly ask for further reasons for
reviewing what is known about PEs at present, the actual
stimulus to survey it arose in writing the psi-missing paper
which I gave at the last Review Meeting. In that paper (17)
it came out clearly that psi-missing and position effects were,
under some conditions, very much intertwined. In some cases
position effects seemed to have led to psi-missing, while on
the other hand the question arose as to whether psi-missing
might not be at least a partial explanation of position effects,
if not in fact an entirely sufficient one.

The questions raised by this mutual involvement of the
two topics called for a review of the present status of PEs
in psi research, and also, of course, the relation of these
effects to psi-missing.

HISTORICAL SKETCH

It was probably Richet (23) who first called attention
to the falling-off of scoring rate in long runs of clairvoyance
tests. Jephson (9) made quite a point of the decline of scoring rate in short runs of five trials in guessing playing cards.
Estabrooks (2) presented the first clear-cut case of PE declines in his runs of 20 trials in the GESP guessing of playing cards.

In the early Duke experiments (16), PEs appeared almost immediately after the adoption of routine card-guessing
tests and the use of standard record sheets. The earliest
case I recall was found in the series of 100-trial runs made
by the subject HLF in guessing the suit of playing cards.
The distribution of hits in the run showed a comparatively
straight decline of scoring rate from the first 20-trial segment to the last. Other declines of this kind followed; and
later on, when the runs were standardized at a length of 25
trials each, subjects who were given long series of routine
tests began to show U-curves of hit distribution within the
run. Not only did these curves become a fairly well marked
characteristic in the ESP experiments; but later, with the development of dice-throwing tests for PK, similar U-curves
appeared in the run structure of these tests as well (16).
End segments of the runs were generally higher in scoring

rate than the middle segments, giving the whole run a more
or less U-shaped curve when the hit distribution was graphed.

As the recurrent character of these PEs stood out sufficiently for a general impression (the time was the mid-
1930s), a natural satisfaction was felt when the effect was
observed in one experimental series after another. However,
the dominant concern among research workers then had to be
the production of the strongest direct evidence of ESP possible.
In the heat of the controversy that followed the first Duke
publication on ESP, such questions as the nature, consistency,
and conditions producing PEs could be given little time and
attention.

It is true, the position-effect data were evaluated statistically so as to take some advantage of the regular drop-
ping-off in scoring. In the case of the HLF work mentioned
above, for example, it was found that the critical ratio of
the difference (CR_d) between the first two segments and the
last two was significant even though the total score for the
entire experiment was not. As a matter of fact, it became
a practice to look for and evaluate top-bottom differences,
since there was a rather general trend of this type in the
work being reported. Sometimes the left-right division of
the record page also showed a decline that furnished a basis
of differentiation and a significant CR.

More important still, the diagonal decline from the
upper left quarter to the lower right proved to be a useful
measurement of significance in psi test data, especially in
the PK work of the 1940s. It will be recalled that this diagonal decline became the highly objective basis for the evaluation of the large available collection of earlier PK researches that had accumulated at the Duke Laboratory. These
diagonal decline analyses are reported in a series of articles
(19, 20, 21) in the Journal of Parapsychology of 1944-45.
This method was called the quarter-distribution analysis, and
it provided very strong evidence for the occurrence of PK.
The point here is that it depended entirely upon PEs for its
superior evidential quality.

In searching for a method of statistical evaluation
adaptable to the U-curve type of PEs, a technique called the
salience-ratio method was devised with the help of Dr. J. A.
Greenwood (5), a mathematician on the Laboratory staff at
the time. The concept of the salience ratio (SR) was based
on terminal salience, the fact that the two end segments

tended to stand out as the highest-scoring (or, in the case of
inverted U-curves, the lowest-scoring) of the five units, making something of a normal U-curve (or an inverted one).
The salience-ratio method was an effective way of evaluating
this terminal salience (essentially a method of playing both
ends against the middle).

Moreover, the SR method applied equally well to the
similar U-curve found to be typical of the five trials within
the segments of the runs.   These segment PEs usually showed
approximately the same terminal salience of the end trials
that was found in the end segments of the run.   Thus the segment SRs (SSRs) served as measures of PEs within the five-
trial sections of the run; and also, by means of a covariation
statistic devised by Greenwood (5), they could be compared
with the SRs of the run as a whole (RSRs).

These covariation tests of the two types of SR were
adequate in themselves as sensitive tests of the presence of
ESP; nothing else conceivably could produce these subtle concomitant tendencies to U-curves in the run and in the segment except the ESP function.   The method made it possible
to obtain evidence of psi in the form of PEs when in many
cases it would not otherwise have been discoverable.   At the
same time, the SR method was more than a mere test of
significance, as the next section will illustrate.   It will be
seen that it was a supplementary technique to the CR$_d$ method and, as such, allowed an easy comparison of types of
measurement.

An Exploratory Experiment in Position Effects

It was with the aid of the salience-ratio method that
in 1941 at the Duke Laboratory the one fairly extensive effort
was made to investigate the U-curve or terminal-salience effect (14).   An outline of the main findings concerning PEs
(drawn from the original 61-page report) will be sketched
here; these results are still relevant today.   The extensive
use of the DT method of ESP testing at that period had considerably accented interest in U-curves; at the same time,
the use of this method with the cards enclosed in sealed
boxes (which delayed the checking process) afforded a very
safe procedure.   The experiment consisted of more than
1,100 runs, about a third of which were made by 14 children
ranging in age from 5 to 13 years; and the rest, by 16 adults,
aged between 21 and 49.

The main objectives of this complex experiment were
to check on the impression that the PEs lowered the scoring
level in psi testing, that it was the structure of the record
sheet that was responsible for the U-curves, and that the
U-curves in the run tended to parallel those of the segment.
There was interest, too, in experimentally making the segments stand out sharply by interposing more interruption between them. Age comparisons were also part of the design;
the earlier PEs encountered had all been produced by adult
subjects.

Writing versus Calling Tests. One of the exploratory
studies of the effects of record-sheet structure on PEs was
the comparison of two methods of response; in one the subject wrote his own guesses on the standard record sheet
(which has the segments marked by a double line), and in
the other he called them aloud for recording by the experimenter (who kept the record sheet out of the subject's view).
In the writing tests the adults gave a significant SR in the
segment though not in the run, and the children gave significance in neither. On the other hand, in the calling tests
neither age group of subjects gave significant SRs. It appeared that the adults were affected by the segmented structure of the record sheet (as they wrote on it) but that the
children were not.

Interruption between Segments. When the subjects
were tested with the run still more definitely interrupted between segments, with the subject having to guess the number
on cards which were interposed at the five-trial intervals in
the target deck, the interruption brought out very marked U-
curves in the segment. The adults gave significant SRs in
both the segment and the run, and even the children gave
quite significant SRs in the segment.

However, when the run was then interrupted by a much
larger task, the effect was apparently overdone. This test
plan required the subject to try to draw the picture on a card
interposed in the deck at the end of every five standard ESP
test cards. This took longer than the mere guessing of a
number and involved more attention. Only the adults gave
significant SRs in this more interrupted series, and they did
it only within the segment.

Summing up, then, the effect of the structure of the
record sheet, the adults gave significant SRs for the segment
in the following order: largest in the series with interruptions

consisting of number-guessing; next highest in the series with
interruption by drawings; third (and about the same as with
drawings), in the writing of responses on the standard record
sheet (divided only by double lines) without interruption; and
fourth, nonsignificant SRs on the calling series. (It should
be remarked that in all these series but the last, the subject
recorded his own guesses and therefore was aware of the
position of the trials in the segments.) All these results
were in segment SRs; only when the series were interrupted
by numbers did the adults give a significant SR both in the
segment and in the run, and the children a significant SR in
the segment.   The tests had obviously accentuated the SRs of
the segment, almost to the point of obscuring the SR of the
run.

CRs versus SRs (Scoring Rate versus PEs).   It was
the children's group, however, that brought out the contrast
between the SRs and CRs; for them, when the SRs were low
the CRs were high.   For example, in the section interrupted
with drawings, the children gave a significant negative deviation by the CR method, but no significance on the SRs measuring the PEs; whereas in the series interrupted by numbers,
the CR was not significant but the SR of the segment was
quite so.   Similarly, the children gave a significant CR on
the uninterrupted series (independently significant on the writing section); but their results gave no significance in the SRs
of either the runs or the segments, either in the writing or
the calling tests.   The dividing lines between segments were
not enough to produce PEs in their written responses.   PEs
were, however, not expected in the calling tests.

Age Comparisons.   In the overall picture, it is quite
clear that the adults were more responsive to the structuring
of the record page than the children, and that when the children did respond to the structuring this was accompanied by
considerable interference with their total deviation.   Consequently, while the total deviation for the entire 1,114 runs
was significantly negative, this effect was almost entirely
contributed by the children and was based on only about half
as many runs as the adults made.

Parallel PEs in Segment and Run.   The similarity of
the curves for the segment and the run was the really outstanding finding of this research.   In consequence of it, the
covariation of the segment SRs and the run SRs is very significant.   The indications were that the same factors were
operating in both structures and were producing a clear-cut
effect.

The similarity (and covariation of SRs) of these curves of hit distributions in segment and run reflects, of course, the lawful nature of the psi process underlying the test data. They both indicate areas of reliability where the usual uncertainties of psi testing have been to an unusual extent eliminated. These U-curves and the covariation of SRs are assurances that, at least under certain conditions, a surprising dependability of psi effect can be attained.

During the early 1940s, other researches besides this particular one using the SR method and covariation showed similar segment-run relations in the PEs. These may be consulted with profit today even though they dealt with PEs only as evidence of ESP (6, 7, 8, 15, 18). It was just this practical usefulness of PEs as psi evidence that produced the large body of PE results now on record. This wealth of data has in turn resulted, of course, from the standardization of testing and recording and the faithfulness of workers in adhering to standard methods.

PEs in PK Test Results. Before the end of the year in which the terminal salience paper was published, this country was plunged into World War II; and with the limited attention it left for parapsychology, the editors of the Journal of Parapsychology decided to release the long-withheld reports on the PK experiments. Preoccupation with these other matters left no time for the pursuit of the position effects in ESP data at the Duke Laboratory. But from the first report on the PK work onward, there was ample indication of PEs in that section of the research data. These were for the most part declines in scoring rate from left to right or from one run to another on the record page; and almost immediately the CR of the difference (between left-right halves or top-bottom) became the same important measure of significance that it had been in the ESP work.

One main difference, however, existed. Because of the long pre-publication period of PK research, there was much free exploration without as much consistent organization as had been possible in the ESP research. Many different kinds of tests were conducted by more than a dozen different individual testers, working in various locations but all keeping in some relation to the Duke Laboratory. The result was that no uniform record sheets such as introduced consistency of PEs for the ESP work were used in any of the early PK experiments. Consequently, any PEs found in those results would be expected to vary with the recording conditions.

As a matter of fact, although PEs were almost universally present throughout the PK researches, they did show wider variety. They were found to be most marked, however, in experiments in which a single subject worked alone and therefore was aware of his progress through the run as he recorded his own results, or where two persons worked together alternating as subject and recorder. Persistence throughout long series seemed to accent the structuring, and close preoccupation with the record sheet greatly intensified the effect of structure. In one remarkable experiment (from the point of view of the PEs) the experimenter-subject (MPR) distributed her hits over the record page in such a way that from at least six different independent break-downs of the data, significant differences based upon declines were found (13).

It must be kept in mind however that none of these experimenters was aware of these PEs in their data. Evidence of PK which years later turned out, from analyses conducted by others than themselves, to be of the very strongest type was hidden in their record sheets, awaiting the period in 1943 when there was time and good reason for turning to look for possible declines. Eventually, as was stated earlier, a general method was found for combining the PE data from all of the available records; this again was the quarter-distribution method which led to the evaluation of the difference between the upper left quarter of the record page (generally high-scoring) and the lower right (usually low-scoring). From this method came one of the strongest blocks of evidence of psi in the field of parapsychology.

THE STATUS OF POSITION EFFECTS TODAY

It may be helpful at this point to bring together the main points that can now be accepted with some confidence concerning the PEs in psi data. These are, by definition, only those effects on the scoring rate that have to do with the subject's reaction to the structure of the test record. This leaves out declines or other effects that may be attributable merely to a long series of tests, long sessions, or to unstructured test operations (for example, those in which the subject does not know the trial position). These are all effects that are not closely related to the record page; the distinctions can be easily drawn. Eliminating these other types of scoring shift in this paper does not, of course, imply a lack of importance.

External Conditions in Position Effects

Within the problem area indicated there is, in addition
to the more or less standard run with its segments as used
in the ESP tests, a variety of lengths, types, and arrangements of run columns on the record page, especially in the
PK work.   Various sizes of record sheets have been used,
some of them containing smaller units or sets.   A set may
have space for 3 runs of 12 trials each or it may have 6
short columns of 6 entries each.   Or it may consist of a set
of 12 x 12 spaces.   Thus far, except for a few broad generalizations, little is known about the relative merit of these
different structures.   For instance, it was found in the quarter-distribution analyses mentioned above that the most significant rate of difference (in the diagonal decline) was obtained within the set rather than for the page as a whole.
Likewise, in the ESP column, the most significant SR was in
the segment instead of in the run as a whole.   It indicates
that, when well marked off, a smaller unit seems to exert
a more effective rate of influence on the PEs than a large
one.

The general findings thus far seem to indicate that
adults are more responsive to structure than children; or
perhaps it would be better to say that, to be equally effective
with children, the structuring needs to be more definitely
marked.   With this in mind, the record sheets used after the
1941 paper had the run of 25 trials broken up into a row of
five short columns of five trials each.   This was done to accent the PEs, as I think it probably did.   However, the interest in it at the time was a practical one, and no comparison with the long-run columns of the old record sheets was
made with the same subjects under similar conditions; so no
firm statement can be made.   The five-column record sheets
were not used after we ceased to rely on the SR for the
main test of significance.

There has been no comparison of the sexes as yet as
to their relative tendencies to produce PEs, but I should
mention that the two most remarkable productions of PEs in
the PK work were both made by women.

As to target range, a qualified statement can be made.
Most of the PEs in the ESP work were produced by the use
of the five-symbol range of the standard ESP test cards, but
the PK work covers a wide variety of target possibilities and
conveys the general impression that the number of dice per

throw or the particular type of target or target combination
(high dice, sevens, single faces, doubles, etc.) has little to
do with the resulting PEs.

Finally, it does not seem to matter whether or not
the subject knows at once about his success on each trial so
far as PEs are concerned. PEs are found both in the PK
and the ESP test results, while the two types of tests differ
radically on whether the subject knows trial-by-trial about
his success. The PK work has always involved immediate
knowledge, while in ESP tests, the subject seldom knows of
results on every trial.

It seems clear that the factors that affect PEs are
mainly those which focus the subject's attention on the structure of the record sheet and that the most effective structures
are those which would most effectively impress themselves
visually upon the subject. In other words, the PEs begin
first in the sensory organization of the record sheet pattern.
This lawfully influences the psi process in its hit distribution
in the test.

The Internal Elements in Position Effects

What goes on inside the subject's ESP responses that
can be so influenced as to produce position effects? Obviously, if nothing takes place but chance guessing in a chance
series, there will be no PEs. Therefore, when any lawful
PE pattern is produced in a proper psi test, it must be because the psi process has intruded its influence into the varying patterns of the chance responses. These chance responses
can, for discussion, be labelled habit guessing, although other elements are also involved. If the subject is entirely
dominated by a simple pattern of habit guessing and falls into a routine system--as, for example, a child may do, repeating the targets over and over in a fixed order--ESP has
little or no opportunity of being expressed. A free opening
in the habit pattern must be found (or made) for its expression; accordingly, it is logical to suppose that the less habit-
driven or the more spontaneous a subject is in his guessing,
the easier it is for the psi process to break through the habit
system. The force or drive given the psi function could also make a difference.

From general observation as well as from general
psychology, it is easy to think that the first trial of a run

(or segment) might be the most advantageous for spontaneity
and that, as the subject went on from there, associative factors of habit guessing would come in more strongly the longer the unbroken series continued. But that observation does
not explain the favoring of the end trial, which is often as
likely to be a hit as the first. However, a kind of psychological salience seems to be shown at both end positions in
a run or column in psi tests just as it is in sensory experiences with structured items. They are said to stand out, or
are salient, or show primacy and terminal effects. Some
will say it is because the ends more easily catch attention,
but why do they? Somehow the terminal trial, like the first,
tends to escape the limitation of habit patterns arriving at
the last trial produces a distinct liberating feeling and this in
itself seems to introduce a slight spontaneity sufficient to allow the subject to elude the pattern association he has carried
along up to that point.

We need not try as yet to be very conclusive about
these explanations. They are matters for study, especially
in relation to their counterparts in memory, learning, and
other cognitive functions which show similar curves.

The advantage of segmenting the run is by now obvious enough. It began by the early discovery in working with
subject HP at Duke that in clairvoyance tests of card guessing he worked best in short runs of five trials. Now of
course the advantage would seem to be that if the run is segmented, the subject has 10 end points in the run instead of
two. But does this really help the total score? That depends on what segmenting does, not only to the end trials of
the segment, but to the middle ones too. This calls for a
new experiment.

I have already recalled the inverse relation between
CRs and SRs (the SRs, of course, representing the measurement of PEs) which the children showed in the 1941 experiment (14). On the face of it, this looks as if, as was suspected in earlier days, the PEs were cutting down the total
psi yield of the run. That still may be the right interpretation, but further research is needed to distinguish more
clearly between the possibilities. In the older work, the
series in which the children got significant CRs but not significant SRs were the same as those which gave the adults
significant SRs. The children did not respond to the segmentation, at least in such a way as to show significantly
measurable PEs. But now it can be seen that another control

is required before a safe interpretation is possible, another
"writing" experiment in which there is no segmentation; conceivably the segmentation may have improved the scoring
level of the children even though it did not give significant
PEs. At any rate, it seems best to leave the question open
as to how far the segmentation of the runs will assist the
subject by giving him more points of enhanced spontaneity,
more "holes in the fence."

What seems apparent now is that finally the position-
effect problems are coming up again and approaching a point
where a range of explorations will be called for to see how
best to liberate the subject from the limitations the test method puts in the way of his psi response. New approaches and
devices may of course be invented to enhance the subject's
free response to the target (that is, his "random behavior"
or spontaneity). If so, it would seem likely that they will
have to be primarily psychological rather than physiological,
pharmacological, or mechanical. But they need not be limited
to visual configuration, as in the segmentation of the test
sheet, or even confined to sensory patterns.

Above all, the PE studies have shown that the influences over the psi scoring-rate that cause PEs involve the
conscious range of the subject's reaction, even though they
actually are unconscious most of the time. When they are
produced, the subject at least knows where the trial is located even though he is not actually thinking of it. Such indications of marginally conscious factors in psi performance
open up a new possibility for extending control over the process. It is plainly in order now to study further the effect
of different kinds and degrees of structuring upon some applications of PEs that are now coming into research interest.

The Relation of Psi-Missing to Position Effects

Even though PEs are in some way the result of the
subject's reaction to the record page structuring, there is
still some question as to how this effect is produced. It
could be simply a matter of the psi-produced hits being concentrated in certain positions, but also the interplay of psi-
missing with psi-hitting could conceivably make up the patterns of the PE curves. For example, HLF's long-run declines already mentioned could have been produced by a gradual shift from psi-hitting in the first section of the run to
psi-missing in the last. At any rate it would be difficult to

eliminate psi-missing with confidence as a possible contributor to PEs in some instances.

At the same time, in spite of these cases of overlapping of PEs and psi-missing, no instance has thus far been
found that has shown psi-missing as playing an essential role
in the production of PEs as defined in this paper. On the
whole, a summary of the evidence at this stage seems to indicate that the two effects are independent of each other in
character, especially in the factors producing them. They
spring from different causal influences, even though they are
sometimes closely associated in results. For example, when
test conditions favor psi-missing, as happened in the terminal
salience research reviewed earlier (14), the same record
sheet that normally produces PEs with the aid of psi-hitting
will usually give inverted PEs both in the run and in the
segment, with all the evidence of psi represented as missing
(negative deviations). (See Figure 1.)

Perhaps the best case for illustrating the independence
of the PEs from psi-missing comes from the PK researches.
Although the PK results are replete with PEs, psi-missing
very seldom appears in close association with them. It frequently does in the ESP records. There is one main difference in procedure which I mentioned earlier: in PK tests the
subject is usually given immediate knowledge of his success
on every trial, while he seldom is in ESP tests. In my psi-
missing review (17), I stated that it seems likely this immediate knowledge of success prevents psi-missing. It obviously does not prevent PEs.

Another way of distinguishing between PEs and negative scoring was illustrated in two of the papers given at
this meeting, one by Sara Feather (3) and the other by Joyce
Jones (10). The curves for the position effects were quite
similar for the scores above the chance mean and those that
fell below. (See Figure 2 for curves from the Feather paper.)
What seems indicated is that the factors making for psi-hitting and -missing in these results appear to be independent
of those producing the curves of position effects.

Here again the PEs and psi-missing are closely associated in the results but the factors producing them are
still distinguishable. The record-sheet structure still produces
the PEs, and the effect of the test conditions on the subject
has to do with the sign of deviation.

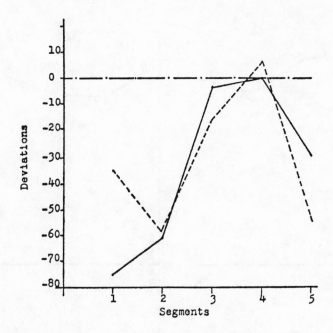

Fig. 1. Graph taken from "Terminal Salience in ESP Performance" (14). Solid line represents segments in the run; broken line, trials in the segment. This series of 1,114 runs was significant both in its total (negative) deviation and in its covariation of salience ratios in segment and run.

A closer look is now possible at what determines which way psi will go--whether as a hit or as a miss--when it does register. This seems to depend on how well the subject can keep the delicate marginal control over the psi process which he apparently has to have to produce a significant positive result. A limited relaxation of this delicate control still allows psi to continue to function, but with a loss of accuracy of direction. It continues to make responses only partly related to the target, actually avoiding the correct response apparently because of what Louisa E. Rhine calls a "blocking effect" (22). I compared it in my earlier paper to a forced attempt at recall where memory is blocked.

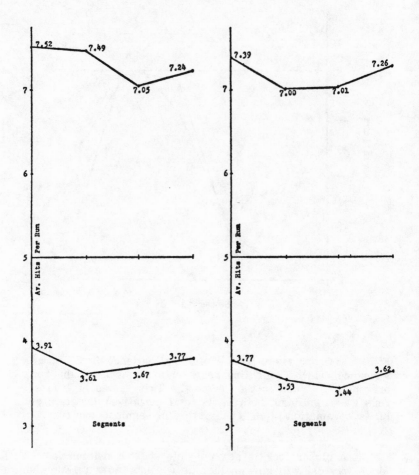

Fig. 2. Data taken from "Position Effects in a Mass Precognition Test" by Sara R. Feather (3). The points on the curves represent the average rate of scoring for the four segments in the run, converted for easy comparison to score averages per run of 25 trials. The upper curves show average scores of 6 hits or above per run, and the lower curves, 5 hits or below. The graphs on the left are based on the data of 966 boys; the ones on the right, 989 girls.

        Thus it can be said with some confidence that the two
main side effects of psi test response, psi-missing and position effects, are often interoperative but, so far as is known,
not interdependent.

                        EVALUATIVE DISCUSSION

        This review of present knowledge should make it pos-
sible to go still further in the consideration of possible uses
of PEs. Enough is now known about the conditions that cause
psi-missing to avoid entangling the two problem areas if it is
desirable to deal with PEs alone. Or psi-missing can be
used in a controlled way, especially by means of the psi-differential effect in the two-aspect type of test. But the problem will be greatly simplified if the interrelations of psi and
chance can be dealt with in test situations over which a degree
of control is possible through the structuring of the subject's
test performance. To this end it becomes eminently worth
while to see what kind of structuring is the best for the purposes of the specific research contemplated.

Position Effects as Openings in the Barrier

        The major suggestion the PEs make at the present
stage is that they may provide a means of by-passing the
habit systems of the subject. At least they seem to indicate
positions of differential penetrability in the barrier of habit
processes through which psi must communicate.

        If so, then it looks very much as though position ef-
fects give a new answer to a question that has been of special
interest in the last year or two--the question of how to single
out before the checkup is made just those trials in the psi
test in which psi "had a chance to function." In other words,
the problem is to screen out the trials on which the subject
was not open to the exercise of psi.

        This question is an old one but it has arisen afresh in
recent years because of work with animals presented at one
of our meetings last year by two French biologists, Duval and
Montredon (1). These experimenters reported results of automatically controlled and recorded precognition tests with mice
in which they found that, from the records, they could distinguish between habit and nonhabit responses of the animals.
They reported that when a mouse was responding from estab-

lished habit, the results were, as should be expected, non-
significant, but when the animal acted contrary to habit and
therefore allowed psi to register, the results were quite significant. From the records, it was possible to make a completely objective selection of these "random behavior" trials,
as the authors called them (those in which psi was a possibility), and these could be scored for success while the larger number of habit responses could safely be deleted from
the analyses. This work has since been continued in the
same laboratory but awaits further replication.

However, the authors of the mouse paper credited the
the idea of sifting out the random behavior trials to a report
of earlier experiments on ESP in cats by Osis and Foster
(11) of the Duke Parapsychology Laboratory. In those experiments it had been observed that the extrachance margin of
success was contributed by those trials in which the animal
broke its side habits. It was in those breaks in the chain of
habit responses that ESP registered.

It had, of course, been common knowledge in psi research that, in order to make a successful ESP response, the
subject had to break through the system of associations that
made up the "stream of consciousness" accompanying the test
performance. That habitual patterns of linkage of symbols in
ESP tests were formed by subjects had often been recognized,
and the general problem had been considered as to how best
to get spontaneous psi expression in spite of the habit system
that prevails in "just guessing." Various efforts to secure
increased spontaneity in the subject were made, for example,
in attempts to introduce competitive games into the testing
program. A brief pilot study of spontaneity was published by
Scherer (24) in 1948 but was not followed up. In a rather
practical way, Forwald (4) made an important step in taking
only the first of each short run of five throws (of dice) for
his test data. He observed that his main success was on this
first throw and adopted the practice of recording but rejecting
the other four trials. Naturally, the first trial would have a
certain spontaneity that successive ones would not, if it could
be kept a fresh start. Pratt, in his analyses (12) of PK records to determine the relative efficiency of the different trials
in the run, brought out a similar point in the work of other
subjects (than Forwald). He found that, after the first trial
in the run, the subject was practically wasting his time so
far as adding to the total deviation was concerned. This continued to be true until the last trial of the run, which again
stood out much like the first when the subject knew it was the
last trial.

In summary, then, it is plain that PEs are roughly like those gaps in the habit barrier found in the ESP tests with cats and mice. The pattern of the record sheet differentiates the relative force of the subject's habit system and certain points (usually ends of some one of the units) stand out.

The way is open now to go on to learn how to make more (or better) openings of this type. The trail may also lead to still other ways of structuring the tests as well as other ways of registering the effects. The researcher can now safely follow Forwald's lead and, with proper design, select his favored trial positions in advance and thus move ahead another step toward psi control. Other devices like sampling techniques and repeated-guessing methods can easily be combined.

In the most general terms, what the PEs seem to be doing is this: they provide a grading system of surface mental processes that automatically differentiate psi and non-psi (chance) positions in the test structure. This works well enough for most subjects to serve as a useful psi test device in itself. For example, it has served as the basis of the SR type of significance test in psi research--an important one in its time. (PEs, of course, contributed much of the psi-differential evidence as well.) All the while that psi workers were in need of just such a selector device for separation of the psi-state trials from the non-psi and were looking enviously at the easy separation allowed by the simpler animal test data, here it was embedded in the large collection of PE material awaiting the moment of recognition.

Further Consequences of the PE Research

Looking ahead to the future research on PEs, the way is now open to pursue not only the investigations leading into the question of just what structures will give the maximal benefit of position, but how far such (potentially) conscious factors as reaction to variations in test structure can be brought more or less directly under the subject's voluntary control. The way seems to be opening finally upon training possibilities for psi control, training that may bear some resemblance to the new discoveries in learning. The latter developments show acquisition of a degree of voluntary control over functions considered to be (like psi) unconscious.

Another question is finally brought back into focus again

that was raised in 1941: whether PEs reduce the CRs or, more generally worded, whether unstructured tests give more psi information than those that produce PEs. Knowing the cause of PEs as well as we now do makes the task of answering the question experimentally a comparatively easy one. But although PEs are now usually more useful than merely having a somewhat larger CR would be, there are researches in which prior importance goes to the CR. It is even of theoretical interest, however, to know whether psi communication is hindered or helped by conditions producing PEs.

To one psi worker at least, the paramount aspect of the PE picture at this stage is the impression of comparative regularity it gives of a process long regarded as the most elusive in nature. Yet, year after year for the nearly forty years since standard tests and record sheets were adopted, these lined sheets of paper were serving as a screening grid on which the psi function displayed certain natural lawful reactions even under all the fenced-in conditions of testing. Here the masses of test data have been sifted for precognition and PK as the evidence has varied and accumulated.

All the while, too, as workers have been pushed and pulled and pressured to abandon such "mechanical" and "quantitative" and "repetitious" methods of testing (and by another group, urged to turn it all over to even more fully mechanized systems of test procedure), fortunately a traceable, usable middle course of practice was found and persistently followed that registered all the more meaningful results because of standardized rules and techniques. And now today these accumulated masses of data have made it possible to see in the long-range perspective of comparative procedures how much was clearly gained by the very methodical adherence to standard test procedures. They show limitations as well as progress; they indicate the cost as well as the gain. The student today can compare the relative fruitfulness of these main lines of test methods with those that earlier were tried and abandoned. Such comparisons, however, are mainly for future guidance. There is no need to justify the past in the case of the PE researches.

In any case, a psi researcher is generally looking ahead from habit, and he can now most probably think of ways to channel and sift the psi process better than could be done in the past. Naturally he will hope to get the general principle behind these position effects and have the larger advantage it always gives the explorer. Happily, this general principle

behind the PEs in psi data, wherever it may lead, is not
likely to demand a new costly and elaborate test approach.
Thus far at least, the approach to the PEs has been over the
humble, unexciting, and even not always appreciated test record sheet itself. One wonders whether, if parapsychology
had started out wealthy enough to have advanced at once to
the use of elaborate expensive apparatus, it would not have
missed the large block of PE information I have briefly reviewed. It is even a fair question whether psi could have
registered well enough without the PE evidence to have made
its way even as far as it has.

REFERENCES

1. Duval, Pierre, and Montredon, Evelyn. "ESP experi-
      ments with mice." J. Parapsychol., 1968, 32,
      153-66.
2. Estabrooks, G. H. "A contribution to experimental
      telepathy." J. Parapsychol., 1961, 25, 190-213.
3. Feather, S. "Position effects in a mass precognition
      test." (Abstract) J. Parapsychol., 1969, 33, 72.
4. Forwald, H. "A continuation of the study of psycho-
      kinesis and physical conditions." J. Parapsychol.,
      1957, 21, 98-121.
5. Greenwood, J. A. "The statistics of salience ratios."
      J. Parapsychol., 1941, 5, 245-49.
6. Humphrey, B. M. "Patterns of success in an ESP ex-
      periment." J. Parapsychol., 1943, 7, 5-19.
7. _____, and Rhine, J. B. "A confirmatory study of
      salience in precognition tests." J. Parapsychol.,
      1942, 6, 190-219.
8. _____, and _____. "The evaluation of salience in
      Dr. Schmeidler's ESP data." J. Parapsychol.,
      1944, 8, 124-26.
9. Jephson, Ina. "Evidence for clairvoyance in card-guess-
      ing." Proc. Soc. Psych. Res., 1929, 38, 223-68.
10. Jones, J. N. "Position effects in ESP tests with one
      subject." (Abstract) J. Parapsychol., 1969, 33,
      73.
11. Osis, Karlis, and Foster, Esther. "A test of ESP in
      cats." J. Parapsychol., 1953, 17, 168-86.
12. Pratt, J. G. "Restricted areas of success in PK tests."
      J. Parapsychol., 1947, 11, 191-207.
13. Reeves, Margaret P., and Rhine, J. B. "The PK ef-
      fect: A study in declines." J. Parapsychol., 1943,
      7, 76-93.

14. Rhine, J. B. "Terminal salience in ESP performance."
     J. Parapsychol., 1941, 5, 183-244.
15. _____. "Evidence of precognition in the covariation
     of salience ratios." J. Parapsychol., 1942, 6, 111-
     43.
16. _____. Extra-Sensory Perception. 2nd ed. Boston:
     Bruce Humphries, 1964.
17. _____. "Psi-missing re-examined." J. Parapsychol.,
     1969, 33, 1-38.
18. _____, and Humphrey, B. M. "A transoceanic ESP
     experiment." J. Parapsychol., 1942, 6, 52-74.
19. _____, and _____. "The PK effect: Special evi-
     dence from hit patterns. I. Quarter distributions
     of the page." J. Parapsychol., 1944, 8, 18-60.
20. _____, and _____. "The PK effect: Special evi-
     dence from hit patterns. II. Quarter distributions
     of the set." J. Parapsychol., 1944, 8, 254-71.
21. _____, _____, and Pratt, J. G. "The PK effect:
     Special evidence from hit patterns. III. Quarter
     distributions of the half-set." J. Parapsychol.,
     1945, 9, 150-68.
22. Rhine, L. E. "Toward understanding psi-missing." J.
     Parapsychol., 1965, 29, 259-74.
23. Richet, C. Thirty Years of Psychical Research. New
     York: Macmillan, 1923.
24. Scherer, W. B. "Spontaneity as a factor in ESP." J.
     Parapsychol., 1948, 12, 126-47.

ADDITIONAL READINGS ON POSITION EFFECTS IN PSI TEST RESULTS

Carpenter, J. C. "Scoring effects within the run." JP 30: 73-83 (Jun 1966).

Crumbaugh, J. C. "Variance declines as indicators of a stimulator-suppressor mechanism in ESP." JASPR 62: 356-65 (Oct 1968).

Joesting, R. and Joesting, J. "Position effects and target material in ESP." Psychological Reports 26(1): 75-78 (1970).

Kelly, E. F., Kanthamani, H., Child, I. L., and Young, F. W. "On the relation between visual and ESP confusion structures in an exceptional subject." JASPR 69: 1-32 (Jan 1975).

Palmer, J. "Scoring in ESP tests as a function of belief in ESP. Part II. Beyond the sheep-goat effect." JASPR 66: 1-26 (Jan 1972).

Pratt, J. G. "Computer studies of the ESP process in card guessing: I. Displacement effects in Mrs. Gloria Stewart's records." JASPR 61: 25-46 (Jan 1967).

_____. "Computer studies of the ESP process in card guessing: II. Did memory habits limit Mrs. Stewart's ESP success?" JASPR 61: 182-202 (Jul 1967).

_____. "Some notes for the future Einstein of parapsychology." JASPR 68: 133-55 (Apr 1974).

_____, Martin, D. R., and Stribic, F. P. "Computer studies of the ESP process in card guessing. III. Displacement effects in the C. J. records from the Colorado series." JASPR 68: 357-84 (Oct 1974).

Price, Alan D. "Subject's control of imagery, 'agent's' mood, and position effects in a dual-target ESP experiment." JP 37: 298-322 (Dec 1973).

Rhine, J. B. "Comments: 'Psi methods reexamined'." JP 39: 38-58 (Mar 1975).

Rogers, D. P. and Carpenter, J. C. "The decline of variance of ESP scores within a testing situation." JP 30: 141-50 (Sep 1966).

Schmeidler, G. R. "An experiment on precognitive clairvoyance. Part II. The reliability of the scores." JP 28: 15-27 (Mar 1964).

_____. "A search for feedback in ESP: Part I. Session salience and stimulus preference." JASPR 62: 130-42 (Apr 1968).

_____. "A search for feedback in ESP: Part II. High ESP scores after two successes on triple-aspect targets." JASPR 62: 255-62 (Jul 1968).

_____. "A search for feedback in ESP. Part III. The preferential effect and the impatience effect." JASPR 63: 60-68 (Jan 1969).

Stanford, R. G. and Brier, R. "Cancellation effects within the test run." In Rhine, J. B. and Brier, R. (Eds.). Parapsychology Today. N.Y., Citadel, 1968. Pp. 54-62.

Chapter 10

HYPNOSIS AND ESP PERFORMANCE:
A Review of the Experimental Literature*

by Charles Honorton and Stanley Krippner

Introduction

The association between parapsychical activity and so-
called altered states of consciousness has been pointed out by
investigators since the time of Myers (43). Observation of
"trance" mediums as well as investigation of spontaneous case
material has suggested a relationship between psi activation
and certain "dissociative" states. For the purpose of this
discussion, altered states of consciousness will be defined in
terms of Ludwig's criteria (38, 39) as:

> ... any mental state, induced by various physiolog-
> ical, psychological, or pharmacological maneuvers
> or agents, which can be recognized subjectively ...
> (or by an objective observer ...) as representing a
> sufficient deviation in subjective experience or psy-
> chological functioning from certain general norms
> for that individual during alert, waking conscious-
> ness. This sufficient deviation may be represented
> by a greater preoccupation than usual with internal
> sensations or mental processes, changes in the
> formal characteristics of thought, and impairment
> of reality testing to various degrees (38, p. 225).

A contemporary analysis of over 7000 spontaneous
cases reported by L. E. Rhine (52), for example, indicates
that psi material is more frequently mediated through dreams

*Reprinted by permission of the authors and publisher from
the Journal of the American Society for Psychical Research
63: 214-52 (July 1969). The preparation of this paper was
made possible through grants provided by the Ittleson Family
Foundation.

227

than in the normal waking state. [Interpretation of spontaneous case material such as this is, of course, limited by the
degree to which the sample may be regarded as representative. Furthermore, no claim is made regarding the evidential status of the cases. While the Rhine study is consistent
with previous investigations of the same type, it is cited (and
was reported) only for the purpose of generating suggestions
concerning the conditions which appear to be conducive to
psi activation in normal life situations.] Sixty-five per cent
of the cases in the Rhine sample were reports of presumptive
psi experiences occurring in the dream state, compared with
only thirty-five per cent which reported psi effects in the waking state. (According to L. E. Rhine's criteria, hallucinatory
cases were classified as waking experiences). Of perhaps
greater interest was the finding that eighty-five per cent of
the dream experiences, but only forty-nine per cent of the
waking cases, provided complete information concerning the
target situation. A chi-square analysis of these data, performed by the present authors, indicates that the difference
between waking and dream reports was significantly related to
the amount of information provided regarding the target (P <
.001). (See Table 1.)

Table 1

REPORTS OF SPONTANEOUS CASES RELATED TO STATES OF CONSCIOUSNESS*

Amount of Information Concerning Target	State		N
	Dreams	Waking	
Complete	3903	1241	5144
Incomplete	696	1279	1975
Total	4599	2520	7119

$\chi^2 = 10.83$ (1 d.f.); P < .001
* Data from L. E. Rhine (52, p. 93, Table 1).

Hypnosis has traditionally been conceptualized as an
artificially-induced "state" (brought about through the imple-
mentation of certain "induction" procedures) in which the subject (S) undergoes an alteration in awareness, becomes hyper-
responsive to suggestions provided by the hypnotist, and is
capable of carrying out tasks which are presumably beyond
his normal, "waking" capability.

Ever since the early days of Mesmer, claims have been made regarding the spontaneous or elicited occurrence of psi effects within or in connection with the hypnotic state. Mesmer and his followers gave public demonstrations of "traveling clairvoyance," in which hypnotized Ss claimed to travel to distant places and purported to describe distant contemporaneous events. A number of early writers described experiments on "community of sensation" wherein hypnotized Ss presumably became aware of tactile or olfactory stimuli presented to the hypnotist (42, 64). Perhaps the most interesting and best controlled of the early claims was represented by Gibert and Janet's experiments on "sommeil à distance," or the induction of hypnosis at a distance (42, 43, 53). The S, referred to as Léonie B., was reported to have entered hypnosis on nineteen out of twenty-five attempts when the hypnotist and witnesses were located at least one-third of a mile away. The time during which hypnotic induction was attempted was determined (by one of the witnesses) on a random basis.

An extensive survey of these early studies has been reported by Dingwall (18). The purpose of the present review is to survey the contemporary experimental literature in the English language dealing with hypnosis and psi test performance. These investigations have been divided into three sections, largely on the basis of procedural similarities: Studies involving a comparison of psi performance in the hypnotic state (or following posthypnotic instructions) and in the waking state; studies in which hypnosis was employed in an attempt to facilitate psi performance, but without the use of a waking control; and attempts to train (i. e., affect a reliable increment in performance) ESP abilities through the use of hypnosis.

In order to clarify some of the problems involved in the interpretation of the reported findings, this review will be prefaced with a brief discussion of methodological problems in hypnosis research. This discussion will emphasize the most prominent contemporary positions regarding the interpretation of hypnotic behavior, the types of (nonhypnotic) controls which are necessary, and some of the main characteristics of hypnosis.

METHODOLOGICAL CONSIDERATIONS IN
CONTEMPORARY HYPNOSIS RESEARCH

Contemporary hypnosis research has developed, in

large part, under the influence of Hull (35). Both from a
methodological standpoint, with the introduction of standard
test suggestions and waking controls, and on an interpretive
level, with emphasis on hypersuggestibility as a key characteristic of hypnotic behavior, Hull's approach has been widely adopted. However, although there has been a proliferation
of experimental research on hypnosis in recent years, little
agreement has been reached by investigators in this area regarding the nature of hypnosis. While the phenomena histor-
ically associated with hypnosis have been fairly well defined
and accepted, the conditions necessary to produce them remain clouded in controversy. The three orientations to be
reviewed constitute different theoretical positions as well as
different methodological approaches to the problems of hypnosis.

Hilgard (28, 29) represents the trance-theorist view
and accepts the traditional concept of hypnosis as an altered
state of consciousness. He has enumerated seven characteristics of the hypnotic state which encompass most of the phenomena traditionally associated with hypnotic behavior:

1. Subsistance of the planning function. The hypnotized subject loses initiative and lacks the
   desire to make and carry out plans of his own.
2. Redistribution of attention.
3. Availability of visual memories from the past,
   and heightened ability for fantasy-production.
4. Reduction in reality testing and a tolerance for
   persistent reality distortion.
5. Increased suggestibility.
6. Role behavior.
7. Amnesia for what transpired within the hypnotic
   state (28, pp. 6-10).

Much of the initial work from Hilgard's laboratory concerned the development of instruments for assessing hypnotic
susceptibility (Stanford Hypnotic Susceptibility Scales, Forms
A and B, 1959 (73); Form C, 1962 (74)) and for the discrimination of different hypnotic abilities (Stanford Profile Scales
of Hypnotic Susceptibility, Forms I and II, 1963 (75)). These
hypnotic susceptibility scales have been extensively researched
in terms of their psychometric characteristics and have en-
joyed wide usage within the field. Through factor analysis,
three factors have been identified in the composition of the
Stanford scales: Loss of voluntary control (represented by
challenge items), motor suggestions (items such as postural

sway), and a cognitive dimension (items involving hallucinations, posthypnotic responses, and amnesia) (28).

Hilgard favors the use of the "same subjects" design
in which the hypnotized Ss serve as their own controls in the
waking state. Hilgard contends that due to the wide individual
differences in hypnotic susceptibility and the high correlation
between waking and hypnotic susceptibility, gains between waking and hypnotic responsiveness to test suggestions would not
be detected with an independent waking control group unless
rather large samples were employed.

Orne (46, 48) has emphasized subjective criteria of
the hypnotic state. Although he too is a trance-theorist and
interprets hypnosis as an altered state of consciousness, he
has been particularly concerned with the multiplicity of implicit and explicit cues which are manifest in the experimental situation and which may contaminate genuine hypnotic effects. Orne (46, 47) has coined the term demand characteristics to refer to implicit cues which the Ss perceive as relating to the investigator's expectations and hypotheses, and
to which they respond. He has illustrated the influence of
demand characteristics in a series of investigations. In one
study, two versions of a lecture and demonstration on hypnosis were given to two separate groups of Ss. For one lecture group, the demonstrator-Ss "spontaneously" (according to
pre-arrangement with Orne) manifested unilateral catalepsy of
the dominant hand. For the other lecture group, the demonstrator-Ss did not exhibit "spontaneous" arm catalepsy. Ss
were then drawn from both lecture groups. As anticipated,
Ss from the group expecting spontaneous catalepsy of the
dominant hand tended to demonstrate it in their experimental
sessions, while those from the other group, with no such expectation, did not.

Since attempts to discover objective indices of the hypnotic state (such as physiological concomitants) have generally
been unsuccessful (4, 5), Orne advocates the adoption of criteria based on subjective characteristics of hypnosis. One of
the important characteristics of hypnotized Ss, which Orne
feels distinguishes them from nonhypnotized Ss, is trance
logic (46). This concept is incorporated into Hilgard's fourth
characteristic listed above, and specifically refers to the tendency for hypnotized Ss to disregard logical inconsistencies
in their perceptions. In another study, Orne (46) gave hypnotized Ss positive hallucination suggestions to the effect that
when they opened their eyes they would see the experimenter's

associate sitting in a chair across the room.   In actuality,
the associate was behind the S.   When S reported seeing the
(hallucination of the) associate, the experimenter instructed
him to turn around and report what he then saw.   Employing
a "real-simulator" design, in which some Ss were actually
hypnotized and others were simulating, and in which the investigator was blind as to which Ss were simulators and which
were real, Orne found that the genuinely hypnotized Ss tended
to report seeing the associate in both places at once, a feat
which did not appear to them, at the time, to be contradic-
tory.   The simulating Ss, however, when confronted with the
same dilemma, denied seeing the associate or said that the
(hallucinated) associate had vanished.   Orne associates trance
logic with primary process thinking.

Orne developed the real-simulator design to demonstrate the "effect of role-play artifact on trance behavior"
(46).   In this design, Ss found through preliminary tests (such
as the Stanford scales) to be satisfactorily susceptible to hypnosis were assigned to the hypnosis group and those who were
insusceptible were asked to simulate.   The experimenter was
kept blind regarding which Ss were in which group.

> The ... use of real and faking Ss in a blind design
> appears to offer several advantages.   It permits a
> rigorous control, in terms of behavior, of inquiry
> procedures designed to elicit demand characteristics.
> In the faking situation, the variable assumed to be
> the cause of the behavior can be omitted.   If such
> behavior still occurs, it can then be accounted for
> adequately by the implicit demands of the situation
> (46, p. 291).

Sutcliffe (66, 67) and others have also advocated the
use of the real-simulator design.

The failure of attempts to isolate physiological indices
or other objective criteria for distinguishing hypnosis--apart
from the Ss' responses to test suggestions--has led several
investigators, notably Barber (4, 5, 6, 7, 8, 9, 10), to question the validity of "hypnosis" as a useful construct in explaining the phenomena.   Barber has reported a lengthy series of
investigations which demonstrate that many of the phenomena
associated with hypnosis can be produced in the waking state
provided that the Ss are given task-motivating pre-test instructions (presumably) similar to those given to hypnotized
Ss.   [The authors are grateful to Dr. T. X. Barber, who

kindly provided them with several important sections of his forthcoming book, A Scientific Approach to Hypnosis (Van Nostrand, 1969).]

Barber indicts the traditional view of hypnosis as an altered state of consciousness on the grounds that the behaviors observed (i.e., increased response to test suggestions) are not independent of the explanatory construct ("hypnosis" when defined as a state of hyper-responsiveness to test suggestions). Furthermore, since objective criteria other than the behaviors to be explained have not been demonstrated, which would require the postulation of a distinct "hypnotic state," Barber rejects the construct "hypnosis" and discounts the efficacy (over other methods) of hypnotic "induction" procedures.

Barber argues that the efficacy of experimental treatments involving hypnosis may not be assumed unless the same treatment is given to a waking control group which has received similar motivational instructions concerning the criterion tasks, and which has the same expectations regarding success. Barber rejects the "same subjects" design because "in striving to comply with what they correctly or incorrectly surmised were the expectations ... of the experimenter, [the subjects] deliberately [give] their best performance under the 'hypnosis' condition and deliberately [give] an inferior performance under the 'waking' condition" (6, p. 448). Accordingly, Barber advocates the employment of an independent control group in which Ss are either randomly assigned to treatment conditions, or one in which they are matched on the basis of suggestibility scores.

This brief survey should serve to indicate some of the more crucial problems involved in the interpretation of hypnotic behavior, as well as the salient features of different methodological approaches. A more detailed discussion of these issues is given by Hilgard (28) and by Barber (6).

Among the many important issues raised in contemporary hypnosis research, several appear to be relevant to the interpretation of the studies to be reviewed in this paper: the method of selecting Ss; the basis of assigning Ss to hypnotic and waking treatments; the degree to which the expectations of the investigators could be communicated to the Ss; the degree of similarity between hypnotic and nonhypnotic treatments in terms of explicit and implicit attitudinal, situational, and motivational influences; the degree of susceptibility

manifested by the Ss in the various treatment conditions; and
the type of instructions or suggestions provided to Ss in the
various treatment conditions.

STUDIES INVOLVING DIRECT COMPARISON
OF ESP PERFORMANCE DURING HYPNOSIS
AND IN THE WAKING STATE

A number of studies have been reported in which direct comparisons have been made between the ESP performance of hypnotized Ss and Ss in the waking state. [For the
purpose of this discussion, "hypnosis" should be understood
to refer to a hypothetical state brought about by what are
traditionally referred to as "induction" procedures. Similarly, use of the term "waking state" is not intended to imply
that hypnosis is a non-waking state, but will be employed to
refer to a non-hypnotized state or condition, not preceded by
hypnotic induction procedures. The use of the term "depth"
or "susceptibility" will be restricted to behavioral or experiential assessment of (a) response to test suggestions (e. g. ,
the Stanford scales) and (b) verbal reports of alterations in
awareness as discussed by Ludwig (38).] or of the same Ss
tested under both conditions. These studies (Grela, 1945;
Fahler, 1957; Fahler and Cadoret, 1958; Nash and Durkin,
1959; Davis, 1961; Casler, 1962; Casler, 1964; Casler, 1967;
Rao, 1964; Honorton, 1964; Honorton, 1966; Honorton, 1969;
Edmunds and Jolliffe, 1965) will be reviewed chronologically
(by investigator).

Grela (1945)

The first systematic investigation of the effects of hypnosis on ESP performance was reported by Grela (26). The
study was designed to assess the effects of positive and negative hypnotic suggestions, and of positive waking suggestions,
on ESP card-guessing performance. Twenty-one Ss participated, eleven of whom were assigned to a hypnosis group and
ten to a waking suggestion group. Separate rooms were employed since a GESP procedure had been adopted, with E
serving as both hypnotist and agent.

Ss in the hypnosis group were selected on the basis
of their responses to a postural sway test. [Weitzenhoffer
and Hilgard (73) reported a biserial correlation coefficient of
.38 between postural sway and the remaining items on the

Stanford Hypnotic Susceptibility Scale, Form A (N= 124).]
Each S participated in three sessions. During the first non-
hypnosis session, no suggestions were given. In the second
session, positive suggestions, "favoring self confidence,"
were given:

> About five ... minutes after you awaken from this
> sleep, you will go through several runs.... You
> [will] believe completely in your ability to record
> your impressions correctly. You know that telep-
> athy is real. You know that it is possible and that
> you can do it yourself. You will not only try your
> hardest to name all of the cards correctly, but you
> will be positive ... that you will do much better
> than before since now you believe that you can and
> are sure you possess the ability (26, p. 198).

For the third session, negative suggestions, aimed at
decreasing the Ss' ESP scoring level, were provided. The
E gave suggestions which "made [the S] ... doubt his ability
to score in ESP tests." The negative suggestions emphasized
(a) the nonexistence of ESP, (b) that the experiment was a
waste of time, and (c) that S would participate but that he
knew he did not possess ESP abilities.

The Ss in the waking suggestion group were given suggestions similar to those given to the hypnosis Ss in the second session, but without prior hypnotic induction. Unfortunately, this group was of doubtful value as a control since the Ss
were not matched with those in the hypnosis group in terms
of susceptibility.

The differences between experimental treatments, and
between experimental and control treatments were not significant. However, the results were in the hypothesized direction, with positive hypnotic suggestion yielding the highest
scoring level (and the only condition independently significant).
Negative hypnotic suggestion yielded the lowest level of scoring. An analysis performed by the present authors (based
on Grela's Table 2) revealed a significant level of consistency
(using each individual S's overall session scores) for higher
scoring in the positive suggestion condition than in the negative suggestion condition (P .05). It would thus appear that
the differing instructions were to some extent effective in
producing the anticipated scoring effects. Unfortunately, however, the hypnosis conditions were not counterbalanced and it
is not possible to determine whether this effect was due to a

genuine treatment difference or whether it was an order effect.

It is also unfortunate that Grela did not provide additional information concerning the induction procedures employed, and that no formal assessment of susceptibility was made. Since the Ss carried out their tasks posthypnotically, assessment of their individual abilities to carry out posthypnotic suggestions would have been desirable (21). Finally, since no assessment was made of the effectiveness of the various types of suggestions employed, it is not possible to determine whether the suggestions were actually accepted by the Ss, nor, if they were accepted, whether the effects of one type of suggestion (positive orientation toward the concept of ESP and the task) were rendered completely ineffective before the administration of other suggestions (negative orientation toward the concept and task). Since the treatment order was held constant across Ss, it is possible that the last condition (negative suggestion) was contaminated not only by its order, but also by the suggestions given in the previous condition, thus accounting for the failure of significant treatment differences to emerge.

It is also obvious from the suggestions given in the positive suggestion condition that strong demand characteristics were available to the Ss (e.g., "... you will do much better than before since you now believe that you can...").

Fahler (1957)

Fahler (22) carried out an intensive exploratory study involving four Ss. Each S completed an equal number of ESP runs under hypnosis and in the waking state. Two Es were present during each of the experimental sessions, each of whom independently recorded the S's responses and checked the number of hits. Before each session, ten closed ESP decks were made up, put in opaque containers, and placed in front of the S. In the waking condition, S called through each of the ten decks without receiving knowledge of results. The same target orders were then employed for the ten hypnosis runs. Altogether, 170 clairvoyance runs were completed in this manner, with 190 precognition (preshuffle) runs interspersed between them.

Overall, the Ss performed at a much higher level during hypnosis (mean= 5. 57) then in the waking state (mean= 4. 96) and the difference between the two conditions was significant (P < .01). [Based on an analysis performed by the present authors. Fahler did not report a difference test between the two groups, presumably due to the possible interdependence of the target orders of the two conditions within each session. This information is provided, therefore, solely for purposes of comparison with other studies of similar design.]

Of possible side-interest is the fact that the precognitive runs yielded a strong bi-directional difference (with psi-hitting in the hypnosis condition and psi-missing in the waking condition), while the clairvoyance runs yielded a difference which was based almost entirely on the psi-hitting performance obtained in the hypnosis condition.

Once again, it is unfortunate that only minimal information was provided in the report concerning the hypnosis procedures (induction techniques, S-selection, and assessment of susceptibility). Furthermore, no information was provided concerning the nature of E's suggestions to the Ss in the hypnosis condition, nor whether explicit suggestions of success were given at all.

Fahler and Cadoret (1958)

A replication of Fahler's initial study, involving three series of experiments, was reported by Fahler and Cadoret (23). Following an exploratory series ("Section A"), two formal experimental series were performed. In "Section B," eleven Ss completed 210 clairvoyance runs, half in the waking state and half during hypnosis. A screening apparatus separated the Ss from the target material. The waking treatment produced a nonsignificant positive deviation. The hypnosis treatment yielded a very high level of scoring (mean= 6.12, P=.0000001). The difference between treatments was also highly significant (P=.0001). The run scores for the hypnosis treatment were consistently higher than those completed in the waking state (P=.003). Treatment order was counterbalanced. No information was given in the report concerning hypnotic induction procedures, susceptibility or selection criteria, or content of suggestions given.

"Section C" represented a more advanced stage of the research. Two Es were present at each session. Twelve Ss were tested, completing an equal number of clairvoyance runs in the waking state and in hypnosis. Each S completed three

runs in each condition per session. The number of sessions
per S ranged from one to seven. Treatment order was counterbalanced. The S and one E were inside a Faraday cage
during the testing sessions. The other E remained outside
the cage and monitored the S's EEG pattern in order to assess
possible relationships between ESP success and changes in
the alpha rhythm. Altogether, 120 runs were completed in
each treatment condition. The waking runs yielded a non-significant negative deviation. The hypnosis runs yielded a highly significant positive deviation (mean= 6.52, P= 10^{-10}). The
difference between treatments was thus highly significant (P <
.000001), as was the run score consistency (P=.00002). Once
again, however, no information is available concerning the
hypnosis procedures.

Although not specified in the text, the summary tables
suggest that seven of the Ss participating in "Section C" also
participated in the previous series ("Section B"). If this was
the case, it is possible that hypnotic reinforcement of whatever suggestions (or instructions) were given to the Ss in
prior sessions may have had an additive effect. In view of
the magnitude of the effects obtained in this study, such a
possibility should perhaps be considered in future studies of
this type. [Previous reviewers (49, 50, 54) have assumed
that no explicit suggestions relative to the Ss' performance
were given. However, no information is provided in the report regarding this question.]

Nash and Durkin (1959)

In the context of a larger investigation, Nash and
Durkin (45) reported a brief series involving two Ss. Each
S completed three hundred trials in the waking state and the
same number during hypnosis, following suggestions for high
scoring. The psi task for each S--in both treatment condi-
tions--was broken down into five types of runs, each of which
was twenty trials in length. The overall results yielded a
difference between the two treatments (waking=+ 7; hypnosis=
-12; P=.07). No information was reported regarding the hypnosis procedure used or the type of suggestions given.

This study suggests that while hypnosis may exert an
influence on the magnitude of ESP deviation, the direction
(sign) of deviation is dependent on other variables.

Davis (1961)

Davis (17) and Van de Castle and Davis (71) reported
a study involving 76 Ss. [The authors are grateful to Dr.
R. L. Van de Castle for his kindness in providing them with
the unpublished Davis manuscript.] The purpose of the study
was to compare the ESP performance of three groups (highly
susceptible-hypnosis, moderately susceptible-hypnosis, and
nonsusceptible-waking) of Ss in five conditions (normal waking,
task-motivated waking, hypnosis, hypnosis with positive suggestions for success, and post-hypnotic performance). The
Ss responded to three decks of 25 cards in each condition.
The targets were dual-aspect in nature, consisting of symbols
and colors.

In the first session, the Ss were tested as a group
and completed the first two conditions (normal and task-motivated waking). The Ss were tested in a group during the second session also, and a test of susceptibility--based largely
on responsiveness to eye catalepsy--was administered. The
three groups were separated at that time, with Ss producing
favorable responses to glove anesthesia comprising the highly
susceptible group; those who responded to other test suggestions but not to glove anesthesia made up the moderately susceptible group, and the third group consisted of Ss who were
considered to be nonsusceptible. The third and last session
consisted of individual testing of the Ss in the first two groups,
who completed the remaining three conditions (hypnosis, hypnosis with positive suggestions, and posthypnotic suggestion).
Induction of hypnosis was accomplished with the use of visual
fixation.

Significant differences emerged for the combined (two)
hypnosis groups between the Ss' waking and (non-suggestion)
hypnosis conditions (P < . 05), for the moderately susceptible
hypnosis group, between waking and posthypnotic performance
(P < . 05), and between hypnosis (with positive suggestions) and
posthypnotic performance (P < . 02). In all cases, with the exception of the last mentioned, the hypnosis scores were higher than the comparison group. Altogether, there were 56 Ss
in the nonsusceptible group who completed 240 runs (mean=
4. 85) in the two waking conditions, and 20 hypnotic Ss (both
hypnosis groups) who completed all five conditions (360 runs;
mean= 5. 12).

The major weakness of this study was that the five
conditions were not counterbalanced, thus permitting contamina-

tion by order effects, and perhaps increasing the demand
characteristics of the experiment. However, if the latter
were the case, one would anticipate higher scoring in the
positive suggestion hypnosis condition.

Casler (1962)

In a preliminary study, Casler (14) investigated the
effects of hypnotic and waking suggestions on two types of
ESP task. One group of Ss was assigned to a hypnosis treatment, the other to a waking-suggestion treatment. In both
groups, the Ss served as their own controls. GESP and
clairvoyance techniques were employed. No significant differences emerged between the two psi tasks, but a definite
difference was observed between the hypnosis and waking-
suggestion treatments. The Ss in the hypnosis group scored
significantly higher following suggestions for high-scoring in
hypnosis than in the waking state (P < .01). The waking-suggestion group did not produce a similar effect.

A follow-up study was then performed with fifteen Ss.
Each of the Ss completed four clairvoyance runs in the waking
state and four in hypnosis. Task order was counterbalanced.
Casler employed the arm levitation induction technique, and
gave informal depth tests consisting of arm catalepsy and
posthypnotic response suggestions. Prior to the beginning of
the ESP task, E gave S suggestions to the effect that he (S)
knew that ESP was "real," and that he could demonstrate it
to a high degree. In order to assess the degree to which
these suggestions were accepted by the Ss, Casler instructed
them to predict the number of hits they expected to obtain on
each run, for both treatment conditions. He reported that Ss
usually estimated their scores to be two to three times higher during hypnosis, although no formal statistical assessment
of the difference between expectations in hypnosis and the waking state was reported. Significantly higher ESP scores were
obtained in the hypnosis condition (mean=5.61) than in the waking state (mean=4.87), with P < .01. No sex or depth effects
were observed, nor was there a relationship between performance and the degree of acceptance of the suggestions for
high scoring.

Casler (1964)

Casler (15) reported a GESP study involving fifteen Ss

in which both S and the agent (A) were hypnotized. Both
were hypnotized by means of the arm levitation technique, and
they were in separate rooms. Each S completed four GESP
runs following hypnotic induction, and four in the waking state
(with A also "awake"). Treatment order was counterbalanced.
The Ss were allowed to instruct A as to the manner in which
they wished her to concentrate on the targets. No direct suggestions for high scoring were given. The hypnosis treatment yielded significantly higher scoring (mean= 5. 43) than the
waking treatment (mean= 4. 72), with P= . 01.

Casler asked the Ss to estimate the number of hits
they expected to obtain on each run and he noted that most
of the Ss gave higher run-score estimates during hypnosis,
but no statistical assessment of the magnitude of this difference was reported. This is unfortunate since it would be of
considerable interest to compare the relative confidence of Ss
with their performance in Casler's various studies involving
different types of suggestions. Casler noted that "one-third
of the male subjects, but none of the females, obtained higher scores in the waking runs than in the hypnosis runs" (15,
p. 132). It was further noted that a similar experiment,
without explicit suggestions for high scoring and employing a
clairvoyance task, failed to produce significant treatment differences.

Casler (1967)

In a further study, Casler (16) attempted to assess the
effects of a different type of suggestion on ESP performance.
He hypothesized that "while ... suggestions aimed at higher
scoring had been successful, greater effectiveness may be expected from specific suggestions that are particularly meaningful to the individual subject (16, p. 125). In order to test
this hypothesis, Casler requested that the Ss themselves,
while in the hypnotic state, generate suggestions which they
believed would increase the level of their ESP performance.
Each of twenty-one Ss completed four clairvoyance runs following induction of hypnosis and four runs in the waking state
(counterbalanced order). Informal depth tests consisting of
arm catalepsy and posthypnotic responses were administered.

A total of 168 runs was completed. A significantly
higher level of scoring was obtained with the hypnosis treatment (mean= 5. 27) than with the waking treatment (mean= 4. 70),
with P < . 025. Unfortunately, no attempt was made in this

study to assess the degree to which the Ss accepted the "self-
generated" suggestions as having a facilitative effect on their
performance.   Since no comparison was possible between the
"self-generated" and explicit positive suggestions employed in
this and Casler's earlier study, it is not possible to assess
the relative effectiveness of "self-generated" suggestions over
those employed in the previous study.   Casler noted that a
number of the suggestions offered by the Ss were ego-oriented
rather than task-oriented, but no significant differences were
observed between the two types of suggestions.

Rao (1964)

In the course of a language-ESP experiment, Rao (49)
completed a brief series employing hypnosis.   One subject
was used and she completed twenty blind matching clairvoyance
runs following hypnotic induction, and the same number in the
waking state.   The first two runs of each session were completed with the S in the waking state, and thus order effects
were not controlled.   A verbal suggestion induction technique
was employed, and Rao reported that S "became extremely
suggestible to the point that auditory and visual hallucinations
could be produced" (49, p. 85).   Rao gave explicit suggestions
that S was completely relaxed and that she "had the right
state of mind to enable her to obtain good ESP scores..."
(49, p. 85).   No tests were reported regarding the degree to
which these suggestions were actually accepted.   The runs in
the hypnosis treatment were carried out by S posthypnotically.

The scores obtained in the hypnosis treatment were
significantly higher (mean= 5. 65) than those completed in the
waking state without such suggestions (mean= 4. 10), with P <
. 02.   Run-score consistency was also significantly greater in
the hypnosis treatment (P < . 02).

Honorton (1964)

Most of the studies reviewed thus far were aimed at
demonstrating higher scoring in hypnosis than in the waking
state.   Honorton reported a study (31) designed to combine
techniques of influencing magnitude of ESP deviation (an experimental manipulation) with methods of predicting the direction of deviation (based on individual differences).   Using a
paper-and-pencil test which had previously been found to separate above and below chance scoring Ss, Honorton hypothe-

sized that suggestions for high scoring, given during hypnosis, would increase the magnitude of the ESP deviation in the direction predicted by the test.   Thus, Ss who were predicted to be "high scorers" were expected to score higher during hypnosis than in the waking state, while predicted "low scorers" were expected to produce lower scores in the hypnotic state.

Six Ss were employed, each of whom completed eight clairvoyance runs in the waking state and the same number following suggestions for high scoring in hypnosis.   The procedure and type of suggestions given were modeled after that of Casler.   The experiment was "blind" in the sense that the Ss' test predictions were not known to E until after the experimental session, and the nature of the predictor-test precluded the possibility that Ss could structure their responses according to their perceptions of the E's expectations.   It would appear that this is the first study in which E and S bias effects have been adequately controlled.   An arm levitation induction procedure was employed, and Ss were asked to estimate the number of hits obtained after each run in order to assess the degree to which the suggestions for high scoring were effective.

Ss predicted to score below chance obtained significantly low scores in the hypnosis treatment (mean=2.83, P < .0003).   Predicted high scorers, and all Ss in the waking condition, obtained chance results.   The difference between predicted high and predicted low scorers in the hypnosis condition was significant (P < .003) as hypothesized.   It was noted that previous research with the same predictor-test had also yielded better results for the predicted low scorers than for the predicted high-scoring Ss.

Honorton (1966)

A replication of the above study was reported by Honorton (32).   Each of twenty Ss completed five clairvoyance runs in the waking state and following suggestions for high scoring during hypnosis.   The suggestions given were similar to those employed in the initial study and were aimed at producing confidence in the Ss regarding the concept of ESP and in their own abilities to produce high ESP scores.   Run-score estimates were obtained in both treatment conditions in order to assess the degree to which these suggestions were accepted by the Ss.   Treatment order was counterbalanced,

and two Es shared the responsibility for the conduct of the
experiment. The study employed a double-blind design in
which neither of the Es nor the Ss were aware of the test
predictions until after the experimental session, thus con-
trolling for E-bias and the influence of demand characteristics. An adaptation of the Eysenck-Furneaux scale was employed in order to assess depth of hypnosis。

The results confirmed those of the previous study:
(a) the predicted low-scoring Ss, but not the predicted high
scorers, produced significantly larger deviations in the predicted direction in the hypnosis condition than in the waking
state (P < . 015); and (b) the difference between the predicted
high and predicted low scorers in the hypnosis condition was
significant (P=. 006)。

Analysis of the run-score estimates for hypnosis and
waking conditions yielded a significant tendency for all Ss to
make much higher estimates in hypnosis than in the waking
state, which indicates that the suggestions for high scoring
were accepted by the Ss。 This finding, however, is not free
from possible contamination by demand characteristics since
the Ss may have perceived the hypnosis condition as one in
which higher scores were expected. No relationship emerged
between depth of hypnosis and degree of success as determined by either hypnosis-waking differences or by differences
between predicted high- and low-scoring Ss.

Honorton (1969)

In an attempt to assess the effects of motivated suggestions for success independent of hypnotic induction, Honorton (33) reported a further study aimed at influencing both
magnitude and sign of ESP deviation。 The design of this
study was similar to that of the preceding hypnosis studies.
However, instead of providing suggestions for successful performance in hypnosis, the E gave the suggestions in the waking state, following administration of the Barber Suggestibility
Scale (8, 10) and in accord with Barber's "waking-imagination"
instructions。 The Ss were given the same type of suggestions
employed in the hypnosis studies, but without hypnotic induc-
tion。 They were told that the experiment involved a relationship between ESP and imagination, and were strongly encouraged to imagine E's suggestions as vividly as possible. Half
of the Ss received the suggestion condition first, and half received the same ESP task without suggestions. Each S thus

served as his own control, and, as in the hypnosis studies, the Ss estimated their run scores in both conditions in order to assess the degree to which the suggestions were accepted.

Two experiments were performed, and differed only in the type of suggestion given. In the first experiment, in which sixteen Ss participated, the same suggestions for high scoring used in the hypnosis studies were employed. The suggestions given in the second experiment differed by stressing the widespread occurrence of ESP rather than the Ss' own abilities to perform at a high level. Fifteen Ss participated in the second study. Significant differences were observed between the suggestion and nonsuggestion conditions for the predicted high scorers in the first experiment (P= .034), but the difference between predicted high and low scorers in the suggestion condition was not significant, and the effect was not generally consistent between Ss. The second experiment, involving suggestions that were less personally involving, did not yield significant treatment differences.

Thus, similar effects to those observed in the hypnosis studies were found in the waking-imagination experiment employing similar suggestions, but the effect was weaker and less consistent. The run-score estimates in both waking-imagination experiments were significantly higher in the suggestion conditions, but, in both studies, were significantly lower than those reported in the hypnosis studies. In addition, the second waking-imagination experiment yielded lower run-score estimates than the first, suggesting that the difference in type of suggestions administered may have resulted in the failure to obtain significant treatment differences in the latter study. A product-moment correlation computed between the ESP scores of the two waking-imagination studies and the Ss' suggestibility scores was not significant and suggested that there is not a strong relationship between level of suggestibility and ESP performance.

Edmunds and Jolliffe (1965)

Edmunds and Jolliffe (20) reported a GESP experiment with four Ss, each of whom underwent a series of approximately twenty pre-experimental hypnosis sessions in order to "familiarize them with the experimenters, the experimental condition, and to condition them to going into the hypnotic state quickly and easily" (20, p. 192). Although the experiment was inspired by the work of Ryzl (discussed below), the description of the pre-experimental hypnosis sessions includes nothing concerning preliminary attempts to "train" psi ability along the lines Ryzl followed, nor is there any description of the type of hypnotic "training" employed by Ryzl, which emphasized the development of visual imagery. During the preliminary period, Edmunds and Jolliffe noted that "the nature of the experiment was outlined to the subjects, and intensive suggestions were repeatedly given that they were developing the ESP faculty" (20, p. 193).

Each S then completed ten sessions of eight GESP runs each. Prior to each session, the Ss were rehypnotized and given instructions that they "possessed the ESP faculty and would be able to perceive the symbols clearly and correctly." As a "rough control," a set of eight waking runs was made by each S before and after the series of hypnosis sessions. No significant effects were reported, either in overall totals or in terms of treatment differences. No information was reported concerning the types of induction procedures used, although informal tests of depth were made. In terms of the investigators' main purpose, it would have been of some interest if they had presented their data in the form of session-by-session breakdowns by S. The number of sessions per S may well have produced an effect in itself, and it would also have been of interest--again in terms of the authors' main hypothesis--if they had presented a comparison of the first and last session for each S.

The main features of the studies reviewed in this section have been summarized in Table 2. It will be noted that ten of the thirteen studies reported significant treatment differences although, as may be seen from the table, several of the studies involved more than one comparison.

FURTHER STUDIES INVOLVING HYPNOSIS AND PSI

In addition to the studies reviewed above, a number of investigations have been reported (Rhine, 1946; Vasiliev, 1963; Stephenson, 1965; Fahler and Osis, 1966; Krippner, 1968; and Honorton and Stump, 1969) in which waking controls were not included or were not directly compared with a hypnosis treatment. In addition, the studies in this section represent for the most part a departure from the standard card-guessing tasks employed in the studies reviewed above, and they tend to represent explorations of novel stimulus-response variables.

Table 2

SUMMARY OF ALL COMPARATIVE STUDIES (1945-1969)

Report	Type of Psi Task	Experimental Conditions Compared	No. of Ss	No. of Runs	P_4	Induction Technique	Formal Depth Tests	Tests of Effectiveness of Suggestions	Controls for Experimenter-Subject Bias
Casler (1962)	DT	+ H – W	15	120	<.01	Arm levitation	No	Yes	No
Casler (1964)	GESP	H – W	15	120	<.01	Arm levitation	No		No
Casler (1967)	DT	+ H – W	21	168	<.025	Arm levitation	No	Yes	No
Davis (1961)	BT	+ H – W / + H – PH	20 / 20	120 / 120	<.05 / .025	Visual fix. / Visual fix.	No / No	No / No	No / No
Edmunds and Jolliffe (1965)	GESP	+ H – W	4	384	n.s.	Not reported	No	No	No
Fahler (1957)	DT, pcg	H – W	4	360	<.01	Not reported	No		No
Fahler and Cadoret (1958)*	BT, DT	H – W	12	240	<.000001	Not reported	No		No
Grela (1945)	GESP	+ PH – W	11	79	n.s.	Not reported	No	No	No
Honorton (1964)	DT	+ H – W / + H – W	4 / 2	64 / 24	n.s. / <.04	Arm levitation / Arm levitation	No / No	Yes / Yes	Yes / Yes
Honorton (1966)	DT	+ H – W / + H – W	9 / 11	90 / 110	n.s. / <.02	Arm levitation / Arm levitation	Yes / Yes	Yes / Yes	Yes / Yes
Honorton (1969)	DT / DT	+ W – W / ++ W – W / + W – W / ++ W – W	6 / 10 / 2 / 13	60 / 100 / 20 / 130	<.05 / n.s. / n.s. / n.s.	Waking Imagination	Yes / Yes / Yes / Yes	Yes / Yes / Yes / Yes	Yes / Yes / Yes / Yes
Nash and Durkin (1964)	DT	+ H – W	2	20**	.07***	Not reported	No	No	No
Rao (1964)	BM	+ H – W	1	40	.02	Verbal suggestion	No	No	No

Note: H = hypnosis; + H = hypnosis with positive suggestions; PH = posthypnotic; + PH = posthypnotic with positive suggestions; W = waking state; + W = waking state with positive suggestions. "Runs" refer to standard 25-trial units with P = .20.
* Confirmatory Section "C." See text.
** Twenty-trial runs with single digit numbers (1-5).
*** + H scoring lower than W.

Rhine (1946)

        Rhine (51) reported an exploratory study involving the
effects of hypnosis on PK performance. [Although the main
purpose of this paper is to review experimental studies involving the effects of hypnosis on ESP, this PK study (the
only reported investigation of the effects of hypnosis on PK)
is included for the sake of completeness.] Five Ss participated, aiming for specific faces (1-6) of 96 dice. Prior to
the hypnosis treatment, each S completed 20 throws of the 96
dice. The Ss were then hypnotized and given instructions that
they would be able to influence the dice by their concentrated
effort. The Ss were not given tests of hypnotic depth and the
criteria of hypnosis were based on hand-clasp, eyelid catalepsy, speech inhibition, and leg catalepsy responses. No information was reported concerning the types of induction techniques employed, the basis of S-selection, nor the degree to
which the Ss accepted the suggestions regarding successful
psi performance. Following administration of the above test
suggestions, the Ss were dehypnotized and carried out their
PK task posthypnotically.

        Although their PK scores were well above chance be-
fore the hypnosis treatment (mean= 4.19), the scores dropped
below chance following the hypnotic suggestions for improved
performance (mean= 3.99). Rhine noted, however, that "an
incidental break in the hypnotic [state] brought about a rever-
sion to high scoring" with two of the Ss. These Ss were rehypnotized and given suggestions that they would participate
in further tests "in a spirit of fun and relaxation." Their subsequent performance was higher than in the pre-hypnosis baseline session (mean= 4.29).

        Several questions naturally arise in connection with this
study. First, since the initial pre- and posthypnotic sessions
were not counterbalanced, the decline in scoring following the
hypnosis session could have been an order (rather than treatment) effect. This would appear to be particularly likely in
PK tasks since chronological declines seem to be a major
characteristic of PK performance. Second, since no formal
assessment was made either of the depth of hypnosis or of the
degree to which the Ss accepted the E's suggestions for improved performance, it is not possible to assess the effectiveness of this study as a test of the effect of hypnosis on PK
performance. If, for example, the Ss were either relatively
unsusceptible to hypnosis or were not strongly influenced by
the E's suggestions for improved performance, significant

treatment differences might not be expected. This latter
point may be particularly relevant to this study since there
appears to be a relationship between susceptibility and posthypnotic behavior (21, 28).

Vasiliev (1963)

A number of Soviet studies--carried out for the most
part in the 1930s--have been reported by Vasiliev (72). Most
of the studies involving hypnosis were concerned with attempts
to induce hypnosis in distant Ss, at randomly determined intervals. These studies appear to represent a more sophisticated version of the earlier studies by Gibert, Janet, and others (18, 42, 43).

In one series, the S and E were in separate but ad-
joining rooms. The F monitored recording instruments which
measured the S's grasp on a rubber bulb (an air kymograph).
The investigator's criterion of hypnosis was apparently the
degree of relaxation, based on compression of the bulb, during "waking" and "induction" periods. Based on this criterion, in a series involving three Ss, sixty-four sessions consisting of 260 trials were completed. Vasiliev reports that
there were only six misses in "hypnotic induction," and
twenty-one misses in (presumably, telepathically) "awakening"
the Ss. The Ss spontaneously "fell asleep" on nine occasions,
and there were eighteen spontaneous "awakenings." The Ss'
reponses were reported to have usually occurred within three
minutes of the E's initial "telepathic" suggestions.

Apparently no attempt was made to elicit similar (psi-
mediated) responses from the Ss in the waking state or with
a nonhypnotized control group. No information was reported
concerning S-selection, induction procedures, assessment of
susceptibility, or the expectations of the Ss concerning the
experiment.

Stephenson (1965)

A series of six exploratory experiments were reported
by Stephenson (65) which were designed to assess the following three hypotheses: "(a) ESP receiving ability is improved
under hypnosis; (b) ESP receiving ability is related to hyp-
notisability; and (c) ESP receiving ability can be developed by
training or learning under hypnosis" (65, p. 77).

These experiments were very exploratory in that the conditions were frequently changed within each series and adequate precautions against sensory leakage were not always observed. In the first series, twenty-five Ss participated and were given card-guessing tasks in the hypnotic state and in the waking state, although no rigid procedure was followed, and the number of trials completed in the two conditions were not equal. Induction procedures varied, but the most common technique involved eye fixation. On the basis of informal depth tests, the Ss' hypnotic performances were classified as light, medium, and deep. No significant treatment differences were obtained. The combined hypnosis and waking trials of the Ss classified as being capable of "light" hypnosis were significant (P=. 0022).

The second and third series were carried out with the Ss in the waking state during the ESP task. They were hypnotized separately only in order to classify them as to susceptibility. Only three Ss participated in the second series, and eight in the third. No significant effects were observed. These series are not, however, directly relevant to the question of hypnotic influence on psi performance inasmuch as they dealt only with classification of levels of hypnotizability and the ESP tasks were completed--without suggestions for success--in the waking state.

The remaining three series, which were loosely based on Ryzl's hypnotic training work, will be discussed in the next section.

Fahler and Osis (1966)

Fahler and Osis (24) reported an experiment in which two Ss, who believed that they were sometimes aware of when their ESP responses were correct, were tested for precognition while in the hypnotic state. Target material consisted of digits from 1 to 10 and the target sequences were generated by an assistant the day following each experimental session. Following the induction of hypnosis, which was described only as involving "verbal suggestion," E suggested to the Ss that "on some trials they might have impressions of correctness or feelings that certain calls were 'different' from the others. " The Ss were instructed to call "mark" whenever this feeling occurred to them. A total of 1950 trials was completed by the two Ss. Their tendencies to call "mark" were strongly associated with psi-hitting (P=. 00000002). The

authors were unable to conclude that the Ss' high level of success in identifying their hits was due to introspective awareness of hitting because of the possibility that they were employing precognitive ESP in a secondary manner.

The brevity of the paper handicaps interpretation of the
reported effect. No description of the induction procedures
was given, nor were attempts to assess susceptibility or degree of acceptance of suggestions for success reported.

Unless the results of this study are attributable to the
coincidental discovery of two very unusually "gifted" Ss, the
findings may be of widespread importance. The claims of
Ryzl concerning the development of a hypnotic training method
based on assisting Ss in discriminating between correct and
incorrect images will be discussed below, but the relevance
of the present study to Ryzl's claims is obvious. In another
vein, it matters little whether the results obtained were due
to the Ss' actual awareness of correct or incorrect responses,
or to a secondary manifestation of ESP. If the effect can be
replicated, it may be possible to employ it in a practical
manner, regardless of its introspective or psi basis. For
example, it might be possible to specify in advance that only
checked ("marked") trials would be counted in the experimental
series, thus greatly increasing the magnitude of the psi-hitting effect.

Krippner (1968)

Krippner (36) reported a study involving a comparison
of waking, dream, and hypnotic imagery in relation to ESP
performance. Each of sixteen Ss produced free-response
imagery in three conditions while an acoustically-isolated
agent concentrated on randomly generated target material (art
prints). Half of the Ss were assigned to a hypnosis treatment and were given Form A of the Stanford Hypnotic Susceptibility Scale (73). The other eight Ss were assigned to
a waking group and were given a test of similar length.
[Form A of the Stanford Scale was administered to the waking group following the experimental session. No significant
differences were observed between the level of susceptibility
of the two groups.] Similar motivational instructions were
given to both groups in order to maximize the similarity between hypnotic and nonhypnotic treatments.

A standardized set of instructions was prepared for

each of the three conditions, in two forms, one for the hypnosis group and one for the waking group. For the first condition, the hypnosis Ss were given the following instructions:

> Many investigators have found that telepathy often
> occurs during periods of hypnosis. . . . While you
> are in the hypnotic trance, I will select a target
> picture and will concentrate on that picture. It is
> very likely that you will be able to think of that
> target even though we are in different rooms. . .
> (36, p. 389).

An alternate form of this statement, emphasizing imagination rather than hypnotic trance, was read to the waking
Ss.

For the second condition, the following statement was
read to both groups:

> Recent experiments at this laboratory show that tel-
> epathic material may appear in a person's dreams.
> In a few minutes, you will have an opportunity to
> rest and to take a nap. The agent will concentrate
> on a target picture that will appear in your thoughts
> and dreams ... (36, p. 391).

The third condition consisted of having Ss in both hypnosis and waking groups keep dream diaries for one week
following the experimental session.

Transcripts of hypnotic and waking images and copies
of the targets were given to judges for blind evaluation of
correspondences. For the hypnosis group, significant correspondences were observed in the second (posthypnotic nap)
condition (P < .001). The waking Ss obtained significant effects in the third (dream diary material) condition (P < .01).
Krippner suggested that hypnosis may have served to "speed
up the processing" of extrasensory material.

Honorton and Stump (1969)

Honorton and Stump (34) reported a study in which
hypnotic dreams were used to elicit psi material. Six Ss
were selected for hypnotic susceptibility on the basis of their
scores on the Barber Suggestibility Scale. Only Ss scoring
in the upper quarter of the distribution were used.

Following induction of hypnosis with the arm levitation technique, the Ss were given suggestions to dream, while in hypnosis, as follows:

> When I count to three, you are going to have a very interesting dream. It will be a very vivid and realistic dream. You will dream about the target in the envelope. It will be as though you are walking right into the picture.... You will participate in whatever action is depicted, and you will observe the picture from that standpoint. You will see everything very clearly because you will be part of it ... (34, pp. 178-179).

Each S was required to produce four different hypnotic dreams with four different target pictures. The target material consisted of art prints enclosed in opaque envelopes. Following each dream period (the Ss were given five minutes per dream), the Ss were instructed to awaken and report their imagery, after which they were rehypnotized through the presentation of a posthypnotic cue, and the procedure was repeated until all four hypnotic dreams had been obtained. Suggestions for increased depth of hypnosis were provided following the posthypnotic cues to return to the hypnotic state.

Both the Ss and independent judges made blind evaluations of target-dream correspondences, assigning ranks of #4 to target-dream pairs with the most correspondence, etc., until the rank of #1, least correspondence, had been assigned. Only direct "hits" (correctly assigned ranks of #4) were considered in the formal analysis of the data. The Ss, ranking their own material, obtained significant correspondences (P=.016), while the independent judges' assessments were nonsignificant. The difference between Ss' and judges' evaluation was almost significant (P=.06). Honorton and Stump suggested that the Ss may have had difficulty reporting their dream material and may have been "unable to adequately verbalize their dream imagery."

While hypnotic dream studies have seldom included waking control groups for comparison, this would be necessary, as Honorton and Stump themselves indicate, before any final conclusions could be drawn regarding the effects of hypnosis, per se, on the results.

"TRAINING" ESP THROUGH HYPNOSIS

Few claims in contemporary parapsychology have generated such widespread interest as those of Ryzl (56, 57)
concerning the development of a method of "training" ESP in
unselected Ss through the use of hypnosis. In the present
section, this "training" method will be reviewed, as will the
more relevant reports dealing with one S whose outstanding
performance Ryzl attributes to the "training" method (Ryzl
and Ryzlova, 1962; Ryzl and Pratt, 1962; Ryzl and Beloff,
1965), and the several attempts by independent investigators
to replicate crucial aspects of the "training" method (Stephenson, 1965; Beloff and Mandleberg, 1966; Haddox, 1966).

Ryzl (1962, 1966)

Ryzl (56, 57) has divided the "training" technique into
three phases. The first phase is based on intensive hypnotic
training, in which the S is trained to carry out increasingly
complex suggestions, culminating with the development of
very complex and vivid visual hallucinations, which Ryzl believes are essential to the later development of ESP. Once
the S "masters" the ability to respond with vivid visual hallucinations, the ESP "training" proper is begun:

> We at first choose the easiest tasks.... We con-
> tent ourselves with the subject having his eyes
> closed.... We ask the subject to distinguish simple
> objects of set shapes--key, hand, scissors, hammer,
> etc., which we put in front of him on a tray....
> We invite the subject to 'have a look' at the object
> without opening his eyes... (56, p. 241).

Thus the "training" procedure moves from the development of non-veridical to veridical hallucinations, with emphasis on visual imagery and free response methods. When initial success is achieved (i.e., when S's imagery contains
suggestive correspondences with the target object), the E attempts to increase S's rudimentary psi ability in the following manner:

> (1) Development of ... new abilities by giving the
> subject increasingly more complicated and difficult
> tasks....
>   (2) We seek to remove the sources of errors
> in clairvoyant cognition.... Our subject has now to

> learn to resist them. Some errors have their ori-
> gin in the suggestions made by the hypnotist....
> The most important thing is to teach the subject
> how to distinguish reliably veridical hallucinations
> from false ones.... Sometimes veridical visions
> are distinguished by greater clarity and distinctness.
> But most often the subject must ... find subjective
> criteria which will help him to recognize veridical
> visions. This is achieved by making with the sub-
> ject many preliminary clairvoyant experiments in
> which his utterances are at once confronted with
> the reality, and the subject is in every case im-
> mediately informed whether he is right or wrong
> (56, pp. 243-244).

The final phase of "training" consists of gradually reducing the S's dependence on E and reducing (and eventually
eliminating) the use of hypnosis. At this stage, carefully
controlled quantitative tests are introduced. Most of Ryzl's
work at this stage has consisted of card-guessing procedures
involving a binary choice (e.g., discrimination of white versus
green sides of the cards).

Ryzl (57) has estimated that approximately five hundred
Ss have undergone this "training" procedure (although many
were discontinued prior to the final stages described above)
and he claims success for approximately ten per cent of
them, although he has reported on work with only two.

Impressive similarities have been noted between the
"training" procedure as described by Ryzl and the methods
employed thirty or more years ago by successful Ss such as
Mary Craig Sinclair, noted by White (76), and by other investigators such as Pagenstecher, noted by Roll (55).

No direct evidence, however, is available to support
Ryzl's contention that his method is effective in training ESP
Ss. Since no baseline data have been reported to ascertain
pre-training performance, and no step-by-step comparison of
possible increments within training, it is not possible to assess the effects of the "training" technique. There are, however, indirect indications that the method had some effect on
the development of Ryzl's S, Pavel Stepanek. First, Stepanek
appears to be one of the most extraordinary Ss in the history
of experimental parapsychology. No other S has been able to
maintain a comparable level of stabilized performance over as
long a period of time as he. No other "star" performer has

exhibited such a degree of flexibility as Stepanek in terms of
working (at his normal level) with teams of unfamiliar Es.
Second, when Stepanek's performance began to deteriorate
(58), Ryzl subjected him to a period of "retraining" after
which the S's high-scoring ability was restored. Some of
the highlights of Stepanek's early career are reviewed below.

Ryzl and Ryzlova (1962)

     In Ryzl's initial report (61) on the development of
Stepanek's ESP abilities, it is stated that he "never had any
psi experiences which he could identify and recognize as such;
but when he was subjected to the hypnosis treatment, he
learned in a few weeks reliably to obtain extrachance scores
in simple quantitative tests" (61, p. 154).

     Stepanek was "trained" to respond to binary targets
(white-black, and later, white-green cards). Each run consisted of ten trials with the card enclosed in an opaque fold-
er. In the first series, Stepanek made his responses while
in the hypnotic state. A total of two hundred runs was completed with a highly significant positive deviation ($P < 10^{-9}$).
The second series was completed with the S in a self-induced
hypnotic state. The target cards were specially prepared for
this series since the S was allowed to make some of his responses unsupervised. The procedure consisted of a repeated-
guessing technique in which S responded to each target several times. Each packet was coded by Ryzl so that it was unnecessary to open it after each response. The dependent variable measured consisted of the "majority vote" for each target; that is, the most frequently assigned response to each
packet. Significant results were obtained when the S worked
unsupervised ($P = .011$) and also when he was under the E's
immediate supervision ($P = .00008$). Ryzl drew the following
conclusions:

          This experiment ... shows that the method which
          involved the use of hypnosis was effective for this
          subject. Whatever explanation of the part the hyp-
          nosis played is favored by further research, the
          comparatively high rate of ESP scoring and the
          minimal decline effects encourage the hope that the
          method is one by which a greater measure of con-
          trol over ESP than shown hitherto can be achieved
          (61, p. 171).

Additional Work with Stepanek

Three experimental series were reported by Ryzl and Pratt (60). In 1100 trials with white-green cards and a two-experimenter level of safeguarding, the S obtained a significant positive deviation (P=.001). An additional 500 trials were performed with the standard ESP cards, with which Stepanek was unaccustomed to working, yielding a significant negative deviation (P < .05).

Two series were reported by Ryzl and Beloff (58) with Beloff serving as main E. In the first series, S worked with five different types of target material: Erotic, religious, "horrorific," self-image, and the standard white-green cards. The results were not significant. In the second series, Stepanek completed 120 runs with the standard white-green target material. The results were significantly below chance (P < .002). Stepanek's performance had been noticeably deteriorating prior to the two Beloff series. It was only after Beloff's visit that Ryzl subjected Stepanek to a "retraining" program, after which his performance was elevated to the previous (high-scoring) level.

In a summary of all experimental work with Stepanek between 1961 and 1964, Ryzl and Otani (59) reported ten experimental series, seven of which were performed entirely by or in collaboration with investigators from other laboratories. Throughout these ten series, the S's level of performance ranged from 5.4 per cent below chance expectation to 13.1 per cent above chance expectation (mean=8 per cent). Further work continues (as of this writing) with Stepanek, but the most relevant studies in terms of hypnosis have been reviewed above.

Attempted Replications of Ryzl's Method

Stephenson (1965)

Stephenson (65) reported three series of experiments designed to test Ryzl's "training" method. The first of these involved seven Ss, although most of the work was carried out with only two Ss. Each of these Ss completed eleven sessions:

> For the first few sessions with each subject Ryzl's method of developing visual hallucinations was followed closely, and all subjects reported some ability

to see commonplace objects and scenes suggested
to them. Then, without any more elaborate training [italics ours], their attention was turned to the
Zener symbols, and they learnt to 'see in the mind's
eye' any one of the symbols without undue effort
(65, pp. 83-84).

The number of ESP card-guessing runs varied from
session to session. A total of 3169 trials was completed
with the Ss in hypnosis. [The number of trials was not stated in the report, and the N cited is based on the expected
values in Table 3 of the report (65, p. 85).] No significant
effects in line with the initial training hypothesis were obtained. An unanticipated (+1) displacement effect was noted
post hoc (P=.027).

The other two series were performed with three Ss
in an attempt to "repeat as closely as possible Ryzl's method
of hypnotic training for ESP":

As advised by Ryzl, [the Ss'] ability to imagine
scenes and objects was developed methodically under
hypnosis, making use of objects around the room
for them to look at with their 'mind's eye.' Zener
card guessing was introduced slowly, starting with
a few runs of ten trials each and rising ... to several hundred trials persession (65, p. 86).

The number of sessions was not specified in the report. Altogether, 2082 trials were completed. [This figure
is based on the expected values given in Table 4 of the report (65, p. 87).] In some sessions a BT clairvoyance technique was employed, and for others, sealed DT. The results
offered no evidence to support "training." However, the 600
trials with the latter technique yielded significantly negative
deviations on both direct (P=.05) and (+1) displacement (P=
.02) scores.

Several points should be mentioned concerning this
study. First, the number of Ss, sessions, and trials involved
was rather small considering that Ryzl claims success for his
method in only about ten per cent of the Ss beginning "training." Second, Ryzl clearly discriminates between hypnosis
training and psi "training," and strongly feels (56, 57) that
restrictive response tasks such as card guessing are detrimental to "training" in the early stages. Third, while attempts were reported concerning the development of visual

hallucinations, no information was given concerning the degree
to which Stephenson's Ss were able to report <u>complex</u> visual
images.   Fourth, no information was reported concerning
another aspect of Ryzl's procedure; namely, direction from
E in the early phases of "training" in the development of S's
ability to discriminate between correct and incorrect responses,
and feedback on early "training" trials.

Haddox (1966)

Haddox (27) reported a pilot study involving an attempt
to "train" the ESP abilities of Ss in a group hypnosis situation.   The Ss were hypnotized "to a trance depth sufficient to
produce positive and negative hallucinations in both the auditory and visual senses" (27, p. 277).   The group sessions
were held on a weekly basis for three months.   At the beginning of each session, the Ss were instructed to dream of
an object placed in front of them.   The Ss made their responses orally, after which they were instructed to open their
eyes and look at the object, and then to close their eyes and
visualize it again.   Three objects were used for each session.
The Ss were then given a 25-trial (P=.20) restricted response
task involving guessing numbers on IBM cards.   The results
of the latter task were analyzed by computer.   No significant
increment in performance was reported.

No information was provided concerning the degree to
which vivid visual hallucinations of the type described by Ryzl
were obtained.   Again, a rather small sample was involved,
and the report does not indicate whether the results were as-
sessed for possible increments on an individual basis or only
for the group as a whole.   In addition, it is not possible to
assess the effects (on the alleged "training" process) of group
testing, where, presumably, the Ss' oral reports could have
served as a source of mutual contamination.   The initial use
of restricted response methods, in which the Ss were explicitly given a set to guess, is also in conflict with Ryzl's admon-
ition:

> [A] target of which the subject is aware impairs
> his concentration and ... while making a selection
> from a limited number of known targets, he is un-
> able to inhibit his conscious thoughts to the same
> degree as when he only passively waits to see what
> [image] will appear (57, p. 526).

Beloff and Mandleberg (1966)

Beloff and Mandleberg (11) reported an attempted validation of Ryzl's technique involving twenty Ss. Each S participated in five preliminary training sessions "involving a
wide variety of hypnotic exercises and some tentative ESP
tests" followed by ten hour-long experimental sessions. No
description was given of the content of the preliminary sessions, although the investigators noted in their discussion
that "none of our subjects were capable of hallucinating with
a degree of realism that would make the experience comparable, subjectively, to an actual perception." (11, p. 248).

Each experimental session was divided into two parts.
During the first part of the sessions, informal psi tests were
given, and during this period the Es freely gave the Ss en-
couragement and feedback as to their degree of success.
During the second part of each session, one trial was completed on each of six psi tasks. Three of the tasks involved
restricted responses (clock cards, block placement, and color
cards; with P=.083, .063, and .20, respectively), and three
involved free responses (word arrangement, picture test, and
object test). While significant results were reported with two
of the restricted response tasks (clock and color cards), no
evidence was obtained suggestive of a reliable increment in
performance.

Once again, however, it is not possible to determine
the degree to which this study may be considered a definitive
replication of Ryzl's claims. Although an ingenious study in
its own right, it does not appear that Beloff and Mandleberg
were successful in eliciting the type of visual imagery which
Ryzl considers to be crucial. Since no information was presented in the report concerning the nature of the preliminary
training sessions, it is not possible to assess the degree of
similarity between Ryzl's approach and that of Beloff and
Mandleberg, and in view of the relatively small proportion of
Ss claimed by Ryzl to be amenable to "training," it would
not be surprising to find no evidence for training in a sample
of twenty Ss with only five training sessions.

Irrespective of the ultimate verdict on the Ryzl "training" method, it does not appear that any of the attempts to
replicate it have taken all of the potentially important aspects
of the method into consideration. To the extent that this
represents an indictment of these studies, however, it must
also represent a failure on the part of Ryzl to clearly specify

objective criteria for several presumptively crucial aspects of his technique.

GENERAL DISCUSSION

Several conclusions would appear to be warranted, at least on a tentative basis, by the studies reviewed in this paper. First, it seems clear that hypnosis does affect psi-performance. Nine of the twelve studies involving direct comparison of ESP performance in hypnosis and the waking state (Table 2, above) yielded significant treatment differences. An additional study (Grela, 1945) yielded significant psi effects only in the hypnosis condition. This would appear to be a rather impressive level of replicability, particularly in view of the fact that seven independent investigators were involved.

Second, it appears that hypnosis affects magnitude (regardless of sign) rather than direction of ESP performance. Two of the nine successful studies yielded significant treatment differences resulting from psi-missing in the hypnosis condition, with chance or non-significant above chance deviations in the waking condition (Honorton, 1964; Honorton, 1966). Nash and Durkin (1959) reported similar results, but they did not reach significance.

Third, it appears that the facilitative effects of hypnosis are not the result of direct suggestions for success. Several of the studies (Casler, 1964; Davis, 1961; Fahler, 1957; Fahler and Cadoret, 1958) reported significant treatment differences without direct suggestions for success. This would suggest that either (a) other variables associated with hypnosis such as reduction of attentive activity (2), relaxation (25), or reduction of reality testing (28, 46), are conducive to psi activation; or (b) the Ss in the studies reviewed responded to implicit demand characteristics (since they served as their own controls), perceiving that the experiment was one in which they were expected to score higher in hypnosis. Several considerations tend to militate against the second interpretation. First, Ss in the Davis study (17) not only performed at a significantly higher level in the hypnosis condition without suggestions for success than in the waking condition, but also scored significantly higher in the posthypnotic condition than in the hypnosis condition involving direct positive suggestions. If the Ss were responding to subtle demand characteristics, in line with the second interpretation, it would

be reasonable to expect that they would perceive the latter
condition as the one in which the highest scores were expected. Second, as discussed above, several of the studies
yielded significantly lower levels of scoring in the hypnosis
condition than in the waking state, even though suggestions
for positive scoring had been given. In the two Honorton
studies (31, 32), both the Ss and the Es were blind as to the
condition in which higher scores were expected. It would
thus appear that the first interpretation--that variables other
than direct suggestion associated with hypnosis are conducive
to parapsychical activation--is more consistent with the data.

While the studies reviewed in this paper were well
controlled in terms of the ESP variables investigated, many
of them failed to control one or more of the variables associated with the interpretation of the effects of hypnosis. Only
four of the studies employed formal measures of hypnotic
susceptibility (Honorton, 1966; Honorton, 1969; Honorton and
Stump, 1969; Krippner, 1968). Only five of the studies involving direct suggestions for success included tests to assess
the degree to which the Ss accepted the suggestions (Casler,
1962; Casler, 1967; Honorton, 1964; Honorton, 1966; Honorton,
1969). Only four of the studies incorporated controls against
experimenter bias and the effects of demand characteristics
(Honorton, 1964; Honorton, 1966; Honorton, 1969; Krippner,
1968). Six of the reports did not furnish sufficient procedural information to allow for independent replication (Edmunds
and Jolliffe, 1965; Fahler, 1957; Fahler and Cadoret, 1958;
Grela, 1945; Nash and Durkin, 1959; Vasiliev, 1963). This
is particularly unfortunate in the case of the Fahler and
Cadoret study, where the treatment difference was of a very
high magnitude. Only three of the studies incorporated task
motivating instructions to the waking control group (Davis,
1961; Grela, 1945; Krippner, 1968).

Further studies will be necessary in order to specify
more directly the role of direct suggestions for success and
different types of direct suggestions, task-motivating waking
suggestions, and level of susceptibility (19, 37). Multiple
variable studies such as those of Grela (26) and Davis (17)
should be performed with factorial designs which would allow
for more appropriate analysis of treatment differences and
assessment of possible interaction effects. There would seem
to be no reason why standardized susceptibility instruments
like the Stanford and Barber scales (10, 73, 74, 75) could not
be incorporated into further studies as standard procedure,
not only for depth assessment per se, but in order to facili-

tate replication through the specification of population parameters.

   While the use of the same-subjects design would seem
to be warranted by the wide individual differences in ESP ability, suitable controls should be taken to preclude, or at least
to allow assessment of, experimenter expectancy and demand
characteristics. One method of doing this has been described
by Hilgard and Tart (30) and involves the manipulation of sub-
ject-expectancy, with one group of Ss expecting hypnosis following a waking condition, and another group of Ss not expecting hypnosis. An alternative method, which is advocated by
Barber (4, 6), would be to employ an independent control
group and either to assign Ss to treatment groups on a random basis, or to match hypnosis and waking Ss in terms of
susceptibility.

   Most of the studies reviewed on pp. 232-238 above
represent novel departures in method and, as such, are more
exploratory than those reviewed in the previous section. The
Vasiliev studies on hypnotic induction at a distance (72) provide further evidence to support the nineteenth-century claims
of sommeil à distance, principally those of Gibert and Janet
(42, 43, 53), although similar findings on a more anecdotal
level have been reported recently by Abrams (1). The air
bulb kymograph which was used as a dependent variable measure would appear to offer an adequate, objective measure of
success. However, in view of the lack of objective criteria
for distinguishing the hypnotic state from the nonhypnotic waking state, as discussed in an earlier section, great caution
must be exercised in the interpretation of such effects. The
incorporation of a motivated waking control and formal assessment of susceptibility would be minimal requirements in
the replication of these studies.

   The studies reported by Krippner (36) and by Honorton
and Stump (34), involving free response material, should be
replicated--the latter study with a suitable waking control.
A combination of the approaches employed in these two studies,
extended to include electrophysiological monitoring, might be
fruitful in the comparison of relative success of hypnotically-
induced and nocturnal dreams as vehicles of psi-mediation
(40, 68, 69). Further studies along these lines could be directed toward the development of an experimental analogue
to Tyrrell's concept of "mediating vehicles" of psi (70). With
the use of the Stanford Profile Scales, for example, Ss could
be selected for specific hypnotic abilities (e.g., dreams and

hallucinatory behavior or motor automatisms) and appropriate
psi tasks could be incorporated in order to assess specific
hypotheses concerning the processing of parapsychical material. Similar approaches have been reported by Blum (12,
13), Muhl (41), and others in the experimental exploration of
psychodynamics.

The implications of Ryzl's claims concerning training
of psi abilities with hypnosis demand that further attempts be
made to replicate his work. Since these attempts should incorporate all the main aspects of Ryzl's procedure if a final
verdict is to be reached concerning the validity of his claims,
the type of control condition chosen is particularly important.
The most appropriate procedure would involve an independent
control group. The use of the Stanford or Barber susceptibility scales would drastically reduce the number of unsusceptible Ss in the initial stages of the experiment. Free response
methods such as those employed by Krippner (36) and by Honorton and Stump (34) would allow quantification in the initial
phases of "training" with minimal disruption of the basic procedure and without requiring Ss to establish guessing sets
which Ryzl believes to be detrimental to "training." Formal
measures should be developed or adapted from other sources
to assess the quality of visual imagery, and techniques such
as those described by Blum (12, 13) and by Naruse (44) could
be adopted to increase the effectiveness of the pre-ESP training phase.

Although attempts to relate hypnosis to certain personality variables have generally been unsuccessful (5), Shor (62,
63) and As (3) have reported moderate correlations between
hypnotizability and scales of naturally-occurring "hypnotic-
like" experiences. In light of the apparent facilitative effect
of hypnosis on ESP performance, it would be of some interest
to investigate the possible relationship between these inven-
tories and ESP performance.

While many problems of both methodological and interpretive importance remain to be resolved, it would appear
that hypnosis provides one of the few presently available techniques for affecting the level of psi test performance.

REFERENCES

1. Abrams, S. "Extrasensory Behavior." Paper presented
        at the Seventh Annual Convention of the Parapsycho-

logical Association, Oxford, 1964.

2. Amadeo, M., and Shagass, C. "Eye Movements, Attention, and Hypnosis." Journal of Nervous and Mental Disease, Vol. 136, 1963, 139-145.

3. As, A. "Hypnotizability as a Function of Non-Hypnotic Experiences." Journal of Abnormal and Social Psychology, Vol. 66, 1963, 142-150.

4. Barber, T. X. "'Hypnosis' as a Causal Variable in Present-Day Psychology: A Critical Analysis." Psychological Reports, Vol. 14, 1964, 839-842.

5. _____. "Empirical Analyses of 'Hypnotic' Behavior: A Review of Recent Empirical Findings." Journal of Abnormal Psychology, Vol. 70, 1965, 132-154.

6. _____. "'Hypnotic' Phenomena: A Critique of Experimental Methods." In J. E. Gordon (Ed.), Handbook of Clinical and Experimental Hypnosis. New York: Macmillan, 1967, 444-480.

7. Barber, T. X., and Calverley, D. S. "'Hypnotic Behavior' as a Function of Task Motivation." Journal of Psychology, Vol. 54, 1962, 263-389.

8. _____. "'Hypnotic-Like' Suggestibility in Children and Adults." Journal of Abnormal and Social Psychology, Vol. 66, 1963, 589-597.

9. _____. "Empirical Evidence for a Theory of 'Hypnotic' Behavior: The Suggestibility-Enhancing Effects of Motivational Suggestions, Relaxation-Sleep Suggestions, and Suggestions that the Subject will be Effectively 'Hypnotized.'" Journal of Personality, Vol. 33, 1965, 256-270.

10. Barber, T. X., and Glass, L. B. "Significant Factors in Hypnotic Behavior." Journal of Abnormal and Social Psychology, Vol. 64, 1962, 222-228.

11. Beloff, J., and Mandleberg, I. "An Attempted Validation of the 'Ryzl Technique' for Training ESP Subjects." Journal S. P. R., Vol. 43, 1966, 229-249.

12. Blum, G. A Model of the Mind. New York: Wiley, 1961.

13. _____. "Hypnosis as a Tool in Psychodynamics Research." In J. E. Gordon (Ed.), Handbook of Clinical and Experimental Hypnosis. New York: Macmillan, 1967, 83-109.

14. Casler, L. "The Improvement of Clairvoyance Scores by Means of Hypnotic Suggestion." Journal of Parapsychology, Vol. 26, 1962, 77-87.

15. _____. "The Effects of Hypnosis on GESP." Journal of Parapsychology, Vol. 28, 1964, 126-134.

16. _____. "Self-Generated Hypnotic Suggestions and

Clairvoyance." International Journal of Parapsychology, Vol. 9, 1967, 125-128.

17. Davis, K. R. "The Effect of Hypnosis upon Scoring
Ability in Tasks Involving Extrasensory Perception."
Unpublished M. A. Thesis, University of Denver,
1961.

18. Dingwall, E. J. (Ed.). Abnormal Hypnotic Phenomena.
London: Churchill, 1967. (4 Vols.)

19. Ducasse, C. J. "Hypnotism, Suggestion, and Suggestibility." International Journal of Parapsychology,
Vol. 5, 1963, 5-24.

20. Edmunds, S., and Jolliffe, D. "A GESP Experiment
with Four Hypnotized Subjects." Journal S. P. R.,
Vol. 43, 1965, 192-194.

21. Edwards, G. "Duration of Post-Hypnotic Effect." British Journal of Psychiatry, Vol. 109, 1963, 259-266.

22. Fahler, J. "ESP Card Tests with and without Hypnosis."
Journal of Parapsychology, Vol. 21, 1957, 179-185.

23. Fahler, J., and Cadoret, R. J. "ESP Card Tests of
College Students with and without Hypnosis." Journal of Parapsychology, Vol. 22, 1958, 125-136.

24. Fahler, J., and Osis, K. "Checking for Awareness of
Hits in a Precognition Experiment with Hypnotized
Subjects." Journal A. S. P. R., Vol. 60, 1966, 340-
346.

25. Gerber, R., and Schmeidler, G. R. "An Investigation
of Relaxation and of Acceptance of the Experimental
Situation as Related to ESP Scores in Maternity
Patients." Journal of Parapsychology, Vol. 21,
1957, 47-57.

26. Grela, J. J. "Effect on ESP Scoring of Hypnotically
Induced Attitudes." Journal of Parapsychology,
Vol. 9, 1945, 194-202.

27. Haddox, V. "A Pilot Study of a Hypnotic Method for
Training Subjects in ESP." Journal of Parapsychology, Vol. 30, 1966, 277-278. (Abstract.)

28. Hilgard, E. R. Hypnotic Susceptibility. New York:
Harcourt, Brace, and World, 1965.

29. _____. "Individual Differences in Hypnotizability."
In J. E. Gordon (Ed.), Handbook of Clinical and
Experimental Hypnosis. New York: Macmillan,
1967, 391-443.

30. Hilgard, E. R., and Tart, C. T. "Responsiveness to
Suggestions Following Waking and Imagination Instructions and Following Induction of Hypnosis."
Journal of Abnormal Psychology, Vol. 71, 1966,
196-208.

31. Honorton, C. "Separation of High- and Low-Scoring
     ESP Subjects through Hypnotic Preparation." Jour-
     nal of Parapsychology, Vol. 28, 1964, 251-257.
32. _____ . "A Further Separation of High- and Low-
     Scoring ESP Subjects through Hypnotic Preparation."
     Journal of Parapsychology, Vol. 30, 1966, 172-183.
33. _____ . "A Combination of Techniques for the Separa-
     tion of High- and Low-Scoring ESP Subjects: Ex-
     periments with Hypnotic and Waking-Imagination In-
     structions." Journal A. S. P. R. , Vol. 63, 1969,
     69-82.
34. Honorton, C. , and Stump, J. P. "A Preliminary Study
     of Hypnotically-Induced Clairvoyant Dreams." Jour-
     nal A. S. P. R. , Vol. 63, 1969, 175-184.
35. Hull, C. L. Hypnosis and Suggestibility. New York:
     Appleton-Century, 1933.
36. Krippner, S. "Experimentally-Induced Telepathic Ef-
     fects in Hypnosis and Non-Hypnosis Groups." Jour-
     nal A. S. P. R. , Vol. 62, 1968, 387-398.
37. LeCron, L. "Hypnosis in the Production of Psi Phe-
     nomena." International Journal of Parapsychology,
     Vol. 3, 1961, 65-78.
38. Ludwig, A. M. "Altered States of Consciousness."
     Archives of General Psychiatry, Vol. 15, 1966,
     225-234.
39. Ludwig, A. M. , and Levine, J. "Alterations in Con-
     sciousness Produced by Hypnosis." Journal of
     Nervous and Mental Disease, Vol. 140, 1965, 146-
     153.
40. Moss, C. S. The Hypnotic Investigation of Dreams.
     New York: Wiley, 1967.
41. Mühl, A. Automatic Writing. New York: Helix Press/
     Garrett Publications, 1963.
42. Myers, F. W. H. "On Telepathic Hypnotism and its
     Relation to Other Forms of Hypnotic Suggestion."
     Proc. S. P. R. , Vol. 4, 1886-87, 127-188.
43. _____ . Human Personality and its Survival of Bodily
     Death. London: Longmans, Green, 1903. (2
     Vols.)
44. Naruse, G. "Hypnosis as a State of Meditative Concen-
     tration and its Relationship to the Perceptual Pro-
     cess." In M. V. Kline (Ed.), The Nature of Hyp-
     nosis. Baltimore: Waverley Press, 1962, 37-72.
45. Nash, C. B. , and Durkin, M. G. "Terminal Salience
     with Multiple Digit Targets." Journal of Parapsy-
     chology, Vol. 23, 1959, 49-53.
46. Orne, M. T. "The Nature of Hypnosis: Artifact and

Essence." Journal of Abnormal and Social Psychology, Vol. 58, 1959, 277-299.

47. _____ . "On the Social Psychology of the Psychological Experiment with Particular Reference to Demand Characteristics and Their Implications." American Psychologist, Vol. 17, 1962, 776-783.

48. _____ . "Hypnotically Induced Hallucinations." In L. J. West (Ed.), Hallucinations. New York: Grune and Stratton, 1962, 211-219.

49. Rao, K. R. "The Differential Response in Three New Situations." Journal of Parapsychology, Vol. 28, 1964, 81-92.

50. _____ . "Hypnosis and Yoga: Their Bearing on Psi Research." Unabridged manuscript of paper read at the International Conference on Hypnosis, Drugs, Dreams, and Psi; Le Piol, St. Paul de Vence, France, June 9-12, 1967, sponsored by the Parapsychology Foundation, Inc.

51. Rhine, J. B. "Hypnotic Suggestion in PK Tests." Journal of Parapsychology, Vol. 10, 1946, 126-140.

52. Rhine, L. E. "Psychological Processes in ESP Experiences, I. Waking Experiences." Journal of Parapsychology, Vol. 26, 1962, 88-111.

53. Richet, C. "Further Experiments in Hypnotic Lucidity or Clairvoyance." Proc. S. P. R., Vol. 6, 1889-90, 66-83.

54. Roll, W. G. "ESP and Memory." International Journal of Neuropsychiatry, Vol. 2, 1966, 505-521.

55. _____ . "Pagenstecher's Contribution to Parapsychology." Journal A. S. P. R., Vol. 61, 1967, 219-240.

56. Ryzl, M. "Training the Psi Faculty by Hypnosis." Journal S. P. R., Vol. 41, 1962, 234-252.

57. _____ . "A Method of Training in ESP." International Journal of Parapsychology, Vol. 8, 1966, 501-532.

58. Ryzl, M., and Beloff, J. "Loss of Stability of ESP Performance in a High-Scoring Subject." Journal of Parapsychology, Vol. 29, 1965, 1-11.

59. Ryzl, M., and Otani, S. "An Experiment in Duplicate Calling with Stepanek." Journal of Parapsychology, Vol. 31, 1967, 19-28.

60. Ryzl, M., and Pratt, J. G. "Confirmation of ESP Performance in a Hypnotically Prepared Subject." Journal of Parapsychology, Vol. 26, 1962, 237-243.

61. Ryzl, M., and Ryzlova, J. "A Case of High-Scoring ESP Performance in the Hypnotic State." Journal of Parapsychology, Vol. 26, 1962, 153-171.

62. Shor, R. E. "The Frequency of Naturally Occurring 'Hypnotic-Like' Experiences in a Normal College Population." International Journal of Clinical and Experimental Hypnosis, Vol. 8, 1960, 151-163.

63. Shor, R. E., Orne, M. T., and O'Connell, D. N. "Validation of a Scale of Self-Reported Personal Experiences which Predicts Hypnotizability." Journal of Psychology, Vol. 53, 1962, 55-75.

64. Sidgwick, E. M., and Johnson, A. "Some Experiments in Thought-Transference." Proc. S. P. R., Vol. 8, 1892, 536-596.

65. Stephenson, C. J. "Cambridge ESP-Hypnosis Experiments (1958-64)." Journal S. P. R., Vol. 43, 1965, 77-91.

66. Sutcliffe, J. P. "'Credulous' and 'Skeptical' Views of Hypnotic Phenomena: A Review of Certain Evidence and Methodology." International Journal of Clinical and Experimental Hypnosis, Vol. 8, 1960, 73-101.

67. _____. "'Credulous' and 'Skeptical' Views of Hypnotic Phenomena: Experiments on Esthesia, Hallucination, and Delusion." Journal of Abnormal and Social Psychology, Vol. 62, 1961, 189-200.

68. Tart, C. T. "The Hypnotic Dream: Methodological Problems and a Review of the Literature." Psychological Bulletin, Vol. 63, 1965, 87-99.

69. _____. "The Control of Nocturnal Dreaming by Means of Posthypnotic Suggestion." International Journal of Parapsychology, Vol. 9, 1967, 184-189.

70. Tyrrell, G. N. M. "The 'Modus Operandi' of Paranormal Cognition." Proc. S. P. R., Vol. 48, 1946-49, 65-120.

71. Van de Castle, R. L., and Davis, K. R. "The Relationship of Suggestibility to ESP Scoring Level." Journal of Parapsychology, Vol. 26, 1962, 270-271. (Abstract.)

72. Vasiliev, L. L. Experiments in Mental Suggestion. Church Crookham, England: Institute for the Study of Mental Images, 1963.

73. Weitzenhoffer, A. M., and Hilgard, E. R. Stanford Hypnotic Susceptibility Scale, Forms A and B. Palo Alto: Consulting Psychologists Press, 1959.

74. _____. Stanford Hypnotic Susceptibility Scale, Form C. Palo Alto: Consulting Psychologists Press, 1962.

75. _____. Stanford Profile Scales of Hypnotic Susceptibility Forms I and II. Palo Alto: Consulting Psychologists Press, 1963.

76. White, R. A. "A Comparison of Old and New Methods of Response to Targets in ESP Experiments." Journal A. S. P. R., Vol. 58, 1964, 21-56.

ADDITIONAL READINGS ON HYPNOSIS AND PSI

Cade, C. M. "Psychical research experiments under hypnosis: A report on work in progress by the Hypnosis Committee. Part I. 'Screening' of subjects and preliminary tests." JSPR 47: 31-47 (Mar 1973).

Chapman, J. D. "Instrumentation, hypnosis, and ESP." Osteopathic Physician, 41: 63-70 (Apr 1974).

Glick, B. S. and Kogen, J. "Clairvoyance in hypnotized subjects: Some positive results." Psychiatric Quarterly 47: 276-84 (No. 2, 1973).

Hernandez-Peon, R. "A unitary neurophysiological model of hypnosis, dreams, hallucinations, and ESP." In Cavanna, R. and Ullman, M. (Eds.). Psi and Altered States of Consciousness. N.Y., Parapsychology Foundation, 1968. Pp. 178-93.

Honorton, C. "Significant factors in hypnotically-induced clairvoyant dreams." JASPR 66: 86-102 (Jan 1972).

Nicol, J. F. "Classic experiments in telepathy under hypnosis: A historical survey." In Cavanna, R. and Ullman, M. (Eds.). Psi and Altered States of Consciousness. N.Y., Parapsychology Foundation, 1968. Pp. 8-16.

Parker, A. "Hypnotically-induced clairvoyant dreams: A partial replication and attempted confirmation." JASPR 64: 432-42 (Oct 1970).

Ryzl, M. "Training methods for psi induction." In Cavanna, R. and Ullman, M. (Eds.). Psi and Altered States of Consciousness. N.Y., Parapsychology Foundation, 1968. Pp. 55-65.

Servadio, E. "Hypnosis and parapsychology: A short historical survey." In Cavanna, R. and Ullman, M. (Eds.). Psi and Altered States of Consciousness. N.Y., Parapsychology Foundation, 1968. Pp. 17-23.

Tart, C. T. "Hypnosis, psychedelics, and psi: conceptual models." In Cavanna, R. and Ullman, M. (Eds.). Psi and Altered States of Consciousness. N.Y., Parapsychology Foundation, 1968. Pp. 24-41.

Van de Castle, R. L. "The facilitation of ESP through hypnosis." Amer. J. Clinical and Experimental Hypnosis 12: 37-56 (1969).

Chapter 11

STATE OF AWARENESS FACTORS
IN PSI ACTIVATION*

by Charles Honorton

Introduction

I shall limit myself to the "input" variety of psi function which involves the acquisition of information by an organism through apparently nonsensory channels. This is usually (though somewhat misleadingly) termed "extrasensory
perception." As a scientific problem, ESP poses two fundamental questions: How is the information "delivered" to the
organism--that is, how is it propagated or otherwise made
available? And once the information is available, how is it
mediated into awareness or transformed into an overt response?

Beyond showing the inadequacy of simple radiation and
transmission models, parapsychological research has thus far
made little progress toward an understanding of the "delivery
system." I believe there will continue to be little progress
in this area until there is more interdisciplinary involvement:
a convergence of physical, biological, and behavioral science

*Reprinted by permission of the author and publisher from
the Journal of the American Society for Psychical Research
68: 246-56 (July 1974).
    This paper was presented by Mr. Honorton at a sym-
posium, "Parapsychological (Psi) Processes: Toward a Conceptual Integration," held at the annual convention of the
American Psychological Association, Montreal, August 27-31,
1973. The other participants in this symposium were Drs.
Montague Ullman (Chairman), E. F. Kelly, Robert L. Morris, Gertrude R. Schmeidler, and Rex G. Stanford. --Ed.
    The financial support of the Foundation for Para-Sen-
sory Investigation (Mrs. Judith Skutch, President), New York
City, is gratefully acknowledged.

on what appears to be a <u>psychophysical</u> problem. It is, of
course, just this problem which has made psi phenomena
anomalous and controversial, and the controversy will doubt-
less continue until a serious search for explanation overtakes
the desire to explain away.   This will require us to adopt
the strategies of science rather than the mentality of the
magician.

Much greater progress is evident with respect to the
question of psi mediation and processing. Previous speakers
in this symposium have drawn our attention to the fact that
psi capacities are much more widely distributed than was
earlier believed.   Dr. Morris has reviewed recent animal
work which strongly suggests psi capacities in at least several infrahuman species.   Dr. Stanford's discussion of spontaneous cases and experimental reports bearing on "nonintentional" psi suggests that extrasensory factors may play a
much more pervasive role in our own species than was previously believed, albeit on an unconscious level.   And Dr.
Schmeidler, one of the foremost pioneers of process-oriented
psi research, has reviewed experimental work indicating
some ways in which human psi functions are modulated by
personality and attitudinal factors.

In coming now to a discussion of state of awareness
factors in psi functioning, we shall be particularly interested
in these questions: Are there specific subjective states,
strategies, and techniques which are particularly conducive
to psi functioning? If so, what factors do they share in common and is it possible to delineate specifically psi-conducive
characteristics? Finally, can ESP performance be reliably
augmented through "state-specific" practices and training
techniques?

SOME PSI-CONDUCIVE STATES

Laboratory demonstrations of ESP seldom involve the
vividness, dramatic detail, or feelings of conviction which
frequently accompany reports of spontaneous psi experiences.
The "psi state" question brings out a basic disparity between
our most popular experimental approaches and the spontaneous phenomena which should be serving as their model.

While most experimental ESP effects have been obtained
with subjects (Ss) functioning in states of presumed "ordinary"
wakefulness (Rao, 1966), spontaneous experiences of psi seem

predominantly to occur in altered states of consciousness
(ASCs) involving withdrawal of attention from external (sensory) stimuli and a concomitant shift toward internally-generated stimuli (thoughts, feelings, images). ESP has peren-
nially been associated with dreams and reverie states, as
well as with deliberately induced ASCs such as hypnosis and
meditation (Dingwall, 1967-68; Mishra, 1969; Rhine, 1962).

However, for nearly forty years parapsychology has
been wedded to a thoroughly behavioristic methodology. While
the forced-choice (restricted response, "guessing") paradigm
provides a simple and convenient methodology, it has usually
been practiced within a context of massed and unrewarded
trials. Guessing sets implicitly discourage Ss from attending to individual trials, much less to subtle internal cues
which may be available to guide correct responses. Nor are
Ss given much opportunity to explore alternative response
strategies. Consequently, little attention has, so far, been
directed toward the manner in which individual ESP responses
are mediated into consciousness (White, 1964).

With the advent of sophisticated psychophysiological
techniques (e.g., REM-sleep detection, biofeedback) which
provide us with greater access to internal processes, there
has been a resurgence of interest in internal state of awareness factors in ESP success. Along with this development
there has been an increased use of free-response designs
which can provide closer approximation to the conditions in
which psi occurs spontaneously. After briefly reviewing some
of the initial fruits of this research, I will suggest a tentative framework which may be useful in guiding further research
and conceptualization. In discussing psi-conducive states, I
will focus primarily upon relaxation, hypnosis, and dreaming.

Relaxation

I think almost every parapsychological investigator has
observed that Ss are more successful when they are relaxed.
In most cases, the association between ESP and relaxation
has been based on "clinical" impressions or the Ss' demeanor.
Gerber and Schmeidler (1957), in an ESP study with hospital-
ized patients, obtained significant scores from those who were
rated (by the experimenter) as "relaxed and acceptant," but
not from those rated "not relaxed and not acceptant." The
difference between the two groups was also significant.

More recently, Braud and Braud (1973, 1974) have reported several studies involving pictorial free-response target
material. The Ss completed Jacobson's progressive relaxation exercises and reported imagery which, when rated blind-
ly against the targets, showed a highly significant degree of
correspondence. A successful independent replication has already been reported by Stanford and Mayer (1974).

Hypnosis

There have been twelve experimental studies comparing ESP card-guessing performance in hypnotic and waking
conditions (reviewed by Honorton and Krippner, 1969). Nine
of the twelve produced significant hypnosis/waking differences.
Pooling the results of these studies, Van de Castle (1969)
computed a probability of ten billion to one for the difference
between hypnotic/waking ESP scores. These studies further
indicate that hypnotic increments in ESP scoring are not attributable to direct suggestions for "high scores," and suggestibility has not been found to correlate significantly with
ESP success (Honorton, 1969; Stanford, 1972).

The contribution of relaxation and attentional factors
to hypnotic increments in ESP has been examined in a recent
hypnotic dream study involving clairvoyant responses to pictorial free-response targets. Ss were trained to gauge subjective changes in relaxation and attention by calling out numbers denoting increasing degrees of relaxation and internaliza-
tion of attention. These state reports were elicited prior to
hypnotic induction and during each hypnotic dream in which
Ss attempted to incorporate target-related content. Ss with
high state reports obtained significantly more target identifi-
cations ("hits") than those with low state reports; and Ss with
strong, internally-directed shifts in state were significantly
more successful than those with little or no shift in state.
Overall, the magnitude of state shift was significantly greater
for these Ss than for those in a "waking-imagination" control
group who produced only chance results (Honorton, 1972a).

This shift-in-state effect was also found in a biofeedback study in which Ss were trained to alternately increase/
decrease EEG alpha (Honorton, Davidson, and Bindler, 1971).
An "alpha state" model has been developed which links alpha
activity to a state of relaxed, internally-directed attentiveness;
as we shall see, however, this relation is not nearly as universal as was initially suggested (Kamiya, 1967). As in the

hypnotic dream study described above, Ss gave state reports.
Pooled across Ss, the state reports were significantly related
to increments in alpha and to decrements in both eye movements and (frontalis) muscle tension, so that we may claim
a degree of construct validity for the state reports (Honorton,
Davidson, and Bindler, 1972). In a second session, the Ss
completed ESP card-guessing runs, alternately while increas-
ing/decreasing alpha, and giving state reports. The overall
ESP results were not significantly different for high/low
alpha conditions. However, only half of the Ss conformed to
the "alpha state" model (i.e., high alpha=relaxed, internal-
ized; low alpha=aroused, externalized). For these Ss, the
high alpha runs were significantly above chance and also significantly higher than the low alpha runs.

Dreaming

Dreaming is the most common ASC and also the most
frequently reported mediator of spontaneous ESP experiences.
In this connection, one of the most interesting findings to
emerge from electrophysiological studies of dream recall is
the relative imperviousness of dream consciousness to the
direct incorporation of external stimuli, suggesting that the
dreamer is to a large extent isolated from his external (sensory) environment (Tart, 1965).

Dreaming accounts for between thirty-seven and sixty-
five per cent of the spontaneous ESP experiences reported in
several international surveys (Green, 1960; Prasad and Stevenson, 1968; Rhine, 1962). In the most extensive of these
surveys (Rhine, 1962), cases were divided into two groups
based on whether the information received with regard to the
target situation was complete or fragmentary. Eighty-five per
cent of the dreams were regarded as complete, compared to
less than half of the waking experiences (hallucinatory or intuitive cases). This difference is significant and suggests an
interaction between the percipient's state of consciousness and
the quality of his psi "perception."

Experimental dream studies were initiated in 1964 at
Maimonides Medical Center by Ullman (Ullman, Krippner,
and Vaughan, 1973). Extrasensory stimuli were programmed
in conjunction with Ss' episodic dream periods, detected
through conventional electrophysiological monitoring techniques.
At the onset of each dream period, an agent located at a distance was signaled to begin looking at a randomly selected

target picture in an attempt to telepathically influence S's
dream content. Dream reports were elicited from the S at
the end of each dream period. Blind matching of dream
transcripts against target pictures has produced statistically
significant correspondences in nine out of twelve formal studies completed thus far. Overall results for all pilot sessions,
conducted over a six-year period (but not as part of the formal series), were also highly significant.

In one study utilizing a modification of the usual methodology, a special sensitive participated in a sixteen-night
comparison of psi and sensory dream incorporation. On each
odd-numbered night (1, 3, 5 ... 15) he attempted to precog-
nitively dream about a target program which would be randomly selected and shown to him on the following even-num-
bered night (2, 4, 6 ... 16). The degree of target incorporation was highly significant for the precognitive nights,
but not for the nights following actual sensory exposure to
the target programs. For this S, at least, extrasensory
stimuli appeared to be more readily incorporated into his
dreams than sensory stimuli (Krippner, Honorton, and Ullman, 1972).

SENSORY ISOLATION

There is a consistent pattern in these findings which
suggests that psi receptivity is facilitated by a reduction in
sensory input and processing. Relatively weak psi impressions may be more readily detected and recognized during
periods in which the sensory "noise level" (including body
tension) is minimized. When sensory inputs are attenuated,
the number of irrelevant stimuli bombarding the S are also
attenuated, thereby increasing his ability to detect, recognize,
and respond appropriately to psi stimuli. The essence of
this model was stated very concisely by Patanjali in the ancient Yoga Aphorisms: "Just as the pure crystal takes color
from the object which is nearest to it, so the mind, when it
is cleared ..., achieves sameness or identity with the object
of its concentration" (Prabhavananda and Isherwood, 1953).

Encouraging support for this model has recently come
from two studies in the Maimonides laboratory involving sensory isolation techniques. In the first study (Honorton,
Drucker, and Hermon, 1973), Ss gave intermittent state reports while confined in a suspended sensory isolation cradle.
Toward the end of the S's confinement, an agent located in

another room attempted to influence S's spontaneous imagery
by concentrating on a randomly selected target picture.
While the overall results were not significant, Ss who gave
high state reports obtained a significant degree of target incorporation. Ss with low state reports produced chance
matchings. The shift-in-state relation, noted earlier in connection with the hypnotic dream and alpha feedback studies,
was present to a significant degree in this study also.

In the second study (Honorton and Harper, 1974), a
homogeneous visual field (Ganzfeld) and continuous auditory
stimulation were employed to regulate perceptual inputs and
to maintain them at relatively constant levels while the Ss
followed instructions to "think out loud" by giving continuous
imagery reports. An agent, in another room, viewed a series
of thematically-related, stereoscopic pictures during a randomly determined "sending" period. The target programs
were correctly identified in 43 per cent of the cases, which
is significantly above the expected chance level of 25 per
cent.

Additional (though presently somewhat more tenuous)
support for the sensory withdrawal model is available in the
disparate areas of personality and animal research. Eysenck
(1967), in a survey of ESP-personality correlates, hypothesized
that extraverts should do better on psi tests than introverts,
who Eysenck believes are in a state of greater cortical arousal. This has, in fact, generally been the case (Kanthamani
and Rao, 1972). Schmeidler and LeShan (1970) found an interaction between a waking-state card-guessing task and
Rorschach-derived "barrier-penetration" scores, which are
believed to reflect individual differences in responsiveness to
internal processes. In the recent animal work involving
shock-avoidance (Levy, 1972), the animals have consistently
been found to be most successful when they are least active
(i. e., when they make fewer inter-trial jumps between the
two halves of the test cage) and when the preceding trial did
not involve stimulation (shock). We should expect that cu-
rarized animals, in an ESP feedback setup, would do even
better.

It is relatively easy to control external sensory stimuli which may compete with psi impressions, but it is much
more difficult to control internally-generated districtions.
What we have seen in most of the free-response designs described above is an attempt to superimpose psi influences on
the idiosyncratic imagery of unselected Ss who vary tremen-

dously in their ability to articulate internal processes. In
addition to the work already mentioned, there are a number
of other studies involving measures of individual differences
in sensitivity to internal processes which have been found to
interact with ESP scores in forced-choice tasks. These include frequency of spontaneous dream recall (Honorton, 1927b;
Johnson, 1968), creativity (Honorton, 1967; Schmeidler, 1964),
and instructional sets to "attend to subjective cues" (McCollam and Honorton, 1973). We might predict, on the basis
of such findings, that Ss who are able quickly to learn control of cortical or autonomic functions via feedback will be
more successful in ESP tasks than those who are unable to
gain control over these functions. We might even expect that
Ss who are especially sensitive to internal processes will be
the most suitable candidates for ESP training techniques since
training would presumably be contingent on cue-utilization,
which in turn is a function of internal sensitivity (Buchsbaum
and Silverman, 1970).

PROSPECTS FOR PSI-TRAINING

I will now briefly outline some ideas concerning the
feasibility of developing reliable ESP training techniques
based on considerations discussed above. Are there "psi cues"
which can be developed to discriminate reliably between correct and incorrect ESP responses? As already noted, conviction is a frequent attribute of spontaneous psi experiences
(Rhine, 1962). But it has been rare in experimental card-
guessing studies, and with good reason: few such studies
have incorporated measures for detecting conviction. In
those experiments which have incorporated conviction measures, Ss were instructed to give "confidence calls" on trials
they believed most likely to be correct. While trials with
confidence calls have usually been associated with more hits
than trials without them, there has been little exploitation of
this finding due to the possibility that confidence calls are
merely additional or secondary ESP responses rather than a
reflection of a weak but genuine discriminative function.

A recent series of studies in the Maimonides laboratory suggests that confidence calls are more than secondary
ESP responses (Honorton, 1970, 1971; McCollam and Honorton, 1973). In these studies the Ss gave confidence calls
during a clairvoyant guessing task. They were then given
these instructions:

> Now we're going to try something ... different.
> Rather than guessing 'down through' the pack and
> making confidence calls, I'm going to turn each
> card over after you make your guess and I'll tell
> you whenever you're right ... pay special attention
> to your correct guesses and see if you can begin to
> discriminate between those that are right versus the
> ones that are wrong. In doing this ... take note
> of any internal differences in feeling, attention,
> method of calling, etc. ... feel free to modify your
> guessing strategy; freely explore the conditions ...
> associated with hits ... (Honorton, 1970, p. 406).

One group of Ss (experimental group) received contingent (correct) feedback for each correct response in accordance with these instructions, while another group (control group) received noncontingent (false) feedback. Ss in both groups then completed another clairvoyant guessing task with confidence calls. The hypothesis, confirmed in each of the three studies, was that Ss given contingent feedback would show significant increments in correct confidence calls, while those given noncontingent feedback would not. Unexpectedly, two of the three studies also showed significant overall scoring increments in the experimental group following the feedback manipulation.

In the most recent of these feedback studies (McCollam and Honorton, 1973) post-experimental interviews were conducted to discover what criteria Ss used to determine their confidence calls. Their responses fell into four groups: (a) Visual or auditory images, (b) nondescript "intuitive" feelings of correctness, (c) multimode impressions involving two or more types of cues, and (d) no discernable cues (for Ss in this group confidence calls were merely an additional guessing task). Ss who reported multiple cues showed significantly larger post-feedback increments in correct confidence calls than those who reported no discernible cues.

Thus far, cue-utilization in psi-conducive states has been explored in only one published study. Fahler and Osis (1966) worked with two hypnotized Ss who performed a precognitive guessing task over a series of experimental sessions. They were given suggestions that "on some trials they might have impressions of correctness or feelings that certain [guesses] were 'different' from the others." On such trials they gave confidence calls. Sixteen per cent of the confidence call trials were correct, compared to about seven per cent of

the non-confidence call trials. This difference is associated
with a probability of fifty million to one.

The advantages of a combination of internal and external cue-detection devices (e. g. , confidence calls and immediate feedback) with hypnosis or other psi-conducive states have
not yet been systematically tested, though they are strongly
suggested by the Fahler-Osis experiment.

The points of convergence with yogic descriptions in-
vite a more thorough examination of Eastern techniques.
Those described in Patanjali's Yoga Aphorisms, for example,
appear to be sophisticated and systematic, and may well be
fertile ground for parapsychological hypothesis-testing and
conceptualization. The most recent psychophysiological studies
in voluntary control of autonomic processes by yogis illustrate
the potential for cross-fertilization between the empirical sciences of the West and the experiential sciences of the East
(Anand, Chhina, and Singh, 1961).

REFERENCES

Anand, B. , Chhina, G. , and Singh, B. "Some aspects of
    electroencephalographic studies in yogis. " Electro-
    encephalography and Clinical Neurophysiology, 1961,
    13, 452-456.
Braud, L. W. , and Braud, W. G. "Further studies of re-
    laxation as a psi-conducive state. " Journal of the
    American Society for Psychical Research, 1974, 68,
    229-245.
Braud, W. G. , and Braud, L. W. "Preliminary explorations
    of psi-conducive states: Progressive muscular relaxa-
    tion. " Journal of the American Society for Psychical
    Research, 1973, 67, 26-46.
Buchsbaum, M. S. , and Silverman, J. "Perceptual corre-
    lates of consciousness: A conceptual model and its
    technical implications for psi research. " In R. Cavan-
    na (Ed.), Psi Favorable States of Consciousness. New
    York: Parapsychology Foundation, 1970. Pp. 143-
    169.
Dingwall, E. J. (Ed.) Abnormal Hypnotic Phenomena. New
    York: Barnes and Noble, 1967-1968. (4 vols.)
Eysenck, H. J. "Personality and extrasensory perception. "
    Journal of the Society for Psychical Research, 1967,
    44, 55-71.
Fahler, J. , and Osis, K. "Checking for awareness of hits in

a precognition experiment with hypnotized subjects."
Journal of the American Society for Psychical Research,
1966, 60, 340-346.

Gerber, R., and Schmeidler, G. R. "An investigation of relaxation and of acceptance of the experimental situation
as related to ESP scores in maternity patients." Journal of Parapsychology, 1957, 21, 47-57.

Green, C. E. "Analysis of spontaneous cases." Proceedings
of the Society for Psychical Research, 1960, 53, 97-
161.

Honorton, C. "Creativity and precognition scoring level."
Journal of Parapsychology, 1967, 31, 29-42.

_____ . "A combination of techniques for the separation of
high- and low-scoring ESP subjects: Experiments with
hypnotic and waking imagination instructions." Journal
of the American Society for Psychical Research, 1969,
63, 69-82.

_____ . "Effects of feedback on discrimination between
correct and incorrect ESP responses." Journal of
the American Society for Psychical Research, 1970,
64, 404-410.

_____ . "Effects of feedback on discrimination between
correct and incorrect ESP responses: A replication
study." Journal of the American Society for Psychical
Research, 1971, 65, 155-161.

_____ . "Significant factors in hypnotically-induced clairvoyant dreams." Journal of the American Society for
Psychical Research, 1972, 66, 86-102. (a)

_____ . "Reported frequency of dream recall and ESP."
Journal of the American Society for Psychical Research,
1972, 66, 369-374. (b)

_____ , Davidson, R., and Bindler, P. "Feedback-augmented EEG alpha, shifts in subjective state, and ESP
card-guessing performance." Journal of the American
Society for Psychical Research, 1971, 65, 308-323.

_____ , _____ , and _____ . "Shifts in subjective state
associated with feedback-augmented EEG alpha." Psychophysiology, 1972, 9, 269-270. (Abstract.)

_____ , Drucker, S., and Hermon, H. "Shifts in subjective
state and ESP under conditions of partial sensory depri-
vation: A preliminary study." Journal of the American Society for Psychical Research, 1973, 67, 191-
196.

_____ , and Harper, S. "Psi-mediated imagery and ideation in an experimental procedure for regulating perceptual input." Journal of the American Society for
Psychical Research, 1974, 68, 156-168.

_____, and Krippner, S. "Hypnosis and ESP performance: A review of the experimental literature." Journal of the American Society for Psychical Research, 1969, 63, 214-252.

Johnson, M. "Relationship between dream recall and scoring direction." Journal of Parapsychology, 1968, 32, 56-57. (Abstract.)

Kamiya, J. "Operant control of the EEG alpha rhythm and some of its reported effects on consciousness." In C. T. Tart (Ed.), Altered States of Consciousness. New York: Wiley, 1969. Pp. 507-517.

Kanthamani, B. K., and Rao, K. R. "Personality characteristics of ESP subjects. II. Extraversion and ESP." Journal of Parapsychology, 1972, 36, 198-212.

Krippner, S., Honorton, C., and Ullman, M. "A second precognitive dream study with Malcolm Bessent." Journal of the American Society for Psychical Research, 1972, 66, 269-279.

Levy, W. J. Jr. "The effect of the test situation on precognition in mice and jirds: A confirmation study." Journal of Parapsychology, 1972, 36, 46-55.

McCollam, E., and Honorton, C. "Effects of feedback on discrimination between correct and incorrect ESP responses: A further replication and extension." Journal of the American Society for Psychical Research, 1973, 67, 77-85.

Mishra, R. The Textbook of Yoga Psychology. New York: Julian Press, 1969.

Prabhavananda, Swami, and Isherwood, C. How to Know God: The Yoga Aphorisms of Patanjali. New York: New American Library, 1953.

Prasad, J., and Stevenson, I. "A survey of spontaneous psychical experiences in school children of Uttar Pradesh, India." International Journal of Parapsychology, 1968, 10, 241-261.

Rao, K. R. Experimental Parapsychology. Springfield, Illinois: Thomas, 1966.

Rhine, L. E. "Psychological processes in ESP experiences. I. Waking experiences." Journal of Parapsychology, 1962, 26, 88-111.

Schmeidler, G. R. "An experiment on precognitive clairvoyance. IV. Precognition scores related to creativity." Journal of Parapsychology, 1964, 28, 102-108.

_____, and LeShan, L. "An aspect of body image related to ESP scores." Journal of the American Society for Psychical Research, 1970, 64, 211-218.

Stanford, R. G. "Suggestibility and success at augury--

divination from 'chance' outcomes." Journal of the
American Society for Psychical Research, 1972, 66,
41-62.

_____, and Mayer, B. "Relaxation as a psi-conducive
state: A replication and exploration of parameters."
Journal of the American Society for Psychical Research,
1974, 68, 182-191.

Tart, C. T. "Toward the experimental control of dreaming:
A review of the literature." Psychological Bulletin,
1965, 64, 81-91.

Ullman, M., Krippner, S., and Vaughan, A. Dream Telepathy. New York: Macmillan, 1973.

Van de Castle, R. L. "The facilitation of ESP through hypnosis." American Journal of Clinical Hypnosis, 1969,
12, 37-56.

White, R. A. "A comparison of old and new methods of response to targets in ESP experiments." Journal of
the American Society for Psychical Research, 1964,
58, 21-56.

ADDITIONAL READINGS ON PSI-CONDUCIVE
STATES OF CONSCIOUSNESS

Beloff, J. "ESP: The search for a physiological index. "
    JSPR 47: 403-20 (Sep 1974).
Braud, L. W. and Braud, W. G. "The influence of relaxa-
    tion and tension on the psi process. " (Abstract) RP
    2: 11-13, 1973.
Braud, W. G. "Psi-conducive states. " Journal of Communi-
    cation 25: 142-52 (Win 1975).
    _____, Wood, R., and Braud, L. W. "Free-response
    GESP performance during an experimental hypnagogic
    state induced by visual and acoustic ganzfeld techniques:
    a replication and extension. " JASPR 69: 105-13 (Apr
    1975).
Brown, B. "Auto-control of consciousness: The next revo-
    lution. " P. A. Proc. 7: 81-95, 1970.
Cavanna, R. (Ed.). Psi Favorable States of Consciousness.
    N. Y., Parapsychology Foundation, 1970.
    _____, and Ullman, M. (Eds.). Psi and Altered States
    of Consciousness. N. Y., Parapsychology Foundation,
    1968.
Chapman, J. D. "Instrumentation, hypnosis and ESP. "
    Osteopathic Physician 41: 63-70 (Apr 1974).
Chari, C. T. K. "Psychophysiological issues about EEG
    alpha activity and ESP. " JASPR 64: 411-20 (Oct 1970).
Ehrenwald, J. "Psi phenomena and the existential shift. "
    JASPR 65: 162-72 (Apr 1971).
Honorton, C. "ESP and altered states of consciousness. "
    In Beloff, J. (Ed.). New Directions in Parapsychol-
    ogy. London, Elek Science, 1974. Metuchen, N. J.,
    Scarecrow Press, 1975. Ch. 2.
    _____. "Psi-conducive states of awareness. " In Mitchell,
    E. D. and others. Psychic Exploration. N. Y., Put-
    nam's, 1974. Ch. 27.
    _____. "Relationship between EEG alpha activity and ESP
    in card-guessing performance. " JASPR 63: 365-74
    (Oct 1969).
    _____. "Signal increasing in ESP. " Osteopathic Physician
    41: 131-36 (Apr 1974).
    _____, and Barksdale, W. "PK performance with waking
    suggestions for muscle tension versus relaxation. "
    JASPR 66: 208-14 (Apr 1972).

_____, and Carbone, M₀ "A preliminary study of feed-
back augmented EEG alpha activity and ESP card-
guessing performance." JASPR 65: 66-74 (Jan 1971).
_____, Tierney, L₀, and Torres, D. "The role of men-
tal imagery in psi-meditation." JASPR 68: 385-94
(Oct 1974)₀
Kanthamani, H₀ and Kelly, E. F. "Awareness of success
in an exceptional subject." JP 38: 355-82 (Dec 1974)₀
Kreitler, H. and Kreitler, S₀ "Optimization of experimental
ESP results." JP 38: 383-92 (Dec 1974)₀
Krippner, S₀ "Dreams and other altered states of conscious-
ness." Journal of Communication 35: 173-82 (Win
1975)₀
LeShan, L₀ "Psychic phenomena and mystical experience."
In Mitchell, E₀ D₀ and others₀ Psychic Exploration₀
N₀Y₀, Putnam's, 1974₀ Ch₀ 24.
Lewis, L₀ and Schmeidler, G. R. "Alpha relations with non-
intentional and purposeful ESP after feedback." JASPR
65: 455-67 (Oct 1971)₀
McCreery, C₀ Science, Philosophy and ESP. London, Ham-
ish Hamilton, 1969₀
Masters, R. "Consciousness and extraordinary phenomena."
In Mitchell, E₀ D₀ and others₀ Psychic Exploration.
N₀Y₀, Putnam's, 1974₀ Ch₀ 26.
Morris, R₀ L₀ and others₀ "EEG patterns and ESP results
in forced choice experiments with Lalsingh Harribance."
JASPR 66: 253-68 (Jul 1972)₀
Osis, K. and Bokert, E₀ "ESP and changed states of con-
sciousness induced by meditation." JASPR 65: 17-65
(Jan 1971).
Rush, J₀ H₀ New Directions in Parapsychological Research.
N₀Y₀, Parapsychology Foundation, 1964. (Parapsy-
chological Monographs No. 4).
_____. "Parapsychology's century of progress." In An-
goff, A₀ and Shapin, B₀ (Eds₀). Parapsychology Today: A Geographic View. N₀Y₀, Parapsychology
Foundation, 1973₀ Pp. 205-23₀
Schmeidler, G₀ R₀ "High ESP scores after a Swami's brief
instruction in meditation and breathing." JASPR 64:
100-03 (Jan 1970)₀
_____. "Mood and attitude on a pretest as predictors of
retest ESP performance." JASPR 65: 324-35 (Jul
1971)₀
_____₀ "Studying individual psi experiences." JP 34:
197-209 (Sep 1970)₀
Stanford, R₀ G₀ "'Associative activation of the unconscious'
and 'visualization' as methods for influencing the PK

target. " <u>JASPR</u> 338-51 (Oct 1969).

_____。 "EEG alpha activity and ESP performance: A replicative study. " <u>JASPR</u> 65: 144-54 (Apr 1971).

_____. "Response Factors in extrasensory perception。" Journal of Communication 25: 153-61 (Win 1975).

_____, and Lovin, C. A. "EEG alpha activity and ESP performance。" <u>JASPR</u> 64: 375-84 (Oct 1970).

_____, and Stevenson, I。 "EEG correlates of free-response GESP in an individual subject。" <u>JASPR</u> 66: 357-68 (Oct 1972).

Tart, C。 T。 "On the nature of altered states of consciousness with special reference to parapsychological phenomena. " <u>RP</u> 2: 163-218, 1973.

Chapter 12

SCIENTIFIC, ETHICAL & CLINICAL PROBLEMS IN THE "TRAINING" OF PSI ABILITY*

by Rex G. Stanford

From a purely scientific perspective, parapsychologists, of all people, should welcome the discovery of a method for training a high and reliable level of psi performance. On the other hand, the ability to reliably produce ESP would immediately raise serious and troubling questions about the possible applications to which such reliable ESP might then be put.

The idea of training psi ability has great popular appeal as well as scientific interest. There now exist numerous commercial organizations which offer courses that are claimed to train individuals to use their ESP, not to mention other supposed mental powers such as the ability to control bodily processes and to prevent illness in oneself and others. One such mind-control program, it is reported, grossed ten million dollars during just four years of its operation (McConnell, 1973). There can be no doubt but that a considerable segment of our population is subject to easy infatuation with promises of expanded mental powers, and the purveyors of such courses make their claims appear credible and respectable by cloaking them in scientific-sounding terminology regarding cortical rhythms and biofeedback.

The pitch for such courses typically states that there are levels of mental function (associated, it is said, with alpha and theta rhythms) at which the mind has capacities of which we are normally unaware and over which we normally exert no conscious control. These capacities include psychic powers and control over mental and physiological processes. The claim is typically made that such a course trains one to function at these levels (whatever that means) and thus en-

---

*Published by permission of the author.

288

ables one to use techniques which allow conscious control
over capacities such as psi and the many facets of the organism's function. The courses are clearly inspired by
popularized ideas about biofeedback and "alpha (or theta)
states," even though such courses usually do not actually
train students through biofeedback techniques.

Before discussing the validity of the parapsychological
claims of the mind-control type course, it will be useful to
consider the laboratory evidence on the training of ESP and
on EEG rhythms and ESP performance. (Studies included in
the tabulations that follow are listed in the reference section
of this paper. They will, for the most part, not be cited
individually.)

Training ESP

The laboratory attempts to demonstrate ESP training
have been based upon a simple feedback paradigm: Give subjects an ESP task, let them know immediately after each trial
what was the target for that trial (or simply tell them whether the response was correct or incorrect), and they should
consequently increase their level of performance on the ESP
task. A convincing argument for studying this paradigm has
been given by Tart (1966).

In practice this approach has generally made no assumptions about what the subject is supposed to learn through
this feedback procedure, but has simply assumed he will
learn something which will produce an increment in performance. In such studies the subject is given no specific instructions which would guide him toward examining particular cues
which might be useful. In all such studies the target material has been very simple and the response mode has been
forced-choice.

Three experiments (Honorton, 1970; Kreiman & Ivinsky, 1973; McCallam & Honorton, 1973) have produced significant evidence of increased ESP performance when post-
feedback ESP trials are compared with prefeedback ESP trials.
However, sixteen other experiments have failed to show an
increment in ESP performance associated with immediate feedback. (A number of the reports of these studies did not actually provide a statistical comparison of possible effects of
feedback, but in such instances I have made my own statistical comparison based upon data supplied.) Some of these six-

teen experiments showed significantly positive ESP performance under a feedback condition, especially when preselected
subjects were studied, but the same studies showed no evidence of an increment in performance associated with feedback. Several of the studies tabulated showed a decrement
in performance within the feedback condition. Further, it
is likely there have been a number of failures to show a
learning effect which have not been published. I know of
several. Many parapsychologists have used electronic random event generators for ESP testing, and they have generally used these machines to supply immediate feedback; but no
experimenter has reported feedback-related increments associated with subjects' use of such a machine. An "exception"
is a single experimenter, whom I will not name, who insists
on testing numerous subjects with such a machine and then,
after the fact, selects out of the data of those subjects showing, individually, a "significant" increase in performance.
He suggests these data demonstrate these subjects were learning ESP. Such a maneuver is, however, just statistical
sophistry.

        One of the studies which did produce positive results
related to feedback (McCallam & Honorton, 1973) also produced anomalies which call into question a learning interpretation of such work. The number of feedback trials given subjects actually decreased the difference of pre- to post-feedback ESP performance, and level of feedback ESP performance
did not correlate significantly with pre- to post-feedback ESP
differences.

        Such studies can be fairly summarized by saying that
increases of performance following immediate feedback are
exceptions rather than the rule, and even in the instances in
which such an effect has been observed, the results are
equivocal of interpretation.

        This summary of the ESP-feedback work did not in-
clude the rather well-known work of Ryzl on "training" ESP
subjects while under hypnosis (Ryzl, 1966). Ryzl's ESP training efforts were more pragmatic than experimental in orientation and were apparently aimed at producing some good ESP
subjects, rather than experimentally assessing his training
method. Thus, for example, we lack reports from Ryzl on
before- and after-training comparisons, and he did not use
control groups which would have helped him infer what was
really happening with his "training." We also know that subjects whom he was able to successfully "train" were only a

small proportion of those on whom he tried his technique. His training method, involving hypnosis, hypnotically-induced visual imagery ("hallucinations"), and free-response ESP tasks with immediate feedback is unique and probably deserves further study. Reported unsuccessful efforts to "replicate" this work (Beloff & Mandleberg, 1966; Haddox, 1966; Stephenson, 1965) and to further study the supposed training effect have involved less than full methodological replications of Ryzl's technique.

There have been few attempts in ESP-feedback studies to test specific principles of learning, although such efforts might prove very valuable. Most unfortunately, as noted earlier, such work has, with rare exceptions, not attempted to specify (theoretically or empirically) what is supposed to be learned. Exceptions are the work of Honorton (1970, 1971) and McCallam and Honorton (1973) in which a major thrust of the work was to learn whether subjects were actually learning to discriminate responses likely to be correct from those less likely to be correct. In the McCallam and Honorton study an effort was also made to learn specifically what kinds of cues subjects used for making such discriminations. Such efforts are commendable, and it is likely that work in ESP training will advance only when experiments are designed around concepts concerning what the subject presumably can learn from such feedback, or when, at the very least, such work attempts to measure what it is the subject may really be learning, if anything.

Though almost all ESP-feedback studies have used rather monotonous, repetitive forced-choice ESP tasks, experimenters' instructions to subjects seem never to have focused on the principle of learning to discriminate one target from another, and the number of target classes used has often been quite large (typically five). Subjects are not told whether they are to try to develop methods for discriminating the presence of one target-class from another, or whether they are supposed to be learning some internal state favorable to psi, or perhaps should be learning to discriminate psi-mediated from non-psi-mediated internal cues, or something else, or perhaps some combination of these. Nor, in my opinion, have experimenters seriously enough considered the role of inhibitory factors in such studies, for subjects have often been required to make extremely long series of calls in a highly repetitive, dull, and probably tiring task.

Few experimenters have heeded the warning of Tart

(1966) that reinforcement of merely chance successes will not
be conducive to ESP performance, and in much work the non-
psi probability of a correct response (or "hit") is one-fourth
or one-fifth.   The feedback work has also rather neglected
the supposed role of reinforcement in learning.   It is perhaps
all too readily supposed that adequate reinforcement occurs
merely by subjects' knowing they have made one more hit in
a series of calls involving a sizeable non-psi hit probability.
One cannot expect a hit to be very reinforcing under such
circumstances, especially since hit rates greatly exceeding
mean chance expectation are rare in such studies.

Although a few studies have attempted to learn whether immediate feedback in a forced-choice setting can increase
subjects' degree of insight about success (as reflected in the
accuracy of trials on which subjects indicate they are very
confident of success) (Honorton, 1970, 1971; McCallam &
Honorton, 1973), no immediate feedback study has actually
combined such confidence-checking with immediate feedback
on the same ESP trials.   Since a number of studies have
shown that a feeling of confidence on certain trials may be
associated with better performance on those trials (cf. Honorton, 1970), it would seem reasonable to give subjects immediate feedback on the same series of trials on which they
are doing this form of confidence rating.   This might facilitate discriminative learning regarding psi-relevant internal
cues.

In conclusion, the forced-choice feedback work has
given little reason for optimism that it can provide an ESP
training method, but further work in that area might be warranted if it involves some changes in methodology and more
incisive conceptualization.

New approaches should in the meantime be explored.
Since certain altered internal states (so-called altered states
of consciousness) have proven psi-conducive (cf. Honorton,
1974) and since subjects seem strongly reinforced when they
succeed on free-response picture-perception targets, an attempt at training ESP performance might usefully combine
these two pieces of information.   Subjects might be trained
to develop and maintain in themselves such internal states
during ESP testing with pictorial target materials to which
they would respond in the free-response manner.   They would
be shown the target picture at the end of each trial.   Such a
program would provide a laboratory analogue of the circumstances under which many so-called psychics claim to have

developed their ESP ability.   Currently I am developing a research project which will study this particular ESP-training paradigm.

Interestingly, the typical mind-control type course seems built around a strategy similar to that just proposed, an effort to train a psi-favorable state and to further train persons to work within it using free-response ESP tasks.

Studies of Alpha Rhythms and ESP Performance

Some observers have suggested that biofeedback training for the production of alpha rhythms might be one way of training a psi-favorable internal state.   Honorton, Davidson, and Bindler (1971) used biofeedback to train subjects either to generate or to suppress occipital alpha rhythms, and these subjects were given forced-choice ESP tests during both alpha generation and suppression.   Since no single physiological parameter is known to reliably and uniquely pinpoint a particular kind of internal state (Johnson, 1970), it is perhaps not surprising that subjects did not show meaningful differences in ESP performance during alpha generation as contrasted with suppression.   It is of interest, however, that when subjects both generated alpha rhythms and reported marked alterations in their internal state, they did particularly well on the ESP task.   It would seem that training to produce an internal state which is psi-conducive will have to involve more than training a single parameter, be it alpha density or any other, contrary to claims often made to the public by certain commercial mind-training enterprises.   The Honorton, Davidson, and Bindler work shows that alpha training does not, of itself, induce an internal state which is sufficient for ESP performance.

The incorrectness of the popular belief that marked alpha abundance is sufficient indication of a psi-conducive state is further underscored by the substantial amount of correlational work on alpha parameters and ESP performance. The results of the alpha-ESP work can be summarized as follows:

1.   When subjects with high occipital alpha densities are contrasted with those showing low alpha densities, there is no consistent evidence supporting the hypothesis that subjects with a high alpha density are more successful at ESP tasks than those with a lower alpha density.   There have been

seven such between-subject comparisons. One of the seven studies showed a significant positive alpha density-ESP correlation; four showed no significant relationship; and two of the studies showed significant negative correlations of ESP performance and alpha density.

2. When a given subject shows a relatively great occipital alpha density will he produce better ESP performance than when he shows a relatively low alpha density? There have been nine such comparisons. Two of these showed a significant positive relationship (one of the two involved a free-response picture-perception ESP task and a single subject); seven showed no significant relationship; and none showed a significant negative relationship.

3. Three studies (Morris, Roll, Klein & Wheeler, 1972; Stanford & Palmer, 1974) used the rather different approach of seeing whether level of ESP performance predicts occipital alpha abundance. In the two experiments reported by Morris et al. a single outstanding ESP subject was shown to produce reliably greater occipital alpha densities when he produced high scores than when he produced chance scores on forced-choice ESP tasks. Stanford and Palmer showed that unselected volunteer subjects who produced free-response picture-perception ESP scores above mean chance expectation produced reliably greater alpha densities (in fact, three times greater, on the average) than did subjects who scored at or below mean chance expectation. This was true even though alpha density did not itself reliably predict ESP scores. That ESP scores might predict alpha abundance more efficiently than alpha abundance predicts ESP scores makes sense if the presence of marked occipital alpha rhythms is indicative of an internal state that is helpful to but is not sufficient for ESP performance. The three experiments cited tentatively support such a conclusion, but considerable more research is needed. The Honorton, Davidson, and Bindler (1970) study discussed earlier, involving biofeedback training of alpha rhythms and ESP testing, also supports this conclusion.

4. Two studies (Stanford, 1971; Stanford & Lovin, 1970) using unselected subjects yielded significant positive correlations of forced-choice ESP performance and degree of upward shift in mean alpha frequency (in Hz) from a pretest relaxation period to the ESP task. Another study (Stanford & Stevenson, 1972) involving a single subject and a free-response picture-perception ESP task produced a significant positive correlation of ESP scores and upward shift of mean alpha fre-

quency from a pretest meditation period to the ESP image-reception period. These three studies suggest that a mentally quiet, passive state (associated with slowed alpha rhythms) is valuable as a stage-setting for ESP performance but that when the subject must attempt to use or be aware of extrasensory information he must become more attentive, causing some upward shift in alpha frequency. Perhaps the previously quiet, passive state must now shift slightly to become a passive, quiet, but attentive state which might be termed "calmly alert." Such EEG findings complement the altered states work (cf. Honorton, 1974) which suggests that an undistracted mind with an inward-directed focus of attention facilitates ESP performance.

The Status of Unpublished Research on Alpha-ESP Training

Various organizations are now claiming to train persons to enter an "alpha state" or "alpha level"--whatever that is--in which the trainee can supposedly learn to demonstrate various remarkable mental powers. Usually such organizations create the appearance that they are scientifically oriented benefactors of the future "evolution" of this planet--an evolution which they propose will be mental and psychic in character. They use language which appears scientific to the layman, but which is really pseudo-scientific. For example, talk of an "alpha state" or "alpha level" as though it were something definitive and scientifically established as a functional entity is highly misleading. The way that such organizations usually conceptualize brain function in relation to mental function is extraordinarily naive and should provide suitable bed-time fairy-tale material for the psychophysiologist.

Often such organizations or their founders claim they have done years of "research" on these problems and have solved them in ways which provide immediate applicability. Though they assure potential students that this research has shown they can train psi abilities, it is curious that such research seems never to have been published in scientific, refereed journals. Indeed, exactly what the "scientific research" is that was supposedly done seems never to be clearly specified anywhere.

In a book (McKnight, 1972) endorsing the claims of what is probably the earliest and most financially successful of these organizations, that providing Silva Mind Control, I recently discovered the intriguing suggestion that Silva had done years of research on his method but modesty had apparently prevented his publishing it and thereby being admired by future generations (p. 9). If modesty was the reason, it certainly did not deter Silva himself from stating, later in the book, that his method opens up for us a dimension ("Alpha") which can increase IQ, promote better health, increase problem-solving potential, and allow communication with God (pp. 86-87). Finally he states (p. 87) that anything is possible within this "dimension."

Published Research on the Validity of the Parapsychological Claims Regarding the Silva Mind Control Method

It is claimed that this method makes possible, among other things, the ability to use ESP quite deliberately, and this claim includes the ability to make psychic diagnoses of the physical and mental conditions of persons, this being known as "working a case." There have been no reports in the parapsychological journals, or other scientific journals, to my knowledge, which support the claims of Silva Mind Control regarding ESP. Nor has such support been forthcoming for the parapsychological claims of any of the similar methods which have so rapidly multiplied in the wake of Silva's financial success.

The available evidence is, in fact, negative. At the Sixteenth Annual Convention of the Parapsychological Association there were two reports, involving three studies, devoted to an examination of the claims regarding Silva Mind Control.

Alan Vaughan undertook a study of these claims at the request of a graduate of the Silva Mind Control program. He (1974) studied twenty-one Mind Control graduates using procedures which took into account the graduates' normal way of proceeding in doing their psychic readings. He did not force them into arbitrary or unaccustomed procedures. Nonetheless, the graduates produced results not reliably different from mean chance expectation. The actual outcome was slightly below mean chance expectation.

Robert Brier, Barry Savits, and Gertrude Schmeidler (1974) reported two studies of the "case working" ability of Silva Mind Control graduates. In each study they used five graduates of Mind Control who were apparently enthusiastic enough about the outcomes of the course to want to show what they could do in an actual study. Again, in both studies, the graduates as a group failed to demonstrate their supposed ability.

It is of interest that even if such studies had validated the claim that the graduates could do psychic diagnosis, this would not have proved that they gained the ability through Silva Mind Control training. A different kind of study involving before- and after-course ESP testing would be required to examine that claim.

Some Causes for Concern about Such Courses

1. If graduates of mind-control type courses have not been reliably trained to use ESP, and clairvoyant diagnosis in particular, may not the graduates of such courses pose a threat to individuals who are in need of medical help but who may not seek it because of a reassuring "psychic diagnosis" from such a graduate?

2. How useful would such an ability be, anyway, even if it were genuine, if its practitioner did not have the medical training to recognize a very specific condition and to properly label it? Would not such an ability be positively dangerous unless it were used under the direct supervision of a physician?

3. Is it proper to make claims for such courses which go counter to the available scientific evidence?

4. Often in such courses the student is supposed to be trained to enter a mental level such that he can "program" other persons' physiological or mental processes at will. It would appear that students often emerge from such courses believing that they can directly heal and help other persons through psychic means. This, too, might pose a serious danger if they promise to treat persons who are seriously ill. Such persons might forego or postpone medical treatment out of a belief that the graduate can help them. I have heard of no scientific reports bearing on the validity of such claims deriving from mind-control type courses.

5. Aside from whatever dangers may exist for persons who come into contact with such course graduates there may be some reason for concern about the effects of such courses upon the mental health of at least a certain proportion of the students.

This potential danger derives in part from the fact that many students come out of such courses seriously believing that the course has delivered what it was claimed to deliver. In interviews with many graduates of such courses I have had the impression that they were amazed at the supposed psychic diagnosis they did which allowed them to graduate from the course. Most graduates, however, seem unaware of how difficult it is to evaluate the likelihood that such a diagnostic reading is genuinely psychic, especially under the conditions in which they are typically given in such a course.

In such courses the student psychic diagnostician is often given the first name and initial, sex, age, and geographic locale of the target person. Additionally, many graduates have told me that they had multiple opportunities to psychically read someone until a reading was felt to be a success, and then they were graduated from the course. Most students seem not to think of their failures which preceded the success and do not reflect on the implications of such failures for the reliability of the results of the training. Nor do they seem to ask themselves why they should be permitted to graduate after a single success instead of being asked to do more successful readings to prove they have been reliably trained. The typical student also does not seem bothered by the fact that in giving the reading he is usually face-to-face with someone who knows the condition of the target person. He does not realize that subtle or even not-so-subtle sensory cues cannot be ruled out. Nor does he realize that it is not always easy to know when one is being sensorially cued by another person. Similarly, the student does not stop to think that the examination process for such courses could not in principle permit a judgment of whether he or students in general have really been trained in ESP performance. They do not realize that such an inference would, at the very least, require pre-course testing for ESP ability but that students are not given the opportunity to see how well they can do before being "trained." Most of them assume that ESP is impossible to do at will without special training.

Students do not realize that the examination process simply gives them an opportunity to try to use ESP in an optimism-inducing, highly supportive setting which has been shown, in the laboratory, to be psi-conducive even when subjects have not been "trained." Thus they do not realize that even if they show some ESP ability in this setting, it proves nothing about their having been trained to use ESP reliably.

Therefore any success they have is attributed to the efficacy of the training procedure.

Granted the inability of the typical student to adequately evaluate the parapsychological outcome of his training, granted the high-powered salesmanship, the morale-boosting atmosphere, and that the student has paid a considerable sum for such a course, it is little wonder that many persons leave the course feeling it has been a success. They graduate believing themselves capable of using ESP and other psychic powers consciously and reliably.

As a parapsychologist I have come into contact with many persons who have graduated from such courses. Many retain reasonable, objective perspectives on what happened to them in the course and on what had been the long-term result. On the other hand, a small proportion of those who have undergone such training come out of the course believing themselves endowed with almost unlimited capacities to manipulate other people by psychic means and they seem fixated on these possibilities. Some mind-control type courses include the claim that graduates can not only use ESP but can influence others mentally and physically and can even influence inanimate matter. It is my considered opinion that some such courses encourage and support bizarre and unrealistic ideation in the student and that this might seriously exacerbate the psychological instability of persons who enter the course in an initially unstable state of mind.

Recently Dr. David Rogers, a clinical psychologist from the University of North Carolina at Chapel Hill, described to the Parapsychological Association some experiences which may be relevant. Rogers reported that he has had several patients whose severe psychological manifestations were precipitated by their having been told by a careless experimenter that their ESP-test results showed them to "have ESP" when, in fact, the scores were not particularly interesting. If that can happen under such circumstances, then the effects upon certain persons of the mind-control type procedures might be more serious, for the claims implanted in the mind of the student are much more bizarre and may have even less of a foundation.

Some Final Thoughts

The existence and great commercial success of the

expensive mind-control type courses with their bizarre and
unsubstantiated claims would seem to indicate that many persons have some strong needs which are not otherwise being
met.   No doubt some of those who enroll have a strong but
frustrated need for power, possibly even a pathological need
of that kind.   Such persons would naturally focus their interest in such courses on the claims that one can learn to
manipulate other people, and I have met several individuals
who have been in such courses who seemed to have a pathological fixation on such imagined powers.   On the other hand,
I suspect that many, if not most, persons who become involved in such courses do so out of more healthy, growth-
oriented needs, such as needs to know more about themselves,
their own minds, the nature of man and about the extent of
human capability.   Or perhaps such persons need to understand some puzzling possibly psychic events which they themselves have experienced.   Perhaps some persons with these
needs derive benefit from taking such courses, just as parapsychologists have noticed persons who seem to benefit from
the self-exploration afforded in certain parapsychological
studies which we conduct in our laboratories.   What seems
undesirable about the commercial programs are the unrealistic claims which are made for the training and the undesirable consequences which they may have for persons who accept them.

It is unfortunate that there exist in our society few if
any noncommercial institutions which can meet the experiential and self-exploration needs which seem to attract many
persons to the mind-control type courses.   Ordinary psychotherapy is not an adequate substitute, and the possibilities
supplied by the humanistic psychology movement have not yet
provided sufficient opportunities for individuals to explore, in
a safe, supervised way, one of the most deeply exciting and
intriguing aspects of human experience--psi interaction.

Few individuals can have their first perceptual-cogni-
tive psi experience without it having a strong impact on their
self-concept and perhaps their world-view.   In our present
age in which many of our past solutions to our personal and
social problems seem impotent, it is little wonder that some
persons are seeking to explore the realm of psi experience
in the hope that they may gain some valuable restructuring of
their personal constructs.   Whether such experience will really have that kind of value is something we cannot answer at
this time.   But it does seem that persons are interested more
than ever before in self-exploration and feel that this explora-

tion should not stop at the usual sensory boundaries but should extend into extrasensory experience and the transpersonal possibilities involved in that.

Might it be possible for parapsychologists and others concerned about these matters to somehow aid in the development of more systematic, safer opportunities for individuals to explore their psi capacities and to do so without commercial exploitation and without their being given unrealistic expectations? This is a topic with many ramifications, and it will not be possible to explore it further in this paper. Suffice it to say that the very existence and popularity of the mind-control type course should alert us to some very real human needs which somehow are not being met through other institutions. Parapsychologists and other concerned persons can and probably should do more than they have been doing to help persons safely and constructively meet such needs. Education about and the publicization of scientifically founded criticisms of the excessive claims of mind-control type organizations is a necessary corrective, but it does not of itself provide a viable alternative for persons who seek personal exploration of human possibility.

REFERENCES

Beloff, J. , & Mandleberg, I. "An attempted validation of the 'Ryzl technique' for training ESP subjects. " Journal of the Society for Psychical Research, 1966, 43, 229-249.

R. Brier, B. Savits, & Schmeidler, G. "Experimental tests of Silva Mind Control graduates. " In W. G. Roll, R. L. Morris, & J. D. Morris (Eds.), Research in Parapsychology 1973. Metuchen, N. J. : Scarecrow Press, 1974. Pp. 13-15.

Cadoret, R. J. "An exploratory experiment: continuous EEG recording during clairvoyant card tests. " Journal of Parapsychology, 1964, 28, 226. (Abstract.)

Dagel, L. T. , & Puryear, H. B. "The effect of immediate reinforcement in a two-choice GESP test. " Journal of Parapsychology, 1969, 33, 339. (Abstract.)

Dale, L. A. , Taves, E. , & Murphy, G. "Research notes. " Journal of the American Society for Psychical Research, 1944, 38, 160-170.

Haddox, V. "A pilot study of a hypnotic method for training subjects in ESP. " Journal of Parapsychology, 1966, 30, 277-278. (Abstract.)

Haraldsson, E. "Subject selection in a machine precognition
    test." Journal of Parapsychology, 1970, 34, 182-191.
Honorton, C. "Relationship between EEG alpha activity and
    ESP in card-guessing performance." Journal of the
    American Society for Psychical Research, 1969, 63,
    365-374.
_____. "Effects of feedback on discrimination between
    correct and incorrect ESP responses." Journal of the
    American Society for Psychical Research, 1970, 64,
    404-410.
_____. "Effects of feedback on discrimination between cor-
    rect and incorrect ESP responses: A replication study."
    Journal of the American Society for Psychical Research,
    1971, 65, 155-161.
_____. "State of awareness factors in psi activation."
    Journal of the American Society for Psychical Research,
    1974, 68, 246-256.
_____, & Carbone, M. "A preliminary study of feedback-
    augmented EEG alpha activity and ESP card-guessing
    performance." Journal of the American Society for
    Psychical Research, 1971, 65, 66-74.
_____, Davidson, R., & Bindler, P. "Feedback-augment-
    ed EEG alpha, shifts in subjective state, and ESP
    card-guessing performance." Journal of the American
    Society for Psychical Research, 1971, 65, 308-323.
Johnson, L. C. "A psychophysiology for all states." Psy-
    chophysiology, 1970, 6, 501-516.
Kreiman, N., & Ivnisky, D. "Effects of feedback on ESP
    responses." Cuadernos de Parapsicologia, 1973, 6
    (No. 2), 1-10.
Lewis, L., & Schmeidler, G. R. "Alpha relations with non-
    intentional and purposeful ESP after feedback." Jour-
    nal of the American Society for Psychical Research,
    1971, 65, 455-467.
McCallam, E., & Honorton, C. "Effects of feedback on dis-
    crimination between correct and incorrect ESP re-
    sponses: A further replication and extension." Jour-
    nal of the American Society for Psychical Research,
    1973, 67, 77-85.
McConnell, R. A. "Parapsychology and the occult." Journal
    of the American Society for Psychical Research, 1973,
    67, 225-243.
McElroy, W. A., & Brown, W. "Electric shocks for errors
    in ESP card tests." Journal of Parapsychology, 1950,
    14, 257-266.
McKnight, H. Silva Mind Control Through Psychorientology.
    Laredo, Texas: Institute of Psychorientology, Inc.,
    1972.

Morris, R. L. , Roll, W. G. , Klein, J. , & Wheeler, G.
"EEG patterns and ESP results in forced-choice ex-
periments with Lalsingh Harribance. " Journal of the
American Society for Psychical Research, 1972, 66,
253-268.
Murphy, G. , & Taves, E. "Current plans for investigations
in psychical research. " Journal of the American So-
ciety for Psychical Research, 1942, 36, 15-28.
Rao, K. R. , & Feola, J. "Alpha rhythm and ESP in a free
response situation. " In W. G. Roll, R. L. Morris,
& J. D. Morris (Eds.), Research in Parapsychology
1972. Metuchen, N. J. : Scarecrow Press, 1973.
Pp. 141-144.
Ryzl, M. "A method of training in ESP. " International
Journal of Parapsychology, 1966, 8, 501-532.
Schmeidler, G. R. , & Lewis, L. "A search for feedback
in ESP: Part II. High ESP scores after two suc-
cesses on triple-aspect targets. " Journal of the
American Society for Psychical Research, 1968, 62,
255-262.
Schmidt, H. "Precognition of a quantum process. " Journal
of Parapsychology, 1960, 33, 99-108.
_____ . "Clairvoyance tests with a machine. " Journal of
Parapsychology, 1969, 33, 300-306.
_____ , & Pantas, L. "Psi tests with internally different
machines. " Journal of Parapsychology, 1972, 36, 222-
232.
Stanford, R. G. "EEG alpha activity and ESP performance:
A replicative study. " Journal of the American Society
for Psychical Research, 1971, 65, 144-154.
_____ , & Lovin, C. "EEG alpha activity and ESP per-
formance. " Journal of the American Society for Psych-
ical Research, 1970, 64, 375-384.
_____ , & Palmer, J. "EEG alpha rhythms and free-response ESP performance. " In W. G. Roll, R. L.
Morris, & J. D. Morris (Eds.), Research in Parapsychology 1973. Metuchen, N. J. : Scarecrow Press,
1974. Pp. 48-50.
_____ , & Stanford, B. E. "Shifts in EEG alpha rhythm as
related to calling patterns and ESP run-score variance. "
Journal of Parapsychology, 1969, 33, 39-47.
_____ , & Stevenson, I. "EEG correlates of free-response
GESP in an individual subject. " Journal of the American Society for Psychical Research, 1972, 66, 357-
368.
Stephenson, C. J. "Cambridge ESP-hypnosis experiments
(1958-64). " Journal of the Society for Psychical Re-

search, 1965, 43, 77-91.
Targ, R., & Hurt, D. B. "Learning clairvoyance and precognition with an ESP teaching machine." Proceedings of the Parapsychological Association, 1971, 8,
9-11.
Tart, C. T. "Physiological correlates of psi cognition."
International Journal of Parapsychology, 1963, 5, 375-
386.
_____. "Card guessing tests: Learning paradigm or ex-
tinction paradigm?" Journal of the American Society
for Psychical Research, 1966, 60, 46-55.
Taves, E., & Dale, L. A. "The Midas touch in psychical
research." Journal of the American Society for Psych-
ical Research, 1943, 37, 57-83.
_____, _____, & Murphy, G. "A further report on the
Midas touch." Journal of the American Society for
Psychical Research, 1943, 37, 111-118.
Vaughan, A. "Investigation of Silva Mind Control claims."
In W. G. Roll, R. L. Morris, & J. D. Morris (Eds.),
Research in Parapsychology 1973. Metuchen, N. J.:
Scarecrow Press, 1974. P. 51.
Wallwork, S. C. "ESP experiments with simultaneous elec-
troencephalographic recordings." Journal of the So-
ciety for Psychical Research, 1952, 36, 697-701.

ADDITIONAL READINGS ON THE
"TRAINING" OF PSI ABILITY

Braud, W. G. "Psi-conducive states." Journal of Conscious-
ness 25: 142-52 (Win 1975).
Honorton, C. "ESP and altered states of consciousness."
In Beloff, J. (Ed.). New Directions in Parapsychol-
ogy. London, Elek Science, 1974. Metuchen, N. J.,
Scarecrow Press, 1975. Ch. 2.
_____. "Psi-conducive states of awareness." In Mitch-
ell, E. D. and others. Psychic Exploration. N. Y.,
Putnam's, 1974. Ch. 27.
Kanthamani, H. and Kelly, E. F. "Awareness of success in
an exceptional subject." JP 38: 355-82 (Dec 1974).
Kelly, E. and Kanthamani, B. "A subject's efforts toward
voluntary control." JP 36: 185-97 (Sept 1972).
Kreiman, N. and Ivnisky, D. "Effects of feedback on ESP
responses." Cuadernos de Parapsicologia 6: 1-10 (No.
2, 1973). Abstract in JP 37: 369 (Dec 1973).
LeShan, L. The Medium, the Mystic, and the Physicist.
N. Y., Viking, 1973.
Ojha, A. B. "Amount of knowledge in ESP and guessing
situations." Journal of General Psychology 71: 307-
12 (Oct 1964).
Pratt, J. G. "In search of the consistent scorer." In
Beloff, J. (Ed.). New Directions in Parapsychology.
London, Elek Science, 1974. Metuchen, N. J., Scare-
crow Press, 1975. Ch. 5.
Ryzl, M. How to Develop ESP in Yourself and in Others.
San Jose, Cal., The Author, 1973.
Targ, R., Cole, P., and Puthoff, H. "Development of tech-
niques to enhance man/machine communication." Men-
lo Park, Cal., Stanford Research Institute Project
2613 Report, 1974.
_____, and Hurt, D. "Use of an automatic stimulus gen-
erator to teach extrasensory perception." Proc. IEEE
International Symposium on Information Theory, 1972.
Tart, C. T. The Application of Learning Theory to ESP
Performance. N. Y., Parapsychology Foundation,
1975.
Thouless, R. H. "Experiments on psi self-training with Dr.
Schmidt's precognitive apparatus." JSPR 46: 15-21
(Mar 1971).

Van de Castle, R. "The facilitation of ESP through hypnosis."
    American Journal of Clinical Hypnosis 12: 37-56 (No.
    1, 1969).

PART IV

THEORIES OF PSI PHENOMENA

INTRODUCTION

It is often said that in order for parapsychology to achieve scientific acceptability it would have to provide a theoretical framework within which psi made sense. Parapsychology is criticized because it consists mainly of studies of anomalous facts which in themselves are at variance with everything else that science has revealed about the universe.

Nevertheless a number of theoretical models of psi operation have been proposed. The first paper in this section, "Consideration of Some Theories in Parapsychology" by K. R. Rao, is one of the best summaries of the major theories that have been set forth. Although it is not a recent paper, the theories described are still useful, and the additional readings point out many new approaches, including a new review by Rao himself.

In Part I, "Psi and Animal Behavior" by Robert Morris presented a survey of the evidence for psi ability in animals. In "Psi Phenomena and Biological Theory," John L. Randall reviews the implications of the evidence for anpsi as regards biological theory. His stated purpose is "to explore the possibility that psi, like electricity, may be all around us unobserved." He discusses psi in terms of its biological role in living organisms and in shaping evolution.

In order to progress, parapsychologists are in need of models of psi operation which will aid in the design of fruitful experiments and which will make sense of the results

obtained.   Although one of the most commonly used parapsychological terms is "extrasensory perception," it has not
been established that perception is the best model with which
to view cognitive forms of psi.   Roll's paper is a well-con-
sidered argument in behalf of using memory, rather than perception, as a model for psi operation.

Although too few scientists in other fields take the existence of psi seriously, there can be little doubt that if real,
psi phenomena have vastly important implications for the other
sciences: psychology, as would be expected, but also biology
and physics.   It is also obvious that parapsychology cannot
exist in a vacuum.   The future goal of parapsychology includes integrating what is known about psi with physics and
biology.   By the same token, a sophisticated physics and biology must take psi into consideration.   In the last paper in
this section, C. T. K. Chari shows how all attempts to create a physical theory to account for psi have failed thus far.
He points out the biological and physical implications of psi
and calls for an integrated approach by all three disciplines
if we are ever to understand truly the nature of man and
the world in which he lives.

Chapter 13

CONSIDERATION OF SOME THEORIES
IN PARAPSYCHOLOGY*

by K. Ramakrishna Rao

The scientist who is, at this stage, averse to accepting the evidence for ESP reminds us of the dogmatic professor of philosophy who refused to look at the planets through
Galileo's telescope. It is a mistake, however, to think, as
G. N. M. Tyrrell put it, that the human mind has been in-
stinctively so adapted as to deal only with the world revealed
by the senses and that consequently it is genetically prone to
disbelieve in ESP. Rather, the human mind has from time
immemorial kept pace with, and adapted to, the panorama of
startling facts, however antagonistic they may be to its prior
notions. It once even committed a "rape of the senses" by
accepting the Copernican hypothesis. And presumably it would
not hesitate to do so again when confronted with the fascinating facts of ESP if the parapsychologists could only put forward an intelligible explanation of these mysterious phenomena
of the human mind. It is therefore of importance to seek a
plausible theory that would account for ESP or at least to
formulate a working hypothesis that would justify present researches and stimulate future work. As a first step forward
in doing so, it is always interesting to see what has already
been said regarding the modus operandi of ESP; and it is with
this intention that the author proposes to review critically
some of the published theories dealing with it.

---

*Reprinted by permission of the author and publisher from
the Journal of Parapsychology, 25: 32-54 (Mar 1961).
       In the following pages no attempt is made to cover all
aspects of ESP. The notable exclusion is precognition, since
it involves many challenging notions that require lengthy and
independent treatment. The reader who is interested in the
theories of precognition may refer to the author's book, Psi
Cognition (Tagore Publishing House, Tenali, India).

I

A PHILOSOPHER'S VIEWS ON TELEPATHY

H. H. Price is one of those open-minded philosophers who accepted the theoretical challenge of ESP and sought to explain it.

Telepathy, according to Price, is not a form of knowing. Knowing, he says, has an "all or none" character. There is no intermediary stage between knowing and not-knowing; we either know a thing or do not. But in telepathy the percipient's impression may be partly true and partly false. Moreover, the percipient's experience seems to take no notice of the success or failure of his call. If telepathy is a form of knowing, there ought to be some difference in the experience when he calls the right card and when he calls the wrong one. Price says that he has no objection to calling telepathy a form of cognition. But he contends that telepathy is not knowing others' thoughts; rather, a telepathic experience is caused by a similar experience in others. "Telepathy," says Price, "is more like infection than like knowledge" (14).

The telepathic rapport observed by many investigators shows that individual minds have something in common. Price points out that the continuous telepathic rapport between two minds makes it foolish to argue for the plurality of minds. Between one mind and another there are no clear-cut boundaries. The division of minds is not "absolute and unconditional, either." The illusion of the individual mind arises out of the superficial nature of self-consciousness.

Price thinks that the unconscious portion of one mind may interact with that of another. Thus he is led to an assumption of the "collective unconscious." The collective unconscious which connects all the apparently individual minds is responsible for telepathic cognition. The collective unconscious, according to Price, is not an "entity" or a "thing" but a "field of interaction." Thus telepathy is possible because minds are not casually isolated entities. Unconscious events in one mind may produce unconscious events in other minds.

Price says that the human mind has developed a repressive mechanism which suppresses the continual flow of telepathic impact from one mind to another because there is

a biological need for such a mechanism. Otherwise the
thoughts, emotions, and feelings of all minds would be constantly received by everyone, and life would very likely become chaos, and action impossible. Psychoanalysts have indicated that the repressive mechanisms are partly in abeyance
during the states of relaxation and dreaming. If telepathic
influences are suppressed by similar mechanisms, they should
come through more often in the same mental states. Price
points out that in fact many spontaneous cases of telepathic
nature occur during dreams. The existence of a repressive
mechanism, he says, is also suggested by the fact that most
mediums enter into a state of dissociation which releases the
functioning of their abilities (13).

Price also makes a suggestion regarding the explanation of clairvoyance. He says that the unconscious part of
our minds may be capable of perceiving everything, however
remote in space, for the simple reason that the unconscious
may be in contact with all things. But we do not see all
things at once because the nervous system and the sense organs may be preventing us from doing so; and this process
is, of course, biologically relevant to us. Occasionally, however, when the physiological mechanism allows it, these unconscious contacts may actualize themselves in the conscious
in the form of psi experiences.

Price's theory leaves the essential intricacies of the
modus operandi of ESP unexplained. His suggestion about
the causal interaction of the unconscious portions of our minds
is helpful in explaining telepathy, but Price does not explain
in a detailed way the nature and implications of such an interaction. His contention regarding the repressive mechanism
is not new, for others, beginning with Bergson (1), have advocated a similar conception. An important omission in
Price is that he does not seem to suggest any clue to the
mysterious riddle of the "selecting process" in ESP; that is,
how one is able to select a particular telepathic communication out of the numerous impacts that are constantly present
in the unconscious. It is difficult to conceive how the repressive mechanism serves as a selecting agent.

II

COMPOUND THEORY OF C. D. BROAD

C. D. Broad uses the concept "paranormal" to include

such psi phenomena as clairvoyance, telepathy, precognition,
and psychokinesis. According to Broad, there are certain
synthetic principles which help to integrate various aspects
of human experience. These he calls the "basic limiting
principles." An event is paranormal if it seems prima facie
to conflict with any of these principles. For instance, a
clairvoyant event is paranormal because it contradicts the
basic limiting principle that: "It is impossible for a person
to perceive a physical event or a material thing except by
means of sensations which that event or thing produces in the
mind" (5).

Broad's definition of the paranormal is one of the most
analytical definitions in the field of parapsychology, but one
wonders if it is not simply a negative description of what the
paranormal is not, rather than a positive assertion of what it
is. However, this criticism should not belittle the importance
of Broad's analysis since what we know of psi is indeed
precious little.

As early as 1925, Broad put forward a hypothesis to
explain the mind-body relation (4). Convinced, as he is, of
the possibility and the reality of psi as revealed in the spontaneous material and the phenomena of trance mediumship,
he directed his hypothesis not only to explain the mind-body
relation, but also to accommodate for the paranormal and the
possibility of survival. According to this hypothesis, which
he calls the "compound theory," the mind is not a single substance. It is a compound of two substances, and neither of
them by itself has the characteristics of mind. These two
substances, as he called them in 1925, are the "psychic factor" and the "bodily factor" (4). In his Examination of Mc-
Taggart's Philosophy (2), he called the former the "psycho-
genic factor," and in his more recent California address,
"Human Personality and the Possibility of Its Survival" (3),
he calls it the " Ψ component. "

Such acts as perception, reasoning, and remembering
are not the functions of either of the factors by itself. Just as
a chemical compound possesses characteristics that do not belong individually to either of the constituents, the functions of
the mind are not to be found in either of its constituent elements.

Broad goes on to say that the psychic factor could persist even after the cessation of the body after death. When
a psychic factor is united with a body, it functions as a mind.

So a discarnate psychic factor will not have consciousness.
But when a psychic factor is united with a body, certain
traces are formed. If it so happens that a psychic factor
after its dissolution from the body with which it has so long
been associated comes into contact with any one of the living
organisms, as would be in the case of an entranced medium,
the newly formed mind of the medium may, in virtue of the
impressions this psychic factor had in the form of traces,
recall the experiences of the deceased person with whose
body the psychic factor had an occasion to associate.

It is possible to extend this hypothesis and argue that
the psychic factor has also the ability to psi-cognize or psi-
kinetize without being conscious of their effects. However,
we then have to assume that the psychic factor goes out to
reach for the object or thought in psi cognitive operations or
that it is in constant touch with all things and thoughts at all
times. If we assume the former, we have to argue that when
a thought, memory, or an experiential event is extrasensorially transferred from one person to another, as in telepathy,
the psychic factor in the mind of the former must have come
into contact with the body of the latter replacing its mind
temporarily. But this could be possible, so far as we know,
only if one of the persons involved in the situation were deceased or if he temporarily lost his mind or were at least
in the state of deep sleep. That this is not the case in successful ESP experiments and even in some spontaneous cases
argues against the plausibility of this alternative. If we admit the second possibility, that of universal and ominiscient
ESP, there would be no need for any traces in the psychic
factor in order to recall the experiences, since it is actually
in touch with all that is.

It is interesting to note that the logical modus operandi of psi as could be deduced from Broad's compound theory
is practically the same as Rhine's hypothesis of 1934 wherein
he speaks of the "going out" function of the mind.

III

RADICAL POSITIVISM AND THE
ASSOCIATION THEORY OF TELEPATHY

Whately Carington sought to formulate a working philosophy of psychical research which he styled "radical positivism." His fundamental postulate is that what is meaningful

must be verified by sensation or introspection. He says that
an analysis of our perceptions reveals to us that the real or
the meaningful in them is only sense data. Hence the real
are the sense data which he calls "cognital." Carington now
proceeds to put forward a novel conception of the mind in
terms of cognita and cognitum sequences. He argues that
to regard the mind as something other than the sense cognita
is entirely metaphysical and has no meaning. "The mind,"
he says, "is an immense assemblage of discrete particles"
(9). Individual minds are the "condensations" formed of cognita. They are not completely "discrete" and "isolate," but
are so formed as to possess a common something which may
be called the common unconscious or subconscious (9).

Carington thinks that this new conception of mind af-
fords a simple and meaningful explanation of the perplexing
phenomenon of telepathy. When two or more individuals are
faced with similar circumstances they are likely to have similar thoughts or mental images. For example, two persons
looking at the sea or thinking about it are likely to imagine
boats, waves, or beaches. In a telepathic experiment the
agent concentrates on a target (for example, a picture). The
idea of this target is probably associated with various thoughts
and ideas about the telepathy experiment. The percipient is
likely to have similar thoughts and ideas. Now, granted that
the minds of the agent and percipient are related in the common unconscious or subconscious, it is likely, says Carington, that the idea of the target will be brought to the percipient's mind because of its association with the idea of the
experiment in the agent's mind. Carington argues that the
principle of association of ideas renders this view plausible
(7).

He advances the following line of reasoning in favor
of his association theory of telepathy. It is demonstrated
by Soal and his associates that the subjects in a telepathy
experiment can do well with particular agents alone, which
means that the subject and the agent have something in common that binds them together. This implies that there are
close bonds of association and similarities between the minds
of the percipient and his agent. This is evident also in spontaneous telepathy which usually occurs between near relatives
and close friends who have common interests.

Carington introduces the concept of "K-ideas" to render the association theory of telepathy more intelligible. The
K-idea is a connecting link, or an associative bond, between

the agent and the percipient. The greater the number of K-ideas, the greater would be the probability of success in telepathy experiments. Carington explains the function of K-ideas by the following analogy. If an individual who is sailing in a boat wishes to send a heavy object to a person who is in another boat, he would naturally tie a rope to the object and throw the free end to the other boat. Now, the two boats are like the minds of the agent and the percipient; the rope is the connector or the K-idea, and the tying of the rope is the formation of an associative bond (7).

The association theory lacks adequate experimental evidence to show that the increase in the strength and number of K-ideas necessarily increases the rate of scoring in ESP experiments. Soal and Bateman (18) have experimented with Mrs. Stewart, a very successful subject, in order to test this implication of Carington's theory. They presented Mrs. Stewart with a photograph of the agent and later with a detailed sketch of the objects in the agent's room to increase the strength of K-ideas. The results of these experiments (the Cambridge-Richmond distance series) were statistically insignificant, and the most that can be said is that they failed to strengthen Carington's theory. The enormous success recorded in certain other card-guessing experiments, which did not appear to foster the formation of associative bonds between the agent and percipient, also stands against Carington's theory. Finally, Carington's theory gives no explanation for the clairvoyant mode of ESP, though Carington himself considered that it is inherently impossible to distinguish between telepathy and clairvoyance (8).

IV

TYRRELL'S THEORY OF THE SUBLIMINAL SELF

According to G. N. M. Tyrrell, human personality at the conscious level is a special adaptation to a certain kind of life steered by the senses. Psychical experiences (ESP, etc.), as well as clinical psychology and mystical experiences, suggest a region of human personality beyond the conscious. This unconscious portion of our personality, which is capable of receiving telepathic and other extrasensory types of communication, is what Tyrrell, along with Myers, calls the "subliminal self" (22).

Telepathy, according to Tyrrell, consists in some sort

of cognitive relationship between the subliminal selves of two
individuals. "The subliminal or extraconscious region of the
self," he says, "contains an enormous range of things, high
and low, transcendental and trivial. All are obliged to pass
through the bottle-neck at the threshold if they are to reach
the normal consciousness, and in doing so, all make use of
the principle of mediation by means of constructs" (23).

Now, according to Tyrrell, the communications and
perceptions received at the subliminal level are pushed into
consciousness in a symbolic guise or in a distorted form as
a mental image or the like. The "tools" by which the unconsciously received psi cognitions are externalized in consciousness are called by Tyrrell the "mediating vehicles."
These vehicles include dreams, sensory hallucinations, automatic writing, mental images, or strong emotion. Tyrrell
rightly attaches great significance to this process of mediation. In telepathic dreams, the unconsciously received telepathic contact is exhibited in the same way as the content of
normal dreams (21).

In psi cognitions, according to Tyrrell, human personalities are able to overcome the space-time barriers because
the subliminal selves, which enter into paranormal cognitive
relations, do not exist in space and time. Subliminal selves
do not exist in the world of our sense perception but "elsewhere" where space and time have no domain.

Tyrrell says that he can give no clear description of
this "elsewhere." He argues that language is incompetent to
deal with things like this. Even as to the nature of subliminal selves he gives no lucid description apart from believing
in their existence. He writes: "Extrasensory faculty may
result from the circumstance that subliminal selves are neither singular nor plural; neither one nor many in their nature,
but simply inconceivable" (22).

Tyrrell's views regarding the modus operandi of telepathy may be summarized as follows: In a telepathic cognition,
the subliminal selves of the agent and the percipient are in a
kind of relationship so that the subliminal self of the percipient has a "propositional awareness" of the agent's subliminal
impressions. Telepathic cognition results if the percipient's
subliminal awareness regarding the agent is manifested in the
consciousness of the percipient by means of a mediating vehicle.

Tyrrell's theory is based on many unwarranted assumptions. His exposition of the nature of the subliminal self is ambiguous and vague. Even granting the reality of subliminal selves, we fail to see how these subliminal selves enter into that relationship by virtue of which one self can have the propositional awareness of another's subliminal impressions. His conception of the unknown "elsewhere" sounds mystical and does not provide any plausible explanation for the transmission of subliminal impressions from one self to another.

The major contribution Tyrrell made consists in his re-emphasizing the process of mediation. His conception of mediating vehicles and his contention that both telepathic dreams and normal dreams exhibit the same form in externalizing the unconscious contents promises a new and important field of ESP research which might unravel the complexities of this mystifying phenomenon of the human mind.

V

JAN EHRENWALD AND THE PSI LEVEL
OF PERSONALITY

Freudian analysis of human behavior has emphasized how the picture of reality may be distorted by instinctive drives and complexes. Freudians have recognized the subliminal forces of the personality. Their conceptions of the unconscious and the id are much nearer to the idea of psi-functioning than most other concepts of human personality. As the psychoanalysts postulated the id-level of functioning, so Dr. Ehrenwald, a psychiatrist himself, seeks to explain ESP by conceiving of a third level of personality functioning which he calls the "psi-level" (10). According to Ehrenwald, psi is a particular part of psychic reality, as is the id. The familiar laws of nature, with their dependence on space and time, which govern the personality at the ego- and the id-levels are not applicable to psi-functioning. Ehrenwald says that "psi is a medium common to all humanity whether or not we are aware of it."

He suggests two important factors that determine the manifestation of psi impulses in consciousness: (1) Impulses of high emotional tension are more likely to manifest in consciousness than those of lower emotional tension; and (2) the greater the degree of intellectual organization and complexity,

the less is the likelihood that these impulses will break
through the barriers that separate the psi from the ego.

Ehrenwald's conception of the psi-level of personality
functioning has very little to say regarding the modus operandi of ESP.   It particularly fails to render intelligible the
process by means of which telepathic or clairvoyant impressions are received at the psi-level.

VI

J. B. RHINE'S THEORY

This less known hypothesis rests on two assumptions:
(1) That some agency of mind which can function to some extent independently of the physical world is operative in ESP;
and (2) that this agency has the capacity to "go out" to meet
the object which is outside the organism it occupies.

According to Rhine (15), psi phenomena suggest the
existence of mind that under certain circumstances and to
some extent can function independently of the physical limitations of the material body.   Relation to space has been considered an invariable characteristic of physical operations.
All our perceptual experiences, as far as they relate to the
material world, are organized into the framework of space.
But with regard to ESP, space apparently has no influence,
and the inverse square laws, etc. , are inapplicable to it,
for no reliable relation has been found between the distance
of the percipient from the target or agent and the success
or failure of the percipient's calls in ESP tests.   In view of
this strange phenomenon and of the evidence of precognition,
unknown to the physical world, Rhine goes on to suggest,
there might well be some other energy, one peculiar to mind,
which is radically different from material energies.   He considers that the source of these distinctive results must be
sought in the nature of the mind capable of such effects.

Further, the success in ESP experiments is relatively
independent of the nature of the thing to be cognized.   It does
not make any difference to the percipient's success whether
the target of his guess is something material like an ESP
test card, or a thought, as in the case of pure telepathy.
Several outstanding subjects in ESP experiments have averaged
about the same in telepathy and clairvoyance tests.   Thus, in
ESP experiments, successful results are obtained with a di-

versity of stimulation, ranging from a material object to a
mental image and even to an object that will exist only at a
future time. In sensory experience, on the contrary, we find
different stimuli giving rise to different types of experience.
Hence, argues Rhine, the only way to render these facts intelligible is to recognize the need of a mental function capable of action independent of the limitations that define physical
reality.

Rhine goes on to make another important suggestion.
He says it appears that the mind "goes out" to perceive extrasensorially. It is not that the mind receives the different
patterns of energy emanating from the objects in order to interpret them but that the mind of the percipient takes the initiative to ESP. Thus the mind's relative independence of the
material universe consists in this appearance of mental causality, which is supported by the observation that space and time
have shown no limiting effect on psi ability (15). [Rhine has
offered these suggestions only tentatively in his first book,
Extrasensory Perception. But this hypothesis represents a
dominant trend in parapsychical speculations.]

In later publications--for example, in New World of
the Mind (16)--Rhine considers the possibility of a mental
energy operative in psi phenomena, an energy not subject to
the familiar conditions of space-time-mass that identify and
belong to physical reality. This energy, like the more familiar energies, is convertible to other forms, and in this way
its operations can be detected by its secondary effects. The
cognitive (ESP) effects of psi result from converting parapsychical energy to the physiological energy of the brain system; the psychokinetic effects of psi result from conversion
of parapsychical energy so that it acts on a material system,
such as rolling dice. The question is left whether psi may
not operate in an energetic order that in itself has no space-
time. Rhine emphasizes the unifying interaction of the mind
with the physical world, even while calling attention to the
valid distinctions parapsychology has established.

VII

THE "SHIN" THEORY OF
R. H. THOULESS AND B. P. WIESNER

The hypothesis of Thouless and Wiesner (19) starts
from the similarity between the normal and paranormal pro-

cesses, and suggests that these two processes are not radically different and that in either case no unusual entity is operative. There is no actual representation of the cognized object in either psi cognition or normal sense perception. In all the spontaneous manifestations of ESP, the symbolic or distorted representation of psi cognitions is evident. In normal sense perception also the image of the object that is cognized is not perceived directly. It is true, of course, that the content of a cognition resembles the object in most cases, but the immediate causal antecedent of our sense perceptions is not the object but the nervous system and the brain. Hence, both psi cognition and sense perception are but the results of processes in the brain and the nervous system.

"In normal thinking and perceiving," Thouless and Wiesner say, "I am in the same sort of relation to what is going on in the sensory part of my brain and nervous system as that of the successful clairvoyant to some external event, and that this relation is established by the same means" (19). In an act of perception, according to their view, we are not aware of the immediate cause of our perceptions, the cause being the changes in the brain and nervous system. So also, a successful clairvoyant is not aware of the object of his cognition, which is the immediate "causal ancestor" of his cognition. Then normal perception differs from clairvoyance in that the former is mediated by the brain and nervous system. In the case of clairvoyant perception a direct contact between the subject and the object is established.

Shin and Psi Cognition

Thouless and Wiesner (along with some of the nineteenth century thinkers, notably Braid) assume that there is some entity which is involved in our processes of volition and perception, which they call "Shin." Shin is almost like the soul, but they prefer to avoid the usage of the concept "soul," as it carries a certain connotation which is partly outside the field of parapsychology. Shin is always operative in sensory as well as extrasensory cognitions. It is constantly being informed of our sensory perceptions. Its cognitions are received from the perceptual side and its volitions are activated on the motor side. In normal perceptions, Shin is mediated by the brain and nervous system, and in psi cognitions, such as clairvoyance, it is directly connected with the object.

Sensory stimuli emanating from the object act on the sensory part of the nervous system. Shin is informed by the processes in the nervous system, and, in turn, Shin controls the motor part of the nervous system. On the other hand, in the processes of clairvoyance, direct connections are established between Shin and the object, without the intervention of the brain and the nervous system. Thus psi cognitions are not supernormal, but, as Thouless and Wiesner put it, are "exo-somatic forms of processes which are normally endosomatic."

Thouless and Wiesner define telepathy as a "process of Shin acting on, or being acted on by, a nervous system other than its own." In every normal act of perception Shin is informed of the processes in its own nervous system. Thouless and Wiesner suggest that it might so happen sometimes that Shin develops contacts with some nervous system other than its own and is thus aware of processes of that other nervous system. Telepathy, then, would be like any other process of perception except that it would involve cognitive relations with a nervous system which is outside the body in which Shin is residing.

Thouless and Wiesner point out that a volitional effort in ESP tends to inhibit success. They seek to interpret this in support of their hypothesis. Thus they argue that the volitional efforts put forth are likely to direct Shin activity to the habitual sensory modes of perception and, consequently, prevent Shin's direct contact with the object. This is, however, a questionable argument. Many successful clairvoyants, particularly mediums, claim to exercise a lot of volitional effort to achieve success. Miss Johnson, who showed ESP to a marked degree, did this "successfully, but not without great nervous strain," says Tyrrell (20). Rhine's brilliant subject Pearce scored all the twenty-five cards when Rhine goaded him by betting on the outcome (15). Thouless and Wiesner think that the action of the nervous system may inhibit psi-functioning. But volitional effort need not put the nervous system into action; on the other hand, it may control its activity. As pointed out by Craig Sinclair, concentration and relaxation may be equally necessary for success. Mrs. Sinclair means perhaps the same when she says, "a part of concentration is complete relaxation" (17).

The hypothesis of Thouless and Wiesner is essentially a development of Rhine's. However, this is disguised by their use of the term "Shin" and their failure to touch upon an im-

portant implication of their Shin theory. They say that the
direct contact of Shin with the object, without the mediation
of the brain and the nervous system, is the necessary condition of clairvoyant cognition and that the direct contact of
Shin with the brain and the nervous system other than its own
is telepathy. Now it may be asked How is the percipient's
Shin able to reach the object which is outside the body it occupies? The laws of causation do not permit us to assume
that Shin sits inside and yet is capable of perceiving distant
objects without any causal connections in between.

        C. D. Broad's analysis (6) of causal objection to pre-
cognition applies mutatis mutandis to the Shin activity.
Therefore it is evidently impossible for Shin to perceive objects unless the radiating patterns of energy emanating from
the object are reflected without sensory aid on Shin, or Shin
is assumed to be capable of forcing itself on the objects external to the organism and extending in space, without itself
being subjected to the laws of space. The known laws of
nature render the first alternative impossible. Hence, the
only way to make the operation of Shin in psi processes consistent with the known order of reality is to assume that
Shin, a part of it, or an agent of it goes out to the object
to perceive extrasensorially.

        This is essentially what Rhine means when he says
that the mind or an agent of it "goes out" to perceive extrasensorially (15); or, alternately, when he later adds that the
mind may function through an energy form not conditioned to
time-space-mass relations (16). The difference between
Rhine and Thouless consists in the use of different terms,
"mind" and "Shin," and perhaps Thouless and Wiesner are
justified in giving currency to the new term "Shin" since it
is not vitiated by any previous metaphysical connotation, as
is the case with the term "mind."

                                VIII

                      FLEW'S "GUESS WORK"

        Antony Flew expresses his concern over the "mind
talk" of some parapsychologists that their findings provide
evidence for metaphysical dualism (11). This, according to
him, is "philosophical sensationalism" which is due in part
to the misunderstanding of the "logic of terms" in which psi
is popularly described, and partly because of the setting up

of inappropriate explanatory models.   Flew directs his comments especially against Rhine whose "mind terminology"
worried him considerably.   He complains that Rhine "mis-
construes its logic" by thinking that the mind is a kind of
object, something more than human capacities, feelings, and
aspirations.   For the readers of the Journal of Parapsychology, Dr. Rhine does not stand in need of any defense, for he
never meant by mind, as far as I can see, an objective entity distinguishable apart from its functions.   I am sure that
Flew would not deny that some of these functions seem to defy the known laws of space and time.   I must confess, however, that some of Dr. Rhine's own statements can be easily
misconstrued to indicate a naive metaphysical dualism which
I abhor no less.   That this is not a correct expression of
his views is evident from many statements he has since made.
Those who are not still convinced of this may profitably refer
to his editorial in the December, 1945, issue of the Journal
of Parapsychology.

          The concept of ESP, Flew argues, suggests an explan-
atory model of perception, but ESP is very different from
perception in essential respects.   He goes on to say that such
paradoxes as Dunne's concept of time are patently due to taking seriously the perceptive models of ESP.   If we cannot
explain ESP on the model of perception, how else could we
do it?   Flew thinks that it is more fruitful to consider ESP
as a "species of guess work" (11).   But one fails to see,
even granting an explainable connection between the subject's
guesses and some other psychological factors associated with
it, what purpose this new model would serve for ESP.   As
Mundle succinctly points out, Flew's "guess work" model
could neither describe nor explain the facts of ESP any more
appropriately than the perception model of the parapsychologists (12).

                              DISCUSSION

          It would appear that each of the theories discussed
above finds it necessary to assume a hitherto unknown "entity" operative in all our psi cognitions--whether it be the
collective unconscious, subliminal self, mind, or Shin--which
is capable of breaking through the barriers of space and
time.   Moreover, its extrasensory awareness ("propositional"
or "perceptual") of objects or of thoughts and the processes
involved in its operations fall beneath the threshold of the subject's consciousness.

If the assumed entity is isolated as well as distinct from and independent of human personality, the problem arises: How does this entity interact with conscious personality so as to manifest its non-sensory awareness of objects in consciousness in the form of images thoughts, etc. ? No known analogy provides any basis for the solution of this problem. However, if the functions of the assumed entity are ascribed to some portions of personality, the problem becomes simple and an intelligible solution is possible. As Tyrrell (21) suggests, the "mediating vehicles" such as dreams, automatic writing, sensory hallucinations, etc. may be regarded as analogous to the repressed consciousness--as the "tools" by which ESP impressions are manifested in consciousness. In this context, Jan Ehrenwald's conception of the psi-level of personality functioning seems very significant (10).

An important problem on which the aforesaid theories seem to disagree concerns the way in which extrasensory perceptions are received at the psi-level. There are two important views regarding the operation of the psi personality: (1) that this portion of our personality is in touch with all objects, however remote they may be in time and space; and (2) that it has the ability to function independently of the body and to extend itself in space without itself being subjected to the laws of space. The first view leads to two serious consequences. First, if the personality is in touch with all objects, how is it that we are able to know so very few things extrasensorially? It is commonly said that human beings have developed a repressive mechanism which prevents them from knowing extrasensorially. However, it remains to be seen how, if it exists, this repressive mechanism operates. Secondly, it has to be explained how the subject in a card-guessing experiment is able to hit the target which is one among twenty-five similar cards. It is pointed out that the desire of the subject may be responsible for the selection of the target card. But desire and will are functions that, so far as we know, belong to the brain and nervous system and not to a distinct psi function. Further, some investigators have observed negative ESP effects, although their subjects exercised their will to guess the right card.

The second view, however, does not entail these difficulties. The relaxation of the brain and nervous activity is conducive to ESP success because the psi division of the total personality is at liberty to initiate contact with the desired object. Or if space and time do not exist for the realm of purely mental energetics, there is no "travel" to be done, as there is no separation.

But if psi is considered an aspect of personality, it
is no more nonphysical than man himself, and it is as much
physical as his personality. Psi function is then not any
more different from other aspects of personality than an atom
is different from a molecule or an electron from an atom.
We would seem to have overstated our case when we stress
the nonphysicality of ESP. On the one hand, if by nonphysical we mean something different in certain respects from
what is merely regarded as physical, just as memory is different from the function of an electronic brain, there would
be no dispute about it. But that this is not the sense in
which it is used is fairly obvious.

On the other hand, if we mean by nonphysical something nonmaterial in the sense of possessing no known characteristics of such psychological functions as perception,
thought, and desire, our assumption would seem to be quite
contrary to the spirit of investigations which are solely designed to find out the physical, physiological, and psychological conditions that would help or hinder the manifestation of
psi. We may not know precisely what psi is; but surely it
is something that happens in a physical world and is known
through physical media. Whether or not psi fits into the
world we know, it is something inescapably "co-extensive"
with the physical world.

I am sure that this is a fairly obvious position, and
many parapsychologists do not dispute its truth, even if they
hold that psi is nonphysical. The controversy, it seems to
me, is wholly due to the misuse of certain concepts. And
what we need in parapsychology today is a close examination
and scrutiny of the parapsychological concepts. Philosophers
would contribute a great service to this infant science, if,
instead of throwing in ideas that make a mystery out of a
muddle, they would help to organize a conceptual framework
within which the parapsychologist could paint the picture of
his fascinating field.

A moment's reflection, for instance, would show how,
once we assume that psi is nonphysical and nonsensory, we
land ourselves in paradoxes and confront formidable questions.
The physical nature of man, as far as his cognitive aspect is
concerned, consists in his dependence on the senses for any
information about the world external to him. It is claimed
that psi is nonsensory. The absence of any need of orientation, the failure to locate any other sense, and the lack of
any known stimulating energy have been considered to indicate

its nonsensory nature. And the alleged ineffectiveness of time
and space is regarded as conclusive proof that psi is nonphysical. It may be noted, however, that the absence of the
need of orientation etc. , does not warrant the conclusion that
psi is nonsensory or nonphysical. It is not antecedently improbable that the function of the senses and the nervous system are different from what we know of them in normal
modes of sensory communication.

       If psi is considered to be devoid of any relation to the
human senses, some formidable questions arise. The colors,
sounds, etc. , are not inherently present in the objects themselves. They depend on our modes of cognition for their existence. Now, if a percipient in a clairvoyant experiment is
assumed to come into direct contact with the object, and the
senses have no function whatsoever to perform in the whole
process, would not the objects in such a situation appear differently, i. e. , without color, etc. ? The question whether
there could be any psi cognitions without the appropriate senses
is interesting and one that is worth while to investigate. Can
a man who was born blind record equal success on visual as
well as auditory targets?

       All figures involve space relations, and ESP subjects
have been found successful with figures as their targets.
Would it not then involve us in a contradiction to assume that
pictures and figures can be known by a process to which space
relations do not make any sense? If space is unreal in the
region of psi, can any subject make any possible distinction
between a square and a cross in a pack of ESP cards? It
is reported that caffeine has a positive effect and sodium
amytal a negative effect on ESP scoring. What does this
mean? Does it not mean that better results could be obtained
by physically stimulating the organism and that physiological
processes have a significant role to play in the functioning of
psi? If fatigue is detrimental, relaxation conducive, and
motivation essential for psi success, cannot we expect to understand, if not account for, psi by means of certain known
concepts?

       Most of the nonphysical hypotheses seem to stem from
an argument somewhat similar to the following. Psi is either
physical or nonphysical. If it is physical, it is subject to
the known physical laws. Since psi cannot fit into the framework of the known order of nature, it is nonphysical and can
be explained only by assuming a nonphysical entity operating
within and influencing the physical world. The main function

of this nonphysical entity is to provide us with a means of over-riding the physical limitations of the physical laws. Consider, for example, the alternatives of a possible cognitive relation between the subject and its object. In order that there could be a cognitive relation between the subject and its object, either the object should be capable of forcing itself on the subject, or the subject itself should be able to reach the object, or the subject and the object should be in continuous contact with each other in virtue of the fact that they are parts of an interrelated system.

The first alternative would amount to a "physical" hypothesis. Since the object in a clairvoyant situation is avowedly a material something, the only way it could make its impact felt on the subject is to emanate energy patterns that could be received by the subject. Since no such energy pattern which could travel in any known medium is discovered, this hypothesis would seem to be far-fetched. In the second alternative the subject is assumed to be capable of forcing himself on the objects external to him and extending in space without his being subject to the laws of space. We find a number of hypotheses based on this assumption throughout the literature of parapsychology. For example, Dr. Rhine suggested in his very first book that the mind or an agent of it "goes out" to perceive extrasensorially. He argues that the mind's relative independence of the material universe consists in its "going out," and it is this "going out" that makes space and time more or less ineffective. It is obvious how an impassable gulf is created between the mind and matter in order to account for the relation between the subject and object in a situation where there is perfect harmony between the two even granting the dichotomy. The third alternative, instead of endowing everyone with this mysterious agency, postulates one universal nonphysical something in which all the physical things can participate and share its potentialities. A typical example is H. H. Price's hypothesis of a "collective unconscious." He thinks that the collective unconscious is a "field of interaction" where minds meet to exchange information. It may be possible, he argues, that our minds are in contact with all things, thus enabling us to perceive everything. It is evident how Price is endeavoring to relate the subject and the object to explain a physical relation in a nonphysical way.

It would seem that this way of looking at psi leads us nowhere. Firstly, the question whether psi is physical or nonphysical does not seem to throw any light on its nature. And

secondly, it is paradoxical to consider psi as a species of
perception and at the same time nonsensory. There is no
evidence that psi involves perceptual awareness. If this is
agreed upon, one need not look for the transmission of waves,
or the establishment of nonphysical relations between the subjects and their cognitive objects. Nor is there any evidence
that psi is nonsensory.

If we ignore the physical-nonphysical dualism, one may
wonder how we could possibly define parapsychology, as most
of our theoretical talk has assumed this dichotomy, more or
less. It seems to me that an essentially functional and natu-
ralistic definition is possible and would be fruitful at this stage
of parapsychology. We deal in parapsychology with behavior.
We assume that it is observable and measurable. May not
we, then, define parapsychology as a branch of psychology
which deals with those aspects of cognitive and kinetic behavior that do not seem to involve any hitherto known modes of
sensory participation? We may find one of these days, if
we can trust the yogic practices, that psi is after all a function of and is generated by the exercise of primordial imagination.

In concluding this paper, I want to make it clear, in
the first place, that I am not arguing for the physicality of
psi. To do so is quite contrary to the position I have taken
in the preceding pages. I do not see how we could, at this
stage of our research, meaningfully define either physicality
or nonphysicality in relation to psi without making dubious
assumptions that lead us to paradoxical positions.

In the second place, my reference to imagination should
not be construed as a hypothesis I am prepared to defend,
even though psi, in its cognitive aspect, would seem to me
more like imagination than perception. My purpose in bringing in imagination here is only to show the inadequacy of perception as an explanatory model of psi cognitions.

In perception, the object to be perceived is an active
agent. The size, color, and surroundings of the object affect perceptions. But this does not seem to be the case with
psi cognitions, which, in this report, are more like imagination. We know that excessive imagination, at least in certain
cases, could produce hallucinations, day dreams, etc. , which
are also found to be the tools by which spontaneous psi cognitions are manifested. The perceptive model creates an

artificial distinction between telepathy and clairvoyance which, on the model I am suggesting, would be imagination directed towards the thoughts of certain persons and towards objects and events respectively. But even if we can accept imagination as a closer parallel to ESP than perception, we have to recognize that it would be imagination plus something more than what that term ordinarily connotes.

Finally, if psi is more like imagination, there is no need to assume that psi is nonphysical, for the nonphysicalistic hypothesis derives its force from the perceptive model on which psi is unwarrantedly based. If the argument simply is that psi is nonphysical because it transcends space and time, then it can also be argued that psi is as much physical as thought and imagination, for you can imagine physical things however remote they may be in space and time.

But the nonphysicalists would argue, I presume, that psi is nonphysical insofar as it is perception and at the same time it transcends space and time, which makes it nonsensory and nonphysical. In other words, the whole force of the hypothesis that psi is nonphysical is based on the assumed similarity of psi to perception. But this is a questionable assumption.

Having said this, I must confess, however, that parapsychologists have the "right to believe" that their phenomenon is nonphysical if this has any useful consequences to them and if their position does not conflict with their actual findings or retard their experimentation. I have only tried to point out some of the logical difficulties this position would entail, and the undesirable consequences it may have on the planning and conducting of psi experiments. It is for the individual investigator to judge the fruitfulness or the uselessness of these suggestions.

REFERENCES

1. Bergson, H. Mind Energy. New York: Henry Holt, 1920.
2. Broad, C. D. Examination of McTaggart's Philosophy. (Two volumes.) Cambridge: Cambridge University Press, 1933, 1938.
3. _____ . Human Personality and the Possibility of Its Survival. Berkeley: Univ. of California Press, 1955.

4. _____. Mind and Its Place in Nature. New York:
      The Humanities Press, 1951.
5. _____. Religion, Philosophy, and Psychical Research.
      New York: Harcourt, Brace & Co., 1953.
6. _____, and Price, H. H. "The Philosophical Impli-
      cations of Precognition." Aristotelian Society, Sup-
      plementary Volume 16, 1937.
7. Carington, W. Thought Transference. New York:
      Creative Age Press, 1946.
8. _____. "Comments on Dr. Rhine's 'Telepathy and
      Clairvoyance Reconsidered.'" Proc. Soc. Psych.
      Res., 1946, 48, 8-27.
9. _____. Matter, Mind and Meaning. New Haven:
      Yale University Press, 1949.
10. Ehrenwald, J. New Dimensions of Deep Analysis. Lon-
      don: Allen & Unwin, 1954.
11. Flew, A. G. N. "Minds and mystifications." The
      Listener. Sept. 27, 1951; Oct. 4, 1951.
12. Mundle, C. W. K. "Some philosophical perspectives
      for parapsychology." J. Parapsychol., 1952, 16,
      257-72.
13. Price, H. H. "Psychical research and human person-
      ality." Hibbert Journal, 1949, 47, 105-13.
14. _____. "Some philosophical questions about telepathy
      and clairvoyance." Philosophy, 1940, 15, 363-74.
15. Rhine, J. B. Extrasensory Perception. Boston:
      Bruce Humphries, 1935.
16. _____. New World of the Mind. New York: William
      Sloane Associates, 1953.
17. Sinclair, U. Mental Radio. Monrovia, Calif.: Upton
      Sinclair, 1930.
18. Soal, S. G., and Bateman, F. Modern Experiments
      in Telepathy. New Haven: Yale Univ. Press,
      1954.
19. Thouless, R. H., and Wiesner, B. P. "The psi pro-
      cess in normal and 'paranormal' psychology."
      Proc. Soc. Psych. Res., 1947, 48, 177-96.
20. Tyrrell, G. N. M. Science and Psychical Phenomena.
      New York: Harpers, 1938.
21. _____. "The modus operandi of paranormal cogni-
      tion." Proc. Soc. Psych. Res., 1947, 48, 65-120.
22. _____. Personality of Man. West Drayton, England:
      Penguin Books, 1948.
23. _____. "Reason, inspiration and telepathy." Hib-
      bert Journal, 1947, 45, 327-33.

ADDITIONAL READINGS ON SPECIFIC MODELS
OF PSI PHENOMENA

Dobbs, A. "The feasibility of a physical theory of ESP."
In Smythies, J. R. (Ed.). Science and ESP. N. Y.,
Humanities Press, 1967. Ch. 10.

Ehrenwald, J. "Parapsychology and the seven dragons: A
neuropsychiatric model of psi phenomena." In Schmeidler, G. R. (Ed.). Parapsychology: Its Relation to
Physics, Biology, Psychology and Psychiatry. Metuch-
en, N. J., Scarecrow Press, 1976.

Gauld, A. "The 'super-ESP' hypothesis." PSPR 53: 226-
46 (Pt. 192, Oct 1961).

Heywood, R. The Sixth Sense. Rev. ed. London, Pan
Books, 1961. Appendix: "Some explanations and hypotheses." (Orig. publ. in U. S. under title: Beyond
the Reach of Sense. OP.).

Kreitler, H. and Kreitler, S. "ESP and cognition." JP 38:
267-85 (Sep 1974).

LeShan, L. The Medium, the Mystic, and the Physicist.
N. Y., Viking, 1974.

Morris, R. L. "Building experimental models." Journal of
Communication 25: 117-25 (Win 1975).

Mundle, C. W. K. "The explanation of ESP." In Smythies,
J. R. (Ed.). Science and ESP. N. Y., Humanities
Press, 1967. Ch. 8.

_____. "Strange facts in search of a theory." PSPR 56:
1-20 (Pt 207, Jan 1973).

Rao, K. R. Experimental Parapsychology. Springfield, Ill.,
Charles C. Thomas, 1966. Ch. 6.

Roll, W. G. "The psi field." P. A. Proc. No. 1: 32-65,
1964.

Scott, C. "Models for psi." PSPR 53: 195-225 (Pt 192,
Oct 1961).

Stanford, R. G. "Concept and psi." RP 2: 137-62, 1973.

_____. "An experimentally testable model for spontaneous
psi events. I. Extrasensory events." JASPR 68:
34-57 (Jan 1974).

_____. "An experimentally testable model for spontaneous
psi events. II. Psychokinetic events." JASPR 68:
321-56 (Oct 1974).

Tart, C. T. "Models for the explanation of extrasensory
perception." Int. J. Neuropsychiatry 10: 37-56 (Spr

1968).

_____. "Preliminary notes on the nature of psi processes."
In Ornstein, R. E. (Ed.). The Nature of Human Consciousness. N. Y., Viking, 1974. Ch. 41.

Chapter 14

PSI PHENOMENA AND
BIOLOGICAL THEORY*

by John L. Randall

For several thousand years electricity was known to
mankind only in the form of the spontaneous phenomenon of
the lightning flash, and the curious behaviour of small pieces
of amber when rubbed with a silk cloth. Even when scientists such as Galvani and Volta managed to bring electricity
into the laboratory, it still remained nothing more than a
curiosity, a spare-time occupation for the leisured amateur.
Who could have foreseen, in those days, that the very nature
of matter itself would turn out to be electrical? Yet today
we know that even an apparently uncharged piece of matter
is nevertheless composed of electricity.

There is a striking parallel here to the situation in
parapsychology. Thanks to the pioneering work of Dr. Rhine
and his colleagues we have now reached the stage where psi
can be studied in the laboratory; but we have not yet discovered how it fits into the natural world. Until we do so, it
is unlikely that the world at large will regard psi as anything more than a minor curiosity. It is the purpose of this
paper to explore the possibility that psi, like electricity, may
be all around us unobserved. It will be suggested, in fact,
that psi is constantly active in every living organism and has
played a major part in shaping the course of evolution.

Mechanistic Biology

At first sight, present day biological theory does not
seem to leave much room for psi. The rapidly advancing

*Reprinted by permission of the author and publisher from
the Journal of the Society for Psychical Research 46: 151-
65 (Sept. 1971).

sciences of genetics and molecular biology have made it possible to elucidate the innermost structures of cells, and the
cracking of the genetic code has left many people with the
feeling that all the basic processes of life are now known, and
it only remains for the biologists of the future to fill in the
details. Life, it appears, is essentially mechanistic, so that
organisms can be satisfactorily regarded as self-regulating
machines. There is no further need for such metaphysical
concepts as "will," "purposiveness" or "consciousness." As
a recent writer puts it (9):

> The vitalist theory, undermined in the first instance
> by Wöhler's synthesis of urea, hastened by Büchner's
> isolation of the first cell-free enzyme, now awaits
> its final overthrow by the first in vitro synthesis of
> the hereditary material, indistinguishable in all re-
> spects from the product of the cell.

It is worth pointing out, however, that a similar spirit
of breezy confidence was felt by the physicists of the 19th
century; they too believed that their science had reached the
stage of being able to account for most of the phenomena of
the physical world. Yet within a few years the whole scheme
of Newtonian mechanics, virtually unchallenged for two hundred years, was to be swept aside with the advent of Relativity and the Quantum Theory. The revolution was brought
about by a very small number of apparently unimportant facts
which did not quite fit into the classical scheme. Again, the
resemblance to the situation in parapsychology is an obvious
one.

Although most of the 'official' biological text-books
manage to convey the impression that the mechanistic view
of the origin and evolution of life is universally accepted a-
mong men of science, this is in fact far from being the case.
In the summer of 1968 Arthur Koestler organised, in the
Austrian village of Alpbach, a symposium of scientists who
were "critical of the totalitarian claims of the neo-Darwin-
ian orthodoxy." The symposium seems to have been sparked
off by a remark of Dr. Thorpe to the effect that there is "an
undercurrent of thought in the minds of perhaps hundreds of
biologists" who find it difficult to believe in the currently accepted reductionist theories of life and of mind. The papers
and discussions of the sixteen distinguished scientists who
took part have since been published in book form (18), and
provide a fascinating insight into some of the theoretical problems which are at present engaging the attentions of leading

thinkers in the life sciences.   In this paper I propose first
to examine some of these problems, and then to suggest possible ways in which parapsychology may point towards their
solution.

The Origin of Life

Sir Frederick Gowland Hopkins, the discoverer of vit-
amins, once described the origin of life as "the most improbable and the most significant event in the history of the universe. " In recent years the work of Miller and others has
shown that many of the basic materials of living matter could
have arisen by the action of lightning flashes upon the primitive atmosphere of the earth.   Nevertheless, it is still a very
big step from the synthesis of amino-acids to even the simplest of living cells, and in general there seems no reason
to disagree with Hopkins' view.   Thorpe has discussed the
matter in some detail (24, p. 37):

> The event which produced living matter must have
> been highly improbable even under primordial con-
> ditions.   Assuming that an aqueous solution of amin-
> o-acids had been formed, the next problem is how
> could these be built up into complex proteins or
> enzymes?   Assuming that the concentration of each
> free amino-acid is kept at one M, the equilibrium
> concentration of a protein with 100 residues (MW
> about 12,000) is $10^{-99}M$ which represents 1 mole-
> cule in a volume of 10^{50} times the volume of the
> earth.   This appears to rule out the possibility of
> the formation of any protein by mass action, even
> in the presence of a catalyst....   Thus the simul-
> taneous formation of two or more molecules of any
> enzyme purely by chance is fanatically improbable.

This question of the likelihood of the spontaneous formation of life has been considered by many writers, from
several different points of view.   One method of approach is
in terms of the Second Law of Thermodynamics (or the "Law
of Morpholysis, " as Clark (8) has called it).   This law states
that all physical systems tend towards a state of maximum
entropy, that is, a state of maximum disorder.   The continuous rise in complexity and orderliness which we observe in
the living world certainly seems to be in direct defiance of
this law.   Schroedinger (22) attempted to explain this by saying that organisms feed on "negative entropy," that is, they

extract order from their surroundings, but this would appear
to be nothing more than an alternative description of the process rather than an explanation. Julian Huxley (7), in his
preface to Teilhard de Chardin's Phenomenon of Man openly
refers to evolution as an "anti-entropic process" without apparently realising that such a description is equivalent to an
admission that living things defy the laws of physics, and
thus throws him straight into the arms of the Vitalists! Recently attempts have been made to answer the thermodynamic
objections to the mechanistic theory by pointing out that classical thermodynamics was developed for closed physical systems, whereas what we really require is a thermodynamics
for open systems--an "irreversible thermodynamics." It is
argued that in an open system we may well have a state of
decreasing entropy. The difficulty still remains, however,
of explaining how such open systems came into existence in
the first place. Bertalanffy is clearly not satisfied with present-day attempts at explanation:

> According to well-known experiments, the formation
> of amino acids and other organic compounds is well
> possible in an artificial 'primeval atmosphere,' en-
> ergy being provided by electric discharges. It
> may also be that, given the necessary time, even-
> tually macromolecules, including self-duplicating
> DNA molecules have formed by chance in the or-
> ganic "soup" of the primeval ocean. What is at
> present quite inexplicable is why and how organic
> substances, nucleoproteins, or coacervates should
> have formed, against the second principle--systems
> not tending toward thermodynamic equilibrium but
> 'open systems' maintaining themselves at a distance
> from equilibrium in a most improbable state. This
> would be possible only in the presence of 'organis-
> ing forces' leading to the formation of such systems.
> Before such systems had emerged, selection could
> not even start to act. (my italics) (18, p. 73-4).

An alternative way of looking at this problem is provided by Information Theory. In order to construct any pat-
terned system, whether it is a house, the picture on a television set, or a virus particle, it is not sufficient merely
to have the necessary raw materials. A certain quantity of
information is required so that the materials may be assembled in the correct order. Engineers express the quantity of
information in terms of binary units, or "bits." Thorpe (24),
following Linschitz and Morowitz, estimates the information

content of a bacterial cell to be of the order of 10^{12} bits,
and points out that even the information content of an amoeba
must be "several orders that of the information store of the
most advanced computer" (p. 38). If the solar system developed by condensation from a "primordial nebula," whence
came the tremendous amount of information which we find in
living creatures? A gas is the most <u>random</u> system known
to science; the amount of information contained in the chaotic
movements of gas molecules is negligible; yet according to the
mechanistic theory we are to suppose that the living world
with all its complexities (and this includes man with his cities,
his transport and communications systems, and his space
rockets!) has arisen from purely chance events occurring in
a slowly cooling gaseous system. The mechanist is forced
to assume that, somehow, the information was all there to
start with:

> Ordered matter has thus evolved through a hier-
> archy of stages of self-assembly. Due to repeated
> reproductive cycling and infrequent but multitudinous
> mutations, <u>information available</u> at <u>the</u> <u>outset</u> has
> expanded to permit a vast array of diverse types
> of informational macromolecules and derived sys-
> tems. These systems collectively represent what
> we recognise as life. (12, my italics)

This is in fact a modern version of the preformation-
ist myth; all the properties of living matter were already
present, presumably in some sort of coded form, in the very
atoms from which the solar system was formed. This will
seem hardly conceivable to anyone except a determined mechanist. It is certainly not conceivable to Thorpe, who writes:

> If we consider the process of cosmic evolution
> from a primordial nebula through the solar system
> allowing, in its turn, organic evolution to take
> place ... we can say that the result has been, in
> the universe as we know it, a stupendous increase
> of order--that is to say, a stupendous increase of
> information. (24, p. 38)

It would seem then, as though something very important has been omitted from the mechanistic picture of life.
It would, of course, be rash to place too much weight upon
calculations of information content and probability; nevertheless, as Burt points out (6) they do "set up a strong pre-
sumption against any completely mechanistic hypothesis of the
origin of life."

Natural Selection

If biological theory fails to account satisfactorily for
the origin of life, to what extent can it account for its subsequent development?   The orthodox view is that all the forms
of living organisms have arisen as the result of natural selection acting upon random mutations, but there are an increasing number of biologists who feel that this cannot be the
whole story. Sir Alister Hardy, in his book The Living
Stream (16) describes a number of phenomena which are very
difficult to account for in orthodox terms. It is obviously
not possible to discuss all of these here, but we must consider some of the more important ones, since they may indicate processes involving psi activity.

The first of these is the problem of homologous organs, which, says Hardy, is "absolutely fundamental to what
we are talking about when we speak of evolution," yet which
now appears to be inexplicable in terms of modern biological
theory.   The older text-books on evolution make much of the
idea of homology, pointing out the obvious resemblances between the skeletons of the limbs of different animals. Thus,
the "pentadactyl" limb pattern is found in the arm of a man,
the wing of a bird, and the flipper of a whale, and this is
held to indicate their common origin. Now if these various
structures were transmitted by the same gene-complex, varied
from time to time by mutations and acted upon by environmental selection, the theory would make good sense. Unfortunately this is not the case. Homologous organs are now
known to be produced by totally different gene complexes in
the different species. The concept of homology in terms of
similar genes handed on from a common ancestor has broken
down, says Hardy. The most striking evidence on this point
comes from Morgan's experiments with the fruit-fly Drosophila; when a pure line of flies containing the eyeless allele
is inbred, within a short time perfectly formed eyes appear,
produced apparently by a kind of co-operative effort on the
part of the other genes. Koestler has a pointed comment to
make on this phenomenon:

> The traditional explanation of this remarkable phe-
> nomenon is that the other members of the gene-
> complex have been 'reshuffled and recombined in
> such a way that they deputise for the missing norm-
> al eye-forming gene. ' Now re-shuffling, as every
> poker player knows, is a randomising process. No
> biologist would be so perverse as to suggest that the

new insect-eye evolved by pure chance, thus repeating within a few generations an evolutionary process
which took hundreds of millions of years. Nor does
the concept of natural selection provide the slightest
help in this case. The recombination of genes to
deputise for the missing gene must have been coordinated according to some overall plan.... (17,
pp. 133-4).

Something similar to this is also suggested by D'Arcy
Thompson's work in the shapes of animals, quoted by Hardy.
Thompson found that the shapes of animals belonging to the
same zoological group are often related to one another in a
simple mathematical way; the shape of one species can be
obtained from the shape of another by a simple distortion of
the spatial coordinates according to definite mathematical
laws. This again suggests some overall "plan" rather than
the result of random mutations selected by a changing environment.

Few people today would deny that natural selection
must have played some part in the evolution of life. The
well known work of Dr. Kettlewell with the peppered moth,
and many of the examples of animal camouflage described by
Hardy, provide clear evidence of the selective effect of the
environment on at least the external features of organisms.
The difficulty lies in the creativeness of evolution.

Whereas Darwinian selection will account for many of
the differences between varieties of the same species ("micro-
evolution") it is difficult to see how it can account for the
emergence of entirely new species with a higher degree of
organisation. Waddington wrote in 1958:

... a new gene mutation can cause an alteration
only to a character which the organism had had in
previous generations. It could not produce a lob-
ster's claw on a cat; it could only alter the cat in
some way, leaving it essentially a cat. (1)

Dr. R. E. D. Clark, in an earlier book, put the matter even more strongly:

... it is easy to imagine that, occasionally, mutations might help individuals to adapt themselves to
their surroundings, after which the mutants may replace their fellows as a result of natural selection.

But to go further and to imagine that a series of such changes, however long continued, would in the end create new and highly complex mechanisms, so making organisms more complex than they were before, would seem to be highly ridiculous. (8)

Nowadays the orthodox Darwinian would reply to this by pointing out that new species can arise through the physical separation of existing ones. Once a population is separated into two by some geographical barrier, random mutations and natural selection acting separately on each half will eventually cause the two to become so unlike that they can no longer interbreed, that is, they become two species instead of one (Hardy, 16, pp. 96-97). This argument is very persuasive, as far as it goes. It explains quite neatly how one species could become two, but it does not explain why either of the two should show any increase in complexity above that of the original. The problem here is not why species differ from one another, but why in the course of evolution they show a continuous increase in organisation. Why should a purely random process--mutation--combined with another presumably random process--environmental change--lead to a steadily increasing amount of order in the living world?

L. L. Whyte, in a book published in 1965, challenged the generally accepted view that mutations are entirely random with respect to the direction of evolution (26). He suggested that a process of internal selection operates on the mutated genes long before they have a chance to become permanently established in the species, so that deleterious genes are eliminated or forced to back-mutate, while advantageous ones are permitted to survive. Again, we seem to be back with the concept of an overall species plan to which new mutations must be made to conform, at least within certain limits.

This survey of some of the problems of present day biological theory can perhaps be summarised as follows:

(I) Both in the origin of life and in its subsequent evolution we are confronted with a tremendous increase in information content which cannot be satisfactorily accounted for by any mechanistic theory. The source of this information, and the method by which it enters the evolutionary stream are unknown.

(II) There appears to be some sort of overall plan for

the development of species (and probably of individuals also),
so that minor deviations from the main line of development
are corrected.   Unhelpful mutations may be removed or com-
pensated for before they are able to express themselves in
bodily form (i. e. phenotype). Again the method by which
this is done remains obscure.

A Definition of Psi

        Let us now see whether parapsychology can contribute
anything of value to the problems we have been considering.
Suppose we examine a typical PK placement experiment, in
which dice are "willed" to fall on one side of a dividing line
rather than the other.   As the experiment proceeds it is clear
that the dice are behaving in a non-random manner; they have,
in fact, received information from the human agent, and are
behaving according to that informational input to an extent
which could not reasonably be attributed to chance.   Of course,
there is still a large element of randomness in the antics of
the dice; but by applying the appropriate mathematics we detect sufficient orderliness for us to infer that information has
been added to the system.   We might almost say that the dice
have come alive for the duration of the experiment; they are
exhibiting non-random purposive behaviour, which is usually
regarded as a characteristic of living organisms.   Now I wish
to suggest that there is operationally no difference whatever
between this kind of experiment and a "telepathy" experiment
in which information is transferred to a human percipient.
We are accustomed to regard the human percipient as "alive"
and the dice in the PK experiment as "inanimate," but "alive-
ness" is surely a matter of degree, not of kind.   We judge
whether something is alive or not by the extent to which it
displays goal-directed behaviour.   While the PK experiment is
in progress the dice have become, in effect, very primitive
organisms, responding to the agent's intentions in the same
way as the paramecia in Richmond's experiments (21), or the
cats in Osis' experiments (19).   We can imaging these experiments conducted over the whole range of targets, beginning
with inorganic objects such as dice and proceeding up the evolutionary scale to man.   At what point are we to say that the
experiment ceases to be one in psychokinesis and becomes a
telepathy experiment?   Do we call it "telepathy" when the organism at the receiving end is a cat, or do we reserve that
distinction for the higher apes and man?   The question begins
to appear rather artificial and meaningless!

I propose, therefore, that we accept the following principles:

(I) A psi phenomenon is said to have occurred whenever information is transferred to a physical system without the use of any known form of physical energy.

(II) There is no essential difference between the various forms of psi phenomena encountered in the laboratory, the apparent differences arising only out of the experimental set-up.

If these principles are accepted, it becomes clear why psi phenomena are regarded as "paranormal." In all normal instances of information-transfer, a certain minimum amount of energy is transferred also. As far as we know, there is no energy transfer in psi. Attempts to detect carrier waves in telepathic experiments have always failed, and there is no reason to suppose that there is any increase in total energy content in a PK experiment either. Even in large scale PK-type phenomena, such as are alleged to occur in "poltergeist" cases, it is probable that the energy for the movement is drawn from the surroundings, not from the human "agent," if such there be. I suggest, therefore, that in all these cases information is fed into the system without any increase in energy content; the energy that is already present is redistributed, contrary to the Second Law of Thermodynamics, to bring about the desired effect.

Psi in the Living World

We may now begin to see some connection between this curious psi process and some of the biological problems discussed earlier. In the origin and evolution of life, we are confronted with (in Thorpe's phrase) a "stupendous increase of information"; is it too far fetched to see some connection between this and, say, the Soal-Goldney experiment, where the transfer of information was such that it would occur by chance only once in 10^{31} such experiments? Bertalanffy, in the passage quoted earlier, stated that the formation of open thermodynamic systems would be possible only in the presence of organising forces; in laboratory experiments of the PK type we are confronted with an organising force at present unrecognised by orthodox science. There is at least a possibility that parapsychology has discovered the missing factor needed to construct a general theory of life.

The task of weaving all these threads into a coherent, all-embracing theory is a frightening one, and what follows here cannot be regarded as anything more than a first, tentative attempt. It will have more than succeeded in its purpose if it stimulates others, with a deeper knowledge of the various disciplines involved, to produce a better theory. With that disclaimer, I shall proceed to lauch out into deep water!

It is clear that psi phenomena cannot be accounted for in terms of present day physical science; we shall therefore have to postulate the existence of a distinctly extra-physical entity in the Universe. I suggest the following postulates as a basis for further consideration:

(1) That there exists in the Universe an entity, distinct from matter but capable of interacting with it, which (to avoid emotive phrases) I will call the psi-factor.

(2) When interaction with the psi-factor is not occurring, matter obeys the second law of thermodynamics, that is, it does not spontaneously organise itself into increasingly complex forms.

(3) We infer that psi-interaction has taken place whenever the information content of a physical system shows an increase which cannot be attributed to chance or to the transfer of information (and therefore energy) from another physical system.

(4) In the beginning of life, psi-interaction took place with the primeval molecules in the seas of the cooling earth. These molecules had information fed into them by the psi-factor, thus leading them to arrange themselves in ordered patterns like the dice in a PK experiment. (If the transfer of information was as slow as it is in a laboratory experiment, it may well have taken a very long time to produce the necessary "build-up" of orderliness for the first living cell to appear.)

(5) Throughout evolution, the tendency has been to produce organisms which are self-regulating, so that the necessity for intervention by the psi-factor is reduced to a minimum. Nevertheless, psi-interaction may possibly occur when a structure is required which is so highly improbable as to be unlikely to occur by chance.

(6) Most of the higher organisms have now developed

satisfactory mechanical systems of self-repair to cope with
injury or disease. Occasionally, however, psi may intervene
here to bring about paranormal healing. Psi acting within
the organism in this way might be called endosomatic psi,
and the type of external psi studied by parapsychologists could
be termed exosomatic psi.

I do not think it matters greatly that we cannot specify the exact nature of the entity behind the psi phenomena--
the "psi-factor" as I have called it. We do not know the
real nature of the electron, or any of the other entities of
physics, but we are able to set up equations which describe
their interactions with one another very precisely. In the
same way, the important thing is to find out where and when
psi operates in the natural world, so that we can begin to
understand the development of life and apply our knowledge to
the healing of disease. It may be that we shall have to accept the psi-factor as one of the irreducible facts of the Universe; but although we cannot explain it, we can study its interactions with matter.

These proposals will seem startling to many parapsychologists, and probably horrifying to most biologists! It
will no doubt be objected that this is simply the old Vitalism
in a slightly newer dress. However, a theory must be judged
by its conformity to the facts, not by its historical antecedents.
We do not disbelieve in atoms because Democritus thought of
them, nor do we accuse the founders of the Quantum Theory
of trying to revive Newton's outmoded corpuscular theory of
light. The older vitalism of Bergson and others failed to
carry conviction because it lacked the necessary evidence; at
the time when Bergson wrote about the élan vital, Duke University did not exist and the word "psychokinesis" had not
yet been invented. It is a mistake to import hypothetical entities into science until there is adequate evidence for them--
even the elusive neutrino had to show some interactions with
matter before it could be accepted by the physicists. In the
same way, the "vital force" acting within the living world
needed to be demonstrated in the laboratory before it could
carry conviction. By the time such demonstration was
achieved, in the Duke PK experiments, vitalism was already
being swept away by the rising tide of mechanistic biology.
But as we have seen in the first part of this paper, mechanistic biology has failed to account satisfactorily for the phenomena of life, so that it is important to re-open the question in the light of the facts discovered by the parapsychologists.

Biological Experiments with Psi

        When an ordinary piece of iron is placed in a mag-
netic field, it becomes itself magnetised and thus increases
the strength of the field in its own vicinity. In a similar
way, we can imagine that the universal psi factor ("psi-at-
large") which I have supposed to be responsible for the origin and development of life also operates more strongly in
the vicinity of its own creations. Thus we would expect a
highly complex organism such as man to be associated with
a "psi-field" capable of imparting information to biological
or biochemical systems in its neighbourhood. The evidence
for biological effects of this kind is quite impressive, although it is scattered throughout the literature, and few people seem to have noticed its significance. Thus there is the
work of Sister Justa Smith, of Rosary Hill College, Buffalo,
who found that the "force" emanating from a healer's hands
accelerated the action of the proteolytic enzyme trypsin, the
acceleration being equivalent to a magnetic field of 13,000
gauss (23). Ascending the scale of organic complexity, we
find evidence that human psi can affect the behaviour of a
variety of animals, ranging from the protozoa of Richmond
(21) to the cats and dogs of Osis and Bechterev (19, 3).
Even more striking are the experiments conducted by Dr.
Barry in 1965, showing that psi effects can inhibit the growth
of parasitic fungi (2).

        Work with plants is experimentally more difficult to
carry out than work with animals, yet here, too, we find an
impressive build up of evidence in favour of a real psi effect.
The work of Paul and Mme Vasse in 1948 (25) has been confirmed by the more recent work of Dr. Grad. Like Sr.
Smith, Grad used as his subject a man who claimed to have
healing powers; by a series of carefully controlled experiments Grad was able to show that wounds made in the skin
of mice healed more quickly after treatment by this man
(13). This would seem to indicate that the effect, whatever
its nature might be, somehow accelerates the processes of
cell division. Grad therefore proceeded to conduct further
experiments using barley seeds as the target material, and
obtained some clearly significant results (14, 15). More recently still, Brier has obtained results with plants which seem
to indicate that psi can affect the electrical processes occurring within the plant as a result of its life activities (5).

Prospects for Future Research

The work of all these experimenters has passed largely unnoticed outside the field of parapsychology; yet its implications are tremendous. If we are to accept the results
of these experiments we must admit that we now have direct
evidence of the existence of a force in nature which is capable of affecting enzyme systems and altering the rates of
cell-division; a force which may well have played a vital part
in the evolution of life. Bergson, Driesch, McDougall, and
all the "vitalists" of a previous age would have been thrilled
to see the results of such work as this! The exploration of
the biological functions of psi is only just beginning, and the
field has far too few workers; nevertheless, what has been
achieved so far opens up exciting prospects. One of the crucial questions with respect to evolution has not so far been
tested (as far as I know), namely: can psi bring about mutations? The factors which cause mutations in nature are still
largely unknown; natural radioactivity is insufficient to account for the number which are known to occur and which
must have occurred in the past to account for evolutionary
progress. It would be of the greatest interest to discover
whether the same force which can promote wound healing in
mice can also induce mutations in Drosophila or bacterial cultures, and the experiment should not be too difficult to perform.

So far we have been concerned with psi acting on systems outside the body--"exosomatic" psi as I called it earlier. It seems very likely that psi also plays an important
part within the body, but to separate such internal psi effects
from the normal biochemical processes will not be easy.

The evidence of psychosomatic medicine is very suggestive of such an effect, though it is hard to be sure in any
given case that the results are not due to some as yet un-
discovered hormonal mechanism. In a recent book on psychosomatic medicine (4), Dr. Stephen Black reports some of
the startling results he has obtained by the use of hypnosis.
These seem to show that psychological factors can profoundly
affect the progress of diseases which a generation ago would
have been regarded as purely physical. Most surprising of
all, a number of congenital conditions such as Brocq's congenital ichthyosis, linear naevus, and pachyonychia, are reported as having been cured by hypnotherapy. What is one
to make of such cases? Has the gene-complex been altered,
or have certain biochemical systems which act as "messen-

gers" for the genes been blocked?   At present we have no
answers to these questions.   It is at least possible that some
of these phenomena may involve an endosomatic form of psi.

   One of the first parapsychologists to suggest a function for psi within the body was W. E. Cox, who in 1957 suggested that psi might have some effect upon the sex of offspring (10).   He produced some evidence to support his hypothesis, but the results could not be regarded as conclusive.
It would be fairly simple to test his idea experimentally.   A
questionnaire could be sent to newly-married couples asking
them to state which sex they would prefer their first-born
child to be.   When the children had been born, a statistical
analysis would show whether there was any correlation between the parents' wishes and the sex of the child.

Practical Applications?

   In this paper I have been largely concerned with the
theoretical implications of psi phenomena for biology.   It
should not be forgotten, however, that these discoveries may
well have practical applications of enormous value to mankind.   The work of Grad on wound healing has already been
referred to, and there is a considerable amount of evidence
both anecdotal and experimental, which suggests that psi may
one day be of great importance in the field of medicine.   In
1968 two workers at the University of Chile's Parapsychology
Laboratory reported significant results in an experiment designed to detect a psi effect on mouse tumours (11).   Ninety
mice were inoculated with a tumour, and then divided into
three groups: With Group A the experimenter tried to increase the growth of the tumour by PK, with Group B she
tried to retard it, and Group C were left as control.   It was
found that there was significant retardation of tumour growth
in Group B (P < 0.001), but the tumours in Group A had not
been accelerated (perhaps because the task was an evil one,
and distasteful to the agent).   Results such as these encourage the hope that one day we may see a science of "applied
parapsychology" at work in our hospitals and clinics.

   On July 30th 1964, a day of celebration was held at
Duke University to commemorate the founding of the FRNM.
In his closing address on that occasion, Dr. Rhine pointed
out that it is parapsychology that must now take the initiative
in bridging the gap between itself and the other sciences:
"We will move out from where we are to these inter-connect-

ing linkages. We will command the bridges and take the of-
fensive in the explorations that are needed ... the time has
come when we can confidently cease to defend our boundaries
and proceed to cross them" (20). Although most biologists
may not realise it yet, the experiments I have described a-
bove show that the invasion of biology has already begun--
and neither biology nor parapsychology can ever be quite the
same again.

REFERENCES

1. Barnett, S. A. (Ed.). A Century of Darwin. London,
        Heinemann, 1958.
2. Barry, J. "General and comparative study of the psycho-
        kinetic effect on a fungus culture." J. Parapsychol.,
        1968, 32, 237-243.
3. Bechterev, W. "'Direct Influence' of a person upon the
        behaviour of animals." J. Parapsychol., 1949, 13,
        166-76.
4. Black, Stephen. Mind and Body. London, William Kim-
        ber, 1969.
5. Brier, R. M. "PK on a bio-electrical system." J.
        Parapsychol., 1969, 33, 187-205.
6. Burt, C. "Evolution and Parapsychology." J. Soc.
        Psych. Res., 1966, 43, 391-422.
7. de Chardin, Teilhard. The Phenomenon of Man. Lon-
        don, Collins, 1959.
8. Clark, R. E. D. Darwin: Before and After. London,
        Paternoster Press, 1948.
9. Clowes, Royston. The Structure of Life. London,
        Penguin Books, 1967.
10. Cox, W. E. "The Influence of 'applied psi' upon the
        sex of off-spring." J. Soc. Psych. Res., 1957,
        39, 65-77.
11. Elguin, G. H. and Onetto, B. "Acta psiquiat. piscol."
        Amer. Lat., 1968, 14, 47.
12. Fox, S. "In the beginning ... life assembled itself."
        New Scientist, 1969, 41, 450-452.
13. Grad, Bernard, Cadoret, Remi J., and Paul, G. I.
        "An unorthodox method of treatment in wound heal-
        ing in mice." Int. J. Parapsychol., 1961, 3, 5-
        24.
14. Grad, B. "A telekinetic effect on plant growth. I."
        Int. J. Parapsychol., 1963, 5, 117-33.
15. _____. "A telekinetic effect on plant growth. II."
        Int. J. Parapsychol., 1964, 6, 473-98.

16. Hardy, A. C. The Living Stream. London, Collins, 1965.

17. Koestler, A. The Ghost in the Machine. London; Hutchinson, 1967.

18. _____, and Smythies, J. R. (Eds.). Beyond Reductionism. London, Hutchinson, 1969.

19. Osis, K. "A Test of the occurrence of a psi effect between man and the cat." J. Parapsychol., 1952, 16, 233-56.

20. Rhine, J. B., et al. Parapsychology: From Duke to FRNM. Durham, N. C., Parapsychology Press, 1965.

21. Richmond, N. "Two series of PK Tests on paramecia." J. Soc. Psych. Res., 1952, 36, 577-88.

22. Schroedinger, E. What is Life? Cambridge University Press, 1944.

23. Smith, Sr. J. "Paranormal effects on enzyme activity." Paper read at 11th Convention of the Parapsychological Association, and abstracted in J. Parapsychol., 1968, 32, 182.

24. Thorpe, W. H. Science, Man, and Morals. London, Methuen, 1965.

25. Vasse, P. and M. "Influence de la pensée sur la croissance des plantes." Revue Metapsychique, Nouvelle Série, 1948, 2, 87-94.

26. Whyte, L. L. Internal Factors in Evolution. London, Tavistock Publications, 1965.

ADDITIONAL READINGS ON BIOLOGY AND PSI

Eisenbud, J. "Evolution and psi. " JASPR 70:35-53 (Jan 1976).

Hardy, A. "Biology and ESP. " In Smythies, J. R. (Ed.). Science and ESP. N. Y. , Humanities Press, 1967. Ch. 6.

_____ . "Psychical research and civilization. " PSPR 55: 1-21 (Pt 199, Dec 1966).

Kreitler, H. and Kreitler, S. "ESP and cognition. " JP 38: 267-85 (Sep 1974).

Morris, R. L. "Biology and psychical research. " In Schmeidler, G. R. (Ed.). Parapsychology: Its Relation to Physics, Biology, Psychology, and Psychiatry. Metuchen, N. J. , Scarecrow Press, 1976.

_____ . "The psychobiology of psi. " In Mitchell, E. D. and others. Psychic Exploration. N. Y. , Putnam's, 1974. Ch. 9.

Poynton, J. C. "Parapsychology and the biological sciences. " In Angoff, A. and Shapin, B. (Eds.). Parapsychology and the Sciences. N. Y. , Parapsychology Foundation, 1974. Pp. 116-34.

Randall, J. "Biological aspects of psi. " In Beloff, J. (Ed.). New Directions in Parapsychology. London, Elek Science, 1974. Metuchen, N. J. , Scarecrow Press, 1975. Ch. 4.

Zorab, G. "Modern genetics and psi phenomena. " In Angoff, A. and Shapin, B. (Eds.). Parapsychology and the Sciences. N. Y. , Parapsychology Foundation, 1974. Pp. 198-208.

Chapter 15

ESP AND MEMORY*

by W. G. Roll

Introduction

The relationship between extrasensory perception (ESP)
and familiar biological and psychological processes has been
the subject matter of several parapsychological investigations.
A particularly fertile area of research has been the study of
the connection between ESP and motivational factors as explored, for instance, by G. R. Schmeidler[70] and M. Anderson and R. White.[2] Perhaps the most convincing argument
for the reality of ESP is that it is affected by psychological
needs in much the same ways as better understood perceptual and cognitive functions are affected.

Aside from that, we know very little. We do not even
know whether extrasensory perception can rightly be called a
form of perception. There seems to be no sense organ for
ESP and the process appears to leave no characteristic experience in consciousness in the manner say, of vision and
hearing. The only obvious similarity between sensory and
extrasensory perception is that both are usually responses
to external events. Also, both are at least to some extent
influenced by motivational factors.

In addition to being influenced by external stimuli and
psychological needs, sense perception is influenced by a person's memory record. Without memories of previous experiences, we could not interpret our sense-data. A man
who has been blind from birth and who recovers his eyesight,

*Reprinted by permission of the author and publisher from
Biological Psychiatry 2: 505-21 (Sept. -Oct. 1966).
Thanks to Dr. J. G. Pratt, Professor H. H. Price,
Dr. C. T. Tart, and Mr. R. Morris for valuable suggestions
made in the writing of this paper.

does not know what he sees till he can interpret his visual
sense-data, say, by touch.   He learns to identify the new
sensations by means of the old, remembered, ones.   This
paper will be concerned with the question whether memory
also plays a role in ESP.

For the purposes of this discussion, we may distinguish four memory functions: learning, retention, remembering, and forgetting.   Learning is the process of acquiring information; retention is the process by means of which this
information persists through time; remembering is the process whereby the information is manifested in the present;
and forgetting is the process whereby it is temporarily or
permanently lost.

The term "memory trace" is used for the hypothetical
change in the cortex or elsewhere by which information is
stored.

The ESP process has been pictured as consisting of
three aspects: source, channel, and receiver.   In an experiment, the source is the ESP target, for instance, a
series of ESP card symbols (star, circle, square, cross,
waves).   If the target is not known to anybody at the time of
testing, this is an experiment in "clairvoyance," or ESP of
objective physical events.   If the target is in the mind of
some person, we are dealing with "telepathy," with ESP of
mental events.   If the card order will be determined only
after the subject has made his responses, this is a test in
"precognition."   These differences do not necessarily reflect
differences in the ESP process.   For instance, it is possible
that telepathy is in fact clairvoyance of brain events in the
person who thinks of the target and that "precognition" scores
are produced by clairvoyance and psychokinesis.   However,
these possibilities need not concern us here.   We shall also
not discuss the ESP channel, the means whereby ESP information reaches the receiver from the source.   It is a matter for lively debate in parapsychology whether or not ESP
stimuli are comparable to known physical stimuli, such as
electromagnetic radiation.   I believe they are,[62] but this
problem is outside our present scope.   We shall consider
mainly the ESP receiver, more particularly we shall ask,
what are the characteristics of the ESP response?

Memory Traces as ESP Responses

An ESP card test is in certain obvious respects a

memory test. It is part of the experimental procedure to
familiarize the subject with the five ESP cards or whatever
the targets will be, so that he can remember them during
the test itself. If he forgets any of the symbols, he is not
likely to do as well as if he remembered them all. (If he
is such a poor learner that he can only remember one card
and always responds with it, he will score at chance, assuming that the target series is random and does not contain an
excess of the favored symbol.) If it is essential that the subject should remember the five ESP symbols, it is just as
essential that in the test itself, he must forget or ignore the
order in which they were initially shown to him as well as
the order of his previous guesses. This applies to any learning situation. To learn something new, the old often must
be forgotten: "learning involves forgetting."

It appears that in the common card tests and in other
experiments where a limited range of targets is used, the
responses are, in a sense, memory responses. Before the
ESP guessing begins, certain memory traces are laid down
which are then aroused during the test itself. However,
though the acquisition of the memory trace is established by
sensory perception, its arousal is caused by external ESP
stimuli--at least if a significant score is obtained in the test.
It appears as if the effect of ESP stimuli is to revive memory traces, much as do other external stimuli in sense perception.

In the search for clues about the nature of ESP, the
investigator may get important insights by looking beyond controlled scientific research. A study of the more informal
material, however, gives essentially the same picture as the
ESP card tests. F. W. H. Myers,[38] the English pioneer in
parapsychology, was one of the first to notice that in ESP
hallucinations ("apparitions") "mind has been at work upon the
picture--that the scene has not been presented, so to say,
in crude objectivity." Another English investigator, G. N. M.
Tyrrell,[80] thought that "the apparitional drama" is worked
out on unconscious regions of the personalities of the agent
and the percipient. These regions, it appears, may be the
memory records of the persons involved. H. F. Saltmarsh,[68]
another English researcher, concluded from his study of Mrs.
Warren Elliott, that "the contents of the subliminal memory"
were used for her ESP responses. The late French parapsychologist, René Warcollier,[87] described the process this
way: "the images which appear to the mind of the percipient
under the form of hallucinations, dreams, or more or less

well-formed images, spring exclusively from his own mind,
from his own conscious or subconscious memory. There is
no carrying of the visual impression from the agent to the
percipient, any more than there is actual carrying of a letter
of the alphabet from the sending apparatus of a telegraph office to the receiving office. The transmission of the message
consists in making the same letter appear, but it already exists at the receiving apparatus, along with all the others, before the transmission took place." The Polish investigator,
Edouard Abramowski,[1] gave a succinct description of ESP
when he said that "the telepathic process, in its psychological
essence, is ... only a process of cryptomnesia."

More recently, W. H. C. Tenhaeff,[78] the Dutch parapsychologist, commenting on the behavior of his "paragnosts"
in free response tests, was reminded "of persons thinking
intently of a word or a name which they have learned or heard
before, or of an event they have witnessed in the past."
L. E. Rhine,[60] in her study of spontaneous cases of precognition, noted that many of the people who had such experiences "marvelled at the fact that the precognitive experience
was just like 'remembering' the future."

It appears not only that a person's memory traces influence his ESP responses, but, more fundamentally, that his
ESP responses consist of revived memory traces. This is
not to say that ESP is only remembering. There is an external stimulus but the way this affects a person's awareness
or behavior in ESP is by first affecting his memory traces.
What is experienced or expressed in ESP is not something
"new" but rather memories of past events. The mechanism
whereby the appropriate memory traces are revived in ESP
is, we may assume, the same that is used in normal perceptual and cognitive functions. However, ESP appears to
rely even more strongly on memory than, say, visual perception, for in ESP there are no sense-data at all, but only
revived memory traces. In a way, memory images are the
"sense-data" of ESP. If we wanted another term for ESP,
we might call it "estrasensory remembering."

The theory that ESP responses consist of memory
traces we might call the "memory theory of ESP." H. H.
Price,[51] the English philosopher, refers to it as the "ecphorising theory of psi cognition" (ecphorise: to revive or rouse
from latency) and contrasts it with the "sixth-sense theory"
according to which ESP is an original source of ideas. Price
notes that the ecphorising theory conforms to David Hume's

view that all ideas have been acquired either from normal
perception or from normal introspection. He finds it more
economical and plausible than the sixth-sense theory.

In the next few pages, I shall discuss some of the
findings in parapsychology in the light of this theory. It will
be seen that a number of apparently unconnected discoveries
about ESP fall into place and that some facts which hitherto
have resisted interpretation now make sense.

The Laws of Learning and ESP

It has long been known that certain conditions facilitate
learning. These are described in the "laws of learning."
The best known are the laws of recency, frequency, and
vividness (or intensity). In other words, recent events, all
other conditions being equal, are more likely to be remembered than events in the more remote past; frequent events
are more likely to be remembered than infrequent ones; and
vivid or emotionally intense events have an advantage over
bland and emotionally neutral ones. If the memory theory of
ESP is correct, we expect ESP responses to be expressed in
terms of memory traces that are recent, frequent, and vivid.
In other words, ESP stimuli are likely to trigger memory
traces that are already prepared to "fire." (We are not here
concerned with the question which target events have the
greatest stimulating power, but only with the question which
of the perceiver's memory traces are likely to be activated
in an instance of ESP.)

In some of the material reported by the Dutch parapsychologist, W. H. C. Tenhaeff,[78] the memory basis of
ESP comes out clearly and illustrates some of the laws of
learning. For instance, his subject, "Beta," stated correctly that a visitor came from the Dutch town of Wageningen.
Beta's reason for making this statement was that he received
a mental image of the agricultural college at Wageningen, a
building he had often seen in the past, a good illustration of
the law of frequency. The law of vividness is also represented in this material. For instance, the image of a German Weinstube where Beta and his father had an argument
with the owner came to mind and suggested, correctly, that
the name of another visitor was "Wijntje" ("wijn," Dutch for
"wine"). Childhood events are often more intense than later
ones and may be recalled more easily, though many years
remote. The introspections of Beta and of Gerard Croiset,[77]

the most famous of Tenhaeff's subjects, provide many examples where ESP responses consisted of memories of childhood events.   Similar observations have been made by E. D.
Dean[15] in his ESP experiments with the plethysmograph.
The scoring was best when the names Dean used as targets
belonged to people whom the subject had seen recently and
who were emotionally important to him.

Associative Habits and ESP

If a memory trace is aroused in the course of normal
perceptual or introspective activities, it may, in turn, arouse
other memory traces which are associated with it but unrelated to the situation at hand.   For instance, the perception
or idea of a table, may make us think of a chair and this,
in turn, of a particular person seated on a chair.   Such
associations are one of the main characteristics of mental
life, though we are often unaware of their existence.   The
conditions which facilitate the formation of these connections
are described in the "laws of association." Some of these
are similar to the "laws of learning" (the laws of recency,
frequency, and vividness).

If the effect of an ESP stimulus is to arouse a memory trace, then we should expect that other memory traces
associated with the former will also be evoked, not because
of their relationship to the ESP stimulus but because of their
relationship to the first memory trace.   Such associative effects emerge strongly in ESP card tests.   For instance, J. G.
Pratt and S. G. Soal[49] found striking evidence for guessing
habits when they analyzed the responses of Mrs. Gloria Stewart, a highly successful ESP subject.   Soal[74] elsewhere suggested that the reason the five ESP symbols (star, circle,
square, cross, and waves) have been so successful in ESP
tests is that there are fewer preestablished associations between them in the minds of most subjects then between, say,
playing cards or numbers.   For the same reason, nonsense
syllables are used in learning tests.   However, with repeated
usage, associations are likely to be formed and it is possible
that this is related to the decline to chance observed in so
many high-scoring subjects after extended testing, including
those of Soal.

The suggestion has been made by C. T. Tart[76] that
such extinctions of ESP capacity are due to the parapsychologist's failure to follow basic procedures for teaching skilled

behavior, in particular to his failure to give immediate rewards for correct responses or punishments for incorrect ones.   Tart notes that in ordinary learning situations if reward and punishment cannot be clearly associated with correct and incorrect responses by the organism, the desired behavior is not learned, or if already present, is extinguished.

In addition to this gradual extinction of ESP in the course of time, declines are often observed during individual tests, sometimes with an upswing toward the end resulting in a "U-curve." These resemble the learning curves found in serial learning trials.   In ESP card tests such curves have been found, for instance, by R. Cadoret,[9] W. A. McElroy and R. K. Brown,[35] K. Osis,[42] J. B. Rhine,[55] and S. G. Soal.[74]   J. G. Pratt[48] and J. B. Rhine[58] attribute the tendency to score best in the first and last segments of the experimental series to less interference from guessing habits in these parts of the run.   In a series of 42 tests I did in England, a subject took a memory test, using an exposed sequence of 25 ESP cards and then did three ESP runs. There was a sharp initial decline in the memory curve with the typical up-swing toward the end.   The ESP scoring was also highest in the beginning of the run but there was no final salience[61] (see Figure I).

At the same time as memory traces are the means for expressing ESP, they may also be a factor in suppressing it.   The ESP response contains the seed of its own destruction.   If it is true that guessing habits block ESP, we should expect that conditions which disrupt guessing habits would improve ESP.   We should also expect that persons who are less prone to such habits than others are better ESP subjects. There are several studies which seem to bear this out.   In the course of ESP experiments with cats, K. Osis and E. B. Foster[43] obtained the best scores shortly after a habit response was broken.   In a previous test with cats, Osis[42] found that "novelty in the situation helped prevent habit formation and thus offered more opportunity for a psi (i. e. parapsychological) effect." R. Cadoret's[9] scores were higher when he read or sang to himself between guesses, and R. L. Van de Castle's[84] subject scored best when the responses were interrupted by long intervals during which she could smoke, talk, read, or listen to the radio.   She also did better with ESP cards and colors as targets than with drawings, letters, and numbers.   The author suggested that "the associative value of a stimulus may be inversely related to its effectiveness as an ESP target." Similarly, in J. G.

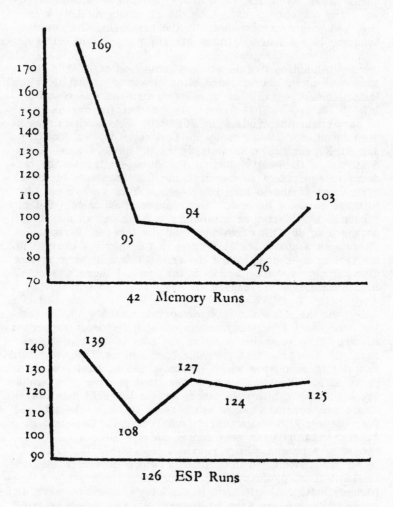

Figure I.
Distribution of Scores in Memory and ESP Tests

The decline between the first and second segment in the memory tests represents odds of several thousands to one against chance. In the ESP tests the odds are fifty to one (CR d:ff. = 2. 19)

van Busschbach's[83] experiments with school children, the
rate of success with arithmetical symbols and colors as the
targets was higher than with words.

In my experiments in England referred to earlier,[61]
a study was also made of the relationship between ESP scores
and the tendency repeatedly to call certain sequences of ESP
symbols or to call certain symbols especially often. Indications were found of an inverse relationship between ESP and
these habits.

Response bias is a function not only of the material to
be learned but also of the learner's mentality. People who
are rigid or compulsive in their behavior and thinking are
not as good learners as those who are capable of a more
flexible approach. Consequently, we should expect that good
ESP subjects are those whose memory traces have less rigid
internal relations. J. G. van Busschbach[83] thought that
young children gave better results than older ones because
they were more capable of "spontaneous giving-way to intuition." A. O. Ross, G. Murphy, and G. R. Schmeidler[65]
found that children with an "unreflective originality" scored
better than those who were constrained. In experiments with
an intelligence test which measured the "mental alertness of
a student," B. M. Humphrey[28] got a positive correlation with
ESP scores. W. A. McElroy and R. K. Brown[35] found that
the ESP scoring was best in runs where the subjects received
electric shocks for errors (although the shocks did not result
in a reduction of ESP errors) and suggested that the shocks
had an "excitement value," favorable for ESP. Improved
scores after electroshock have been claimed by H. J. Urban[82] and in tests by Schmeidler,[69] cerebral concussion patients appeared to be superior ESP subjects. By disrupting
habit responses the cortical disturbances may have created
openings for ESP.

In a study where children were instructed to look for
"hidden" figures in drawings, G. R. Schmeidler[71] found that
the best subjects also were the highest ESP scorers. She
suggests that "there is a common factor between ESP ability
and the ability, while taking a new look at some situation ...
to shift one's way of looking so as to notice obscure cues
not previously observed." Perhaps the common factor is lack
of constraint in the association that a subject superimposes on
his perceptions.

Learning Performance and ESP

If memory traces are vehicles for ESP impressions, we expect a person with good recall ability to perform well in ESP and, conversely, a good ESP subject to perform well in memory tasks. Some observations reported in the literature bear this out. E. Osty,[44] the French physician and parapsychologist, thought that good ESP subjects have exceptional memories. One of his subjects could recall verbatim the statements he had made in a previous session. The Russian physiologist, V. M. Bekhterev[4] obtained high ESP scores with an 18-year-old girl who had good visual and kinetic memory and Eduoard Abramowski and Jeanne Hirschberg[1] reported that among their (Polish) subjects those who were best at recalling "forgotten" material also were the best telepathic subjects. Similar observations were made about some of the English "mediums." William James[30] and Sir Oliver Lodge[33] noticed that Mrs. Piper had a good memory in her trance state. C. D. Thomas[79] and Mrs. W. H. Salter[67] commented similarly about Mrs. Leonard. J. G. Pidding-ton,[47] in a discussion of automatic writing, was struck by "the remarkable tenacity of the script memory, for it often involves the repetition of little catchwords from a script written, it may be, many years earlier and perhaps never seen again by the automatist." W. H. C. Tenhaeff[78] has found that his subjects "show a most remarkable hypermnesia with respect to all sorts of data given at earlier sessions."

Young people seem to do best in learning tests and the same may be true of ESP, as noted by J. B. Rhine,[58] and R. White and J. Angstadt.[90] Fatigue, whether induced naturally or by drugs, tends to depress scores in serial learning tasks and in ESP card tests.[55,57] Rhine[55] observed that the ESP scores of Zirkle dropped markedly when he was given sodium amytal. It was also noted that his recall of recent events was impaired. S. R. Feather[24] found that subjects who did well in memory trials also scored well in ESP and those who did poorly in memory had low ESP scores.

Parapraxes and Psi-Missing

One of the peculiarities of ESP is the tendency of some subjects consistently to go below chance expectancy. Instead of positive deviations, fewer scores are produced than chance allows. In some experiments the subjects have been instructed to avoid the target and consciously to aim for

negative scores.   More often this avoidance tendency appears
to be unconscious: the subject, though consciously trying to
score positively, nevertheless, produced negative deviations,
or what is called "psi-missing."   Needless to say, it is in-
admissible to use negative scores, or positive ones for that
matter, as evidence for anything unless the experimenter has
predicted such scores beforehand for the experiment in question.   Many tests have been conducted with the purpose of
analysing the results for negative scores.   I shall refer to
some of these shortly.

If the theory about the memory basis for ESP responses
is correct, we may gain insight into the nature of psi-missing by regarding it as a memory phenomenon.   The errors
of memory, known as "parapraxes," such as slips of the
tongue and pen, resemble psi-missing.   Parapraxes generally
seem to be due, not simply to chance actions, but to needs
which are unknown to the persons in question.   David Rapaport[53] calls parapraxes "unsuccessful attempts at forgetting."
They result from "prohibited strivings" which, unable to enter consciousness, distort ideas or actions.   "Parapraxes
are memory phenomena embedded in thought processes: instead of the emergence of a memory fitting the chain of
thoughts, either the memory fails to emerge or one not fitting
the chain of conscious thoughts emerges, or the relevant
memory forms a compromise with a seemingly irrelevant
memory.   This compromise results from the interplay of the
prohibited but upsurging strivings and others which strive to
prevent it from entering consciousness."[53]   Parapraxes have
been experimentally produced.   For instance, a subject was
given a post-hypnotic suggestion to the effect that he would
be bored by a conversation but would attempt to conceal his
boredom.   At one stage he closed the door to the room and
when asked what he was doing, replied, "Why, I just shut
the bore."[53]

If negative ESP scores are to be regarded as parapraxes, they are instances where the relevant memory trace,
say, of the symbol "star" which corresponds with the ESP
target "forms a compromise with a seemingly irrelevant
memory," say, with "circle," thus making for an incorrect
response.

The parapraxes of memory occur when there is a conflict between the demands of an actual situation and a psychological need.   If negative ESP responses are parapraxes, we
expect they, too, will be found in conflict situations.   This

appears to be the case.   For instance, G. R. Schmeidler[70]
found that subjects who said they did not believe there could
be evidence for ESP in a given experiment tended to score
negatively while the believers scored positively.   Here, we
have a clear conflict between a person's belief and the actual
situation in which he finds himself: the subject has agreed
to undertake a task which he believes to be impossible.   In
tests with school children by M. Anderson and R. White,[2]
the conflict is of a different nature.   The teachers who administered the ESP tests were rated by the children into
liked and disliked categories.   It was found that while the
children scored positively with liked teachers, the tests with
the disliked teachers gave negative deviations.   Again, there
is a conflict between the task at hand, namely, to respond
correctly to the ESP symbols, and the psychological situation,
namely, the negative relationship to the person in charge of
the tests.   Other examples where a conflict between the demands of the ESP test and its psychological setting was associated with psi-missing are reviewed by K. R. Rao.[52]

Symbolism

A symbol is an object or activity which represents
something else.   Symbols play an important part in our mental life.   Sometimes we are consciously aware of the connections between a thing and its symbol; other times, we are
not.   "Symbolization," D. Rapaport[53] says, "is a representation, or in other words reproduction, of an idea in visual
images using the available memory-traces for this purpose. "

Most parapsychologists who have studied cases of os-
tensible ESP outside the laboratory, such as ESP dreams or
tests using free response methods have observed that ESP is
often symbolic.   Among those who have paid special attention
to this are E. Osty,[44] L. E. Rhine,[60] and W. H. C. Tenhaeff.[77,78]   There are several examples in the excerpt from
Tenhaeff referred to earlier.[78]   For instance, mental images
of fjords were a symbol of Norway for Beta and an image of
a bottle of wine was a symbol for a name, the first part of
which means "wine" in Dutch.   The latter example illustrates
that a person does not always know what a symbol represents.
The association that first came to mind was wine drinking,
which led to an ESP error; only afterwards was the "correct"
association seen.   One thought or image may be represented
by several symbols.   Symbolic representations have also
been found in card tests.   R. Cadoret and J. G. Pratt[8]

found evidence in what they called "the consistent missing effect" that the subject substituted another of the four ESP card designs for the one that was target. For instance, if the card was "circle," the subject might say "cross" or "square" instead.

There appear to be several reasons for symbolism in familiar mental processes. For instance, prohibited strivings may be represented in consciousness by images whose meaning the person is hiding from himself. This type of substitution is similar to those that are found in parapraxes and are likely, in ESP tests, to lead to psi-missing. Another reason for symbolic ESP responses may be, simply, a deficiency in the percipient of available memory traces corresponding with the target. If the target idea can be represented by a symbol, then at least the general meaning may be conveyed.

The Unconsciousness of ESP

One of the features of ESP which sets it off from such sensory modalities as vision and hearing is the absence of any introspective characteristics whereby ESP responses can be identified for what they are. There appears to be no way in which we can recognize an ESP impression before it is compared with some actual state of affairs, such as the series of cards used as targets. ESP is sometimes "conscious" insofar as it may be associated with an experience in awareness, such as a mental image, but it is "unconscious" insofar as the person who experiences the image apparently cannot, at the time, be certain that it is due to ESP. The absence of an introspective guide is one of the greatest impediments to the practical use of ESP. If we could know when an impression was due to ESP, this would greatly improve the prospects for practical application, even if such impressions were rare and erratic. However, the images and other forms of expression that ESP assumes do not, by themselves, give any clues about their parapsychological origin. This, of course, is to be expected if ESP responses consist of memory traces. Since memory traces are the products of sensory perceptions and other familiar psychological processes, introspectively, they reflect these rather than the ESP stimulus that evokes them.

W. Carington,[10] the English parapsychologist, in tests with drawings as ESP targets, found that his subjects could

not distinguish their correct responses from incorrect ones.
Similarly, B. Shackleton, the highly successful subject of
S. G. Soal,[74] failed to distinguish card hits from misses.
My experience with English college students was the same.[61]
Also in card experiments in the United States, for instance
by B. A. McMahan and E. K. Bates,[36] C. E. Stuart,[75] and
by J. L. Woodruff and R. W. George,[92] the subjects were
unable to identify their hits.

So-called mediums and sensitives are often thought to
produce more striking evidence of ESP than card-calling subjects.   However, they do not seem to be better at distinguishing right responses from wrong ones.   E. Osty[44] observed
some 45 years ago that "it is impossible to judge of the origin and the quality of ... information at the time of a seance." As J. B. Rhine[58] says, "the psi process itself
leaves no identifying trace in the subject's mind to make it
known as a psi experience."

There are a few experiments which seem to contradict this observation.   In ESP card tests by B. M. Humphrey
and F. Nicol[29] and by L. Eilbert and G. R. Schmeidler,[20]
the subjects appeared to succeed when asked to identify which
of their previous responses were ESP responses.   In these
experiments, however, there was actually no evidence for
ESP in the guesses the subjects estimated.   The only paranormal material were the estimates themselves.   The hypothesis advanced by Schmeidler, that her subjects did not
show awareness of ESP but simply made a second ESP guess
as to which earlier (chance) guesses matched their targets,
seems to be the most economical explanation for both experiments.   The same applies to the studies by C. B. Nash and
C. S. Nash,[39] C. B. Nash,[40] and G. R. Schmeidler[72] where
there was evidence of ESP in the calls which the subject
afterwards identified as ESP responses.   Unless it can be
determined whether the correct guesses which the subjects
identify are only their ESP hits, and not also their chance
hits, we cannot know whether a subject is introspectively
aware of the occurrence of ESP or is only making another
ESP response when he correctly says that a previous guess
matched its target.

This, however, is not to say there are no ways to
identify ESP responses at the time they are made.   If a subject's guessing habits are known, it may be possible to identify ESP responses when these interrupt the guessing habits.
For instance, in the cat experiments by Osis and Foster,[43]

ESP scores were found when a guessing response had terminated.   When a sequence of responses is interrupted which
is known to be due to subjective associative factors, this may
be the place to look for psi.   The psychoanalysts, J. Ehrenwald[19] and J. Eisenbud[21] report that in this way they have
distinguished ESP images from subjective ones in their patients' dreams.

In her studies of "conviction of ESP," L. E. Rhine[59]
noted that the percipient sometimes seemed to know when his
experience had a psi origin.   Since there is nothing to suggest that this awareness stems from a peculiar quality in-
herent in the ESP impression, I suggest it is due to the observation by the percipient of a contrast between the ESP experience and its context.   A psi basis is inferred when the
experience is inconsistent with previous mental or overt activities.   That this is the correct interpretation is suggested
by the fact that ESP experiences in the waking state are more
likely to carry conviction than ESP impressions in dreams.
If a person suddenly receives an "irrational" impression, for
instance, that "something is wrong at home," he is more
likely to take notice than if this occurred in a dream where
it is not unusual to experience (apparently) unconnected or
irrational thoughts and images.   In other words, when memory traces which are aroused by ESP are identified, this is
because the person was aware that no familiar external or internal stimulus was present which could have aroused them.
ESP responses may be identified, not because they possess
something which ordinary memory traces lack, but on the
contrary, because they lack something which ordinary memory
traces often possess, namely, an obvious stimulus.

Hypnosis, Memory, and ESP

In the effort to control ESP or to increase the yield,
several experimenters have used hypnosis.   There are two
schools of thought in parapsychology regarding the efficacy of
hypnosis and allied states.   Some investigators believe that
hypnosis and dissociated states facilitate the emergence of
ESP; others find them ineffective.   G. Pagenstecher,[45] a
German physician practicing in Mexico, discovered the ESP
abilities of his patient, Mrs. Maria Zierold, only after he
had hypnotised her (to cure her insomnia).   Similarly, the
Swedish psychiatrist, J. Björkhem,[6] found marked ESP abilities in hypnotised subjects who showed none in their waking
state.   Again, most of the mediums studied by members of

the Society for Psychical Research in England[27,68,73,79,86]
worked in more or less pronounced trance states, usually
self-induced.   L. E. Rhine, [60] in her analyses of non-experimental instances of ESP, found that "realistic" cases, that
is, cases where there was the closest correspondence with
the events, usually occurred in dreams rather than waking
states (but she did not find a greater number of ESP cases
in the dreaming state than the waking).   In recent experiments by M. Ullman, S. Krippner, and S. Feldstein[81] with
drawings as targets and free verbal responses, the subjects
were asleep at the time of testing.   Gardner Murphy[37] concluded that dissociated states are helpful to ESP because they
entail "freedom from inhibitory conscious factors" and "removal from contact with the conscious system of ideas."   A
similar view has been expressed by M. P. Reeves, [54] and
R. White[89] concluded from her survey of the older experimental material that the "first general requirement is to
achieve a state of complete relaxation."

        However, when we turn to the tests with ESP cards
and similar materials, we do not find the same emphasis on
dissociated states.   J. J. Grela[25] and J. Beloff and I. Mandleberg[5] did not find that hypnosis was an aid to ESP.   J. B.
Rhine, [56] in a summary of the experimental material on this
subject, concluded that there is no indication that hypnosis
improves ESP.   Add to this that high-scoring subjects such
as Soal's[74] were not in any kind of trance.   A study of the
experimental literature, on the contrary, indicates that wakefulness and alertness, sometimes approaching a high pitch of
excitement, supported with rewards and other forms of reinforcement, are associated with success.   It would be going
too far to say that the issue is clear cut.   Thus J. Fahler, [22] J. Fahler and R. Cadoret, [23] and L. Casler[12,13] report that hypnosis increased their subjects' card-hitting output.   The work of M. Ryzl[66] falls into a different category.
His hypnotic training procedure is used only with subjects
who show evidence of ESP in initial tests.   These subjects
then participate in a lengthy training program in which Ryzl
attempts to promote their experiences of mental images in
ESP test situations.   Once their ESP performance has been
stabilized, however, hypnosis need no longer be used.   Thus
his remarkable subject, P. Stepanek, is not hypnotised during card testing.

        There are many kinds of hypnotic procedures and sug-
gestions and perhaps some of these can affect ESP card-calling tests.   At the present, however, we are concerned only

with the limited question whether the hypnotic state as such facilitates scoring. Ryzl's work with Stepanek and most of the other card tests do not suggest that hypnosis is likely to increase the output of serial ESP tests but that it may help in the free impression kind of ESP experiment.

We can summarize these contrasting findings by saying that in situations where the subject describes his mental images and impressions in free verbal statements, hypnosis and other dissociated states appear to facilitate ESP. On the other hand, in serial ESP tests, where there is a restricted choice of responses such as the five ESP symbols, it is doubtful whether hypnosis or other states of dissociation improves the scores.

This apparent inconsistency is resolved if we regard the ESP response as a memory response. If we ask what effect hypnosis has on memory, we find it does not improve scores in the type of serial learning tests that resemble card calling but that it does improve recall of memories of meaningful past events such as those that make up the memory traces used for ESP responses of the free impression type.

R. W. White, G. F. Fox, and W. W. Harris[91] found that there was no improvement under hypnosis of the recall of the nonsense syllables used in serial learning tasks but there was a significant gain for meaningful verbal material. This finding was confirmed by B. G. Rosenthal.[64] The observation that hypnosis helps recall of material of this nature agrees with the commonly known fact that childhood and other early memories are more likely to return during sleep and other periods of dissociation than during periods of heightened consciousness. There is no conflict then between the adherents of ESP tests under hypnosis or other dissociated states and those who prefer waking state tests as long as the target material is adapted to the subject's state. The difficulties only arise if we expect good results from a card-calling subject merely by hypnotizing him or if we expect that a subject in tests with free verbal material will do better if we keep him wakeful and alert. It does not take much reflection to see that on the one hand, the five ESP symbols can easily be remembered under most conditions, while the memory traces that may be required to convey an unlimited target range must themselves cover a wide variety of events, and that the emergence of such a wide selection of memory traces usually only occurs in dissociated states where we are removed from the demands of everyday life.

Memory Traces as ESP Stimuli

There are strong indications that the ESP response is formed by the percipient's own memory traces. There is also some indication that in telepathy, where the source of information is another brain or mind, memory traces play a role in the transmission of information. Parapsychologists have not in recent years been as interested in the nature of ESP transmission as in the reception end of the process. The findings that suggest a relationship between memory and ESP transmission are mostly of older date.

René Warcollier,[87] who also mentioned the importance of memory traces for the ESP response, found that material in the unconscious of the telepathic agent is transmitted better than material on which he concentrates his attention. E. Osty[44] concluded that the further removed from the agent's attention the item is, the more likely it is to serve as a telepathic stimulus. Transmission of something on which attention is focused is, he said, "very rare indeed." More frequent is the communication of material which is within the range of consciousness but not actually thought of at the time. Most common is the communication of material which "lies, as if statically, in the reservoirs of memory." A report by the Russian Committee for the Study of Mental Suggestion, headed by V. M. Bekterev[85] stated that an image "to which the voluntary and deliberate attention of the sender was not directed was more easily transmitted to the percipient."

In England, S. G. Soal[73] reported that the medium, Mrs. Blanche Cooper, produced the best results when Soal was not thinking about the target. Similarly, Mrs. A. W. Verrall,[86] discovered only a few cases where the medium's correct statements corresponded with what the agent was thinking about at the time, more often they corresponded with ideas that were at the back of his mind. In an experiment with Mrs. Piper, R. Hodgson[27] instructed her to report on the activities of a third party at that moment. Instead, she described in great detail that person's activities on the previous day. E. R. Dodds[17] and C. D. Broad[7] also have commented on the greater incidence of the transmission of material that is not in the foreground of consciousness. [It is not certain that these investigators always took account of the fact that on any one occasion there will be a great number of items in the memory record of a person and only a few at the center of attention. If the probability of responding to all items is the same, on the basis of chance expectancy we an-

ticipate more hits on material in the memory record than on
material in consciousness.   The observations by these authors
are not offered as proven facts but as suggestions that should
be tested in properly designed experiments.]

     If the memory traces of the telepathic agent are used
in ESP transmission, we expect that the "laws of learning"
and the other characteristics of the memory process affect
the transmission process in the same way we found that they
affected the reception.   W. Carington[11] discovered that drawings which had been frequently shown to the agent seemed to
make better targets than others.   G. Pagenstecher[45] and J.
Björkhem[6] found that events which were accompanied by strong
emotions tended to be transmitted more easily than emotionally neutral events.   R. Heywood[26] also noted that the medium
responded to her "emotional memories" and mentioned the
problem facing a medium of "being swept down the stream of
a sitter's associated thoughts or memories."   Telepathy, it
appears, is an interaction between the memory records of
both agent and percipient.

The Brain, RNA, and ESP

     The existence of a relationship between memory and
ESP makes discoveries about memory of possible interest to
the parapsychologist.   Two recent discoveries may have implications for our understanding of ESP, namely the findings
that certain brain areas and certain chemicals play a role in
memory processes.   W. Penfield[71] has shown that memories
of past events can be elicited in human subjects by electrical
stimulation of the temporal lobes when these are exposed during brain operations.   On the other hand, when the electrodes
are applied, say, to the visual cortex, the patient only experiences meaningless sounds or sights.   Penfield calls the
area of the brain connected with memory the "interpretive
cortex."

     If memory traces are part of the ESP reception sys-
tem and if the interpretive cortex specializes in the retrieval
of memory traces, it is possible that it also plays a part in
the ESP process.   The interpretive cortex in that case would
function as an "ESP cortex," having a similar relation to
ESP stimuli as the visual cortex and optic nerve have to light
rays.

     Memories of the past are not necessarily destroyed by

destroying even large parts of the interpretive cortex; however, injury or diseases that affect the interpretive cortex as a rule also affect recall ability.   For instance, epileptic fits which are due to discharges in the interpretive cortex are often preceded by compulsive recall, say, of a childhood event.   The normal behavior of epileptics also often shows persevering and compulsive features characteristic of impaired learning ability. [46] It would be interesting to know how such persons perform in ESP tests.

In addition to the relationship between memory and macroscopic brain structure, there is evidence that molecular brain patterns affect learning and remembering.   For instance, the long-term administration of yeast ribonucleic acid (RNA) is said to improve impaired ability to remember in humans and to increase the rate of learning in animals. [16]

If the amount of RNA or other molecules in the brain facilitates learning and recall, we expect it may also facilitate ESP.   However, as in any other attempt to influence ESP performance, the conditions we introduce must be adjusted to the test.   RNA could only be expected to aid ESP in the case of a subject who is attempting to respond to targets which correspond to temporarily forgotten memory traces, the recall of which may be restored by ingestion of RNA.   RNA is not likely to be of use in tests, say, with the five ESP symbols, unless the memory of the subject is so poor that without it, he cannot recall even these.

The Nature of Memory Traces

It has been shown that the ESP response can be understood in terms of the familiar processes of memory.   These, however, are not themselves fully understood.   In particular, we do not know what a memory trace is nor where it is stored.   The discovery that RNA facilitates learning and remembering has stimulated the hope that the RNA molecule is itself the long-sought-after memory trace.   W. Dingman and B. M. Sporn[16] have cautioned, however, that we still lack grounds for identifying memory traces with RNA molecules. Before this step can be taken, it must be shown that changes in RNA metabolism caused by learning last as long as the memory in question can be demonstrated and that the destruction of the altered RNA state results in permanent loss of the memory.   K. S. Lashley[32] found that large parts of the cortex of rats can be destroyed without impairing the animals'

recognition of shapes.   Similarly, in man, large parts of the
cortex can be destroyed, including the interpretive cortex,[46]
without permanently abolishing memories of past events.
These facts appear to argue against the hypothesis that memory traces consist of localized structures in the brain such
as specific RNA molecules.

        Some findings in parapsychology suggest that the capa-
city to store information exists also in inanimate physical
systems.   If this is true, an examination of these findings
may give us some insight into the retention aspect of memory.

        The parapsychological phenomenon that may be rele-
vant to this question is "psychometry," or as research on
this form of ESP is also known, "object association" or
"token object" tests.   In such an experiment the subject
seems to obtain information about events in the past by holding, or being in the physical proximity of, an object which
has been in the neighborhood of these events.   The tests are
usually in the form of free association experiments in ESP
in which the subject says anything that comes to his mind in ·
connection with the past history of the object.   The method
has been widely used by the mediums studied by members of
the English Society for Psychical Research,[27,68,73,79,86]
by the "paragnosts" of W. H. C. Tenhaeff,[77,78] and others.[6,45]   F. W. H. Myers[38] said that "objects which have
been in contact with organisms preserve their trace; and it
sometimes seems as though even inorganic nature could still
be made, so to say, luminescent with the age-old history of
its past. "   Sir Oliver Lodge,[34] the English physicist who was
one of the pioneers in the development of wireless telegraphy,
remarked that "it appears as if we left traces of ourselves,
not only on our bodies, but on many other things with which
we have been subordinately associated, and that these traces
can thereafter be detected by a sufficiently sensitive person. "
N. Kotik,[3] an early Russian investigator, found he could
transfer the "psychic energy" from a person's brain to a
piece of paper and use this paper to develop corresponding
ideas in another person.   G. Pagenstecher,[45] who found a
remarkable psychometry subject among his patients, used
pumice stones and other objects for his studies of their
"stored vibrations. "

        The idea that there can be a close causal relationship
between ESP and material objects is foreign to the thinking
of many present day parapsychologists.   Nevertheless, the

effect appears to have turned up in card testing experiments. For instance, in the tests by G. W. Fisk and D. J. West[88] where packs of sealed cards were sent to the subjects, the subjects tended to avoid scoring on the cards West had handled though they were unaware of his participation in the experiments and though West did not know when his packs were being used. This avoidance tendency was similar to one West often had observed when he personally directed the testing. But here he seemed to inhibit the subjects' ESP by means of the cards themselves. Conversely, it appears that cards which have been endowed by the experimenters with favorable psi traces make better ESP targets. M. Ryzl and J. G. Pratt[66] discovered that P. Stepanek scored particularly high on two cards which seemed to differ from the rest only in that they were the cards that corresponded to the first two numbers on the experimenter's code sheet and might therefore have stood out more strongly in their minds. However, Ryzl and Pratt had no way of knowing during the experiment which particular cards the subject was guessing. Evidently, Stepanek responded directly to the cards' psi traces. The authors noted the similarity between this effect and those found in psychometry testing.

Findings such as these open up the possibility that in other card experiments the subjects also responded to such traces rather than to the familiar physical properties of the cards. Card experiments directed at this problem by M. Johnson[62] and myself[63] have shown that some subjects respond to blank cards whose only differences appear to be their different past histories. The hypothetical change caused by an event in an object or in some medium or "field"[62] surrounding it, whereby information about this event is stored, has been termed a "psi trace."

The similarity between psi traces and memory traces has been noted by the Australian physicist, Raynor Johnson:[31] "Rocks cannot remember--but they may hold a memory (in their associated psychic aether), which the mind of a man in favorable circumstances can cognize." The German embryologist, Hans Driesch,[18] suggests that in remembering the brain has the same function as the object used in object association experiments. Similarly, C. B. Nash,[41] in his Presidential Address to the Parapsychological Association, suggested that the same process is involved in remembering as in ESP of past events ("retrocognition").

The theory that memory traces are a special form of

psi traces, we may call the "psi trace theory of memory. "
Such a theory would explain the apparent lack of cortical
localization of memory traces.   Once a memory trace has
been formed by physical events in a brain (e. g. by a special
RNA configuration) it can be communicated to another part of
that brain (and there evoke corresponding RNA configurations)
as in remembering, or to other brains, as in ESP. H. H.
Price[50] theorizes along such lines when he suggests that ESP
hallucinations ("apparitions") of the kind which are said to
recur in special places may be due to mental images which
have lost their connection with the mind in which they originated and have become attached to a region of physical space.
Here they create a "psychic atmosphere" which, when it over-
laps with the psychic atmosphere of a person sensitive to it,
may cause him to see an "apparition. "

The proposal that information about past events can
actually be stored in physical objects is likely to strike one
as highly implausible.   What, after all, could be the physical
structure which could contain such information?   If we address ourselves to this question, we discover that physicists
have in fact postulated structures in the universe which could
do exactly this, that is, could contain information about past
events.   The "world-line" of relativity theory is such a
structure.   A world-line can be described, simply, as the
spatial path of an object over a period of time.   However,
world-lines are not only a means of representing the location
of an object in space and time, they are held to have real
existence.   If this is indeed the case, then the concept of
world-lines may help to provide an explanation of the retention capacity of inanimate matter and perhaps also of animate
matter.   C. B. Nash[41] suggests that "Memory ... is auto-
scopic retrocognition by means of the world-lines of particles
in the brain. "   We might similarly say that in object association, the subject follows the world-lines of the object into its
past and in this way obtains information about events that
happened in its neighborhood.   The test of a concept lies in
its predictive powers.   It might be worth the effort to explore
with physicists what the empirical consequences would be of
regarding psi traces and memory traces as world-lines.   At
the present, however, it will be enough to indicate this as a
possible area of exploration.   Whether or not this approach
is fruitful, it is consistent with the general rapprochement
between the physical and life sciences.   For instance, A. A.
Cochran[14] has found that the wave properties of inanimate
matter are highly predominant in protein, the most important
substance of living matter, and that the most abundant chem-

ical elements in protein, carbon and hydrogen, are also the
elements with the highest degree of wave predominance.
Perhaps we shall similarly find that what we might call the
"trace properties" of living matter are also found in inanimate matter and perhaps even predominate in these substances.

Epicrisis

        If we distinguish between the learning, retention, re-
membering, and forgetting aspects of memory, the ESP response can be described as an instance of remembering
something that the organism learnt in the course of its past
sensory experiences or other familiar activities. This part
of the ESP process is an ordinary psychological or biological
one. It is only because there is evidence that the evoked
memories are relevant to some actual event which the person
could not have known about by sensory or rational means that
we are dealing with a parapsychological phenomenon. A survey of ESP investigations conducted at different times and in
different parts of the world supports the theory that the ESP
response consists of the percipient's own memory traces and
is, therefore, subject to the same "laws" and conditions that
affect learning and remembering. As other cognitive and
perceptual functions, ESP involves forgetting. In order to
respond to something new, the organism must be able to "forget" the old, either permanently or temporarily.

        Except in the limited case of telepathy, I have not dis-
cussed the nature of psi stimuli. In telepathy, it appears
these are often the memory traces of the telepathic agent.
In other forms of ESP, the subject may respond to traces
associated with inanimate systems. The apparent existence
of psi traces suggest that retention is a property of inanimate
as well as of animate matter.

        The mechanism whereby ESP stimuli reach the percipi-
ent may be similar to those that govern known physical processes. The evidence suggests that ESP, as sense perception, is the result of an interaction between a biological organism and its physical environment.

REFERENCES

1.   Abramowski, E.   Le Subsconscient Normal, Librairie
        Felix Alcan, Paris, 1914.

2. Anderson, M. and White, R. "A Survey of Work on ESP and Teacher-Pupil Attitudes," J. Parapsychol., 22:246-268, 1958.

3. Bekhterev, V. M. "Further Observations of 'Mental' Influence of Man on Behavior of Animals," Conference of the Inst. of Study of Brain and Physic Activities, Feb. 2, 1920 (Private translation from the Russian at the Foundation for Research on the Nature of Man, Durham).

4. _____. "Collective Reflexology," Leningrad, 1921 (Private translation).

5. Beloff, J. and Mandleberg, I. "An Attempt to Validate the 'Ryzl Technique' for the Training of ESP," J. Soc. Psychical Rsch., 43:727, 229-249, 1966.

6. Björkhem, J. Det Ockulta Problemet, Lindblads Forlag, Uppsala, 1951.

7. Broad, C. D. Religion, Philosophy and Psychical Research, Routledge and Kegan Paul, London, 1953.

8. Cadoret, R. J. and Pratt, J. G. "The Consistent Missing Effect," J. Parapsychol., 14:244-256, 1950.

9. _____. "Effect of Novelty in Test Conditions on ESP Performance," J. Parapsychol., 16:192-203, 1952.

10. Carington, W. "Experiments on the Paranormal Cognition of Drawings," Proc. Soc. Psychical Rsch., 46:277-344, 1941.

11. _____. Telepathy; An Outline of Its Facts, Theory and Implications, Methuen, London, 1945.

12. Casler, L. "The Improvement of Clairvoyance Scores by Means of Hypnotic Suggestion," J. Parapsychol., 26:77-87, 1962.

13. _____. "Self-Generated Suggestions and Clairvoyance." Convention Paper. Eighth Annual Convention of the Parapsychological Association, New York, Sept. 9-11, 1965.

14. Cochran, A. A. "Mind, Matter and Quanta," Main Currents, 22:79-88, 1966.

15. Dean, E. D. "Plethysmograph Recordings as ESP Responses," Int. J. Neuropsychiatry, 2:439-446, 1966.

16. Dingman, W. and Sporn, M. B. "Molecular Theories of Memory," Science, 144:26-29, 1964.

17. Dodds, E. R. "Why I Do Not Believe in Survival," Proc. Soc. Psychical Rsch., 42:147-172, 1933-34.

18. Driesch, H. Psychical Research (transl. by T. Besterman), G. Bell and Sons, London, 1933.

19. Ehrenwald, J. New Dimensions of Deep Analysis: A Study of Telepathy in Interpersonal Relationships, Allen and Unwin, London, 1954.

20. Eilbert, L. and Schmeidler, G. R. "A Study of Certain

Psychological Factors in Relation to ESP Performance." J. Parapsychol. , 14:53-74, 1959.

21. Eisenbud, J. "Analysis of a Presumptively Telepathic
Dream," Psychiatric Quarterly, 22:103-135, 1948.

22. Fahler, J. "ESP Card Tests With and Without Hypnosis," J. Parapsychol. , 21:179-185, 1957.

23. _____, and Cadoret, R. J. "ESP Card Tests of
College Students With and Without Hypnosis," J.
Parapsychol. , 22:125-136, 1958.

24. Feather, S. R. "A Comparison of Performance in
Memory and ESP Tests," in Parapsychology from
Duke to FRNM by J. B. Rhine and Associates,
Parapsychology Press, Durham, 1965.

25. Grela, J. J. "Effect on ESP Scoring of Hypnotically
Induced Attitudes," J. Parapsychol. , 9:194-202,
1945.

26. Heywood, R. "The Labyrinth of Associations," J. Soc.
Psychical Rsch. , 42:227-229, 1964.

27. Hodgson, R. "A Further Record of Observations of
Certain Phenomena of Trance," Proc. Soc. Psychical Rsch. , 13:284-584, 1897-98.

28. Humphrey, B. M. "ESP and Intelligence " J. Parapsychol. , 9:7-16, 1945.

29. _____, and Nicol, F. "The Feeling of Success in
ESP," J. Amer. Soc. Psychical Rsch. , 49:3-37,
1955.

30. James, W. "A Record of Observations of Certain
Phenomena of Trance," Proc. Soc. Psychical Rsch. ,
6:443-557, 1889-90.

31. Johnson, R. C. The Imprisoned Splendour, Hodder and
Stoughton, London, 1953.

32. Lashley, K. S. Brain Mechanisms and Intelligence,
Chicago University Press, Chicago, 1929.

33. Lodge, O. "A Record of Certain Phenomena of Trance
2, Part 1," Proc. Soc. Psychical Rsch. , 6:443-
557, 1889-90.

34. _____. "Report on some Trance Communications
Received Chiefly Through Mrs. Piper," Proc. Soc.
Psychical Rsch. , 23:127-285, 1909.

35. McElroy, W. A. and Brown, R. K. "Electric Shocks
for Errors in ESP Card Tests," J. Parapsychol. ,
14:257-266, 1950.

36. McMahan, E. A. and Bates, E. K. "Report on Further
Marchesi Experiments," J. Parapsychol. , 18:82-
92, 1954.

37. Murphy, G. "Psychical Research and Personality,"
Proc. Soc. Psychical Rsch. , 49:1-15, 1949.

38. Myers, F. W. H. Human Personality and Its Survival of Bodily Death, Longmans, Green, and Co. , London, 1903.

39. Nash, C. B. and Nash, C. S. "Checking Success and the Relationship of Personality Traits to ESP," J. Amer. Soc. Psychical Rsch. , 52:98-107, 1958.

40. _____ . "Can Precognition Occur Diametrically?," J. Parapsychol. , 24:26-32, 1960.

41. _____ . "Physical and Metaphysical Parapsychology," J. Parapsychol. , 27:283-300, 1963.

42. Osis, K. "A Test of the Occurrence of a Psi Effect Between Man and the Cat," J. Parapsychol. , 16: 233-256, 1952.

43. _____ , and Foster, E. "A Test of ESP in Cats," J. Parapsychol. , 17:167-186, 1953.

44. Osty, E. Supernormal Faculties in Man (transl. by S. de Brath), Methuen, London, 1923.

45. Pagenstecher, G. "Past Events Seership: A Study in Psychometry," Proc. Amer. Soc. Psychical Rsch. , 16:1-136, 1922.

46. Penfield, W. "The Interpretive Cortex," Science, 129: 1719-1725, 1959.

47. Piddington, J. G. "Forecasts in Scripts Concerning the War," Proc. Soc. Psychical Rsch. , 33:439-605, 1923.

48. Pratt, J. G. "The Meaning of Performance Curves in ESP and PK Test Data," J. Parapsychol. , 13:9-23, 1949.

49. _____ , and Soal, S. G. "Some Relations Between Call Sequences and ESP Performance," J. Parapsychol. , 16:165-186, 1952.

50. Price, H. H. "Haunting and the 'Psychic Ether' Hypothesis," Proc. Soc. Psychical Rsch. , 45:307-343, 1939.

51. _____ . "Memory and Paranormal Cognition. " Convention Paper. Seventh Annual Convention of the Parapsychological Association, Oxford Univ. , Sept. 3-6, 1964.

52. Rao, K. R. "The Bidirectionality of Psi," J. Parapsychol. , 29:230-250, 1965.

53. Rapaport, D. Emotions and Memory. Science Editions, Inc. , New York, 1961.

54. Reeves, M. P. "A Topological Approach to Parapsychology," J. Amer. Soc. Psychical Rsch. , 38:72-82, 1944.

55. Rhine, J. B. Extra-Sensory Perception, Bruce Humphries, Boston, 1935.

56. _____. "Extrasensory Perception and Hypnosis."
        In Lecron, L. M. Experimental Hypnosis, p. 359-
        375, Macmillan, New York, 1952.
57. _____, Humphrey, B. M., Averill, R. B. "An Ex-
        ploratory Experiment on the Effect of Caffeine Upon
        Performance in PK Tests," J. Parapsychol., 9:
        80-91, 1945.
58. _____. New World of the Mind, William Sloane,
        New York, 1953.
59. Rhine, L. E. "Conviction and Associated Conditions in
        Spontaneous Cases," J. Parapsychol., 15:164-191,
        1951.
60. _____. "Frequency of Types of Experiences in Spon-
        taneous Precognition," J. Parapsychol., 18:93-123,
        1954.
61. Roll, W. G. "Theory and Experiment in Psychical Re-
        search," unpubl. B. Litt. Thesis, Oxford Univ.,
        1959.
62. _____. "The Psi Field." Presidential Address.
        Seventh Annual Convention of the Parapsychological
        Association, Oxford Univ., Sept. 3-6, 1964.
63. _____. "Token Object Matching Tests: Third Ser-
        ies," J. Amer. Soc. Psychical Rsch., 60:363-379,
        1966.
64. Rosenthal, B. G. "Hypnotic Recall of Material Learned
        Under Anxiety and Non-Anxiety Producing Conditions,"
        J. Exper. Psychol., 34:369-389, 1944.
65. Ross, A. C., Murphy, G., Schmeidler, G. R. "The
        Spontaneity Factor in Extrasensory Perception,"
        J. Amer. Soc. Psychical Rsch., 46:14-16, 1952.
66. Ryzl, M. and Pratt, J. G. "The Focusing of ESP upon
        Particular Targets," J. Parapsychol., 27:227-241,
        1963.
67. Salter, Mrs. W. H. "Some Incidents Occurring at
        Sittings with Mrs. Leonard Which May Throw Light
        upon Their Modus Operandi," Proc. Soc. Psychical
        Rsch., 39:306-332, 1930-31.
68. Saltmarsh, H. F. "A Report on the Investigation of
        Some Sittings with Mrs. Warren Elliott," Proc.
        Soc. Psychical Rsch., 39:47-184, 1929.
69. Schmeidler, G. R. "Rorschachs and ESP Scores of
        Patients Suffering from Cerebral Concussion,"
        J. Parapsychol., 16:80-89, 1952.
70. _____, and McConnell, R. A. ESP and Personality
        Patterns, Yale University Press, New Haven, 1959.
71. _____. "ESP and Tests of Perception," J. Amer.
        Soc. Psychical Rsch., 56:48-51, 1962.

72. _____. "An Experiment on Precognitive Clairvoyance, Part V. Precognition Scores Related to Feelings of Success," J. Parapsychol., 28:109-125, 1965.

73. Soal, S. G. "A Report on Some Communications Received Through Mrs. Blanche Cooper," Proc. Soc. Psychical Rsch., 35:471-594, 1925.

74. _____, and Bateman, F. Modern Experiments in Telepathy, Faber and Faber, London, 1954.

75. Stuart, C. E. "An Analysis to Determine a Test Predictive of Extra-Chance Scoring in Card-Calling Tests," J. Parapsychol., 5:99-137, 1941.

76. Tart, C. T. "Card Guessing Tests: Learning Paradigm or Extinction Paradigm?," J. Amer. Soc. Psychical Rsch., 60:46-55, 1966.

77. Tenhaeff, W. H. C. Psychoscopic Experiments on Behalf of the Police. Conference Report No. 41, First Int. Conference of Parapsychological Studies, Utrecht, Holland, 1953.

78. _____. Proceedings of the Parapsychological Institute of the State University of Utrecht, No. 3, January, 1965.

79. Thomas, C. D. "The Modus Operandi of Trance Communication According to Descriptions Received Through Mrs. Osborne Leonard," Proc. Soc. Psychical Rsch., 38:49-100, 1928-29.

80. Tyrrell, G. N. M. Science and Psychical Phenomena. Apparitions. University Books, New York, 1961.

81. Ullman, M., Krippner, S. and Feldstein, S. "Experimentally-induced Telepathic Dreams: Two Studies Using EEG-REM Monitoring Technique," Int. J. Neuropsychiatry, 2:420-438, 1966.

82. Urban, H. J. Parapsychological Research at a Psychiatric Clinic. Conference Report No. 18, First International Conference of Parapsychological Studies, Utrecht, Holland, 1953.

83. van Busschbach, J. G. "An Investigation of Extrasensory Perception in School Children," J. Parapsychol., 17:210-222, 1953; "A Further Report on an Investigation of ESP in School Children," J. Parapsychol., 19:73-81, 1955; "An Investigation of ESP Between Teacher and Pupils in American Schools," J. Parapsychol., 20:71-80, 1956.

84. Van de Castle, R. L. "An Exploratory Study of Some Variables Relating to Individual ESP Performance," J. Parapsychol., 17:61-72, 1953.

85. Vasiliev, L. L. Experiments in Mental Suggestion, In-

stitute for the Study of Mental Images, Church
Crookham, Hampshire, England, 1963.

86.   Verrall, Mrs. A. W.   "Notes on the Trance Phenomena
      of Mrs. Thompson," Proc. Soc. Psychical Rsch.,
      17:164-244, 1901-3.

87.   Warcollier, R.   Experimental Telepathy (transl. by
      J. B. Gridley from La Telepathie, 1921), Boston
      Soc. for Psychical Rsch., 1938.

88.   West, D. J. and Fisk, G. W.   "A Dual ESP Experi-
      ment with Clock Cards," J. Soc. Psychical Rsch.,
      37:185-189, 1953.

89.   White, R.   "A Comparison of Old and New Methods of
      Response to Targets in ESP Experiments," J.
      Amer. Soc. Psychical Rsch., 58:21-56, 1964.

90.   _____, and Angstadt, J.   "Student Preferences in a
      Two-Classroom GESP Experiment with Two Stu-
      dent-Agents Acting Simultaneously," J. Amer. Soc.
      Psychical Rsch., 57:32-42, 1963.

91.   White, R. W., Fox, G. F. and Harris, W. W.   "Hyp-
      notic Hypermnesia for Recently Learned Material,"
      J. Abnor. and Soc. Psychol., 35:88-103, 1940.

92.   Woodruff, F. L. and George, R. W.   "Experiments in
      Extra-Sensory Perception," J. Parapsychol., 1:18-
      30, 1937.

ADDITIONAL READINGS ON MEMORY
AND PSI PHENOMENA

Barrington, M. R. "A free response sheep/goat experiment using an irrelevant task." JSPR 47: 222-45 (Dec 1973).

Feather, S. R. "A quantitative comparison of memory and psi." JP 31: 93-98 (Jun 1967).

Heywood, R. "The labyrinth of associations." JSPR 42: 227-29 (Mar 1964).

_____, and Stevenson, I. "The connections between previous experiences and an apparently precognitive dream." JASPR 60: 32-45 (Jan 1966).

Honorton, C. and Harper, S. "Psi-mediated imagery and ideation in an experimental procedure for regulating perceptual input." JASPR 68: 156-68 (Apr 1974).

Kanthamani, H. and Rao, H. H. "A study of memory--ESP relationships using linguistic forms." JP 38: 286-300 (Sep 1974).

_____, and _____. "The role of association strength in memory-ESP interaction." JP 39: 1-11 (Mar 1975).

Kreitler, H. and Kreitler, S. "ESP and cognition." JP 38: 267-85 (Sep 1974).

Parker, K. "Relationship between immediate memory and ESP scores." Paper given at the Southeastern Regional Parapsychological Association Conference held Jan. 10 and 11, 1975. (Abstract) JP 39: 35 (Mar 1975).

Pratt, J. G. "Computer studies of the ESP process in card guessing: II. Did memory habits limit Mrs. Stewart's ESP success?" JASPR 61: 182-202 (Jul 1967).

Stanford, R. G. "Extrasensory effects upon 'memory'." JASPR 64: 161-86 (Apr 1970).

_____. "Response factors in extrasensory performance." Journal of Communication 25: 153-61 (Win 1975).

Tenhaeff, W. H. C. Telepathy and Clairvoyance. Springfield, Ill., Charles C Thomas, 1972.

Chapter 16

THE CHALLENGE OF PSI:
New Horizons of Scientific Research*

by C. T. K. Chari**

Dr. J. B. Rhine (1972), in a suggestive article, has
explored the several complex relations parapsychology bears
to the main divisions of science. I wish to underline, in
the context of his remarks, the immense challenges as well
as the immense opportunities psi offers to contemporary science and contemporary philosophy of science.

Is a Physicalistic Theory of Psi Feasible?

I must, in the first place, insist that there is no known
physicalistic theory which covers, even in principle, the man-
ifold aspects of psi. In two recent papers (1970a, 1972b), I
have examined in some technical detail many of the proposed
theories--notably those of A. C. Garnett, G. D. Wasser-
mann, J. M. J. Kooy, Ninian Marshall (see my remarks in
Chari, 1964), Durk Pearson (as reported by Douglas Dean),
H. A. C. Dobbs, and I. J. Good--and stressed their utter
inadequacy if they are intended as "explanations" of psi.

Ruderfer (1968) has put forward a neutrino theory of
ESP. The suggestion is not new. In an earlier note in this
Journal (1957), I remarked that the theory was advanced in
1957 by an All-India Radio engineer, V. V. L. Rao. Ignoring for the time being the problematic role of neutrinos in
biopsychological information processing, I must ask whether

*Reprinted by permission of the author and publisher from
the Journal of Parapsychology 38: 1-15 (Mar 1974).
**I acknowledge support from the Parapsychology Foundation
Inc., of New York and I owe much to the steady encourage-
ment I have received from Dr. J. B. Rhine over the years
in my rambles through the world of psi.

particles with a proper mass* of zero and traveling with the
maximal velocity of light can ever cross the "barrier of the
future," i.e., annul the relativistic distinction between the
"forecone" and the "aftercone," and account for precognition.
In very few of the cosmological models (and they are not the
prevailing ones) can the neutrino "travel against the arrow
of time" (Narlikar, 1962). The "rate of flow of information"
varies in the steady-state De Sitter, Page, Milne, Einstein,
and Dirac cosmologies.

Tachyons (so christened by Gerald Feinberg in 1967
though E. C. G. Sudarshan had invoked them earlier in 1962),
particles with an imaginary proper mass and traveling with
a velocity greater than that of light, have been recently proposed as possible "carriers" of "precognitive ESP information" (see my remarks in Chari, 1972b, postscript). I shall
waive the by no means negligible questions whether tardyons
(so named by Olexa-Myron Bilaniuk), that is, particles with
a mass greater than zero and traveling with a velocity less
than that of light, in the human brain or elsewhere, can be
converted into tachyons while maintaining other relationships
in the relevant system constant, and also whether consciousness can control the speed and direction of the hypothetical
"superliminal" particles. I focus attention on what seems a
more serious difficulty. On the basis of a mathematical
analysis carried out by Bilaniuk in the 1971 issue of the Mc-
Graw-Hill Yearbook of Science and Technology, Isaac Asimov
finds that, whichever side of the "luxon wall" (i.e., the relativistic barrier presented by the finite velocity of light) we
are on, would seem to be the tardyon universe for us; only
the "other side" would appear to be the tachyon world. There
would seem to be perfect mathematical symmetry between the
two worlds. If so, the speed limit remains for us and the
problem of precognitive ESP has not been lightened by even
a feather-weight. Incidentally, the speed of light constitutes
a limit also for the fastest sequential computer.

I should like to add that much the same theoretical
situation would seem to prevail if, by changing the signs in
the CPT (charge-parity-time) theorem, we postulate two mathematically symmetrical worlds, matter and anti-matter (Stannard, 1966). There would be no cogent reasons for supposing interaction, especially recurrent interaction, between the

---

*The term "proper mass" is used in Bilaniuk's sense; it re-
places the older term "rest mass."

two worlds.   In the cosmology proposed by Alfvén (1967), a
particle of matter and one of anti-matter annihilate each other.   In the cosmology of Oskar Klein quasars are anti-matter worlds but protected from annihiliation, in the possible
interaction with the opposite world next door, by a sort of
glowing curtain of limited collisions.   Martin Gardner (1967)
sums up the present stage of scientific knowledge by saying
that two different time-arrows cannot be carried by the same
individual or by the same brain in the same world without
jeopardizing the whole theory.   The "psitron" theory of the
late H. A. C. Dobbs can claim no unequivocal support from
the logic of quantum mechanics or from the mathematics of
EEG rhythms (Chari, 1972b).

        I admire V. A. Firsoff for his bold critiques (e. g. ,
1965, 1969) of cosmological models.   But I fear that his
"mindons" carry but little promise for parapsychological research.   I am inclined to agree with Arthur Koestler (1973)
that all these labored attempts to lodge psi in a physicalistic
framework are disabled by something like the "fallacy of mis-
placed concreteness. "

The Problem of Precognition

        Satosi Watanabe (1961) complained that Rhine took too
narrow a view of physics in envisaging a nonphysical ESP.
Can Watanabe, or somebody else for that matter, suggest
in some detail how the ambitious program of fitting psi into
the known laws of physics is to be implemented?   In a recent
international symposium (1971a), I have argued the information-theoretic case for temporal asymmetry in the universe.
Professor Adolf Grünbaum (1963, pp. 287-88) finds that the
"temporal asymmetry of recordability" makes cases of bona
fide precognition "overwhelmingly improbable, " but he gen-
erously adds that if evidence of sufficient quality and quantity
is forthcoming for so bizarre a phenomenon, he for one is
prepared to "envision such alterations in the body of current
orthodox scientific theory as may be required. " Herbert
Feigl (1963, pp. 240-41), too, in a volume dedicated to Rudolf Carnap, admitted that if psi phenomena were firmly established, "our conception of the basic laws of nature may
well have to be revised at least in some essential aspects. "
Parapsychologists have no further argument with philosophers
of science if it is only more evidence that is required.

        Professor C. W. K. Mundle (1973), in his presidential

address to the S. P. R. , makes a somewhat strange plea when
he counsels us to "explain precognition away" (italics not
mine) in view of the paradoxes in which it threatens to land
us.   Any parapsychologist who is content to remain a thor-
ough-going empiricist, cheerfully leaving all theories aside,
must continue to insist obstinately on "noninferential pre-
records" however much they flout all current theories of the
universe.   Rhine (1972, p. 104) pertinently observes, "The
point of importance here is that obviously no physical principle can furnish a reasonable explanation of the significant
results in the many years of precognition experiments...."

T. S. Kuhn's "Scientific Revolutions"
and Parapsychology

Dr. R. H. Thouless (1971) and others have drawn the
attention of parapsychologists to T. S. Kuhn's book (1962)
which assigns a crucial role to "scientific revolutions" in all
notable advances made in scientific theory.   What are the
implications of this view for the philosophy of science and
for parapsychology?   What are we to make of Kuhn's "anomalies"?   R. Suszko (1968) thinks that the postulated universe
of the new paradigm, in a scientific revolution, may be an
overset of the universe of the older paradigm.   The older
scientific language may be embedded as a subset in the newer language.   On this view, scientific languages are (in principle at least) "open" and, in any scientific revolution, change
to accommodate newer sets and newer relations.

J. Giedymin (1968), however, points out that Kuhn's
"revolutions" perhaps make the growth of scientific knowledge
more than merely cumulative.   There may be radical dis-
continuities of languages in scientific revolutions which negate
Suszko's suggested inclusion of sets.   If that may conceivably
hold for scientific revolutions in general, I submit that it may
hold a fortiori for a radical and revolutionary discipline like
parapsychology, the empirical language of which cannot be re-
constructed into the available axiomatic, semantic, and pragmatic rules of orthodox scientific theory.   Precognition, in
my considered opinion, calls for an unprecedented revolution
in our modes of interpreting the status and functions of sym-
bol-using sentient organisms in the universe.   As Rhine
(1956, p. 205) has remarked, psi phenomena represent a
"Copernican order of revolution" which is without parallel in
psychology.

Some Problems of "Psi Physics"

        Instead of asking whether present-day physics can con-
tribute to a new understanding of psi, it may be more profitable for us to ask whether psi can hint at some re-interpretation of present-day physical theory. As Rhine (1972) phrases
the challenge and the opportunity, "this means, of course,
that whatever psi is, it interoperates with the natural physical order." Can psi, for instance, foreshadow some new
grasp of the issues involved in the still hotly contested "quantum-mechanical theory of measurement"? Methodology and
revolutionary re-interpretation are not easily separated in a
discipline like parapsychology. To assert that the science of
psi furnishes reliable data but no theory is to miss the challenge.

        Helmut Schmidt's experiment (1971) to test precognitive
psi in effect couples the consciousness of an observer to a
quantum-mechanical process. What is the role of consciousness in the experimental set-up? W. Klip (1967) mooted the
question but confined its scope to a possible PK effect.
J. H. M. Whiteman, who has written on the profounder aspects of psi as well as of the mystical life (1961), is content
with saying that the "state vector" of a quantum-mechanical
system stands for "a potentiality which cannot be represented
in terms of specific actualized structures" (1967, p. 340).
It seems to me that this view does not represent any significant advance over Heisenberg's version of the "Copenhagen
interpretation" of quantum mechanics.

        I have debated, in more than one context (Chari, 1966b,
1966c, 1969, 1971b, 1972b), several alternative technical interpretations of the "quantum-mechanical theory of measurement." The basic issue is that superposition disappears in
the process of measurement and that the Schrödinger wave
becomes somehow nonlinear (Amai, 1963; Burgers, 1963;
Wigner, 1963). Attempts to eliminate the conscious observer
and replace him by an unconscious recording device, plausible
as they are at the first glance, lead to difficulties (Shimony,
1963). An infinite regress can be apparently terminated only
in the consciousness of an observer. The apparent result is
embodied in the so-called paradox of "Wigner's friend" (Jauch,
1968, pp. 187-88, 191). The hypothesis (Green, 1958; Landé,
1960) that reduction of the "wave packet" occurs when a mac-
rosystem interacts with a microsystem, i. e., that the interaction is somehow irreducibly stochastic, seems insufficient.
J. M. Jauch (1964) proposed to dispense with consciousness

and the irreducible interaction of macrosystems and microsystems. He introduced a "classical" property postulated as
common to macrosystems and microsystems in the shape of
an "Abelian set of observables." As a discerning reviewer
in Mathematical Reviews (May, 1966) pointed out, the alleged
correspondence between the "Abelian set" and physical "observables" was not demonstrated by Jauch. In a later systematic exposition (1968), Jauch says that physical theory
should be interested as much in the aesthetic form of the constructs (presumably the "Abelian set") as in any correspondence with experience. My impression is that the "subjectivity"
of the "quantum theory of measurement" remains in Jauch's
theory and restricts us to certain observables alone, i.e.,
those prescribed by the "Abelian set." Not all self-adjoint
operators, Jauch grants, are observable.

In a symposium on the philosophy of science conducted
not long ago, two sharply opposed views about the epistemology of quantum mechanics were presented: on the one hand,
there was the view of E. H. Hutten (1968, p. 142) that the
observer as "the creator of information" plays a central role
in physics and, on the other hand, Mario Bunge's view (1968,
pp. 146-47) that "physics has had enough of the psyche."
Dr. John Beloff (1973) has argued, and very persuasively,
that subliminal processes in some ways behave extraordinarily
like ESP. In other ways, I suspect, ESP is radically different. It must be confessed that ordinary mental processes like
the resolution of perceptual and conceptual vagueness and the
evocation of alternative strategies in decision-making (White,
1969) provide no analogies to the quantum-mechanical resolution of a "wave packet" (Shimony, 1963). A "psi physics,"
as Rhine (1972) calls it, cannot be constructed with these
mental processes only.

In a "psi physics," minds and material systems do not
simply co-exist; nor do they interact only in the manner of
Karl Popper's (1966) "plastic control" system with "statistical
clouds." E. P. Wigner (1962, 1963, 1964) holds that the evolution of conscious states does not obey the known quantum-
mechanical laws. Non-linearity in wave mechanics, he thinks,
may be a sign of the presence of life and consciousness.
Can parapsychology make sense of these suggestions, coming
as they do from one who has been called "the conscience of
modern physics"? G. Ludwig (1954) and others have argued
that quantum mechanics is valid only in micro-descriptions
and has no unlimited validity in macro-descriptions. Wigner
(1962), however, maintains that there is no sharp line between

macro-description and micro-description (see my discussion, Chari, 1966a, pp. 388-90). Interaction between psi and the natural physical order, Rhine (1972) hazards, "necessarily implies the existence of a more general <u>common</u> <u>principle</u> as a basis of interoperation" (italics not <u>mine</u>). I suggest (1971a, 1971b) that the differential equations of physics, interpreted as "laws," may have as their limits more general stochastic equations signifying more general processes. The theory of Markov chains can be treated as a limiting case of statistical theory. A strongly continuous Markov process can always be generated, but only by a suitable choice of the characteristic function. Meanwhile Rhine has provided what appears to me at least a guiding idea of some value. Where "psi physics" will lead us in the labyrinth of the universe we cannot yet foresee. It may be profitable to explore the probability space of experimental psi with entropic concepts (Schmidt, 1973).

Problems of "Psi Biology"

"Psi biology" also seems to me to open up new vistas. J. L. Randall (1971, 1972), in an excellent review of the research on ESP and PK in animals, remarks that the newer experiments (inaugurated by "Duval" and "Montredon") are entirely self-operating and virtually eliminate possible human influences on the organisms. Dr. Rhine (1972, pp. 109-10) says with justice that "there is a need for a more comparative study of psi in different species, to see whether there has been progress or decline of psi ability with evolution. In the background of such a research for evidence of psi in different species there will always be the pertinent question as to what the value of this ability has been to biological survival. "

Dr. John Poynton (1973) of the Biology Department of the University of Natal, Durban, South Africa, in a survey of the implications of parapsychology for the biological sciences, is inclined to dismiss as "free-wheeling speculation" Sir Alister Hardy's hypothesis (Hardy, 1953, 1965, 1966) of a "psychic pool of experience" acting as a "species blue print" in biological evolution, and also J. L. Randall's conjectures (1972) about a "psi factor" interacting with a material world and turning living beings into essentially "open, " information-gathering systems. I am afraid that I do not see that Dr. Poynton offers us any constructive suggestion of his own in his speculation on "self-organizing systems" which are

"potentially open" to "non-physical influences." Can we formulate more specific working hypotheses taking us beyond the
vaguely conceived vitalistic "dynamo-psychism" of Geley
(1920) and an earlier generation of parapsychologists?

The recent experiments of Levy and McRae (1971)
seem to imply that the ESP of animals is alerted in unfamiliar or disoriented situations. There would appear to be significant links between these animal psi experiments and the
new science of comparative behavior or ethology (Eibl-Eibesfeldt, 1970; Klopfer & Hailman, 1967). D. E. Berlyne (1960)
showed that a rodent like the rat displays a characteristic
tendency to be curious about a novel environment and to explore it and, at the same time, a tendency to be fearful of
it. Both responses are adaptive, and a balance between
the two is undoubtedly attained through natural selection.
From the experiments of Beach and Jaynes (1954), of Denenberg and Whimbey (1963), we may infer that the adaptive
behavior is also reached through experience. The degree of
fear manifested by an adult rodent introduced into a strange
environment can be substantially influenced by early weaning,
by handling through early life, or even by preweaning with
different mothers. These findings suggest that animal psi
may function, not only as a genotypic influence (as Alister
Hardy holds) but also as a phenotypic influence. Suppose G
is gene, E is environment and $(\Psi)GE$ is their interaction as
influenced by psi (Ψ), then a plausible symbolism for phenotypic behavioral variance may be

$$\sigma_P{}^2 = \sigma_G{}^2 + \sigma_E{}^2 + (\sigma_{\Psi GE})^2.$$

It is worth comparing the symbolism with T. Dobzhansky's
(1962) "coefficient of heritability" (h) for identical (I) and
fraternal (F) twins set down in terms of the variances (V's):
V_F-V_I/V_F. ESP, if it occurs in identical twins, may not
be simply "inherited" but may be a function of the environmental transactions as well.

The earlier "mnemic" theories of life, Ewald Hering's
Ueber das Gedächtniss als eine allgemeine Funktion der or-
ganisirten Materie, 1870, Samuel Butler's Life and Habit,
1878, and Richard Semon's Die Mneme, 1904, deserve to be
reviewed in the light of the new "psi biology." Experiments
with human subjects have suggested to more than one investigator that psi bears an affinity, if not identity, to memory
functions. To postulate "psi genes," as suggested by a perceptive Rumanian medical student, Miklós (1973), may not

perhaps be necessary, for that would shift the emphasis from my (Ψ)GE to the more tangible and more localizable G's.

Berlyne (1965) characterizes exploratory animal behavior in its several phases--orientation, locomotion, investigation--as culminating in what he calls "epistemic behavior." If I am right, psi in animals contributes to "epistemic behavior." Randall (1971) emphasizes, and rightly, the "informational increase" that appears to be associated with the operation of psi in living organisms. Statistical variance (V or σ^2) is closely analogous to the "information" of information theory (Chari, 1966c). One, therefore, wonders whether an ensemble of evolving organisms which interact with their environments can be represented by varying values of a "biological information" to which psi makes decisive contributions. More than one DNA conformation has been found to exist and display the basic Watson-Crick double helical structure. The left-handed structure seems to be excluded on stereochemical (and other?) grounds (Watson, 1968) even if diffraction patterns alone do not specify the screw-sense of the helix. The interatomic distances involved are sometimes very small. A "quantum psi biology" is not perhaps precluded (Elsasser, 1966; Shimony, 1965).

Reductionism, the Mind-Body Dualism, and Survival

I venture to think that parapsychology goes very much beyond the "reductionism vs. non-reductionism" (Koestler & Smythies, 1969) and computer vs. mind (Chari, 1968, 1970b, 1970c, 1972a) debates which have figured in much recent literature on scientific theory. The classical emergentism propounded in the twenties of this century by S. Alexander (1920) was a far step from reductionism. Yet Alexander could say brazenly that his entire metaphysics presupposed the nonoccurrence of telepathy. If holism, organicism, and emergentism are to come to terms with psi, they must be reformulated.

Contrary to the view held in some influential quarters, parapsychology has to do with problems which are more fundamental and far-reaching than the much-debated "body-mind" identity/or liaison (Borst, 1970; Feyerabend & Maxwell, 1966; Hampshire, 1966; Radner & Winokur, 1973), with its possible implications, positive or negative, for survival and reincarnation research. It is quite mis-leading to represent this research, legitimate though it remains and will remain as the

goal or the climax of parapsychology. The apparent postmortem or ante-mortem existence, in some undefined and
attenuated space-time, of a few isolated clusters of experiences and/or personal memories (even a million such cases
are a drop in the ocean of human mortality), which is all
that the most careful survival or reincarnation research can
support, stops far, far short of solving problems which a-
rise in the rest of parapsychology. It is fallacious to represent ESP and survival as necessarily exclusive and rival -
hypotheses, even though it is true that most survival data
could be comfortably accommodated by a rightly-conceived
ESP functioning in the life-setting. Survival, if it is not a
solipsistic dream-state, presupposes a very comprehensive
ESP. It is safe to say that until explicit solutions to the
more compelling problems of "psi physics" and "psi biology"
have been spelled out, the problem of human survival cannot
be posed effectively for science and philosophy, let alone
solved. We need, as Rhine (1972) has said with prophetic
wisdom, a science of the total man.

Conclusion: The Magnitude
of the Challenge of Psi

In concluding this note, I contend (in reply to a query
put to me by Dr. Rhine) that the issues about parapsychology
should be of concern, not to a few specialists recruited from
a few disciplines (though admittedly specialist knowledge is
invaluable in any pioneering field of research), nor even to a
few privileged cultures, whether occidental or oriental, with
their claimed unique perspectives (e. g. , the "scientific-in-
dustrial outlook" or the "religious-moral other-worldly outlook"). As I have remarked (1966a) in a festschrift for
W. E. Hocking, the parapsychological issues are vital to humanity at large, which confronts a world of new political and
economic conflicts and is perplexed about its status and role,
while anxious to know more about the increasingly strange
universe which none of the creeds quite anticipated. Eugene
Osty (1928), a former Director of the Institut Métapsychique
at Paris, hoped that the new science of metaphysics, when it
won general acceptance and attained a stature of its own,
would reduce much of the older metaphysics of mankind to
crude and dubious speculation conducted without adequate data.
Is it too much to say that we need this optimism today?

REFERENCES

Alexander, S.   Space, Time and Deity (2 vols.).   London:
      Macmillan & Co., 1920.
Alfvén, H.   "Antimatter and cosmology."   Scientific Ameri-
      can, 1967, 216, 106-14.
Amai, Saburo.   "Theory of measurement in quantum mechan-
      ics."   Progress of Theoretical Physics, 1963, 30,
      550-62.
Beach, F. A., & Jaynes, J.   "Effects of early experience
      upon the behavior of animals."   Psychological Bulletin,
      1954, 51, 239-63.
Beloff, J.   "The subliminal and the extrasensory."   Parapsy-
      chology Review, 1973, 4 (No. 3), 23-27.
Berlyne, D. E.   Conflict, Arousal and Curiosity.   New York:
      McGraw-Hill Book Co., 1960.
_____.   Structure and Direction in Thinking.   New York:
      John Wiley, 1965.
Borst, C. V. (Ed.).   The Mind-Brain Identity Theory.   Lon-
      don: Macmillan & Co., 1970.
Bunge, M.   "The Maturation of Science" in Problems in the
      Philosophy of Science.   (I. Lakatos, Ed.).   Vol. 3.
      (Proceedings of the International Colloquium in the
      Philosophy of Science, London, 1965.) Amsterdam:
      North-Holland Publishing Co., 1968.
Burgers, J. M.   "The measuring process in quantum theory."
      Reviews of Modern Physics, 1963, 35, 145-50.
Chari, C. T. K.   "A postscript to 'Quantum Physics and
      Parapsychology.'"   Journal of Parapsychology, 1957,
      21, 73.
_____.   "ESP and the 'theory of resonance.'"   British
      Journal for the Philosophy of Science, 1964, 15, 137-
      40.
_____.   "Human Personality in East-West Perspectives"
      in Philosophy, Religion and the Coming World Civiliza-
      tion.   (Leroy S. Rouner, Ed.).   The Hague: Martinus
      Nijhoff, 1966.   (a)
_____.   "Information theory, quantum mechanics and
      linguistic duality.'"   Dialectica, 1966, 20, 67-88.
      (b)
_____.   "On information-theoretic approaches to ESP."
      International Journal of Parapsychology, 1966, 8, 533-
      53.   (c)
_____.   "A note on some computer programmes and re-
      cursive unsolvability."   Methodology and Science, 1968,
      1, 127-29.
_____.   "Logical Issues About the Canonical Formalism in

Classical and Quantum Mechanics" in Modern Logic:
Its Relevance to Philosophy. (Daya Krishna, D. C.
Mathur, and A. P. Rao, Eds.). New Delhi: Impex
India, 1969.
_____. "An evaluation of some field-theoretical approaches
to psi." Psychocosmos, 1970, 1, 1-19 (Mimeographed).
(a)
_____. "Issues about machine translation and undecidabil-
ity." Pensiero e Linguaggio in operazioni, 1970, 1,
407-11. (b)
_____. "Undecidability in metamathematics and linguistic
theory." Methodology and Science, 1970, 3, 37-41.
(c)
_____. "Informo-Dynamics and the Anisotropy of Time"
in Time in Science and Philosophy (An International
Study of Some Current Problems). (Jiři Zeman, Ed.).
Prague: Academia, 1971. (a)
_____. "Towards generalized probabilities in quantum
mechanics." Synthèse, 1971, 22, 438-47. (b)
_____. "A Critique of the Cybernetic Approach to Mind"
in The Concept of Mind. (T. E. Shanmugam, Ed.).
Bombay: Popular Prakashan, 1972. (a)
_____. "Precognition, probability and quantum mechanics."
Journal of the American Society for Psychical Research,
1972, 66, 193-208. (b)
Denenberg, V., & Whimbey, A. E. "Behavior of adult rats
as modified by the experiences their mothers had as
infants." Science, 1963, 142, 1192-93.
Dobzhansky, T. Mankind Evolving. New Haven: Yale Uni-
versity Press, 1962.
Eibl-Eibesfeldt, I. Ethology: The Biology of Behavior. New
York: Holt, Rinehart, & Winston, 1970.
Elsasser, W. Atom and Organism. Princeton, N.J.:
Princeton University Press, 1966.
Feigl, H. "Physicalism, Unity of Science and the Founda-
tions of Psychology" in The Philosophy of Rudolf Car-
nap. (P. A. Schilpp, Ed.). LaSalle, Ill.: The Open
Court Publishing Co., 1963.
Feyerabend, P. K., & Maxwell, G. (Eds.). Mind, Matter
and Method. Minneapolis: University of Minnesota
Press, 1966.
Firsoff, V. A. "Is the universe expanding?" Discovery,
1965, 26, 18-21.
_____. Letter to the editor. The Observatory, 1969,
87, 119.
Gardner, M. "Can time go backward?" Scientific American,
1967, 216, 98-108.

Geley, G.   From the Unconscious to the Conscious.   London:
    W. Collins, 1920.
Giedymin, J.   Comments in Problems in the Philosophy of
    Science.   (I. Lakatos, Ed.).   Vol. 3.   (Proceedings of
    the International Colloquium in the Philosophy of Sci-
    ence, London, 1965.)   Amsterdam: North Holland
    Publishing Co., 1968.
Green, H. S.   "Observation in quantum mechanics."   Il
    Nuovo Cimento, 1958, 9, 880-89.
Grünbaum, A.   Philosophical Problems of Space and Time.
    New York: A. Knopf, 1963.
Hampshire, S. (Ed.).   Philosophy of Mind.   New York:
    Harper & Row, 1966.
Hardy, A.   "Biology and psychical research."   Proceedings
    of the Society for Psychical Research, 1953, 50, 96-
    134.
_____.   The Living Stream.   London: W. Collins, 1965.
_____.   "Psychical research and civilization."   Proceed-
    ings of the Society for Psychical Research, 1966, 55,
    1-21.
Hutten, E. H.   Comments in Problems in the Philosophy of
    Science.   (I. Lakatos, Ed.).   Vol. 3.   (Proceedings
    of the International Colloquium in the Philosophy of
    Science, London, 1965.)   Amsterdam: North-Holland
    Publishing Co., 1968.
Jauch, J. M.   "The problem of measurement."   Helvetica
    Physica Acta, 1964, 37, 293-316.
_____.   Foundations of Quantum Mechanics.   Reading,
    Mass.:   Addison-Wesley Publishing Co., 1968.
Klip, W.   "An experimental approach to the interpretation of
    the quantum theory."   Journal of the Society for Psych-
    ical Research, 1967, 44, 181-87.
Klopfer, P. H., & Hailman, J. B.   An Introduction to Ani-
    mal Behavior: Ethology's First Century.   Englewood
    Cliffs, N.J.:   Prentice-Hall, Inc., 1967.
Koestler, A.   "The perversity of physics."   Parapsychology
    Review, 1973, 4, 1-3.
_____, & Smythies, J. R. (Eds.).   Beyond Reductionism:
    New Perspectives in the Life Sciences.   New York:
    The Macmillan Co., 1969.
Kuhn, T. S.   The Structure of Scientific Revolutions.   Chi-
    cago: University of Chicago Press, 1962.
Landé, A.   From Dualism to Unity in Quantum Mechanics.
    Cambridge: University Press, 1960.
Levy, W. J., & McRae, A.   "Precognition in mice and
    jirds."   Journal of Parapsychology, 1971, 35, 120-31.
Ludwig, G.   Die Grundlagen der Quantenmechanik.   Berlin:

Julius Springer, 1954.

Miklós, J.   Personal communication.   (1973)

Mundle, C. W. K.   "Strange facts in search of a theory."
Proceedings of the Society for Psychical Research,
1973, 56, 1-20.

Narlikar, J. V.   "Neutrinos and the arrow of time."   Proceedings of the Royal Society (London, Series A),
1962, 270, 553-63.

Osty, E.   "Metaphysics and Philosophy" in Philosophy Today.
(E. L. Schaub, Ed.).   Chicago: The Open Court Publishing Co., 1928.

Popper, K. R.   Of Clouds and Clocks.   St. Louis, Missouri:
Washington University Press, 1966.

Poynton, J.   "Parapsychology and the biological sciences."
Parapsychology Review, 1973 (No. 2) 10-12; 23-26.

Radner, M., & Winokur, S.   Minnesota Studies in Philosophy
of Science, (Vol. 4).   Minneapolis: University of Minnesota Press, 1973.

Randall, J. L.   "Psi phenomena and biological theory."   Journal of the Society for Psychical Research, 1971, 46,
151-65.

_____.   "Recent experiments in animal parapsychology."
Journal of the Society for Psychical Research, 1972,
46, 124-35.

Rhine, J. B.   "Parapsychology" in The New Outline of Modern Knowledge.   Alan Pryce-Jones (Ed.).   London:
Victor Gollancz, 1956.

_____.   "Parapsychology and man."   Journal of Parapsy-
chology, 1972, 36, 101-21.

Ruderfer, M.   Letter to the editor.   Journal of the American Society for Psychical Research, 1968, 62, 84-86.

Schmidt, H.   "A Quantum Process in Psi Testing" in Progress in Parapsychology.   (J. B. Rhine, Ed.).   Durham, N.C.: The Parapsychology Press, 1971.

_____.   Personal communication.   (1973)

Shimony, A.   "Role of the observer in quantum theory."
American Journal of Physics, 1963, 31, 755-73.

_____.   "Quantum Physics and the Philosophy of White-
head" in Philosophy in America.   (Max Black, Ed.).
London: George Allen & Unwin, 1965.

Stannard, F. R.   "Symmetry of the time axis."   Nature,
1966, 211, 693-95.

Suszko, R.   "Formal Logic and the Development of Knowledge"
in Problems in the Philosophy of Science.   (I. Laka-
tos, Ed.).   Vol. 3.   (Proceedings of the International
Colloquium in the Philosophy of Science, London,
1965.)   Amsterdam: North-Holland Publishing Co.,
1968.

Thouless, R. H. "Parapsychology During the Last Quarter
        of a Century" in Progress in Parapsychology. (J. B.
        Rhine, Ed.). Durham, N. C. : Parapsychology Press,
        1971.
Watanabe, S. "Comments on Key Issues" in Dimensions of
        Mind. (Sidney Hook, Ed.). New York: Collier
        Books, Inc. , 1961.
Watson, J. D. The Double Helix. London: Atheneum, 1968.
White, D. J. Decision Theory. London: George Allen &
        Unwin, 1969.
Whiteman, J. H. M. The Mystical Life. London: Faber
        & Faber, 1961.
_____ . Philosophy of Space and Time. New York: Hu-
        manities Press, 1967.
Wigner, E. P. "Remarks on the mind-body question" in
        The Scientist Speculates. (I. J. Good, Ed.). Lon-
        don: Heinemann, 1962.
_____ . "The problem of measurement. " American Jour-
        nal of Physics, 1963, 31, 6-15.
_____ . "Two kinds of reality. " The Monist, 1964, 48,
        248-64.

ADDITIONAL READINGS ON SCIENTIFIC
THEORIES AND PSI

Beloff, J. "Parapsychology and its neighbors." JP 34: 129-42 (Jun 1970).

Cahn, H. A. "Methodological postulates for science and the paranormal." In Angoff, A. and Shapin, B. (Eds.). Parapsychology and the Sciences. N.Y., Parapsychology Foundation, 1974. Pp. 31-51.

Chauvin, R. "To reconcile psi and physics." JP 34: 215-18 (Sep 1970).

Dean, E. D. "Parapsychology and Dr. Einstein." P. A. Proc. No. 4: 33-56, 1969.

Ellis, D. "The chemistry of psi." In Angoff, A. and Shapin, B. (Eds.). Parapsychology and the Sciences. N.Y., Parapsychology Foundation, 1974, Pp. 209-224.

Firsoff, V. A. "Life and quantum physics." Parapsychology Review. 5(6): 11-15 (Nov-Dec 1974).

Koestler, A. "Out on a tightrope: Parapsychology and physics." RP 1: 201-16, 1972.

Kreitler, H. and Kreitler, S. "ESP and cognition." JP 38: 267-85 (Sep 1974).

Margenau, H. "ESP in the framework of modern science." JASPR 60: 214-27 (Jul 1966).

Nash, C. B. "Physical and metaphysical parapsychology." JP 27: 283-300 (Dec 1963).

O'Regan, B. "The emergency of paraphysics: theoretical foundations." In Mitchell, E. D. and others. Psychic Exploration. N.Y., Putnam's, 1973. Ch. 19.

Panati, C. "Quantum physics and parapsychology." Parapsychology Review 5(6): 1-5 (Nov-Dec 1974).

Puthoff, H. and Targ, R. "Psychic research and modern physics." In Mitchell, E. D. and others. Psychic Exploration. N.Y., Putnam's, 1974. Ch. 22.

Roberts, R. B. "A theory for psi." In Schmeidler, G. R. (Ed.). Parapsychology: Its Relation to Physics, Biology, Psychology, and Psychiatry. Metuchen, N.J., Scarecrow Press, 1976.

Ruderfer, M. "Letter to the editor commenting on Chari's discussion of the neutrino theory of ESP." JP 38: 338-40 (Sep 1974).

Rush, J. H. "Parapsychology's century of progress." In Angoff, A. and Shapin, B. (Eds.). Parapsychology

Today: A Geographic View. N. Y. , Parapsychology
Foundation, 1973. Pp. 205-23.
_____ . "Physical aspects of psi phenomena. " Paper de-
livered at ASPR Symposium, New York City, May
18, 1974.
Scriven, M. , Broad, C. D. , Pratt, J. G. and Burt, C.
"Physicality and psi: A symposium and forum discus-
sion. " JP 25: 13-31 (Mar 1961).
Walker, E. H. "Consciousness and quantum theory. " In
Mitchell, E. D. (Ed.). Psychic Exploration. N. Y. ,
Putnam's, 1974. Ch. 23.
Whiteman, J. H. M. "Quantum theory and parapsychology. "
JASPR 67: 341-60 (Oct 1973).
Young, A. M. "Toward a theory of ESP. " In Muses, C.
and Young, A. M. Consciousness and Reality. N. Y. ,
Outerbridge and Lazard, 1972. Ch. 3.

Note: As this volume was in the final stages of production,
the Parapsychology Foundation published an important
conference proceedings which should be added to the
above list:

Oteri, L. (ed.). Quantum Physics and Parapsychology.
N. Y. , Parapsychology Foundation, 1975.

PART V

CRITICISMS OF PARAPSYCHOLOGY

INTRODUCTION

From the very beginning parapsychologists have had to
deal with more than their normal share of criticisms, due to
the unprecedented nature of their claims. Much of this criticism has had a salutory effect on parapsychology, for it has
led to more sophisticated experimental designs and to the
adoption of high standards of evidence which are more strin-
gent than those generally employed in other behavioral sciences.

Over the years a number of surveys of these criticisms, often with replies to specific criticisms, have been
published in the parapsychological literature as well as outside it. One of the most recent of these surveys is the one
by Champe Ransom which is the lead selection in this section.
He has revised and edited his paper for inclusion in this an-
thology. Of the items in the list of additional readings, particular attention should be given to Honorton's "Error Some
Place."

Not by any means are all critics of parapsychology
outside the field. Parapsychology has critics within as well,
and their criticisms are especially valuable because they are
offered by persons who are thoroughly familiar with the field,
as critics outside parapsychology generally are not. Moreover, they are tendered in full recognition of the importance
of psi phenomena, which makes for a sensitivity and a sophistication that persons with only a superficial knowledge of the
field cannot possibly achieve. The second paper in this sec-

tion is by one of these inside critics, Dr. James Crumbaugh.
Although he has been interested in parapsychology since his
student days he has never been reconciled to the fact that
most parapsychological experiments are not repeatable, not
even by the original experimenter.   In his paper he outlines
the full extent of the repeatability problem in parapsychological research.

The final paper in this section is also by a parapsychologist, the most famous one of all--J. B. Rhine.   His
article, "Telepathy and Other Untestable Hypotheses," could
also have been placed in Part I, since it is on basic forms of
psi, or in Part IV, since it also represents a certain way of
viewing psi phenomena.   It has been placed with criticisms,
however, because he argues that many of the basic areas of
psi studied by parapsychologists, such as out of the body experiences, survival, retrocognition, psychometry, and even
telepathy, are not capable of being investigated since there is
no way to rule out the possibility that they are due to clairvoyance.   Dr. Rhine's position represents an extreme point
of view and illustrates how one form of psi may be used to
explain away another form of psi.   But even if, as he argues,
such apparent phenomena as out of the body experiences, survival, retrocognition, psychometry, and telepathy cannot be
experimentally verified, nonetheless they have an experiential
quality which makes each qualitatively different from other
forms of psi.   We need new tools for dealing with and perhaps even conceptualizing these experiences which persist in
occurring in their own particular forms even if theoretically
they can be reduced to something else.   A more sophisticated
phenomenology of psi may provide insights which could allow
us to go beyond the stalemate described by Dr. Rhine.   The
sources cited in the Additional Readings appended to Rhine's
paper are not strictly relevant to the point of view presented
in that paper, since his view is unique in the field.   The
additional readings center mainly on the next best thing, which
seemed to be papers dealing with the question of the nature
of clairvoyance, telepathy, and other forms of psi phenomena.

Chapter 17

RECENT CRITICISMS OF PARAPSYCHOLOGY:
A Review*

by Champe Ransom

INTRODUCTION

This report attempts to list the major criticisms brought against the experimental work in parapsychology during the past twenty years. Parapsychologists will be familiar with all of these criticisms, but I hope the viewpoint will be a fresh one (my background is in law, not parapsychology), and perhaps it will be of value to them to have all the recent criticisms gathered together in one place. The report is intended primarily, however, for the lay person who is curious about ESP and wonders what objections to parapsychology research have been voiced by the scientific community.

The questions which prompted this study were: Why does the scientific community in general reject or ignore the evidence gathered by parapsychologists? After looking at the evidence, should a reasonable person be persuaded that the phenomena bear further investigation--if not belief--or are there valid objections to the methods and underlying assumptions of the parapsychologists which considerably weaken the evidence? Gathering and briefly discussing the objections is one way to begin answering these questions.

My first surprise as I began this study was to find that the scientific world's rejection of or indifference to parapsychology is not as complete as I had thought. The scientific journals treat the subject seriously and more frequently

*Reprinted, with changes by the author, by permission of the author and publisher from the Journal of the American Society for Psychical Research 65: 289-307 (July 1971). This research was supported by a grant from the Parapsychology Foundation, New York.

than I had expected, and the list of natural and social scientists who are professionally interested in psi phenomena is
impressive. It was revealing to find that, in 1955, over
ninety per cent of a group of psychologists (associate members of the American Psychological Association admitted in
1950 and 1955) replying to a questionnaire, considered the
investigation of ESP a legitimate scientific undertaking (33).
In 1969 the American Association for the Advancement of Science accepted as an affiliate member the Parapsychological
Association, made up primarily of professional researchers
in parapsychology. (This was after several rejections in
previous years, it should be noted.) These comments should
not be taken to mean that there is general scientific approval
of the methods and conclusions of parapsychology, but only
that the rejection or indifference is not complete.

The second surprise was to find that most scientists
are unfamiliar with the actual findings of parapsychology.
The Warner survey of the attitude of psychologists toward
ESP indicated that most of the respondents (whether they believed or disbelieved in ESP) had based their opinions on
newspaper and magazine reports and hearsay rather than on
a study of the experiments themselves as reported in the scientific journals. In a brief review of the state of ESP research, Berelson and Steiner state that "the majority of psychologists, most of whom have not studied the subject are
not convinced" (1964, p. 126) [my emphasis]. Meehl and
Girden in Encyclopaedia Britannica say of professional scientists that "... very few are acquainted with the [parapsy-
chological] research, most of which appears in journals with
which they are not familiar" (1966, p. 322). Indifference to
or rejection of the findings of parapsychology may be in order
but not, it seems to me, before a fair study of those findings.
The same is true of acceptance of the findings. There is
every evidence that the authors of the criticisms which I
shall now cite have studied the research data. The criticisms
are as follows:

1. Successful experiments conducted by parapsychologists are not repeatable.
2. The possibility of fraud in an experiment precludes
regarding that experiment as conclusive evidence for ESP.
This possibility existed in the parapsychological experiments
which cannot be explained by other normal means.
3. Parapsychologists use improper mathematical methods.
4. Psi phenomena are, a priori, impossible.

    5.   Parapsychologists interpret the evidence of their
research improperly by drawing conclusions which are un-
supported by the evidence.
    6.   The alleged phenomena are not amenable to scien-
tific investigation, they have not been fitted into a theoretical
framework, and they have shown no relevance to the rest of
scientific knowledge.
    7.   The experimental designs used by parapsycholo-
gists often permit recording errors and the use of sensory
cues (consciously or unconsciously).   To the extent that improved designs are used, scores drop to the chance level.
    8.   Parapsychologists are not in agreement among
themselves as to the quality of the evidence.
    9.   Parapsychologists are biased in favor of the ex-
istence of psi phenomena.

    Some of the criticisms overlap, some are the cause
or result of another, and some contain material which could
be divided into two criticisms.   I have arranged the material
into these nine sections for discussion purposes only.   The
criticisms are arranged roughly in a descending scale according to the frequency with which they are heard.

    The listing of a criticism indicates merely that it has
been voiced within the period covered by the report and not
that it is regarded as a strong or uncontested criticism.   The
report is designedly one-sided; there is no attempt to answer
the criticisms or to guide the reader to answers already published.   The comments after each section in this part of this
paper are not intended to be an evaluation of the material,
but are merely some miscellaneous thoughts which I hope
will promote discussion.   Occasionally, I have made a few
comments in rebuttal when I thought this would clarify one of
the criticisms.

CRITICISMS

1.   Nonrepeatability

    "Obviously successful ESP experiments are not repeat-
able and thus do not meet a basic requirement of all scientific experiments" (Cohen, 1966, p. 550).

    This seems to be one of the most frequent criticisms
brought against the experiments in parapsychology.   Parapsychologists and critics alike admit the lack of repeatability

and the necessity for it.   West, a parapsychologist, in discussing the best experiments in extrasensory perception,
says, ''... they fall short of the requirements for universal
scientific conviction for several reasons, the chief one being
that they are more in the nature of demonstrations than repeatable experiments.... No demonstration, however well
done, can take the place of an experiment that can be repeated by anyone who cares to make the effort'' (1966, p. 17).

Nicol (1966), Hansel (1966), Brown (1957), Evans
(1969), Mann (1963), Berelson and Steiner (1964), and Murphy
(1961), to name both parapsychologists and critics, have all
pointed out the importance of and the lack of repeatability.

Hansel adds a subcriticism by pointing out that some
parapsychologists deny the necessity of confirming experiments by repetition.   Perhaps this would be better worded
by saying that some parapsychologists maintain they already
have repeatability--in the sense that there have been numerous different experiments with positive results.   The more
usual definition of repeatability, however, involves the notion
of a single experiment which can be replicated in any laboratory as many times as desired with essentially the same results.   Since parapsychologists in general stick to this definition, acknowledge the importance of repeatability and admit
that it has not been attained, this subcriticism of Hansel's
will not concern us further here.

If parapsychologist and critic agree on the fact of nonrepeatability, they surely do not agree on its implications.
The critic says, ''You have not verified your claim; there is
nothing there to be verified. '' The parapsychologist replies,
''No, if a result cannot be replicated, it does not necessarily
follow that the effect was never there.   It could also be that
the phenomenon involved is elusive and that we have not yet
discovered all the factors which produced it in the successful
experiment. '' I have detected a note of exasperation on the
part of some critics when they are faced with the explanations
(excuses?) of the parapsychologists for the lack of repeatability.   When a previously high-scoring ESP subject scores at
the chance level whenever he is tested by a skeptical investigator, the parapsychologist explains that the phenomenon does
not operate in a hostile atmosphere.   If the atmosphere is
friendly and the former high scorer still scores at chance
level, the parapsycholgist explains that boredom or fatigue
(of the subject or experimenter) inhibits the phenomenon from
operating.   Hansel objects, ''If fresh characteristics are postu-

lated in this manner, it is possible to survive almost any
form of criticism. An experimental result cannot be confirmed or refuted since ESP does not operate in front of critics. After tightening up his experimental conditions, an investigator cannot disclaim the findings of his earlier work;
failure in the later work reveals that he has lost his enthusiasm" (Hansel, 1966, p. 238). Wilson echoes this: "... parapsychologists tend to rationalize away negative results as
due to a lag in motivation or some other factor, and to accept occasional unusual results ... as positive evidence."
(Wilson, 1964, p. 380).

    Comments. Since there is no way to tell whether the
failure to demonstrate an alleged phenomenon is due to the
nonexistence of the phenomenon or to the mismanagement of
the underlying factors which produce it, there is really no
way to tell whether this criticism is fatal. The explanations
of the parapsychologist may describe the true reason for the
nonrepeatability of the experiments. If the alleged phenomenon depends on mood, for example, we would expect the experimental results to be exactly as erratic as they have been,
until the proper mood was discovered and was able to be
evoked in subject and experimenter. But the search for unknown (and perhaps nonexistent) factors could go on forever--
one critic says it has gone on long enough: "... while pro-
tagonists of ESP could reasonably plead for breathing space
to identify the elusive variables which lie at the root of this
unreliability, most scientists now feel that they have had
their chances and failed to deliver the goods" (Evans, 1969,
p. 640).

    I am not certain how Dr. Evans knows that this is
what most scientists think about parapsychologists, or when
in science one closes the door and says, "time's up," but it
is true that researchers have worked for many years and
failed to come up with enough knowledge of the alleged phenomena to produce the necessary repeatable experiment. Can
the small number of researchers and the limited amount of
funds be blamed?

    Discussion of the criticism regarding repeatability
should include consideration of the various roles that it plays
in different sciences (compare geology and physics, for example) and of any modification of the definition of a repeatable
experiment that has taken place in science generally over the
years. Also, consideration should be given to the fact that
there is not a complete lack of repeatability in parapsychology.

Crumbaugh (1966) estimated that there is somewhere between twenty-five and fifty per cent repeatability in any ESP experiment.

2. Conclusive Evidence vs. the Possibility of Fraud

"It cannot be stated categorically that trickery was responsible for the results of these experiments, but so long as the possibility is present, the experiments cannot be regarded as satisfying the aims of their originators or as supplying conclusive evidence for ESP" (Hansel, 1966, p. 241).

The charge here is not that fraud accounts for the successful ESP experiment but simply that if fraud (or anything else, for that matter) is a possible alternative explanation for the result, then that experiment cannot be offered as conclusive proof of ESP. The critic then goes on to show that, in all of the experiments which have been offered as conclusive, there was a possibility that fraud could have occurred. It should be made clear that, under this criticism, it is not necessary to prove that fraud occurred or even to present any evidence that it occurred; it is sufficient to demonstrate that it could have occurred.

The fraud referred to here can be on the part of the subject, the experimenter, or both. Both Hansel and Price have suggested methods by which Soal in the Soal-Goldney experiment could have cheated with the assistance of several confederates. To the objection that is is improbable that a reputable scientist would engage in such a conspiracy, the critic would reply that, under this criticism, the objection is immaterial. The point is not that fraud was likely but that it was possible. No matter how "unlikely" the alternative explanation, as long as it remains a possibility then the experiment can just as well be considered proof of the alternative explanation as proof of ESP. This criticism, then, is not really a denial of the claim that there is evidence for the existence of ESP but rather it is a rejection of the claim that there is conclusive proof for its existence.

Comments. To me there is something unsatisfactory in leaving the matter in limbo like this. The important question is not whether cheating was possible in a certain experiment, but whether or not someone actually cheated. If cheating did not in fact occur, the fact that the experimental design made cheating possible is of no concern. It is only because

we may have no way of knowing whether someone actually
cheated that we have to adopt the next best standard, that of
considering the possibility of cheating.   But, though we cannot have proof of whether someone cheated or not, we can
have evidence one way or the other.   Is there any direct
evidence of fraud?   Is there any direct evidence of an honestly conducted experiment?   In short, if you have a situation
where fraud or ESP are the only explanations for an experimental result, the result is evidence for (not proof of) ESP
to the degree that the evidence for an honestly conducted experiment outweighs the evidence for fraud; and it is evidence
for (not proof of) fraud to the degree that the evidence for
fraud outweighs the evidence for an honestly conducted experiment.

These comments are prompted by the fact that Hansel
and Price, after correctly pointing out that if two explanations are possible neither one is proved, seem to be uninterested in the question of where the weight of the evidence lies.

The necessary corollary to the question of the possibility of fraud is the question of the evidence for or against
the actual occurrence of fraud.   Answering the latter question
will determine whether one should tentatively favor the fraud
explanation or tentatively favor the ESP explanation in regard
to a certain experiment.

Two more thoughts.   First, this criticism does not
apply to all parapsychologists since many are not claiming
that the evidence is conclusive in the first place.   "They
[parapsychologists] do not claim that their results compel
belief in ESP, only that the results compel attention to the
strong possibility of ESP" (Stevenson, et al., 1969, p. 745).
Second, the challenge that "fraud was possible" is, in a way,
an insurmountable one, since the critic can always claim that
everyone involved in the experiment in question was lying a-
bout any or all of the details.   Even if an experiment was
repeated, it could be claimed that it is possible that all the
experimenters were fraudulent.   This impasse shows, again,
the importance of dealing with the question of direct evidence
of fraud in addition to the question of the possibility of fraud.

3.   Improper Mathematical Methods

"... how insecure is the support these elaborate statistics and gigantic probabilities in parapsychology afford"
(Boring, in Introduction to Hansel, 1966, p. xx).

Although the Institute of Mathematical Statistics in
1937 approved in general the validity of the statistical analysis of ESP research, the 1966 edition of Encyclopaedia Britannica states that "many scientists remain unimpressed by and
are even scornful of the statistical methodology of parapsychology" (Meehl and Girden, 1966, p. 322).

Concern with the mathematical methods used in parapsychology has been expressed by Boring (1955), Berelson
and Steiner (1964), Brown (1957), Smith and Canon (1954),
Rogosin (1962), and Bridgman (1956).

The concern seems to be based not so much on the
idea that parapsychologists are misusing a perfectly good tool
as on the idea that probability arguments and statistical significance, even when correctly used, are inadequate tools to
prove what the parapsychologists are trying to prove by them.
Thus Bridgman's "I am unwilling to accept the genuineness of
any phenomenon that leans as heavily as does ESP on probability arguments" (1956, p. 17). And Boring's "... the
parapsychologists are forced to rely on the shaky evidence of
statistical significances..." (1961, p. 150).

Brown describes the psychical research experiment as
"degenerate" since it is a pure probability experiment (1957,
p. 134).

These critics maintain that statistical significance alone
cannot be used to prove the reality of a phenomenon but only
to point to where repeatability can be found. Thouless replies,
"We should like that sort of evidence [from repeatability] better but, in its absence, we must make our judgment as to the
reality of ESP on the kind of evidence [statistical] that is
available" (1963, p. 109).

Brown goes further than most other critics by asserting
that the apparent successes of experimental parapsychology
are really the failure of probability theory: "They [the results of psychical research] comprise, in fact, the most prominent empirical reason for beginning to doubt the universal applicability of classical frequency probability" (1957, p. 110).

Comments. The layman will have a hard time trying
to evaluate this criticism, especially after reading statements
such as Eysenck's concerning modern telepathy experiments
that "the highest authorities on mathematical statistics have
explicitly given their blessings to the methods of analysis

currently used" (1958, p. 127).   Rawcliffe, a strong critic on
other grounds, has spoken of the "excellent mathematical su-
perstructure" used by American parapsychologists and the
"general excellence of much of their statistical evaluations"
(1959, p. 442).   The non-mathematician is unable to assess
the conflicting statements and thus must regard the question
as raised but unanswered.   A statement by a society of mathematicians may be in order once again.

4.   The A Priori Argument

"... ESP is incompatible with current scientific theory"
(Price, 1955, p. 360).

Some critics (and over sixteen per cent of the respondents in the Warner survey mentioned above) base or partially
base their rejection of the evidence of parapsychology on a
priori grounds.   In other words, they regard the antecedent
improbability of psi phenomena as being so great that no
amount of evidence for the existence of the phenomena would
be considered convincing.

As T. R. Willis has put it, "The conclusions of modern science are reached by strict logical proof, based on the
cumulative results of numerous ad hoc observations and experiments reported in reputable scientific journals and confirmed by other scientific investigators: then, and only then,
can they be regarded as certain and decisively demonstrated.
Once they have been finally established, any conjecture that
conflicts with them, as all forms of 'extra-sensory perception' plainly must, can be confidently dismissed without more
ado" (quoted in Burt, 1967, p. 62).

Here we are dealing with the idea that there are a
number of fundamental concepts in science that seem completely self-evident or that have become evident by an overwhelming amount of data gathered by science.   Any data which
conflict with these fundamental concepts are likely to be inaccurate.   That is, it is more plausible to hold that the conflicting data are wrong than that the fundamental concepts
(which are backed up by a greater amount of data) are wrong.
The data of parapsychology seem to contradict these fundamental concepts.

"In effect, parapsychologists are claiming that miraculous, and as far as we can see lawless, phenomena are part

of the structure of the universe in which we live.... If this
is so, then our complexly interlocked sciences of physics,
chemistry and biology are rotten to their foundation and the
logic of science is a mockery" (Slater, 1968, p. 1479).

Comments. The pure form of this criticism states
that "no amount of evidence can prove something that conflicts with everything else we have learned." A modified
form might be stated as: "A greater amount of evidence
is required to prove something that conflicts with everything
else we have learned than is required to prove something
that conforms with everything else we have learned."

If the former meaning is used, then the question is
raised of how any possible radically new concepts in science
can be discovered. This approach would seem to say that
the "big picture" has already been obtained and that everything from now on must fit into this picture or be ignored.
But has not the history of science shown this attitude to be
presumptuous every time? Do the Einsteins adopt this attitude? Not all of them, apparently, since Albert Einstein
himself wrote an introduction to Upton Sinclair's Mental Radio
(Springfield, Illinois, Thomas, 1962) in which he expressed
the feeling that the book contained interesting evidence of
phenomena that should be looked into seriously.

In my opinion, the critic of parapsychology is in his
weakest and most unscientific position when he advocates rejection of the evidence on a priori grounds. According to
William James, "Science means, first of all, a certain dis-
passionate method. To suppose that it means a certain set of
results that one should pin one's faith upon and hug forever
is sadly to mistake its genius, and degrades the scientific
body to the status of a sect" (1897, p. 319).

If it is true that science, by definition, is a discipline
which must always question its own findings and that it can
contain no final or absolute truths, then the scientist must
go where the evidence leads without deciding beforehand what
can and cannot be.

In courts of law evidence is not excluded merely because it conflicts with other evidence; its weight may be lessened by the accumulation of other evidence to the contrary,
but it is never excluded on this basis. So, by this example,
the fact that psi phenomena prima facie contradict the laws
of physics does not make the evidence for psi phenomena in-

admissible. The effect that this contradiction does have, however, is to lessen the weight of the evidence; and this leads us to the second possible meaning of this criticism.

How much more evidence is required to prove something that is unlikely than to prove something that is likely? Obviously, this depends on how "unlikely" the something (in this case psi phenomena) is. Some would argue that a revolution has taken place in physics which has reduced the certainty of fundamental concepts. What appeared to be "finally established" has been questioned anew and, in the process, the antecedent improbability of psi phenomena has been reduced. Cyril Burt claims, "... it would be easy to show that every one of the 'basic requirements of science,' which, as the behaviourists allege, would be violated by the theories of mentalism and parapsychology are just as freely violated by the hypotheses of contemporary physics ... the so-called 'laws of Nature,' as is now generally recognized, can claim validity only within a certain limited range" (1967, p. 108).

In my opinion it is reasonable to place a greater burden of proof on parapsychology than on other disciplines. The difficult question is, how much greater?

5.   Improper Interpretation of the Evidence

"All you have got yet for extrasensory perception is an observed difference between two frequencies, between hits and misses, and a great deal of ignorance as to what causes the difference" (Boring, 1961, p. 114).

"Unexplained cases are simply unexplained. They can never constitute evidence for any hypothesis" (Hoagland, 1969, p. 625).

Even if we admit, say some commentators, that you parapsychologists have come up with evidence for something, we cannot agree with your exaggerated interpretation of what it is. Your generalizations transcend your observations.

These critics maintain that the data gathered by parapsychology experiments are as yet unexplained, and that the experimenters are jumping to conclusions when they talk of extrasensory perception. "... as long as the ESP experimenter is more interested in trying to prove such preconceived metaphysical 'theories' as telepathy, clairvoyance and

nonsensory perception, instead of trying to find a rational explanation of his experiments, his efforts, sincere though they
may be, are doomed to frustration and failure" (Rawcliffe,
1959, p. 490).

Bridgman says that parapsychology, with its lack of
repeatable experiments, contains the only instance that he
knows of where it is claimed that nonchance should be capi-
talized simply because it is nonchance (1956, p. 17).

Comments. This criticism applies well to some parapsychologists and hardly at all to others. One parapsychologist may regard telepathy, clairvoyance, and precognition all
as proven beyond a reasonable doubt and even go on to talk
about the "spiritual nature" of man; while another may consider the evidence for precognition very weak, the evidence
for other psi phenomena strong but not conclusive, and re-
fuse to condemn or support any philosophical system on the
basis of this evidence. Antony Flew, the British philosopher
(who believes that the research has yielded enough results
to establish the reality of some unfamiliar factor), says that
" 'psi-gamma' can--at present at least [1953]--be defined only
as 'the factor which gives rise to significant deviations from
mean chance expectation in a series of guesses. ' If we use
the term to mean more than this, then the results so far recorded have not established the existence of psi-gamma: if
'psi-gamma' is to entail any reference to the putative unknown
means or mechanism by which significant correlations are
achieved, then there are not sufficient grounds for believing
that psi-gamma genuinely occurs... " (1953, p. 118). Such
a cautious statement as this does not seem subject to the
criticism of this section.

There does seem to be a split among the parapsychologists into those who have drawn conclusions about the
nature of man and the universe from the research data and
those who have refrained from doing so. Much of the criticism of parapsychology has been directed, not at the excellence of the evidence, but at the interpretation of the evidence made by the former group of parapsychologists. In
my opinion, parapsychologists need not set out to "prove"
anything--they should investigate the alleged phenomena and
follow the evidence where it leads. As yet no one knows
where it will lead.

But what of the parapsychologist who takes the more
cautious view--how does this criticism apply to him? The

difference between the critic and this type of parapsychologist would seem to be that the critic describes the data of parapsychology as "empty correlations" and seems uninterested, while the parapsychologist describes them as "significant correlations" and wonders why the scientific community is not interested.   Hoagland calls the findings "unexplained" and dismisses them; Thouless says, "... the unexplained finding is the point of potential advance.   Parapsychology is such a region of unexplained findings" (quoted in Rhine, et al., 1968, p. 191).

Discussion of whether the findings are empty correlations would, of course, have to include consideration of the "lawfulness" that parapsychologists claim they are finding in the data, such as sheep-goat differences and decline effects.

6.   Lack of Theoretical Framework, Relevance to other Sciences or Amenability to Scientific Investigation

The quotations in this section illustrate a variety of reasons for scientists' general non-interest in parapsychology. These criticisms do not deal with rejection of the evidence, but with the practical and philosophical reasons for indifference to it.

"... any skepticism voiced by most biologists and psychologists toward extrasensory perception is based primarily on the omission by the proponents of the latter of any attempt to correlate these phenomena with known ones, and, on the weakening, through such omission, of the convincingness of their evidence" (Rashevsky, 1955, p. 195).

Nicol, a parapsychologist, says about the same thing when he lists as one of the major reasons for scientific difficulty with ESP recognition, "The seeming irrelevance of the subject to other sciences" (1966, p. 26).

Davis points out that if ESP is not of a physical nature (as it would appear not to be from the fact that physical stimuli are eliminated in the experiments) then it must be of a metaphysical nature, and that metaphysical problems are not the traditional areas for scientific research (1970, p. 278).

Skinner, in reply to the assertion that demonstration of psi phenomena may be inhibited by the use of testing machines or the presence of hostile investigators, has stated, "The methods of science cannot be applied to a phenomenon which is defined as unsuitable to scientific study" (1948, p. 458).

Szasz, after explaining the science is, in a sense, nothing but theory, says that "In the realm of psychical research ... there is still nothing that would deserve to be called a theory..." (1957, p. 106). He maintains that science does not simply deal with facts but rather with systems of relationships, and that parapsychology could only be considered a science if it started being concerned with finding out how its phenomena occurred.

Boring pointed out that in order to have a meaningful scientific experiment there must be a standard of reference or a control and that since there is no reliable way to turn ESP on or off, there is no way to distinguish between control and experimental observations in parapsychological research. He continues, "If ESP has no definition, that is to say, if its definition is negative [communication without the use of ordinary sensory channels] and is thus no definition at all, if it has no specifications of conditions that will tell you when ESP is working and when it is not, why then belief in the existence of ESP has to be a matter of faith and preference, since there can be no proof" (Introduction to Hansel, 1966, p. xvi).

Price says, "So little is claimed, and this little is demonstrated only to such restricted audiences and under such carefully controlled conditions and with so many excuses for failure available that it is quite difficult to prove that the little is actually nothing" (1955, p. 366).

Finally, Stevens objects that "The signal-to-noise ratio for ESP is simply too low to be interesting" (1967, p. 3).

Comments. In summary, these critics feel that the alleged phenomena are, at best, too rare, elusive, and irrelevant for scientists to become interested. At worst, the phenomena involve matters which science is incapable of studying.

7.   Inadequate Experimental Design

"My opinion concerning the findings of the parapsychologists is that many of them are dependent on clerical and statistical errors and unintentional use of sensory clues, and that all extrachance results not so explicable are dependent on deliberate fraud or mildly abnormal mental conditions" (Price, 1955, p. 360).

This criticism covers several different types of flaws in the research, all of which, presumably, could be corrected by properly designed experiments.

Rawcliffe says, "... it is on the question of safe-guards against sensory cues that all ESP experiments are shown to be at fault" (1959, p. 455). He admonishes the parapsychologists for not knowing enough about sensory hyperacuity to guard against its conscious or unconscious use by subjects during experiments.

Rashevsky warns us to be suspicious of the findings of parapsychology on the grounds that subjects have outwitted experimenters many times in the past: "Given the number of frauds that have been exercised successfully on critical observers, what is the probability that we are dealing with fraud again?" (1955, p. 194).

As the parapsychologist has, in answer to these criticisms, designed experiments with better controls, the scores of the subjects have usually dropped to a chance level. Not only is this true in the individual experiment, the critics say, but it describes the whole history of parapsychology. In the early days--the days of poor experimental design--there were many successful ESP experiments; as the test conditions were improved throughout the years there was a progressive decline in successful experimentation.

Comments. Discussion of the "experimental improvement/scoring decline" argument should consider the possibility that (a) not all the early successful experiments were poorly designed and not all the later, adequately designed experiments were unsuccessful; and (b) the decline in successful experiments could be due to factors other than improvements in design--for example, the nature of certain experimental techniques may inhibit the operation of the phenomena.

The experimenter, it seems to me, must be able to fully control for sensory cues, fraud, and recording errors in many of his experiments, for if this were not the case he would seldom, if ever, obtain chance results. The chance

score demonstrates not only that no psi was present, but
also that no sensory cues, fraud, or recording errors were
present to a significant degree.   So this criticism might be
reworded--how is it that the researcher (apparently) knows
how to and does control these factors in some experiments
and yet (apparently) fails to control them in others?

8.   Disagreement over the Quality of the Evidence

"Proof for the existence of ESP must obviously depend
on conclusive experiments, but only a small number of all
such experiments are considered to fall into this category,
and parapsychologists are not agreed among themselves which
of the experiments should be regarded as conclusive" (Hansel,
1966, p. 23).

Which experiments do the parapsychologists regard as
producing the best evidence for psi phenomena?   According
to several critics, the parapsychologists will not, or cannot,
answer this question unequivocally.   Experiments listed as
conclusive by one parapsychologist may be seriously questioned or completely ignored in the listing of another parapsychologist.   This is more serious when one realizes that
there are only a very few experiments listed by any parapsychologist as conclusive.

In Extrasensory Perception after Sixty Years (Rhine,
et al. , 1966) the parapsychologist authors examine over 140
experiments and come up with only six which they regard as
being fairly conclusive.   In Modern Experiments in Telepathy
(Soal and Bateman, 1954), other parapsychologists, discussing experiments conducted during the same period, approve
unequivocally of only one of these six experiments, reject or
give limited approval to three, and fail even to mention the
remaining two.   Nicol presents us with this comparison and
concludes that "... psychical researchers of undoubted authority do not agree among themselves as to whether some
of the leading experiments are conclusive evidence for para-
normality" (1966, p. 29).

Another criticism which is voiced occasionally (especially when parapsychologists claim that it is the total result of all the experiments that is convincing rather than the
result of a so-called conclusive experiment) is that parapsychologists use the "faggot theory" in order to bolster the
strength of their evidence.   This theory states that multiple

pieces of evidence, each piece of which is suspect on one or more grounds, are convincing in their totality.

Comments. Three of the experiments which survived pretty well the scrutiny of both of the books mentioned above are the Pearce-Pratt, the Pratt-Woodruff, and the Soal-Goldney experiments. Yet Stevenson, defending against Hansel's criticism of the Pearce-Pratt series, says that it is only Hansel who considers these experiments vital, while the parapsychologists consider them "just another good experiment" (1967, p. 259). The implication here is that there are plenty of strong ESP experiments, and even if someone finds some holes in the Pearce-Pratt series, that will not make much difference. The layman is left with the question of just which experiments the parapsychologists are banking on.

9. Bias in Favor of Psi Phenomena

"To view the modern ESP movement in perspective, one must realize that it is basically a cult--a cult of the supernatural in technical dress. The perpetuation of all such cults depends ultimately on irrational beliefs and the ignoring or 'explaining away' of rational criticism" (1959, p. 437).

"People want to believe in an occult something" (Boring in Introduction to Hansel, 1966, p. xvi).

Care must be used here to distinguish between comments directed at the general public and those directed at parapsychologists. Though Rawcliffe maintains that parapsychologists are so blinded by their own yearning for the occult that their experiments cannot be trusted, the other critics seem to be making comments about the public in general and not to be singling out parapsychologists.

Comments. The fact that credulity can explain the belief in ESP of many people tells us nothing about the extent of credulity in parapsychologists or about the degree to which it affects their research. Experimenter bias is a problem in every area of scientific investigation, but there is no evidence that I know of to show that parapsychology has more than an average amount of it. This criticism, then, has been infrequently heard in the past twenty years and, to my knowledge, no one has presented evidence in support of it.

CONCLUDING COMMENTS

This report is an "exploratory" review of the criticisms. It should not be regarded as a detailed examination
of the "case against parapsychology," nor has the "case for
parapsychology" been presented. All of these criticisms
have been dealt with in the parapsychological journals and
some, in my opinion, have been answered adequately there.

I think it is important to note that some of the critics
are saying there is nothing for parapsychologists to study and
that the research should cease, while others are saying there
is something to study but that the methods and interpretations
of parapsychology need improvement. (I suggest that the history of the ESP controversy shows a shift from the former to
the latter type of criticism, but this has not been determined
by and is outside the scope of the present report.) Also, I
think it should be remembered in reviewing criticisms that
different parapsychologists hold different views so that when
a criticism is made against some interpretation given the
findings by parapsychologist A, this criticism cannot be automatically applied to parapsychologist B nor to the whole field
of parapsychology.

The reader may be interested in some of the miscellaneous impressions that I have about critics and parapsychologists after doing this research: I am somewhat dissatis-
fied with some of the critics in their demonstration of a "will
not to believe" in psi phenomena (no matter what the evidence), and with the tendency of some to base their criticisms on the early work of parapsychology and to ignore the
more recent research. One should not get the impression
that the critics are unanimous in their criticisms--some of
the literature is taken up with one critic demolishing a particular argument of another critic. Also, some of the literature is taken up with praise, by a critic, for certain areas
of parapsychology.

As for the parapsychologists, I must credit them with
displaying a healthy amount of self-criticism. Though I have
not quoted them extensively in this report, parapsychologists
have recognized and discussed every criticism listed, in
many instances before an "outside" critic has done so. Reading the parapsychological journals and books by parapsychologists will put one in touch with nearly all that is being said
in the way of criticism. On the other hand, I am really not

so sure that reading the critics will put one in touch with nearly all the important parapsychological research.

Of course, it is not enough that the parapsychologists recognize and discuss the criticisms. They must, if the questions about parapsychology are ever to be resolved, answer the criticisms to the satisfaction of the scientific community. This has not yet been done.

REFERENCES

Berelson, B., and Steiner, G. A. Human Behavior: An Inventory of Scientific Findings. New York: Harcourt, Brace & World, 1964.

Boring, E. G. "The Present Status of Parapsychology." American Scientist, Vol. 43, January, 1955, 108-117.
_____. "The Spirits Against Bosh." Contemporary Psychology, Vol. 6, May, 1961, 149-151.

Bridgman, P. W. "Probability, Logic, and ESP." Science, Vol. 123, January 6, 1956, 15-17.

Brown, G. S. Probability and Scientific Inference. New York: Longmans, Green, 1957.

Burt, C. "Psychology and Parapsychology." In J. R. Smythies (Ed.), Science and ESP. New York: Humanities Press, 1967. Pp. 61-141.

Cohen, D. "ESP: Science or Delusion?" The Nation, May 9, 1966, 550-553.

Crumbaugh, J. C. "A Scientific Critique of Parapsychology." International Journal of Neuropsychiatry, Vol. 2, September-October, 1966, 523-531.

Davis, H. Letter. American Psychologist, March, 1970, 278-279.

Evans, C. "Long Dream Ending." New Scientist, March 20, 1969, 638-640.

Eysenck, H. J. Sense and Nonsense in Psychology. Baltimore: Penguin Books, 1958.

Flew, A. A New Approach to Psychical Research. London: Watts, 1953.

Hansel, C. E. M. ESP: A Scientific Evaluation. (Introduction by E. G. Boring.) New York: Scribner's, 1966.

Hoagland, H. Editorial. Science, Vol. 163, February 14, 1969, 625.

James, W. The Will to Believe. New York: Longmans, Green, 1897.

Mann, J. Frontiers of Psychology. New York: Macmillan, 1963.

Meehl, P. E., and Girden, E. "Parapsychology." Ency-
    clopaedia Britannica, 1966.
Murphy, G. Challenge of Psychical Research. New York:
    Harper & Row, 1961.
Nicol, J. F. "Some Difficulties in the Way of Scientific
    Recognition of Extrasensory Perception." In G. E. W.
    Wolstenholme and E. C. P. Millar (Eds.), Extra-
    sensory Perception. New York: Citadel Press, 1966.
    Pp. 24-37.
Price, G. R. "Science and the Supernatural." Science, Vol.
    122, August 26, 1955, 359-367.
Rashevsky, N. "Review of S. G. Soal and F. Bateman's
    Modern Experiments in Telepathy." Bulletin of Atomic
    Scientists, May, 1955, 193-195.
Rawcliffe, D. H. Illusions and Delusions of the Supernatural
    and the Occult. New York: Dover Publications, 1959.
Rhine and others. Extrasensory Perception After Sixty Years.
    Boston: Bruce Humphries, 1966.
Rhine, J. B., and Brier, R. (Eds.). Parapsychology Today.
    New York: Citadel Press, 1968.
Rogosin, H. "Review of G. Murphy's Challenge of Psychical
    Research." Contemporary Psychology, Vol. 7, Janu-
    ary, 1962, 14-15.
Skinner, B. F. "Card Guessing Experiments." American
    Scientist, Vol. 36, July, 1948, 456-462.
Slater, E. Letter. British Journal of Psychiatry, Vol. 144,
    November, 1968, 1479-1480.
Smith, K. and Canon, H. J. "A Methodological Refinement
    in the Study of ESP, and Negative Findings." Science,
    Vol. 120, July 23, 1954, 148-149.
Soal and Bateman. Modern Experiments in Telepathy. Lon-
    don: Faber, 1954.
Stevens, S. S. "The Market for Miracles." Contemporary
    Psychology, Vol. 12, January, 1967, 1-3.
Stevenson, I. "An Antagonist's View of Parapsychology. A
    Review of Professor Hansel's ESP: A Scientific Eval-
    uation." Journal A. S. P. R., Vol. 61, July, 1967,
    254-267.
_____, and others. Letter. British Journal of Psychi-
    atry, Vol. 115, 1969, 743-745.
Szasz, T. S. "A Critical Analysis of the Fundamental Con-
    cepts of Psychical Research." Psychiatric Quarterly,
    Vol. 31, 1957, 96-108.
Thouless, R. H. Experimental Psychical Research. Balti-
    more: Penguin Books, 1963.
Warner, L. "What the Younger Psychologists Think about
    ESP." Journal of Parapsychology, Vol. 19, December,

1955, 228-235.

West, D. J.   "The Strength and Weakness of the Available
Evidence for Extrasensory Perception. " In G. E. W.
Wolstenholme and E. C. P. Millar (Eds.), Extra-
sensory Perception.   New York: Citadel Press, 1966,
Pp. 14-23.

Wilson, W.   "Do Parapsychologists Really Believe in ESP?"
Journal of Social Psychology, Vol. 64, 1964, 379-389.

Postscript: Since writing this paper, I have discovered several more recent criticisms of parapsychology, the sources
of which I would like to note (although the material, in my
opinion, does not present any different types of criticism from
those already presented here):

Christopher, M.   ESP, Seers and Psychics.   New York:
Crowell, 1970.

_____ .   Mediums, Mystics and the Occult.   N. Y. , Crowell,
1975.

Maddox, J.   Editorial.   Nature, Vol. 255, January 24, 1970,
p. 313.

ADDITIONAL READINGS ON CRITICISMS
OF PARAPSYCHOLOGY

Angoff, A. and Shapin, B. (Eds.). A Century of Psychical Research: The Continuing Doubts and Affirmations. N.Y., Parapsychology Foundation, 1971. (See especially papers by E. J. Dingwall and D. J. West.)

Beloff, J. "Belief and doubt." RP 1: 189-200, 1972.

_____. "Parapsychology as science." IJP 9: 91-97 (Sum 1967).

Eisenbud, J. "Some notes on the psychology of the paranormal." JASPR 66: 27-41 (Jan 1972).

Hanlon, J. "Uri Geller and Science." New Scientist 64: 170-85 (Oct 17, 1974). (See also discussion in the issues of Oct 31, Nov 7, Nov 14, Nov 21, Nov 28, and Dec 5.)

Hansel, C. E. M. "A critical review of experiments with Mr. Basil Shackleton and Mrs. Gloria Stewart as sensitives." PSPR 53: 1-42 (Pt 190, May 1960).

_____. "ESP: deficiencies of experimental method" [Correspondence]. Nature 221: 1171-72 (Mar 22, 1969).

Honorton, C. "Error Some Place." Journal of Communication. 25: 103-16 (Win 1975).

_____, Ramsey, M. and Cabibbo, C. "Experimenter effects in extrasensory perception." JASPR 69: 135-49 (Apr 1975).

LeShan, L. "Parapsychology and the concept of the repeatable experiment." IJP 8: 133-46 (Win 1966).

_____. "Some psychological hypotheses on the non-acceptance of parapsychology as a science." IJP 8: 367-86 (Sum 1966).

Medhurst, R. G. and Goldney, K. M. "William Crookes and the physical phenomena of mediumship." PSPR 54: 25-157 (Pt 195, Mar 1964).

_____, and Scott, C. "A re-examination of C. E. M. Hansel's criticism of the Pratt-Woodruff experiment." JP 38: 163-84 (Jun 1974).

Pratt, J. G. "Comments on the Medhurst-Scott criticism of the Pratt-Woodruff experiment." JP 38: 185-201 (Jun 1974).

_____. "Reply to Dr. Scott." JP 38: 207-14 (Jun 1974).

Rhine, J. B. "Comments: A new case of experimenter un-

reliability. "   JP 38: 215-25 (Jun 1974).
_____ .   "Comments: 'Security versus deception' in para-
psychology. "   JP 38: 99-121 (Mar 1974).
Rollo, C.   "Thomas Bayes and the bundle of sticks. "   PSPR
55: 23-64 (Pt 200, Dec 1967).
Sage, W.   "ESP and the psychology establishment. "   Human
Behavior 1: 56-59 (No 5, 1972).
Scott, C.   "The Pratt-Woodruff experiment: Reply to Dr.
Pratt's comments. "   JP 38: 202-06 (Jun 1974).
Scriven, M.   "The frontiers of psychology: Psychoanalysis
and parapsychology. "   In Colodny, R. G. (Ed.).
Frontiers of Science and Philosophy.   Pittsburgh,
University of Pittsburgh Press, 1962.   Ch. 3.
Soal, S. G.   "A reply to Mr. Hansel. "   PSPR 53: 43-82
(Pt 190, May 1960).
Stevenson, I. and Roll, W. G.   "Criticism of parapsychol-
ogy: An informal statement of some guiding prin-
ciples. "   JASPR 60: 347-56 (Oct 1966).

Chapter 18

A SCIENTIFIC CRITIQUE
OF PARAPSYCHOLOGY*

by James C. Crumbaugh

Scientific parapsychology is now slightly over a generation old. The present-day story really begins with the
work of J. B. Rhine at Duke in the early 1930's. To be
sure, there were scientific antecedents such as the French
physiologist, Charles Richet,[29] who in 1884 anticipated Rhine's
basic methodology: the testing of subjects by having them
guess a sequence of events which is set by chance ratios,
and statistical evaluation of the presence of an extra-chance
factor in the guessing. Richet used playing cards (which
Rhine later replaced with his five "ESP" symbols). The
Richet experiments made little impact, however, save in the
circles of the then newly organized (1882) Society for Psychical Research in London and among isolated scientists and
other individuals already sympathetic to the claims of psychic
(later termed by R. H. Thouless, English psychologist "psi")
phenomena. There were some well-known British figures
such as physicists Sir William Barrett, Sir William Crookes,
Sir Oliver Lodge, and physician Sir Arthur Conan Doyle (the
Sherlock Holmes creator more oriented toward fiction than
science), but in America only a very few genuine scientists
--such as William James, the Harvard physiologist-philosopher-
psychologist who fathered American psychology, and William
McDougall, the English-American physician-psychologist who
was Rhine's mentor at Duke--actually believed in even the
possible rare occurrence of what have now become known as
parapsychological phenomena.[19]

While the picture in American science today is by no
means so vastly different as one might expect after a generation of research (if the parapsychological claims are indeed

*Reprinted by permission of the author and publisher from
Behavioral Psychiatry 2: 523-31 (Sept-Oct 1966).

valid), the changes that have occurred have largely followed
the impetus of Rhine's experiments.

The work of the Duke laboratory was introduced in
1935 with Rhine's monograph, Extrasensory Perception, [24]
but it was his second book, New Frontiers of the Mind in
1937[25] which caught the public eye.   His studies were the
first to apply the scientific method to the field in a systematic, consistent and tenacious attempt to obtain sufficient and
adequate data to gain acceptance by the scientific world.
The major phenomena (mental telepathy and clairvoyance) he
subsumed under the term, extrasensory perception or ESP.

In the early years there was heated controversy, and
American scientists divided themselves quickly into "for" and
"against" camps.   The "unconvinced" platform held 91% of
the votes according to a survey of American psychologists by
Warner and Clark in 1938. [36] A less extensive questionnaire
sent the same year by the present writer suggested that the
skeptics constituted about 97%. [7] A second survey by Warner
14 years later[35] indicated that the "ESP is unproven" camp
was losing, though it still held some 83% of the chips.

Compared to the British, it was more difficult for
American psychologists--dominated as they were by the extreme mechanism of Watsonian behaviorism and its various
subsequent afterbirths--to accept the possibility of these
phenomena, which have with few exceptions been considered
to represent nonmechanistic or "nonphysical" events in nature.

I entered the parapsychological scene in 1938 with a
Master's thesis on extrasensory perception.   At the time of
performing the experiments involved, I fully expected that
they would yield easily all of the final answers.   I did not
imagine that after 28 years I would still be as much in doubt
as when I had begun.

I repeated a number of the then current Duke techniques, but the results of 3,024 runs of the ESP cards--as
much work as Rhine reported in his first book--were all
negative. [6] In 1940 I utilized further Duke methods with high
school students, again with negative findings.

A number of other experimenters had of course repeated Rhine's experiments, some obtaining positive and others negative results.   The number of repetitions which failed
of verification always seemed, however, to be greater than
those that succeeded.

The subsequent literature adequately answered, in my
opinion, all of the criticisms leveled at the Duke research
except one vital point (to be discussed later).

The first and foremost center of early attack was upon
Rhine's statistical methods, though these objections came
from would-be mathematician-psychologists rather than from
professional mathematicians.   The latter supported Rhine almost from the first, for he had taken his techniques directly
from their tutorage, and in 1937 this issue was virtually end-
edby a statement from the American Institute of Mathematical
Statistics endorsing the ESP mathematics (26, p. 54).   It did
not, however, change many psychologists' opinions.

And, more important, it did not solve the problem of
exactly what interpretive conclusions may properly be drawn
concerning the validity of the ESP hypothesis from finding the
presence of an extra-chance factor in data that have been
quite adequately and carefully treated by legitimately applicable statistics.   This point will be considered later.

Following the failure of the initial attack (upon Rhine's
statistics), a second major assault was launched on the
grounds of poor experimental control of such extraneous variables as sensory cues, recording errors, and the like.
Many of these criticisms were justified in some of the early
Duke experiments, but Rhine set about to answer them one
by one, and in the course of a few years had produced studies
(or could point to the studies of others) which were virtually
foolproof in all of these areas.

A third cause of critical rejection of positive ESP results by many scientists was the fact that ESP violated a
priori the sacred framework of mechanistic science; that is,
it could not be logically explained as consistent with natural
law.   While most experimentalists pay lip service to the importance of evaluating experimental results strictly on the
soundness of the experimental procedures involved, they usually feel quite unconsciously that whenever results that cannot
be rationalized within the framework of systematic science are
obtained, something must be wrong with the experimental work
itself.   Though this is often correct, the error can also be--
and in the history of science often has been--on the other side
of the coin: in the theoretical assumptions of the current scientific systems.   Such names as Galilei, Pasteur, Mesmer
and Einstein come immediately to mind, and the list could be
greatly extended.

In spite of the treacherous and costly fallacy of drawing a priori or deductive conclusions from a posteriori or inductive data, however, the temptation seems overpowering for many of even the top scientists. Witness the case of D. O. Hebb, one of the most creative names in physiological psychology today, who has chosen by his own admission this route with reference to ESP:

"Why do we not accept ESP as a psychological fact? Rhine has offered enough evidence to have convinced us on almost any other issue where one could make some guess as to the mechanics of the disputed process.... Personally I do not accept ESP for a moment, because it does not make any sense.... I cannot see what other basis my colleagues have for rejecting it.... My own rejection of (Rhine's) views is--in a literal sense--prejudice."[15]

That to take this sort of position is to build upon the sands is shown by a more recent Russian opinion which, while remaining utterly mechanistic as required of loyal communists, accepts the existence of ESP and offers a purely physical interpretation of it.[31] Roshchin (the writer) does not specify the actual mechanism involved, but shows that one can postulate such and that many other phenomena for which a physical basis is now known were once rejected because they "could not be true" from a physical standpoint.

If we rejected evidence for any effect which we cannot at the time fit consistently into the picture of current scientific theory, we would still be rejecting the value of aspirin. It seems that physicians do not yet know just how it works, but few would doubt that it does.

This third cause of rejection of ESP--on a priori grounds--cannot stand as scientifically valid and need not trouble us further. Rhine has, however, partially brought this criticism upon himself by his refusal to accept the requirement of a repeatable experiment as essential to proof of the ESP hypothesis. (This will be discussed later.) Failure here relegates parapsychology to observational rather than experimental science, where Hebb's position is more reasonable.

If one wishes to reject an hypothesis but finds nothing wrong with the evidence for it, he may then turn to an ad hominem argument--the dishonesty of the experimenters. So this was the fourth line of criticicism of the ESP results,

though it came, as might be expected, after most other avenues of attack had been exhausted. Price[22] suggested that
deliberate fraud on the part of the investigators is the explanation of experiments that cannot be attributed to error or
competence.   And more recently a Russian scientist, Kitaygorodsky, has stated that "there can be only one answer.
The successful experiments are simply a matter of dishonest
researchers or mediums."[16]

The only immediate rejoinder to this type of argument
--an argument which can, of course, always be applied to
any scientific findings out of harmony with whatever one wishes
to believe--is to point to the number and quality of experimenters who have produced the results in question.   In the case
of ESP the positive findings come from so large a number of
experimenters representing such a variety of disciplines that
most critics do not take this kind of criticism seriously.
Still there is only one way to rule it out completely, and that
is to produce an experimental procedure which can be employed
by almost all qualified experimenters with very similar findings.

And that brings us to the fifth and last major line of
criticism of ESP results, the only criticism not yet adequately
met by present data, and the one which I contend is crucial
and must be met before the great bulk of scientists will swing
over to acceptance of the ESP hypothesis.   This is the failure
of ESP experimenters to produce a truly repeatable experi-
ment--one which can be replicated in almost any laboratory
as many times as desired with essentially the same results.
Repeatability has long been a cornerstone among the requirements of sound methodology in all experimental science.

Rhine has consistently rejected this criterion, admitting
that it cannot be met by parapsychologists at present, but arguing that the only type of repeatability necessary is that
furnished by the numerous positive experiments.[28]

In addition to Rhine, Murphy[33] has pointed to observational sciences like geology and biology, many of whose phenomena cannot be reproduced consistently in an experimental
laboratory.   One type of example would be the observed
phylogenetic relationships upon which the theory of evolution
is based.   We can easily reproduce the evolutionary process
in the laboratory through experiments with Drosophila Melan-
ogaster, the common fruit fly.   But this does not prove man's
evolution, which is an a priori inference based on observational

rather than experimental data. If this theory were not in
logical harmony with the main body of science, we would
reject it for the same reason Hebb rejects ESP. So until
ESP data become fully repeatable and therefore fully experimental, Hebb cannot be criticized too severely. His error
is that he apparently accepts ESP data as experimentally adequate yet still refuses them a priori.

     Since the exact conditions which produce ESP are un-
known, experiments that fail are presumed by Rhine to have
failed to hit upon these conditions, while those which succeed
are presumed to have found them. This argument may, of
course, represent the true facts; but on the other hand the
real facts may be otherwise: There may be some unknown
error in the positive experiments which is just as elusive
and subtle as the true conditions for the production of ESP
are presumed to be in the negative results. We cannot know
which is the true situation until the conditions for the occurrence of ESP can be specified accurately enough to yield a
consistently repeatable experiment. Until then the only justi-
fiable scientific position must be one of suspended judgment
on the basis of inconclusive evidence.

     If one accepts ESP as proven without its having met
the criterion of repeatability or of specification of conditions
necessary for its control, one is accepting proof based purely
on statistical grounds. Now statistics alone can never "prove"
the existence of anything, no matter how impressive the statistical results may be. Statistics only state the mathematical odds that an extra-chance factor is present in the results.
The criterion of any given odds which may be accepted as
evidence of this extra-chance factor is always arbitrary.
The conventional criterion of the "1% level of confidence"
means merely that on the average if 100 similar samples of
data were gathered and if there really is no extra-chance
factor, one would obtain a chance deviation as great as that
actually obtained from the average expected by chance in only
one of these 100 samples. If one took 1,000 such samples,
he should get by pure chance 10 samples that deviate from
chance expectation as much as the deviation actually obtained.
But these 10 samples might be included in the first 100
samples drawn and there might be none in the remaining 900
samples.

     In any given samples of data treated by statistics, we
can never be absolutely certain just what did and did not occur by chance. Thus in an ESP experiment the correct hy-

pothesis is not, "If odds of 100 to 1 (or any acceptable criterion) are obtained in the experimental results, ESP exists. "
The correct hypothesis is, "If these odds are obtained and
if ESP exists, then it probably occurred in this experiment,
and the probability is given by the obtained odds. "

As the late R. A. Fisher, dean of statisticians,
pointed out years ago, "Very long odds.... are much less
relevant to the establishment of the facts of nature than would
be a demonstration of the reliable reproducibility of the phenomena. "[13] Dr. Malcolm Turner, a statistician formerly on
the staff of the Duke Laboratory, once pointed out to me that
since the majority of ESP experiments have probably been
done by persons predisposed to a belief in ESP, and since
many such persons are not scientifically trained and tend to
discard and not to report negative results (and, it might be
added, since the parapsychological journals have tended to
report all positive experiments even where controls are poor
but to publish only brief notes of negative studies or to reject
them on grounds of methodological errors), it is impossible
to evaluate all of the ESP experimentation that has ever been
done. But if it were possible to do this, it might be that the
positive findings represent only the number of spurious or
"extra-criterion of chance" deviations to be expected in this
amount of data by chance. A similar point has been made
by Leuba. [17]

At the time of my own experimentation I was aware
of all of this, but it was the following incident which cinched
my resolution never to accept the ESP (or any other experimental) hypothesis as proven until the criterion of a truly repeatable experiment can be met.

In the summer of 1954, having renewed my ESP experimentation following interruption by World War II, I was
on the staff of the Duke Laboratory under a research grant
from the Parapsychology Foundation. Even though my own
experimentation had continued to yield negative results, I had
been impressed almost to the point of conviction by some of
the studies in the literature. There were two in particular
which, while not among those Rhine considered to be the best
advocates of the case for ESP, seemed to me from the written reports as very well done and just about fool-proof.

I discussed my reactions to these experiments with
other members of the Duke staff, and was quite amazed to
learn that neither experiment had a good reputation there. In

one case there were rumors that the scoring had not been
done by the student scorers as the professor believed and reported in the literature; and in the other--a case of phenom-
enally high ESP scores of one subject in a distance experi-
ment--it was reported that the subject was known to have
considerable psychopathology and that she had access to the
home of the experimenter where the ESP target cards were
kept, and it was suspected that she had gained sensory knowledge of them before making her calls.

Whether the aspersions cast upon either of these experiments were true is beside the point.   The reports jolted
deeply my confidence in the ability of any experimenter to
report with absolute accuracy exactly what he has done.   Often what he actually did may deviate in unrecognized ways
from what he thinks he has done.   Both of the aforementioned
experimenters were probably completely honest and believed
they reported exactly what happened.   But in both there were
those close to the experiment who believed the true events
occurred--unknown to the experimenters--somewhat differently.

I recalled at this point the words of E. G. Boring in
a personal communication to me in response to my 1938
questionnaire on attitudes toward the validity of ESP.   In re-
fusing to answer the questionnaire, Boring stated, "I doubt
that an evaluative judgment of whether this or that research
is valid should ever be sponsored on the basis of published
reports alone. "   The wisdom of this statement was now clear,
and from that point on I made my personal criterion of acceptance the production of a genuinely repeatable experiment.

So I set out to find a repeatable experimental design.
Nicol and Humphrey[20] and Schmeidler[32] had produced data
that suggested a relationship between ESP ability and factors
of personality and attitude of belief in ESP.   Believers got
better scores than disbelievers, and selfconfident subjects
scored higher than insecure individuals.   And Rhine had in-
sisted that the enthusiasm and confident belief of the experimenter was a major factor in stimulating subjects to score
significantly.

I reasoned that if both experimenters and subjects
were fractionated on such variables, self-confident believer
experimenters should get far superior results with similar
subjects than insecure disbeliever experimenters would get
with subjects like themselves.   I obtained grants from the

Parapsychology Foundation of New York to spend a summer
at the Duke Laboratory studying Rhine's techniques and then
to return to the college where at that time I taught psychology
and to set up experiments along the above lines.

The first experiment (1955) yielded marginally significant results favorable to ESP, but a repetition (1956) was
negative, and the results of the two together were at chance
level. [8] I had hoped to interest other laboratories in repeating the same design, but Rhine and others showed an interest
in a design of Anderson and White, [2] which following the lead
of van Busschbach, [34] indicated that school children made significantly higher ESP scores when the tests were administered
by teachers they liked and who liked them than when given by
teachers with whom the children shared a mutual dislike.
This design had some successful repetitions. [1,3]

Therefore several years later at another institution I
interested two of my graduate students in repeating the Anderson and White design.   One repetition, that of Deguisne, [10]
seemed to support the ESP hypothesis, while the other, that
of Goldstone, [14] did not.   Since then further repetitions elsewhere have been ambiguous: e.g., Rilling et al. [30]

Today, as far as I can see, the repeatability issue is
left about where it started: Only a portion of repetitions of
any ESP experiment are successful, somewhere between 25%
and 50%. [21]

Hoping to end this deadlock, I issued a challenge to
all parapsychologists to face up to the repeatability issue. [9]
I suggested they select a single experimental design which
offered promise of becoming repeatable and which at the same
time permitted full control of all conditions, and that they en-
list the support of all laboratories interested in parapsychology in large-scale mass repetitions of this design.   It should
be possible, if the ESP hypothesis is valid, to find a design
which would yield at least a majority of successful repetitions.

To all of this Rhine dissented, [28] denying as always
the necessity of satisfying the criterion of repeatability.   So
far nothing of consequence has been done on this issue, though
some parapsychologists--like Murphy, [33] one of the field's top
names--have emphasized its importance.

The result of this situation is that the vast majority
of experimental scientists have simply ignored psi research.

In my opinion the only development which could interest them would be the discovery of a truly repeatable experimental design by which they could obtain reasonably consistent positive ESP results in their own laboratories.   And until a far larger share of the best scientific brains are recruited in the study of psi capacities (again assuming that they are valid), it is very unlikely than an understanding of their nature and their control will be worked out.

For my part, while scientifically I feel I must suspend judgment on the ESP hypothesis pending the appearance of a repeatable experiment, the evidence to date leads me to a strong suspicion that it is valid.   Suspicion is not science; it is nevertheless interesting and often valuable to speculate beyond that which is proven.

And to speculate further, the enigmatic and illusive way in which psi capacities avoid being pinned down causes me to suspect that if they do exist as valid phenomena they also bear characteristics which may make it forever impossible to demonstrate them by the criteria of mechanistic science.

While most parapsychologists assume psi phenomena are not governed by mechanistic laws, they use the technique of mechanistic science--the experimental or inductive method--to study them.   Although this method is the only known means of proof in the usual scientific sense, there may be an inconsistency in its use here: It may turn out that (a) these phenomena exist, (b) they are governed by nonmechanistic laws, (c) nonmechanistic laws can never be discovered by mechanistic methods, and (d) such laws therefore cannot be known with scientific certainty but must be forever inferred by nonrational or intuitive means.

This is a philosophically dignified way of acceding to the religionist's dogma that the ultimate questions of the nature of man and the universe can never be understood by science (a view to which most scientists also subscribe), but must be assumed on the basis of faith rooted in a freely chosen system of values (which, of course, to the religionist are in turn determined by his particular theological system).

In other words, parapsychology may really fall within the province of religion rather than science. If its phenomena are actually nonmechanistic, it would appear likely that this is so.   But because the phenomena may in reality be a part of mechanism, as some parapsychologists--and apparently an increasing number--believe, and further because there is a possibility that even if they are nonmechanistic they can still be studied successfully by mechanistic techniques as Rhine seems to assume, there is every good reason to go all out in pressing to the limit the application of the experimental method to their solution. And this is the reason for my insistence on a concerted attack upon the problem of repeatability.

If the latter goal can be achieved, it will change the entire complexion of mechanistic science and the attendant view of the nature of man and probably of the universe. And with this change will come a new birth in philosophy, social and political science and economics--as well as in psychiatry and the mental health professions. Indeed, it will profoundly affect all who deal with man, which includes just about everybody.

We may pause to speculate upon the implications for psychiatry in particular. Eisenbud,[12] Ehrenwald,[11] Ullman, and Meerloo are among the psychiatrists who have led in studying the relationships between psi capacities and psychopathology.[33] No one has so far suggested a practical application of psi phenomena in the treatment of mental or emotional disorders, but important possibilities for common areas of study are indicated. For example, parapsychologists have concluded that their phenomena operate--exclusively, so far-- on the unconscious (though at least partially voluntary) level of awareness (27; pp. 86-89). Further, some of the phenomena of psychopathology, such as visual and auditory hallucinations, may be interpreted at least in some instances either as psi manifestations or as psychiatric aberrations, or possibly as both. And some psychiatrists feel that patients who have--or think they have--psi experiences exhibit particular types of regressive personalities, which means that reports of such phenomena may be valuable in diagnosis. Thus there are many points of common interest between the two disciplines, and therefore very logical reasons for each to be concerned with the phenomena of the other.

And there are still more important reasons why an interest should exist on the part of virtually all disciplines in arriving at a satisfactory answer to the question of the validity of psi phenomena. Man stands as at no other time in his entire history at the crossroads in his choice between two systems of values based on opposite concepts of the nature of man.

One holds that man is fully reducible to mechanism and Pavlovian reflexiology. This is the thesis of Marxist dialectical materialism and congruent with the entire social and economic thinking of communism, and collectivism.

The other regards man as more than mechanism, as irreducible to its concepts, as existing in a unique dimension of values which transcend the material world. This view is congruent with the concepts of individualism and its socio-economic correlates, the interpretation of man upon which America was founded.

Between these two diametrically opposed value systems modern man must choose, choose quickly, and bear the responsibility for his choice. Any field of study which offers the hope of clear evidence upon which presently faltering multitudes may base a sound decision is a vital field. Parapsychology is such an area of study.

REFERENCES

1. Anderson, Margaret. "Clairvoyance and teacher-pupil attitudes in fifth and sixth grades," J. Parapsychol., 21:1-11, 1957.
2. _____, and White, Rhea. "Teacher-pupil attitudes and clairvoyance test results," J. Parapsychol., 20:141-157, 1956.
3. _____, and _____. "A further investigation of teacher-pupil attitudes and clairvoyance test results," J. Parapsychol., 21:81-97, 1957.
4. Coover, J. E. Experiments in Psychical Research, Stanford Univ. Press, Stanford, Calif., 1917.
5. _____. "Metapsychics and the incredulity of psychologists," in Murchison, C. (ed.), The Case for and against Psychical Belief, Clark Univ. Press, Worcester, Mass., 1927.
6. Crumbaugh, J. C. An Experimental Study of Extra-sensory Perception, unpublished Masters' thesis in psychology, Southern Methodist Univ., 1938.
7. _____. "A questionnaire designed to determine the attitudes of psychologists toward the field of extra-sensory perception," J. Parapsychol., 2:302-307, 1938.
8. _____. "Are negative ESP results attributable to traits and attitudes of subjects and experimenters?" (abstract), J. Parapsychol., 22:294-295, 1958.

9. _____. "ESP and flying saucers: A challenge to parapsychologists," Amer. Psychologist, 14:604-606, 1959.

10. Deguisne, A. "Two repetitions of the Anderson-White investigation of teacher-pupil attitudes and clairvoyance test results: Part I, high school tests," J. Parapsychol., 23:196-207, 1959.

11. Ehrenwald, J. Telepathy and Medical Psychology, W. W. Norton & Co., New York, 1948.

12. Eisenbud, J. "Psychiatric contributions to parapsychology: A review," J. Parapsychol., 13:247-262, 1949.

13. Fisher, R. A. Letter to Hyman Rogosin quoted (p. 267) in the ESP symposium at the A.P.A., J. Parapsychol., 2:246-272, 1938.

14. Goldstone, G. "Two repetitions of the Anderson-White investigation of teacher-pupil attitudes and clairvoyance test results: Part II, grade school tests," J. Parapsychol., 23:208-213, 1959.

15. Hebb, D. O. "The role of neurological ideas in psychology," J. Personal., 20:39-55, 1951.

16. Kitaygorodsky, A. "The fruits of education," Moscow Literary Gazette, Nov. 26, 1964, trans. by Natalia Iljinsky, reprinted in J. Parapsychol., 29:45-50, 1965.

17. Leuba, C. "An experiment to test the role of chance in ESP research," J. Parapsychol., 2:217-221, 1938.

18. Lodge, O. The Survival of Man, Moffat Yard & Co., New York, 1909.

19. Murchison, C. (Ed.). The Case for and against Psychical Belief, Clark Univ. Press, Worcester, Mass., 1927.

20. Nicol, J. F. and Humphrey, Betty. "The exploration of ESP and human personality," J. Amer. Soc. for Psych. Res., 47:133-178, 1953.

21. _____, and _____. "The repeatability issue in ESP-personality research," J. Amer. Soc. Psychical Res., 49:125-156, 1955.

22. Price, G. W. "Science and the supernatural," Science, Aug. 26, 1955.

23. Reiss, B. F. "A case of high scores in card guessing at a distance," J. Parapsychol., 1:260-264, 1937.

24. Rhine, J. B. Extrasensory Perception, Bruce Humphries, Boston, 1935.

25. _____. New Frontiers of the Mind, Farrar and Rinehart, New York, 1937.

26. _____. New World of the Mind, William Sloane
    Associates, New York, 1953.

27. _____, and Pratt, J. G. Parapsychology, Charles
    C. Thomas, Springfield, Illinois, 1957.

28. _____. "How does one decide about ESP?" Amer.
    Psychologist, 14:606-608, 1959.

29. Richet, C. Thirty Years of Psychic Research, Mac-
    millan & Co., London, 1922.

30. Rilling, M. E., Pettijohn, Clare and Adams, J. Q.
    "A two-experimenter investigation of teacher-pupil
    attitudes and clairvoyance test results in the high
    school classroom," J. Parapsychol., 25:247-259,
    1961.

31. Roshchin, A. "Don't be afraid of facts," Moscow Lit-
    erary Gazette, Nov. 26, 1964, trans. by Natalia
    Iljinsky, reprinted in J. Parapsychol., 29:51-53,
    1965.

32. Schmeidler, G. R. "Separating the sheep from the
    goats," J. Amer. Soc. Psychic Res., 39:47-50,
    1945.

33. Schreiber, Flora Rheta, and Herman, M. "What psy-
    chiatry is doing about ESP," Science Digest, 32-
    36, Feb. 1966.

34. van Busschbach, J. G. "An investigation of extra-
    sensory perception in school children," J. Parapsy-
    chol., 17:210-214, 1953.

35. Warner, L. "A second survey of psychological opinion
    on ESP," J. Parapsychol., 16:284-295, 1952.

36. _____, and Clark, C. C. "A survey of psycholog-
    ical opinion on ESP," J. Parapsychol., 2:296-301,
    1938.

37. _____, and Raible, Mildred. "Telepathy in the psy-
    chophysical laboratory," J. Parapsychol., 1:44-52,
    1937.

ADDITIONAL READINGS ON THE
REPEATABILITY PROBLEM

"Advancement toward control and application." In Rhine,
J. B. and Associates. Parapsychology from Duke to
FRNM. Durham, N. C., Parapsychology Press, 1964.
Ch. 5.

Beloff, J. "Belief and doubt." RP 1: 189-200, 1972.
_____. "Parapsychology as science." IJP 9(2): 91-97
(Jun 1967).

Braud, L. W. and Braud, W. G. "Further studies of relaxation as a psi-conducive state." JASPR 68: 229-
45 (Jul 1974).

Braud, W. G., Wood, R. and Braud, L. W. "Free-response
GESP performance during an experimental hypnagogic
state induced by visual and acoustic ganzfeld techniques:
a replication and extension." JASPR 69: 105-13 (Apr
1975).

Crumbaugh, J. C. "Are negative ESP results attributable to
traits and attitudes of subjects and experimenters?"
Unpublished MS. 1959.
_____. "ESP experiments with students and the repeata-
bility issue." Parapsychology 5: 1-6 (No. 1, 1963-
64).
_____. "Parapsychology and the repeatability issue."
Research Journal of Philosophy and the Social Sciences
1965 2(1): 60-64.

Eisenbud, J. "Psi and the nature of things." IJP 5(3):
245-73 (Sum 1963).

Honorton, C. "Effects of feedback on discrimination between
correct and incorrect ESP responses: A replication
study." JASPR 65: 155-61 (Apr 1971).
_____, Ramsey, M., and Cabibbo, C. "Experimenter ef-
fects in extrasensory perception." JASPR 69: 135-49
(Apr 1975).

Kahn, S. D. "'Myers' problem' revisited." In Schmeidler,
G. R. (Ed.). Parapsychology: Its Relation to Physics,
Biology, Psychology, and Psychiatry. Metuchen, N. J.,
Scarecrow Press, 1976.

Kanthamani, H. and Kelly, E. F. "Awareness of success in
an exceptional subject." JP 38: 355-82 (Dec 1974).

Kelly, E. F. and Kanthamani, B. K. "A subject's efforts
toward voluntary control." JP 36: 185-97 (Sep 1972).

Kreitler, H. and Kreitler, S. "Optimization of experimental
    ESP results." JP 38: 383-92 (Dec 1974).
LeShan, L. "Parapsychology and the concept of the repeat-
    able experiment." IJP 8(1): 133-47 (Win 1966).
Lykken, D. T. "Statistical significance in psychological re-
    search." Psychological Bulletin 70: 151-59 (No. 3,
    1968).
McCallam, E. and Honorton, C. "Effects of feedback on
    discrimination between correct and incorrect ESP re-
    sponses: A further replication and extension." JASPR
    67: 77-85 (Jan 1973).
McCreery, C. Science, Philosophy and ESP. London, Faber
    and Faber, 1967.
Murphy, G. "The problem of repeatability in psychical re-
    search." JASPR 65: 3-16 (Jan 1971).
Pratt, J. G. "Some notes for the future Einstein for para-
    psychology." JASPR 68: 133-55 (Apr 1974).
Ransom, C. "Recent criticisms of parapsychology: A re-
    view." JASPR 65: 289-307 (Jul 1971). See especial-
    ly pp. 290-93. (This paper appears in this book as
    chapter 17.)
Rao, K. R. Experimental Parapsychology. Springfield, Ill.,
    Charles C Thomas, 1966. Ch. 6.
Rhine, J. B. "Editorial: Repeatability and reliability."
    Parapsychology Bulletin, n. s. No. 18: 2 (Aut 1970).
Schmeidler, G. R. "Exploring the parameters of research
    variables." JP 23: 238-50 (Dec 1959).
_____ (Ed.). Extrasensory Perception. N.Y., Atherton,
    1969.
_____. "Mood and attitude on a pretest as predictors of
    retest ESP performance." JASPR 65: 324-35 (Jul
    1971).
_____, and Craig, J. G. "Moods and ESP scores in
    group testing." JASPR 66: 280-87 (Jul 1972).
Stanford, R. G. "EEG alpha activity and ESP performance:
    a replicative study." JASPR 65: 144-54 (Apr 1971).
_____. "Response factors in extrasensory performance."
    Journal of Communication 25: 153-61 (Win 1975).
_____, and Mayer, B. "Relaxation as a psi-conducive
    state: A replication and exploration of parameters."
    JASPR 68: 182-91 (Apr 1974).
Thouless, R. H. "Parapsychology during the last quarter
    of a century." JP 33: 283-99 (Dec 1969).
Van de Castle, R. L. "Is there a madness to our methods
    in psi research?" P. A. Proc. 8: 40-46, 1971.
West, Donald J. "ESP the next step." PSPR 54: 185-202
    (Pt 196, Jan 1965).

White, R. A. and Angstadt, J. A.   "A review of results and
    new experiments bearing on teacher-selection methods
    in the Anderson-White high school experiments. "
    JASPR 59: 56-83 (Jan 1965).
Whiteman, J. H. M.   "Letter to the editor on the concept
    of repeatability in scientific experimentation. "   JASPR
    66: 227-29 (Apr 1972).

Chapter 19

TELEPATHY AND OTHER
UNTESTABLE HYPOTHESES*

by J. B. Rhine

For almost a century both scientific and lay interest
in the idea of telepathy (or extrasensory thought-transference)
has been, in some countries at least, more widespread than
in any other type of psi or parapsychic ability. The idea
that one person can, in some extrasensorial way, become
aware of another person's thought is generally accepted as
fact by most of those giving any credence to the findings of
parapsychology. Among the many spontaneous parapsychic
happenings in everyday life that are reported, the cases considered to be telepathic in nature are among the most familiar.

Some research workers in parapsychology, however,
are in doubt as to whether the effects usually attributed to
telepathy--either in the experimental situation or in spontaneous experiences--can be reliably concluded to be due to this
hypothetical subtype of psi ability. While these research
workers would not reject a general parapsychic explanation
of such results, they would question whether the effects can
be said to be telepathic, as that term is used. After nearly
a century of inquiry about telepathy, even though such inquiries have been scattered, it is extraordinarily curious that
this question still presents so sharp a challenge. On this account and because of the very important implications of the
concept of telepathy, it is time to review what we can find
on the nature of this difficulty.

There is another reason, too, for this review, or rather for its timing. For some years I have been giving special
attention to finding ways by which the quality and conditions

*Reprinted by permission of the author and publisher from
the Journal of Parapsychology, 38: 137-53 (June 1974).

of the slow-moving field of psi research can be reinforced
and its general scientific acceptability upgraded and expedited.
This I have often mentioned before, sometimes in the context
of telepathy. What I say in this review, however, also has
a broadly sweeping application to a series of other, more or
less major, issues in parapsychology quite as well as to the
problem of telepathy itself. As may be seen, a common circumstance is involved here: all the problems to be considered
are without exception logically untestable by an experiment
that could give an unambiguous result. This discussion, then,
is part of an attempt to see in the example of telepathy a
range of problems about which parapsychologists have had a
long period of uncertainty. But I will proceed with telepathy
first, since this is the best and most familiar example of the
group it represents here. Naturally, I am not unaware of
the severe challenge this step gives to some of the most dedicated workers in or around the field as a whole; but in the
interest of progress it is unavoidable, I think, that it be made.
I will return to this aspect after the discussion of telepathy.

THE MEANING OF TELEPATHY

As a first step, let us look into the original definition
of the term "telepathy." When Frederic W. H. Myers introduced the term in the Proceedings of the S. P. R. (Barrett,
Massey, Moses, Podmore, Gurney, & Myers, 1882) he also
presented along with it the term "tel-aesthesia" (meaning the
same as the French word "clairvoyance"), intending these two
terms "to cover all cases of impression received at a distance without the normal operation of the recognized sense
organs [p. 147]." But he added, "No true demarcation, in
fact, can as yet be made...." Twenty-one years later, however, in Human Personality (Myers, 1903) he wrote, "It has
become possible, I think, to discriminate between these two
words somewhat more sharply than when I first suggested
them in 1882. Telepathy may still be defined as 'the communication of impressions of any kind from one mind to another independently of the recognized channels of sense' [p.
xxii]." This mind-to-mind exchange was the definition that
became general for telepathy, and is to be found in the major works on the subject (such as those of S. G. Soal and
R. Warcollier, among others).

Myers, however, in Vol. II of Human Personality
(1903, pp. 195-96), pointed also to the possibility of the direct action of one person's thought upon the brain of another,

the percipient.   This would be a type of psychokinesis, but
that term had not then been introduced into the language of
parapsychology.   However, Thouless and Wiesner (1948)
recognized this possibility as one of the ways in which thought
might be transferred from one person to another extrasensorially, and considered the experimental work on psychokinesis
(PK), already reported by that date, as furnishing an experimental foundation for such a possibility of direct action of
mind on matter, in this case the brain.

But Thouless and Wiesner also went on in the same
article to suggest still another possible explanation of what
was called telepathy, one that was based mainly on recent
research in card-guessing tests for clairvoyance.   The percipient might, they argued, become clairvoyantly aware of
the state of the brain (or other organs) of the agent or sender when the latter was reported to be thinking of the target
idea to be transmitted.   These authors did, of course, consider the original Myers hypothesis of telepathy (the direct
mind-to-mind transfer of thought) but commented that "there
seems no reason to postulate such a process since we can
regard telepathy more simply...." (i.e., by way of the other
two hypotheses--clairvoyance and PK--as just explained).
Still more recently Thouless (1972) took a stronger stand
against the mind-to-mind type of transference: "I should of
course agree that no experiment proves the reality of mind-
to-mind transmission.   It seems to me to be a metaphysical
and not a scientific proposition [p. 243]."

TELEPATHY AND SPIRIT SURVIVAL

So far, this review has to do only with how the word
"telepathy" is to be defined.   Myers, who was primarily interested in the question of postmortem survival of personality
(PMS), saw in the frequent human experiences of what appeared to be thought transference indications of a possible
mode of communication that could function between the living
and the dead.   He was assuming that a brain was not necessary for the discarnate telepathic communicator.   Either the
mind-to-mind concept, which was his view of telepathy, or his
mind-to-brain alternative (which today we would think of as
PK) would meet Myers' need for a possible explanation of
communication between a discarnate mind and a living brain.

However, by the time Thouless and Wiesner wrote in
1948, the PMS problem had run into a great deal more diffi-

culty than it had encountered in Myers' mind, although he
had anticipated some of it with remarkable clarity. Various
research workers in parapsychology realized that messages
which mediums represented as coming from spirit sources
could have been unconsciously received (by means of the
medium's extrasensory abilities) from living persons or from
other mundane records, both sources also available to the
medium's ESP. This alternative explanation does not rule
out the possibility of PMS, but proof would require experimental tests that are not designable from the scientific knowledge of today.

The significant point here is that Myers, in his acceptance of PMS, had what was for him a conclusively established
finding that in turn needed telepathy as a principle of communication. The concept of communication with discarnate
spirits did logically require telepathy as a means of direct
mental interchange, or else (as per Thouless and Wiesner)
a combination of clairvoyance and psychokinesis. Which one
of these alternatives was the actual means of exchange was
not a question in Myers' day; and as we have seen, Thouless
was ready by 1972 to dismiss the original mind-to-mind idea
of telepathy as not a scientific problem, one that could not be
solved. But then (unlike Myers in his time) Thouless did not
consider PMS to be scientifically established; so he did not
face the same intellectual necessity Myers must have had to
consider (i.e., in accepting PMS he assumed a world of in-
corporeal human beings supposedly able to communicate with
each other as well as with the living). Today, however,
Thouless is willing to let the term "telepathy" apply to the
clairvoyance-psychokinesis (or general psi) basis of exchange
between persons.

On the other hand, some of us think this definition
would only confuse the issue. It would amount to applying
the name "telepathy" to phenomena that could well be the result of other subtypes of psi, while the Myers concept of
telepathic exchange would be dropped from further scientific
consideration as an unnecessary hypothesis.

THE SEARCH FOR A DEFINITIVE TEST

Before attempting a firm decision on the way telepathy
should be defined let us review the main steps in the experimental researches that have been conducted under the name
of telepathy. It is interesting to see the degree to which the

local cultural interests of the time (such as the attention
given to the PMS issue) influenced the conception of the problem, the methods of testing, and the interpretation of the results. For example, the early experiments in Britain dealing with extrasensory abilities were almost exclusively tests
of thought-transference (called telepathy, of course, when
that term was introduced). Professor William Barrett and
Frederic Myers, who were among the outstanding leaders in
British psychical research of the late nineteenth century,
were also actively interested in the PMS question. Other
early contributors to telepathy research, such as Eleanor
Sidgwick and Professor Oliver Lodge, were hardly less concerned.

On the French side of the Channel, however, where
interest in parapsychology was comparably great at that stage,
the major emphasis and attention were given to the ability
which Myers called "telaesthesia" (and which was also called
"clairvoyance," "lucidity," and "cryptaesthesia," among other
terms) rather than to telepathy. But at the same time, much
less respect and favor were shown for the PMS question
among French intellectuals than was expressed in England.
Professor Charles Richet (1923) and other French experimenters who contributed to the evidence for ESP did so almost entirely by way of clairvoyance tests. America, on the
other hand, had a close cultural relationship to Britain; accordingly the combination of interest in telepathy and in mediumship that occupied the early British psychical researchers
prevailed in the U.S. up until 1927.

However, at the beginning of the experiments at Duke
University, the research workers had the advantage of observing the national cultural differences between Britain and
France in their approach to parapsychology. But they also
had in mind the different precautionary requirements of the
two problems. In contrast to the simplicity of the tests for
clairvoyance, telepathy test procedures were obviously complex. The mere fact of having to deal with the control of
two subjects (agent and percipient) instead of one, as in clairvoyance, was a considerable obstacle to the desired safeguarding of experimental procedures.

Furthermore, the somewhat unguarded way in which
telepathy tests had for a half-century been conducted in various countries allowed equal opportunity for the subject to use
clairvoyance instead of (or along with) telepathy. This uncertain background required a completely new approach in any

case. It was necessary to test for telepathy without keeping
any objective record identified with the mental target of which
the agent or sender was thinking. Such a physical record
would be accessible to the subject's clairvoyant ESP. It was,
at the time, somewhat startling to realize that actually no
test for telepathy which excluded clairvoyance had yet been
reported! It is true that telepathy seemed the more plausible
hypothesis of the two in the cultural setting of the time. On
their part, however, French psychical researchers had no
comparable problem; they could more easily conduct clairvoyance tests without at the same time exposing the subject to
possible telepathic exchange, and they generally did so.
(That is, in card-guessing tests of clairvoyance the experimenter did not know the target card until later.)

The first concern at the Duke Laboratory was to set
up the best possible controls against sensory functions, and
accordingly clairvoyance tests were given preference over
those for telepathy. However, the attempt was also made to
test the telepathy hypothesis under conditions that excluded
clairvoyance as a counterexplanation.

In the first Duke report, Extra-Sensory Perception
(Rhine, 1934), the results of the card-guessing tests of clairvoyance mainly offered evidence from more and better controlled tests of that sub-type of psi capacity. However, progress was reported also on the "pure telepathy" tests (as
they were called) which for the first time provided a situation in which there was no objective record of the sender's
knowledge or thought of the target symbol. This thought was
to be "guessed" by the percipient subject before it was recorded by the agent. A different method had to be devised
so as to permit the recording and the checking of results (and
also to allow independent checking, which was considered an
essential safeguard). This recording was most effectively
safeguarded with the use of a set of numbered cards coded
in advance to represent the sender's thought-symbols which
the percipient subject would attempt to guess. Thus a step
forward was made toward a "pure telepathy" test, and from
the results of these tests it appeared that the scoring rate
was as high without the use of accompanying target cards as
it had been with them (i.e., in the older "telepathy" tests).

But this advance in method was only a temporary gain.
By the time Extra-Sensory Perception was published, the experimental program had advanced into the testing of precognition and psychokinesis. Thereupon it became necessary to

reconsider again the conditions necessary for a test of pure
telepathy (i. e. , a test controlled to exclude other types of
psi).   The precognition results offered a new counterhypothesis
to telepathy in these experiments.   They showed that one subject (H. P.) who had done well in the clairvoyance tests was
also able to predict significantly the order of cards in a pack
as it would be after the pack was reshuffled.   Accordingly,
this precognitive ability could presumably be used by the subject in a pure telepathy test to foresee the target record as
it would be after being decoded.   Obviously, then, if any recording of the telepathy targets was ever to be made, the control against precognition would not be effective.   The subject
in the telepathy test could use precognition, even when clairvoyance was ruled out by the new test procedure.   Accordingly, another method was needed for a pure telepathy test, a
method in which there was never to be a detailed objective
record; only the end results in the form of total trials and
successes would be recorded.   The target series were forever to remain in the category of existing only in the sender's subjective thought processes.

    And yet it was necessary that this memory be inde-
pendently checked by the double-blind procedure introduced
and used in major researches at the Laboratory from 1933
onward.   Elizabeth A. McMahan and Betty M. Humphrey,
along with other staff members of the Laboratory, worked
out a design for a pure telepathy test of this type, and later
S. G. Soal developed still another method on comparable
lines.   Both the American and British workers reported significant results (McMahan, 1946; Soal & Bateman, 1954, pp.
247-66).

    This more advanced test of pure telepathy was con-
sidered to be another forward step in sustaining interest in
the question of telepathy.   The experimental difficulties involved, however, were rather formidable, and the experiment required exceptional motivation.   This special motivation owed much of its stimulus to the international reactions
that developed in the mid-forties and aroused a strong
(though friendly) competitive interest between the research
workers in the United Kingdom and the U. S.   As a first step,
the U. K. colleagues had challenged the clairvoyance findings
reported at Duke, claiming that the hypothesis of precognitive
telepathy could explain them.   The American claims of an experimental distinction between the pure telepathy results and
those credited to pure clairvoyance were under some question.
The effect of these exchanges (Rhine, 1945, 1946) was to improve the test design for both sub-types of psi.

NO SATISFACTORY TEST

But while the other subtypes of psi were increasingly clarified by experiment, the status of the telepathy hypothesis still remained inconclusive. Soon thereafter, in 1948, as I have indicated, Thouless and Wiesner published their analysis of the alternatives to the Myers hypothesis of a direct mental exchange in telepathy. They proposed the two alternative psi hypotheses to explain the results of telepathy studies, either of which appears adequate to account for present findings. These will have to be excluded to establish telepathy, as I have long been indicating. In fact, in 1950 in my Myers Memorial Lecture in London (Rhine, 1950), I ended a summary of the work on telepathy by saying, "We have nothing on the record that we can, without hesitation and ambiguity, call evidence of telepathy ... [p. 20]" (or mind-to-mind exchange). And so far as I know, even today there is nothing that alters that summary. Accordingly the problem of mind-to-mind telepathy is about where it was in 1950, awaiting the possibility of a stage in the future at which it may, if there is sufficient reason, be reconsidered.

Dr. Thouless has, as I have noted, suggested that we define telepathy as the ESP of the mental state or activity of another person, the condition being that the agent or sender would have no external target to identify the thought to be transmitted. As already indicated, it has seemed to me that this is not a clear enough definition to serve a useful purpose. It simply means GESP, or GP (general psi). Consider the case, let us say, of a sender thinking of a cavity in his tooth; the tooth could just as well be the target for clairvoyance as if it were a card in the sender's hand. The telepathy category for such internal targets, or thoughts about them, would seem to be as indecisive as it has been for external ones.

Why, then, should we cling to the mere name if the original telepathy hypothesis no longer serves the purpose for which Myers invented it, especially since even after this long period of time, no secure evidential support for that hypothesis has been found? Even though it cannot be dismissed as an impossible idea, the hypothesis that the mind can, in extrasensorial communication with another mind, act independently of other subtypes of psi, remains only an interesting speculation, one that cannot be confirmed by any known method.

To Myers, of course, it was a very different matter.
Such exchange was for him a logical consequence of his acceptance of the case for spirit survival, and it would in turn
be at least highly relevant to the PMS hypothesis if telepathy
itself were ever to be independently verified.   Today, however,
the question, like that of PMS itself, belongs on the list of
unsolvable issues in parapsychology, issues inactivated because, like many great questions in other sciences, they are
simply not yet conceivably answerable by reliable methods.

CONSEQUENCES OF SHELVING TELEPATHY

What effect will this removal of the telepathy problem
or the concept of mind-to-mind exchange from the active list
have on the rest of the field?   One reassuring answer can,
I think, be given without hesitation; namely, that it will mean
no loss of any of the rightful (and already validated) territory
of parapsychology.   No well observed data and no confirmed
conclusions drawn from such data will have to be sacrificed
if the active pursuit of telepathy is suspended.   For the most
part the same records, whether of case material or of test
results, can be retained and valued, and even the word
"telepathy" can be kept in use with quotes added.   A telepathy
test will of course be understood to mean a GESP or GP test,
and there the question should be left for the present.

This decision about telepathy in no way disqualifies the
evidence that psi ability of some type does function between
persons (e.g., the acceptable evidence of GESP, including
the so-called "pure telepathy" tests).   All this work is as
good as ever in its support of the case for psi.   It is simply
not acceptable as proof that mind-to-mind telepathy occurs;
but for that matter, interest in isolated subtypes of psi has
considerably declined and the concept of the unity of psi has
become more acceptable.   It now appears that telepathy, if
it should be found to occur, would be only one of the phenomena of the unitary psi process, not the independent function
it was once thought to be.

Perhaps the most immediate advantage in shelving the
telepathy problem will lie in the clarified scientific policy it
will exemplify in the logic of psi research.   The firming-up
of the psi test design in this way should help parapsychology
to make better sense to the scientific mind at large.   It recognizes that we cannot adhere faithfully to sound methods and
hard logic and still continue to be overtolerant of preferred

but untestable hypotheses which have been carried along un-
discriminatingly from a period now long outgrown.

The most serious consequence at present of having to
set the telepathy problem aside is that this removes from
active consideration an idea that favors the PMS hypothesis.
Telepathy between the minds of the living left less of a gap
for such transfer of thought between living and discarnate
minds. But this does not alter the facts, although it may
help to keep the question alive.

OTHER UNSOLVABLE PROBLEMS IN PARAPSYCHOLOGY

As I stated earlier, quite a list could be made up of
research problems in parapsychology for which, as in the
case of telepathy, no intelligently designable test is available
now. These all ought to be cleared away, I think, and their
ambiguous nature labelled for what it is. This is necessary
in order to give priority to the problems of the field that can
effectively be undertaken today. No matter what other invit-
ing values a problem may have, feasibility of solution is obviously a primary essential.

Telepathy, PMS, and Mental Projection

As a basis for discussion of this matter I will begin
with a comparison of the problems of telepathy and PMS,
mainly because their relation has already been briefly discussed. Also, they are still among the most popular topics
of parapsychology research; for example, in a recently published critique of the field by the McGill University psychologist Dr. D. O. Hebb (1974), these two hypotheses received
first emphasis and Dr. Hebb stated that he remains unconvinced on them both.

I do not know Dr. Hebb's difficulty; but, as already
indicated, I myself find this basic weakness: in both these
cases the evidence supporting the hypothesis being tested applies
equally well to one of the counterhypotheses. With both telepathy and PMS the test results leave two possible (and reasonable) hypotheses; this has been said for more than a quarter of a century and there has been no serious challenge to
this view. What I now add is a more imperative point--that
this pursuit of unclear and indecisive research problems is
not only inefficient, but it is also not the way to give para-

psychology a respected image among fellow-scientists. Unfortunately, these two claims are only selected examples
from a numerous classification.   Let us look briefly at a few
other types of debatable problems belonging to this category
of the unsolvable.

As the third illustration of these confusing problems,
I will mention the so-called out-of-the-body experience.   This
is the old but currently popular idea of mental (or spirit)
projection by a living person to another location outside his
own body, an idea essentially similar in ambiguity to those of
telepathy and PMS.   In fact, the very same difficulty arises
when we ask: How can it ever be proved that the subject
who claims to have projected himself mentally out of his own
body and traveled to some other physical location has not
simply imagined that he has traveled there?   The only meaningful evidence offered us consists of claims of psi effects
supposed to have been produced by the traveling mind; but
the interpretation is always ambiguous.   On the one hand, it
may be pure imagination with ESP and PK simply operating
(as they well may) at a distance; on the other, if the mind
can and does "travel," it still depends on psi ability to give
the evidence that is reported.   How could a clear distinction
be drawn to show that some personal agency did travel in
space to the new location and that it was there that it exercised whatever psi ability was registered?   That is the question to be answered, and no one has yet offered a definitive
design for a way of obtaining an answer.

In all these cases there is an unrecognized assumption.
In this one it is that we do not yet know that a mind needs
to (or even can) travel to another physical location in order
to exercise a psi effect there.   The individual's parapsychic
system may have no space-time-matter limitations--certainly
none has been acceptably demonstrated.   Accordingly, for the
present at least, it is impossible to make a conclusive distinction between the hypothetical assumption of "projection"
and the imaginary experience of mental travel.

Let us look for a moment at these three mentalistic
hypotheses (telepathy, PMS, and mental projection) together,
since they are essentially in the same category of inconclu-
siveness of test design; that is, there is always, so far as
we know at present, an equally logical alternative hypothesis.
The great question involved in all three of them is whether
the mind can act independently of the body (brain), as these
questions assume, and (1) make direct contact with a sender's

mind (telepathy); (2) leave its body and travel in space (projection), or (3) interact mentally with a discarnate personality (PMS). For adequate proof, the mind would have to do something empirically observable that could be clearly distinguished from the known types of psi ability attributable to the subject. As it is, in all three types this cannot now be shown to occur (i.e., psi can account for everything) and the question is thus necessarily left up in the air. The best thing we can do, therefore, is to get on with the more soundly productive types of psi research that will eventually make possible a more informed attack on all these currently unsolvable problems.

Other Futile Hypotheses of External Personal Agency

Various other somewhat similar questions remain that can readily be grouped together loosely with the three already considered. Among them are still other hypotheses of spirit agency, not necessarily discarnate. However, not enough scientific attention has been given these, I think, to warrant more than a brief mention as to where they belong. The religious doctrine of reincarnation is one of the more familiar of these; but it is surprising too how many claims have been made of mediumistic communication with the inhabitants of other planets, with theological realms, and such. What these all have in common is that, like the more familiar type of spiritualist mediumship, the reports of contact with states, transitions, or regions that have no more definitive evidential basis than the subject's own imagination (however much they may be supported by evidence of some kind of psi manifestation) cannot, so far as I can see, yield the acceptable proof of independent agency that is necessary. This is essentially the same defect as in the three preceding cases. Even if the evidence were acceptable by conclusive psi research standards (which is so far not at all the case) it would still be alternatively explainable by means of psi contact with the sources used in the checkup. We may as well face this experimental fact and cease to ease wishfully past it. This is an essential checkpoint of scientific objectivity.

Yet it could not be said about any of these hypotheses that no method will ever be discovered or invented that could allow a reliable test and thus solve such problems. It is not impossible--or to me even inconceivable--that this should one day occur. All that might be needed for such an advance would be that one or more subjects develop reliable enough tracer-sensitivity to identify reliably the sources of information received.

Unclear "Retro" Problems

Another problem that invited experimental attention in the 1920's (although of a much earlier origin) was the popular clairvoyant object-association test, misnamed "psychometry." It has also been identified as "retrocognition." Before much time was given it in the laboratory, however, it was recognized back in the 1930's that this test of the ability to "visit" and clairvoyantly cognize events in the past was not logically sound;or better stated, it was not a solvable problem. The defect was again the familiar one, that the design of the test was inconclusive. The subject's retrocognitive responses could not be separated experimentally from his possible ESP of the very same existing sources of knowledge the experimenter needed in the checkup. Accordingly, since there is no logically tenable way of identifying retrocognition, the test was regarded as essentially just one possible form of contemporaneous clairvoyance.

Later on, with the advent of controlled researches in psychokinesis, a parallel variety of "retro" questions have also been proposed. In recent years some ideas concerning a backward-PK effect have been conceived and have actually been put to test. As with retrocognitive ESP, there have also been some significant results; but again the question of interpretation remains. "Retrokinesis" was the first name used; and later the term "retroactive PK" was used. So far, the outline of the basic procedure goes like this: first the target series was recorded by the experimenter on tape (magnetic or punched), so it could be replayed exactly later on. (The experimenter did not try to influence it either time.) Sometime, perhaps a week later, the subjects were selected and each was asked to try to influence this mechanically determined order of targets as it was replayed, although he was not told it was not actually the usual random order as in a normal test of PK.

Now then, can anybody say with confidence what was going on here? Were the subjects showing backward PK? (This is, of course, not the question of how retro-PK could work; no one knows how precognition works, or just cognition.) Rather, the question here is the same, in fact, that we have been asking repeatedly: How could one tell from this design whether, as an empirical fact, retroactive PK did occur--whether the subjects did, as was intended, influence the already recorded target order? One counterhypothesis is that it was the experimenter who exerted the influence, and

that he used precognition (of what the targets would be later
on for the intended subject) to guide his own PK ability in
making up the record of the original random order. So the
idea that it was the subject who retro-PK'd that original
order is obviously only one of the possible hypotheses and
(although this is not the main point) a less conceivable one
at that. In fact the subjects were not yet chosen for the tests
when the target series was recorded.

If, as seems preferable, the results are interpreted
as due to precognitive PK (i.e., the effect was registered in
the recording of the original random order), this would only
raise another double-header question as to whether the (still
unselected) subjects even had anything at all to do with the
result; the experimenter could have done it all himself. With
no more discriminative rational design behind the test than
is so far discernible, this type of experiment adds up to another shot in the parapsychological dark. It too belongs, as
much as many an older one, on the already crowded shelf of
baffling, unsolvable problems.

Some of these problems that qualify for the bad-risk
shelf have admittedly been of some value up to a point. The
beginning researches have in many cases shown at least that
psi of some sort was present; and perhaps something else
may have been learned incidentally. But this is a poor return, a weak argument, for a field of scientific research already a century old and in critical need of using the best scientific logic obtainable.

On the other hand, there is no such thing as absolute
certainty in research in any science. There is some risk in
every research undertaking. But a look through the literature
of this field will reveal that for the most part the major
questions successfully explored have given interpretable experimental answers, answers that have allowed the progressive advances of knowledge on which parapsychology is building. In fact there is a reasonably definable distinction: the
good-risk problems have been those that, without making any
important untestable assumptions, could be answered empirically by significant results from tests of a single essential
hypothesis. While, as in all the sciences, the answers are
not always final, those obtained in psi research are well on
a par with the more comparable experimental behavioral
branches of study. One by one these more secure problems
were sifted out of the vast unsorted mixture of existing heterogeneous claims, and the selection has become the basis of a
rather clearly definable field of science.

At the same time, we still have to cope with further problems of fact, method, and interpretation, some that are only now emerging in parapsychology. As a matter of fact, it now appears (as I stated in the Comments section in the September issue) that there may be new limits of experimental method (for the present anyhow) not hitherto encountered; but then too (fair to say) there may be future discoveries coming up that will provide the means of solving these present problems. Such, of course, is always the risk and hope in the sciences; that is the essential challenge. Yet, while we will try to deal with these further difficulties of method and design, using all available help, a very large part of the necessary preparation will consist of ridding the field without any further delay of these older uncertainties of problem selection considered here.

Discerning persons today are more and more looking appraisingly at the great potential of the findings of this research field--some with a view to joining it, others with the urge to support it, and still others wishing to give it what it needs in some effective way. It should be possible to assure them that the psi researcher today is more than ever discriminating and far-seeing in this first requirement of the explorer--that he know clearly and well what it is that he is attempting to do and how to interpret the results if his experiment is successful.

The telepathy example, after nearly a century of trial, seems to offer an important lesson for the psi research worker, the necessity of selecting a clearly researchable problem; first, one that does not assume anything the method itself cannot test; and, second, one that with significantly positive results can be expected to answer the one question singled out for the test as designed. The lesson of working always with clear and sharp issues, if fully learned and applied at this stage of parapsychology, could multiply the rate of advance for the field as a whole more rapidly than anything else to be compared.

REFERENCES

Barrett, W. F.; Massey, C. C.; Moses, W. S.; Podmore, F.; Gurney, E.; & Myers, F. W. H. "Report of the literary committee." Proceedings of the Society for Psychical Research, 1882, 1, 116-75.
Hebb, D. O. "What psychology is about." American Psy-

chologist, 1974, 29, 71-79.

McMahan, E. A. "An experiment in pure telepathy." Journal of Parapsychology, 1946, 10, 224-42.

Myers, F. W. H. Human Personality. (2 vols.) New York:
Longmans, Green, & Co., 1903.

Rhine, J. B. Extra-Sensory Perception. Boston Society for
Psychic Research, 1934. (Republished: Boston, Bruce
Humphries, Branden Press, 1973.)

_____. "Telepathy and clairvoyance reconsidered." Jour-
nal of Parapsychology, 1945, 9, 176-93.

_____. "A digest and discussion of some comments on
'Telepathy and Clairvoyance Reconsidered.'" Journal
of Parapsychology, 1946, 10, 36-50.

_____. "Telepathy and Human Personality." (The tenth
Frederic W. H. Myers Memorial Lecture.) Society
for Psychical Research, London, 1950.

Richet, Charles. Thirty Years of Psychical Research. New
York: The Macmillan Company, 1923.

Soal, S. G., & Bateman, F. Modern Experiments in Telepathy. New Haven: Yale University Press, 1954.

Thouless, R. H., & Wiesner, B. P. "The psi process in
normal and 'paranormal' psychology." Journal of
Parapsychology, 1948, 12, 192-212.

_____. Remarks in "News and Comments." Journal of
Parapsychology, 1972, 36, 241-50.

ADDITIONAL READINGS ON
TELEPATHY AND CLAIRVOYANCE

Kanthamani, H. and Kelly, E. F. "Card experiments with a special subject. I. Single-card clairvoyance." JP 38: 16-26 (Mar 1974).

Krippner, S. "Telepathy." In Mitchell, E. D. and others. Psychic Exploration. N. Y., Putnam's, 1974, Ch. 4.

Morris, R. L. "Building experimental models." Journal of Communication 25: 117-25 (Win 1975).

Mundle, C. W. K. "Strange facts in search of a theory." PSPR 56: 1-20 (Pt 207, Jan 1973).

Nash, C. B. "Note on precognition of the percipient's calls as an hypothesis to telepathy." JP 39: 21-23 (Mar 1975).

Rhine, J. B. "Comments: 'Psi methods reexamined'." JP 39: 38-58 (Mar 1975).

Schmeidler, G. R. "Are there two kinds of telepathy?" JASPR 55: 87-97 (Jul 1961).

Schmidt, H. "Clairvoyance tests with a machine." JP 33: 300-06 (Dec 1969).

Stanford, R. G. "Clairvoyance." In Mitchell, E. D. and others. Psychic Exploration. N. Y., Putnam's, 1974. Ch. 5.

_____. "Concept and psi." RP 2: 137-62 (1973).

_____. "An experimentally testable model for spontaneous psi events. II. Psychokinetic events." JASPR 68: 321-56 (Oct 1974).

APPENDICES

APPENDIX A

PARAPSYCHOLOGICAL PERIODICALS

Since one of the purposes of this book is to encourage students of parapsychology to read the periodical literature of the subject, a brief description of the major English-language periodicals, arranged in alphabetical order, and how they may be obtained, is provided below.[1]

International Journal of Parapsychology (IJP)

v. 1, Summer, 1959 - v. 10, Winter, 1968. This quarterly journal was published by the Parapsychology Foundation, 29 West 57th Street, N.Y. 10019.

The International Journal of Parapsychology was a scholarly journal whose main purpose was to link parapsychology with other disciplines such as psychology, physics, anthropology, pharmacology, religion, etc. Most issues contained abstracts of the articles in English, French, German, Italian, and Spanish, evidence of the publisher's intention to make it international in scope. Theoretical articles and exploratory essays predominated although review articles and experimental reports were also published. Each issue contained several book reviews.
Volumes 1-10 are available from University Microfilms (Ann Arbor, Mi 48106) for $60.00.
Separate indexes were published by the IJP for vols. 1-3, 4, 5, 6, and 8-10.

---

[1]Additional information on these and other parapsychological periodicals may be found in R. A. White and L. A. Dale, Parapsychology: Sources of Information. Metuchen, N.J., Scarecrow Press, 1973, pp. 203-17.

Journal of Parapsychology (JP)

v. 1, 1937 to date. Published quarterly in March,
June, September, and December by Parapsychology Press,
Box 6847, College Station, Durham, North Carolina 27708.

The JP is a scholarly journal primarily devoted to the
publication of experimental reports. It also publishes criticisms, methodological and review articles, some theoretical
papers, and book reviews. Since 1958 most issues contain a
valuable section entitled "Parapsychological Abstracts," which
provides half-page abstracts of articles on parapsychology ap-
pearing in other parapsychological periodicals, both English
and foreign, articles in non-parapsychological journals, some
books, and unpublished manuscripts.
A subscription for one year is $8.00, or $2.00 per
issue. Johnson Reprint Corp., (111 Fifth Ave., N.Y. 10003),
has the rights to reprint vols. 1-12 (1937-1948). Some back
issues from vol. 13 to date may be obtained from Parapsychology Press at $9.00 per volume, or $2.25 per issue. It
is also available on microfilm from University Microfilms
(Ann Arbor, Mi 48106).
The JP prepares an index and table of contents listing
for each volume. The contents from v. 1, 1937, through v.
16, 1952, was published in the September, 1953, issue. JP
is abstracted in Psychological Abstracts and is indexed in
Social Sciences Index.

Journal of the American Society for Psychical Research
(JASPR)

v. 1, 1907 to date. Published quarterly in January,
April, July, and October by the American Society for Psychical Research, 5 West 73rd Street, N.Y. 10023.

This is a scholarly journal which publishes experimental reports, theoretical and review articles, and reviews
of current books.
It is free to members. Individual issues are $3.00
apiece and are available from the Society. Back issues of
vols. 35-54, 1941-1960, are available from Johnson Reprint
Corp. (111 Fifth Ave., N.Y. 10003) at $230 for a paper-
bound set; $11.50 per paperback volume. Also available
from University Microfilms (Ann Arbor, Mi 48106): Vols.
1-42, 1907-1948, for $143.00; 1949, to date, available at
$4.00 per volume.

The JASPR publishes its own name and subject index and table of contents listing for each volume. It is abstracted in Psychological Abstracts and indexed in Social Sciences Index. It is also included in Social Science Citation Index and its contents are listed in Selected List of Tables of Contents of Psychiatric Periodicals.

Journal of the Society for Psychical Research (JSPR)

v. 1, 1884 to date. (vols. 1-34 were restricted to members only.) Published quarterly in March, June, September, and December by the Society for Psychical Research, 1 Adam and Eve Mews, London W8 6UQ, England.

The JSPR is a scholarly periodical publishing experimental reports, spontaneous case reports, theoretical papers, mediumistic reports, and reviews of books and individual periodicals.

JSPR is free to members. Available to others at £5 per year and £1.50 per issue. Some bound volumes and individual issues from v. 35 on are available from the Society. Reprints of v. 1-43 (1884-1966) may be obtained for $200.00 from AMS Press (156 E. 13th Street, N.Y. 10003).

Each volume has its own name and subject index and table of contents listing. The Society has also issued a list of the principal contents of the Journal from v. 35, 1949 to v. 45, 1969. The JSPR is indexed in a 4-volume index to its publications published by the Society for Psychical Research and covering the years 1884 to 1970. It is abstracted in Psychological Abstracts.

Parapsychology Review (PR)

v. 1, 1970 to date. Published bimonthly by the Parapsychology Foundation, 29 West 57th Street, N.Y. 10019.

This non-technical newsletter is international in scope. It has a magazine-type format and contains photographs. It publishes directory-type information and news of persons and organizations associated with parapsychology. It carries some articles, usually based on papers presented at the Foundation's annual international parapsychology conferences, and several book reviews.

PR costs $8.00 per year and $.85 per issue. Some back issues are available from the Foundation.

An annual index is published with the January-February issue of the following year and it is abstracted in Psychological Abstracts.

Proceedings of the Society for Psychical Research (PSPR)

v. 1, 1882 to date. Published irregularly by the Society for Psychical Research, 1 Adam and Eve Mews, London W8 6UQ, England.

PSPR is a scholarly periodical which publishes major research reports, addresses of the presidents of the SPR, critical reviews, and lengthy theoretical papers.

PSPR is free to members; price to non-members varies by size. Single issues are still available from the Society (members pay half price). AMS Press (56 East 13th Street, N.Y. 10003) plans to reprint vols. 1-53, 1882-1962: $325.00.

A list of the contents of PSPR from 1882-1969 is available from the Society. The contents of 1882-1933 are listed in Fodor's Encyclopedia of Psychic Science. The SPR has also published a four-part index to its publications, including PSPR from v. 1-v. 54 (1966). Vols. 3-11 (1920-1949) of PSPR were indexed in Social Sciences and Humanities Index (then known as the International Index). It is also indexed in British Humanities Index and abstracted in Psychological Abstracts.

Research in Parapsychology (RP)

v. 1, 1972 to date. Published annually by Scarecrow Press, Metuchen, N.J. 08840.

This annual supersedes the Proceedings of the Parapsychological Association and is the record of the annual convention of the Parapsychological Association (P.A.), the professional parapsychological society. It provides abstracts of papers delivered at the annual convention, and the full texts of the presidential address and the invited speaker's address (usually by an expert in a scholarly field other than parapsychology). It provides the best existing record of what is happening in experimental parapsychology in any given year.

Nos. 1-8, under the title Proceedings of the Parapsychological Association are available from the Psychical Research Foundation (Duke Station, Durham, N.C. 27706). Nos.

1-5 are $3. 50 each (hardcover) and $1. 95 (paper). Nos. 6-8 are available in paper only at $3. 00 each. Special price for first four numbers is $12. 00; $6. 00 (paper). The hardcover edition of No. 5 and paperback edition of No. 1 are no longer in print. Back copies of Research in Parapsychology may be ordered from Scarecrow Press.

Each volume of both Proc. P. A. and RP has detailed subject and author indexes. Cumulative author and subject indexes for the 8 years of Proc. P. A. was published in No. 8, 1971.

APPENDIX B

LOCATING ARTICLES IN
NON-PARAPSYCHOLOGICAL PERIODICALS

To locate articles on parapsychology in non-parapsychological journals, such as the ones in Behavioral Psychiatry included in this book, it is necessary to use general and specialized indexing and abstracting services, some of which are found in most libraries of any size. An alphabetical list of the titles of indexes and abstracts likely to contain references to articles on parapsychology is as follows: Biological Abstracts, British Humanities Index, Index Medicus, Index of Psychoanalytic Writings (edited by Grinstein), Psychological Abstracts, Readers' Guide to Periodical Literature, and Social Sciences and Humanities Index (expanded in 1974 and separated into two indexes: Humanities Index and Social Sciences Index, the latter being the one more likely to index parapsychological articles). It is also useful to consult the section, "Parapsychological Abstracts," published in most issues of the Journal of Parapsychology.

APPENDIX C

INFORMATION ABOUT AUTHORS

CHARI, C. T. K. Born in 1909 in Trivellore, India, he received an M. A. and a Ph. D. from Madras University in 1932 and 1953, respectively. He was a Lecturer in Philosophy at American College, Madura, from 1933-1940 and then moved to Madras Christian College as an assistant professor, 1940-1956, an associate professor, 1956-1958, and in 1958 became Chairman of the Department of Philosophy and Psychology. He has been active in Indian philosophical and psychological associations. He has published books on philosophy and many articles on philosophy, psychology, and parapsychology. The latter have appeared in Indian, British, and American parapsychological periodicals. He is interested in the relation of parapsychology to philosophy, physics, mathematics, and mysticism.

CRUMBAUGH, JAMES C. Born in 1921, Crumbaugh obtained his M. A. in psychology at Southern Methodist University in 1938, in partial fulfillment for which he carried out an ESP research project. He obtained his Ph. D. in psychology in 1953 from the University of Texas. He has held teaching positions at Memphis State College, MacMurray College, and since 1964 has been a staff psychologist at the VA Hospital in Gulfport, Mississippi. Although Dr. Crumbaugh's interest in parapsychology has spanned many years, he has never succeeded in obtaining significant results in a psi experiment. Therefore he has played the role of skeptic, stressing the importance of the experimenter and the necessity for repeatable experiments in parapsychological research. In addition to his own research he has supervised work in parapsychology carried out by his students. His articles on parapsychology have appeared in both parapsychological and psychological journals.

HONORTON, CHARLES R. Born in 1946 in Minnesota, as an undergraduate at the University of Minnesota Honorton was research coordinator for the Minnesota Society for Psychic

465

Research in 1965 and 1966. In 1966 he became Research
Fellow at the Institute for Parapsychology, FRNM, and in
1967 he joined the research staff of the Division of Parapsychology and Psychophysics, Department of Psychiatry, Maimonides Medical Center, in Brooklyn, where he is now Senior
Research Associate. He has served on the Council of the
Parapsychological Association, and has held offices as Secretary, Vice-President, and President (1975). He is also a
member of the Board of Trustees of the American Society
for Psychical Research. Honorton's major concern has been
with finding ways of facilitating psi by altered states of consciousness and other means.

KRIPPNER, STANLEY CURTIS. Born in 1932 in Edgerton,
Wisconsin, Krippner obtained a B. S. (1954), M. A. (1957),
and Ph. D. in psychology (1961) from Northwestern University.
He was actively interested in parapsychology as a student,
and while at Northwestern arranged for J. B. Rhine to give
lectures at the university on two different occasions. He began his career as a speech therapist and in 1961 was made
Director of the Child Study Center at Kent State University.
In 1964 he became Director of the Dream Laboratory at Maimonides Medical Center in Brooklyn. In addition from 1966
to 1972 he lectured in the graduate school of Wagner College
and for some years has been Director of Research for the
New York Institute of Child Development. In 1972 he assumed
his present positions as senior research associate for education and training in the Division of Parapsychology and Psychophysics at Maimonides Medical Center and as adjunct and
visiting professor at the Humanistic Psychology Institute,
California State College at Sonoma, and the University of
Puerto Rico.
        He is a Fellow of the American Society of Clinical
Hypnosis and was Chairman of the first three International
Conferences on Humanistic Psychology, 1970-72. He also
chaired the first western hemisphere conference on acupunc-
ture, Kirlian photography, and the human aura. He co-edited
the proceedings of the latter conference under the title, Gal-
axies of Life (1972; paperbound edition: The Kirlian Aura,
1974). He has also co-authored, with Montague Ullman, a
Parapsychological Monograph entitled Telepathy and Dreams
(1970) as well as a book (with Ullman and Alan Vaughan) entitled Dream Telepathy (1973). He has published over 200
articles in psychological, psychiatric, educational, and parapsychological journals and edits the new journal, Psychoener-
getic Systems.

Dr. Krippner is interested in the relation of parapsychology to personality. In recent years he has been involved
in creating bridges between parapsychology and psychology and
between Western parapsychologists and their counterparts in
the U. S. S. R. and other Communist countries of Europe.

MORRIS, ROBERT L. Born in Canonsburg, Pennsylvania in
1942, Morris got a B. S. in psychology from the University
of Pittsburgh in 1963 and a Ph. D. in biological psychology
from Duke in 1969. While a student Dr. Morris held a
three-year summer research fellowship in parapsychology at
FRNM. He was a postdoctoral research fellow at Duke's
Center for the Study of Aging and Human Development from
1966 to 1971 when he joined the staff of the Psychical Research Foundation as Research Coordinator. In 1974 he went
to the University of California at Santa Barbara to set up a
tutorial program in parapsychology. He has been active on
the Council of the Parapsychological Association and was its
president in 1974. He has published several articles in parapsychology and zoology journals and has contributed to several
parapsychology anthologies. He edited Arno Press's reprint
series entitled "Perspectives in Psychical Research. " His
main parapsychological interests concern biological aspects
of psi and anpsi. He has also been involved with a systematic review and revaluation of parapsychological findings, terminology, and interpretations.

NASH, CARROLL B. Born in 1914 in Louisville, Kentucky,
Nash obtained his M. S. in 1937 and his Ph. D. in 1939 from
the University of Maryland. His parapsychological career has
paralleled his career as a college professor. He was an instructor in zoology from 1939 to 1941 at the University of
Arizona where he also conducted his first psi experiments.
He has also taught biology at Pennsylvania Military College
(1941-1944), American University (1944-45), and Washington
College (where he chaired the Biology Department) from 1945-
48, until taking his current position as Chairman of the Biology Department at St. Joseph's College (from 1948 on).
In 1956 he organized and has since directed the Parapsychology Laboratory at St. Joseph's College in Philadelphia. He
has served on the Council of the Parapsychological Association as well as an officer, and was president in 1963. For
many years he has taught a college-level course in parapsychology in the Evening Division at St. Joseph's. He has experimented widely and has published numerous reports in

parapsychological journals as well as papers on biology and
zoology. He is particularly interested in precognition and
psychokinesis and in personality variables and psi.

OSIS, KARLIS. Born in 1917 in Riga, Latvia, Osis obtained
his Ph. D. in psychology from the University of Munich in
1950. The title of his dissertation was "A Hypothesis of Extrasensory Perception. " After coming to the United States
he joined the staff of the Parapsychology Laboratory, Duke
University, as a Research Associate from 1951 to 1957. In
1957 he became Director of Research at the Parapsychology
Foundation, a position he held until 1962, at which time he
was appointed to the position he still holds as Director of
Research at the American Society for Psychical Research.
He has served on the Council of the Parapsychological Association, and has held several offices, including the presidency in 1961. He has written a monograph, Deathbed Observations by Physicians and Nurses (1961) and has published
many articles in parapsychological journals. His primary
research interests are deathbed experiences and the light they
shed on the possibility of survival, creativity and psi, distance and ESP, out of the body experiences, and experiments
with mediums using a linkage design.

PRATT, JOSEPH GAITHER. Gaither Pratt was born in 1910
in Winston-Salem, North Carolina. He obtained both an M. A.
degree (1933) and a Ph. D. (1936) in psychology at Duke University. In 1932 he became a research assistant in the Duke
University Parapsychology Laboratory where he worked with
J. B. Rhine until 1963, when he assumed his present position
on the research staff of the Division of Parapsychology, Dept.
of Psychiatry, University of Virginia, where he also holds the
rank of full professor. In addition to numerous articles on
parapsychology, Dr. Pratt has written two books: Parapsychology: an Insider's View of ESP (rev. ed. , 1966) and ESP
Research Today (1973). He has co-authored two more: Extrasensory Perception after Sixty Years (with J. B. Rhine
and others, 1949) and Parapsychology: Frontier Science of
the Mind (with J. B. Rhine, rev. ed. , 1962). He has also
authored a Parapsychology Foundation monograph, On the
Evaluation of Verbal Material in Parapsychology (1969). He
has been very active as an officer of the Parapsychological
Association and as a member of the Board of Trustees of the
American Society for Psychical Research, where he also
serves as Chairman of the Publications Committee. He is

one of parapsychology's most versatile investigators, having
at one time or other studied such diverse phenomena as position effects, poltergeists, pigeon homing, the focussing effect
of Pavel Stepanek, computer applications to parapsychological
data, work with high scoring subjects, and psychokinesis. In
his student days he discovered the famous ESP subject, Hu-
bert Pearce, and he has had an abiding interest in the discovery and ways of testing high scoring subjects ever since.

RANDALL, JOHN L. Born in 1933 in Warwick, England,
Randall took an honours degree in chemistry with a minor in
biology at Leicester College of Technology and obtained a
Graduate Certificate in Education from Leicester University.
He taught in secondary schools for four years before taking
his current position as a biology master at a boy's grammar
school, Leamington College. He has conducted psi experiments with his students and has assisted in introducing parapsychology in a General Studies Course for Sixth Formers.
In addition to his experimental work he has made theoretical
contributions and is interested in the philosophical implications of psi.

RANSOM, CHAMPE. Born in San Diego, California in 1936,
Ransom became a seaman in the Merchant Marines after high
school. He obtained his B. A. degree from Lawrence University, majoring in history, in 1961, and a J. D. degree from
St. Mary's University School of Law in 1966. From 1966 to
1970 he served as a legislative counsel to the state legisla-
ture in Juneau, Alaska. His interest in parapsychology was
kindled during his final year in law school and he became a
research assistant at the Division of Parapsychology, University of Virginia, for three years, beginning in 1970. At present he is an editor with Michie Company, a law book publisher in Charlottesville, North Carolina. He is representative
of a certain type of parapsychologist whose active interest in
the field is blended with a healthy skepticism.

RAO, KONERU RAMAKRISHNA. Born in 1932 in Enikepadu,
Krishna District, Andhra Pradesh, India, Rao obtained his
M. A. in philosophy from Andhra University in 1955 for a
thesis on parapsychology and taught philosophy there from
1953 to 1958. He was a Fullbright Scholar and Rockefeller
Fellow from 1958 to 1960 while obtaining an M. L. S. from the
University of Chicago and also completing his Ph. D. disserta-

tion.   Returning to Andhra University, he received his Ph. D.
degree and was appointed University Librarian, and soon became involved in administrative details which left little time
for pursuing parapsychological interests.   However, from
1962 through 1965 he accepted a position as Research Associate at the Duke University Parapsychology Laboratory where
he proved to be a gifted experimenter and completed several
fruitful investigations.   Upon returning to India he was asked
to set up a combined Department of Psychology and Parapsychology at Andhra University.   The new department was inaugurated in 1967 with Rao as Chairman, a position he still
holds.   He has served on the Council of the Parapsychological
Association and was its president in 1965.   He has written a
survey of parapsychology in book form, Experimental Parapsychology (1966), and his Master's thesis was published under the title, Psi Cognition (1957).   He has also co-authored
a Parapsychology Foundation monograph and has published
many experimental papers in parapsychological journals.   Rao
is interested in the application of yoga and other Eastern techniques to the study of ESP and has been actively engaged in
elucidating the bidirectionality of psi, both experimentally and
theoretically.

RHINE, JOSEPH BANKS, was born in 1895 in Juniata County,
Pennsylvania.   He obtained a B. S. (1922), M. S. (1923), and
Ph. D. (1925) from the University of Chicago.   His doctorate
was in botany.   Dr. Rhine was a research fellow in plant
physiology at Boyce Thompson Institute, 1923-24, and was an
instructor in plant physiology at Western Virginia University
the following two years.   In 1926 he went to Harvard to investigate the Margery mediumship and to work with Walter
Franklin Prince.   In 1927 he went to Duke University to pursue parapsychological studies with William McDougall, Chairman of the Psychology Dept. , who asked him to stay as an
instructor in philosophy and psychology.   Rhine became a professor in psychology in 1929.   In the same year he became
director of the Parapsychology Laboratory at Duke, which
he helped to found.   He also founded the Journal of Parapsychology, which for many years was the major vehicle for the
publication of experimental parapsychology reports.   He continued as director of the Laboratory until 1962, when he was
forced to retire from Duke University, and then established
the Laboratory's successor, the Institute for Parapsychology,
an independent research organization, which is a division of
the larger Foundation for Research on the Nature of Man
(FRNM).   Rhine is currently the Executive Director of FRNM,

which is also the owner of the Parapsychology Press, which publishes books on parapsychology and the Journal of Parapsychology. Rhine has justly earned the title, "father of experimental parapsychology." He made "ESP" a household word, was responsible for the widespread application of statistical methods in parapsychological research, and was the first to obtain largescale evidence of ESP in the general population. He also pioneered laboratory investigations of psychokinesis and precognition. More than any other single person he has been responsible for what measure of academic and scientific recognition parapsychology has achieved, and his laboratory, together with its successor, has trained the majority of scientists working in parapsychology today. Although he purposely has left the handling of the Parapsychological Association (the professional society of parapsychologists) to others, he was responsible for founding it. He has published numerous articles not only in parapsychological periodicals but in professional journals of related fields and in general magazines. He has also written several books: Extrasensory Perception (1935), New Frontiers of the Mind (1937), Extrasensory Perception after Sixty Years (with others, 1940), Reach of the Mind (1947), New World of the Mind (1953), Parapsychology: Frontier Science of the Mind (with J. G. Pratt, rev. ed., 1962), Parapsychology Today (Editor, with R. Brier, 1968), and Progress in Parapsychology (Editor, 1971).

ROLL, WILLIAM G. Born in Bremen, Germany, in 1926, Roll obtained his B. A. degree from the University of California at Berkeley in 1949 and received a B. Litt. from Oxford University in 1960 for a thesis on the subject of parapsychology. He was president of the Oxford University Society for Psychical Research from 1952-1957. From 1957 to 1960 he was a Research Associate at the Duke University Parapsychology Laboratory. He then founded a private research organization, the Psychical Research Foundation, to conduct research on the problem of survival, and from the beginning has served as its director. He edits Theta, the Foundation's quarterly bulletin, and has published a book, The Poltergeist (1973), as well as many journal articles. He has often served on the Council of the Parapsychological Association and has held several of its offices, including the presidency in 1964. He edited the Proceedings of the Parapsychological Association for the 9 years of its existence as well as the first two years of its successor, Research in Parapsychology, through 1973. He has been actively involved

with all aspects of survival research, has made studies of
special sensitives, and is an acknowledged expert in the investigation of poltergeist phenomena. From his student days
he has been interested in explicating his "psi field theory."
He is also interested in altered states of consciousness and
psi.

SABINE, WILLIAM H. W. Born in 1903 in Claughton, England, Mr. Sabine was educated in private schools and became
a writer and editor in the historical field, as well as an
editor and book dealer. In 1947 he came to the United States
and now lives and works in Hollis, New York, where he is
a book and print dealer. His principal historical work is the
three-volume Historical Memoirs of William Smith, which he
edited, and which is being published by Arno Press. Mr.
Sabine has had many spontaneous psi experiences throughout
his life, particularly precognitive ones. Some of these experiences were published in his book, Second Sight in Daily
Life (1949). The accounts of his experiences have the special distinction of having been recorded immediately. He describes himself as "a percipient and recorder in the field of
spontaneous paranormal phenomena."

STANFORD, REX G. Born in Robstown, Texas, in 1938,
Stanford received a B.A. (1963) and a Ph.D. (1967) in psychology from the University of Texas at Austin. Stanford
comes from a family in which spontaneous psi occurrences
are not unusual. This factor provided impetus for his interest in parapsychology, together with a strong realization of
the importance of the scientific investigation of psi for man's
understanding of his world. While doing his graduate work,
Stanford spent the summers of 1964 through 1967 on the staff
of the Institute of Parapsychology, FRNM. In 1968 he taught
psychology at Western Carolina University and in September,
1968, he went to the University of Virginia as a research
associate in the Division of Parapsychology, School of Medicine. In 1973 he became an Assistant Professor of Psychology at St. John's University where he teaches psychology and
is actively engaged in conducting and supervising parapsychological research. Dr. Stanford has published many significant experimental and theoretical articles in the Journal of
Parapsychology and Journal of the American Society for Psychical Research. He has also written chapters for several anthologies. He has been active in the Parapsychological Association, serving as Vice-President in 1970 and 1971 and as

President in 1973. He is a member of the Board of Trustees
of the ASPR. His major interests in parapsychology are the
development and experimental testing of models for spontaneous (nonintentional) psi events, mediational factors in extrasensory response, models of ESP receiver optimization, and
the basic nature of psi events beyond their psychological and
biological functioning.

VAN DE CASTLE, ROBERT L. Born in 1927 in Rochester,
N.Y., he obtained a B.A. from Syracuse University, and an
M.A. in Psychology from the University of Missouri in 1953
for a research project in ESP. He joined the research staff
of the Parapsychology Laboratory, Duke University, from
1954 to 1956 and in 1959 obtained his Ph.D. from the University of North Carolina. After teaching psychology at the University of Idaho and the University of Denver, he conducted
dream research with Calvin Hall at the Institute of Dream
Research in Miami. Together they published The Content
Analysis of Dreams (1966). In 1967 he assumed the position
of Director of the Sleep and Dream Laboratory at the University of Virginia until 1975, when he took a leave of absence, though remaining as a Professor of Clinical Psychology in the Department of Psychiatry. Since 1969 he has
served on the Council of the Parapsychological Association
where he held several offices, including the presidency in
1970. He has written several chapters on parapsychology in
books and has contributed many articles to the journal literature. He was himself an outstanding subject in the dream/
ESP experiments conducted at the Maimonides Medical Center,
earning the title "prince of the dreamers." His parapsychological research interests are centered in anthropological investigations of psi, ESP and dreams, and psychological correlates of psi test results.

APPENDIX D

ABBREVIATIONS OF PARAPSYCHOLOGY PERIODICALS
CITED IN THE ADDITIONAL READINGS

IJP   International Journal of Parapsychology

JASPR   Journal of the American Society for Psychical Research

JP   Journal of Parapsychology

JSPR   Journal of the Society for Psychical Research

PASPR   Proceedings of the American Society for Psychical Research

PR   Parapsychology Review

PSPR   Proceedings of the Society for Psychical Research

RP   Research in Parapsychology

NAME INDEX

Abramowski, E. 354, 360
Abrams, S. I. 263
Allison, L. W. 195
Amadou, R. 197
American Institute of Mathematical Statistics 408, 426
Anderson, M. L. 351, 362, 432
Angstadt, J. 360

Barber, T. X. 232-33, 244, 263, 264
Barrett, W. F. 424, 442, 445
Barry, J. 345
Bateman, F. 5, 6, 194, 315, 416
Bates, E. K. 364
Bechterev, W. 345, 360, 368
Beloff, J. 254, 257, 260-61, 291, 366, 387
Bendit, L. J. 124
Bergson, H. 344, 346
Bertrand, A. 122
Bestall, C. M. 82, 86
Besterman, T. 98, 192
Bindler, P. 275-76, 293, 294
Björkhem, J. 365, 369
Black, S. 346
Bleksley, A. E. H. 193
Boring, E. G. 407, 408, 411, 414, 431
Braud, L. W. 275
Braud, W. G. 275
Bridgman, P. W. 408, 412

Brier, R. 296-97, 345
Broad, C. D. 311-13, 322, 368
Brown, G. S. 404, 408
Brown, R. K. 357, 359
Burlingham, D. 129
Burt, C. 337, 411
Burt, F. P. 192

Cadoret, R. J. 81, 86, 120, 127-28, 155, 234, 237-38, 261, 262, 357, 362-63, 366
Callaway, H. 99
Canon, H. J. 408
Carington, W. C. 6-7, 194-95, 196-97, 313-15, 363-64, 369
Carpenter, J. C. 166, 172
Casler, L. 234, 240-42, 261, 262, 366
Cavanna, R. 128
Chari, C. T. K. 308, 382-96, 465
Chauvin, R. 74
Cheek, D. B. 125
Clark, R. E. D. 339-40
Clowe, C. W. 38
Cohen, D. 403
Cooper, B. 368
Coover, J. E. 192
Cox, W. E. 58, 61, 150-51, 347
Croiset, G. 355-56
Crookes, W. 424
Crowe, C. 25
Crumbaugh, J. C. 400, 406, 424-37, 465

Daba, S. 100
Dagel, L. T. 171
Dale, L. A. 56
Davidson, R. 275-76, 293, 294
Davis, H. 413
Davis, K. R. 234, 239-40, 261-62
Dean, E. D. 356, 382
Deguisne, A. 432
Deutsch, H. 129
Dingwall, E. J. 229, 274
Dobbs, H. A. C. 382, 384
Dodds, E. R. 98, 368
Doyle, A. C. 424
Driesch, H. 198, 346, 372
Drucker, S. 277-78
Dunne, J. W. 323
Durkin, M. G. 234, 238, 261
Duval, P. 82-83, 86, 170, 219-20

Edmunds, S. 234, 245-46, 262
Egerton, F. 99
Ehrenwald, J. 124-25, 130, 317-18, 324, 365, 434
Eilbert, L. 364
Eisenbud, J. 129, 131, 365, 434
Elliotson, J. 122
Estabrooks, G. H. 205
Evans, C. 404-05
Eysenck, H. J. 278, 408

Fahler, J. 234, 236-38, 246, 250-51, 261, 262, 280-81, 366
Feather, S. 76, 79, 216, 218, 360
Feigl, H. 384
Feinberg, G. 383
Feldstein, S. 366
Firsoff, V. A. 384
Fisher, R. A. 430
Fisk, G. W. 42, 372

FitzHerbert, J. 123, 130
Flammarion, C. 26, 35
Flew, A. 322-23, 412
Fodor, N. 126, 130
Forwald, H. 58-60, 172, 220-21
Foster, A. 100
Foster, E. B. 80, 84, 150, 170, 220, 357, 364-65
Franke, W. (F. Gurtis, pseud.) 38-41
Frazer, J. 96-97
Freeman, J. 149, 151
Freud, S. 129-30
Fry, T. 145, 151-52, 158

Gardner, M. 384
Garnett, A. C. 382
Geley, G. 389
George, R. W. 364
Gerber, R. 274
Gibson, L. 152
Gillespie, W. H. 131
Girden, E. 402, 408
Goldney, M. K. 342, 406, 417
Goldstone, G. 432
Good, I. J. 382
Gorer, G. 100
Grad, B. 124, 345, 347
Green, C. E. 276
Greenwood, J. A. 161, 162, 206-07
Grela, J. 234-36, 261, 262, 366
Gross, H. 152
Gurtis, F., pseud. see Franke, W.

Haddox, V. 254, 259, 291
Hallett, S. J. 150
Hallowell, I. 99
Hansel, C. E. M. 404-05, 406, 407, 416, 417
Hardy, A. 338, 339, 388, 389
Harper, S. 278

Hauri, P. 114-15
Hebb, D. O. 427, 429, 450
Hermon, H. 277-78
Heywood, R. 369
Hilgard, E. R. 230-31, 233,
   234, 262
Hirschberg, J. 360
Hoagland, H. 411, 413
Hodgson, R. 368
Hollos, I. 129-30
Honorton, C. 140, 227-70,
   272-84, 289, 290, 291, 292,
   293, 294, 295, 399, 465-
   66
Huby, P. M. 128
Hull, C. L. 230
Humphrey, B. 54, 153, 359,
   364, 431, 447
Hutton, J. H. 100
Huxley, J. 336

Ivinsky, D. 289

Jacobson, E. 275
James, W. 360, 410, 424
Janet, P. 122, 229, 263
Jensen, A. 195
Jephson, I. 205
Johnson, A. 191
Johnson, G. M. 321
Johnson, M. 279, 293, 372
Johnson, R. 372
Jolliffe, D. 234, 245-46, 262
Jones, J. 216
Jourdain, E. F. 28-37, 44-
   45
Jung, C. G. 121, 198

Kitaygorodsky, A. 428
Klein, J. 294
Knowles, F. W. 122
Koestler, A. 334, 338-39,
   384, 390
Kooy, J. M. J. 382
Kotik, N. 371
Kreiman, N. 289
Krippner, S. 140, 227-70,

   275, 366, 466
Kuhn, T. S. 385

Lang, A. 98
Lashley, K. S. 370-71
Laubscher, B. J. 100
Leonard, G. O. 360
LeShan, L. 278
Lodge, O. 360, 371, 424,
   445
Long, J. K. 72
Lorenz, K. 8
Lovin, C. 294
Ludwig, A. M. 227, 234

McCollam, E. 279-80, 289,
   290, 291, 292
McConnell, R. A. 56-57,
   288
McDougall, W. 346, 424
McElroy, W. A. 357, 359
McMahan, E. 152, 364, 447
MacRobert, R. G. 126
Maeterlinck, M. 77
Mandleberg, I. 254, 260-61,
   291, 366
Mangan, G. L. 7-8, 193-94
Marais, E. 77
Marsh, M. C. 194, 195
Marshall, N. 382
Matthew, K. 85
Matthews, G. V. T. 75
Mayer, B. 275
Mead, M. 116
Meehl, P. E. 402, 408
Meerloo, J. A. M. 434
Mesmer, F. A. 229
Michie, D. 193
Miklos, J. 389-90
Mishra, R. 274
Moberly, C. A. 28-37, 44-
   45
Montredon, E. 82-83, 86,
   170, 219-20
Morris, R. L. 71, 73-93,
   273, 294, 307, 467
Mundle, C. W. K. 5-6, 384-
   85

Murphy, G.   359, 366, 404,
   428, 432
Myers, F. W. H.   12-13, 15,
   22, 27-28, 227, 353, 371,
   379, 441-42, 443-45, 448-
   49

Nash, C. B.   155, 192-93,
   234, 238, 261, 262, 364,
   372, 373, 467-68
Nash, C. S.   364
Nicol, J. F.   364, 404, 413,
   416, 431

Olivier, E.   35
Orne, M. T.   231-32
Osis, K.   80, 84, 86, 127,
   140, 148, 170, 180-202,
   220, 246, 250-51, 280-81,
   341, 345, 357, 364-65,
   468
Osmond, H.   128
Osty, E.   360, 362, 364,
   368, 391
Otani, S.   257

Pagenstecher, G.   255, 365,
   369, 371
Palmer, J.   294
Parker, A.   146-47
Patanjali   277, 281
Pearson, D.   382
Pederson-Krag, G.   130
Penfield, W.   369-70
Piddington, J. G.   360
Piper, L. E.   360, 368
Pobers, M.   101
Podmore, F.   194
Pope, D. H.   101
Poynton, J.   388-89
Prasad, J.   276
Pratt, J. G.   2, 50-67, 74,
   75, 81, 139, 155, 220, 254,
   257, 356, 357, 362-63,
   372, 417, 469
Price, G.   406, 407, 409,
   414, 415, 428

Price, H. H.   310-11, 327,
   354-55, 373
Prince, R.   99
Puharich, A.   128
Puryear, H. B.   171

Randall, J. L.   333-49, 388,
   390, 469
Ransom, C.   399, 401-21,
   469
Rao, K. R.   87, 149, 151-
   52, 234, 242, 273, 307,
   309-30, 362, 469-70
Rao, V. V. L.   382
Rapaport, D.   361, 362
Rashevsky, N.   413, 415
Rawcliffe, D. H.   409, 412,
   415, 417
Reeves, M. P.   366
Reik, T.   78
Reitler, R.   85-86
Rhine, J. B.   52, 54, 55,
   76, 79, 83, 139, 140,
   142-77, 191, 204-24, 246,
   248-323, 327, 347-48,
   357, 360, 364, 366, 382,
   385, 396, 387, 388, 391,
   400, 416, 424-30, 432,
   441-56, 470-71
Rhine, L. E.   52, 155-56,
   157-58, 169, 217, 227-
   28, 274, 276, 279, 354,
   360, 365, 366
Richet, C.   121, 205, 424,
   445
Richmond, N.   83-84, 341,
   345
Rilling, M. E.   432
Rogers, D. P.   166, 299
Rogosin, H.   408
Roll, W. G.   1-2, 3-18,
   255, 294, 308, 351-80,
   471
Rose, L.   101-03
Rose, R.   101-03
Ruderfer, M.   382
Rush, J. H.   195, 198

Rushton, W. A. H.   131
Ryzl, M.   245, 254-59, 264,
    290-91, 366-67, 372

Sabine, W. W. H.   2, 22-48,
    472
Salter, Mrs. W. H.   360
Saltmarsh, H. F.   353
Sanders, M. C.   149
Savits, B.   296-97
Scherer, W. B.   220
Schmeidler, G. R.   148, 149,
    153, 162, 167-68, 195,
    197, 273, 274, 278, 279,
    296-97, 351, 359, 362,
    364, 431
Schmidt, H.   171, 386, 388
Schroedinger, E.   335-36
Schwarz, B.   130
Scott, W.   23
Selous, E.   77-78
Servadio, E.   128, 129
Shackleton, B.   364
Shulman, R.   191-92
Sidgwick, E. M.   191, 345
Silva Mind Control   288, 295-
    97
Sinclair, M. C.   255, 321
Skinner, B. F.   413-14
Smith, J.   345
Smith, K.   408
Soal, S. G.   5, 6, 192, 194,
    197, 314, 315, 356, 357,
    364, 368, 406, 416, 417,
    442, 447
Stanford, R. G.   140, 166,
    273, 275, 288-304, 472-73
Stekel, W.   129
Stepanek, P.   255-57, 366-67,
    372
Stephenson, C. J.   246, 249-
    50, 291
Stevenson, I.   127, 276, 294,
    407, 417
Stewart, G.   315, 356
Stuart, C. E.   364
Stump, J. P.   84, 246, 252-

53, 262, 263, 264
Sturge-Whiting, J. R.   31
Szasz, T.   414

Tart, C. T.   263, 276, 289,
    291-92, 356-57
Tenhaeff, W. H. C.   354,
    355-56, 360, 362, 371
Thomas, C. D.   360
Thompson, D.   339
Thorpe, W. H.   334, 336-
    37, 342
Thouless, R. H.   42, 319-
    22, 385, 408, 424, 443-
    44, 448
Timm, U.   156
Tinbergen, N.   73
Turner, M. E.   148, 180,
    184-88, 430
Tyrrell, G. N. M.   171,
    198, 263, 309, 315-17,
    321, 324, 353

Ullman, M.   72, 128-29,
    276-77, 366, 434
Urban, H. J.   120-21, 125-
    26, 359
Usher, F. L.   192

Van Busschbach, J. G.   357,
    359, 432
Van de Castle, R. L.   72,
    95-118, 239-40, 275,
    357, 473
Vasiliev, L. L.   198, 246,
    249, 263
Vasse, C.   345
Vasse, P.   345
Vaughan, A.   276-77, 296
Verrall, Mrs. A. W.   368

Warcollier, R.   194, 353-
    54, 368, 442
Warner, L.   402, 425
Wasserman, G. D.   382
Watanabe, S.   384
Weitzenhoffer, A. M.   234

West, D. J.   42, 123, 126-
    27, 193, 197, 372
White, R. A.   79, 255, 274,
    351, 360, 362, 366, 432
Whiteman, J. H. M.   386
Wiesner, B. P.   319-22, 443,
    448
Wigner, E. P.   386-87
Williams, L.   102
Whyte, L. L.   340
Wilson, C. W. M.   128
Wood, G. H.   81, 86
Woodruff, J. L.   364, 417

Zierold, M.   365

SUBJECT INDEX

An Adventure (Moberly and Jourdain) 28-37, 44-45
Age and psi 108, 208-09, 212, 214-15, 360
Agent, role of in psi testing 110-12, 368-69
Alpha rhythms and psi 275-76, 293-95
Altered states of consciousness and psi 227-28, 230-33,
    273-79, 365-67; see also Alpha rhythms and psi; Dreams
    and psi; Drugs and psi; Hypnosis and psi; Sensory isola-
    tion and psi; Trance
Animals, clever see Clever animals
Anpsi 71, 73-94, 341, 345
Anpsi--Bibliography 91-94
Anthropology and psi 71, 95-119
Anthropology and psi--Bibliography 116-19
Association theory of telepathy 313-15

Biology and psi 333-50, 388-90

Chris (dog) 79, 81
Clairvoyance 1, 236-38, 240-45, 252-53, 256-59, 311, 443,
    445-48, 453, 456-57
Clever animals 78-79, 81
Clever Hans (horse) 78
Cognition and psi 312-13, 319-22, 325-27, 328, 354-65
Collective unconscious and psi 310, 327
Confidence calls in ESP testing 250-51, 279-81, 292, 363-
    65
Consistent missing 155-58, 362-63
Control of psi 172-74, 204-05, 219-23, 433; see also Train-
    ing of psi ability
Conviction and psi 273, 279, 363-65; see also Confidence
    calls in ESP testing
Criticisms of parapsychology 399-457
Criticisms of parapsychology--Bibliography 419-23
Cuna Indians 103-16

Deathbed experiences 127
Decline effects see Position effects

Development of psi ability see Training of psi ability
Diagnosis, paranormal 114-15, 120-21, 297-98
Differential effect 149-51, 162-64, 242-45
Distance and psi 140, 180-203
Distance and psi--Bibliography 199-203
Divination, primitive 99-100
Dreams and psi 12-16, 128-31, 227-28, 252, 276-77; see
    also Hypnotic dreams and psi
Dreams, hypnotic see Hypnotic dreams and psi
Drugs and psi 127-28
Dual-aspect tests see Differential effect

ESP--Theories see Psi phenomena--Theories
Evolution and psi 42, 335-47, 388-90
Evidence for psi see Criticisms
Experimenter as the actual subject 10, 85, 87, 454

Faith healing see Medicine and parapsychology
Feedback in psi testing see Learning and ESP
Fraud 406-07, 427-28
Free response experiments 194-95, 251-53, 274, 292, 362,
    366-67

GESP 1, 234-36, 240-41, 245-46, 251-52
Golden Bough (Frazer) 96-97

Habit patterns in ESP testing 213, 219-22, 356-59
Hallucinations and psi 23-25, 27-38, 44, 126-27, 254-59,
    324, 353-54
Hit distribution in psi tests see Position effects
Hive behavior 77-78
Homing 74-76
Hypnosis 228-34
Hypnosis and psi 229, 234-71, 275-76, 365-67; see also
    Hypnotic dreams and psi; Hypnosis-at-a-distance
Hypnosis and psi--Bibliography 265-71
Hypnosis-at-a-distance 122, 140, 229, 249, 263
Hypnotic dreams and psi 252-53

International Journal of Parapsychology 459
Journal of Parapsychology 460
Journal of the American Society for Psychical Research
    460-61
Journal of the Society for Psychical Research 461

Learning and ESP 280-81, 289-92, 355-60; see also Train-
    ing of psi ability

Lumen (Flammarion) 26, 35

Maimonides Medical Center 120, 128-29
Medicine and parapsychology 120-38, 347; see also Diagnosis,
    paranormal; Psychiatry and psi phenomena
Medicine and parapsychology--Bibliography 132-38
Memory and psi 14, 38, 41-42, 44-45, 351-81
Memory and psi--Bibliography 374-81
Memory, inherited 41-42
Mind-body relationship 312-13, 319-22, 390, 451-52
Mind-control courses 288-89, 295-301; see also Silva Mind
    Control

Out-of-the-body experiences 451

Paranthropology see Anthropology and psi
Parapsychological Association. Proceedings. see Research
    in Parapsychology
Parapsychology Review 461-62
Periodicals, parapsychological 459-63
Physics and psi 61, 382-88
Plants and psi 345
Position effects 6-7, 53-57, 146-49, 174, 204-26, 357-58
Position effects--Bibliography 223-26
Possession 99, 126
Precognition 1-2, 3-21, 28, 236-27, 250-51, 322, 384-86;
    see also Psychokinesis and precognition
Precognition--Bibliography 17-21
Precognition and retrocognition 28, 38, 43-45
Preferential effect see Differential effect
Primitive belief systems 95-97
Primitives and psi see Anthropology and psi
Proceedings of the Parapsychological Association see Re-
    search in Parapsychology
Proceedings of the Society for Psychical Research 462
Psi-conducive states 261-64, 272-87, 292-95, 365-67; see
    also Altered states and psi; Training of psi ability
Psi-conducive states--Bibliography 281-87
Psi fields 11-13, 16-17, 345, 371-74
Psi-missing 139, 142-79, 205, 215-19, 237, 360-62; see
    also Consistent missing
Psi-missing--Bibliography 174-79
Psi phenomena 1, 3, 261-64, 272-73, 279-81, 312-13, 317-
    29, 342-45
Psi phenomena--Theories 42-45, 307-32, 342-47, 351-74,
    382-98, 441-57
Psi-trailing 76-77

Psi-training see Training of psi ability
Psychiatry and psi 72, 124-26, 128-31, 434
Psychokinesis 2, 50-70, 121, 206, 210-11, 248-49, 341-42
Psychokinesis--Bibliography 62-70
Psychokinesis and precognition 4-5, 9-10, 13-14, 16, 453-
    54
Psychometry 371-72
Psychotherapy and psi see Psychiatry and psi

Relaxation and psi ability see Psi-conducive states
Repeatability in psi research 86-87, 403-06, 428-34
Repeatability in psi research--Bibliography 438-40
Research in Parapsychology 462-63
Response bias see Habit patterns in ESP testing
Response factors in psi testing 213-23, 356-60, 368-69;
    see also Habit patterns in ESP testing
Retrocognition 2, 22-49, 453
Retrocognition--Bibliography 49
Retrocognition and precognition see Precognition and retro-
    cognition

Salience ratios 161, 206-10
Second Sight in Daily Life (Sabine) 43-44
Sensory isolation and psi 277-79
Sex and psi test results 107-10
Silva Mind Control 295-97
Spontaneous psi phenomena 4-10, 22-45, 227-28, 273-74,
    276, 362, 366
Statistics of parapsychological research 158-67, 206-07,
    407-09, 426, 430-34
Stress and psi 151-54
Survival 41, 312-13, 390-91, 443-44, 450-52

Telepathy 1, 42, 310-11, 313-15, 316-17, 441-52, 455-57
Thinking animals see Clever animals
Training of psi ability 139-40, 245-46, 251, 254-61, 264,
    279-81, 288-306; see also Learning and ESP; Mind control
    courses
Training of psi ability--Bibliography 301-06
Trance 99, 227, 230-33
Two-aspect test conditions see Differential effect

Unorthodox healing see Medicine and parapsychology

Variance in psi test results 165-66

Worth, Patience 38, 41

How to Read Character

a New Illustrated Handbook
of Phrenology and Physiognomy

for Students and Examiners
with a Descriptive Chart

by SAMUEL R. WELLS

CHARLES E. TUTTLE COMPANY
Rutland, Vermont & Tokyo, Japan

PUBLISHER'S FOREWORD

———◆◆◆———

THE theory of pherenology, popularized in the United States by Orson and Lorenzo Fowler, has been discredited by many biological scientists in view of today's medical and psychological advances, but the belief still has many advocates and supporters. In fact, the very important physiological advances that disparage many of Franz Joseph Gall's original theories also serve to substantiate many of his suppositions regarding human conduct and its cause-and-effect relationships.

The physiology of the brain is still not completely understood, although many of its qualities are, such as the knowledge that the brain is larger and more complicated in proportion to the strength and variety of the faculties manifested, and that deficiency of the brain is connected with a low degree of mental power. Interest in phrenology will continue as man continues his study of why we behave like human beings.

It is for this reason, as well as for reasons of sheer human interest (to say nothing of humor) that this curious and often surprising book has been brought back into print. Certainly a new audience of readers will find many things in it to enjoy and to ponder as well.

PREFACE.

HE first Phrenological CHART ever produced was printed on a single sheet, the size of our common note paper, and was sold for a cent. It simply gave the names of the organs then discovered by Dr. GALL. The next was larger, and gave both the names and definitions of the organs; still later, the charts of Drs. GALL and SPURZHEIM embraced all the above, together with some account of the Temperaments. But as it was with the inventors of the steam-engine, the locomotive, and the steamboat, so it has been with phrenologists. Each succeeding author is supposed to have availed himself of all that has been proved to be true and useful, adding thereto his own observations and experiences. Thus the improved charts of to-day are as unlike those first printed as are the modern steamers, locomotives, and engines to those first invented.

During our thirty years' experience in the practical application of scientific rules to character reading, we have used many different charts, revising old ones year after year, and adding one improvement after another. The present work embodies our latest and best ideas on the subject, so far as they can be set forth in this condensed and popular form.

It contains not only all of the PHRENOLOGY of previous charts or hand-books for self-instruction, but it embraces much more of PHYSIOLOGY and PHYSIOGNOMY than any former book of the kind.

In this Illustrated Hand-book we have endeavored to incorporate just that kind of matter best suited to both the EXAMINER and the EXAMINED, and to put it in the smallest possible compass compatible with completeness of statement and ample illustration. We have endeavored to be systematic in our arrangement, succinct and clear in our expositions, and popular rather than technical or professional in our style. We do not claim that this work is free from error. Our knowledge of Anatomy, Physiology, Chemistry, Astronomy, etc., will, we doubt not, increase with our years and with more careful study ; so we intend it shall be with our knowledge of Phrenology and Physiognomy. We hope to revise this and all our other works when time may permit. We ask examiners and readers to kindly point out errors and to suggest improvements, that we may correct the former and incorporate the latter in future editions.

That this little work may be the means of encouraging the reader to correct any errors of judgment or improper habits he may possess—to cultivate and develop all the higher qualities of mind and heart— and to make the most of his opportunities and of himself, is the desire of

THE AUTHOR.

NEW YORK, *January*, 1869.

INTRODUCTION.

THE BRAIN AND THE SKULL.

THE HUMAN SKULL.

SOME knowledge of the structure of the human brain, and of its appearance when exposed, as well as of the general forms of the skull, will be useful to the learner. We can here merely give very brief descriptions, referring those who desire further information to our larger and more elaborate works.

The human brain is an oval mass filling and fitting the interior of the skull, and consisting of two substances, a gray, ash-colored, or cineritious portion, and a white, fibrous, or medullary portion. It is divided, both in form and function, into two principal masses—the cerebrum and the cerebellum.

BRAIN EXPOSED.

The cerebrum is divided longitudinally into two equal hemispheres, and each of these, in its under surface, into three lobes. But the most remarkable feature in the structure of the cerebral globe is its numerous and complicated convolutions, the furrows between which dip deeply down into the brain. By means of these foldings the surface of the brain is greatly increased, and

BRAIN IN THE
SKULL.*

---

* The side and top of the cerebrum are seen in this engraving. A A. The scalp turned down. B B. Edge of the base of the skull, the top having been sawed off and removed. C. Dura Mater, a part of the lining membrane of the skull raised up from the brain. D. Left hemisphere of the brain. E. Right hemisphere. F. The longitudinal cleft or fissure which divides the hemispheres.

In the next engraving the brain is fully exposed.

power gained with the utmost economy of space; for it is a demonstrated fact, that in proportion to the number and depth of these convolutions is the mental force. "The mind's revolvings," as Wilkinson

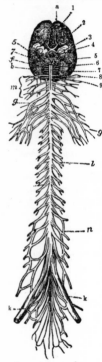

beautifully expresses it, "are here represented in moving spirals, and the subtile insinuation of thought, whose path is through all things, issues with power from the form of cerebral screws. They print their shape and make themselves room on the inside of the skull, and are the most irresistible things in the human world."

The cerebellum lies behind and immediately underneath the cerebrum, and is about one-eighth the size of the latter organ. It is divided into lobes and lobules, and consists of a gray and a white substance, like the cerebrum, but differently disposed, the white portion being internal in the cerebrum and external in the cerebellum, in which, also, both substances are disposed in thin plates instead of convolutions.

Extending from the base of the brain to the atlas or bony pivot on which the head rests, is the medulla oblongata. It is conical in shape, and may be considered as merely the head or beginning of the spinal cord, which continues it, and, in fact, extends the brain down the vertical canal, and by means of the nerves which it gives off, and which pass through notches between the vertebræ, connects it with every part of the body. There are generally reckoned eleven pairs of nerves arising from the brain, and thirty-one from the spinal marrow. It is thus seen that the whole nervous apparatus is included in the mental system, and that the

SPINAL CORD AND NERVES.*

brain, as the organ of the overruling mind should be, as it unquestionably is, is omnipresent in the human body.

Now, as is the soul which is incarnate in it, so is the brain in texture, size, and configuration; and as is the brain, so is its bony casement, the cranium, on which may be read, in general forms and special elevations and depressions, and with unerring certainty, a correct outline of the intellectual and moral character of the man.

---

* *a.* The brain. *b.* Cerebellum. *f.* Medulla oblongata. *g, g.* Nerves distributed to the arms. *k, k.* Great sciatic nerve, distributed to the lower limbs. *l.* Dorsal nerve. *n.* Lumbar nerve. *m.* Plexus of cervical nerves. 1. Olfactory nerve. 2. Optic nerve. 3, 4, 5, 6. The third, fourth, fifth, and sixth nerves. 7. Portio dura of the seventh nerve. 8. Auditory nerve and par vagum. 9. Hypoglossal nerve.

The heads of the sexes differ in shape as much as do their bodily forms. The engravings here presented are from two skulls in our possession, and were copied by daguerreotype, and show their relative size and shape. The first is from the skull of a man, and is a fair specimen of the male head. It rises high from the opening of the ear, *a*, to Firmness, *b*. It is large in the social region, particularly at Amativeness, *c*. The phrenological organs of force, pride, energy, and self-reliance are predominant. The second

is of a well-balanced female skull, and is fine, smooth, and even. The leading developments are at *d*, in the region of Philoprogenitiveness, Adhesiveness, and Inhabitiveness, while at *b* and *c* it is much less than in the male. At *e*, Benevolence, and at *f*, Veneration, the female is rela-

MALE SKULL.

FEMALE SKULL.

tively more developed, but less so at Firmness and Self-Esteem, *b*.

The skulls of races and nations also differ widely in form, and these differences are found to correspond with known differences of character. In the Caucasian it will be seen that the forehead is prominent and high, the coronal region elevated, and the back-head moderately projected. The facial angle, measured according to Camper's method, is about 80°. It indicates great intellectual power, strong moral or spiritual sentiments, and a comparatively moderate development of the propensities. The special organs in which the Caucasian brain most excels, and which distinguish it

CAUCASIAN SKULL.

from those of all less advanced races, are Mirthfulness, Ideality, and Conscientiousness, the organs of these faculties being somewhat smaller in savage and barbarous tribes.

There is a contrast between the Caucasian skull and those of the North American Indian and the Negro, but not nearly as great as

INDIAN SKULL.

some scientists have reported. One of the most distinctive traits of the aboriginal American skull is roundness. This quality is manifest in every aspect, but more so in the vertical and back views than in the

NEGRO SKULL.

one here presented. Great breadth immediately above the ears and in the region of Cautiousness and Secretiveness, and the lofty coronal region, are also prominent characteristics. The forehead is broad and very prominent at the lower part, but tends to retreat. The back-head in the region of the affections is, in general, developed, but there is sometimes a large and sharply defined occipital protuberance.

The Negro cranium has a tendency toward being longer and narrower. In the side view the frontal region may be less capacious than in the Caucasian, the forehead more retreating, and the occiput comparatively more full. The facial angle is about 70°, the jaws being large and sometimes projecting. The top view shows the facial bones compressed laterally, but projecting considerably in front. However, much study remains in this respect, nor, in view of recent findings, can it be assumed that one race or ethnic group holds a distinct intellectual advantage over another. The opportunity for development often brings astounding results.

We might carry these comparisons still farther, and show that each nation has its peculiar type of skull, the English differing strikingly from the French, and the American from both, and so on, but space will not here permit, and we must refer the reader to " New Physiognomy " for additional particulars on this and kindred topics.

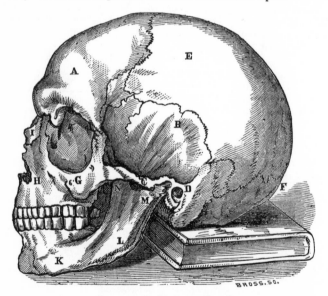

BONES OF THE HEAD AND FACE.*

---

* A. Frontal bone. B. Temporal bone. C. Zygoma. D. Mastoid process. E. Parietal bone. F. Occipital bone. G. Malar bone. H. Superior maxillary bone. I. Nasal bone. K. Inferior maxillary bone. L. Angle of the jaw. M. Condyles. N. Connoid process.